D1034058

In Praise of *Comprehensive Functional Verification: The Complete Industry Cycle*

As chip design complexity continues to increase, functional verification is becoming the dominant task in the development process. The book does an excellent job of describing the fundamentals of functional verification. The reader of this book will learn the details of the verification cycle and the methods employed by verification engineers to ensure a bug-free design release.

Fadi A. Aloul, American University of Sharjah, UAE

This book provides the most comprehensive treatment of functional verification to date. The authors have used their extensive experience to provide an industrial perspective on issues and challenges that verification engineers could face. The book is valuable to both novice and experienced verification engineers.

Baback Izadi, State University of New York—New Paltz

This book is a comprehensive tour of the industrial verification cycle. The authors have paid particular attention to the coverage of recent advances in the field, and introduced them gradually in a chain of well-organized chapters. This, along with the abundance of illustrative examples and case studies, make it an ideal text for a university course on functional verification.

Nazanin Mansouri, Syracuse University

This book provides a comprehensive overview of verification principles and techniques. The extensive use of examples and insightful perspective on practical verification challenges make this book ideal for introducing hardware verification concepts to undergraduate computer engineering students.

Vijaykrishnan Narayanan and Mary Jane Irwin, The Pennsylvania State University

Verification now dominates digital design flows, as teams struggle to efficiently ensure their systems work correctly. Despite the tremendous importance of verification, no book has adequately covered the material needed to guarantee the quality of complex electronic systems. Wile, Goss, and Roesner present an insightful introduction to functional verification technology, including theoretical issues and practical techniques. This excellent text promises to benefit both the student and practicing engineer in becoming more effective in addressing modern verification challenges.

Greg Peterson, University of Tennessee

This is an excellent reference for those needing an in-depth treatment of functional verification but also a much needed text for courses which focus on this complex and difficult topic. It goes beyond the normal coverage of functional verification topics by including two chapters on formal verification, a topic often skipped or barely mentioned in other texts. The message "verification is tough" has been heard often at recent Design Automation Conferences. This book is a powerful response to that very important message.

Hardy J. Pottinger, University of Missouri—Rolla

COMPREHENSIVE FUNCTIONAL VERIFICATION

VERIFICATION

THE COMPLETE INDUSTRY CYCLE

Author Bios

Bruce Wile, IBM Distinguished Engineer, is ASIC Chief Engineer for IBM Systems and Technology Group. In this position, he leads the development of the current and next generation server chip set. Mr. Wile worked in functional verification for 18 years, where he started his career in 1985 after graduating from the Pennsylvania State University. He has worked as a verification engineer on many chips and systems, starting with IBM's S/390 ES/9000 series' cache and storage controller unit, and thereafter working on processors, IO devices, and entire systems. Throughout his verification career, he has held both team lead and management positions. In 2000, Mr. Wile was named the Verification Lead for all IBM server chips, where, he was responsible for driving verification technology deployment and execution across the entire IBM line of server products. Mr. Wile has several patents and published papers. He is passionately involved with engineering, science, and math educational efforts, working with all levels of secondary schools as well as universities.

John C. Goss, an Advisory Engineer, is a verification team lead for IBM Systems and Technology Group. In this position, he leads the system simulation efforts the current and next generation server processor chips. Mr. Goss has worked in the field of functional verification his entire career, since 1993. He graduated from Pennsylvania State University with his BS in Computer Engineering and a minor in Computer Science. Shortly after joining IBM, he then pursued his Masters degree in Computer Engineering at the North Carolina State University where he graduated in 1996. He has worked as a verification engineer on many chips and systems, starting with IBM's networking division. He worked on a series of ASIC's that were used in IBM's networking gear including a network processor. In 2002, he has assumed responsibility of system verification in one of IBM's next generation server processor chips. In addition to his position at IBM, Mr. Goss also is an adjunct professor at North Carolina State University where he has been teaching functional verification to graduate students since 2001.

Wolfgang Roesner is an IBM Distinguished Engineer and the Verification Lead for the IBM Systems and Technology Group. He currently leads both the verification technology teams as well as the verification execution teams on IBM's next generation server chips and systems. Dr. Roesner started his IBM career in Boeblingen, Germany, developing HDL compilers and simulators. After a temporary assignment to be part of the development of the first POWER processor chip, he decided to stay with the Austin, TX based teams and projects. During the last fifteen years, his verification tools have been used on every CMOS microprocessor system including the POWER and PowerPC systems and IBM's large zSeries servers. IBM's verification technologies range from software- and hardware-based simulation engines to testbench languages and formal and semi-formal verification tools. Since 2003, Dr. Roesner is also responsible for the verification teams of the next generation server chips. He has published numerous papers and has been an invited speaker to several technical conferences.

COMPREHENSIVE FUNCTIONAL VERIFICATION
THE COMPLETE INDUSTRY CYCLE

Bruce Wile

John C. Goss

Wolfgang Roesner

ELSEVIER

AMSTERDAM • BOSTON • HEIDELBERG • LONDON
NEW YORK • OXFORD • PARIS • SAN DIEGO
SAN FRANCISCO • SINGAPORE • SYDNEY • TOKYO

Morgan Kaufmann is an imprint of Elsevier

MORGAN KAUFMANN PUBLISHERS

Publisher   Denise E.M. Penrose
Publishing Services Manager   Simon Crump
Project Manager   Brandy Lilly
Project Management   Graphic World NY
Developmental Editor   Nate McFadden
Cover Design   Chen Design
Text Design   Julio Esperas
Technical Illustration   Dartmouth Publishing, Inc.
Copyeditor   Graphic World NY
Proofreader   Graphic World NY
Indexer   Graphic World NY
Interior printer   The Maple-Vail Book Manufacturing Group
Cover printer   Phoenix Color

Morgan Kaufmann Publishers is an imprint of Elsevier.
500 Sansome Street, Suite 400, San Francisco, CA 94111

This book is printed on acid-free paper.

© 2005 by Elsevier Inc. All rights reserved.

Designations used by companies to distinguish their products are often claimed as trademarks or
registered trademarks. In all instances in which Morgan Kaufmann Publishers is aware of a claim,
the product names appear in initial capital or all capital letters. Readers, however, should contact the
appropriate companies for more complete information regarding trademarks and registration.

No part of this publication may be reproduced, stored in a retrieval system, or transmitted in any
form or by any means—electronic, mechanical, photocopying, scanning, or otherwise—without prior
written permission of the publisher.

Permissions may be sought directly from Elsevier's Science & Technology Rights Department in
Oxford, UK: phone: (+44) 1865 843830, fax: (+44) 1865 853333, e-mail: *permissions@elsevier.com.uk*.
You may also complete your request on-line via the Elsevier homepage (*http://elsevier.com*) by
selecting "Customer Support" and then "Obtaining Permissions."

Library of Congress Cataloging-in-Publication Data
Application Submitted

ISBN: 0-12-751803-7

For information on all Morgan Kaufmann publications,
visit our Web site at www.mkp.com or www.books.elsevier.com

Printed in the United States of America
05 06 07 08 09   5 4 3 2 1

Working together to grow
libraries in developing countries

www.elsevier.com | www.bookaid.org | www.sabre.org

ELSEVIER   BOOK AID
             International   Sabre Foundation

Throughout this book, we place the verification team at the forefront of technical performance. Over the years we've been influenced by many outstanding individuals on our verification and verification tools teams. The information in this book is truly a compilation of that which we've learned, together with these teammates. We wish to acknowledge their camaraderie, support, and dedication to producing bug-free designs.

We wish to thank our families for their continued support throughout this long stretch of time when we stared at our laptop screens at night and on weekends while the only words they heard from us were, "yes . . . I think" and "say again?"

Finally, we must express our gratitude to Nate McFadden, whose tireless work shepherded this book through the creative process. His advice, guidance, and enthusiasm kept us on course.

FOREWORD

Complex electronic designs pervade almost every aspect of modern life. We take for granted the existence of cell phones, or antilock brakes, or medical imaging devices, not to mention the ubiquitous PC. As users or customers, we also take it for granted that these devices will function correctly. The impact of an undetected functional failure can range from mild annoyance to major catastrophe, and the cost—to individuals, to companies, to society as a whole—can likewise be immense.

The danger is compounded by the fact that the relentless march of semiconductor process technology allows us to produce increasingly complex designs, which contain an increasing number of bugs. With shorter design cycles and increased competitive pressure to get products to market, verification is often the critical path to production. The authors of the 2003 International Technology Roadmap for Semiconductors were moved to describe verification as "a bottleneck that has now reached crisis proportions".

For that reason alone, this book would be welcome. But there are many other reasons. The authors bring to their task a wealth of practical verification experience and a strong academic background—a rare combination. Their focus on the verification cycle *as a process* is particularly important in placing verification in the proper context—as the authors state: "results and learning from the current project feed the verification plans and implementation for the next project". The only way to stay on top of the growth in complexity is to continuously learn and improve, so that verification becomes a systematic and sustainable process.

A unique feature of this book is that it is designed be used in conjunction with hands-on functional verification exercises. The authors have collaborated with major Electronic Design Automation (EDA) companies to create exercises based on RTL design implementations of a four-operation calculator. These implementations come complete with functional errors for the student to find, using an industrial-strength verification environment. As in real life, successive implementations of the calculator provide increasing complexity and additional verification challenges. Not only will the student learn how to look for and find bugs in these designs, he or she will do so using the tools that they will later use to attack real-life verification problems of their own. Unfortunately, the latter will not come with a handy web-based set of solutions, as these exercises do!

Part II of the book covers the three pillars of Simulation Based Verification: testing, checking and coverage. A good simulation environment, or "testbench," provides the mechanisms for stimulating the design with some mixture of directed and randomized tests; provides a language and tools for creating checkers at all the appropriate levels of the design; and provides a means for collecting and analyzing coverage data to tell the verification engineer what has, and more importantly what has not, been tested.

I particularly commend the discussion of coverage in Section 6.2. Coverage is an important and much misunderstood part of the verification cycle. A colleague of mine with a great deal of experience in this area once summarized his opinion as follows: "the value of coverage lies in the act of analyzing it and driving it up." Coverage analysis often results in surprises—complex designs, by their very nature, are difficult to grasp, and our intuition is a poor guide to the interactions that are occurring as we simulate the design. Coverage analysis, if done properly, challenges our assumptions and makes us stop and think about what we might otherwise take for granted. Testing without coverage is like driving a car with a blindfold—you may think you know where you are going, but where you end up is not where you intended to be!

The discussion of "Pervasive Function Verification" in Chapter 9 is another good example of the authors sharing their practical experience of what it takes to get a product to market. In the real world, it is not enough just to verify the correctness of mainline functionality, though this is where most of the focus is applied. A product also needs to be tested, manufactured, debugged and maintained, and very often this involves mechanisms that are orthogonal to the rest of the design. After all, if the part won't come out of reset, it doesn't matter that the function units are logically correct!

I am particularly pleased to see the emphasis that the authors place on formal verification in Part III. Although it is not always possible to apply formal methods, when they *can* be applied they provide a level of certitude that dynamic simulation (in general) cannot—as the authors state, "A formal proof is the most desirable verification of a property." In the past decade, formal verification has gone from being largely of academic interest to becoming an indispensable tool for attacking certain classes of problems. For example, formal verification is the *only* practical way of assuring the correctness of an implementation for the huge data space specified by the IEEE 754 floating point standard. Verification engineers should have both formal and dynamic verification tools in their toolbox, and should know how and when to apply the right tool to the problem at hand.

The Case Studies in Chapter 15 provide an all-too-rare glimpse "behind the curtain" at the kinds of problems that are seldom, if ever, discussed in public. Every experienced validator could cite a similar set of examples, and every novice can learn from these cases. The authors are to be commended for their willingness to discuss their successes *and* their failures for the benefit of the verification community as a whole.

This book is a must-read for the novice validator, but even the most grizzled veteran will find it an excellent addition to his or her library. It has my highest recommendation.

Bob Bentley
Intel Corporation

CONTENTS

Part II: Simulation Based Verification

5   HDLs and Simulation Engines   141

6   Creating Environments   199

7   Strategies for Simulation-Based Stimulus Generation   259

8   Strategies for Results Checking in Simulation-Based Verification   313

9   Pervasive Function Verification   355

10   Re-Use Strategies and System Simulation   391

Part IV: Comprehensive Verification

13   Completing the Verification Cycle   539

14   Advanced Verification Techniques   579

PREFACE

Within the chip hardware design process, there are multiple verification efforts. These efforts include functional verification, timing verification, test verification, and equivalence checking. The most time consuming of these is functional verification. Functional verification ensures that the logic in a chip and system performs operations correctly under all circumstances as stipulated by the specification of that design. Functional verification engineers perform their work on a software model of the hardware design prior to fabrication of the chip. They measure their success based on the functionality of the first pass of fabricated hardware.

There is no single formula for functional verification success. There is no golden code to employ consistently on every design. Every hardware design has unique subtleties. Like a sculptor staring at a block of wood and visualizing its final form, the verification engineer requires experience and insight to craft a precise environment essential for exploring and verifying that design.

While experience is important for a successful verification effort, so is a core understanding of verification theory, strategy, and available methods. Over the last 20 years, a strong verification team has become the keystone to hardware development efforts. Yet hiring engineering (or programming) college graduates into the verification field remains challenging. Through the early 1990s, the extent of most engineering graduates' exposure to verification came from a few days of simple testbench writing during their design class labs. In fact, most engineering graduates never hear about the verification career path until they come to work on a major hardware design effort.

To combat the gap in base verification knowledge in our new engineers, we developed a two-week class on the fundamentals of functional verification. The course content included an introduction to verification, and separate sections on simulation-based verification and formal verification. The class became a staple for the education of new verification engineers as well as experienced engineers looking to sharpen their skills.

It was not long before we took the base verification education package to our contacts at various universities. Soon, our material had seeded multiple undergraduate level classes on functional verification. We even found our class lab exercises—Calc1, Calc2, and Calc3—worked well in the university lab environment. We collaborated with the universities, providing guest lecturers on specific verification topics, bringing a feel for the industry challenges to the classrooms. As invigorating as it is to provide classroom lectures, the most rewarding outcome from the university partnerships is watching top engineering talent emerge with the skills and desire to pursue a career in functional verification.

The same classroom syllabus provided us with the original outline for *Comprehensive Functional Verification: The Complete Industry Cycle*. Much of that foundation remains in this book, including the Calc exercises. However, we have added considerably more depth, including extensive discussions on the development of a verification plan, the anatomy of a simulation environment, the inner workings of a simulation engine, the underlying practical usage of formal verification, system-level and pervasive verification, and management of a verification project. To provide an industry perspective on real issues and challenges, we augment verification theory with practical examples and real-world case studies. The result is a comprehensive text on functional verification.

THE VERIFICATION CYCLE

The unifying theme throughout *Comprehensive Function Verification: The Complete Industry Cycle* is the concept of the verification cycle. Functional verification is a structured, cyclical process, and this book follows this concept. The process is a cycle because results and learning from the current project feed the verification plans and implementation for the next project. This book follows the cycle from planning to implementation, through regression and the feedback stage, called escape analysis. Like the functional verification effort itself, we devote the most attention to the implementation stage of the cycle.

STRUCTURE OF THE BOOK

This book is organized in five parts. Part I contains an overview of functional verification, including background concepts, verification planning and strategy, and basic exercises. It also introduces the concept of the verification cycle as well as hierarchical verification, the practice of breaking down large designs into verifiable components. Parts II and III focus on the two main functional verification methods: simulation based verification and formal verification. Part IV concentrates on latter stages of the verification cycle, including regression and escape analysis, as well as advanced verification techniques. The book concludes with Part V, a collection of case studies, which highlight concepts from the verification cycle and processes.

BASIC KNOWLEDGE NEEDED FOR THIS BOOK

This book's discussions and exercises assume a basic understanding of computer engineering concepts. We use the two standard hardware design languages, Verilog and VHDL, throughout the book, so some familiarity with these languages is helpful. The reader should also have an understanding of logic design architecture and system structures. Finally, a background in programming is important, as major parts of the verification environment rely on programming constructs.

EXERCISES AND SUPPORTING MATERIALS

Comprehensive Functional Verification: The Complete Industry Cycle should be used in conjunction with hands-on functional verification exercises. To support this hands-on approach, we have collaborated with the major Electronic Design Automation (EDA) companies to create exercises based on RTL design implementations of a four-operation calculator: Calc1 and Calc2. Both Calc implementations come complete with functional errors for you to find using your verification environment. The Calc2-based exercise extends the first exercise based on Calc1, as Calc2 is a substantially more complex design. This progression follows the standard industry practice of increasing complexity with each new generation of the design. Of course, along with complexity comes additional verification challenges!

Links to the Calc1 and Calc2 vendor implementations and a link to a third, even more challenging Calc3 exercise, are available on-line. Access to these and other related materials, including exercise solutions and figures from the book, may be found at www.mkp.com/companions/0127518037.

ACKNOWLEDGEMENTS

We would like to acknowledge many people who helped create this book. First and foremost are the reviewers who gave us invaluable feedback, namely, Hardy J. Pottinger (University of Missouri—Rolla), Nazanin Mansouri (Syracuse University), Fadi A. Aloul (The American University of Sharjah, UAE), Vijaykrishnan Narayanan (The Pennsylvania State University) Baback Izadi (The State University of New York–New Paltz), Yuval Caspi (Yuval Caspi Consultants), Steven P. Levitan (University of Pittsburgh), Sean Smith (Denali Software, Inc.), and Scott Taylor (Intel).

We would also like to give additional special thanks to Professor Nazanin Mansouri and Yuval Caspi for their contributions of exercise material.

We created the Calc exercises featured in this book over a period of years. Multiple users have suggested both design and specification updates based on their experiences. However, in order to meet teaching deadlines for Calc3, Lance Hehenberger provided invaluable assistance in creating portions of the original Calc3 designs.

Finally, we want to thank our partners at Mentor Graphics, Synopsys, and Verisity Design for their work on creating implementations of the Calc1 and Calc2 examples. All were extremely supportive of this project from the start, and we are deeply grateful for their generous assistance.

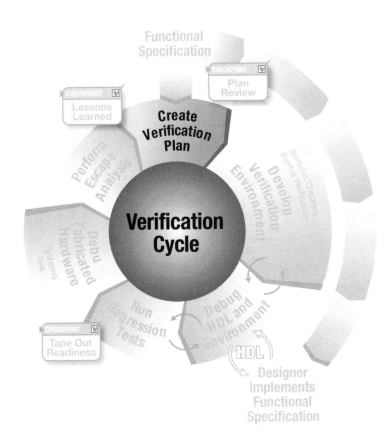

PART I

INTRODUCTION TO VERIFICATION

Functional verification plays a key role in meeting an aggressive chip design schedule and achieving cost and quality goals. Because functional verification is a critical part of all complex chip designs, to achieve these lofty targets the functional verification team must have a deep understanding of the chip design and a robust process. This process is the Verification Cycle. The process is cyclic, providing feedback from past projects, allowing the verification team to continually improve their process and environment.

Part One begins by describing the verification challenges and introducing the Verification Cycle. Chapters 2 and 3 describe basic verification strategies central to all techniques and the simulation-based components commonly used throughout the Verification Cycle. Chapter 4 details the verification plan—the first part of a project cycle—containing the strategy, methods, and requirements for the project.

CHAPTER 1

VERIFICATION IN THE CHIP DESIGN PROCESS

Functional verification has become a major challenge in the chip and system design arena. As engineers place more and more function in increasingly dense chips, the discipline required for successful chip and system verification has advanced. As a result, the verification engineer, little known 10 years ago, has become a treasured member of the chip design team.

This chapter introduces verification tasks, illustrated with basic examples; their challenges; and the defined process behind functional verification. These challenges require a controlled verification process, with continuous feedback for improvements. This chapter also introduces the two fundamental methods, simulation and formal verification, which the book describes in detail as the foundations of functional verification.

1.1 INTRODUCTION TO FUNCTIONAL VERIFICATION

Silicon chip technology powers many of today's innovations and newest products. Rapid technology advancement fuels ever-increasing chip complexity, which in turn enables the latest round of amazing products. These chips touch many aspects of our everyday life, from the pocket-sized combination cell phone, pager, and digital camera to the high-end server that searches an online bookseller's database, verifies credit card funds, and sends the order to the warehouse for immediate delivery. Expectations for these chips grow at an equal rate, despite the additional complexity. For example, consumers do not expect the chips that monitor safety processes in our cars to fail during the normal life of the vehicle. Nor is it acceptable to be denied access to our on-line brokerage accounts because the server is down. Thus, it has become a major engineering feat to design these silicon chips correctly.

An enormous amount of engineering goes into each of these chips, whether it is a microprocessor, memory device, or entire system on a chip (*SoC*). All types of chips have a set of challenges that the engineers must solve for the final product to be successful in the marketplace.

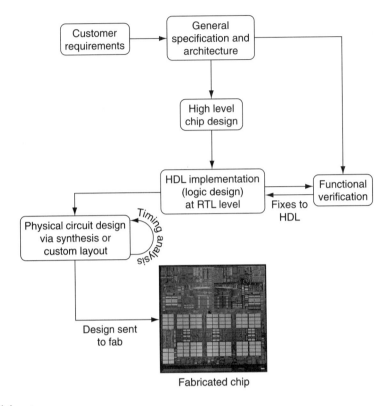

■ **FIGURE 1.1**

The chip design process. All silicon design starts with the customer's requirements, which drive the general specification and architecture. The chip components then take shapae during the high-level design stage, followed by the register transfer level (RTL) implementation in a hardware description language (HDL; usually Verilog or VHDL). Circuit design and timing analysis are based on the HDL, whereas functional verification explores the state space of the logic design to compare the implementation against the specification and design intent.

Figure 1.1 shows a chip's design flow, which starts with the customer's requirements. Those requirements include (but are not limited to) function, chip size, chip power consumption, and processing speed. Requirements are compiled and prioritized during the concept and high-level design phase, in which designers architect the chip's main internal components and goals. As the chip design process progresses, engineers face challenges to balance goals that often conflict: higher chip performance may require faster cycle times, but that will raise power consumption; faster cycle times may require adding more stages in the logic, but that increases chip complexity and area.

Throughout the chip design process, *design automation* (DA) tools accurately predict chip area, timing, and power aid the engineers. After an engineer creates logic, written in a *hardware description language* (HDL), DA tools can synthesize that logic into appropriate gates that correspond to the original design. Verilog and VHDL are the two most common HDLs. But two questions remain: (1) what if the HDL did not express the correct function in the first place, and (2) what if the designer missed a critical corner condition? Detecting incorrect function has become one of the trickiest challenges in the entire chip design process. This is the challenge of functional verification.

Functional verification ensures that the design performs the tasks as intended by the overall system architecture. It differs from circuit level validation in multiple ways. First, verification engineers work predominantly on the *register transfer level* (RTL) of the design rather than on the gate level. RTL is a more abstract way to specify the logic design than are the low-level ANDs and ORs of the gate level. RTL languages (HDLs) allow the designer to specify the behavior by using higher-level constructs such as Boolean equations and IF-THEN-ELSE structures. Second, although the main challenge for the circuit designers is to fit the gates into the available chip area and ensure that timing goals are met, it is the verification engineer's role to ensure that the design is functionally correct in the first place.

To illustrate the role of functional verification, consider the design of a simple traffic light controller. After a few minor accidents at the corner of Elm and Main streets in Eagleton, the town council commissions the installation of a traffic light. A careful study of the traffic survey leads the council to specify that the light should stay green for 1 minute in each direction when the intersection is busy. Workers are to install sensors to detect traffic on both streets.

The town council grants the contract for design and installation of the light to a local company, Eagleton Signal Controllers and Parking Engineering Solutions (ESCAPES). The ESCAPES SoC team quickly creates the algorithm for the traffic light controller, as shown in Figure 1.2.

The next step in the design process is to write the HDL. The ESCAPES team uses VHDL to code the algorithm as defined (Figure 1.3).

The algorithm and VHDL match, but they contain a flaw. Cars that approach the intersection on Main Street trigger the "Main Street Traffic?" sensor, and cars that approach on Elm Street trigger the "Elm Street Traffic?" sensor. The design team maps an exact translation of this algorithm to a circuit layout. However, the Eagleton council intended the traffic light to have a concept of fairness for the cars approaching the intersection from any direction; that is, the traffic light must allow all cars to proceed through the intersection within a realistic timeframe. In this flawed design, continued traffic on Main Street would indefinitely lock out the Elm Street traffic, leading, of course, to a nightmare on Elm Street. It is the job of the verification engineer to uncover these design flaws, ensuring that the final product acts as intended.

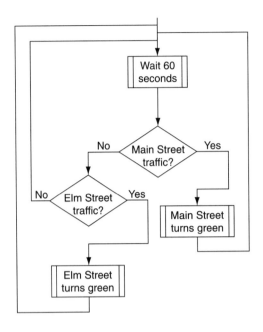

■ **FIGURE 1.2**

Algorithm for a traffic controller as written by the Eagleton Signal Controllers and Parking Engineering Solutions (ESCAPES) system-on-a-chip (SoC) team.

Despite the flawed HDL, the design team can translate the VHDL to a circuit design. Figure 1.4 shows the circuit design for the traffic light and accurately represents the original VHDL. The circuit design meets the timing, power, and chip area targets; however, without appropriate verification, the algorithm flaw would go undetected until testing at the intersection.

1.2 THE VERIFICATION CHALLENGE

Chip designs can easily consist of hundreds of thousands of lines of HDL. A verification engineer's job is to seek out problems in the HDL implementation, flagging flaws or *bugs* when the HDL does not act according to specification. A verification engineer exposes these bugs by running complex simulations on the design. The verification engineer faces two major challenges: dealing with enormous state space size and detecting incorrect behavior.

```
library ieee;
use ieee.std_logic_1164.all;

entity traffic is
 port(
  clk          :in std_ulogic; --Clock
  reset        :in std_ulogic; --Async Reset
  timer_pulse      :in std_ulogic; --The timer pulse, '1' indicates timer expiration
  Main_Street      :in std_ulogic; --Indicates when traffic is present on Main St.
  Elm_Street       :in std_ulogic; --Indicates when traffic is present on Elm St.
  Light_Direction   :out std_ulogic_vector(1 downto 0) --"01" Indicates that Main St. should be green
                          --"10" Indicates that Elm St. should be green
  );
end traffic;

architecture rtl of traffic is

 signal current_state_din, current_state_dout : std_ulogic_vector(1 downto 0);

begin --rtl

 --purpose: Determines when the light should change
 --type  : combinational
 --inputs : timer_pulse, Main_Street, Elm_Street, current_state_dout
 --outputs: current_state_din
 dataflow_proc: process(timer_pulse, Main_Street, Elm_Street, current_state_dout)
 begin --process change_light
  current_state_din <= current_state_dout;
  --When the timer expires, evaluate the traffic situation
  if timer_pulse = '1' then
   if Main_Street = '1' then
    current_state_din <= "01";
   elsif Elm_Street = '1' then
    current_state_din <= "10";
   end if;
  end if;
 end process dataflow_proc;

 Light_Direction <= current_state_dout;

 --purpose: creates the registers for current state
 --type  :sequential
 --inputs : clk, reset, current_state_din
 --outputs: current_state_dout
 reg_proc: process(clk, reset)
 begin --process register
  if reset = '0' then        --asynchronous reset (active low)
   current_state_dout <= "01";
  elsif clk'event and clk = '1' then -- rising clock edge
   current_state_dout <= current_state_din;
  end if;
 end process reg_proc;

end rtl;
```

■ **FIGURE 1.3**

VHDL for the traffic light algorithm.

1.2.1 The Challenge of State Space Explosion

The scale of the state space is the first verification challenge. Typically, HDL contains thousands of latches, large arrays (RAM), and combinatorial logic, all of which control the behavior of the chip. The chip inputs manipulate the internal logic, causing it to act on the applied stimulus.

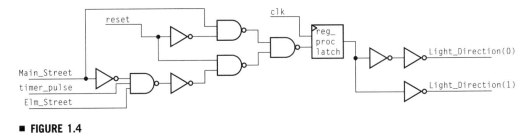

■ **FIGURE 1.4**

Circuit design of the flawed traffic signal showing the logic gates translated from the VHDL in Figure 1.3.

These inputs transform the current state of the chip, defined by the stored values in the latches and arrays, into the next and future states of the chip. At a given point in time, a chip can be in any one of an enormous number of possible current states.[1] Furthermore, the next state of the chip, determined by the current state and the current inputs, can be any of the possible states. To verify exhaustively that a chip is functionally correct, the verification engineer would have the daunting task of checking that each possible current state and each possible input combination yields the correct next state.

In the case of the traffic light mentioned above, there are just 2 bits of internal latches, yielding 4 possible current states, and 5 input pins, yielding 32 possible input combinations. Exhaustive verification of the entire state space of this simple example would yield just 128 combinations (32 input scenarios × 4 current states).

However, even simple computer designs may have huge state space problems that make the task of checking the combinations of current state and next state impossible. Consider the video portion of a DVD player with six possible inputs: "nothing pressed" (remain in current state), "play," "pause," "stop," "fast forward," and "reverse." Internally, the DVD player uses five states: "stopped," "playing at normal speed," "paused," "forward at 2× speed,", and "reverse at 2× speed." Figure 1.5 shows the effect of the inputs on these five states.

Pressing a button on the DVD remote (corresponding to the inputs) causes the video to superimpose the name of the button in the top left corner of the video output. Therefore, one other video state must be considered: the current state of the screen (video output). The screen is 1024 pixels wide by 768 pixels high and has "true color" (32 bits per pixel), for a total of $(2^{32})^{(1024 \times 768)}$ possible discrete states. To calculate the combina-

---

[1] The number of possible states is 2^n, where n is the total number of bits of latches and arrays.

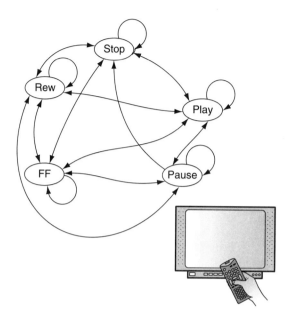

■ **FIGURE 1.5**

The DVD state machine transitions. The ellipses represent the five states; the arrows show the effect of pressing particular buttons on the remote control.

tions of current-screen states to next-screen states, square the number of screen states: $[(2^{32})^{(1024 \times 768)}]^2$. However, because each pixel has no effect on any other pixel, it is only necessary to verify that each pixel can display all 2^{32} possible colors, limiting the state space and keeping calculations in the realm of workstation computability.

Therefore, the bounded number of possible current states of the DVD video design is as follows:

number of pixels × number of possible pixel colors × number of internal state machines, or
$$(1024 \times 768) \times 2^{32} \times 5 = 16,888,498,602,639,360$$

However, to verify exhaustively that the chip is correct, all transitions from current state to next state must be considered. The number of possible next states of the DVD video design is based on

number of pixels × number of possible pixel colors × number of possible inputs, or
$$(1024 \times 768) \times 2^{32} \times 6 = 20,266,198,323,167,232$$

Therefore, to exhaustively verify the chip, the correctness of all transitions from all possible current states to all possible next states must be checked, or

$$16,888,498,602,639,360 \times 20,266,198,323,167,232 = 3.4 \times 10^{32}$$

Even with a simulation engine that could verify 1,000,000 transitions every second, this task would still take more than 10,853,172,947,159,498,300 years. Want to hang around?

In this same example, the DVD video chip illustrates the extreme of state space explosion. The introduction of array space and a number of internal states produces too many possible combinations to verify exhaustively.

To combat state space explosion, verification engineers break the problem down into smaller pieces. A typical chip may have 100,000 latches, imbedded arrays, and hundreds of input pins. Rather than verify the entire chip at once, the verification team will carve out subcomponents of the design and verify these pieces separately. Once the smaller, more manageable pieces are verified, the team stitches the chip subcomponents back together and ensures that they work.

Furthermore, many of the possible states of the chip and many of the possible input combinations are defined as *illegal* based on design specifications. An illegal state is a state that the design should never enter. The traffic light example mentioned above has just 64 legal combinations, as two of the internal states are unused and are therefore invalid. Illegal states cut down the size of the current states that must be evaluated by the verification engineer.[2]

1.2.2   The Challenge of Detecting Incorrect Behavior

The second verification challenge is detecting when the design violates the expected behavior or specification. With all of the possible transitions from one state to the next, the verification engineer must be able to identify whether or not the design acted correctly based on the current state and input.

Rather than focusing on each of the possible states of the hardware, verification engineers validate the logic at a higher level of abstraction: inputs are grouped into valid command and data sets, and the verification engineer concentrates on the behavior of the design based on the functional input stimulus.

---

[2] Verification engineers cannot ignore illegal states in certain chip designs, specifically those chips that must be tolerant of errors. Illegal states can occur because of many factors, including erroneous input, alpha particles flipping a latch, or circuit failures. The verification task may require ensuring that the hardware can recover from these unexpected conditions.

TABLE 1.1 ■ Examples of functional stimulus and a possible verification method: Type of logic→ stimulus → method of validating results

Type of design	Functional-based stimulus	Example of result validation	Special challenges
Microprocessor	Instruction stream loaded into memory	Do the resulting registers have the correct values after each instruction?	Have all possible combinations of instruction sequences been verified?
IO device	Header data followed by destination address, data, and checkbits	Does the proper data move to the correct outbound port?	Can the IO device handle hundreds of possible traffic generation sources?
Memory controller in a multiprocessor server	Requests for data and store commands from multiple processors to a large array space	Is the correct data retrieved and stored?	Is systemwide coherency maintained?
Digital video converter	Streaming-encoded video	Does the video appear correctly on a monitor?	How do we know if a pixel is wrong?

In the traffic signal example, a verification engineer will expect certain behavior from the design. Stimulus is applied to the design by manipulation of the five input signals, and the output, Light_direction, is monitored. When Light_direction is "01" (Main Street traffic is flowing) and Elm Street traffic is detected, the verification engineer expects that the light will change direction when the timer_pulse rises. This may or may not flag the flaw in the design, depending on whether or not Main Street traffic is still detected. Furthermore, the verification engineer can look inside the design and place checks on internal components. In our example, the verification engineer should assert that the current_state_dout latch must never enter a state of "00" or "11."

Table 1.1 describes four real-life examples of functional verification, as well as the particular nuances and special challenges associated with verifying each logic type. Each example requires a method for activating the design (stimulus) and a method for checking that the design acted correctly (result validation). The first example, a microprocessor, may have hundreds of instructions that can operate on the values in the *general-purpose registers* (GPRs). When each instruction completes, the verification engineer can check that the appropriate target register contains the correct value. It is equally important to check that the logic did not update another register erroneously.

In simplest terms, then, the verification challenge comes down to two fundamentals:

1. **Drive the state transitions and input scenarios**

2. **Flag any incorrect behavior exhibited by the design**

Verification engineers attack the challenge by using two fundamental methods: (1) *simulation-based verification* and (2) *formal verification*, or verifying the design adheres to protocols by using formal proof engines.

In simulation-based verification, the verification engineer applies stimulus to a software model of the design. The *sim model* runs in conjunction with a simulation engine, which accurately reflects the behavior of the design. As inputs are applied, the simulation engine evaluates the design's reaction to the specific inputs on the current state, and updates the internal state of the design accordingly. The simulation engine is often run on a desk-side workstation (a general purpose computer), and the verification engineer uses the user interface to query the behavior of the model to check for results and to flag incorrect behavior.

Formal verification, a newer technique, is a great complement to simulation. Rather than verifying possible input sequences and internal-state machine values individually or in sequence, formal verification proves that a protocol, assertion, or design rule holds true for all possible cases in the design. The major drawback of formal verification is that it can only verify a limited size design. Because all possible values in a design are checked, formal verification engines can consume enormous amounts of computer resources, even on small designs. For this reason, formal verification most often is applied to portions of the entire design rather than the whole so the engine can digest the design and return results in a reasonable timeframe.

This book covers the strategies used to verify complex hardware designs. It describes techniques to apply stimuli and identify errors while running simulation, as well as methods to perform formal verification. The verification engineer must be a sleuth, keeping an open mind about the possible problems that may occur in the design. A top-notch verification engineer is invaluable to the design team, combining experience on how to uncover design flaws with the ability to develop tests and checks that guarantee the success of the fabricated chip.

1.3 MISSION AND GOALS OF VERIFICATION

Design teams manage the process of developing computer hardware by balancing *the triple constraints*:

- **Schedule:** Computer product success depends heavily on hitting the marketplace at the right time. Delays in getting products to market can be deadly for a company, as, more than in any other industry, a disproportionate amount of revenue goes to the product that gets to market first.

- **Cost:** At the same time, a company must endeavor to maximize the profit created by a digital hardware product. A key profit lever is to keep the manufacturing and development expense for a product at a minimum.

   An expanded look at the verification cycle, as pictured in Figure 1.6, shows that after silicon fabrication, engineers perform testing on the entire system using fabricated hardware running end-user applications. Frequently, bugs missed by verification are discovered by engineers during this *systems testing*, causing design updates and re-fabrication of the hardware. These changes costs money and time, as fabrication facilities charge additional money for re-doing a chip, and some chips, depending on the technology used, may take up to 2 months to process. After a completed systems test, the company manufactures the product and ships it to customers. Customers provide the company with feedback about the product, which, in turn, feeds the requirements for follow-up products. Examples of customer feedback include requests for new features or higher quality.

- **Quality:** Customers expect that delivered products will meet quality standards. Component failures invoke warranty costs, which affect the company's bottom-line. Furthermore, if the marketplace perceives that a product is of poor quality, it can have a devastating effect on the company.

Finding the correct balance of schedule, cost, and quality will depend on the product. However, the balancing act is tricky, as optimizing for two of the constraints will often hurt the third. For example, maximizing quality while minimizing schedule often inflates product cost.

Figure 1.7 shows how the costs of undetected bugs grow over time. If a bug is uncovered early during verification, it costs little to fix: the designer reworks the HDL and the verification team shows that the update fixed the original problem. A bug found in a systems test, however, may cost hundreds of thousands of dollars: hardware must be refabricated and there is additional time-to-market. Finally, and most costly, a customer discovering a bug not only invokes warranty replacement or upgrades but may tarnish the image of the company or brand of products—a problem from which the company may never recover.

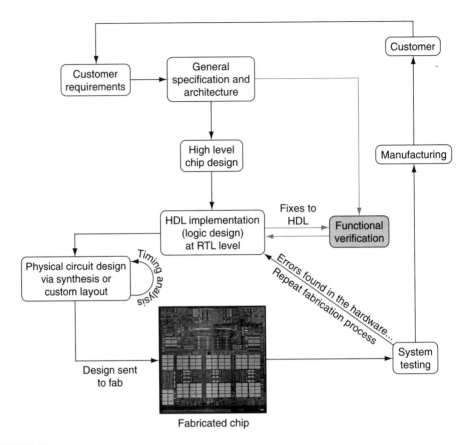

▪ **FIGURE 1.6**

An expanded look at the design process includes the systems testing on the real hardware, manufacturing, and delivery to the customer. A well-verified chip avoids the re-fabrication step and proceeds right to manufacturing. Avoiding the re-fabrication loop saves both time and product cost.

Verification is the single biggest lever that affects all three of the triple constraints. A chip can be fabricated sooner rather than later if the verification team is able to remove errors quickly and efficiently. Furthermore, costs of re-fabricating a chip multiple times ("re-spins") can drive development expenses to an unacceptable level and negatively affect the product schedule. A solid verification effort reduces the number of re-spins and removes latent problems, which, if not discovered by verification and a systems test, can show up in customer environments and cause quality problems.

Because verification has such a strong effect on the triple constraints, it is prudent to track verification productivity. The design team measures verification productivity by two factors: schedule time and quality of bugs found.

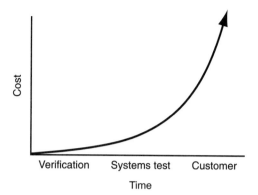

■ **FIGURE 1.7**

The cost of undetected problems grows over time. There is little cost in finding and fixing a problem in verification, but there is a huge cost if the customer finds the problem.

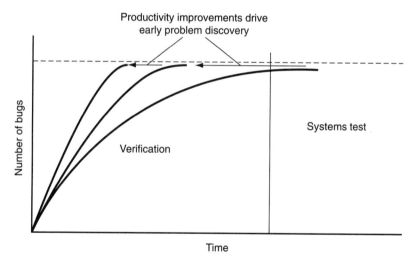

■ **FIGURE 1.8**

Increasing verification productivity reduces schedule and costs. The figure shows three possible "bug curves." The longest one stretches into the systems test, where engineers find the last bugs on the hardware. Improvements in verification, depicted by the two other curves, will drive the bug discovery earlier, reducing schedule and costs.

Project teams track productivity with respect to schedule time by measuring the steepness of the "bug curve," as shown in Figure 1.8. An efficient verification team with a robust process will remove bugs at a faster pace than will a less effective team and process. Therefore, it is a good practice to maintain a history of bug curve rates from each project to track improvements in verification productivity.

The second measure of verification productivity, quality of bugs found, is a more qualitative evaluation than is measuring bug curve rates. The verification team measures the quality of a bug by analyzing the scenario and test case that uncovered the design flaw: the more difficult, esoteric, or complex the scenario, the higher the quality of bug. A productive verification team should find any "easy" or low-quality bugs early in the verification schedule. Throughout the process, the average complexity of the design flaws that the verification team uncovers should grow. Simple bugs found late in the verification cycle signal that the verification environment and test plans need to be analyzed.

1.3.1 Verification Engineer "Musts"

A strong verification team is an invaluable asset to a company that develops hardware. The mission of the verification team is to remove all of the functional design problems as quickly as possible. To do this, verification engineers must gain specific skills. Successful verification engineers must understand the design, must be able to work closely and cordially with designers, must understand the strengths and weaknesses of the variety of verification tools at their disposal, and must be able to use these tools efficiently to uncover the bugs in the design.

Verification requires detailed knowledge of the design that is being verified (the *design under verification*, or *DUV*). Understanding of the design comes at two levels: the specification level and the implementation level.

The specification dictates the overall function of the design. It includes the *architecture*, the inputs and outputs, and the performance requirements. The architecture is the main specification of the device: for a microprocessor, this is the instruction set and definitions; for an I/O device, this is the protocols. The architecture is well documented and often globally published. The inputs and outputs of the DUV define the chip or system pins and include the required timings and protocols. The performance requirements of the DUV include the desired throughput of the design, processing speed, and bandwidth, as well as associative cache size and cache.

The implementation of the design deals with the internal constructs used to perform the specification. This is known as the *microarchitecture* of the design. Implementation components include the following:

- Queues and buffers that hold data and commands
- Internal state machines
- Pipelines
- Data and control flows

Designers or system-level architects (in the company or in industry) write the specifications of the design, documents that are available for the verification engineer to study and are the arbiter when design questions arise. Less formal documentation exists for implementation details, and this information must come from the designers. If necessary, verification engineers must extract the implementation details by interviewing the designers. These implementation details are needed so appropriate verification tests that stress the many structures within the design can be created.

Throughout a project, the verification engineer must have a strong relationship with the designer team. This does take some finesse, as it is the verification engineer's role to find a designer's mistakes and oversights.

Consider the words used when reporting a bug back to the designer. A verification engineer might state, "I found another bug in your design, and I need a fix right away." Depending on the verification engineer's tone, this could be an insult to the designer. It is also important not to jump to conclusions about the design. Very often, "alleged" design bugs are not a design deficiency but are problems in the test-case stimuli or checking components. A more tactful approach would be to say, "I think I've uncovered an interesting condition in the design. Can you take a look at this?"

With the wealth of techniques available for verification, it is important for a verification engineer to understand the strengths and weaknesses of each method. Some methods may be very effective on small portions of the design but not on large chips (e.g., formal verification). Other methods might require long lead times to create the code necessary for the environment. A verification engineer must also understand the tools that assist in gauging the state space covered by the testing. Each of these tools must be evaluated for

- Effectiveness of approach for this design implementation
- Effect of the approach on simulation throughput
- Amount of time required to create the verification environment

Finally, when a verification approach is selected, the verification engineer must be able to create the verification environment, ensuring that the required functional test scenarios occur and that the checking is complete. This requires proficiency in multiple verification techniques, all of which rely on the verification engineer's knack for sniffing out bugs in the design.

1.4 COST OF VERIFICATION

Functional verification is essential to the hardware design process. The benefits of the verification effort appear throughout the design process, but the team measures its success by results in system testing. So how does the development team gauge just how many resources to put into verification? Too few resources and the hardware will need multiple passes through the fabrication process, which costs orders of magnitude more dollars in time-to-market and development expenses than would allocation of enough verification resources. At the same time, a design team does not want to over-invest in any area, including verification, as overinvestment would indicate costly redundancy. Therefore, the development team must strike the right balance.

Verification resource costs fall into three areas: engineering costs, DA tools, and time. A successful verification effort requires appropriate investment in all three areas.

1.4.1 Engineering Costs and the Need for an Independent Verification Team

Verification engineering cost is a measure of the number of people performing verification. Some design teams employ separate verification engineers, whereas other teams use their logic designers to perform verification after writing their HDL. However, there are clear advantages to using an independent verification team and not having the design team play a dual role. Some of these advantages are listed here.

Verification is a separate vocation that requires different skills than does logic design. The ability to create the scenarios and checkers needed to find bugs is detective work unlike the skills needed to create HDL that meets logical and physical requirements. The multiple disciplines of verification are a full-time job to master—and once mastered, the verification engineer's worth to the design team remains in the verification realm.

A second reason for an independent verification team is these verification engineers will not be biased by the thought process that goes into the design. There is a certain catch-22 in verifying one's own logic design. If a designer overlooked a case while creating the logic, the same designer should not be expected to write a test scenario for that missed case.

Finally, when creating logic, a designer makes assumptions about the design. It is the verification engineer's job to judge separately the verification environment requirements without the bias of the designer's assumptions. Interface protocol specifications should come from an independent designer or from master documentation, rather than from the designer whose logic is under test.

However, for many reasons, the design team is crucial to the verification effort. First, designers are the initial line of defense against bugs. Designers should perform a suite of verification tests that ensures a level of quality before delivering HDL to the verification team. No designer wants to "throw HDL over the wall" to the verification team, only to have it "thrown back" because of typographical errors, simple bugs, or an HDL compile failure.

Designers also have keen insight into tricky areas of the logic. As the designer writes the HDL, there are complex parts that cause him or her to pause and think through multiple scenarios and different implementation choices. The designer should highlight these areas of the design to the verification team as potential sources of bugs. Methods of identifying these areas include assertions statements, e-mails to the verification team, and suggestions for functional coverage metrics.

A final key element for designers to assist in the verification effort is through accurate and timely documentation. Documentation is an essential part of the design job. Important documents for the verification engineer include interface specifications and details on the internals of the design such as queue depth, pipeline length, array sizes, and state machine transitions. This information guides the verification team in creating complete test plans and executing their work.

Design management teams often calculate the engineering cost of verification by the ratio of logic designers to verification engineers. This ratio can vary in industry from about $1:1$ to $1:4$ (four verification engineers for every designer). Accounting for the difference in these ratios is tricky. Investment in sophisticated DA tools can differ across design teams; where there is less investment, more verification engineers are needed. In addition, active participation in verification by the design team as "the first line of defense" can drive down the number of required verification engineers. Other factors such as business pressure will alter the equation. For example, a small company in a highly competitive market such as network processors must get their new products correct on the first fabrication pass, and hit the market with a new product every 6 months. A failure in verification can put this small company out of business. For this company, it is better to hire additional verification engineers than risk missing a bug.

1.4.2   DA Tools

This book will cover multiple methodologies for functional verification. Behind each of these methods is DA software that assists the verification engineer in finding bugs.

The basic building blocks of DA tools for verification are simulation engines and formal verification engines. Simulation engines allow the verification engineer to drive stimulus into a software model of the HDL. The engine, which compiles the HDL, will "simulate" the effects of stimulus on the HDL over time. The simulation engine calculates the values of internal latches, wires, and arrays and presents these values to the user. Formal verification engines are conceptually different from simulation engines. Whereas simulation engines allow the user to create discrete scenarios and check multiple properties concurrently within the logic, formal verification engines check a single property against all possible input scenarios. A formal verification engine uses mathematical proofs to verify the single property against all inputs. The two methods are complimentary, and verification engineers must be trained to use each.

Other DA tools build on the two basic engines. Software includes

- ▪ "Coverage" tools that assist in evaluating the effectiveness of the scenarios driven into the logic during simulation

- ▪ Trace viewers that show graphical (waveform) representations of the scenarios and the values of the latches, arrays, and wires in the HDL

- ▪ High-level verification languages that assist the verification engineer in writing complex simulation environments

- ▪ Test case generation software that can create multiple simulation test cases based on abstract templates

- ▪ Simulation farm control software that allows simulation jobs to be run across multiple workstations simultaneously and collects the test scenario results

- ▪ Assertion-based tools that assist in debug, allowing a bug to be flagged at the moment it occurs and enabling the engineer to know exactly where the HDL failed

Electronic DA (EDA) vendors supply these tools to the industry. DA software costs generally are based on licensing fees. A verification team must procure enough software licenses to run the peak number of verification jobs. If, for example, a company allocates 100 workstations for running simulation cycles, 100 simulation engine licenses are required; otherwise, workstations will be idle.

1.4.3   Time

The amount of time spent on verification is key in the overall cost equation. Design teams must balance engineering costs and DA software licensing with schedule time. If a design team has an aggressive schedule (based on fabrication passes, experience, and industry benchmarks), then more verification skills and software will be required to meet the goals. If the verification team is not allocated enough resources for the allotted schedule, either the schedule will slip or the results seen in the fabricated hardware will be poor. Time IS money in the equation.

All of these factors lead to a key management requirement for successful verification: **commitment**. Engineering management must invest in the appropriate verification skills (including experienced leaders) and software tools to meet goals. The complexity of the hardware designs requires nurturing of the verification teams as well as the design team. Long-term careers in verification must be encouraged. The best hardware teams have separate and clear career paths for verification engineers to reach high technical ranks within the company.

1.5 AREAS OF VERIFICATION BEYOND THE SCOPE OF THIS BOOK

There are multiple verification disciplines within hardware design, including functional verification, timing verification, and test verification. This book focuses on functional verification and does not cover the other areas.

However, test verification is worth a comparison to functional verification, as the two are sometimes grouped together despite different requirements and personnel skills. Test verification focuses on the ability to detect manufacturing defects quickly as chips come off the manufacturing line. Current practices in test verification include driving random patterns within the chip and collecting the output patterns. Test engineers choose patterns to stimulate a maximum number of circuits inside of the chip. Test tools assist in predicting the output patterns based on the inputs. These patterns are run on the manufactured chips, allowing defective ones to be discarded.

Also included in the field of test verification is built-in self test (BIST). Test engineers create BIST engines for both arrays (ABIST) and logic (LBIST). The goals behind both types of BIST are the same. After manufacturing, process engineers activate the BIST engines inside the chip. The engine drives patterns through the logic or arrays, and compares the resulting patterns against the predicted pattern. If the patterns do not match, the manufacturing process may need to be tuned in order for the chips to be fabricated correctly.

Even though test verification and functional verification are often grouped together, the two disciplines have little in common. A chip that successfully runs through test verification may still add 1 + 1 and get three if the chip had poor functional verification. Test verification only confirms (to a high probability) that the manufactured chip is equivalent to the circuit design specified to the manufacturing process. It makes no statement about the logical functionality of the chip itself.

Furthermore, the theory behind functional verification and test verification are different. Test verification aims to create patterns that flag bad circuits; therefore, patterns that exercise a broad number of circuits in a short interval are optimal. However, functional verification bugs are much more insidious, in that the circuits are defect-free but the combination of specific circuits—which together define a function in the design—may give a wrong result in specific scenarios across a long interval.

On a different front, this book will briefly detail some specific DA tools but will not compare strengths and weaknesses of competing DA companies' offerings. The book demonstrates some of these tools as possible choices for specific verification challenges.

1.6 THE VERIFICATION CYCLE: A STRUCTURED PROCESS

Structure is necessary in any complex field. In verification, structure comes from a well-defined process. The verification process identifies the required steps toward developing a bug-free chip release. Because the verification team enhances their environment based on previous experiences, the process is called the verification cycle.

Generally, verification teams stay together across multiple products. The verification cycle shadows the product cycle, allowing verification engineers to incorporate enhancements into the methodology continuously. Verification engineers gain experience through multiple passes of this cycle.

Figure 1.9 shows the stages of the verification cycle. The cycle proceeds in a clockwise direction, starting from the functional specification, a key delivery to both the design and verification teams. As the team starts development of the verification environment, they reach the first checkpoint. After completing the verification plan based on the specifications, the entire engineering team reviews the plan to look for enhancements.

Two stages in the process provide feedback to previous stages. These stages are the debug and regression stages in which the verification team detects problems either in the HDL or in their environment code. As regression winds down, the team prepares the product for fabrication. This is the second checkpoint in the cycle, when the design and verification teams review all of the verification work against the tape-out criteria.

The cycle proceeds through the manufacturing and systems test. Once the team receives fabricated hardware, they evaluate the quality of their verification effort through escape analysis, which provides feedback into the process to plug holes in the verification environment. The final checkpoint in the cycle, lessons learned, uses escape analysis and the entire verification cycle experience to compile a list of items to improve on as they start the cycle again.

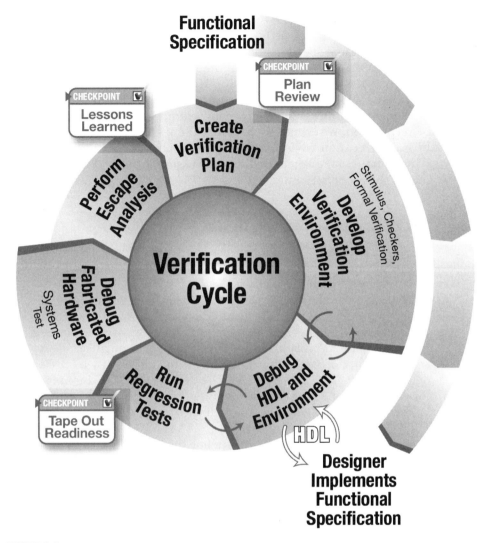

■ **FIGURE 1.9**

Each spin of the verification cycle starts with the functional specification. This process gives a structure to the verification tasks and provides feedback for continuous improvements. Tasks around the inner circle are the stages of the verification cycle. Strategic checkpoints assure process compliance.

1.6.1 Functional Specification

The functional specification describes the desired product. It contains the specification of the interfaces with which it communicates, the function that it must perform, and the conditions that affect the design. In the case of a processor, the functional specification describes the interfaces to memory and IO, the architecture it must obey, and details of the surrounding system. The system architect determines the functional specification.

The functional specification is the foundation of the verification cycle. While the designers implement the functional specification in HDL (shown to the outside of the Debug HDL and Environment stage), verification engineers incorporate the functional specification into the verification environment. This may seem redundant, but it is the foundation of verification. A second implementation of the functional specification by the verification environment forms the cross-check in the cycle. This redundancy ensures that the designer's assumptions and implementation match the architect's intent.

1.6.2 Create Verification Plan

A verification plan is crucial because it presents a detailed description of the verification effort. It answers the questions "what am I verifying?" and "how am I going to verify it?"

The verification leaders write the verification plan, using the logic designers and system architects as consultants during the process.

Unless the design is simple, a hierarchical approach to verification is required. This approach allows the verification engineer to work on smaller components before building up to the system level (for more detail, see Chapter 2, Section 2.1). The verification plan contains sections for each component at each level of the hierarchy.

Verification plans include many of the following elements:

- Specific tests and methods—define the type of environment that the verification engineers will create (see Chapters 3–4, 7–12).

- Required tools—list the software necessary to support the described environment. This list may drive requirements on the software procurement team or on internal software development teams (Chapters 5, 6).

- Completion criteria—define the measurements that indicate that verification is complete (Chapter 13).

- Resources (people, hardware, and software) required and schedule details—tie plan to program management by estimating the cost of verification.

- Functions to be verified—list the functions that will be verified at this level of verification.

- Functions not covered—describe any functions that must be verified at a different level of the hierarchy. The verification of these functions will be specified in a different section of the verification plan.

Chapter 4 contains an in-depth look at the components of a quality verification plan.

The team reviews the final verification plans with the architects and designers. This is the first checkpoint in the cycle. The designers and architects compare the verification plans with the design specification and internal structures, suggesting enhancements and modifications to the verification environment plans.

1.6.3 Develop Environment

Once the verification plan is in place, construction of the verification environment begins. Verification engineers spend the majority of their time on this stage of the cycle. As such, much of this book describes methods for developing verification environments. Major components in the verification environment are stimuli and checking for simulation-based environments, as well as rules generation for formal verification environments.

The verification environment is the set of software code and tools that enable the verification engineer to identify flaws in the design. The software code tends to be specific to the design, whereas the tools are more generic and are used across multiple verification projects.

There are many different types of environments, including deterministic, random based, formal based, and test case generators. Each of these environments has different mechanisms to create stimuli and check results against the DUV. In all cases, a reference model cross-checks the behavior against the design intent. The verification team creates the reference model to implement independently the design specification. A reference model makes a prediction of the test case results based on the test case stimulus. The verification team builds the knowledge of the function and design into the reference model. The reference model provides the checking components with the predicted data. The checking components compare the predicted data to the actual data from the DUV.

The environment is continually refined throughout the verification cycle. Refinements include fixes and additions to the software code.

1.6.4 Debug HDL and Environment

The next step of the verification cycle integrates the verification environment with the HDL. This is when verification engineers begin to debug the hardware by running tests. As these tests run, verification engineers find anomalies and examine them. Examination reveals the failure source, which will be either in the verification environment or in the HDL design. The anomaly occurs because the verification environment has predicted different behavior than has the HDL. This is the payoff of the redundant path in the cycle.

If the error is in the verification environment, the verification engineer updates the software to correct the predicted behavior. Otherwise, the HDL has a bug that the design team must correct. Once fixed, the verification engineer reruns the exact same test. This ensures that the update corrects the original anomaly and does not introduce new ones. The team applies this iterative approach until all tests pass.

Chapter 8 details the debug process.

1.6.5 Regression

Regression is the continuous running of the tests defined in the verification plan. This is a required step in the verification cycle for two main reasons. The first reason is that verification environments often have elements of randomization, which drive different input scenarios each time the team runs the test. The second reason is that the team must repeat all tests after fixes have been applied to the design.

The failure occurrence rate drops as the verification cycle reaches the regression stage. To uncover hard-to-find bugs, verification teams leverage large workstation pools, or "farms," to run an ever-increasing number of verification jobs. The randomization built into the environment enables new test scenarios on each of the jobs.

When the team finds a bug during regression, they use the same process as during HDL and environment debug. The bug is isolated and fixed, and then the verification team re-runs the exact same test.

With chip fabrication on the horizon, the verification team must reflect on the environment to ensure that they have applied all valid scenarios to the design and performed all pertinent checks. This is the tape-out readiness checkpoint.

Chapter 13 contains full details on the regression process.

1.6.6 Fabricate Hardware

The design team releases the hardware to the fabrication facility when they meet all fabrication criteria. Releasing a chip to the fabrication facility, or *fab*, is also known as the *tape-out*, a reference to the past when the design team stored the chip's physical design information onto magnetic tape and sent it to the fabrication facility. The chip design team uses a checklist, or *tape-out criteria*, to track all of the items, both physical and logical, that they must complete before sending the design to manufacturing. Verification is a major part of the checklist, being the independent judge of the logical capabilities of the chip. The verification team creates and maintains their portion of the tape-out criteria, initially basing it on the test plan. This tape-out criteria is the formalized requirements for the verification cycle.

With all the hard work that goes into preparing a design for manufacturing, this stage is a good time to celebrate a milestone in the process.

At this point, the failure occurrence rate in the regression stage has dropped to near zero, indicating that the verification environments have exhausted their bug-finding capability. However, environments that include randomization parameters continue in the regression stage after the design is sent to manufacturing. During the time between tape-out and receiving parts back from manufacturing (about 2 months' duration), continued regression using randomization parameters may uncover further logical bugs. In complex designs, random-based verification environments continually create logical states in the design or scenarios that were never encountered before tape-out. Occasionally, one of these new states yields a bug, making the continued regression worthwhile. Designers integrate fixes for bugs found after the initial tape-out into revised HDL code, which will also contain fixes for any problems found during the hardware debug of the systems test.

1.6.7 Debug Fabricated Hardware (Systems Test)

The design team receives the hardware once the chip fabrication completes and the manufacturing test of the chip has been applied (this validates that there are no physical defects that may affect the function). The hardware is then mounted onto test vehicles or into the planned systems for these chips. At this point, the hardware debug team (which often consists of designers and verification engineers) performs the hardware bring-up. During hardware bring-up, further anomalies may present themselves.

Again, the design and verification teams must investigate these anomalies. The overall verification goal is to avoid finding bugs on the real hardware, as it is very expensive. Debugging on the real hardware is much more difficult than in a verification environment, mainly because the real hardware does not provide the full tracing capabilities of the verification environment. If an anomaly is determined to be a functional bug, the design team must fix it. There may be multiple options for fixing the bug, which include using system microcode to avoid the failing condition. However, if the fix must be made in the hardware, re-fabrication is required.[3]

1.6.8 Escape Analysis

If bugs are uncovered during the hardware bring-up, then the verification team must perform escape analysis. This often overlooked but critical part of the verification cycle ensures that the verification team fully

---

[3] Often hardware fixes can be contained to the metal layers or to wires on a chip. If this is the case, then the re-fabrication process may not require rebuilding certain masks. This is a less expensive and shorter process than when a fix requires latches or arrays to be modified or added.

understands the bug and the reasons why it was not discovered in the verification environments. The verification team must reproduce the bug in a simulation environment, if possible, to confirm they understand the bug and to assess how the bug got through the verification stage and into the real hardware. The team cannot assert that the bug fix is correct without reproducing the original bug in verification.

Chapter 13 describes the analysis process on the bugs that "escape."

The escape analysis assessment feeds back to the beginning of the verification cycle, as the verification team learns from escapes. Future hardware benefits from the learning, as verification test plans and environments are continually improved. This is the lessons-learned checkpoint.

1.6.9 Common Verification Cycle Breakdowns

Breakdowns in the verification cycle result in time-consuming and costly re-spins of the chip. Too often, teams do not follow the entire verification cycle. A few of the more common verification errors made by design teams or their management are listed here. These errors lead to breakdowns and sub-optimal chip or system development efforts.

The first breakdown is when the verification engineer uses a functional description based on the design implementation rather than on the functional specification. When this occurs, the redundancy path breaks, leading to a verification effort that simply proves that the HDL design is equal to itself. The functional specification must come from a higher-level source than the HDL.

Underdeveloped verification plans can foul-up a design effort. The verification plan is the road map for the environment implementation. It is also the communication vehicle to other verification engineers and the design team. Skipping or skimping on the verification plan inevitably causes engineers to overlook functional testing on portions of the design. The plan review checkpoint protects against this failure.

Similarly, an underdeveloped or late-to-arrive specification will cause verification breakdowns. As with the problem of underdeveloped verification plans, the design team needs to create and document the specification prior to writing HDL. The specification provides both designers and verification engineers with valuable information needed for implementation.

Another common breakdown occurs if the verification team skips the escape analysis step of the cycle. There are lessons to be learned from the mistakes. Because most escapes occur on very difficult or esoteric problems, there is no shame in discussing the holes in the verification environments. However, one of the more common reasons that a verification team might skip escape analysis is that the team disbands and the members take on different jobs. Even in this case, the team should give the next set of verification engineers the benefit of escape analysis. We are destined to repeat our mistakes when we do not learn from them. This is the intent of the lessons-learned checkpoint

Too often, management does not employ a large enough verification team. Without the needed number of verification engineers, the team cannot complete a robust verification plan on the required schedule. This breakdown will cause morale problems and execution failure.

A final breakdown worth highlighting occurs when the project team sends the design to manufacturing based on the schedule rather than on tape-out criteria. Occasionally, the drive to maintain a schedule over-shadows quality. However, in the end, both schedule and quality suffer when the team does not meet the design tape-out criteria. The second checkpoint, tape-out readiness, brings rigor and a quantitative assessment needed to protect against this process breakdown.

1.7 SUMMARY

Functional verification is a necessary step in the development of today's complex digital designs. In the past, chips were simple enough that a good designer could review and debug a chip with relative success. At the same time, schedules were not so competitive, so that companies were not concerned about the chips needing a multitude of passes through the fabrication facility before the product shipped to customers. Now, chip complexity and product competitiveness have increased to the point that design teams require partners, the verification engineers, to find the multitude of bugs that lurk in their RTL designs.

Verification engineers must understand the specification and internal microarchitecture of the DUV. They couple this knowledge with pro-gramming skills, RTL comprehension, and a detective's ability to find the scenarios that uncover bugs. The entire design team relies on the verification engineers' success, as no other group can more positively influence the costs, schedule, and quality of a product.

Verification engineers face two major challenges in their work. The first is the creation of a comprehensive set of stimuli, a task made diffi-cult by the enormous state space of complex chip and system designs. The second challenge is to identify incorrect design behavior when encountered during verification of the DUV. Together, driving stimulus and checking for bugs are the pillars of functional verification.

The foundation under these two pillars is the well-defined verification cycle. Verification teams use the cycle to create a repeatable, closed-loop practice upon which they base their work. The cycle requires careful planning, communication, consistency checks, and feedback loops to ensure that the design is solid when released to the fabrication facility. The process includes creation of test plans, writing and running verifi-cation tests, debugging, and analysis of the holes in the verification environments. This book describes the details of the verification cycle and the methods verification engineers use to ensure quality design releases.

1.8 EXERCISES

1. What relevance do scenario creation and checking for incorrect behavior have on functional verification?

2. What prevents verification engineers from creating test benches for every possible scenario in a DUV?

3. Describe the role of functional verification within the chip design process.

4. How do the costs of verification compare to the savings? What impact would under-spending on verification have on the triple constraints?

5. From which stage (or stages) of the verification cycle are these activities?

   (a) Write code to drive and check the DUV
   (b) Understand the interesting scenarios and corner cases in the DUV
   (c) Contemplate what improvements need to be made to the verification environment based on hardware results
   (d) Contemplate what improvements need to be made to the verification environment as the bug rate drops
   (e) Find bugs by using a simulation engine
   (f) Find bugs by using an oscilloscope
   (g) Discuss design intent and specification with designer and architect
   (h) Discuss a miscompare between the HDL and the reference model with the designer
   (i) List the tools needed for verification
   (j) Create a reference model to check the design's behavior

6. Which of the following should verification engineers do, and which should they avoid?

   (a) Talk to designers about the function and understand the design
   (b) Rely on the DUV designer's description for input/output specification
   (c) When creating checkers and reference models, look at the HDL implement for hard-to-predict cases

(d) Try to think of situations the designer might have missed
(e) Focus on exotic scenarios and situations
(f) After receiving a bug fix, move on to the next job in the test plan
(g) Try to fill all queues during simulation
(h) Focus on multiple events at the same time
(i) Move on to the next product after the initial tape-out because the work is complete

CHAPTER 2

VERIFICATION FLOW

The verification team spends the majority of their time in two stages of the verification cycle: (1) develop verification environment and (2) debug hardware design language (HDL) and environment. These two stages are at the heart of verification work, and at their foundation are hierarchical verification and the strategies for driving and checking designs under verification (DUVs).

A basic practice with a complex problem is to break the large problem into smaller, more manageable challenges. Verification accomplishes this by using the existing hierarchical structure of the design. Rather than verifying an entire system from the start, the verification team will first attack the smaller building blocks of the system before advancing to larger portions.

No matter where in the hierarchy a verification engineer works, the basic strategy of driving stimuli and detecting errors is vital to verification. With driving stimuli and detecting errors as the underlying requirement, it is useful to understand the roots of today's verification methodologies. Early verification methodologies had little automation for stimulus or checking. However, the design complexity explosion demanded continuous and dramatic changes to the available verification techniques.

This chapter starts by describing how the verification team creates the right hierarchical partitions for the design. Then, basic driving and checking strategies are discussed, providing a guide for the sources of these basic verification building blocks. Together, these concepts form the structure upon which verification engineers build successful environments. The chapter ends with a brief summary of the evolution of the verification methodologies, from the early and simple test patterns to complex test case drivers and formal verification.

2.1 VERIFICATION HIERARCHY

Designers of today's complex chips do not create "flat" HDL. Instead, designers divide the system and chips into logical units. These logical units usually, but are not required to, follow the architecture for the

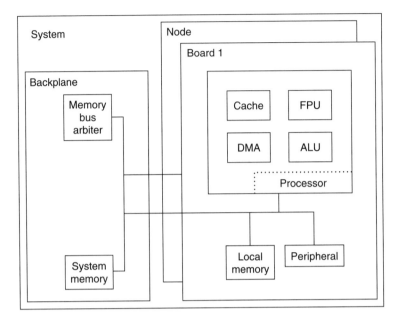

▪ **FIGURE 2.1**

A block diagram showing the multiple components of a large system. This system contains multiple processor boards, or nodes, hooked together with a backplane containing a bus adapter and system memory.

system and chip. This common practice is called *hierarchical design.* Hierarchical design allows a designer to subdivide a complex problem into more manageable blocks. The design team combines these more manageable blocks to form bigger blocks; these blocks are merged until the chip or system is complete. Figure 2.1 shows an example of a large, complex system.

Can verification capitalize on this inherent design style? The answer is "absolutely!" The same factors that drive the design team to break a complex chip into simpler components also suggest that verification teams take advantage of the same hierarchical designs.

2.1.1   Levels of Verification

Because designers divide the logic into hierarchical components, verification takes advantage of the same hierarchical boundaries, or "levels." There can be many levels of verification. Presented here are some typical levels, but actual implementations may have more or fewer levels depending on the complexity of the design. The following list represents some potential levels, from lowest to highest:

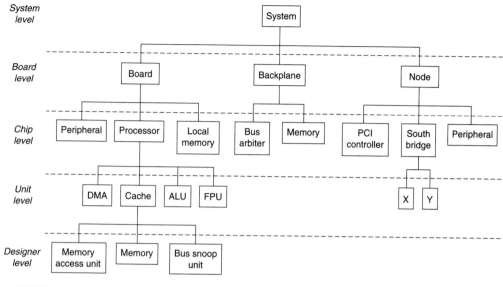

■ **FIGURE 2.2**

A hierarchical diagram of the multiple node system from Figure 2.1 showing the system built from the lower-level components. The designer level contains the HDL building blocks. For space reasons, the figure only shows the lowest level of the cache unit. However, every chip has units, and every unit has designer level HDL. Each of the next levels—unit, chip, board, and system—stitch together multiple lower-level blocks.

1. Designer

2. Unit

3. Core

4. Chip

5. Board and system

6. Hardware/software coverification

Figure 2.2 shows how the above hierarchical verification levels correspond to the large, complex system shown in Figure 2.1.

Each of these levels of verification has strengths and weaknesses. Although most projects do not require all of these levels, complex designs need at least two levels of verification. Verification teams choose levels based on their unique design features and the complexity of the logic within the hierarchy.

Designer-Level Verification

The designer level (also called macro) is the lowest level. This level is often verified by the designer, hence its name. This level may be simply a "smoke test" in which the designer "certifies" the design's use for the "real" verification environment. The designer level of verification ensures that the design will load into the simulation engine and that the basic functions are correct.

The designer level tends to be very dynamic, especially at the beginning of a project. At this level, interfaces and functionality tend to change often. During the design phase, engineers often uncover problems that make altering or moving functions across HDL macro boundaries necessary, which, in turn, causes interfaces to change.

Because of the high number of designer level blocks in a system, it is not feasible to have a verification engineer verify each block independently. However, the blocks at the most risk should have an independent verification effort.

Because of the small size of these blocks, verification engineers often use formal verification (for more detail, see Chapters 11, 12) at this level. At higher levels of the hierarchy, with thousands of latches, formal verification tends to hit a state space explosion problem, rendering the tool cumbersome above the designer or unit level.

Unit-Level Verification

In large and complex designs, unit-level verification is needed. In the system diagram of Figure 2.2, the DMA, ALU, FPU, and cache blocks are all units. The unit contains multiple designer level pieces of HDL that are stitched together into units. Interfaces and function are more stable than at the designer level, because units tend to have formalized specifications and physical or timing contracts to which designers adhere. Because interfaces and specifications are more stable, the verification team can create a more advanced environment (using randomized stimuli and autonomous checking).

To facilitate verification, the design should be partitioned so that the units have fully contained functions. These verification requirements are synergetic with the hierarchical design partitioning, which facilitates larger design efforts. Although the purpose of the unit level is to verify fully the functionality of the unit, there may be certain functions that the verification team cannot verify here, such as function split across multiple units.

Once the unit level is verified, the verification engineer can proceed to higher levels of verification, knowing that the unit's basic functionality is correct. The higher levels must then verify that the connectivity and interface protocols to and from the unit are correct; that is, the neighboring units contained in higher levels correctly implement the unit.

Core-Level Verification

A core is a special, reusable unit which requires a complete functional specification with stable interfaces. Designers may use a core multiple times within a system and across multiple systems. They may create the core internally, or obtain it from an external source.

The verification of a core is a double-edged sword. The positive is that once verified, reusing a core should not add a burden to the verification effort. For example, a core that the engineering team reuses 10 times in a design needs just one strong verification effort, saving the need to verify it nine other times. The drawback to core-level verification is that because designers may use cores in many different applications across a system or multiple systems, the usage of each instance may be different. This drives a broader verification effort because the verification team may not know all of the actual interface and application parameters in which the design team will place the core. Engineers can be very creative when it comes to using a core, exercising it in ways different from the primary intentions. Therefore, the verification team must think outside the box when verifying a core, allowing for a broader range of input scenarios than the core's initial use. Thus, the bounds in which the verification team works on a core are less defined and put a bigger burden on the team to verify the core in a more aggressive manner, as they must dream of "weird" scenarios.

When the core will be used by outside design teams, the verification team must employ a well-defined process, as engineers shy away from cores they do not trust. The key question when designing and verifying a core that other design teams will use is, "How do I gain my customers' confidence?" This is where a well-defined process helps. The verification cycle for a reusable core includes a regression suite, well-documented specification (functions and interfaces), coverage items (to help indicate what has been verified), and possibly verification scenarios (these scenarios are the ones in the regression suite). The well-documented specification teaches the end-user about the core, and the verification scenarios indicate the bounds and depth of the core verification effort. The regression suite exists for when designers make changes to the core. When this occurs, the verification team runs this suite of verification tests to ensure that this fix or enhancement did not cause any other problems within the core. Chapter 10 covers verification reuse in full detail.

Chip-Level Verification

The chip level is composed of multiple units. At this level, there are very well defined interface boundaries. The purpose of this verification is to ensure that the units are properly connected and that the design adheres to all unit interface protocols. However, there may also be functions that could not be validated at the unit level; these functions require full testing at the chip level. An example of this is chip reset, in which the verification team simulates the entire start-up sequence of the chip.

The well-defined interface of a chip creates a huge advantage for the verification team at this level. Designers must solidify the physical chip pin definitions early in the design process, giving the verification team a stable base on which they can create chip level test suites. Although lower-level environments and designs tend to evolve throughout the project, chip-level verification requires less maintenance.

Board- and System-Level Verification

A board is a collection of chips that may also contain some discrete, "glue" logic (AND gates, OR gates, etc.). Many times, designers place this glue logic into a small field programmable gate array (FPGA), providing an inexpensive and modifiable interchip connection. The purpose of this level of verification is to confirm the chip interconnection, integration, and board design.

The definition of a system is different across industry segments and product lines. In some cases, a chip could be a system (in which case, the chip and system levels are the same); in other cases, the system is a multiframe server with hundreds of chips. For verification, the basic definition of a system is a logical partition of independently verified components.

The verification focus at the system level is that of interaction rather than particular functions buried inside a chip or unit. As a result, a verification team working on a large application-specific integrated circuit (ASIC) will assume that previous verification efforts on its units and cores specified, documented, and fully verified the lower levels below the system level. Because the focus is on component interaction, the verification engineer assumes that the individual chips, cores, or units are functionally correct.

Hardware/Software Coverification

The hardware/software coverification level marries the system level hardware with the code that runs on the hardware. The code may be device drivers, system boot code, microcode, or application software that runs on the hardware engines. The purpose of this level of verification is to find bugs due to inconsistent understandings of the specifications between the hardware designers and the code architects and programmers.

To run the hardware and software together, hardware and software engineers must rigorously verify both components. Methods of software verification are beyond the realm of this book.

2.1.2 What Level To Choose?

Choosing which verification levels to use is not as easy as it may seem. Although six levels of hardware verification were described above, most verification projects will use an appropriate subset of these levels based on the design details. A single system on chip (SoC) may need unit-level verification on certain new blocks, followed by a chip/system-level effort. On the other hand, a complex server would need verification at the designer, unit, chip, system, and coverification levels.

There are technical factors that help teams decide which levels to choose for a given design. These factors are highlighted here.

- *Always choose the lowest level that completely contains the targeted function.* The smaller the model, the more direct control the verification engineer has over creating the required test scenarios. A test that exercises the board in Figure 2.2 does not need a system-level model containing the node and the backplane. These extra design pieces have a negative effect on simulation engine performance without providing any benefit to the test.

- *Each verifiable piece should have its own specification document.* This helps keep interfaces and the function more stable, as well as allows everyone on the team to be "reading from the same sheet of music." If functions and interfaces change often, then verification environments must change as well (with recoding each time).

- *New or complex components need focus.* If a portion of function is new (versus function inherited from previous designs) or complex, then the verification team should isolate this function and create an environment to test it. Complex functions often have arbitration logic or multiple requestors vying for a single resource. This type of function lends itself to creation of robust, focused verification environments.

- *The appropriate level of control and observability drives decisions on which levels to verify.* The lower the verification level, the more control the verification engineer has on the interface inputs, and the more observability on the outputs. This comes at a price of additional effort. Robust designer-level verification on all macrocomponents in a large system is not realistic, as more effort is required to construct each environment for each macro. Instead, only the complex macros have individual verification, leaving the less risky components to the higher levels. When dealing with higher levels of verification (chip, board, system), the team implicitly verifies the smaller components at the cost of lower control and observability.

- *Function may dictate verification levels.* Verification engineers cannot verify certain functions at the lower levels. Often, this is because a function spans multiple components. Although the verification environment can test each component individually, the

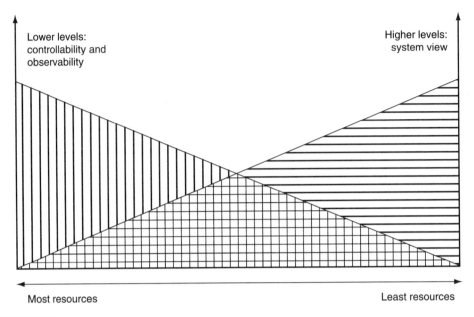

Lower levels of the verification hierarchy provide the verification engineer with more control over the smaller environment. Higher levels provide a systemwide view, but lose the tight control. The trade-off for the control is that, because there are more designer or unit levels (compared with one system), the total staffing requirements for the lower levels is higher than the system level.

environment can prove only portions of the whole function. At a higher level, the team assembles all of the components and verifies the entire function. The trace/debug function is an example of this.[1] Trace/debug logic usually spans across many smaller blocks, capturing signal and latch data from across the entire chip.

From a business standpoint, verification resources are in demand and management must allocate them wisely. It may be desirable to verify every designer block, but resources may make this unfeasible. Alternatively, proposing to take the available resources and serialize the designer-level verification effort would break the schedule. Figure 2.3 illustrates the trade offs.

Bug Rates and the Levels at Which They Are Found

The amount of controllability and observability that the verification engineer has directly correlates to the ability to find bugs in the design.

---

[1] Design teams use the trace/debug function to debug the fabricated hardware. When testing on the actual hardware, engineers must obtain information about the internal states of the machine in order to debug errors. The trace/debug functions capture the state of a set of internal signals and latches across a small window of time (a few hundred cycles). It is critical for the verification team to verify the trace/debug function or it may not work when the chip is fabricated.

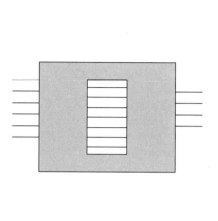
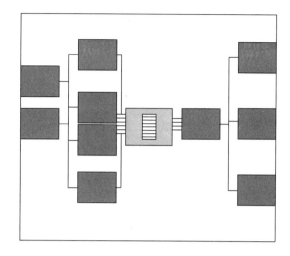

(a) Filling the buffer at the designer level...   (b) ... is easier than at the core level

■ **FIGURE 2.4**

At the designer level, verification engineers can manipulate the HDL inputs and create corner conditions in the logic. It is harder to create these cases at higher levels as the other portions of the design effect the stimulus.

Controllability indicates the ease at which the verification engineer creates the specific scenarios that are of interest. If a design contains a bug but the input scenario conditions that create the bug never occur, the verification engineer will not discover the bug in simulation. *Controllability and the verification level of hierarchy are closely related.* The higher the level of the hierarchy, the less controllability the verification engineer has. Verification engineers have greater controllability at lower levels because there are fewer dependencies on the surrounding units to cause the scenario.

As an example, a verification engineer wants to create a buffer-full condition in a macro within a core. If the level of hierarchy is the designer level, in which just the macro exists in the simulation environment, the verification engineer simply controls the input signals by pushing data into the buffer without ever popping the data. However, at the higher core level of verification, it is much harder to create this condition because the core level inputs are further from the buffer, and the behavior of the surrounding macros and units may continuously pop data from the buffer unless a very specific core level event occurs. This makes it difficult to fill the buffer. Figure 2.4 depicts these two cases: in Figure 2.4a, the verification engineer can directly control the state of the buffer; in Figure 2.4b, the control is indirect because of all of the surrounding logic.

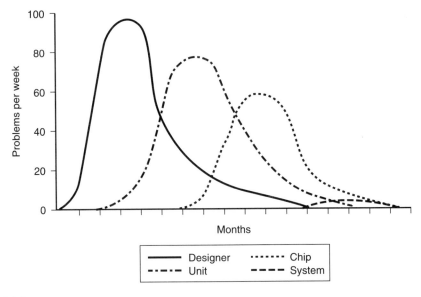

▪ **FIGURE 2.5**

Lower levels of verification tend to uncover more bugs because they occur earlier in the design cycle and because verification of each designer or unit level occurs in parallel with the others. It is an efficient practice to wait until the bug rate begins to drop in a lower level before moving to the next level.

Observability is the other aspect in discovering bugs. Observability indicates the ease with which the verification engineer can identify when the design acts appropriately versus when it demonstrates incorrect behavior. Lower levels of verification are conducive to observability because bugs are more likely to manifest themselves on the outputs. At the higher levels, it is often harder to observe interesting bugs without internal observation points.

The increased ability to find bugs at the lower levels dovetails with the design cycle as well. Each designer on the team works at a different rate and pace. Therefore, not all macros in a project are ready for verification simultaneously. Designer- or unit-level verification may be available on early blocks long before an entire chip is ready for verification. As a result, it is good practice to progress the verification focus from the lower levels to the higher levels over time. This practice typically yields bug rates and trends as shown in Figure 2.5.

Another Word on the Cost of Bugs

Figure 1.7 compared the cost of finding a bug in verification to finding the bug in hardware or the customer environment, showing that the longer a bug goes undetected, the more costly it is to fix. There is a saying that holds true: "Pay me now, or pay me later—with inflation." Similarly, this trend holds true across the levels of verification, further augmenting the business and technical need for a hierarchical approach to verification.

A bug found at the designer level has little cost. The designer has the algorithms and decision process of the HDL fresh in his or her mind, and finding a bug quickly may drive the designer to implement the function differently, long before physical design or timing of the macro occurs. That same bug found at chip or system level has moderate cost because it will require more problem isolation and debug time. Furthermore, the designer may no longer be able to reimplement the function in a more effective manner because the required rework of physical design on this and other macros would break the schedule.

2.2 STRATEGY OF VERIFICATION

The above discussion of controllability and observability illustrates that the verification engineer divides work into two separate tasks: driving (controllability) and checking (observability) the design under test. The two tasks correspond to the following basic questions a verification engineer must ask:

1. Am I driving all possible input scenarios?

2. How will I know when a failure has occurred?

These tasks are separate but must work together to succeed. A verification engineer captures a bug if the design inputs aggravate the failing condition *and* if a checker flags an illegal state. One is inadequate without the other. Driving all possible combinations of inputs cannot uncover a bug if the checkers fail to identify the bad condition. Likewise, checking for all possible failures is futile if the drivers fail to stimulate the conditions that cause the failure. As shown in Figure 2.6, drivers and checkers are the yin and yang of verification.

The following sections give a brief overview of how driving and checking work together to uncover bugs. The principles of driving and checking are expanded in Chapters 7 and 8.

2.2.1 Driving Principles

What does it mean to "drive all possible input scenarios"? Although driving all possible input scenarios is trivial with a two-latch design, it is very hard to gauge completeness of input scenarios in a complex design. And what does it mean to "know when it fails"? How can we know if a complete set of checkers are in place?

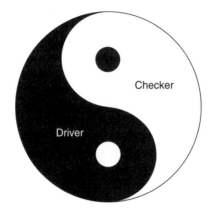

▪ **FIGURE 2.6**

Finding a bug in the design under verification requires both the stimulus components, or drivers, and checking components. A verification engineer cannot find a bug without creating the failing conditions and detecting incorrect hardware description language behavior. Therefore, driving and checking are the yin and yang of verification.

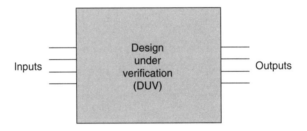

▪ **FIGURE 2.7**

Black box verification is the most common simulation style of verification. Under the black box style, verification engineers manipulate the inputs and check the outputs but do not observe or set signals or latches inside the design under verification.

To analyze these questions, first look at the "black box" in Figure 2.7. The black box is a piece of HDL, which is called a black box because verification engineers do not look inside the design implementation. The verification engineer does look at its inputs and outputs, their definitions, and their functions. The actual behavior of the black box and its outputs will depend on the inputs supplied to it over time and the function it performs. Given a set of input stimuli, the function of the black box will yield specific, predictable values over one or more machine cycles.

The black box may have complete documentation, or not. The amount of documentation required and the quality of documentation varies by the designer, the company policy, and the size of the black box. Larger pieces of design (which are higher in the design's hierarchy) tend to have more documentation. Smaller portions of HDL (lowest levels of the hierarchy) tend to have embedded documentation but not separate functional descriptions.

When charged with verifying a piece of design, the verification engineer should first read whatever documentation exists for that design. The first task is to understand all input and output lines. The verification engineer must then understand the design's function and thereby be able to predict the outputs based on the inputs. This is the design's specification.

It is important that the verification engineer obtain the input descriptions from a source other than the author of the HDL under test. This source might be an industry standard specification (such as a Peripheral Component Interconnect (PCI) protocol) or another designer whose HDL outputs are the inputs to the HDL under test. This is significant because the verification engineer must maintain independence in understanding the design inputs in order to break the redundancy path. If the DUV designer authors the input specification, the verification engineer would duplicate any incorrect input understanding that the DUV designer has and bugs may be missed. If the interface specification must come from the designer whose logic is under test, the verification engineer should ensure that other designers sign off on the contents as matching their expectations of what their logic will drive into the DUV.

With the input definitions understood, the verification engineer begins to plan a stimulus strategy. Often, a design has a large number of input signals. In this case, the verification engineer will group multiple signals together based on their logical function. For example, a memory design's command and address busses function hand in hand to access or store data at the intended memory location. Other memory DUV input signals might support different functions such as resetting the design. Grouping signals and busses together is important because the verification engineer will develop separate driving strategies for each set of grouped input signals.

In developing a stimulus strategy, the verification engineer must always remember the goal is to maximize the scenarios that the verification environment creates. For control signals, this means ensuring that the environment exercises all possible commands and modifiers. For data busses, the environment should create a wide assortment of possible data patterns. It is especially important for the environment to exercise *edge* cases when data patterns are choosen. Edge cases create odd, exception, or end conditions in the design such as storing to the last address in memory or causing an overflow in an adder.

Driving the Black Box

Figure 2.8 briefly describes four inputs, including a wire name and bit width, for our black box. Even with the limited description of the inputs

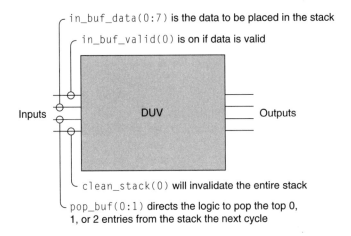

in_buf_data(0:7) is the data to be placed in the stack

in_buf_valid(0) is on if data is valid

Inputs

DUV

Outputs

clean_stack(0) will invalidate the entire stack

pop_buf(0:1) directs the logic to pop the top 0, 1, or 2 entries from the stack the next cycle

▪ **FIGURE 2.8**

A DUV has inputs and input descriptions. This DUV has four sets of input signals, each with an English language description of the purpose of the signals.

of this black box, the verification engineer can start to understand the design by ascertaining the following details:

- There is a stack inside.
- The stack is at least two deep.
- The stack is 8 bits wide.
- Only one entry can be written at a time.

However, there are still plenty of unknowns about this black box. For example, even though it is clear that there is a stack inside the design, the current description does not indicate whether the stack protocol is last in, first-out (LIFO) or first in, first out (FIFO). Other unknowns about the design include the following:

- How deep is the stack?
- What conditions indicate a full stack?
- When do the contents become valid?
- What is the behavior if a read and write occur on the same cycle? Is that even allowed?
- How long does it take to reset the stack?
- Do the entries get zeroed-out or just marked invalid?
- What happens if a read operation occurs when the stack is empty?

TABLE 2.1 ■ The verification team should include these scenarios in the test plan for the black box in Figure 2.8

Stimulus cases	Description
Writing and not writing	Writing data to the stack is obvious. However, the verification engineer must include in the test plan cases in which data are not written to the stack for multiple cycles.
Writing and reading	The inputs appear to allow for simultaneous reads and writes to the stack.
All three possible reads	There are three different decodes (none, 1, or 2) described for pop_buf(0:1) and the verification engineer must create all three cases.
Reading when there is nothing in the stack	The correct function of the design in this case has not been defined yet. Regardless of whether or not the design will return no data or an error, the verification engineer must include this case in the test plan.
Writing when the stack is full	At this point, both the depth of the stack and the correct function when data is written to a full stack is not defined. The test plan still must include this scenario.
Reading from the stack and resetting it (clean_stack)	Concurrent conflicting operations, such as reading from the stack and resetting the contents of the stack are often a source of bugs.
Writing to the stack and resetting it (*clean_stack*)	Again, this concurrent conflicting operation must be included in the test plan.
All bits of data	The test plan should include verifying that each bit of the width of data (8 bits) can be either '0'b or '1'b, and that each line in the stack correctly holds the 8 bit value.
Temporal cases such as writing back-to-back with a double read on the first cycle (starting with an empty stack).	Temporal cases, where stimulus evolves over multiple cycles, are always the most difficult to create—and most often where bugs lurk.

- In case of reading two entries, how are the two data items returned? Back to back or one at a time?

- What happens if pop_buf(0:1) is set to "11"b (e.g., three reads)?

Despite these unknowns, the verification engineer can begin to contemplate the types of scenarios that he or she must drive into the logic. This simple input definition allows the test plan to begin. Table 2.1 lists stimulus that the verification team should include in the test plan for the black box.

Because of the close ties between driving stimuli and checking outputs, the verification engineer must next look at the outputs of the black box before completing the stimulus strategy. However, before returning to the black box example, the fundamental verification checking strategies must be discussed.

2.2.2 Checking Strategies

Stimulus and checking are tightly coupled. Although the verification stimulus engines drive inputs, it is the checker's job to ensure that the DUV behaves correctly based on the stimulus. A DUV behaves correctly when it abides by the design specification and intended function.

There are four main sources of checkers. The design and architecture teams document these sources in various specifications, and the verification engineer must understand each of these sources to create environments that contain complete checking. The four sources are as follows:

- The inputs and outputs of the design

- The context of the design

- The microarchitecture rules of the design

- The architecture of the design

Checkers Based on Inputs and Outputs

A fundamental source of checkers is the outputs of the DUV because any bug in the design will at some point manifest itself at the outputs of the design. With robust drivers, most bugs will show up as a *miscompare* on an output of the design. A miscompare occurs when the actual DUV data does not match the expected data from the checker.

To predict the correct outputs—and to flag *incorrect* outputs—the verification engineer must understand the output specification. Output documentation comes in many forms, such as an industry standard specification (e.g., a **PCI** protocol) or an informal interface between two designers. As discussed, the verification engineer should work from a definition of the output that is independent from the designer whose HDL is under test.

The verification engineer writes code to check the values of the outputs at all times during simulation. It is equally important to check for a correct value on a bus when the verification engineer expects a specific output as it is to check that there is no value on the bus when the bus should be idle.

The verification engineer's checking code uses the inputs to predict the outputs. Outputs are a function of the inputs, so the verification code must understand the function to correctly predict the outputs. The actual implementation of the function in verification code is usually simpler than in the HDL, as the verification code is not burdened by require-

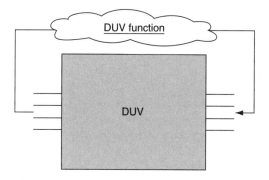

■ **FIGURE 2.9**

A fundamental source of output checking is the DUV inputs. The verification engineer creates checkers for output signals based on the inputs and an understanding of the DUV function.

ments on latch counts and physical timing. Further simplifying the verification code is that the environment, unlike the HDL, does not have to handle all possible input cases when the verification engineer knows that the environment will only drive specific values.

Figure 2.9 shows that verification engineers create checkers for output signals based on the DUV function and properties and on the input stimulus. A function might be as simple as "when a command is sent on the input, a response is expected on the third cycle." This property might actually generate multiple checks: a countdown from three to make sure the response appears on the output at the correct time, and a check that the actual response is correct. In addition, there should be a check that the response bus remains idle on all cycles except when the verification environment predicts a response. The inputs and the function of the design dictate the value of the response.

Checkers Based on the Context of the Design

When verifying HDL at the lower levels of the design hierarchy, it is important for the verification engineer to understand the design's higher-level functionality, or design context. A verification engineer must understand the big picture, even when focusing on a specific portion of the design.

In Figure 2.10, HDL A and HDL B are two portions of the design that work together to perform a higher-level function. For example, the higher level of DUV hierarchy in Figure 2.10 might be an instruction decode unit within a microprocessor. The function of HDL A might be to parse an incoming instruction stream into individual instructions, and the function of HDL B might be to group a few instructions together to feed a parallel (superscalar) pipeline in the neighboring execution unit.

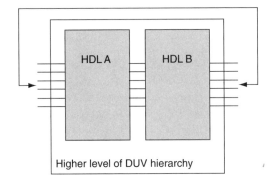

Higher level of DUV hierarchy

▪ **FIGURE 2.10**

When verifying lower levels of hierarchy such as individual HDLs, the verification engineer derives checkers from an understanding of the function, properties, and context of the larger design. In this figure, functions of the higher level of hierarchy imply checking on the individual outputs of HDL A and HDL B.

The execution unit's inputs would be wired to the outputs of this decode unit.

In this example, it is important to understand the overall function of the decode unit while verifying an individual portion such as HDL A. A design context property or function would be that the decode unit design should feed only valid instructions (op-codes) to the execution unit. When verifying HDL A by itself (macro-level hierarchy), the verification engineer needs to know all valid op-codes, and that invalid op-codes should cause exceptions and not be passed on signals that drive HDL B. The test plan for verifying HDL A would include tests that imbed invalid instructions in the stream.

Verification engineers derive design context checking for HDL B as well. Knowledge of the number of parallel execution paths in the super-scalar pipeline and the types of instructions that are valid in each path is required to verify HDL B. HDL B must group the instructions according to these design context rules, as the outputs feed the execution paths. For example, the execution unit might contain a fixed-point arithmetic pipeline, a floating-point arithmetic pipeline, a branch execution pipeline, and a store pipeline. It would be illegal to have floating-point operations fed to the fixed-point unit. The verification of HDL B must ensure that this never occurs.

Checkers Based on Microarchitecture Rules of the Design

Verification teams derive many checkers from properties based on the *microarchitecture*, or internal structures of the design, so verification engineers must understand the internals of the design. This applies to driving techniques as well as checking because it is equally important for

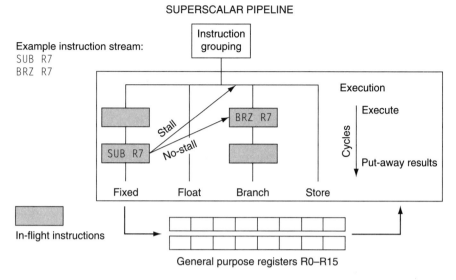

SUPERSCALAR PIPELINE

Example instruction stream:
SUB R7
BRZ R7

Instruction grouping

Execution

Execute

Stall

No-stall

BRZ R7

SUB R7

Cycles

Put-away results

Fixed   Float   Branch   Store

In-flight instructions

General purpose registers R0–R15

■ **FIGURE 2.11**

The architecture and microarchitecture of the design under verification provide a source of checkers. This figure shows a superscalar pipeline with four pipes: Fixed, Float, Branch, and Store. The ability or inability of in-flight results to feed prior stages of a pipeline will affect instruction grouping, as shown by the stall or no-stall arrows. In all cases, as defined by the architecture, the BRZ R7 instruction must use the results of the SUB R7 instruction.

the verification engineer to know if, during the course of simulation, the stimulus has filled a buffer (driving) as it is to know if there has been a buffer overrun (checking).

Checks based on the microarchitecture can come from many sources, including these common ones:

- Invalid state machine values

- Invalid state machine transitions

- Overrun or underrun queues and buffers

- Bad timing on control signals

- Invalid data

However, the above list is an oversimplification of the specific implementation of most microarchitecture-based checkers. Figure 2.11 shows the microprocessor's superscalar pipeline briefly described in the previous section. Here, the instruction grouping HDL feeds instructions to our four parallel executing pipelines. Depending on the contents of the instruction stream, the pipeline can execute one, two, three, or four instructions in parallel.

A superscalar pipeline such as this one will have many checkers based on the implementation details. One example of checkers is how the design handles shared resources within the pipeline such as the general-purpose registers (GPRs). If the microprocessor places the results of a fixed-point operation in a register (e.g. the subtract result goes to register R7 in the figure) that the following instruction, branch if zero (BRZ), will use, then we have resource contention on R7. If the design under verification is the execution unit, then the verification engineer can write checkers that monitor for correct behavior in the case of shared resources. The figure shows two possible implementations. The lower arrow represents the case in which one pipeline (fixed point) forwards results to another pipeline (branch) simultaneous to the write of R7. The upper arrow represents a different implementation, in which a pipeline stall occurs because the BRZ instruction must wait for the logic to write the results of the SUB to R7 before execution can continue. The verification engineer must write checkers to verify the correct behavior in either case.

It is interesting to note that if the design under verification is the instruction grouping design (rather than the execution unit), the verification team must check the above example of stalling the pipeline based on register resource conflicts. In this case, the checker is a design context based checker of the instruction grouping design. The verification engineer requires an understanding of the input restrictions in the neighboring execution unit. The design context dictates that if a branch follows a subtract and uses the same register, the design cannot group the instructions together.

Checkers Based on the Architecture of the Design

Most verification checkers have their roots in the design *architecture*. Although the microarchitecture defines the structures that compose the design, the architecture dictates how the design must act. Industry standards groups and companies publish architecture specifications for public protocols, programmable processing units, and system structures. Hardware designs must abide by these specifications. The architecture lends itself to being the verification engineer's main source of checkers because of the strict requirements on documenting the architecture.

Again using the microprocessor superscalar pipeline shown in Figure 2.11 as an example, the architecture dictates the behavior of all instructions that pass through the pipeline. The example instructions behave similarly across practically any microprocessor architecture. The subtract (SUB) instruction must correctly operate on the operands (not specified on our example) and store the results in R7. The BRZ instruction must test the contents of R7 and branch to the target instruction address (again, unspecified in our example) if the contents equal zero. The verification engineer must predict the results of the instruction stream and check that the design results are correct. Furthermore, because all microprocessor architectures dictate that the BRZ instruction must test the contents of R7 after any previous instructions (in this case, the SUB instruction) have updated R7, the checking must also verify this. In this case, a well-constructed test case would ensure that either

- R7 be initialized with a nonzero value, and the result of the SUB instruction writes zero into R7

- R7 be initialized with a zero value, and the result of the SUB instruction writes a nonzero value into R7

With this setup, the results of the branch (taken or not taken) will allow for direct observation of whether the BRZ instruction waited for execution logic to write the results of the SUB instruction to R7 before testing for a zero value. Otherwise, if zeros overwrite zeros or nonzeros overwrite nonzeros, it is difficult to observe from the outputs of the execution pipeline if the pipeline implementation obeyed the architecture.

Architecture documents exist for all industry standard design protocols, such as Infiniband, all types of PCI, and Ethernet. All microprocessors have strict architecture rules that dictate their behavior as well. Programming applications are written based on these documents, so the verification engineer's highest priority is to check that the design follows the architecture in all cases.

2.2.3 Checking the Black Box

We return now to our black box example. Figure 2.12 defines the outputs of the black box. Each of the four output wires has an associated bit width and wire name. The short descriptions of the function that accompanies each wire begin to answer some of the open questions about the design:

- In case of double-read, entries come simultaneously.

- The logic within the black box indicates when the stack is full.

- The input driver must retry when overflow occurs, as the data is discarded.

Yet there are still many unknown details about the design. More documentation is required to understand the following:

- How deep is the stack?

- How soon after a write do the stack contents become valid?

- What is the behavior if we read and write the same cycle, and can we even do this?

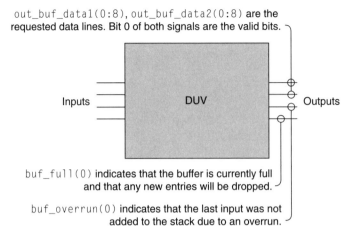

out_buf_data1(0:8), out_buf_data2(0:8) are the requested data lines. Bit 0 of both signals are the valid bits.

Inputs   DUV   Outputs

buf_full(0) indicates that the buffer is currently full and that any new entries will be dropped.

buf_overrun(0) indicates that the last input was not added to the stack due to an overrun.

▪ **FIGURE 2.12**

Checking the design under verification requires an understanding of the output signal definitions. This figure shows four output signals (two of them are bundled and two are single-bit signals) with their accompanied English language descriptions.

- How long does it take to reset the stack?
- After a reset, are the entries zeroed-out or just marked invalid?
- What if a test performs a read when the stack is empty?
- Is the stack a FIFO or LIFO?
- Must the design return data from a single read on bus1?

The design or architecture team produces a specification of our black box design. This documentation reveals the following:

- The stack is seven deep.
- A new stack entry is valid for reading the next cycle.
- The stack reset completes the cycle after a clean command, and the design ignores inputs arriving simultaneous with a clean command.
- The clean command turns the valid bit off on all seven entries.
- No data are returned for a read if the stack is empty.
- The stack is a FIFO.

Furthermore, the documentation provides an explanation for usage of the buf_full and buf_overrun signals. The buf_full and buf_overrun outputs are both required because buf_full becomes active the cycle after

TABLE 2.2 ■ The verification team must check these cases for the black box example

Checker	Checker source	Checker implementation
The design returns the correct data	Inputs and outputs, architecture	A fundamental check on the black box is that the returned data matches the sent data. The verification code must keep an independent copy of all design under verification (DUV) data in order to check the data outputs coming from the stack.
Buffer overflow	Microarchitecture	The verification code must keep a count of how much data is in the design. This allows prediction and checking of the buf_full(0) and buf_overrun outputs.
Stack become valid at the right time	Microarchitecture	The design description stipulates that the driver may read data from the stack the cycle after it sends it. Therefore, the verification team should write a checker to verify that the data is not valid too early (the same cycle it was written) and that it can be read the following cycle.
Check all outputs all of the time	Design context	Other designs that use the outputs of this black box depend on these outputs always being correct. It is not sufficient only to check for valid data after a read operation. The out_buf_data1 and out_buf_data2 wires should never contain valid data unless the driver performed a read and there was data in the stack. Similarly, the buf_full and buf_overrun wires should only be active when the verification code predicts a full or overrun condition.

The table lists the checker as well as the type of checker (source).

the design receives the data that fill the stack. It is possible for the input driver to send another byte of data to the cycle so that the buf_full signal wire becomes active. In this case, the design raises the buf_overrun signal on the following cycle, and the design drops the "eighth" byte of data.

With all of this information in hand, the verification engineer can write a test plan that specifies the checkers. Table 2.2 suggests some of the checkers, the checker source, and an implementation.

Verification Checking Should Not Reimplement To Design

The verification engineer must remain independent while maintaining a close working relationship with the design team. This is especially important when checking code for verification is being created. Although the verification engineer is privy to the design implementation, the checking code should not mirror the design algorithm.

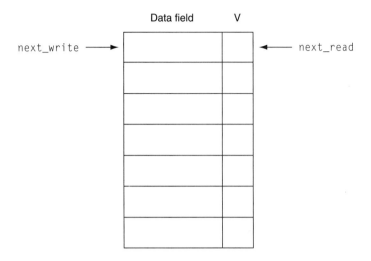

■ FIGURE 2.13

The seven-deep stack hardware description language for design implementation uses a data field, a valid bit (V), and two pointers. The pointers track the position for the next write to the buffer and the next read (oldest entry).

The verification engineer must always start with the assumption that the design implementation is **wrong**. If the checking code mirrors the design, the potential exists for the checkers to implement a bug in the same fashion that the design did. This breaks the redundancy path and would cause the bug to go undetected, as both the design and checker results match.

To demonstrate this, consider the HDL design implementation of the stack inside the black box example. Figure 2.13 shows the seven-deep stack with two pointers, a next_read pointer and a next_write pointer. The next_read pointer indicates which position to read when the inputs drive the next read command, and the next_write pointer indicates which position to put the next byte of data received from the inputs. The V column is the valid bit for each entry. If next_read and next_write point to the same entry, then the stack is either empty or full, depending on the state of the valid bit. The design implements a wrap condition when either pointer is incremented beyond the seventh position.

As described in Table 2.2, verification checking code must keep track of the data, as well as the number of entries currently in the stack. Checking code written in C could create a seven-deep stack and use pointers as in the design. However, the better, simpler way is to create a linked list. This creates a checking structure with a different and independent implementation than the HDL design. Verification engineers can take advantage of the fact that they do not synthesize their code and do not have to meet timing or physical goals; they must only compile it for

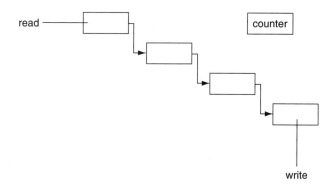

■ **FIGURE 2.14**

The verification code uses a different, and easier to implement, method for tracking the contents of the data. Rather than building a physical stack (as required in hardware), the verification engineer can utilize a "virtual" stack implemented as a linked list. The different implementation provides an optimal checking method uninfluenced by the design implementation.

simulation. As such, many verification teams use programming languages rather than HDLs to implement their drivers and checkers. The choice of a different style source code further divorces the verification implementation from the HDL.

Figure 2.14 shows the linked list checker implementation. The simple linked list has a head and a tail. The code increments a counter for each write operation and decrements it for each read. A null pointer value indicates an empty list, as would a counter value of zero. This strategy allows the checking code to quickly access the top of the stack for read operations and then remove the data from the stack (and release the memory). Write operations trigger memory allocation and append the data to the end of the linked list. This implementation is simple, effective, and independent from the design approach.

2.2.4 Putting It All Together

The previous sections introduced strategies for driving and checking a design. Verification engineers find bugs with robust drivers that aggravate the error condition and with complete checking that flags a miscompare in the design.

Uncovering complex bugs requires intricate drivers and checkers. Consider the following bug in the black box stack example:[2]

---

[2] This example works backward and is for illustration purposes only. During the course of normal verification, the verification engineer is not "given" a bug description and then asked to create the drivers and checkers that find it. However, this backward challenge does occur during the reproduction stage of escape analysis (Chapter 13).

The design description states that when the driver asserts the input signal clean_stack(0) to "1," the design should clear all the data valid bits inside the stack design. For simplicity, the design should set the next_write pointer and next_read pointer to the top of the stack. If the driver asserts in_buf_valid(0) to "1" (with data) the same cycle as the clean_stack, the logic resets the pointers as intended but erroneously puts the data in the stack. This case only occurs when the stack has six valid entries when the clean_stack and in_buf_valid are set, as the bug is in the logic that is trying to set the buf_full output. As a result, somewhere in the stack there is a valid bit set to "1"b that should not be on.

What does it take to find this bug? What scenario must the drivers create? What checkers must be in place to flag the erroneous behavior? Finding this bug is not trivial.

First, the driver must create a specific sequence of events. Over the course of a test case, enough writes to the stack need to occur so that there are exactly six entries loaded. Then, the test case must set the clean_stack and in_buf_valid signals simultaneously. At this point, the stack has an erroneous value, but the bug has not manifested itself on the outputs. If a second clean_stack operation occurs over the course of the next few cycles, then the design would clear its erroneous behavior and the bug would go undetected. To detect this bug, the stack needs to accumulate six new entries without another clean_stack operation. Only then would the internal pointers move to the erroneously valid entry.

The checkers that would highlight this bug are more straightforward than the driver scenario, but equally important. The bug could show up in any one of the following three ways.

The first is a miscompare on the buf_ful output signal. The buf_full comes on because the next_write points to an entry marked valid (but should not be valid). Because there is supposed to be only six entries in the seven-deep stack, the checker flags the bug.

The second way that the bug could manifest itself is as incorrect data on the out_buf_data1 or out_buf_data2. This occurs when the HDL responds to a read request by sending the data in the stack position of the erroneously set valid bit. The checking code predicts the output data will be the first data written after the clean_stack occurred, but the HDL returns different data and the environment finds the bug.

The final way that the checkers may discover the bug is when the HDL sets the buf_overrun output signal too soon. This would occur when the HDL's write pointer detects that it is pointing to a valid entry when another write comes in. Once again, there is supposed to be only six entries in the seven-deep stack, but the HDL incorrectly has all seven entries marked valid.

Is it reasonable to believe that the best, most experienced verification engineer would know to create this exact scenario? Maybe. However, today's hardware designs are orders of magnitude more complex, and the bugs are even more devious. A verification engineer can never envision

■ **FIGURE 2.15**

The three simulation commandments edict robust stimulus, complete checking, and the rule for moving to the next verification level.

all of the possible failing mechanisms in a complex design. To combat the problem of increasing complexity, verification technology has advanced to assist the verification engineer in uncovering even the most difficult bugs.

The essence of verification lies in the fundamental completeness of the stimulus and checking components, and the use of these components across verification levels. This foundation is so important that it comprises the three simulation commandments shown in Figure 2.15. The commandments edict the highest quality of stimulus, checker, and monitor components and the appropriate time to move from one verification level to the next.

2.2.5 The General Simulation Environment

Verification methodologies continue to evolve. In earlier days of hardware design, engineers first performed verification on the fabricated hardware itself. As the designs became more complex, design automation teams created simulation engines to model the behavior of the design. Although Chapter 5 fully describes simulation engines, a description of the general simulation-based verification environment, which became the springboard for the evolution of the methodology, now follows.

Figure 2.16 shows the flow of the general simulation-based verification environment. The verification engineer writes a test case and supplies environmental data, such as initial values, to the simulation engine, and the designer supplies the logic description in the form of an HDL. In this picture, the test case is generic. No matter what the form of the

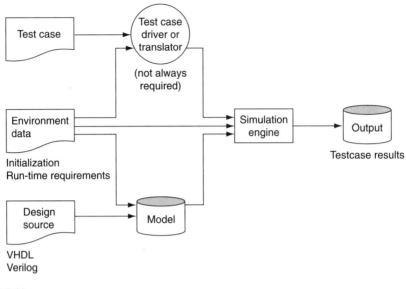

■ **FIGURE 2.16**

A typical simulation-based verification environment uses a test case, environmental data, and hardware description language source code as inputs to the simulation engine.

test case, the environment presents it to the simulation engine either directly or indirectly through a compiler or test case driver. The environmental data may be required for both the test case driver and simulation engine. A step called model-build compiles the HDL into a simulation model, which is the format that the simulation engine uses to step through cycles and reproduce the behavior of the design.

Simulation engines provide many types of outputs. All simulation engines have the ability to produce traces of the activity that took place within the design during the simulation run. Designers and verification engineers use waveform viewers to read the trace output files. Depending on the type of test case, other output files include data on miscompares identified by the verification code, as well as text-based results files.

2.2.6 Verification Methodology Evolution

With the advent of simulation engines, the engineers drove simple, single scenario test cases into the simulation model. The engineers observed the behavior of the design by looking at a trace generated by the simulation engine. Meticulous scrutiny of the trace revealed unwanted behavior within the design. This type of deterministic verification is called test patterns and is shown at the start of the verification methodology evo-

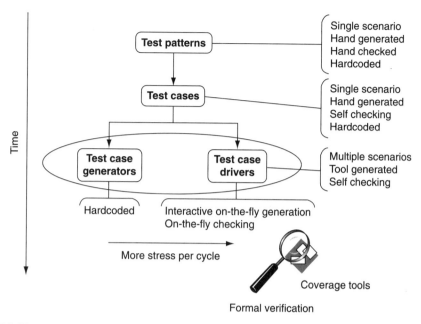

■ **FIGURE 2.17**

Verification environments continue to evolve. Early test cases had simple, handwritten stimulus and had no automated checking. The evolution brought complex stimulus and checking, along with coverage tools to the simulation-based environment. Additionally, verification engineers have added formal verification tools to their arsenal of bug-finding tools.

lution in Figure 2.17. The engineering teams hand-generated each test pattern to perform a specific scenario, and hand-checked the results via the simulation trace. Test patterns are deterministic or static, and require routine maintenance when design changes occur that render the test pattern invalid. Without maintenance, the team may lose the intent of the test pattern.[3]

The process of scrutinizing traces of simulation outputs in search of bugs is tedious and error prone. As verification methodology evolved, self-checking test cases replaced the test patterns. Test cases were still hand-generated and contained a single scenario; however, they differed from test patterns in that the test case polls the simulation engine while the scenario is running on the model and compares selected values from the design with expected values from the test case. The design

---

[3] The design methodology also evolved because of complexity issues. Early designs were captured at the gate level, but it became clear that the designers needed a level of abstraction to capture the intent of the design, without worrying about each gate. Register Transfer Level design languages such as VHDL and Verilog were created to facilitate the design process against the onslaught of complexity.

engineer bases the expected values on his or her understanding of the design function.

Engineers needed more and more test cases to accomplish their tasks on the newer designs. Engineers began to specialize in the creation of test cases, and the verification career was born.

At this point, verification engineers and designers wrote most test cases in the register transfer level (RTL) language (e.g. VHDL or Verilog). Test cases written in RTL are called test benches. Today, teams still use the test-bench methodology for simple designs or for verifying a single macro (designer-level verification). It is possible to create robust test benches that drive multiple scenarios; however, it is clear that although RTL is great for describing hardware design, it is not optimal for creating test cases.

Test Benches Evolve into Test Cases

As verification engineers looked at the onslaught of required test cases, it was apparent that they needed further design automation to keep pace with the growing design complexity. Verification engineers invented *test case languages* to facilitate writing the input scenarios and checks required for the given scenario. Test case languages varied from design to design, but they generally captured the intent of the test scenario at a level of abstraction higher than the bits and bytes that the verification engineer needs to drive and check.

Although a verification engineer may create a test case language for any type of DUV, a microprocessor test case is a special case in which the engineer can use a test case language to create instruction streams. A microprocessor test case example follows to illustrate the power of a test case language.

Figure 2.18 shows a simple microprocessor test case language. The test case defines initial values; a short, two-operation instruction stream; and end-of-test case checks. This test case initializes four GPRs: GPR0, GPR1, GPR5, and GPR6. The two instructions, ADD and OR, use the initialized GPRs as data operands and write the results into GPR2 and GPR7. Note that the end-of-test case checks not only verify that the design writes correct instruction results to GPR2 and GPR7 but also verify that the operand GPRs remain unchanged.

Figure 2.19 shows a reusable test case translation program for the microprocessor test case in Figure 2.18. The translation program allows the verification engineer to focus on the scenarios that must be verified rather than address the mundane task of initializing every byte in the model or driving inputs. The verification engineer leaves these tedious tasks to the test case parser, loader, mnemonic translator, and end checking program routines. A simple routine such as the mnemonic translator demonstrates how raising the level of abstraction eases the burden of creating test cases. The mnemonic (such as ADD and OR)

```
***Test case ADD OR***
***Initializations***
INIT GPR0 "00000008"X
INIT GPR1 "00000005"X
INIT GPR5 "A5A5A5A5"X
INIT GPR6 "5A5A5A5A"X
***Instructions***
START ADDR "00005000"X
INSTR ADDR "00005000"X OP ADD GPR0 GPR1 GPR2
INSTR ADDR "00005002"X OP OR GPR5 GPR6 GPR7
***Results***
ENDCHECK GPR0 "00000008"X
ENDCHECK GPR1 "00000005"X
ENDCHECK GPR2 "0000000D"X
ENDCHECK GPR5 "A5A5A5A5"X
ENDCHECK GPR6 "5A5A5A5A"X
ENDCHECK GPR7 "FFFFFFFF"X
```

■ **FIGURE 2.18**

A simple simulation test case language for microprocessor verification initializes internal design under verification latches, defines an instruction stream for stimulus, and provides end-of-test-case values for results checking.

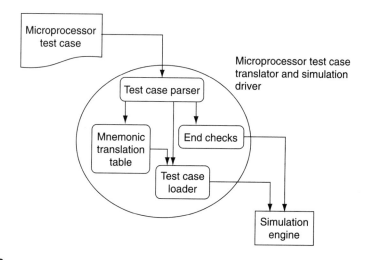

■ **FIGURE 2.19**

A test case environment allows the verification engineer to create multiple test cases by raising the abstraction level for the verification engineer.

is a programming level representation of a multibit code that "instructs" a processor to perform a specific operation. Rather than requiring the test case writer to memorize the multibit op-code for each instruction, the test case language uses the user-friendly mnemonic. Furthermore, the use of mnemonics in the test case makes for easy test case readability.

With the test case translation routine in place, the verification engineer can quickly modify the ADD operands to verify the design of the adder. The verification engineer pays special attention to creating test cases with operands that hit corner cases such as overflows. The verification engineer would also write test cases that verify that any GPR can be used for the ADD instruction, as well as the case in which the results of the ADD overwrite one of the operands. The verification and design teams can conceive of dozens of test cases to verify the adder, as well as any other of the hundreds of instructions. That is thousands of test cases required to verify single instructions. Thousands more test cases are needed to verify that every instruction can follow every other instruction. Writing each of these test cases by hand would be an overwhelming task, even for a large verification team.

Test Case Generators and Test Case Drivers

With the need for so many test cases, verification teams realized they needed further advances in test case automation. At this point in the evolution, verification engineers invented two separate technologies that revolutionized simulation-based verification.

The first technology was a direct result of the overwhelming number of test cases required to verify a design such as a microprocessor. Rather than hand-generating (at a keyboard) individual test cases for each scenario, verification and tools designers created expert software systems that use test case templates as inputs. These expert systems have built-in knowledge of the microprocessor architecture. This raises the abstraction for the verification engineer to the next level. Now, rather than calculating each operand needed to verify that the adder overflow works, a template with keywords such as OVERFLOW tells the test case generator the desired type of test case. A single template can create hundreds of different test cases, all with similar attributes. Templates can be very specific or very generic. For example, a template might call for a specific instruction (e.g., ADD), or it could specify a choice of any instruction that uses the fixed-point unit of the microprocessor (e.g. ADD, SUB, OR, XOR, AND, Shift Left). Innovations such as test case generators allowed verification engineers to focus on the intent of their test plans rather than spend their time manipulating bits and bytes of inputs.

Automated test case drivers were the second technology developed after basic test cases. Test case drivers differ from test case generators in that test case drivers do not produce a test scenario that can be viewed before simulation. Whereas the test case generator produces many test cases that hit specific cases, the test case driver is designed to understand the input protocols and manipulate the design's inputs on-the-fly during simulation. Test case drivers are interactive programs that continuously interface with the simulation model. Rather than using pregenerated test cases as the source, test case drivers make real-time decisions about what to drive on the DUV inputs. Test case drivers replace the test case

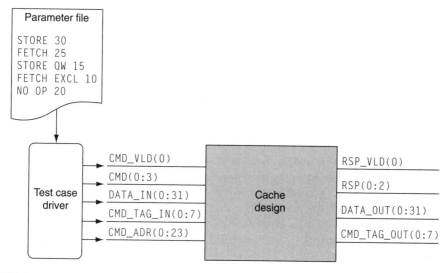

■ **FIGURE 2.20**

Under the test case generation paradigm, the test case driver uses a parameter file to make decisions on input stimulus to the DUV. In this case, the DUV is a cache. This parameter file shows weightings for different cache commands.

generator templates with parameter files, which use probabilities and pseudorandom number generators to bias the controls of the design inputs. These parameter files guide the real-time decisions made by the driver.

Figure 2.20 shows a generic test case generator setup for a few of the inputs to a cache. The biasing in the parameter file directs the test case generator to drive commands based on the specified ratios, or weightings. The parameter file shows only command biasing for illustration purposes; a real cache parameter file would contain many biasing fields, including address ranges and data patterns. When the cache DUV interface allows the driver to send a command, the test case generator chooses one of {STORE, FETCH, STORE QuadWord, FETCH EXCLusive, or NO OPeration} by using a pseudorandom number generator and the weights from the parameter file. In this example, the driver would choose the STORE command 30% of the time on average. The test case generator then manipulates the input lines (valid, command, data, and tag) as dictated by the cache input protocols. Designers must document these protocols and the verification engineer who creates the driver program must understand the precise protocols, but the intent of the driver is to abstract this low-level detail out of test case creation. In all cases, checking code (not pictured) verifies that the DUV provides the correct response for each command and that fetch data matches previous store data for the given address.

Initially, verification engineers wrote test case drivers in general-purpose programming languages such as C or C++. This remains an acceptable and viable solution. Recently, the use of High-Level Verification Languages (HVLs) has further eased the creation of robust verification driver and checker environments. HVLs are described in Chapter 6.

Coverage and Formal Verification

Test case drivers and generators provide the ability to run enormous numbers of test cases. Server farms dedicated to running simulations have grown to handle all of these test cases. However, the creation of pseudorandom, on-the-fly test cases led to the need for more observability of what sequences test cases actually generate. Verification engineers accomplished this by capturing the scenarios that the test cases create. *Coverage* is the collection of information about the scenarios run against a DUV. Coverage metrics allow verification engineers to be sure that their test cases actually hit the scenarios that they intended to create. Coverage metrics also help show the effectiveness of the test case automation by highlighting unexercised areas of the design.

Continuing with the evolution shown in Figure 2.17, effective formal verification engines further expanded the tool kit available to the verification engineer. This technology departs from the use of simulation engines by using automated mathematical proofs to show that a property of the design holds for all cases. Whereas simulation-based techniques show that for a single path in the design (a test scenario) all properties are upheld (checkers), formal verification shows that a single property holds for all paths. The initial drawback of formal verification engines was that the engines could model only very small portions of the design (less than 100 latches). Recent advances continue to improve the size constraints, making formal verification complementary to simulation-based verification techniques. We explain the details of formal verification in Chapters 11 and 12.

Timeframes of the early evolution in verification methods differed from one design company to another. Until the mid 1990s, the main technology available from the EDA industry was simulation engines. Hardware design companies developed test case generation and driver techniques in-house. In contrast, today, the EDA industry provides some of the most advanced engines for both simulation and formal verification methods.

2.3 SUMMARY

As design complexity increases, the design teams break their HDL into logic partitions, which come together in a hierarchy. Verification teams take advantage of the hierarchy in the same manner and split their work into hierarchical levels. The team must decide which hierarchical levels to use on a project, based on its unique features. The team bases their choice of levels on multiple factors, including location of highly complex functions, specification availability, work force, and evolutionary versus new design implementation.

Once the team chooses the levels of hierarchy, each environment must focus on the cornerstone of verification: driving and checking. Robust drivers and complete checkers are both required for effective verification. One is no good without the other.

Robust drivers require an understanding of the inputs to the DUV. The goal for the verification engineer is to create all possible scenarios, but that is not feasible on the largest designs. In any case, the verification engineer must maximize the scenario generation capability of the environment. This process includes driving all possible command and control signals and driving a varied array of values on data signals. Equally important is the creation of edge cases, in which unique exceptions and odd combinations of inputs often uncover bugs in the DUV.

A complete set of checkers comes from multiple sources. One source is the DUV output signals, from which the verification engineer can create basic checks. Another source is the design context, which supplies the verification engineer with a greater understanding of the underlying function. Finally, the architecture and microarchitecture specify the exact behavior that the DUV must exhibit and the design implementation.

Driver and checker practices evolved over time. In their early form, engineers imbedded stimulus in test patterns—hand-coded bit-level DUV inputs. Verification has grown enormously from these simple roots. Advances in test case techniques have raised the level of abstraction, allowing the verification engineer to focus on creating scenarios and results checking through automation. Recent advances brought coverage and formal verification tools into the mix. Each advance in methodology further strengthens the verification engineer's capability at all levels of the hierarchy.

2.4 EXERCISES

1. We return to the town of Eagleton, where the town board has awarded a new contract to the development team at Eagleton Signal Controllers and Parking Engineering Solutions (ESCAPES). The contract stipulates that ESCAPES should design and deliver a parking lot controller for the new, state-of-the-art parking garage.

   The garage is a multilevel structure with 500 parking spots. The town council has decided to base the parking fees on an hourly charge, with a maximum charge for 8 hours. With this in mind, the team at

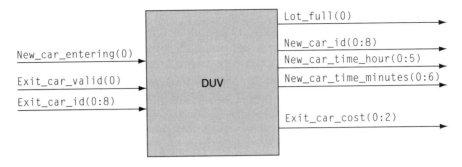

▪ **FIGURE 2.21**

The input and output signals for the parking lot controller design under verification in Exercise 1.

ESCAPES designs a chip with inputs and outputs as depicted in Figure 2.21.

The design team breaks the inputs to the chip into two parts:

1. An indication that a new car is entering the garage (new_car_entering(0))
2. An indication that a car is leaving the garage (exit_car_valid(0) and exit_car_id(0:8)). The controller assigns the 9-bit ID to the car when it enters the garage. Nine bits accommodates the 500-car capacity.

The outputs to the chip are in three parts:

1. A single bit to indicate that the lot is full (lot_full(0)).
2. A set of signals for cars entering the garage. New_car_id assigns the car a 9-bit ID tag. The chip also outputs the time (in hours and minutes) that the car arrived (new_car_time_hours(0:5) accommodates 24 hours, and new_car_time_minutes(0:6) accommodates 60 minutes). The controller also saves the time in an internal array associated with the car identification number.
3. Exit_car_cost(0:2) indicates the number of hours that the car was in the lot (up to 8 hours) and rounded up to the next hour.

As Eagleton's chief verification engineer, you have the job of verifying this chip. What scenarios must your team create? What checks are required? Is the input and output definition sufficient?

2. Figure 2.22 shows the interface of a household temperature controller. The user can set the temperature between 60°F and 100°F. The chip has a mechanical temperature sensor and has the following inputs and outputs:

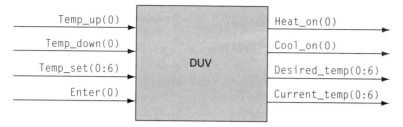

The input and output description for the temperature controller design under verification in Exercise 2.

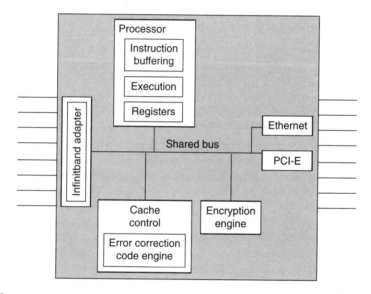

■ **FIGURE 2.23**

Logical connections of the card in Exercises 2 and 3. This card plugs into a system that may have up to 15 more identical cards.

Inputs:

- Temp_up(0) is the request for increasing the temperature by 1°.
- Temp_down(0) is the request for decreasing the temperature by 1°.
- Temp(0:6) and Enter(0) function together to set the temperature to a particular value.

Outputs:

- When asserted, Heat_on(0) turns on the heater.
- When asserted, Cool_on(0) turns on the air conditioner.

- Current_temp(0:6) displays the current temperature.
- Desired_temp(0:6) shows the requested temperature.

The specification for the temperature controller follows. The controller reads inputs at the beginning of each clock cycle. If the homeowner asserts Temp_up(0), the controller must update Desired_temp to the new value (Current_temp + 1) at the beginning of the next clock cycle. Conversely, if the homeowner asserts Temp_down(0), the controller decrements Current_temp.

At any given cycle, the controller asserts Heat_on if [Desired_temp > Current_temp]. Similarly, the controller asserts Cool_on if [Desired_temp < Current_temp]. If [Desired_temp = Current_temp], then the controller sets both Heat_on(0) and Cool_on(0) to "0"b. Finally, the controller never sets Heat_on(0) and Cool_on(0) simultaneously.

You have the job of verifying this chip. What scenarios must you create? What checks must you implement?

3. The card in Figure 2.23 depicts a design that plugs into a backplane. The backplane may contain up to 16 of these cards. Describe the levels of hierarchy and components at each level needed to verify this system.

4. Where would the verification engineer obtain input and output definitions for the Ethernet and PCI-E units shown in Figure 2.23?

CHAPTER 3

FUNDAMENTALS OF SIMULATION-BASED VERIFICATION

This chapter introduces a simple simulation-based verification environment, explores the individual elements (also known as verification components) that comprise the verification environment, and examines the driver and checker concepts that were introduced in Chapter 2 (by discussing the details of the verification components and their interactions).

In addition, this chapter covers the depth to which a verification team needs to understand the functions they are verifying in order to create a robust set of verification components, expands on the black box verification paradigm by introducing two other paradigms that the verification team must understand, and includes a discussion on the extent that the team needs to understand the design intent and implementation.

As the complexities of verification compound, designers can participate and assist in verification by using a new paradigm called assertion-based verification. This chapter gives an overview of assertion-based verification and how it relates to the different verification paradigms.

This chapter concludes by presenting different strategies of testing, discussing how the verification environment is structured and how the verification components interact with one another, as well as how the depth implementation knowledge that the verification team has affects the testing strategy.

3.1 BASIC VERIFICATION ENVIRONMENT: A TEST BENCH

The verification environment models the universe for the design and must support all actions that can happen to the design. The basic environment consists of the design or logic that is being verified, stimulus components, monitor components, checking components, and scoreboard components (some environments may not include a scoreboard). Figure 3.1 shows a diagram of a basic verification environment.

This environment is referred to as a *test bench*. In general, a test bench is all the code used to create, observe, and check a pre-determined

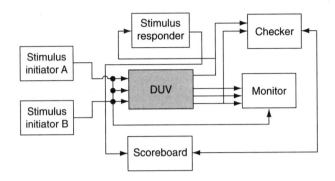

■ **FIGURE 3.1**

Basic verification environment: a test bench. (Some environments do not include a scoreboard.)

("deterministic") input sequence to the design. This pre-determined input sequence may be generated in a direct approach or by a random method. The test bench, or environment, is a closed system, meaning that the top level of the test bench has no inputs or outputs. It is effectively a model of the universe from the design-under-verification (DUV) standpoint.

The verification engineer must create the code for the components of this test bench universe, and the logic designer creates the hardware description language (HDL) for the DUV. These components can be written in the HDL itself, in a language that was designed for verification (HVL, a high-level verification language covered in Chapter 6), or in a general-purpose programming language such as C/C++. In the case of an HVL or programming language, the code communicates to the simulation engine through an application programming interface (API). Occasionally, it is necessary to mix and match the languages in which the components are written. An outside customer's model may even be required in the verification environment.

The challenge for a verification engineer is to create a test bench that stimulates the design with interesting input patterns (ideally, these patterns should cover all the functionality of the design if possible, or at least as much as possible) and calculates the expected responses for the outputs based on those input patterns. The design can be said to be functioning as intended by exercising all the functionality and by predicting and checking all responses.

The sections that follow look at each component in the test bench.

3.1.1 Stimulus Component

The *stimulus component* manipulates inputs to the DUV. Stimulus models are also known as drivers, behaviorals, agitators, irritators, or generators. Typically, the stimulus component code mimics the behavior

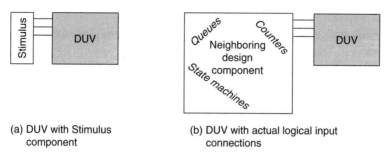

(a) DUV with Stimulus
component

(b) DUV with actual logical input
connections

■ **FIGURE 3.2**

Stimulus component. The stimulus component need not model the real design component.

of a neighboring design entity or entities. In creating the stimulus component, the verification engineer should not model the entire behavior of the neighboring design component; instead, the stimulus component should only mimic the interface inputs to the DUV. This not only makes the simulation code easier to maintain but also allows the stimulus engine to drive the interfaces free of the burden of the realities of the neighboring design component it is mimicking. The stimulus component only needs to concern itself with the behavior of the inputs that affect the DUV, as shown in Figure 3.2.

For example, the real design component (Figure 3.2b) may have an eight-deep queue that, when full, inhibits sending a control signal to the DUV, even if the DUV could accept the control signal. The stimulus component only concerns itself with the availability of the DUV to accept the control signal, not whether the real design component's queue is full (Figure 3.2a).

This is a key concept in verification. The stimulus engine must drive what the DUV is capable of accepting and not restrict itself to what the real neighboring design component might send. This allows the verification engineer to exert a maximum amount of stress on the DUV. If possible, this stress level should exceed that which will ever occur in a customer environment. By exceeding the limits of the design, the verification engineer is more likely to encounter seldom seen occurrences, called *corner cases*, in the DUV. These corner cases otherwise might never be seen until hundreds of trillions of cycles of hardware test. This concept of "over-stressing" the DUV allows the verification engineer to compete with the relatively infinite number of cycles run in fabricated hardware.

All stimulus components must understand the complete interface protocol; that is, they must be capable of mimicking all possible variations of the protocol. This must occur so that the DUV is stimulated in all possible ways. Without full protocol stimulus capability, the model is incomplete.

Sometimes these verification components have configuration settings that allow the model to work in different environments or levels. These settings indicate to the stimulus component how it should behave. For example, given an Ethernet stimulus component, a configuration mode may exist to allow it to only create jumbo Ethernet packets.

It is also interesting to place a model in a mode in which all it does is generate bus traffic that is not used. This just irritates the system with "noise." Then when real bus commands are performed, different results occur because the irritator is running.

A final job of the stimulus component is to track its activity for possible post-simulation analysis of the test case. The stimulus components should record events into a file used for initial test case debugging.

The particular details for both initiators and responders are discussed in the sections that follow.

Deciding What To Model

The verification engineer should use the design specification when deciding on what to model from a behavioral standpoint. If the DUV does not have a specification, the verification engineer should interview the designer of the neighboring design component to understand the protocols. This provides a cross-check of the DUV designer's assumptions. At this level, the verification team should find miscommunications between designers.

The verification engineer should not rely on the DUV designer for interface protocol specification because this breaks the redundancy model built into the verification cycle (discussed in Chapter 1). The designer could misunderstand a part of the agreed on communications scheme and thus bias the stimulus model such that both the HDL and the stimulus component code the incorrect or incomplete behavior. Occasionally, this does occur, and the misunderstanding is not found until the next higher verification level when the two real components exist together. However, as discussed in Chapter 2, there will be less control over this interface at the next level of verification, and the misunderstood scenario may never be created. A second concern with receiving input definitions from the designer of the DUV is that the designer may bias the verification engineer about what will occur on the interface. This could lead the verification engineer to miss stimulating certain boundary conditions.

The deterministic test bench stimulus component mainly has outputs that drive the DUV. The only inputs to these stimulus components will be those necessary for their behavior, such as a clock or reset signal. However, more complex stimulus generation components will have inputs that control the stimulus generation.

There are two types of stimulus models: *initiators* and *responders*. An *initiator* is a stimulus model that will initiate a transaction or transac-

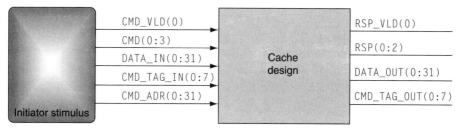

■ FIGURE 3.3

Initiator stimulus.

tions to the DUV; a responder reacts to outputs from the DUV and feeds stimulus back into the DUV.

Initiators

All verification environments, simple simulation based or advanced, require driving the bit-level stimulus into the DUV as defined by the protocols. This portion of the environment requires the verification engineer to have detailed knowledge of the complete interface definition. This is the protocol component of the initiator. As an example, this chapter builds on the cache design shown in Chapter 2 (see Figure 2.20). Figure 3.3 shows that the protocol component needs to drive five separate signals and buses comprising 77 total bits.

In this example, the protocol component must understand the decode values and relative timings required by the cache for initiating a valid request. In this cache design, a 64-bit store request is represented by a "5"x value on the command bus. Up to 15 other request types may exist with different CMD(0:3) decode values. The valid bit must accompany the request, along with the tag, address, and first 32 bits of data. The next 32 bits of data follow on the next cycle. Figure 3.4 shows the trace of a single store.

The protocol component acts as a slave to the generation component. Although the protocol component handles low-level bit manipulation into the DUV, it is the role of the generation component to supply the higher-level request. In the cache example, the generation component dictated the sending of a 64-bit store request to address "01357900"X. In a deterministic environment, this might be the only request sent to the cache. More than likely, however, the test case will contain more requests for the DUV, such as more stores to similar addresses or fetches that collide with the stores. On an interface such as the cache, the generation component will feed the protocol component one request at a time as determined by the simple test case.

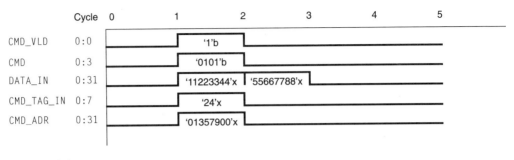

▪ FIGURE 3.4

Cache input timing for a single store request. This figure shows the input signal values driven by the stimulus component into the cache design.

The microarchitecture of the DUV will dictate how the generation component knows when it is legal to supply a new command to the DUV. Invariably there are two ways that any design communicates availability of its resources to a requestor. The two choices are as follows:

1. The requestor knows the depth of the resource and keeps track of it.

2. The owner of the resource supplies an "available" signal to the requestor.

To illustrate this, suppose that the microarchitecture of the cache example contains a buffer than can hold up to eight fetch requests concurrently. If at any time during the test case, the generation component (requestor) sends a request to the DUV such that the cache had nine outstanding fetch requests, then an illegal test case with an overwrite condition occurs. Therefore, the generation component must implement the same resource availability determination as the microarchitecture. Either the generation component must keep count of the number of outstanding fetches in the cache (number of fetches sent minus the number of fetches completed), or the cache must supply a signal indicating that the buffer is full.

In both cases, a feedback mechanism is required to prevent the generation component from illegally initiating a request. Often, the *scoreboard component* of the verification environment (described later in this section) participates in this feedback. In the simplest terms, a scoreboard is a temporary holding location for information that the checker will require (described later in this chapter). The generation component must contain the intelligence to know when resources are available.

Implementation decisions abound even in a simple example such as this cache. Depending on the significance of the CMD_TAG_IN(0:7) line, the test case writer may want control over the values. If this were the case, the generation component would also send the tag with the request. On the other hand, if the tag were used only as an identifier to be escorted along the request path, it would suffice to have the protocol generator supply a unique tag to the DUV with each request. A simple incrementor would satisfy the protocol as long as the protocol generator guarded against duplicate outstanding tags (assuming that the design forbids having duplicate tags in the DUV concurrently). Similarly, there is a decision to be made on the DATA_IN(0:31) values, as they could be randomly generated by the protocol component or strategically chosen by the test case writer.

The separation of the generation and protocol components is important. Most interfaces are not as trivial as this cache example and have multiple concurrent or overlapping interactions and many more control and data signals. Breaking these components apart simplifies the coding of the environment. This structure has other benefits as well: a separate protocol component allows the test case writer to think more about the transactions rather than focus on the bit-level manipulations, and furthermore, a well-defined interface between the generation component and the protocol component allows for substitution of generation components. Simple test bench environments often precede complex random environments. The verification team avoids redundant work by creating stand-alone protocol components, allowing current and future generation components to plug into them. The stand-alone protocol component is also referred to as a *Bus Functional Model* (BFM), a model that performs the bus function.

This type of stimulation of the DUV is called "transaction-based" verification. The basis for the simulation is all types of transactions, generated in a random or directed fashion.

Responders

The second type of stimulus component, responders, reacts to outputs from the DUV and feeds stimulus back into the DUV. The difference between an initiator and a responder is that the responder acts as a slave to the DUV. It will only send stimulus back into the DUV as a result of a request, command, or other demand from the DUV.

Continuing with the cache example, Figure 3.5 shows a main storage memory component that communicates with the cache. The memory receives either a store or fetch command from the cache and must act on that request. The memory itself never initiates communication.

For verification of the cache, the memory is replaced by a main store responder stimulus component. When receiving a store command along with an address and data, the main store will react at the appropriate time with a response. For a fetch command, the main store component will return both a response and the requested data.

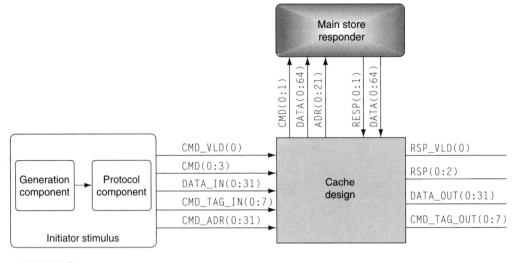

▪ **FIGURE 3.5**

Memory stimulus acting as a responder.

Variability is allowed in the sequence with the responder. In the cache to main store example, there can be variability in the response (successful completion or failure) and in the number of cycles between command and response (if the timing is not fixed allows). However, in simple simulation environments, the test case writer pre-determines the timings and values.

3.1.2 Monitor

A monitor is a model that observes different aspects of the environment. Monitors are self-contained components that observe

- Outputs of the DUV for protocol adherence

- Inputs to the DUV for functional coverage analysis and scoreboard updates

- Internals of the DUV for events of interest to the environment

At a minimum, the monitor must observe the outputs of the DUV. If the DUV does not adhere to the protocol, then the monitor must return an error. The monitor does not drive any signals or wires into the DUV; it only receives inputs and/or callbacks to it. By developing a monitor in this fashion, the verification engineer ensures it is reusable at other levels.

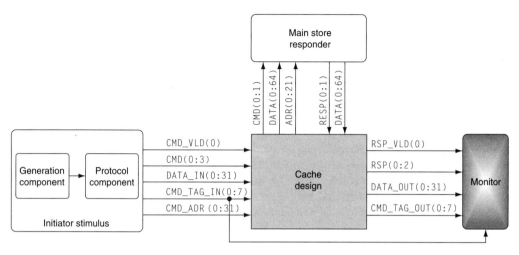

■ **FIGURE 3.6**

Monitor observing the cache design under verification.

Figure 3.6 shows the monitor added to the cache environment. The monitor verifies that the DUV obeys the output protocols at all times. In this case, the monitor must check the following:

- RSP_VLD(0) (the response valid signal) always accompanies a valid response.

- The RSP(0:2) signal, when accompanied by the valid signal, has legal values (e.g., 001 = success; 010 = parity error; 011 = retry due to busy; 100 = illegal command sent; all others are illegal response decodes).

In addition, the monitor may check for the following, depending on the environment and protocols:

- The RSP(0:2) signal never is on in the absence of the RSP_VLD(0) signal. Depending on the protocol, the outputs may be required to be zero unless a valid response is being sent.

- The tag is correct; that is, it matches with a tag sent previously by the initiator component.

When deciding on how to monitor the outputs for protocol adherence, the verification engineer should refer to the specification. Similar to the stimulus model, if the DUV does not have a specification, then at a minimum, the verification engineer should communicate with the architect and the designer of the piece of logic on the receiving side of the

DUV. The independence of the verification engineer is lost if information on how the monitor should work is obtained from the designer, who could misunderstand a part of the correct communication and protocol scheme and thus bias the verification checking.

However, the monitor may need to probe internals of the DUV to collect information to pass on to the checker or scoreboard components. In this case, the verification engineer should limit the internal probes and beware of breaking the redundancy path by relying on the design for too much information.

In all the above scenarios, the monitor can use this information to generate functional coverage data (for more information on functional coverage, see Chapter 6).

In sophisticated environments, the stimulus components may use coverage information (either from internal DUV probes or from DUV inputs) collected by the monitor to adapt the stimulus for a more stressful or diverse DUV simulation (for more information, see Chapter 14). This is called coverage directed generation.

A final job of the monitor is to provide post-simulation information to the verification engineer. The monitor should be able to record interface events to a runtime file, formatting it for readability and debugging assistance.

3.1.3 Checker

A checker is a special type of monitor that only collects DUV outputs. However, it validates that the design is working as intended from a functional standpoint, not just from a protocol standpoint.

The checker tends to be one of the harder components in the environment to get correct, as the verification engineer must implement many functional checks within the component. It is not only challenging to get individual checkers working correctly for all cases but also imperative that the verification engineer conceive of all the required checking. This is fundamental to the question, "How will I know if the design has a flaw?"

In the past, verification engineers performed the functional checking by reviewing the test case traces by hand and looking for specific results on the DUV outputs. Often, the reference model for the DUV was in the verification engineer's head. Although this was an arduous process, the designs were simpler and contained fewer corner conditions and complex interactions. As design complexity increased, verification engineers transferred the intelligence behind the checking from their own knowledge to automated software checker components.

The checker may need knowledge from a monitor or scoreboard to accomplish its task. The checker needs to understand what stimulus has occurred in order to independently predict functional results. Because there may be multiple requests and interaction stimulus in a single test case, the checker needs to correlate input requests with output responses. The checker code compares these expected results against actual outputs of the DUV. If the results match, the test case continues or completes successfully. If the results miscompare, the checker will write a failure message to a debug file, noting the actual and expected results along with other information needed to understand the failure.

Checkers monitor for various types of error types:

- All requests receive responses (no lost data, commands, packets, etc.)

- All outputs match predicted values (response codes, data, packets, etc.)

- No superfluous output activity (outputs that do not correspond to any stimulus)

Remember, the monitor component performs checks that are more mundane:

- Parity and check-bit correctness

- Actual data transfer length corresponds to header transfer length

- Other checking that does not require knowledge from the stimulus components

3.1.4 Scoreboard

A scoreboard is a relatively new term, although the concept has been around for a long time. In the simplest terms, a scoreboard is a temporary holding location for information the checker will require.

A checker can use a scoreboard in two ways. The main difference between the two methods centers on which component does the translation from inputs and expected outputs. The component that performs this function acts as the DUV reference model and contains the checking intelligence.

In the first method, the checker component contains the reference model. The scoreboard's role is to examine the inputs for transactions to occur, capture pertinent information, and store the information for later use. Then when the checker observes some condition on the outputs of the DUV, it makes a call to the scoreboard to get the data (referred to as a *callback*).

The scoreboard implementation depends on the functionality that is contained in the DUV. If the DUV has a simple first in, first out (FIFO) protocol, then the scoreboard would also contain a simple FIFO, and the data returned would be from a callback such as "pop expect from port 1." Or if the DUV had a complex queuing algorithm, then a much more

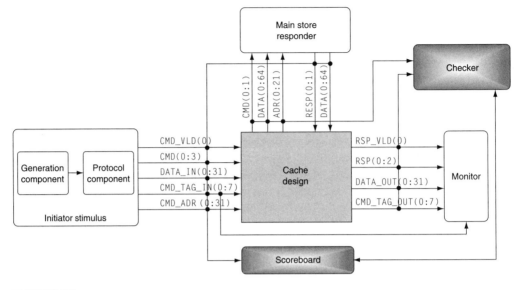

▪ **FIGURE 3.7**

Checker comparing responses.

complex function such as a search based on port number would need to be performed in the scoreboard in order to return the correct data. Once the scoreboard returns the data, the reference model in the checker "transforms the data" into expected results and then compares those results to the actual DUV output signals.

In the second method, the scoreboard is the reference model and does the expected result calculation based on the input stimulus it observes. When the checker observes DUV output events, it then queries the scoreboard for the expected data and performs the compare.

Figure 3.7 shows the checker and scoreboard components added to the cache design verification environment. To illustrate the two reference model cases described above, consider the required checking on a command that fetches data from memory address "01234500"X with a tag of "23"X.

In both cases (in which the checker or scoreboard contains the reference model), the following basic sequence occurs. The scoreboard observes and records the initiator stimulus, sending a fetch command to the cache design. The scoreboard must observe the stimulus on the interface, rather than have the initiator stimulus component write the data to the scoreboard directly. The independence of the scoreboard and stimulus generator is important for component re-use at later levels of the verification hierarchy.

The scoreboard also records other command stimulus. The information about the commands that are outstanding in the DUV is stored in a table. The index into the table is the command tag. Soon after receiving the fetch command, the DUV forwards the fetch to the main store memory. The checker observes this action and queries the scoreboard, ensuring that there was a fetch command to address "01234500"X in the system. When the main store responder component responds to the fetch request with data, the scoreboard writes the data into the table. The cache design finishes the fetch transaction as it drives the response, valid, tag, and data output signals. The monitor verifies that as the RSP_VLD(0) signal is raised, there is a valid decode value on the RSP(0:2) bus.

At this point, the final checks are required. In the case in which the checker component has the reference model, it will query the scoreboard for all data in the table indexed by the value of the tag on the CMD_TAG_OUT(0:7) signal. The scoreboard dumps the data to the checker for the final checks. If the scoreboard has no valid data corresponding to the tag index, then one of the following is true:

- The DUV has corrupted a tag.

- The DUV is returning a tag that has previously been returned.

- The DUV has "made-up" a tag.

- The scoreboard has a bug.

However, in this case, the tag of "23"X has a valid entry in the scoreboard table, and the checker receives the values saved in the table. It is then the checker's job to compile the expected results and compare it to the DUV output data. In some cases, this might entail manipulating the data, depending on the format of the main store responder inputs and the expected outputs of the DUV.

In the case in which the scoreboard contains the reference model code, the checker will still send the scoreboard the tag index. The scoreboard will compile the data, including any reformatting or manipulation, and send the exact expected results to the checker for final comparison to the actual DUV outputs.

In both cases, any failures or miscompare values should be recorded to an output file for debug purposes. Depending on the severity of the observed error, the test case halts after hitting the failure.

Either of the above divisions of work between scoreboard and checker is acceptable. However, it is important that the choice of reference model placement remains consistent. The same paradigm should be followed for all DUV checking throughout the environment.

3.1.5 Design Under Verification

The last component, the DUV, is the center of the verification environment and is also known as the *unit under test* (*UUT*) or the *device under test* (*DUT*). Most of the other components interact with the DUV. If there are bugs in the DUV, the verification team must find them.

The DUV source is the HDL itself. Whether running a simulation or formal verification, the source HDL gets interpreted or compiled into the DUV model (depending on the tools and HDL source used), which the verification team uses for its simulation. The specific interpreter or compiler differs depending on the electronic design automation vendor, but in all cases, the DUV is an accurate representation of the HDL.

The DUV can be from any level of the hierarchy. The DUV in Figure 3.1 can represent a sole designer macro, a logical unit, a chip, or an entire system. Regardless of the level, the verification engineer must customize stimulus and checking components, scoreboards, and monitors to exercise and validate the particular DUV.

The depth at which the DUV is described can be different as well. The source HDL may describe the function at the RTL level, gate level, transistor level, or even behavioral level (non-synthesisable). As seen in Chapter 1, it is the responsibility of the verification team to ensure that whatever form the design takes, the function matches the intent.

The DUV interacts directly with the stimulus and checking components. The stimulus component manipulates the DUV's inputs, and the monitor and checking components observe its outputs. In some situations, monitors and checkers may reside inside the DUV, which could be attributed to the need for additional observation or checking points.

3.2 OBSERVATION POINTS: BLACK-BOX, WHITE-BOX, AND GREY-BOX VERIFICATION

In the cache example above, all of the verification code was restricted to interfacing with external interfaces of the DUV. This is known as black box verification, because the verification environment is "in the dark" about internal details of the DUV. However, some environments may look at signals that are inside the DUV. These environments are grey box or white box environments, depending on the type of internal DUV observation.

3.2.1 Black Box

Most simulation-based environments begin as black box environments. The verification engineers begin reading a specification of the DUV that contains the function and the definition of the external interfaces. As the team writes the verification code, the drivers, monitors, checkers, and scoreboard use only the external interfaces as defined by the specification. The internal signals and constructs remain in the dark.

The key to black box verification is the ability to predict the outputs based on the inputs. To do this, the specification must clearly explain the function of the DUV.

The black box environment has pros and cons. The good points are that structural changes inside the DUV have little impact on the verification code, as the function is independent of implementation. If an internal pipeline had to change because of a timing constraint, there is little to no impact on the verification environment. Furthermore, the ability to predict functional results based on inputs alone ensures that the reference model remains independent from the DUV algorithms.

On the other hand, because the black box environment can only control the inputs and observe the outputs, it lacks control and observation points. There are many cases in which a verification environment can be more robust just by keying off internal signals in the DUV. Similarly, checking ambiguous cases becomes trivial if the scoreboard component monitors internal signals. By using internal signals, the verification engineers can shed some light on the black box.

3.2.2 White Box

The advantages and disadvantages of black box testing are reversed in the white box environment, which provides a full understanding of the internal structures of the DUV. The verification engineer observes and places checking on internal signals, as well as models and predicts the behavior of internal queues, pipelines, state machines, and other portions of the microarchitecture.

The white box environment contrasts with the black box environment through its direct measurement of the DUV. A white box environment will flag a bug at its source, whereas the black box environment captures a failure indirectly as its symptoms appear on the DUV output. More details of the cache design described above can illustrate the white box methods.

Figure 3.8 shows that the incoming command, tag, and address are placed into an eight-deep command queue. In the white box environment, the verification engineer might keep a reference model of the command queue and use that model to constantly check the contents of the queue. If the design has a bug such that a valid entry in the queue was dropped or overwritten, the white box environment checker would immediately flag the flaw. This is a direct capture of the failure where valid data is destroyed. The black box environment would also flag this bug, as the cache design would never give a response to a command that was recorded in the scoreboard. In this case, the checker is indirect, detecting the symptoms (a lost command). Both paradigms are successful.

Assertion checkers, comment-like statements in the HDL that the verification environment or simulation engine monitors, are a second form of white box verification placed in the DUV by the designer. Assertion checkers monitor the behavior for specific invalid cases. Typical assertion checkers flag invalid state transitions, overflowing queues, and other illegal states. Because these checkers observe specific cases within the

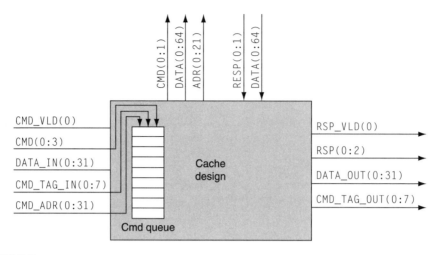

Cache design implementation details and white box checking.

design, they fit the definition of white box verification. Further details of assertions follow in this chapter.

Any form of white box verification has its drawbacks in the amount of maintenance required on the environment. The problem is that the environment is tightly integrated with the implementation: if a signal name changes, the white box checker component must change as well, which can become a maintenance nightmare. Therefore, this type of verification is typically done only at the low levels of the hierarchy.

Verification environments coded in a white box paradigm must also take care to remain independent of the DUV. Despite knowledge of the internal microarchitecture, the verification engineer must not use the HDL algorithms as a source of checking. This would break the redundancy path required to find bugs in the design.

3.2.3   Grey Box

Grey box verification is the combination of both black box and white box verifications. In the grey box environment, the verification engineer monitors or observes some internal signals, which assist in validating the functional specification of the black box level; the rest of the DUV remains "in the dark."

Grey box is typically the model used for most environments, mainly because some prediction of interface level results is nearly impossible without viewing an internal signal. Drawing on the cache design example, there is a case in which two or more fetch commands to the same address can be in the design simultaneously. In time, the main store

```
assert <expression>
   [report <message>]
      [severity <level>]
```

■ **FIGURE 3.9**

General syntax of VHDL assertion statement.

responder returns data to each command. In a black box environment, it is impossible to know if the correct data was returned with each command without "peeking" inside the DUV to see which tag corresponded to each main store fetch request.

There are also certain test scenarios that are desirable but rarely occur without verification intervention inside the DUV structures. Often, designs have counters used to initiate actions on a repetitive basis. In many cases, these counters "go off" after thousands or even millions of machine cycles. Although this may be only milliseconds on real hardware, it is an eternity in simulation cycles. To cause the counter-initiated event multiple times in a single test case, the verification engineer must overwrite the counter to a value close to its limit. This activity falls into the realm of grey box verification.

3.3 ASSERTION-BASED VERIFICATION: AN OVERVIEW

Assertion-based verification is a variant of white box verification and has been gaining much attention in literature and industry during the last several years [1]. Assertions by their very definition target the implementation of a design; they formalize assumptions about conditions inside the design that are supposed to hold true at all times.

The idea of assertions is not new. Software engineers have used the concept for ages. Many programming languages have formalized assertion constructs (e.g., the C language with the assert macro), even though other terms sometimes were used (e.g., invariants). In the context of hardware design, VHDL, even in its first standardization, included a language construct to express assertions (Figure 3.9).

Of course, assertions and verification checkers have related purposes. There is a choice to do the checking of an internal microarchitecture condition in a test bench that is owned by a verification engineer or directly in the HDL by the designer.

In the implementation of the traffic light design introduced in Chapter 1 (Figure 1.3), the encoding of the internal state machine used 2 bits to encode two legal states. As was mentioned in Chapter 1, the assertion that the state flip-flops should never assume illegal values covered by the verification engineer's test bench. However, the fact that the internal state

```
assert (buf_overrun(0)/='1')
    report "Internal Buffer Overflow"
        severity ERROR;
```

■ **FIGURE 3.10**

VHDL assertion example.

encoding is identical to the encoding of the signal Light_direction is an internal implementation detail that is unlikely to be formally documented between design and verification engineers. Even more dangerously, other logic internally downstream from these flip-flops might rely on this assertion. It is therefore vital for the designer to capture such an assumption to protect the downstream logic (Figure 3.10).

One real practical argument for the designer ownership of assertions is the fact that at the designer best understands and considers such internal white box checks at the time the he or she writes the HDL. Good examples are corner conditions and specific illegal encodings of signal states such as

- Illegal states

- Orthogonality of signals or one-hot encodings

- Illegal control conditions

One view of a systematic use of assertion checking is the notion of *defensive HDL design* (Figure 3.11). Every assertion checks a "cone of logic" for boundary conditions and protects the downstream logic by continuously guarding the assumption.

Figure 3.12 shows another implementation level example. This time the HDL assertion actually protects the physical implementation of the logic. It codifies the assumption that two "select" signals (s1, s2), which drive a pass-gate multiplexer implementation, are to be orthogonal. In the absence of the assertion, logic simulation would never detect the functional problem where s1 and s2 are on at the same time. It is the circuit implementation that exploits the orthogonality condition by using a cheaper, faster circuit layout and needs to be protected from destruction by a violation of this assumption. Very clearly, this implementation assumption must be formalized by the design engineer.

3.3.1 The Importance of Assertions

There are several reasons why a modern verification methodology must make heavy use of assertions that are embedded into the HDL design:

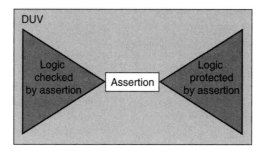

■ **FIGURE 3.11**

Assertion checking as defensive hardware design language design.

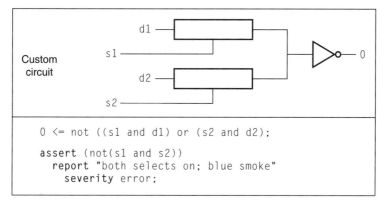

■ **FIGURE 3.12**

Pass-gate mux implementation, exploiting orthogonal select signals.

- White box conditions are best specified and, more importantly, maintained over time by the design team. Many internal assertions could not be known by a verification engineer, but violation of these internal conditions can lead to severe malfunction of the design.

- Unlike non-HDL test bench checkers, formal verification tools (Chapters 11, 12) can process HDL assertions. This opens the potential of *proving* formally that an assertion always holds true, a much more powerful verification result than any amount of pattern-based simulation can ever deliver.

- An uncaught assertion violation can result in an error that is detected in the architecture state of the design downstream after more simulation time. However, catching a problem at the point of an internal assertion violation is always more effective in debugging because the problem is caught at its very source.

- Assertions are cheap. Typically, they are sanity checks that are easily written by the designer, and they do not consume a lot of simulation engine performance.

- Empirical evidence shows that a systematic application of assertions by the design team is able to catch significant amounts (24% to 35%) of the design bugs found overall on large industrial projects [2, 3].

3.3.2 Assertions Express Design Intent

Although the HDL expresses what a design implements, assertions also play an important role in the specification of design intent. For example, in a high-frequency design, finite state machines are usually implemented by a collection of discrete flip-flops and Boolean logic. The Boolean logic implements the state transfer and output functions in the physically most efficient way. Very often, the physical constraints on the design overrule the desire to clearly specify the finite state machine (FSM) functionality in the most abstract and concise way.

In such cases, the HDL looks like a random set of flip-flops and gates, and the original design intent, the FSM, is lost. Using assertions, which specify the legal versus illegal states and the legal versus illegal state transitions, will serve the verification cycle in two ways:

- The original design intent is explicitly expressed by stating what the intended implementation behavior is. It is possible to look at such a set of assertions as an internal implementation specification, encoded in the HDL.

- The verification cycle can utilize an invaluable set of checks that make it possible to verify the implementation specification against the discrete implementation.

It is important to note that the HDLs have mechanisms that allow the expression and checking for design intent even at compile time. Doing the check earlier than simulation, as part of the model build process, has obvious advantages for the strength of verification. Otherwise, the incidental test case must stimulate the design in a way that exposes a violation of design intent.

The most powerful way to express design intent in VHDL is the use of signal data types. VHDL is what is called a strongly typed language. Signals have defined data types, and the VHDL compiler checks type compatibility between signals when the source file is processed. Going back once again to the traffic light example from Chapter 1, the assertion of the illegal state encodings, introduced above, can be completely replaced with the correct use of signal types (Figure 3.13).

```vhdl
library ieee;
use ieee.std_logic_1164.all;

entity traffic is
 port(
  clk                : in std_ulogic; -- Clock
  reset              : in std_ulogic; -- Async Reset
  timer_pulse        : in std_ulogic; -- The timer pulse, '1' indicates timer expiration
  Main_Street        : in std_ulogic; -- Indicates when traffic is present on Main St.
  Elm_Street         : in std_ulogic; -- Indicates when traffic is present on Elm St.
  Light_Direction    : out std_ulogic_vecotor(1 downto 0) -- '01' indicates that Main St.
  should be green

                                                          -- '10' indicates that Elm St.
  should be green

  );
end traffic;

architecture rtl of traffic is
 type state is (main, elm);
 signal current_state_din, current_state_dout: state;

begin -- rtl

 -- purpose: Determines when the light should change
 -- type   : combinational
 -- inputs : timer_pulse, Main_Street, Elm_Street, current_state_dout
 -- outputs: current_state_din
 dataflow _proc: process (timer_pulse, Main_Street, Elm_Street, current_state_dout)
 begin -- process change_light
  current_state_din <= current_state_dout;
  -- When the timer expires, evaluate the traffic situation
  if timer_pulse = '1' then
   if Main_Street = '1' then
    current_state_din <= main;
   elsif Elm_Street = '1' then
    current_state_din_ <= elm;
   end if;
  end if;
 end process dataflow_proc;

 Light_Direction <= '01' when current_state_dout = main else "10";

 -- purpose: creates the registers for current state
 -- type   : sequential
 -- inputs : clk, reset, current_state_din
 -- outputs: current_state_dout
 reg_proc: process (clk, reset)
 begin -- process register
  if reset = '0' then              --asynchronous reset (active low)
   current_state_dout <= main;
  elsif clk'event and clk = '1' then -- rising clock edge
   current_state_dout <= current_state_din;
  end if;
 end process reg_proc;
end rtl;
```

■ **FIGURE 3.13**

VHDL for the traffic light algorithm with enumerated state machine encoding.

```
assert (clock and condition)…;
```

(a) Flat assertion

```
if (clock) then
    ……
    assert (condition) ……;
    ……
end if;
```

(b) Nested assertion

▪ **FIGURE 3.14**

Flat (a) and nested (b) hardware design language assertion.

In this version, the state encoding uses an enumerated type declaration for the two states "main" and "elm." The state transitions move the controller between these two symbolic states. Furthermore, an illegal assignment to a different state value would be a compile error. Using the type declaration makes the design intent explicitly clear and removes one source of potential design errors.

Assertion-based verification moves the specification of checkers earlier into the design cycle. The earlier design intent is captured in the HDL, the more effective verification processes can catch design bugs.

3.3.3 Classification of Assertions

The examples up to this point have used assertions that only check Boolean conditions that have to hold true over all times.

More often than not, a certain condition holds true only after another gating condition is also true. A simple example would be if the condition could only be checked during the time that a certain clock signal was active. There are two ways to handle this complication. Either the pre-condition (e.g. "clock active") can be encoded as a simple term in the Boolean expression or the HDL has already a conditional structure into which the assertion can be embedded, thus exploiting already existing decoding of the pre-condition (Figure 3.14).

The following list attempts to classify assertions according to increasing complexity:

- *Event detection*: The most atomic and simple assertion checks for absence of an event, a "failure condition." Designers encode these events by the flat assertions discussed mostly so far. Such events can be classified as *static*; that is, they do not relate to any other events.

- *Temporal event detection*: More complex assertions will refer to sequence of events over time; that is, several events have to occur before the final asserted event can be checked. Designers encode such assertion events via the embedded (nested) method shown in Figure 3.14. Essentially, the designer embeds the assertion into the logic of a state machine (the sequentially nested context in HDL) that controls the pre-condition for the final Boolean check.

■ *Pre-defined event detection building blocks*: Pre-build a set of assertions for events to occur often in hardware designs. Examples are data structures (buffers, stacks, FIFOs) or control structures (handshake, windows with pre- and/or post-conditions).

Temporal events require a general mechanism to express events (not just assertions) over time. Formal verification tools first pioneered the definition of such specifications. With the standardization of a property specification language (PSL/Sugar), there is now a broadly supported means to express event sequences over time, as assertions available for all forms of verification, not just formal verification [4]. We will discuss PSL/Sugar in Chapter 12.

A popular example of pre-defined event detection building blocks is the Open Verification Library (OVL) library [5]. OVL is a library of HDL building blocks that a designer can embed as an instantiated component into an HDL specification and connect to a set of signals that provide the context for the assertion check.

In light of the development of OVL and PSL/Sugar, designers of HDLs have started to extend the HDLs themselves to provide more than the basic assertion checking support in their languages. SystemVerilog defined its own built-in assertion mechanism that parallels many of PSL/Sugar's capabilities as a direct extension of Verilog [4]. Obviously, this makes the assertion language very specific to Verilog, and it is unavailable for VHDL users.

3.4 TEST BENCHES AND TESTING STRATEGIES

With the test bench environment and components defined, focus is now on the test case. A *test case* constrains the stimulus components such that a specific function (or set of functions) within the DUV is targeted to be exercised. We also call this deterministic testing, or a deterministic test bench, because the targeted function is determined before the test runs. There are also self-checking test benches in which the test bench always performs checking regardless of the stimulus. This allows for the functionality of the DUV to be checked regardless of the test case.

3.4.1 Deterministic Test Benches

Verification teams use deterministic test cases predominantly early in the verification cycle to prove basic DUV functionality. Here, the verification engineer looks to the specification for guidance on the basic commands and protocols to test and monitor, creates deterministic test cases to

TABLE 3.1 ▪ Two-input AND gate

Input A	Input B	Expected Output
0	0	0
0	1	0
1	0	0
1	1	1

pinpoint specific points of contention in the DUV specification, and relies in part on the design engineers for advice on scenarios to exercise.

A very simple example is a "two-input AND gate." There are four deterministic tests for the DUV in Table 3.1.

A verification engineer charged with verifying this two-input AND gate could create four individual deterministic test cases. Alternatively, the verification engineer could decide that the four scenarios are simplistic enough to merge into a single deterministic test case that drives the four scenarios in sequence.

A more interesting deterministic test case involving the cache design would be to ensure that particular sequences of operations maintain data coherency. Coherency dictates that data requestors *always* get the latest copy of the data. This inherently implies that for every address in the system, there is only one current data value associated with that address. In this cache design, a fetch cannot return data that does not represent the latest value for that address. A verification engineer could write many deterministic test cases to verify coherency. One such case is described here.

Figure 3.15 shows a decode mux in front of separate store and fetch queues in the cache design. As commands enter the cache DUV, the design directs the address, tag, and the data (for stores) toward the appropriate logic based on the type of command.

A deterministic sequence to verify coherency might consist of the following inputs:

- Three store commands to various addresses are sent. These commands initially fill three of the four positions in the store queue.

- A fourth store request to address X is sent. This store request is the last in line to be executed

- A fetch request to address X is sent.

Because the fetch request is at the top of the queue and a previous store request is buried in the store queue, this test case is designed to uncover a design flaw that would return fetch data other than that in the store queue. Coherency requires that the fetch request return the latest data, which may be in the store queue rather than in the cache or main

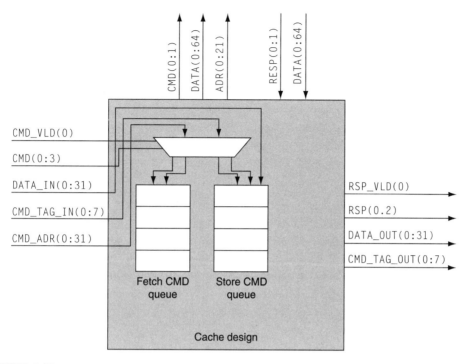

Cache design with separate queues for stores and fetches.

memory. The cache design must deal with this case by one of these means:

- Give stores higher priority than that of fetches, allowing the store queue to drain before processing fetches.

- Do an address comparison of all stores addresses pending based on the fetch address and block the fetch.

- Do an address comparison of all stores addresses pending based on the fetch address and provide a cache and main store bypass by the store queue data that would feed the fetch response data.

3.4.2 Self-Checking Test Benches

Placing the knowledge of the DUV's function into the test bench environment is extremely advantageous as it automates the tedious checking process, which means that a user does not have to scrutinize every test case trace to ensure that it passes the functional criteria.

Because the test bench is the "universe," all the knowledge needed for checking exists in the test bench. The verification engineer codes that knowledge into the checkers and the scoreboard in order to make the environment self-checking. There are different types of self-checking test benches:

- Golden Vectors
- Reference Model
- Transaction Based

Golden Vectors

A golden vectors environment is a simple environment in which some knowledge base of valid output vectors is stored in the scoreboard. The checking component compares the DUV results to this knowledge base by calling the scoreboard and requesting the expected vectors. This can be done either for every cycle or for every transaction (based on the functions). In most cases, the scoreboard is loaded (via a file or some other mechanism) at the beginning of the test with a known set of valid expect traces that correspond to what the stimulus will be generating. The output checker compares the actual DUV results to the golden vector-predicted results. The verification engineer either generates these valid traces manually or generates them by using an external program. Figure 3.16 shows a diagram of this type of environment.

The advantage to this mechanism of checking is that the verification engineer can check all of the predicted result traces before running the simulation. Another advantage is that when the verification team runs a regression (for more detail on regression, see Chapter 13), all the vectors that need to be verified already exist.

A disadvantage to this type of verification is twofold: the creation and the maintenance of the golden vectors. Manual creation of golden vectors is tedious. If a program creates the golden vectors, then that program will require knowledge about the DUV. (The reference model environment explained next tackles this by placing the knowledge directly into the simulation environment). The maintenance challenge is keeping the

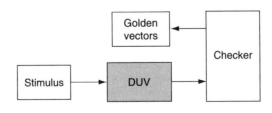

■ **FIGURE 3.16**

Golden vector environment.

golden vectors and stimulus generation synchronized. If the DUV rules change, the verification team must update all of the test cases and golden vectors to reflect the change.

Golden vector checking is best suited for DUVs that have sporadic outputs that correspond closely to the inputs. DUVs that handle just one concurrent command are ripe for golden vector checking as the output is usually easy to predict.

Reference Model

The reference model calculates all expected outputs based on the input stimulus. The reference model re-implements the function of the DUV, usually in a high level programming language or an HVL. Because the reference model calculates the results for each cycle, it is also known as a cycle accurate model.

Unlike the golden vectors approach, the checker component does not request information from the reference model. Instead, the reference model sends information to the checker every cycle based on the program calculations. It is the checker's job to compare this information to the DUV outputs and decide if the output signals match the expected results. Figure 3.17 shows a diagram of this checking paradigm.

The main advantage to the reference model is the level of checking accuracy. Once the reference model is correct (and debugged), the verification team knows that the DUV is correct for every cycle. This comes at a price, as this method has a maintenance overhead. The reference model must know the exact internal timing implementation of the DUV, which is very similar to white box verification except that the reference model has no probes into the design.

Verification teams should chose reference models for checking DUVs that have high activity on the outputs. DUVs with multiple concurrent inputs or internal priority logic to process stimulus are candidates for reference model checking because the prediction of the outputs depends highly on the stimulus sequence. Furthermore, if the internal timings of the DUV changes, it is easier to update the reference model once than to edit all of the golden vector test cases.

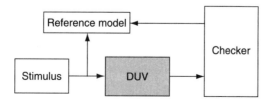

■ **FIGURE 3.17**

Reference model environment.

A variation of the reference model checker is one that is not accurate for every cycle but instead is checked at key points in time. For example, consider an ALU that contains a pipeline with a depth of five. Five cycles after receiving input stimulus to the ALU, the reference model sends predicted outputs to the checker component. This also helps alleviate potential performance disadvantages because the reference model does not have to keep up with all the details, but the reference model does have to know that the pipeline depth is five.

Transaction Based

A transaction-based environment is used for DUVs that have identifiable transactions in which commands and data are acted on and forwarded to appropriate output signals. This allows the verification engineer to structure the environment based on the transaction nature of the DUV. Caches, which act on commands and data, are one example. Many input/output (IO) protocol devices (such as Ethernet and PCI) that forward and route packets of data should use transaction-based checking.

This type of checking environment uses a scoreboard to track commands and data driven on the inputs of the DUV. In this environment, the DUV processes the commands and associated data before forwarding the transactions on the outputs. The DUV may reformat the command and data before forwarding it. Figure 3.18 shows the transaction-based environment.

The scoreboard keeps a record of all "current" transactions that have entered the DUV but have not been completed (or forwarded). The scoreboard must also perform any data reformatting. On observing output signals, the checker component queries the scoreboard, usually with a transaction identifier, and receives the expected data. The checker flags an error if the identifier does not match an outstanding transaction or if the command or data are not as predicted by the scoreboard.

The key in the transaction-based environment is the abstraction level of the command and data. Often, this is simple, as in the Ethernet packet protocol or PCI bus commands. However, DUVs may allow transactions to be spread across many cycles or have other transactions intermixed.

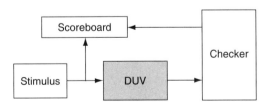

■ **FIGURE 3.18**

Transaction-based environment.

It is the scoreboard's job to package the abstracted transactions into predictable outputs.

The only disadvantage and difficulty to this type of environment is deciding the correct level of abstraction, which is an important decision as it influences both the effectiveness and efficiency of the verification environment. The team should base this decision on the functional stimulus injected into the DUV. When the team defines the right level of abstraction, it becomes easy to define interesting test cases by using sequences of these abstract items, as well as to generate meaningful tests, and it is easier to analyze the test results by looking at the abstract items for debug.

3.5   SUMMARY

In creating the verification environment, the verification team creates many different components. Some of these components are ones that stimulate the DUV, whereas others perform the checking. To allow the checking components to work, monitors are created to observe the DUV's inputs and outputs, and scoreboards are created to store the expected results. These four types of components allow the verification team to create the yin and yang of verification. It allows the verification team to drive the necessary input combinations and check the resulting outputs for those inputs.

However, before the verification team can create any of the components, they must understand the function to be verified. This is especially true when deciding on what type of observability is desired for checking. As seen in the cache design example (Figure 3.8), both the white and black box approaches would have caught the bug where data was destroyed. However, the white box approach has a larger price to pay in terms of maintenance. Because of the high price, white box verification should be used only when necessary. In many cases, the verification engineer would like to have some visibility into the design. The verification team can obtain this visibility by using monitor components that observe some internal portions of the DUV. The drawback is that the verification engineer must learn portions of the implementation.

Assertion-based verification is another approach to adding visibility into the DUV that is gaining much attention in the industry. In this approach, the designer takes on some responsibility by placing assertions within the design. These assertions can be static (event based) or temporal in nature, or they can use a pre-defined set of event-based building blocks. In any event, these assertions provide a mechanism by which some of the logic is checked by the assertion and other logic is protected by the assertion.

Once the verification team understands the functionality of the design and what visibilty depth is needed, they can start to strategize on how to validate the DUV. Validating simple DUVs is straightforward and feasible by using a deterministic testing strategy. However, when the function gets more complex, deterministic testing strategy becomes more of a burden and a self-checking becomes the better approach because it is independent of the stimulus component. As discussed, the verification team must consider three different self-checking test strategies. Each of these has pros and cons, and the verification engineer must choose the appropriate one based on the functions to be verified.

3.6 EXERCISES

1. Why is over-stressing the design so important?

2. What are the two ways of knowing when a resource is available? How does this microarchitecture choice affect the verification environment?

3. Deterministic test cases can be used on simple DUVs such as the 2-bit adder. The problem becomes much bigger with a 32-bit adder. How many deterministic tests would there be now?

4. What kind of verification is applicable for the following (black box, grey box, or white box) and why:

    (a) A 32-bit adder
    (b) An eight-stage CPU pipeline
    (c) An Ethernet to local bus bridge

5. Name the advantages of doing HDL-based assertions.

6. Compare the three types of checking models (golden vectors, reference model, and transaction). When should each be used?

7. Again, we return to the town of Eagleton, where you are the chief verification engineer for the parking lot controller. Given the criteria from Exercise 1 in Chapter 2, perform the following:

    (a) Describe a simple verification environment by using a block diagram, and list the functions required for each component.
    (b) Describe what type of observation points you desire (black box, white box, or grey box).
    (c) Describe the testing strategy for the environment.

CHAPTER 4

THE VERIFICATION PLAN

The verification plan is a decisive factor for success. It defines both the functions that the verification team must attack and how they will do their work. As the first step in the verification cycle, the team derives the entire verification effort from this document. This document is a living document, owned by the entire design team—not by any one person and not by the verification team alone.

This chapter describes the construction and section contents of the verification plan. A verification plan must contain each of these sections, as they provide necessary insight into the upcoming verification task. The chapter concludes with the functional specification of an example design, Calc1. We provide a sample verification plan for Calc1 as a template for future work and as a guide for verifying the Calc1 exercise.

Calc1 is the first of our interactive examples. We invite the reader to download the example source code and verify the design. The Preface contains details for downloading the examples.

4.1 THE FUNCTIONAL SPECIFICATION

The source of the plan is the functional intent and specification. The verification engineer must first understand the design under verification (DUV) before determining how to verify it. The specification is the driving vehicle for this; it becomes the "law." Many times, discrepancies arise between verification and design (these manifest themselves as test case miscompares). In these cases, the team will refer to the specification for the correct behavior.

However, discrepancies can often occur when the specification is unclear or ambiguous on a technical matter. If two people read the same specification issue and interpret it differently, then the specification has a problem. Observe the following example: "A response, R, shall occur when A occurs after B or C." This English language statement is ambiguous because it has two possible meanings. The first is that "R should occur when A occurs after B, or when C occurs"; the second, "the design asserts R when A occurs after either B or C occurs." This is a basic matter of order of operations, which, in English, may not follow mathematical ordering rules. The reader may interpret it in different ways.

In this case, the specification was unclear. Because the specification is the law, the team must settle the discrepancy. It is a simple matter of going back to the architect and having the intent clarified.

The specification and verification plan are not "gentleman's agreements," as both items must exist in written form and apply to the current project. It is not acceptable to use a previous version of the verification plan and specification on a new version of a design. These documents must evolve with the design: if the project is important enough to create another version, then it is important enough to update both the specification and verification plan to reflect the current changes.

However, the reality is not always so black and white. Often the final specification is not complete until the chip ships to manufacturing or even to the customer. The verification team must use the evolving document as the basis of the plan. Other times, designers have workbooks that evolve into the specification. If this is the current specification, then these workbooks are the basis for the verification plan. However, technical insights that affect the system or chip, such as power-on-reset sequences or chip configuration initializations, may be missing from the workbooks. In these cases, the architect must have input on the function of the design. These cases are suboptimal, but do occur in industry.

4.2   THE EVOLUTION OF THE VERIFICATION PLAN

The verification plan is an evolving document. In the beginning, the verification team pours the foundation of their work into this document, however this initial plan may be incomplete. The team will update the plan with details found within the environment and design as the project progresses, sometimes because of new requirements owing to architectural changes or because of missing items found on the design or verification team drive updates.

Figure 4.1 shows how a typical schedule for a design interlocks with the verification cycle. It depicts the portion of the verification cycle from high-level specification and verification plan creation through to the regression stage.

The design and verification cycle interlock follows a "waterfall" flow. Key to the flow is the functional specification development, high-level design, and verification plan. Although some of the subsequent stages of development may overlap to reduce overall schedule, the initial stages lay the foundation for a solid, timely, and executable development cycle. Even so, the verification team will modify and enhance the verification plan throughout the process, as the team will undoubtedly discover the

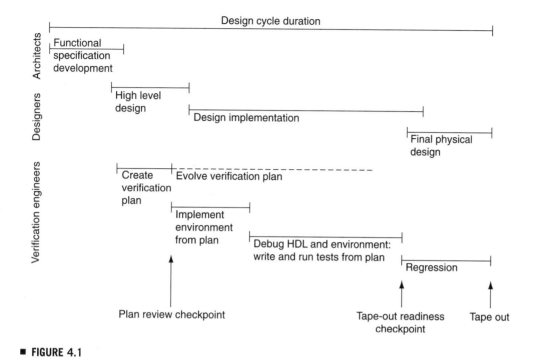

■ FIGURE 4.1

Design and verification cycle interlock. This figure shows a timeline for the first half of the verification cycle.

need for new scenarios and checkers while implementing the environment and debugging the HDL.

A key milestone in any project is a plan review checkpoint, which is intended to "sync up" all the involved players for a design. At a minimum, the reviewing committee includes the designer and verifier of the DUV, the designers and verifiers of its neighboring blocks, and the architect. This review ensures that the design adheres to the interface protocols, that functional models have the correct behavior, and that the plan is complete. This review should occur before any verification code is written. Because the plan is the base for implementing the verification environment, it is important to ensure that the foundation of the environment is correct.

Failure to review the verification plan often results in an incomplete or faulty foundation, which in turn carries on into the verification environment. As a result, the environment may need to be rewritten—a waste of precious time. In other cases, the verification engineer might choose to "bandage" the faulty environment to prevent rewriting; typically when this occurs, the environment is fundamentally flawed, allowing bugs to go undetected. Thus, to maintain the shortest possible schedule, the initial review must gate the implementation phase. The team should continuously review and revalidate the plan throughout the verification cycle, especially if the specification evolves. This is critical to ensure that the plan matches the specification. In addition, there should be reviews that coincide with key milestones such as "ready for the next level of verification" or "ready for fabrication."

Following this process puts the verification plan and execution in lock step with the design cycle, thus reducing the overall design risk by keeping verification in the forefront of the design consciousness.

Another aspect to consider is the integration of all the hierarchical-level verification plans into one cohesive plan. Every block that will have its own environment should have its own verification plan; as a result, there may be numerous owners of these plans or for each verification level. To ensure that all functions are covered, the verification plan and initial review should be a compilation of all these plans. The lead verification engineer for the project usually owns the comprehensive plan, which covers the verification of all functions and indicates at what level the functions are exercised.

4.3 CONTENTS OF THE VERIFICATION PLAN

The verification plan consists of multiple sections, each articulating a critical component of the verification workload. These sections describe both the technical requirements for the verification environments and the project management needs.

The technical requirements of the verification plan fall into the following major headings: *description of verification levels, functions to be verified, specific tests and methods, coverage requirements*, and *test scenarios (matrix)*. These sections describe, in detail, the strategy and construction of the verification environments for the project.

The project management sections of the plan have these major headings: *required tools, risks and dependencies, resources requirements*, and *schedule details*. These sections articulate the software, compute hardware, and personnel required to complete the project on the required schedule.

4.3.1 Description of Verification Levels

The verification team's first decision in verifying a design is to articulate the verification levels. As described in Section 2.1, a system may contain multiple levels of design hierarchy. Depending on the complexity of each level, the verification team must choose to verify levels independently or group levels together into functional components.

The verification team bases their decision to group components together or to first verify some (or each) components independently on two factors. The first factor is the *complexity of the individual component*.

Complex portions of the DUV require their own verification. Proper verification on complex functions usually requires a high level of control and observability. Conversely, the verification team may fold simpler macros that do not require this high level of control and observability into the next level of verification with little risk.

The second factor in grouping components is the *existence of a clean interface and specification* to drive the component. The ability to properly drive interface protocol and check for results is the key to verification and requires a stable, documented interface. If the interface is "a moving target," then the volatility in the design and verification environment should be expected. If it is feasible to verify blocks with unwieldy or unstable interfaces at a higher level, then this may be an appropriate trade-off.

After defining the verification levels, the verification team will create verification plans for each level. The following sections describe the components of a verification plan needed for each level.

4.3.2 Required Tools

The required tools section contains the specification and list of the verification toolset, describing the software (and potentially hardware simulation machines) needed to perform the plan. Some examples of this are as follows:

- Event simulation tools for units
- Cycle simulation tools for chip (for performance reasons)
- Formal verification tools
- Assertion-based tools
- Debuggers
- Emulation hardware
- Acceleration hardware
- Cosimulation software
- High-level verification languages (HVLs)
- Libraries of functions

In some companies, a concrete verification methodology exists, and this section is predetermined. In these cases, the verification plan follows the current methodology, including the default toolset.

There are instances in which a deviation is required from the default toolset. For example, if a system-level simulation environment involves a chip verified separately under a different methodology or toolset, the team may need additional tools to bridge the environments. It might follow then that the team needs a *cosimulation environment*. Cosimulation occurs when the team verifies diverse source code or methodologies at once. This could be between VHDL and Verilog, or it might be between two different HVLs—Specman *e*, SystemC, and/or Vera.

Articulating the required tools is important because they could have a resource or monetary impact. New or different tools will drive more resources or inflate the schedule as the team learns the appropriate usages. Inclusion of tools in the plan also serves to document software purchase requirements from electronic design automation (EDA) vendors, as well as simulation engine estimates.

4.3.3 Risks and Dependencies

This section of the verification plan identifies critical threats to success and delivery requirements that project management needs to track to closure. The complexity of today's designs inherently contains verification risks. The verification team depends on other teams to deliver information, tools, function, and intellectual property in order to achieve success. This section articulates these items.

The verification team manages risk through focusing on avoidance and by creating contingency plans. For instance, there are risks associated with dependence on a new tool: delivery and start-up delays (e.g., late delivery or nonworking functions), integration with established tools, and educational challenges. Contingency plans might consist of using a backup tool or creating an early acceptance test for the tool.

Dependencies range from on-time HDL deliveries to availability of tools and technology. HDL deliveries may come in regularly scheduled packages, in which the design team delivers basic function first, followed by further, more complex functions. The verification team must plan their work based on these deliveries, so the plan must articulate this dependency.

The verification team should highlight the dependency and risks during the initial plan review, thus driving overall acknowledgement of these items and discussion of possible risk mitigation actions.

In a complex design project, there are common risks and dependencies. One of the most common risks in a large design project is the reliance on a separate verification team, such as a local team or an intellectual property (IP) vendor (in a system-on-a-chip design), to preverify a lower-level core before chip- or system-level verification. Receiving a release of a poorly verified core likely leads to debugging a unit-level bug at the system level. In these situations, pinpointing the bug is much more difficult or even impossible.

As mentioned above, new tools and new versions of current tools add risk to a project. As tools continue to evolve in order to keep pace with design complexity, the engineering team must manage new tool deliveries. Problems include occasions when the tool is not available when promised, when quality defects in the tool slow the pace of the verification effort, or when the promised functionality of the tool is not delivered. Worse yet, a new tool, advertised as a seamless integration effort, might end up requiring months of environment changes. Many groups have a *tool freeze* within a project. This is a point after which the team will not entertain new tools (or revisions of tools) because of the risk associated with changes. Beta testing tools is a good practice before new releases. This avoids wasted hours because the new tool has bugs, which requires the team to go back to a previous version. The team must plan for education on new tools as well. Classes and on-site support help alleviate these risks.

Architecture closure is a common risk and dependency item. As mentioned before, the design team rarely supplies the complete and final specification before the start of verification. Often, there are architectural and specification issues that are not resolved when the team writes the verification plan. This is both a dependency and a risk. The team requires closure of architectural items by specific dates in order to meet the schedule. However, the team also runs the risk that they need to overhaul their verification environment because the early assumptions prove to be invalid.

A final common risk and dependency is having the available resources to complete the work on schedule. There may be a unique resource requirement that needs to be listed (e.g., people, machines, licenses). For instance, there may be contention among multiple projects for specific simulation hardware such as emulators. In another case, the verification plan will assume a certain daily simulation cycle throughput during the early phases of the design right through the regression phase. The simulation engines and licenses must be available to meet this throughput. Most important is having the available, skilled verification engineers on a project. These verification engineers are in high demand, with other projects vying for the same limited skill pool. The project must manage the appropriate staffing levels to maintain the desired quality and schedule goals.

4.3.4 Functions to be Verified

This section lists the specific functions of the DUV that the verification team will exercise. Because the plan is crucial in determining success, this is where the verification team articulates the functional requirements. This section identifies *everything* that the team will verify. Any functions omitted (intentionally or inadvertently) may not be verified. During the initial review, it is equally important for the design team to focus on the listed functions as it is to brainstorm on what might be missing. The verification team creates this section of the plan for each level of verification.

The main source of the list of functions is the specification. Each function should have a short description about it, and the team can cross-reference these functions to the specification to help determine if the plan covers all functions in the specification. This list of functions can also be of assistance when disputes arise on the function of something that is being tested, as the team has a quick reference back to the specification for clarification on a function.

The list of functions to be verified must include pervasive functions, operations other than those that may occur under normal running conditions. Pervasive functions include system resets, error handling, and system debug. The verification team often devotes an entire section of the verification plan toward pervasive function (for more detail, see Chapter 9).

This section also describes under what conditions the team will verify all the functions. This is crucial in that it helps define the functions that the verification components need to support. If a component cannot produce the stimulus, then the verification engineer cannot check that function. Even if a check exists, the environment will never exercise the checker because the stimulus is constrained in an inappropriate fashion.

The other purpose of the list of functions is to provide an order of priority. The list should be broken down into different areas:

- Critical functions

- Secondary functions

- Nonverified functions at this level

The *critical functions* are those that the team must verify before using the design elsewhere. These functions provide the base set of tasks and behaviors of the DUV. If the design were a unit, this could be the criterion needed to start the next level of verification. Typically, the functions listed here are the things that will render the chip dead if not met. The critical functions list is like "drawing a line"; if crossed, the team compromises the success of the project.

There are two categories of *secondary functions*: noncritical to tapeout and noncritical to the next level of verification. Functions that are not critical to the initial tape-out include performance-related issues, functions that the designers will enable in later versions of the chip, or function that has software backup. If any one of these functions is broken, the design is not "dead." In these cases, there may be a decision not to delay the design's release to manufacturing while the verification effort continues on these functions. It does not mean that the team will not verify these functions; it just means that the team will verify them after releasing the design to manufacturing.

Schedule dictates the need to classify function as noncritical to the next level of verification. In a perfect world, the next level of verification will not start until the verification team completes the lower level verification plan. This is typically unrealistic in a fast-paced business. To parallelize some of the schedule, the team may choose to verify only the critical functions before beginning the next level of verification. This gives the next level a chance to test and initiate their environment while the lower level continues verification of secondary functions. These functions are typically corner case type criteria that the next level will not expect to hit until later. The owners of the next level must scrutinize this list of functions so as to align expectations. Discovering that some function initially deemed as secondary is actually critical will cause churn in the verification environment. This is another aspect covered by the design teams during the initial review.

The final category, nonverified function, may seem out of place, but it is necessary. *Nonverified functions* indicate functions that the verification team will not exercise at this particular level of verification. There are two reasons to ignore function at a particular level: the first is that the team fully verified the function at a lower level (usually through exhaustive formal verification) and there will be further verification (for a sanity check) in simulation at a higher level, and the second is that the function is not applicable at this level of verification.

Articulating this category of function informs everyone that the team considered these functions and decided that the functions would be verified elsewhere. It is important to note in the plan where the function will be verified.

Architects, designers, and verification engineers all need to focus on this section of the verification plan to identify holes and overlooked functions. By listing nonverified and verified functions together, all parties gain insight into the verification plan.

4.3.5 Specific Tests and Methods: Environment

This section provides the details of the verification environments for each level of verification. It describes if the environment will treat the DUV as a black box, white box, or grey box and provides specifics on the verification strategy, including the amount of randomness or determinism in a simulation environment and the types of checks for a formal verification environment.

For simulation environments, the verification team must document the level of abstraction the components will use. In addition, this section of the verification plan describes the checking strategy.

It is often helpful to include a block diagram showing the universe for the DUV, which is an easy way to indicate the required components in the environment. This description of the environment components is critical because it details the interactions between blocks and the controls a user has on them. In many instances, this is crucial for component reuse (for reuse strategies, see Chapter 10), as it is often desirable to use a component in multiple levels of verification. Each component in the diagram should have its own description, which details how the environment will drive all of the inputs and check the outputs.

Along with a block diagram, the following sections provide a framework for the specific tests and methods for the verification environment.

What Type of Verification?

This section states the choice of black box, white box, or grey box verification, as well as the ramifications of the decision. If the verification team chooses a black box approach, it may not be necessary to have the monitors probe into the design; however, if the team chooses a white box approach, it may require many more monitors for the DUV. The team bases their choice on the following:

- The function to be verified

- How to best exercise the internal structures

- How errors may manifest themselves

- The availability of resources for maintenance (remember, white box style will require more work but may also uncover more bugs)

Most environments are grey box, as the verification team decides to create observation points within the DUV to ensure the handful of interesting aspects occur during simulation. By laying out this approach, it may be feasible to settle on some standard observation points that will not change, thus causing less maintenance because of the stability within the implementation.

Verification Strategy

The choice of deterministic simulation, random-based simulation, or formal verification drives divergent environment components. The verification team bases the choice on the function of the DUV and the available resources. Simple designs with straightforward functionality lend themselves to deterministic test approaches. Complex functions require randomization, because the verification team cannot envision all of the input permutations. In this case, the verification team builds intelligence into the components so they can leverage the speed of their workstation farm through design automation. The team chooses formal verification for small, complex blocks of design for which many permutations exist. The key trade-off between simulation-based randomization and formal verification is that the team will employ formal verification if the formal verification engine can manage the block size. Larger DUV models will require simulation.

The deterministic approach requires the verification engineer to put features into the environment to enable writing all permutations of deterministic tests. The deterministic environment must be sufficiently robust to exercise the DUV function. In this environment, the intelligence in driving stimulus and checking outputs and intent of the test case remains in the verification engineer's mind. The environment enables the uninhibited flow of that intent into the DUV.

The random environment and formal verification choices drive much of the same thinking. Both environments require that the verification engineer allow all possible permutations to occur on the DUV's input interfaces. Although deterministic testing drives a single, legal event, random and formal verification approaches require that the verification engineer explicitly disable illegal stimulus and allow everything else. Rather than considering all of the possible scenarios, the random and formal verification approaches prevent scenarios that the specification prohibits. The random and formal verification environments require the verification engineers to codify their checking knowledge into the checker, scoreboard, and monitor components or into the formal verification rules.

Random Aspects

The decision on random, formal, or deterministic testing affects the functions within the model. Too much randomness can prevent problems from being uncovered, as the tests may not hit interesting cases, and may drive false failures. Conversely, not enough randomness will prohibit the creation of all the interesting tests. A user wants controlled and properly constrained randomness possibly with "unrandomizing" controls built in. Controls to cut back on randomization allow for a more directed random approach. These controls can pursue

- Hangs due to looping

- Low activity scenarios

- Specific directed tests

The random environment may require further specialized *micromodes* to get around an architecture fault or to create a known scenario. A micromode allows the verification engineer to inject a deterministic sequence into the random environment.

Abstraction Level

The abstraction level dictates how the verification environment views streams of control and data bits. At the lowest level, at which the environment components observe and examine each input and output of the

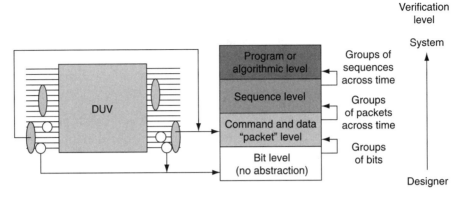

▪ **FIGURE 4.2**

Abstraction levels dictate how the verification components interact with the design under verification.

DUV as bits, there is no abstraction. This level is generally shunned by the verification team as there is little design intent context; instead, teams usually opt to group control and data bits into meaningful functions, raising the level of abstraction. Once chosen, the team uses this level for all checkers, stimulus, scoreboards, and monitors in the particular verification environment.

Figure 4.2 shows various abstraction level choices. Above the bit-level, inputs and outputs join to make meaningful command and data packets. Components create sequences by joining multiple packets together to form a function; multiple sequences create a program or implement an algorithm.

Often, the choice of abstraction level parallels the verification level. Designer-level verification uses bit streams to verify simple blocks. For the unit and chip levels, verification engineers choose the packet or sequence level of abstraction. Program-level abstraction rarely occurs below the system level.

For example, the verification engineer would drive and check a Peripheral Component Interconnect (PCI) model using PCI transactions packets or sequences, not a stream of bits or bytes. Although the verification engineer could think of all the bus transactions in terms of a stream of bits, it complicates the creation, maintainability, and effectiveness of the model. Similar examples hold for microprocessor verification, in which verification engineers can choose to deal in binary instruction encoding, abstract to the mnemonic op-code, write sequences of instructions, or advance to writing programs that run on the microprocessor.

Without the correct abstraction level, it may not be feasible to cover all the interesting scenarios. The correct abstraction level will make it

- Easy to define concise test scenarios based on interesting sequences

■ Able to generate meaningful reports for debug analysis of test results

Checking

The checking strategy falls into place based on the choice of verification type (black box, white box, grey box), the verification stimulus strategy, and the level of abstraction. Still, the team needs to document the choice among golden vectors, reference model, and transaction-based strategies for simulation-based environments. Checking for formal verification environments requires equal thought, but comes in the form of rules and assertions.

The level of abstraction will dictate the required level of context checking. However, the team still needs to think through the multiple sources of checkers (see Chapter 2).

For checking on inputs and outputs, the verification team must examine the output specification and remember to check all outputs. Even if a higher level of abstraction is chosen for the environment, there still will be bit-level checking built into the monitors for parity and basic outputs.

For design context checking, the verification team must understand the larger system or higher level of hierarchy in which the DUV will work. Higher-level or neighboring designs will dictate requirements and checks.

To address microarchitecture checking, the team studies the constructs within the DUV to ensure that checking components will know if the DUV has gone astray. The checkers must know when a queue overflows or when state machines have taken illegal transitions.

For architecture checking, the design must fully adhere to the published standards. Checkers must be in place to guarantee that there are no violations.

The type of stimulus (deterministic versus random) guides the choice between golden vectors and the reference model or transaction-based checking. The available staffing will also drive the decision, especially between a cycle-accurate reference model and the transaction-based checking. Appropriate verification staffing allows for pinpoint accuracy in reference model checking.

The verification team can include details such as the data contents of the scoreboard in this section of the verification plan. The team must understand what information they will track globally within the environment, as well as what data they must check in local output monitor components.

4.3.6 Coverage Requirements

Coverage is the feedback mechanism that evaluates the quality of the verification environment's stimulus generation components. The verification environment provides "quality control" on the DUV; coverage provides quality control on the verification environment. Coverage information is required in any complex simulation-based environment.

This section of the verification plan describes the intended stimulus goals for the environment. The goals should cover all of the functional stimulus requirements and ensure that the stimulus components in the environment do what they should. These coverage goals may include the following:

- The environment has exercised all types of commands and transactions.

- The stimulus has created a specific or varying range of data types.

- The environment has driven varying degrees of legal concurrent stimulus.

- The initiator and responder components have driven errors into the DUV.

Another good practice is to have coverage feedback for all environment checkers to verify that the stimulus exercises all of the checking code. Unexercised individual checks indicate that there is a hole somewhere in the stimulus components or in the plan (for more information on coverage, see Chapter 6).

4.3.7 Test Case Scenarios: Matrix

A good verification plan should list all of the interesting test scenarios that will serve to verify the design. This list is the *test case matrix*. Defining a preliminary matrix is necessary before starting the design and modeling of the verification environment because every potentially valuable test should be enabled. Within the matrix, the verification plan should label each test, give a short description, and contain a cross-reference to the function and coverage lists.

The matrix starts with the basic required tests and then builds on them. The plan groups tests with similar features to form test scenarios, which may have the same configuration, granularity, or verification strategy. The descriptions of the scenario designate the targeted function. The last item on the matrix is a cross-reference to the functional requirements and coverage goals.

This section can produce a huge matrix of tests. Often, the matrix size can explode when there are multiple DUV configurations. If a DUV has 10 basic functional tests and each one is valid in one of three modes (e.g., bus frequency), then the net result is that the matrix will have 30 tests.

A random coverage-based matrix begins with a listing of the targeted functions. The initial description states how the team will constrain the environment to achieve the goals. In a random environment, this translates to driving certain inputs with specific values while leaving other inputs unconstrained (randomly generated values). This set of constraints then determines the scenario.

The test matrix grows as the implementation continues. For complex DUVs, the team cannot define all tests at the start; instead, they add to the test matrix as they determine new scenarios, through either DUV discovery or coverage holes. It is critical to document these new tests in the verification plan, as the team needs to include these tests in the future.

As part of defining a verification plan, the verification team needs to specify the legal values, illegal values, and corner cases of each input data element they want to generate. The following should be kept in mind when creating the matrix: configurations to verify, variations of the data items in the environment (this ties to the abstraction level), important attributes of each data item, interesting sequences for every DUV input port, error conditions, and corner cases.

Corner cases deserve their own section in the test case matrix. The verification team must pay special attention to many out-of-the-ordinary cases, which include the smallest and the largest data elements such as an empty and full queue or first in, first out (FIFO), extreme values such as the largest and smallest packet lengths, and unique time relations such as bus collisions and interrupts during instruction streams.

As the above test scenarios listed, the team should define the range of values for each generated data item, thus helping to define the verification plan and model the input data.

4.3.8 Resource Requirements

With the environment architecture and test scenarios in place, the team can estimate its resource requirements. Resource requirements include not only people but also compute and license resources.

People resource estimates vary based on the type of environment and the experience of the individuals. Reference model checking environments will require more people to implement, but their accuracy and checking capabilities are often worth the investment. However, less resource-intensive solutions such as transaction-based checking may be adequate. Experienced verification engineers will require less time to code and debug the environment. Time should be planned for review of the verification components for all portions of the code, paying special attention to the code of inexperienced verification engineers.

The verification leaders allocate people resources across the verification hierarchy, starting with the lowest level in the plan. The verification assignments will shift as the lower levels complete and the next level of verification in the hierarchy begins. Because there are more total environments at the lower levels (e.g., there are many units in a single chip and multiple chips in a system), the resource plan allocates fewer people per environment at the lower levels and has the verification engineers moving together toward system level. Typically, it takes fewer people to execute a unit environment than a system environment.

Within every environment, the leaders allocate individual verification engineers across the components. Typically, a single verification engineer will write all of the stimulus components at a unit level. The leaders may assign another verification engineer to create the checking for that unit. However, for a complex chip or system, there are too many interfaces for a single verification engineer to write all of the stimulus or checking components, so the team splits the development across multiple people along sensible partitions. In a well-designed verification plan, the plan calls for porting many of the lower-level drivers and checkers to the higher levels of the verification hierarchy. This reuse eases some of the resource requirements.

Aside from engineering resources, it is very important to estimate the required compute resources. This is calculated based on the length of one test scenario and the estimated number of tests to run during the whole verification cycle. These numbers should be consistent with the time and computing resources available for the project (the limiting factor could be central processing units or licenses available to the project), which may drive requests for additional compute or license resources.

When deciding on the length of tests, keep in mind that long tests *might* reach more interesting DUV scenarios, but they are harder to debug when they fail. It may be more beneficial to have many smaller (more focused and easier-to-debug) tests than a few long ones. In practice, a simulation time of 15 minutes to 1 hour provides a good balance of all the above factors, assuming that the environment can create all interesting scenarios within this time span.

4.3.9 Schedule Details

Previous sections of the plan cover the verification of the many different levels of hierarchy and the proposed environments for each. The final portion of verification planning is to document the timeline for each of the verification activities.

As the team creates the schedule details, they must consider all of the other sections of the verification plan. However, the resource section is the most tightly coupled to the schedule details section because the available resources have a direct and obvious impact on schedule. More resources will improve the schedule, and less resources will extend the schedule.

The schedule includes both deliveries to the verification team and verification work items. The first step is to create a high-level schedule before filling in the details. The high-level schedule follows the first half of the verification cycle. It starts with a delivery of the specification and completes with chip release(s) to manufacturing. For each level of the hierarchy, the high-level schedule includes the development of verification environments, the debugging of the HDL, and the regression stage.

A key delivery in the schedule is the first *drop* of HDL to the verification team. An HDL drop consists of enough HDL to perform specific DUV functions. Often, there are multiple drops of HDL in the development cycle. Staggering the drops allows the verification team to make progress on basic functions while the HDL designers work on complex and secondary functions. This parallelization can streamline the schedule; however, it will force the HDL designers to balance their time between creating new HDL and fixing newly discovered verification bugs in previous drops.

The verification leaders must estimate how long it will take to create the basic verification environment. In most cases, this time is closely aligned with how long it takes the designers to create the first HDL delivery. The second time estimate is the duration of the debug portion of the schedule, which begins after the initial delivery of environment and HDL. The estimated duration of this portion of the schedule is based on how long it should take to run through the test matrix. The estimate must account for further HDL delivery dates as well. The remaining timeframe before the chip release to manufacturing is set aside for regression.

Figure 4.3 shows the format of the high-level schedule. In this example, the team chose to execute three levels of functional verification: unit, chip, and system. Verification engineers have singled out four units across three chips for unit simulation environments.

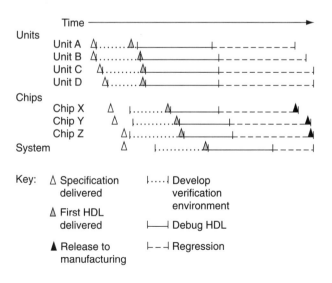

■ **FIGURE 4.3**

High-level schedule showing the first half of the verification cycle. The major checkpoints include design deliveries, environment development, debug, and regression.

Verification proceeds from the lowest level of the hierarchy (in this case, unit level) to the highest. Unit verification precedes chip level, which then precedes system level. Chip-level verification should not start until after the verification of substantial function at unit level. Similarly, system level cannot begin until all three chips have demonstrated solid functionality.

The schedule must allow enough time for each level of hierarchy to test the function before the next level starts. This ensures that the verification team will find bugs at the lowest level possible, easing the debugging burden and capturing bugs at the earliest point in the schedule. A good practice is to start the next level of verification when the bug rate from the lower level has dropped. This ensures that the resources stay focused on the most productive verification level. Figure 4.4 shows a sample bug curve that results when the team follows the schedule guidelines.

The scheduling challenge is to create reasonable estimates of when these events will occur. The typical bug curve in Figure 4.4 looks great in hindsight, but predicting the timing of the bug rate fall-off is no easy task. To assist in schedule estimation, the verification team should use historical references from past projects. By coupling the history of similar projects with the latest enhancements in verification methodologies, the verification leaders can make reliable schedule estimates.

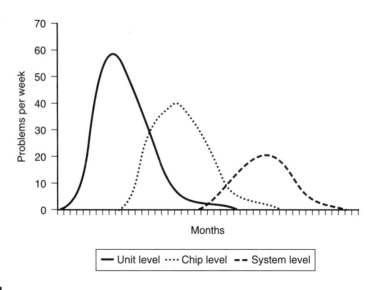

▪ **FIGURE 4.4**

A typical bug curve shows that the lowest levels of verification uncover the majority of bugs because of their granularity and their precedence in the schedule.

4.4 VERIFICATION EXAMPLE: CALC1

Calc1 is a sample DUV used to demonstrate test planning and simple verification. This section describes Calc1 from the view of a verification engineer and then discusses the first step in verifying the design, the creation of a verification plan, and the deterministic test cases required to verify the Calc1 design. Compared to real-world complex designs, Calc1 is very simple although it serves well as an initial training example. The design also serves as a base for more complex verification tutorials.

4.4.1 Design Description

Before creating a verification plan and test cases for Calc1, the verification engineer must understand the design. This section describes the inputs, outputs, and function of the Calc1 design.

Calc1 is a register transfer level (RTL) design implementation of a four-operation calculator. The four operators are Add, Subtract, Shift_left, and Shift_right. The RTL can accept up to four simultaneous operators from its four ports. A single port request sends an operator into the calculator on the command input bus, accompanied by operand data. Each request uses one of four input ports to send the command and operand data. The four ports can each handle a single command in parallel.

Each command will receive a response from the calculator design. Except in the case of an error condition, the response will include the result of the operation. This section describes the exact protocols.

Figure 4.5 shows the input and output signals for Calc1. As with all designs, the RTL must generate or receive a clock signal input. For Calc1, the RTL receives the clock signal on c_clk.

Each of the four Calc1 ports has two separate input busses and two output busses. The first input bus, reqX_cmd_in(0:3) (where X is replaced by port numbers 1, 2, 3, or 4) is a 4-bit bus used to transmit the command to the Calc design. Table 4.1 shows the command and decode values for the 4-bit command bus.

The second input bus, reqX_data_in(0:31), is the operand data bus. Each of the four operation types requires two operands. The requestor ports send operand1 data and operand2 data on sequential cycles, with operand1 data concurrent with the command. Therefore, it takes two cycles to send a complete command and data sequence.

Table 4.2 shows how the Calc1 design operates on the two operands.

The two output lines for each port are the response bus, out_respX (0:1), and result data bus, out_dataX(0:31). The response bus goes active for one cycle when the Calc1 design completes the computation for the port. The number of cycles that it takes to complete an operation depends on amount of activity on the three other ports but will always be at

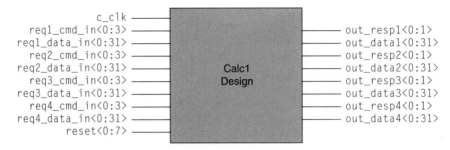

▪ **FIGURE 4.5**

The Calc1 design receives a clock and reset signal, along with a command and data bus from each of the four ports. The outputs include a response and data bas for each port.

TABLE 4.1 ▪ Calc1 command decode values

Command	Decode value
No operation	"0000"b
Add	"0001"b
Subtract	"0010"b
Shift_left	"0101"b
Shift_right	"0110"b
Invalid	All others

TABLE 4.2 ▪ Calc1 operation details

Command	Effect on operands
Add	Result is Operand1 + Operand2
Subtract	Result is Operand1 − Operand2
Shift_left	Result is Operand1 shifted left Operand2 places. Bits shifted out are dropped. Zeros are always shifted in.
Shift_right	Result is operand1 shifted right Operand2 places. Bits shifted out are dropped. Zeros are always shifted in.

For both shift commands, only the rightmost (low-order) 5 bits, reqX_data_in(27:31), of Operand 2 (the shift amount) are used. The calc1 logic ignores bits 0 to 26 of the shift Operand2, allowing the Operand1 data to be shifted any amount from 0 to 31 places (inclusive).

TABLE 4.3 ■ Calc1 response values

Response decode	Response meaning
"00"b	No response on this cycle.
"01"b	Successful response. Response data are on the output data bus.
"10"b	Overflow, underflow, or invalid command. Overflow/underflow only valid for the add or subtract commands. No data on output data bus.
"11"b	Unused response value.

Each port must wait for its response prior to sending the next command!

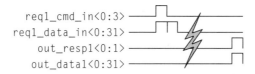

■ **FIGURE 4.6**

A timing diagram of a single port command sequence.

least three cycles. Table 4.3 shows the possible responses for a given operation.

The output data bus, out_dataX(0:31), should only be sampled when out_respX(0:1) contains the successful response decode value ("01"b). At that time, the value on the output bus will contain the result of the operation for that port.

Figure 4.6 shows a timing diagram of the command and response sequence for a single successful command on Port 1. The command and first operand of data appear on the first cycle of the sequence, and the second operand data follows on the second cycle. A few cycles pass, and the response appears on the output of the design, accompanied by the result data.

Each port may have one operation ongoing at a time. Once a port sends a command, it may not send another command until it receives a response for the preceding command. The protocols do not require that a requestor port send a new command whenever the preceding command completes; the port may be idle for any number of cycles in between commands.

TABLE 4.4 ▪ Add and subtract overflow/underflow and successful response examples

Command	Operand1	Operand2	Response	Result data
Add	"80002345"X	"00010000"X	Successful	"80012345"X
Add	"FFFFFFFF"X	"00000001"X	Overflow	None
Subtract	"FFFFFFFF"X	"11111111"X	Successful	"EEEEEEEE"X
Subtract	"11111111"X	"20000000"X	Underflow	None

Each port is independent of the others: all four ports may send commands concurrently or any combination of commands across cycles (with the stated restriction of only one outstanding command per port). Therefore, at any given point, the Calc1 design may work on any number of commands, up to a maximum of four.

If all four ports send commands concurrently, the responses will not be concurrent. Although each port has equal priority, there are limited resources inside the design. Specifically, there is one ALU for adds and subtracts, and a second ALU for shift commands. Hence, if all four ports sent concurrent add commands, the Calc1 logic would serialize the responses, as only one add command could be processed by the ALU at a time.[1]

Internal to the design is a priority logic scheme that sends commands to one ALU or the other, depending on the command decode. Calc1 services commands on a first-come, first-serve basis. Calc1 may service commands that arrive on the same cycle in any order.

The design has a reset bus input used to clear the internal state of the design. During verification, the test case initially should activate the reset to put the design in a cleared state. Setting the reset line, reset(0:7), to "11111111"b activates the reset. This input value needs to be held for seven consecutive cycles in order for the reset to propagate through the design. The test case should set to zero all other input busses except the c_clk while resetting the Calc1 DUV.[2]

Calc1 treats arithmetic operands as unsigned data. The most significant (leftmost) bit, bit 0, is a data bit, not a sign bit. An overflow occurs on an add operation when the high-order bit (bit 0) has a carryout, and an underflow occurs on a subtract operation when a larger number is subtracted from a smaller number. Table 4.4 shows examples.

---

[1] This is microarchitectural information describing the internals of Calc1. The verification engineer may not need this information to drive inputs, but checking components, such as reference models, do require this information. The more a verification engineer understands how the design functions, the better the environment.

[2] The test case must drive the c_clk. However, the value of the c_clk input depends on the type of simulation engine. For event simulation, the stimulus component must toggle c_clk every cycle. For cycle simulation engines, the stimulus component should stick c_clk to "1"b.

4.4.2 Creating the Verification Plan for Calc1

Now that the specification is in place, it is time to create the verification plan for the Calc1 design. Even for a relatively simple design such as Calc1, it is best not to jump into test case writing before thinking through the entire verification plan requirements.

The above design description details the intent of the Calc1 design. It is the verification engineer's job to prove that the actual design implementation matches the intent. Therefore, the verification engineer should not assume the details of the above Calc1 design are correct in the implementation.

Description of Verification Levels

Calc1 is a simple design used as an initial introduction to simulation-based verification (however, verification engineers have successfully applied formal verification to the design as well). Therefore, this design requires verification only at the top level of the DUV hierarchy; furthermore, the available specification only describes the top-level interfaces. Verification at a lower level of hierarchy, such as the ALUs, would require an input and output description of that subunit.

However, if the people resources exist, it is better to do unit-level verification, thus placing the priority logic and ALUs under a microscope of verification and allowing a higher level of control and stress on the design. Furthermore, in real-world designs, it is common for one designer's logic to be available before others' logic. If the priority logic HDL is ready for verification before the ALUs, the priority logic unit-level verification can commence without waiting for the entire chip. This level of verification would add a dependency on the design team to document the unit interfaces.

Required Tools

The tools inventory for Calc1 comprises a single software simulation engine (and license to run it) and one workstation, a waveform viewer, and a test case language or infrastructure. The language or infrastructure must communicate with the simulation engine through the engine's application programming interface (API), which provides the means to drive the inputs, check the outputs, and clock the model of the design, which is simulated by the engine itself.[3]

---

[3] Basic tools such as text editors (to write test cases) need not be included in the required tools section of the verification plan.

Risks and Dependencies

This exercise does not have risks worthy of documentation. In a larger project with a more complex design, there might be risks inherent in the delivery of the specification of esoteric operations (e.g., binary floating point) or in the ability to verify the design in a short schedule. If Calc1 were part of a large system, this section would detail schedule integration factors. The system-level verification cycle depends on the correctness of the Calc1 function so that broader system integration verification can occur without being concerned with the quality of the add, subtract, or shift functions.

The Calc1 exercise also depends on the delivery of the specification (which was delivered above) and availability of the required tools. To perform this exercise, you will need the required tools as documented in the previous section of the verification plan.

Functions to be Verified and Test Scenarios: Matrix

Because Calc1 is simple, we have combined the *functions to be verified* and the *test case scenarios (matrix)* sections of the verification plan. We list the details here in table format with a reference number for cross-checking tests against the verification plan.

Certain test case requirements jump out at the verification engineer. From the Calc1 design description, it is clear that the verification engineer must create the following basic tests as shown in Table 4.5. Beyond the basic functions described in Table 4.5 are a series of tests that involve scenarios that are more complex (Table 4.6). Finally, there are generic tests and checks that are applicable to all verification plans (Table 4.7).

Specific Tests and Methods: Environment

This section describes all of the specifics of the verification environment plans for Calc1. All sections enumerated in the plan's previous sections are described. However, some of the specifics, such as resource requirements, depend on the available team.

TABLE 4.5 ▪ Calc1 basic function tests

Test reference number	Test description
1.1	Check the basic command-response protocol on each of the four ports.
1.2	Check the basic operation of each command on each port.
1.3	Check overflow and underflow cases for add and subtract commands.

TABLE 4.6 ■ Calc1 advanced function tests

Test reference number	Test description
2.1.1	For each port, check that each command can have any command follow it without leaving the state of the design dirty, such that the following command is corrupted, such that the following command is corrupted.
2.1.2	Across all ports (e.g., four concurrent adds do not interfere with each other), check that each command can have any command follow it without leaving the state of the design dirty, such that the following command is corrupted, such that the following command is corrupted.
2.2	Check that there is fairness across all four ports such that no port has higher priority than the others.
2.3	Check that the high-order 27 bits are ignored in the second operand of both shift commands.
2.4.1	Data dependent corner case: Add two numbers that overflow by 1 ("FFFFFFFF"X + 1).
2.4.2	Data dependent corner case: Add two numbers whose sum is "FFFFFFFF"X.
2.4.3	Data dependent corner case: Subtract two equal numbers.
2.4.4	Data dependent corner case: Subtract a number that underflows by 1 (Operand2 is one greater than Operand1).
2.4.5	Data dependent corner case: Shift 0 places (should return Operand1 unchanged).
2.4.6	Data dependent corner case: Shift 31 places (the max allowable shift places).
2.5	Check that the design ignores data inputs unless the data are supposed to be valid (concurrent with the command and the following cycle). Remember that "00000000"X is a data value just as any other 32-bit combination. Here, the check must include verifying that the design latches the data only when appropriate, and does not key off nonzero data.

TABLE 4.7 ■ Generic tests and checks

Test reference number	Test description
3.1	Check that the design correctly handles illegal commands.
3.2	Check all outputs all of the time. Calc1 should not generate superfluous output values.
3.3	Check that the reset function correctly resets the design.

Type of Verification: Black Box, White Box, Grey Box

A verification engineer can create all of the functions listed under the *functions to be verified* section by driving the chip inputs and can check most scenarios by monitoring the chip outputs. This would indicate that black box checking is adequate. However, checkers placed on certain logic functions internal to the design might flag logic flaws faster. These checkers include checks on internal queues or stacks, especially in the priority logic. This would verify that no command leaves the state of the machine dirty (item 2.1 in the list of functions to be verified). In addition, the environment could include checks that verify fairness in the priority logic by monitoring the dispatch of commands to the ALUs (item 2.2 in the list of functions to be verified).

These checkers indicate that grey box verification is appropriate. Therefore, all stimulus will be driven on the chip inputs, and most checkers will monitor the chip outputs. The environment will contain a limited number of checkers on internal logic.

Verification Strategy

Deterministic, random, and formal verification are all viable technologies for Calc1. However, formal verification could have trouble verifying correct ALU results across all 32 bits simultaneously. A full-blown random environment might be overkill for this simple design, as the number of test cases required to verify the functions is limited. Therefore, for the Calc1 exercise, the deterministic verification method is chosen.[4]

Randomization Controls

Given the deterministic test case method, questions such as randomization controls become moot. The test case writer will encode the input values and the expected outputs into the test case itself.

Abstraction Level

The level of abstraction depends on the test case language. If the infrastructure exists, driving the Calc1 at the packet level is optimal for quickly coding test cases. Figure 4.7 shows an example test case with packet-level syntax.

The syntax in Figure 4.7 is very convenient, as the infrastructure that reads and manages the test case handles many mundane tasks, allowing

---

[4] As we advance to the Calc2 exercise in Chapter 7, the number of permutations and the level of complexity quickly exceed the number of deterministic tests that a verification team can reasonably write. Therefore, we leave the example of random-based methods to Calc2.

```
/* Port number   Cmd   Operand1       Operand2       Result         Response*/
   Port1         ADD   "00012345"X    "00054321"X    "00066666"X    Good
   Port2         SHL   "22222222"X    "00000002"X    "88888888"X    Good
   Port1         SUB   "00000001"X    "00000003"X    "00000000"X    Underflow
```

■ **FIGURE 4.7**

A basic Calc1 test case with packet-level abstraction.

the test case writer to focus on the intent of the test case. In the the syntax, the infrastructure environment manages multiple tasks for the test case writer. The first task for the infrastructure is translating the actual command decode values to bits (e.g., ADD = "0001"b). This has a potentially huge added benefit: if the designer ever changes the decode value of the ADD operand (e.g., ADD = "1001"b), all that is required in the environment is a simple modification to the infrastructure. If, instead, the verification engineer codes the operand decode values in the test case itself, then the team must change every test case with the ADD command. The same is true for the encoding of the response value.

The next task for the infrastructure is driving the bit-level values into the Calc1 design. The infrastructure knows to place the operand1 data value on the bus concurrent with the command and to send operand2 data the next cycle.

The infrastructure design also waits for the valid response. The test case writer cannot predict when the response will come back, so the infrastructure waits for the response event and checks the value when it finally appears on the outputs. This enables the next infrastructure task to send the next command to the port when the port becomes available. In the sample test case of Figure 4.7, there are two commands destined for Port 1. The protocol states that only one command may be outstanding at a time on a given port. Therefore, the infrastructure can send the first two commands concurrently (to Port1 and Port2) but must wait for the ADD on Port 1 to finish before initiating the SUB. Without an infrastructure, sending multiple commands to the same port is a very tedious task involving trial and error.

The infrastructure will also take care of resetting the logic and driving the clocks. The infrastructure automatically raises the reset line for seven cycles as required at the beginning of every test case, thus circumventing the need to articulate the reset in every test case. The infrastructure also drives the clocks to the correct values. An even more robust infrastructure might further simplify the test case writing task by including other advanced aspects of verification stimulus generation and checking.

An advanced Calc1 verification environment would include data prediction. If the infrastructure included a golden model that predicts the result and response fields, it frees the test case writer from having to "do the math."

```
SET INPUT "reset(0:7)""11111111"b;
CLOCK 7;
SET INPUT "reset(0:7)""00000000"b;
CLOCK 1;
SET INPUT "req1_cmd_in(0:3)""0001"b;
SET INPUT "req1_data_in(0:31)""00012345"x©

...
CLOCK 3;
EXPECT OUTPUT "out_resp1(0:1)""01"b;

...
```

▪ **FIGURE 4.8**

A bit-level test case for Calc1.

Further functions in an advanced verification environment include generation of random operand data. If desired, the syntax of the test case allows the writer to replace an operand data value with the keyword "random," which tells the packet generator to pick a random number value. This requires data prediction capabilities in the infrastructure.[5] The test case writer maintains deterministic control over the command selection and flow of the test case, but optionally can allow the infrastructure to choose values.

When compared with the packet level of abstraction in the test case of Figure 4.7, the test case in Figure 4.8 shows the tedious nature of bit-level environments. The bit-stream level test case language requires the test case writer to specify all inputs every cycle.

This bit-stream level of abstraction is very tiresome for a verification engineer to write test cases. This test case sample does not even complete the sending of a single Port command. Even worse, the writer must predict when the response will return from Calc1 through trial and error. This entails adjusting the clock value in line 8 to the actual cycle that the Calc1 logic returns the response.

Output Checking

The previous section prescribed the golden vector approach to checking. Under this approach, the verification engineer supplies the expected output values for the deterministic sequences. Unless the team creates an advanced verification infrastructure with predictive data checking, the test case writer imbeds the data and result checking inside the test case.

---

[5] This type of random data generation should not be confused with "random-based verification methodologies" (see Chapter 7). Random-based verification go well beyond random data by using biasing tables to randomly select commands and ports, as well as idle cycles between port commands.

Coverage Requirements

Coverage goals for the Calc1 example are based on the tests defined in the *functions to be verified* section, and the goals require that the verification tests create all of the cases described in that section. These goals are simple because the test scenarios in this design are able to be articulated. However, in robust designs, coverage goals require greater effort and rigor in the verification cycle.

Although there is a detailed explanation of coverage and coverage tools in Chapter 7, the fundamental notion of coverage is to provide feedback and confirmation of what the verification environment has exercised in the DUV. Coverage feedback provides the verification engineer with insight into the actual data of what the test case has done. This data will show either that the test case has met its intent or that the test case failed to exercise the intended function or scenario within the design. For example, in the *functions to be verified* section of the verification plan, test reference number 2.1.1 calls for tests that verify that each command can follow any other command on each port. This statement stipulates a series of 16 pairs of commands on each port for a total of 64 different test scenarios. Coverage feedback will track which of the 64 sequences the test cases have completed.

Resource Requirements

For the Calc1 exercise, the resource requirements call for a single verification engineer. The compute resources call for a single workstation on which the simulation engine runs.

Schedule Details

The schedule details for the Calc1 exercise are straightforward. A verification engineer should expect to complete the Calc1 design example in a single workday.

In the case of the packet-level abstraction, the Calc1 verification engineer depends on the existence and quality of the infrastructure. Usually, the verification engineer must create the infrastructure or at least personalize it for the design under test. If this is the case, extra schedule time is required.

4.4.3 Deterministic Verification of Calc1

With the design intent and the verification plan in place, it is time to begin verifying the Calc1 design. The verification plan called for deterministic testing of the design. For clarity, this description uses a packet level of abstraction to detail the deterministic tests. As stated in the verification plan, the packet level requires an infrastructure to be in place.

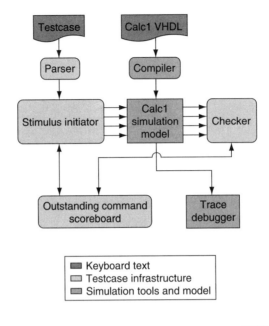

▪ FIGURE 4.9

Infrastructure for sending simple command packets into the Calc1 simulation model.

Figure 4.9 shows the high-level view of the components in the infrastructure. The test case parser reads the text-based commands from the test case and converts them into packet structures for the stimulus initiator. The initiator passes the packets into the model on the designated port, performing the packet to bit-stream conversion. Each command packet requires two cycles to transmit into the Calc1 simulation model as dictated by the design's specification. The stimulus initiator can multiplex across all four ports, sending simultaneous or staggered commands based on the test case. When the interface driver transmits a command packet, it also posts the command to a scoreboard, which keeps track of commands currently under execution by the Calc1 simulation model. As the Calc1 simulation model completes commands, the output checker pulls the expected response and expected data from the scoreboard for comparison to the actual response. If there is a response or data mismatch, the test case execution ceases and the output checker records both the error and the actual versus expected data. Otherwise, the output checker removes the command from the scoreboard, indicating that the stimulus initiator may dispatch a new packet to that port. When the stimulus initiator transmits all of the test case packets and the checker receives all responses, the test case ends successfully.

The infrastructure also takes care of the seven-cycle reset sequence as well as driving the clocks into the model.

```
/* Port number  DelayN  Cmd  Operand1       Operand2       Result         Response*/
    Port1         0     ADD  "00012345"X    "00054321"X    "00066666"X    Good
    Port2         2     SHL  "22222222"X    "00000002"X    "88888888"X    Good
    Port1         3     SUB  "00000001"X    "00000003"X    "00000000"X    Underflow
```

■ **FIGURE 4.10**

Test case syntax with a delay field.

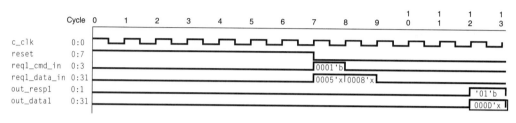

■ **FIGURE 4.11**

The Calc1 DUV trace for test case 1.1.1, an ADD command to Port1.

For this exercise, we will build on the test case syntax introduced in the test case of Figure 4.7, described in the previous section. The new syntax includes an additional field, DelayN, to control the number of cycles between packets (Figure 4.10).

The delay field causes the interface driver to wait N cycles before dispatching the packet. In the above example, the first packet on Port1 (ADD command) will dispatch as soon as the reset completes (cycle 8), and the environment will initiate the Port2 command two cycles later. When the Port1 command completes, the port will remain idle for three cycles before the interface driver initiates the SUB command packet.

With this packet-level infrastructure in place, the verification engineer focuses on the intent of each test case. The first set of test cases in the plan can now be written.

Verification Plan Tests 1.1 to 1.3

Our first test case runs to completion and the simulation engine captures the trace. The response and data are correct, and test case 1.1.1 is successful. Figure 4.11 shows the trace of test case 1.1.1. Similar test cases, 1.1.2, 1.1.3, and 1.1.4, verify the basic command-response flow of each port for the ADD command. However, test case 1.1.4 does not complete in 13 cycles, as the others did. Instead, it runs until the test times out. Figure 4.12 shows the trace for test case 1.1.4.

The out_resp4 wire never returns a valid response. At this point, the verification engineer has potentially found a bug where Port4 hangs.

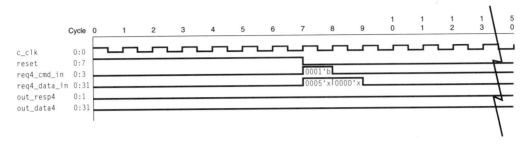

▪ **FIGURE 4.12**

The Calc1 DUV trace for test case 1.1.4, an ADD command to Port4.

After further study of the trace, the verification engineer confers with the designer, and the designer concludes that the priority logic does have a bug. The designer makes a fix and recompiles the model. The verification engineer reruns the exact same test case to validate the fix and concludes that the basic command-response sequence on Port4 now works. For good measure, the verification engineer reruns the first three test cases to ensure that the fix did not break any other logic that had been working. The first bug in Calc1 has been uncovered and fixed.

Test reference number 1.2 of the verification plan prescribes test cases for each operation on each port. Test cases 1.1.1 through 1.1.4 already verified the add operation on each port, so the new test case verifies the subtract operation on each port in parallel.

```
/* Test case 1.2.1 SUB commands on each port                              */
/* Port #  DelayN  Cmd  Operand1        Operand2        Result          Response*/
   Port1   0       SUB  "00000007"X     "00000004"X     "00000003"X     Good
   Port2   0       SUB  "0000000D"X     "00000008"X     "00000005"X     Good
   Port3   0       SUB  "00000010"X     "00000001"X     "0000000F"X     Good
   Port4   0       SUB  "00000012"X     "00000007"X     "0000000B"X     Good
```

The test case runs to completion in 16 cycles. Figure 4.13 shows the trace.

Next, test cases 1.2.2 and 1.2.3 verify the Shift_left and Shift_right operations on each port. Both test cases run successfully against the Calc1 model.

Section 1.3 of the verification plan calls for add and subtract overflows and underflows.

```
/* Test case 1.3.1 Overflow and underflow                                 */
/* Port #  DelayN  Cmd  Operand1        Operand2        Result          Response*/
   Port1   0       ADD  "FFFFFFFF"X     "00000002"X     "00000000"X     Overflow
   Port2   0       SUB  "0000000D"X     "0000000E"X     "00000000"X     Underflow
```

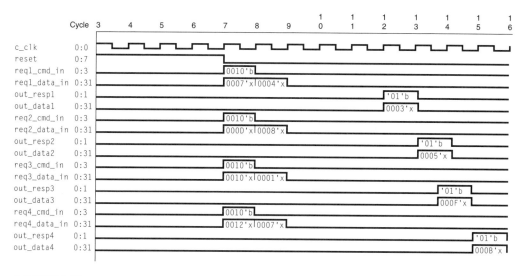

■ FIGURE 4.13

The Calc1 DUV trace for test case 1.2.1, the subtract operation on each port.

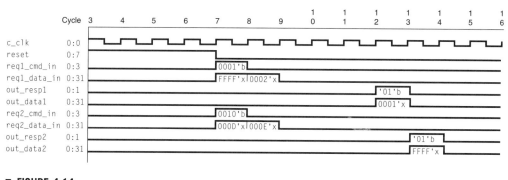

■ FIGURE 4.14

The Calc1 DUV trace for test case 1.3.1, overflow and underflow add and subtract operations.

When test case 1.3.1 runs against the Calc1 model, the test case fails with miscompares on both the result and response values. Figure 4.14 shows the trace.

Rather than responding with the overflow/underflow response of "10"b, the Calc1 model returns a good response. Further examination reveals that the results for both the add and subtract would be correct in 2's complement but that does not match the specification. The verification engineer consults the designer and confirms the second bug. The Calc1 design ignored the carry_out bit from the adder ALU instead of using it to generate the overflow/underflow response. The verification engineer reruns the test case with the fix, and it runs successfully.

Further overflow and underflow test case permutations run against each of the ports and find no more bugs in this area.

4.5 SUMMARY

Throughout the project, the verification plan provides the blueprint for success. It contains the details for all of the environments. Although the plan will inevitably require updates as the project progresses, it contains all of the fundamental information on what will be verified, where it will be verified, and when that verification will occur.

As time progresses, the question "when am I done?" will arise. The team finds many of the answers to the following targets by referencing the verification plan.

- Components written with all required function

- All checkers contain all appropriate checks

- All identified tests written

- All identified tests pass

- All identified coverage goals met

- All bug rates have dropped off

4.6 EXERCISES

1. There are two bugs identified in the Calc1 design (see test case 1.1.1 and test case 1.3.1). Using the Calc1 verification plan as your guide (Tables 4.5–4.7), write the remaining deterministic test cases and identify any remaining bugs. You will need the Calc1 HDL (download from the companion Web site for this book) to create a simulation model using your vendor's engine. Describe any more bugs and indicate the verification plan section under which you found them.

2. List and summarize the sections of the verification plan.

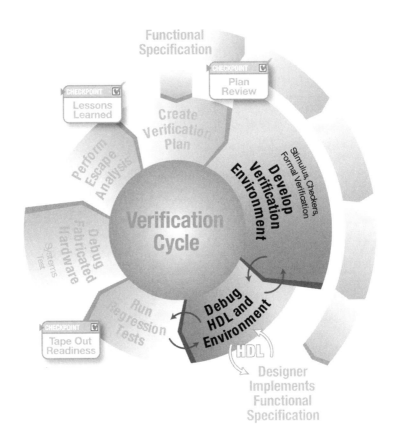

Within the Verification Cycle, the verification team spends most of their time developing the verification environment and debugging the HDL. Having completed the verification plan, the team embarks on creating robust stimulus and checkers in their quest for delivering a bug-free hardware design. Because of the depth of effort needed to develop a verification environment and debug both the HDL and verification environment, Part 2 and Part 3 of this book focus squarely on these two portion of the Verification Cycle.

Simulation based verification is the most widely used method of functional verification. At the heart of this methodology is the simulation engine, which allows the verification team to model the behavior of the design. Other critical tools support the simulation method, including High-level Verification Languages, debugging software and coverage modelers. Within Part 2, Chapter 5 and 6 describe these simulation-based verification tools.

Robust simulation tools provide a platform upon which skilled verification engineers create stimulus and checking components that verify the correct design behavior. Verification engineers have multiple techniques available for creating these components. Chatpers 7 and 8 explain these varying methods, citing multiple examples, including a second Calc design. Chapter 8 also delves into the debug process used when the environment detects a difference between the expected behavior and the actual results from the modeled design.

Simulation extends beyond the basic function of the design as verification engineers employ simulation-based techniques to reset logic, built-in test logic, and system-level verification. Chapter 9 describes simulation methods for non-basic, or pervasive functions, and Chapter 10 explains the many elements of system-level simulation.

CHAPTER 5

HARDWARE DESCRIPTION LANGUAGES AND SIMULATION ENGINES

Before exploring the details of the verification cycle's simulation-based strategies, this chapter and Chapter 6 discuss the typical design automation (DA) tools that are available to the design and verification teams. First, we introduce the major characteristics of hardware description languages (HDLs) and their simulation engines, which provide the heart of the simulation-based verification cycle. Newer DA technologies that allow the formal verification of a DUV are the focus of Chapters 11 and 12.

Design engineers normally use an HDL to define the function and the structure of a design under verification (DUV). Specifying a design in the text format of an HDL, an activity called *design entry*, allows the engineer to document the DUV unambiguously and later execute it as a model in a simulation engine. The HDL version of the DUV is also the basis for the physical implementation of the design. To better support the simulation task, HDLs have features that go beyond the mere description of the design and include the specification of stimulus and checking components, which form an HDL test bench. When we characterize the typical elements of HDLs as design specification tools in this chapter, we compare and contrast the two most popular HDLs, VHDL and Verilog, as prime examples.

Figure 5.1 is used to guide the discussion from design entry through the simulation-based verification cycle. The simulation engine is at the heart of simulation-based verification. It executes the HDL model in conjunction with the HDL test bench elements a user might have coded.

There are a variety of algorithms available to build simulation engines. Because the simulation engine plays such a crucial role in the center of the simulation-based flow, typical architectures of such engines in this are discussed in this chapter. It is important that verification engineers understand the characteristics of such tools at their disposal. Electronic design automation (EDA) developers build tools such as simulation engines around different sets of trade-offs, many of which select between accuracy and speed. The verification team must choose those tools that are most adequate for their given project.

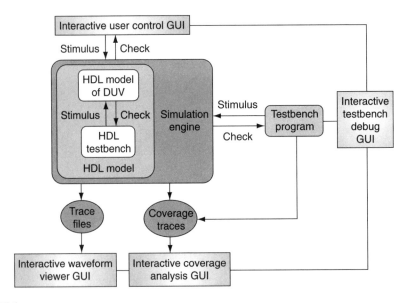

▪ **FIGURE 5.1**

Overview of major simulation tools. The simulation engine executes the design under verification model as well as a test bench specified in a hardware description language. The verification team can stimulate and check the model in two additional ways: through a test bench external to the simulation engine or by an interactive control user-interface. Shaded rectangles show a set of graphical user interfaces typically provided around these tools to improve verification productivity.

Many simulation engines offer an interactive graphical user interface (GUI), which lets the user apply individual stimulus and check commands manually in between simulation steps of the model. Such interfaces, which support a detailed debug mode, are effective mainly on smaller models or very specific debug situations. When working with larger-sized DUVs, the verification engineer lets the simulation engine save the results of a simulation run to trace files, which capture simulated model states over time. As also shown in Figure 5.1, waveform viewer tools let the user browse through these results files in various ways, for example, forward *and* backward in simulation time, to inspect and debug the model behavior in detail. An overview of typical characteristics of such tools is provided at the end of the chapter.

For many verification tasks, the users do not find the test bench features of the HDL sufficient. Therefore, most simulation engines provide open interfaces that support the application of checks and stimuli from a programming or test bench authoring language. The discussion of several test bench languages is the subject of Chapter 6.

It is already apparent from Figure 5.1 that many simulation tools present an interactive GUI to the designer. A very common approach is to integrate the different GUI tasks under one single master GUI, which then gives the user the view of a single integrated HDL and verification development environment even if the implementation underneath consists of separate tools.

All major EDA companies offer many of these tools, often integrated into one GUI framework. The benefit of the Institute of Electrical and Electronics Engineers (IEEE) standardization of the HDLs is that many simulation engines are largely interchangeable with each other. The differentiation comes from simulation speed and value-add features such as the integration of the other simulation tasks: coverage, test bench program support, and user-friendliness for debug.

5.1 HARDWARE DESCRIPTION LANGUAGES

Hardware description languages are the central tools for design engineers to specify the behavior and the functional and physical partitioning of a piece of hardware design. This chapter will not provide a detailed tutorial of one or several HDLs because there are excellent textbooks available on all the popular HDLs [1,2]. Despite the detailed lists of syntax elements and features of the HDLs, this chapter will give a taxonomy of the most important properties of VHDL and Verilog as representatives that together stand for the majority of HDLs in use today. This discussion and the comparison between the two languages should allow readers a foundation from which they can quickly explore actual language details using an HDL textbook.

5.1.1 HDL Modeling Levels

The idea of a formal language to specify the behavior of hardware goes back to the 1960s. Similar to the concept of a programming language, the idea was to use a formal, machine-readable syntax with well-defined semantics to allow the unambiguous specification of a given hardware design. Developers in academia and industry have defined and implemented various HDLs over the decades.

Aside from the pure specification of the design, the main purpose of using an HDL was always to automatically turn the HDL text into a *simulation model*. Figure 5.2 shows the model build flow from HDL to simulation engine. A simulation engine runs the model and lets the verification engineer interact with it at various times during the simulation. Typical interactions during simulation run time are the control of the amount of time to simulate, interrogation of the state of the model, and changing the state of the model. There are different options for the level of integration of the components of the system shown in Figure 5.2. The most integrated system presents the user with a tool that loads files of HDL specifications directly into the simulation engine, making the compilation and model build appear seamless. Other systems give the

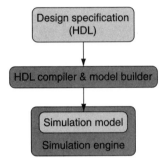

This flow shows how a language-processing program (compiler) reads the hardware description language specification of a design under verification (DUV) and produces a simulation model in the end. The user can execute the compiled model by calling a simulation engine, which loads the model of the DUV and evaluates it.

user access to discrete components in which a compiler translates the HDL into a simulation model file that is stored to disk, and the simulation engine simply loads the pre-compiled model file at the beginning of every simulation run.

The two main hardware description languages used in the industry today are Verilog and VHDL. The IEEE has defined standards for both (VHDL IEEE 1076, Verilog IEEE 1364), and all major EDA vendors support both languages equally well [3, 4]. There are largely historical reasons for the existence of two different standards in this field; however, the two languages focus on different areas of the hardware specification task. A taxonomy of the hardware specification space will help understand the differences between Verilog and VHDL as well as give a framework, to make it easier to characterize future trends in HDL development.

The main attributes of a design at the highest modeling level (Figure 5.3) are its inputs and outputs and the behavior of the DUV. One way to describe the behavior would simply be the specification of the value of input signals and the corresponding value of output signals over time.

Modeling Dimensions

Approaching the specification of input/output (I/O) behavior more systematically, the properties of the design block and its I/Os can be described along four different modeling dimensions (Figure 5.4). For each dimension, we list specification methods ordered by increasing levels of abstraction.

The *temporal dimension* is necessary to describe behavior over time, which is always observable as change of model state. The values of I/O

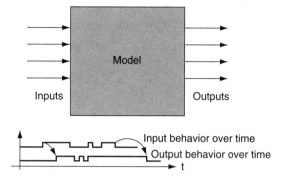

■ **FIGURE 5.3**

At the highest level of abstraction, the designer specifies the outside interface of a design under verification (DUV) and the behavior of the DUV outputs because of DUV input changes over time.

- Temporal dimension
    - Continuous (analog)
    - Gate/wire delay
    - Clock cycle
    - Instruction/transaction cycle — Discrete time
    - Events
- Data abstraction
    - Continuous (analog)
    - "Bit" : multiple values
    - Bit : binary
    - Abstract value — Discrete value
    - Composite value ("struct"/"record")
- Functional dimension
    - Continuous functions (e.g. differential equations)
    - Switch-level (transistors as switches)
    - Boolean logic
    - Algorithmic (e.g. sort procedure)
    - Abstract mathematical formula (e.g. matrix multiplication)
- Structural dimension
    - Single black box
    - Functional blocks
    - Detailed hierarchy with primitive library elements

■ **FIGURE 5.4**

This list of four dimensions allows the discussion of independent aspects of the specification of design under verification (DUV) behavior into separate categories. The temporal dimension deals with the timing relationship of DUV behavior. The data abstraction defines the value sets for DUV signals. The specification of the functional relationships between DUV inputs/outputs belongs into the functional dimension. The structural dimension is relevant when the designer specifies a DUV not by functional behavior but by creating a more complex DUV from simpler building blocks.

signals or state-holding variables inside the DUV represent the state of the model. An analog simulation system lets us specify behavior in *continuous time*, fairly close to the physical model of an electrical circuit. *Gate and wire delays* are more abstract; they are the first example of discrete time in the list of increasing temporal abstraction in Figure 5.4. They measure the time it takes to propagate changes of signal values through the elements of a model. Every change occurs abruptly at the outputs of these elements. The notion of *clock cycle* abstracts time further: on this level, we are only interested in sampling signal values at specific periodic, recurring points in time. Such a cycle might coincide with a clock cycle of a synchronous design. More generally, however, a clock cycle of HDL specification could simply sample signals several times during a real hardware clock cycle. A DUV specification uses the most abstract notion of time when it views changes of model state only as occurrences of *instructions* or *transactions*. The model is still sampled periodically, but the measure of time is abstractly the completion of units of work in the model. Finally, the most abstract notion of time knows only abstract *events*. The only concern at this level is the mere precedence of observed changes of model state.

For the purpose of the level of verification discussed in this book, we will limit ourselves to *discrete time*.

In the dimension of *data abstraction*, it is useful to distinguish five different levels to describe model state. Again close to the physical model of a circuit is the notion of a *continuous* value, typically a voltage measure. At a level more abstract, multi-value simulation engines or HDL signal types allow for granular representations of a signal state as a multi-valued *"bit"*. A multi-valued *bit* signal or variable can assume values besides the strict binary "0" and "1". For example, values like *"u"* or *"x"* specify the states *"un-initialized"* or *"unknown"*, respectively. Other value denotations are useful to distinguish signal strength and are helpful to simulate bus signals with multiple sources. The more abstract binary representation of *bit* is central to the type of verification discussed here. *Abstract values* are much better suited than are simple bits and collection of bits to encode the actual intention of the design and the semantic meaning implied by a signal state. The definition of the symbolically enumerated values *main* and *elm* used in Section 3.3.2 is an example. Figure 5.5 repeats the relevant section of Figure 3.13.

However, integer, floating-point, or text string types are equally suited to serve as abstract values. From this more abstract specification, the bit encoding is a question of implementation. Finally, at the end of the list of data abstractions, *composite values* can package together several abstract values to one structured object, similar to records or C-language-like *structs*, which allow users to refer to complex composite values or states in a very concise way.

```
...
architecture rtl of traffic is
  type state is (main, elm);
  signal current_state_din, current_state_dout : state;

begin  -- rtl

  -- purpose: Determines when the light should change
  -- type    : combinational
  -- inputs : timer_pulse, Main_Street, Elm_Street, current_state_dout
  -- outputs: current_state_din
  dataflow_proc: process (timer_pulse, Main_Street, Elm_Street, current_state_dout)
  begin  -- process change_light
    current_state_din <= current_state_dout;
    -- When the timer expires, evaluate the traffic situation
    if timer_pulse = '1' then
      if Main_Street = '1' then
        current_state_din <= main;
      elsif Elm_Street = '1' then
        current_state_din <= elm;
      end if;
    end if;
  end process dataflow_proc;

  Light_Direction <= "01" when current_state_dout = main else "10";
...
```

■ **FIGURE 5.5**

Enumerated types in VHDL are an example of abstract values for signals.

For the specification of the behavior of a DUV, we can choose from the different abstraction levels in the *functional dimension*. Clearly related to the continuous domain in the dimensions of data abstraction and temporal abstraction is the use of *continuous mathematical functions* such as differential equations. Next, the abstractions of transistors to *switch-level* elements yield a concise model for detailed custom-circuit simulations. So-called gate-level and register-transfer models (explained below) use *Boolean logic* as the base for the specification of functional blocks built from Boolean elements. Further abstracted forms of specification use general programmed *algorithms* to define functionality. For example, a sort algorithm that sorts different key entries in a buffer can concisely use a bubble-sort subroutine regardless of how the real hardware implements the function in Boolean logic later. If our simulation system and HDL support built-in high-level data types and operators, such as matrices and their multiply operators, the behavioral function of a block can be defined most concisely with an *abstract mathematical formula*.

The fourth and final important dimension of our modeling taxonomy is the *structural dimension*. We can describe a design as a single

Temporal				
Continuous	Gate delay	Clock cycle	Instruction cycle	Events

Data				
Continuous	Multivalue bit	Bit	Abstract value	"Struct"

Functional				
Continuous	Switch level	Boolean logic	Algorithmic	Abstract mathematical

Structural		
Single black box	Functional blocks	Detailed component hierarchy

■ **FIGURE 5.6**

Coverage of modeling levels by Verilog. We list the four dimensions of the hardware description language taxonomy vertically with their different modeling levels expanded horizontally. The shaded, overlaid area represents the modeling levels directly supported in the Verilog language.

amorphous *black box* without any structural content, for example, a fast-Fourier-transformation (FFT) design described with abstract mathematical formulas. More typical is the breakdown of a single black box to a set of interconnected *functional blocks* in a refinement step. Although such simple structural refinement implies at least two levels of hierarchy, the most granular structural partitioning uses potentially many levels of *detailed hierarchy*, all the way to a library of pre-defined primitive elements.

Figure 5.6 illustrates how the Verilog HDL covers the dimensions of our HDL taxonomy. Similar to VHDL (Figure 5.7), Verilog covers large parts of the non-analog domain in all dimensions. Verilog has direct built-in support for switch-level modeling, which gives it a clear performance edge over VHDL in this area. VHDL's focus is decidedly on higher-levels of abstractions with its support for user-defined data-types, programming-language-like function overloading, and the support to define complex composite data types with records. On the other hand, VHDL supports switch-level and multi-value logic only specified as open-ended user *packages* without direct language support versus the built-in but fixed capabilities of Verilog. The trade-offs between the languages are generality and flexibility versus performance.

Both languages excel in their flexibility to express structural decomposition and hierarchy as one would expect in an area where an HDL is most fundamentally different from a programming language. After all, it is a central design technique in hardware design to build more complex

Temporal				
Continuous	Gate delay	Clock cycle	Instruction cycle	Events

Data				
Continuous	Multivalue bit	Bit	Abstract value	"Struct"

Functional				
Continuous	Switch level	Boolean logic	Algorithmic	Abstract mathematical

Structural		
Single black box	Functional blocks	Detailed component hierarchy

■ **FIGURE 5.7**

Coverage of modeling levels by VHDL. We list the four dimensions of the hardware description language taxonomy vertically with their different modeling levels expanded horizontally. The shaded, overlaid area represents the modeling level modeling levels directly supported in the VHDL language.

hardware modules from simpler building blocks. The definition of *modules* (Verilog) or *entities* (VHDL) that represent such re-usable building blocks, their instantiation, and the interconnection of the instances via signals is a basic activity of HDL-based logic design.

It is interesting to note that Verilog's built-in support for abstract events has no counterpart in VHDL, in which the designer has to model the occurrence of an event as a change of a signal value.

The IEEE standard called VHDL-AMS (IEEE 1076.1) extends VHDL to cover the continuous domains (time and data values).

Before we extend the HDL review from constructs for modeling the DUV to the support of verification concepts, we use the modeling taxonomy to discuss two important modeling styles, which apply to both VHDL and Verilog. The two styles are *gate-level* and *RT-level* modeling and are the workhorses for functional digital hardware verification today.

Gate-Level Model

A gate-level model is an exclusively structural model that only uses instances of a fixed set of elementary Boolean function library blocks to build the DUV. The interconnect specification of these instances might extend over several levels of a hierarchy. The source for these models is usually a *physical netlist*. Many times such a netlist is the output of a logic synthesis tool that transformed an original HDL design source and mapped the function into an available silicon library of logic primitives

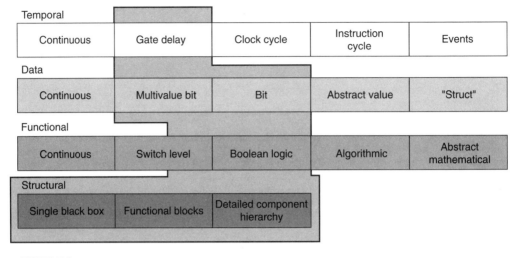

Temporal				
Continuous	Gate delay	Clock cycle	Instruction cycle	Events

Data				
Continuous	Multivalue bit	Bit	Abstract value	"Struct"

Functional				
Continuous	Switch level	Boolean logic	Algorithmic	Abstract mathematical

Structural		
Single black box	Functional blocks	Detailed component hierarchy

▪ FIGURE 5.8

The gate-level modeling style covers the lower levels of abstraction of the modeling taxonomy of the hardware description language. Gate-level models are highly structural and use a gate delay time reference, multi-value signals, and Boolean logic primitive to implement the function of the design under verification.

(Figure 1.1). Such a library of technology-specific building blocks contains HDL models that include information about the timing behavior of the primitives. Many times, engineers verify the implementation timing behavior of the design at the gate-level.

At the gate-level (Figure 5.8), it is standard to use a multi-value bit representation for signals to enable a more detailed verification of non-Boolean function aspects of the DUV. A good example is the so-called power-on-reset (POR) simulation (Chapter 9), which verifies that the DUV can be set into a defined starting state after power on. The multi-value simulation initializes the DUV to a random state, represented by an initial value "u" for all DUV state elements. "u" represents the state *un-initialized*, a symbolic short-hand for any possible Boolean value. POR simulation verifies that there is a controlled input sequence, which moves the DUV from this "u" state to its defined initial state from where it will be ready to execute its specified main function.

The detailed simulation at the gate-level comes at the price of lower simulation performance compared to the register-transfer level (RTL), which we discuss next.

Register-Transfer Model

The RTL style (Figure 5.9) is more abstract but overlaps somewhat with the gate-level model. The intention of an RTL model is to specify the DUV

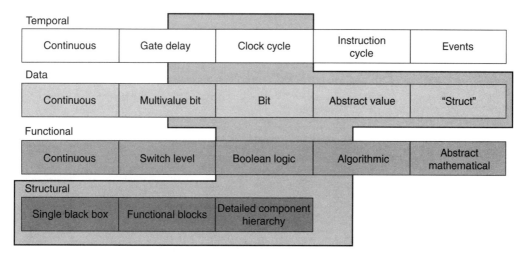

The register transfer level (RTL) modeling style covers more abstracts levels of the modeling taxonomy of the hardware description language. RTL models can be very structural such as gate-level models. However, they typically model the function of the design under verification (DUV) by using Boolean logic, equations, and algorithmic specification using sequential code. Designers use the full range of high-level data abstractions to allow a concise behavioral specification of the DUV.

in terms of state-holding dataflow elements (registers and storage arrays) and how the DUV updates the state between clock cycles. Most typically, the granularity of an RTL model differs from the gate-level in that the structural hierarchy does not reach all the way down to technology library primitives but ends at least at the level of Boolean equations. Modern design methodologies use equations and sequential HDL constructs (*always/process* constructs in Verilog/VHDL) but keep corresponding state-holding elements, latches and flip-flops, identical between the RTL and the gate-level. Keeping the consistent state-elements between the two levels allows formal verification methods to prove Boolean equivalence between the two and reduces greatly the need for the more costly gate-level simulation. Chapter 11 discusses the advantages of formal verification and the equivalence proof between gate-level and RTL models.

The use of higher-level abstractions at the RTL in the description of the combinational function of the DUV allows for a more concise design specification and better simulation performance. The influence of HDL style on simulation performance will be discussed in more detail later in this chapter.

Figure 5.10 shows the role of the RTL specification in the design flow. An RTL specification is the starting point for both verification and physical implementation of a DUV. From this perspective, a gate-level version

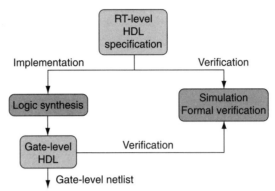

▪ **FIGURE 5.10**

The very large scale integration (VLSI) design flow uses an register transfer level (RTL) model as the source for both verification and implementation. A modern design system supports the automatic mapping of the RTL specification via a logic synthesis tool to a technology library at the gate level. The RTL model is the principal model for verification in this approach. Verification of the gate-level model checks correctness of logic synthesis and dynamic timing properties. The gate-level netlist is input to the physical design process (chip placement and wiring) and finally to chip fabrication.

of the DUV is an implementation of the RTL specification. Although designers can implement the gate-level version manually, it is usually an EDA tool, logic synthesis, which creates the implementation of the DUV automatically. Most of the functional verification of the DUV can occur on the RTL model. Simulation on the gate level provides the verification team with a detailed view of physical parameters such as signal propagation times. Such parameters, unknown at the time the RTL specification is done, can be part of a detailed simulation at the gate-level. In addition, verification that the gate-level and the RTL versions of the DUV are functionally identical is necessary to ensure that the transformation of RTL to gate-level did not introduce inconsistencies.

The Finite State Machine Model of an RTL Specification

Figure 5.11 shows an alternate view of the RTL style of DUV specification. We view the RTL model as a general *finite state machine (FSM)*. All state-holding elements of the DUV represent the state of the FSM, and all RTL code that is concerned with the state changes between clock cycles translates into the combinational state transition function of Figure 5.11.

If all the clocks in the FSM model run at the same frequency, we call the FSM purely synchronous. However, it is possible to have different frequencies for different clocks in the RTL specification. We consider all

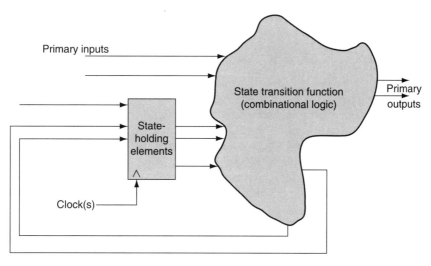

■ FIGURE 5.11

A specific view of a register transfer level specification expresses the notion of a finite-state machine. The finite state machine (FSM) notion combines all state-holding elements of a design conceptually together to a single state vector. The combinational logic of the FSM reacts to changes on the primary inputs of the design or the current state. This results in changes to the primary outputs or the new input values of the state-holding elements. The state updates if any of the clocks are active that synchronize the update of state-holding elements.

logic clocked by the same clock a *clock domain*. We will discuss some aspects of multiple clock domain simulation in Section 5.5.3.

The general state machine model of a DUV will be the basis for many verification tasks and tools throughout this book.

5.1.2 Verification Aspects of HDLs

The use of HDLs in verification is not limited to the simulation of the hardware design specification (the DUV). Modern HDLs also include constructs that support verification tasks. The verification aspects discussed in this section cover two different areas: capturing *design intent* and HDL features for the creation of test benches. This chapter provides only an informal overview of both topics; for detailed coverage, refer to books that focus extensively on these aspects of HDL use: *Assertion-Based Design* [5] covers systematic ways to insert design intent and its benefits for verification, and *Writing Test Benches: Functional Verification of HDL Models* [6] focuses on a methodology to use HDLs to write test benches.

Design Intent

In general, the concept of defining design intent in an HDL description is that there is additional information present in the HDL that the verification cycle can utilize in addition to the functional and structural specification.

Some of the design intent is contained implicitly. A finite-state machine expressed on the RTL with enumerated values for the states and a "case" statement for the state-transfer function captures more about the intent of the design than the gate-level implementation that implements states encoded in Boolean values and the transfer function as a sea of low-level gates. For example, the RTL use of three enumerated values to encode the three possible states of an FSM clearly delineates legal state values (encodings) from illegal ones. On the other hand, the gate-level implementation of the state vector as two flip-flop bits loses the original explicit design intent of three states and leaves it implicit to the state transition function, which does not allow the FSM to reach the illegal state encoding.

The lower-level implementation contains less *semantic structure*. For example, it is clear from the RTL description what the state-holding latches are. If the verification task is to collect information about states reached during a simulation, we can simply look at the set of state-holding elements and capture their values. The design intent of the FSM is clearly visible in the RTL. On the other hand, the gate-level implementation does not clearly distinguish between FSM control state latches and data-flow latches. If the only specification available is gate-level, it is very difficult to retrieve the FSM semantics from a sea of gates.

HDLs also have mechanisms to express functional design intent directly. The main means for this is the ASSERT construct in VHDL (which interestingly has no counterpart in standard Verilog). An ASSERT can be used to clearly specify an *assumption* on the input or an intended *guarantee* on the output of a design. We discuss the importance of assertions in Section 3.3 and the systematic methodology of an *assertion-based verification* process in Chapter 8.

In an ideal world for verification, designers would use the highest levels of abstraction possible in their HDL descriptions and thus provide much implicitly contained semantic structure. Then, verification engineers and EDA tools could retrieve the design intent from the HDL automatically. The tools could tie into specific usage patterns of certain HDL constructs, such as enumerated values and *case* statements to denote FSMs.

However, there is a problem with this direction. A basic goal conflict affects HDL descriptions. On one hand, we want the highest possible abstraction to aid verification, but on the other hand, the HDL needs to satisfy physical design constraints such as timing, area, and power testability. Sometimes these physical goals are diametrically opposed to our desires for verification. Increasing pressure from the physical design constraints in the sub-micron very large scale integration (VLSI) design era morphed typical HDL descriptions to contain more and more structural detail, which increasingly obscures the semantic structure.

It is for this very conflict that methods to *explicitly express* design intent have gained much more attention in recent years. Although the explicit ASSERT has more value than normally utilized, its expressive power is nevertheless limited. More complicated and expressive methods are desirable, and this did lead to a trend of extending the traditional HDLs. The two main examples of language extensions to express design intent are property specification language (PSL) (for more detail, see Chapter 12) [7] and the assertion language part of the new HDL SystemVerilog [8]. All these HDL extensions are clearly annotations to the actual design description, and their common purpose is to capture *design intent* explicitly.

HDL Test Benches

As discussed in Chapter 3, a test bench for a given design has two main tasks (Figure 5.12):

1. Stimulate the primary inputs of a design with drivers.

2. Check interfaces and internal state of the design.

It is good practice to separate test benches into at least two partitions along the lines of these main tasks. Hierarchical verification will be discussed later in this book (Chapter 10), and it will become clear that reusing the investment made into the checkers on interfaces and design internals is needed, as the real designs are connected to the interface of the previously standalone verified design units.

In Figure 5.12, the driver was separated from the checker. The larger model in Figure 5.13 still includes the checker for the design units while replacing the drivers with the neighboring real design.

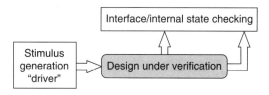

■ **FIGURE 5.12**

A basic hardware description language test bench is represented by the components stimulus generation and checking.

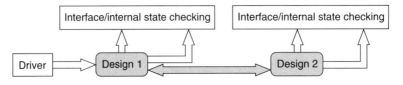

▪ **FIGURE 5.13**

Hardware description language test bench re-use example. We integrate Design1 and Design2 into a larger design under verification and want to re-use as much as possible from the simulation environments used to verify Design1 and Design2 standalone. While Design1 replaces the driver component for Design2, all checker components are re-usable in this configuration, as well as the driver component for Design1.

Using HDLs to implement test benches is especially intuitive in the structural domain. The drivers and checkers are *"connected"* to their target signals by connecting instances of the test bench components into the HDL hierarchy. The strong support for structural specification in HDLs pays off nicely in the case in which a higher-level design replicates a lower-level design unit multiple times. Figure 5.14 illustrates this with a DUV called *System* that contains three instances of a lower-level unit called *Design*. One test bench checker needs to connect to each of the *Design* instances. Once we package *CheckedDesign* in Figure 5.14 as its own HDL module or entity, it is easy to replicate the test bench component *together* with every instance of *Design*. Every co-replicated checker automatically connects to the correct signals of its respective design.

Although this scheme shows nicely how powerful it can be to take advantage of HDL features supporting test bench writing, there is one complication with this method to instrument the *Design*: it forces us to change the HDL specification of our target DUV *System*. This side effect is trivial for the case of a standalone design (Figure 5.12). All that is needed is to create a new level of model hierarchy above the actual DUV. However, once this instrumented DUV is embedded inside a higher-level structure, its HDL must be changed more profoundly. Notice that *CheckedDesign* and not *Design* inside *System* must be instantiated. This might be of little consequence if the HDL for *System* exists for verification only. However, if we want to utilize the *System* HDL for other purposes, such as logic synthesis, timing, or placement, special provisions must be made because it is not a pure design specification anymore.

There are three solutions to manage this intrusive nature of HDL test benches. First, we can use so-called pragmas in the HDL code to mark specifically which instances and signal connections were added for verification only and which other tools, such as logic synthesis, can be ignored. Second, VHDL has configurations that let the user include the test bench component pieces only in verification configurations and exclude them for synthesis or timing analysis. Finally, Verilog has the

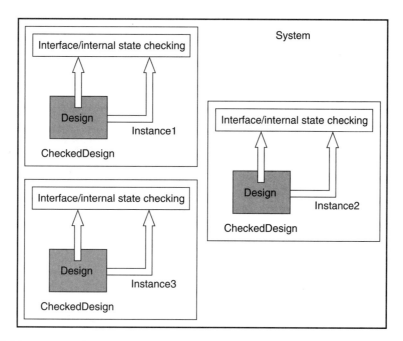

■ **FIGURE 5.14**

Hardware description language (HDL) test bench replication. As we package the design unit Design with its checker component, we can replicate the overall CheckedDesign easily, using standard structural instantiation features of common HDLs.

capability to connect an instance to signals by using hierarchical names, allowing the instantiation of the test bench at the outer level of the model HDL and cross-hierarchy connections to tunnel into the desired model hierarchy (Figure 5.15).

The HDL coding for drivers and checkers does not need to satisfy any of the non-verification constraints imposed on design HDL. Therefore, the full range of HDL constructs is available. Test bench components are the area of heavy use of the higher-level, behavioral HDL constructs, which have little or no application in pure design specifications:

- Abstract data types, records, multi-dimensional arrays
- File I/O
- Subprograms, tasks, fork/join
- Dynamic memory allocation (e.g., for scoreboarding)

Most of the language features listed here are very similar to what programming languages offer. Therefore, a viable alternative to using HDL coding for test benches is the use of a general-purpose programming

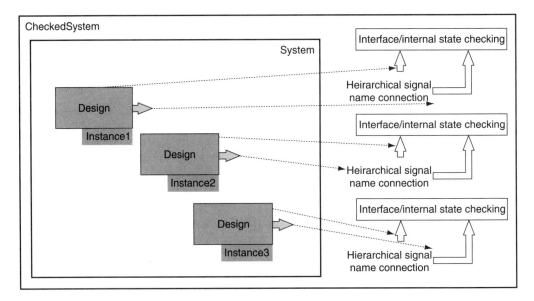

Verilog's cross-hierarchy connection capability allows the instrumentation of the three Design instances with their respective checker components from a level of hardware description language (HDL) hierarchy above System, thus leaving the design specification of System unchanged by the verification task. We place the checker components for every Design instance in the HDL hierarchy level Checked System above System.

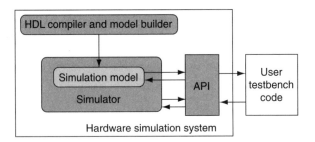

▪ **FIGURE 5.16**

Using a programming language outside the simulation engine that accesses the model via an application-programming interface (API) is an alternative to the use of hardware description language test benches.

language that has access to the simulation model via a programming interface to the simulation engine.

As shown in Figure 5.16, simulation engines usually offer an application-programming interface (API) that lets test bench code written in programming languages interact with the simulation engine and the model. There are even simulation engine-independent standard definitions of such interfaces. Verilog programming-language interface (PLI) is part of the language's IEEE standard. A corresponding activity for VHDL is under way.

The availability of standard interfaces to simulation engines and the desire to improve productivity for verification led to the development of special-purpose verification languages (Vera, e, System C languages), which use the available API or PLI of various commercial simulation engines. The focus on the verification task alone in these languages led to the development of innovative features supporting the verification task (for more detail, see Chapter 6).

The acceptance of these so-called *high-level verification languages* (HVLs) in turn created the motivation for HDL developers to add such features directly into hardware description languages. Many extensions over IEEE Verilog found in SystemVerilog are directly verification related [8].

5.2 SIMULATION ENGINES: INTRODUCTION

After this overview of the key HDL capabilities, the discussion now turns to the principles of simulation engines. Figure 5.1 shows the simulation engine as the primary tool using HDL specifications. There are many simulation engines available on the electronic design automation (EDA) market. This book will not provide usage instructions for any of the commercial tools as these tools are too different from each other to make a generalized user's guide possible. In addition, such a reference would be outdated quickly, and the EDA vendor of choice provides it anyway. Instead, this book will discuss the general principles and look under the cover of these tools. These insights are important to verification engineers because they introduce the different trade-offs and help engineers decide which simulation engine to use in a given project.

The task of a simulation engine is to evaluate an HDL model over time and present its state to the user and programs, which the user attaches to the engine's programming interface. The HDL *language reference manual* (LRM) defines the behavior of the simulation engine. Both VHDL and Verilog have an LRM as a result of IEEE standardization [3, 4]. The VHDL LRM in particular prescribes a detailed model of processing to define the correct and unambiguous execution semantics of the language.

Built into the definition of Verilog and VHDL is the concept of event-driven simulation. It provides an algorithm well suited to support both HDLs across all their features. We will discuss the event-driven simulation scheme in more detail in more detail in a later section (Section 5.3), as well as the different methods to increase simulation throughout (Section 5.4), and we finish the overview of simulation engine technology with a view of cycle-based simulation. Cycle-based simulation is a high-speed alternative to event-driven simulation and relies on a methodology that allows the verification team to accomplish most functional verification on an abstract RTL model. It can also serve to enable the use of hardware accelerator and emulator engines (Chapter 10) and formal verification (Chapters 11, 12). The focus in this chapter is only on software simulation engines and their optimization because of their high importance for every verification project. Chapter 10 will extend the discussion to specialized hardware simulation engines that speed up simulation even more.

The following section highlights some of the general principles guiding the application of simulation engines.

5.2.1 Speed Versus Accuracy

A simulation engine is a central tool for the verification team, which spends a majority of the effort of the verification cycle running simulation. This part of the cycle requires the most compute resources, and therefore, it is easy to understand that the optimization of simulation efficiency is a high priority. The performance of the simulation engine is only one factor of the overall efficiency; however, it is a key factor because a verification team that can run models twice as fast can run double the amount of test cases in the same time and likely find DUV bugs faster.

It is possible to optimize simulation efficiency from two different angles. First, a higher level of abstraction in the HDL specification of the DUV will generally result in faster simulation because the model will contain less detail that the simulation engine has to evaluate. The second method to improve simulation performance is, of course, optimizing the simulation engine itself. The optimization of simulation engine performance has been a key differentiator for EDA vendors for the past 10 years, and only recently have the performance gains achieved every year flattened out somewhat, indicating a maturation of the technology.

Both methods to improve simulation speed can work together in synergy. When a design methodology supports a certain abstract style of HDL specification and it is possible to optimize a simulation engine very specifically toward that style, a significant improvement of speed is possible. The cycle-based simulation method discussed later (Section 5.5) is a classic example of this synergy.

The first HDL simulation engines were quite literal implementations of the ideal execution models defined in the LRMs. They used algorithms designed to support all features of the full HDL languages. With such general-purpose simulation engines, the level of abstraction used to specify the DUV is the biggest factor influencing simulation performance. Figure 5.17 illustrates the basic trade-offs for simulation engine efficiency. Different HDL modeling styles are used to characterize the choice between faster simulation with the RTL abstraction and a DUV model

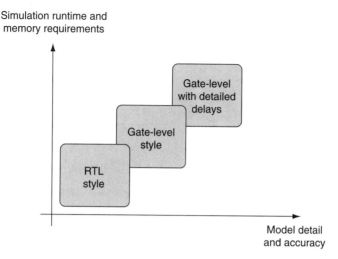

The level of abstraction used to model a design under verification (DUV) has a direct impact on simulation runtime and memory requirements. The more detailed and accurate the modeling style with respect to the DUV implementation, the bigger and slower the simulation model becomes. Abstract register transfer level (RTL) simulation can be much more efficient than a detailed timing-aware simulation on the gate-level. The actual performance difference depends much on the given simulation engine and the exact modeling style used, but can reach factors of 5 to 10 times in runtime and model size.

that exhibits a close relationship with the design implementation, down to the delay characteristics of individual gates.

There is a fundamental goal conflict in verification between speed and accuracy. A simulation engine that is able to simulate more test cases per time can simulate a bigger part of the state space of a design. However, abstraction means that less accuracy and detailed design implementation information are contained in the model. For functional verification to rely safely on an abstract model, the design methodology must cover the verification of the implementation details otherwise.

For example, if the design team uses logic synthesis to implement a synchronously clocked design, the verification team may not need delay simulation if a static timing tool guarantees timing verification during logic synthesis, placement, and wiring. Relieving functional simulation from the detailed delay information can lead to better simulation performance because verification can use a more abstract HDL model. However, if the designers add an asynchronous interface, it might be necessary to run at least some amount of dedicated tests against a detailed delay simulation model, which will simulate more slowly. If the verification team simulates the asynchronous interface without the exact delay information, it will likely miss error scenarios in which the hardware interfaces fail to interact correctly. In this case, the emphasis on a fast simulation model leads to the costly escape of design bugs.

This discussion shows that it is not possible to come to a general verdict whether simulation speed or modeling accuracy is more important. It is necessary to make this choice only after a consideration of the design methodology as a whole and not just with the desire to optimize functional verification in isolation.

5.2.2   Making the Right Methodology Choices

A correctly designed verification methodology makes choices of tools and algorithms in a way that systematically eliminates the risk of verification escapes and optimally uses available resources.

One of the first methodology choices is obviously the HDL itself. As discussed, Verilog and VHDL cover slightly different areas of the HDL space (Figures 5.6, 5.7). If, for example, the verification team needs to simulate parts of a design in switch-level logic to be able to verify transistor level behavior accurately, Verilog appears to be a better choice for performance reasons. On the other hand, the speed advantage on the switch-level side might be less important compared with the capability of designing at a more abstract level using VHDL, if other parts of this design use interfaces that the design team can specify more concisely as packets in user-defined *record* types. The more abstract design specification can avoid design mistakes likely made when constantly designing on the bit level of the implementation.

It is certainly possible to benchmark different simulation engines by using the same HDL source files and the same test cases. Under such constant conditions, a faster simulation engine might well be better. Most often, however, optimization for performance in one case means the exploitation of a special set of parameters to be able to short cut what under other conditions need a more general, slower solution.

It is crucial to keep this importance of the methodology trade-offs in perspective during the following discussion of details of different simulation algorithms. Accuracy and performance are not goals with absolute value. It is a measure of effectiveness of a methodology to cover the maximum amount of verification (i.e., uncovering bugs) with a minimum amount of total people and compute resources.

5.3   EVENT-DRIVEN SIMULATION

The *event-driven* simulation scheme is the most popular and broadly known simulation algorithm and reaches far beyond just simulation of digital hardware designs. Most simulation systems have used discrete event-driven approaches since the 1960s. This simulation scheme is very general, which explains its wide applicability. Every event-driven model consists of a network of blocks interconnected with each other. The interconnections, sometimes called *channels* or *signals*, transport information between the blocks, flowing from block outputs to inputs of other blocks. It is the function of each block to process the information presented at its inputs. This may result in the change of the internal state of a block or in the transfer of new information to the block's outputs. We call such a transfer an *event*. The general event-driven scheme does not define how the user specifies the function of a block. This can occur via a special-purpose simulation language, a programming language, or an HDL. The event-driven simulation engine has a structural view of the model: the block/interconnect topology or *model network*. By using this view of the model network, the simulation engine activates a block whenever an event occurs on its inputs. In this scheme, the engine takes notice of the events propagating through the network, activating only those blocks affected by the event flow. This is the essence of the event-driven simulation scheme. An alternative scheme, for example, could call all blocks of the model network round robin, making sure to activate every block function during every such cycle through the model. The event-driven simulation, on the other hand, activates only those parts of the model that need to process new input data. Skipping the activation of blocks whose inputs show no events promises superior simulation performance, which is the reason why event-driven simulation is so attractive in many areas.

The following section discusses how the functionality and structure of HDL models map to the event-driven simulation algorithm.

5.3.1 Hierarchical Model Network

The earlier HDL discussion (Section 5.1.1) introduced the top-level view of a simulation model, showing the input/output interfaces and a monolithic block for the DUV model itself (Figure 5.3). Only for the simplest models is it possible to specify the behavior of the block also as one monolithic function. It is more natural to refine the model structurally for one or several levels by replacing the top-level block with a set of interconnected blocks on the next level of hierarchy.

Figure 5.18 demonstrates the structural refinement process as a hierarchy tree diagram for an example. *Model A* contains blocks *B*, *C*, and *D* on the next level of detail. Blocks *B* and *C* themselves are partitioned into two or three sub-blocks, respectively. The top level of the hierarchy is the root; the blocks *D*, *B1*, *B2*, *C1*, *C2*, *C3* are the leaf-level nodes. By definition, leaf-level nodes have no further structural refinement, and therefore, their functional specification is contained in one VHDL entity/architecture or Verilog module without any instances of lower-level entity/architectures or modules. The root of every sub-hierarchy (*A*, *B*, *C*) contains the instances of the lower levels and potentially functional HDL code.

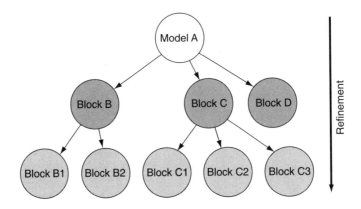

■ **FIGURE 5.18**

A tree structure illustrates on example Model A how HDL specifications can use structural refinement to build from instances of lower level elements. Model A builds on blocks B, C, and D; blocks B and C in turn instantiate components of their own, and block D contains no further structural refinement.

Figure 5.19 shows the same model hierarchy, *Model A*, using a dataflow model network diagram. In addition to the component hierarchy, this representation shows the flow of information, the signal flow between the different model components, and levels of hierarchy. Consider, for example, the first model input *i1*. It is a primary input, an input port of *Model A* itself. A signal *s1* connects this port to the first input port of block B, which in turn drives signal *s2*, which connects to the first port of block *B1*. Inside *B1*, this port drives signal *s3*, the only visible signal inside the diagram of that block.

The blocks of the model interconnected by signals build a network. Because the signals have a specific direction, as shown by the arrows in the diagram, we say the model forms a *directed network*. The signal flow connects the component blocks with each other. The behavioral HDL specification of each block prescribes the application of the values of the input ports to the block's internal computation. The HDL behavior also specifies how output ports, and therefore the connected signals, change as result of such a computation.

It is the task of the simulation engine to compute the values of the model signals over time. The direction of the signals implies a natural order of computation. It is clear that, if signal *s1* changes, the signals *s2* and *s3* should change to keep the values in the network consistent. Because *s3* is an input to *B1*, it is intuitive to assume that *B1*'s behavioral specification needs to be invoked when *s3*'s value changes. Because of this computation, it is possible that signals *s4*, *s5*, and *s6* will subsequently change in value.

Consistent with the discussion of the scope of HDLs earlier, we limit ourselves to models with discrete signal values. Figure 5.20 shows an

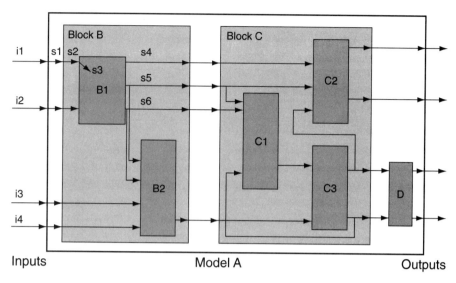

■ FIGURE 5.19

The same example Model A used in Figure 5.18 shown again as a hierarchical dataflow network. Embedding lower level blocks represents the structural hierarchy. In addition, all components have input and output ports. Signals, illustrated by arrows, connect inputs and outputs of the model components to show the data flow between blocks and through the levels of hierarchy.

example of discrete signal waveforms over time as recorded during an HDL simulation. Disregarding the analog extensions of VHDL, HDL simulations use discrete time intervals, meaning that the signal update and block evaluation scheme described above occurs at fixed model time intervals. The finest granularity for these intervals in VHDL is on a time scale of femtoseconds. The time scale for Verilog is more abstract and just a 64-bit number that the user can map to a time scale appropriate for the given DUV.

Changes of signal values designate events in the model. The model time orders events relative to each other; that is, it is important to be able to tell whether a particular event happened before another event or if it caused another event. Therefore, it is possible to look at the discrete time steps in Figure 5.20 as points at which the simulation engine calculates or *samples* the model state.

5.3.2　Model Evaluation Over Time

There are two fundamentally different algorithms to control simulation over time as specified in Table 5.1.

Algorithm 1 is useful only if it is very likely that at every evaluation time there are new values to be calculated. Clearly, compute power would be wasted if the model was simply in a steady state at many evaluation

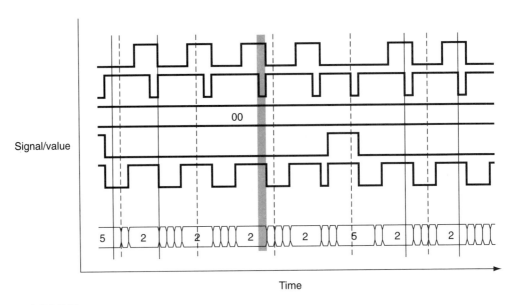

Signal/value

Time

▪ **FIGURE 5.20**

Hardware description language (HDL) model signal changes over time recorded as waveforms. HDL signals have discrete values and change at discrete time intervals. The vertical lines in the waveform display help the user to align signal changes visually. The waveforms show bit-signal values simply by level and illustrate more complex signal values by annotation, like the integer values in the lowest waveform.

TABLE 5.1 ▪ The two basic algorithms for simulation engines to manage model time

Algorithm 1
Evaluate the model at every point in time along the finest time granularity known to the simulation engine.

Algorithm 2
Evaluate signals and blocks only at model times for which events are scheduled.

Algorithm 2 is part of the event-driven simulation scheme.

points, and the simulation engine had to evaluate the entire model only to find out that no signal update work has to be done. Algorithm 2 can only function if the simulation engine has knowledge about which events it has to evaluate at the current time or any point in future model time. The model objects (blocks and signals) need to notify the simulation engine about future changes. This notification about change or update information is called *scheduling*. By using the scheduling information, the simulation engine is able to skip time intervals during which no work is scheduled, a performance advantage for the simulation.

Delayed assignment in Verilog
```
and #27 (z, a, b);     // gate delay "27"
assign #3 z =  a & b; // assign after "3"
```

Wait statement in VHDL
```
oscillator: process is
begin
  clock <= '0';
  wait for 1ns;
  clock <= '1';
  wait for 1ns;
end process oscillator;
```

■ **FIGURE 5.21**

Example for hardware description language constructs in both Verilog and VHDL that schedule future events with the simulation engine. Both Verilog statements specify a delay of a number of model time ticks in the assignment of output signal z. The VHDL process statement contains two wait statements that suspend the execution of this VHDL code and schedule a continuation with the simulation engine at model time 1 ns in the future.

Figure 5.21 shows two classic examples of HDL constructs that contain explicit scheduling information for events the simulation engine has to execute at a future model time.

The Verilog examples in Figure 5.21 specify delayed propagation of a computed signal change: first for a signal connected to the output of a gate primitive and second for a delayed assignment statement. If the simulation engine implements Algorithm 2 above, the HDL model code evaluates the future value of the output signal z and *schedules* this value change with the simulation engine.

The VHDL example in Figure 5.21 illustrates a simple sequential process specifying the function of an oscillator block. The behavioral code for process *oscillator* iterates endlessly between setting the signal *clock* to *"0"* and *"1."* After each update, the process suspends control to the simulation engine for the specified amount of model time.

In both cases, the HDL model code relinquishes control and delegates the scheduled future action to the simulation engine. It is part of the semantic rules in the LRM of both HDLs to support Algorithm 2 in any implementation of a simulation engine.

5.3.3 Event-Driven Control of Model Evaluation

Now that we decided how the engine advances time during a simulation, the next question is how the engine controls the evaluation of model updates.

Going back to the example for a hierarchical network model of Figure 5.21 (shown with mark-ups in Figure 5.22), we assume, as an example, that a specific update occurs on the input *i2*. Several of the key model update events are marked with the numbers 1 to 5 highlighted with shaded circles. The change event of *s1* (*1*) propagates over time in a series

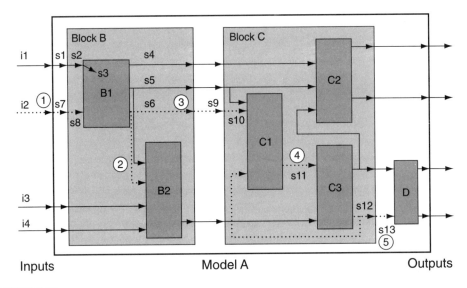

▪ FIGURE 5.22

A change of the signal value on input i2 results in a series of updates to Model A. The dashed arrows show how the change propagates over time. The sequence of signal changes and corresponding key model updates are marked by the numbered circles and discussed below.

of signal changes through the network until it concludes with an output signal change of *s13* (*5*).

Initially, after a series of signal changes (*s7*, *s8*), block *B1* is activated, which results in a change of signal *s6*. This causes a scheduled change, marked as (*3*), of *block B*'s output port, the signal connected to it (*s9*) and the activation of block *B2* (*2*). Note that *B2*'s output does not change at this point because apparently the change on input signal *s6* has no effect of *B2*'s output function. The signal change on *s9* ripples into block *C*, causes the call of *C1* and a change event on signal *s11* (*4*). After the activation of *C3*, the signals *s12* and *s13* change. Because *s12* is also an input to block *C1*, this block has to be activated again. For this example, we assume that the repeated call to *C1* does not cause another output change on *s11*. Note that the re-activation of *C1* results from a topological feedback loop, which could cause repeated calls of the same model blocks. In the example of Figure 5.22, the second activation of *C1* does not cause further signal changes. Similarly, the final update of *s13* and the call to block *D* causes no further update event.

The feedback loop in the topology exhibits how a particular block (*C1*) can be scheduled and re-scheduled because of a wave of updates. The feedback of the signal change of *s12* leads to another evaluation of *C1*. Although the example assumes no further events after that evaluation, it is possible that the behavior of the model exercises the re-scheduling loop between *C1* and *C3* more than once. It depends on the behavior of the blocks whether such a topological loop settles at some point or continues to oscillate forever. The simulation engine or an external intervention by the user has to interrupt an uncontrolled model oscillation.

Throughout the example update sequence in Figure 5.22, block *C2* was never activated, illustrating how the event-driven scheme only evaluates those parts of the DUV model that are affected by changes and successfully avoids the activation of model parts that can be skipped. Still, the topology of the model required massive updates in this case because input *i2* affects many model blocks. However, changing input *i4*, for example, would probably result in only the activation of *B2*, *C3*, and *D*.

Another way to visualize the model updates of Figure 5.22 is to line up the sequence of scheduled model events over time. If the HDL for *Model A* specifies explicit delays for model updates (signals/gate delays or *wait* statements in behavioral code such as in Figure 5.21), the changes will spread out naturally over a range of model time controlled by the DUV specification. The simulation engine itself must order changes dynamically that have no HDL-specified model time delay (*zero delay*). Assuming the HDL of *Model A* does not use any explicit delays (*zero delay* model), we show every successive model event as one discrete step internal to the simulation engine in Figure 5.23. Every evaluation creates a resulting update that the simulation engine schedules to occur at the beginning of the next internal step. At several points in the sequence (after the changes of *s6* and *s12*), the simulation engine schedules more

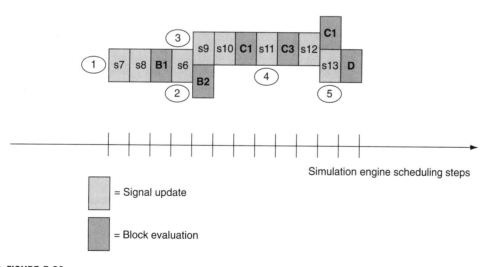

Simulation engine scheduling steps

= Signal update

= Block evaluation

■ **FIGURE 5.23**

The update sequence of Figure 5.22 assuming all zero-delay events. The numbers in the shaded circles refer to the same marked key events in Figure 5.22. The simulation engine orders the events dynamically as they occur on the model. The change events on signals s6 and s12 cause parallel change events.

TABLE 5.2 ■ The essential properties of event-driven simulation

Evaluate model behavior only at those times when model events are scheduled.
Evaluate behavior only for the blocks or signals for which events are scheduled.

than one update in parallel. In a sequential program that simulates this network, it is effectively up to the simulation engine's random choice to decide in which sequence the two model updates really happen; from a user view, the model actions happen in parallel.

We call the described evaluation strategy *event-driven*. Whenever an event occurs, such as the update of a signal, the simulation engine schedules the computation of all the blocks, which are sinks of this signal. If these blocks update their output signals, the changes propagate further in the same way.

We can now combine the two key aspects of the event-driven simulation approach (Table 5.2).

It appears obvious that event-driven simulation is quite efficient because the strategy implies that the simulation engine only does the work necessary to evaluate model changes. Extraneous computations do not occur.

Although we assumed zero-delay in Figure 5.23, the event-driven simulation algorithm is much more general. By using VHDL or Verilog time control constructs, signal updates can have delays of arbitrary amounts of model time. In contrast to Figure 5.23, this simply postpones the model evaluation to another discrete model time step instead of all updates happening at the same model time. Hence, it stretches out the event sequence over simulated time but does not change the basic event-driven update mechanism.

The definition of Verilog and VHDL clearly includes the assumption of an underlying event-driven simulator. Figure 5.24 illustrates this using VHDL with two blocks (processes) connected to each other via the signals *count* and *tick*. Whenever *tick* toggles, *block 1* updates *count*, which triggers *block 2*'s inversion of *tick's* value again.

With Table 5.3, we introduce an example piece of VHDL that specifies the implementation of a 2-bit ripple-carry adder at the low abstraction level of Boolean equations including delayed assignments.

Figure 5.25 shows how a simulation engine could translate the adder VHDL into a network view. For the example, we assume that the network consists of Boolean operator blocks. Another valid translation could have created one network block per VHDL statement, yielding six blocks instead of the fine granularity of 16 blocks in Figure 5.25. The event-driven algorithm of the example engine keeps track of model changes

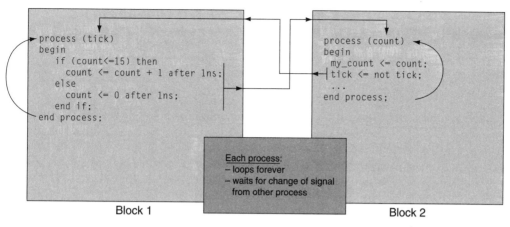

■ **FIGURE 5.24**

Two VHDL example blocks with process statements defining the behavior. Each process iteration causes a signal update that schedules the resumed execution of the other process.

TABLE 5.3 ■ VHDL fragment that defines a 2-bit adder design under verification at the Boolean equation level

(1)	s(0) <= a(0) xor b(0) after 2ns;
(2)	c(0) <= a(0) and b(0) after 1ns;
(3)	s(1) <= a(1) xor b(1) xor c(0) after 2ns;
(4)	c(1) <= (a(1) and b(1))or (b(1) and c(0)) or (c(0) and a(1)) after 1ns;
(5)	sum_out(1 to 0) <= s(1 to 0);
(6)	carry_out <= c(1);

through the network shown. The signals that have label names in Figure 5.25 correspond to the HDL signals in Figure 5.24. Because the engine split the equations to their constituent operator blocks, the network also contains signals that have no user names. The event-driven simulation engine will propagate every change of the input signals *a* and *b* through the network.

The pair of Figures 5.26 and 5.27 shows in detail the event-driven update of the adder model as a result of the arrival of new values at the adder inputs. We show only the first eight simulation steps that lead the model from time 0 ns to 2 ns. This is enough model time to propagate the necessary changes to the output signal *carry_out*. Because the path through the equations driving the *sum_out* vector runs through the assignment statements with a longer delay (statements *1* and *3* in Table 5.3), it will take more simulation steps at model time 3 ns to complete the adder model update. These final simulation steps were left out for space reasons and left as an exercise for the reader.

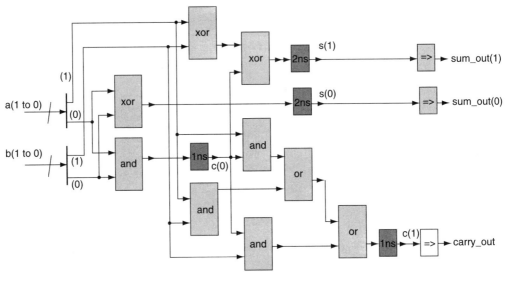

▪ **FIGURE 5.25**

Network view of the 2-bit adder equation logic from Table 5.3. The example simulation engine turns every Boolean operator into its own block in the model network. The delayed assignments turn into the shaded special-purpose blocks. All the signals in the network that have HDL names are marked accordingly.

The HDL specification of the 1-bit adder in this example is modeled at a *Boolean-equation level*. This granularity of detail in the model ties the delay information to a per-equation level. A truly *RTL* model would compress the specification dramatically by using the arithmetic "+" operator (see Figure 5.31). In the opposite direction of less abstraction, a *gate-level* model would have an even finer resolution and reference the Boolean operations in terms of primitives from a technology library (e.g., NANDs, NORs). With many commercial simulation engines, it is possible to leave the gate-level HDL free of timing control constructs and back-annotate the actual physical timing information into the simulation via the loading of the so-called *standard delay format* (SDF) file. Physical design tools can generate SDF files (IEEE standard 1497—1999) at the point when exact technology parameters such as library cell characteristics and placement and wiring information are available.

5.3.4   Implementation Sketch of an Event-Driven Simulation Engine

The properties of the event-driven simulation approach can now be summarized, with a conceptual description of the basic mechanisms of an event-driven simulation engine.

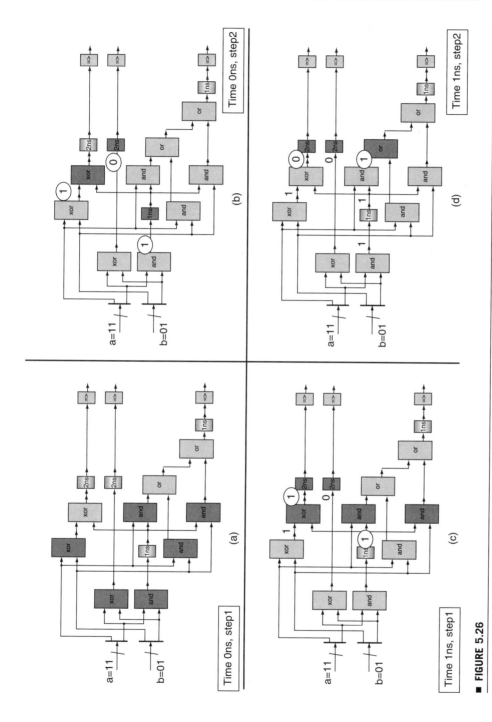

■ **FIGURE 5.26**

The first four simulation steps of event-driven simulation of the 2-bit adder model after the update of the input vectors a and b. For every step, the Boolean operator blocks with shaded background are those scheduled for activation because of inputs changes. Every output that changes because of an active Boolean block in the previous step has a shaded circle. Signal values that change because of simulation activity, remain marked in the subsequent Figures. a and b, The two simulation steps necessary to complete model time 0 ns. The time 1 ns starts with the delayed update of signal c(0). c and d, The first two step at time 1 ns.

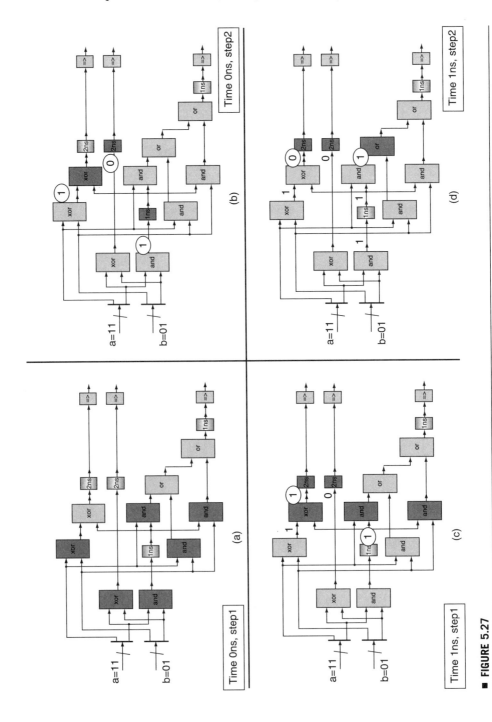

■ **FIGURE 5.27**

The next four steps of the simulation update started in Figure 5.26. a and b, The final steps necessary to complete the update of signal c(1). c and d, The delayed assignment to signal carry_out leads to the steps.

TABLE 5.4 ■ The three basic data structures at the core of every event-driven simulation engine

1. A list of all executable blocks present in the model network
2. A data structure that represents the interconnection of the blocks via signals
3. A value table that holds all current signal values

The simulation engine needs to maintain the following data structures to represent the model network, its interconnect topology, and the current state of the model (Table 5.4).

A central data structure to control activity and time progress in an event simulator is typically the so-called *time wheel* (Figure 5.28). The time wheel is a simple linked list that contains entries for every model time, current or future, for which the engine has scheduled an activity. For any such model time, the simulation engine keeps a *to-do list* of model blocks and signals that are scheduled. The simulation engine always takes the next item from the list for the current time, does the necessary evaluation, and proceeds to the next list item. As we have shown, the result of an evaluation can trigger the addition of list items for the current time (zero-delay) or any future time. Once the list for a current time is empty, the time wheel can "turn" to the next model time for which work is scheduled. As illustrated in Figure 5.28, the engine updates the current model time simply by moving the *current_model_time* reference to the new head of the time wheel list.

For time zero, the start time of simulation, the simulation engine schedules all executable model blocks contained in a model. In VHDL, these are all *processes* and *concurrent assignment* statements. For Verilog, the initial model blocks scheduled at time zero are all *always blocks* and all *continuous signal assignment* statements. This approach makes sure that the simulation properly initializes all model blocks. In addition, Verilog supports a special provision with the *initialize block* that the simulation engine *only* schedules for time zero.

Figure 5.29 shows the core algorithm of an event-driven simulation engine. Users issue a "run" command, either interactively or via a program, which hands control over to the simulation engine. Starting at point 1 in Figure 5.29, the simulation engine takes the next scheduled model block from the to-do list for the current time and call its code. Typically, a block evaluation results in scheduled signal updates. Once the engine is done with all scheduled model blocks, it performs the scheduled signal updates (point 2 in Figure 5.29), which usually add more model blocks into the current to-do list of the scheduling data. As long as signal updates add more model blocks to the to-do list for the current model time, the engine will loop back to point 1 in the flowchart. Once

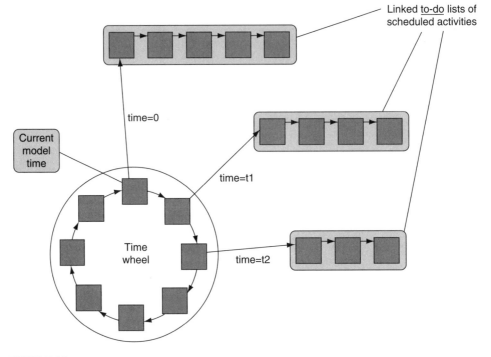

▪ FIGURE 5.28

Conceptual diagram of the central scheduling data structure at the heart of the execution control of an event-driven simulation engine. Every model time with scheduled events has a linked to-do list containing information to enable the engine to execute the event. Every to-do list is anchored at a particular position of the time wheel. The time wheel is a circular linked list in which every entry maintains a pointer to the to-do list for a given model time, which has scheduled activity. The data entry current_model_time simply marks the head of the time wheel list for the current model time.

all block and signal updates have rippled through (point 3 in Figure 5.29), the simulation engine is ready to increment model time, which means advancing the time wheel to the next time for which events are scheduled. Simulation stops when the engine reaches the user-defined model time limit.

Because event-driven simulation has been so widely used, the optimization of its performance is well understood. The algorithm for the simulation engines just described has obvious performance-critical portions. The most prominent area is the management of the to-do lists, the time wheel, and the data that represents the topology of the model. For every event evaluated, the simulation engine must traverse the model topology data to find which blocks or signals it needs to schedule next. Once identified, the simulation engine must find the scheduled time on the time wheel and put the corresponding event on the to-do list for that given time.

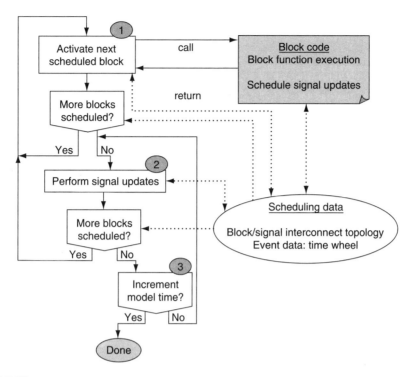

■ **FIGURE 5.29**

The main control algorithm for an event-driven simulation engine. The dashed arrows show data access of the execution algorithm to the scheduling data. The engine starts at model time zero with calls to all initially scheduled model blocks, which schedule signal updates. Afterward, it performs the scheduled signal updates. This might result in more scheduled block activations. Once there are no more scheduled updates for the current model time, the engine moves to the time of the next scheduled events. We use the numbered circles in the flow diagram to anchor the explanation in the text.

Figure 5.30 illustrates the sensitivity of simulation performance in relationship to the granularity of the model. For the case of many small blocks (e.g., the 2-bit adder example above), most time in simulation will be spent on scheduling overhead while the actual block evaluations are trivial. For the cases of large *processes* (VHDL) or *always blocks* (Verilog), the model topology will increasingly be fraught with feedback loops (see Figure 5.22). Although the amount of scheduling activity is low compared with the time spent inside the code of the model blocks, the blocks are evaluated multiple times until the model converges to a steady state.

The activity rate of the model is another big factor for the performance of event-driven simulation, and therefore, Figure 5.30 illustrates it as another dimension. Obviously, a low activity rate helps simulation speed. The primary advantage of event-driven simulation is the ability to skip unnecessary model evaluations; however, a model with few monolithic blocks of sequential code can take less advantage of a low activity rate

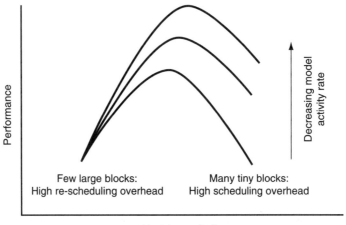

■ FIGURE 5.30

Performance balance for event-driven simulation. The speed of simulation depends on the granularity of the model and the rate of dynamic model changes. A model with few monolithic blocks will likely suffer from a large amount of re-scheduling overhead because of topological feedback loops. The same DUV function modeled with a large number of primitive blocks will degrade in speed because the simulation engine must keep track of a huge amount of scheduling activity. The optimum performance lies somewhere between these two extremes. Less dynamic model activity improves simulation speed more in the case of fine model granularity.

than can a model with finer granularity. Performance gain from low activity is only possible if there are distinct blocks of work that the engine can skip. In contrast, with a model of the finest granularity, the scheduling overhead will again cause loss of efficiency compared with a model that has an optimal balance in model block size.

Overall, event-driven simulation proved to cover a wide range of modeling styles with reasonable performance results, which led to its dominant position in the area of simulation engines. The reader should now have enough technical insight of this technology to be able to understand what trade-offs are available in its use.

5.4 IMPROVING SIMULATION THROUGHPUT

Because of the overwhelming size of the state space of industrial designs, simulation performance is a critical factor for a project. The correct measure for the performance of simulation, however, is not only the speed of a single simulation run but the amount of verification in number of tests, number of cycles, and number of distinct model states visited and checked during simulation per time spent: the *simulation throughput*.

TABLE 5.5 ■ The three main techniques to improve simulation throughput

1. Increase simulation engine performance
2. Run many simulations in parallel
3. Eliminate redundant simulations

There are several ways to improve simulation throughput (Table 5.5).

The parallelization of a project's simulation effort, option (2), is a topic of Chapter 13 (Section 13.1.3), and Chapter 6 (Section 6.2) covers option (3). Several approaches to increase the performance of a simulation engine, option (1), or simply the speed of model simulation are discussed in the remainder of this chapter.

The apparent, technically trivial option is simply to buy a faster simulation engine. However, this alternative is surprisingly complicated. Unlike performance benchmarks for general-purpose computer systems, such as those of Standard Performance Evaluation Corporation (SPEC), simulation engine benchmarks are hard to find [9]. Too many parameters influence simulation engine speed: most are project specific and defy classification with a simple benchmark number; others are HDL style, event activity rate, and the profile of the interaction between test bench and DUV model. In addition, there is the expected reluctance on the side of the EDA vendors to accept a common set of simulation engine benchmarks.

This chapter has discussed how the HDLs cover a wide range of specification styles. HDL style is one factor in the performance profile of a simulation engine. It is entirely possible to optimize a simulation engine largely for gate-level timing simulation with the result of an engine performance profile that does compete well against another simulation engine whose primary target is high-level, programming-language-like HDL. For a verification project that uses mostly gate-level simulation, the first simulation engine might be the optimal choice. If that same project accumulates a set of high-level test bench code in HDL over time, a simulation engine whose performance is more balanced across the full HDL spectrum might be the better long-term alternative. In summary, the verification team should consider simulation engine benchmarks with care and only under clear consideration of the project-specific HDL style.

With that said, the HDL writers have indeed a big influence on the performance of their simulation. Several EDA vendors publish guidelines such as "HDL style to optimize performance." In addition, some simulation engines offer a profiling function, which allows a user to trace in which parts of the model most of the simulation time is spent.

As discussed above, the overhead of scheduling versus the time spent in actual HDL code largely defines the efficiency of an event-driven simulation, meaning that simulations run faster if there are less events

TABLE 5.6 ■ A selection of hardware design language (HDL) style choices to improve event-driven simulation performance

More abstract HDL constructs	Use higher-level built-in operators versus explicit gate/expression level implementations of those functions. Use integer arithmetic instead versus bit-level arithmetic. VHDL: Use standard libraries versus Project-specific versions; simulation engines often have optimized, built-in support for standard libraries.
Two-valued logic	Use binary values over multivalues when possible. Simulation engines often optimize for binary logic operations.
Full data-value operations	Use delay control statements judiciously, i.e., only in modeling situations in which the function is dependent on timing. Use zero-delay specification when possible. Many simulation engines will be able to order events statically at model build time and eliminate runtime scheduling overhead automatically for that part of the model.
Two-valued logic	Consider sequential code (process/always-block, procedure/function) for part of a design in which the order of evaluation can clearly be defined at specification time.

scheduled. Given the same DUV function, there are HDL style choices that allow the user to improve simulation performance. As always, there are trade-offs to observe. If the HDL specification is not only the input for simulation, the user should ensure that a style choice that improves simulation speed does not hurt the other uses of the design source, like logic synthesis results for example.

In Table 5.6 we list some example strategies to improve event-driven HDL simulation speed, partially dependent on the given simulation engine, most of which minimize event creation and scheduling.

Table 5.7 shows several examples for the choices in Table 5.6. The least efficient version, version 3, uses concurrent signal assignment statements with delay clauses (see Table 5.3). Every evaluation causes new events to be scheduled. Depending on the possibly random initial ordering of the assignments, the simulation engine will schedule statements several times before the model settles. Version 2 is more abstract, using built-in arithmetic expressions, full-vector assignments, and no delay clauses. Note that this level of specification is only applicable if the verification team does not really need the accuracy of version 3 to verify the correctness of this design. Version 1 goes a step further by ordering the statements of version 2 statically inside a sequential process block. Except for the output signal updates, no scheduling is necessary for the simulation engine; the whole process is one atomic action for the engine. Furthermore, the engine's model build process is able to apply optimizations that have proven powerful for the compilation of programming languages. For example, the actual model code can keep the value of signal s available in a processor register for further use in the second statement of the process.

TABLE 5.7 ■ Examples for range of abstractions of hardware design language specifications for a 2-bit adder in the order of increasing structural detail but decreasing simulation speed

(1)	process(a, b)
	variable s: std_ulogic_vector(2 to 0);
	begin
	s(2 to 0) := ('0' & a(1 to 0)) + ('0' & b(1 to 0));
	sum_out(1 to 0) <= s(1 to 0);
	carry_out <= s(0);
	end;
	end process;

(2)	sum_out(1 to 0) <= s(1 to 0);
	carry_out <= s(0);
	s(2 to 0) := ('0' & a(1 to 0)) + ('0' & b(1 to 0));

(3)	s(0) <= a(0) xor b(0) after 2ns;
	c(0) <= a(0) and b(0) after 1ns;
	s(1) <= a(1) xor b(1) xor c(0) after 2ns;
	c(1) <= (a(1) and b(1))or (b(1) and c(0)) or (c(0) and a(1)) after 1ns;
	sum_out(1 to 0) <= s(1 to 0);
	carry_out <= c(1);

The overall theme of these optimizations is that we can gain simulation speed if the model specification does not rely on the most general use of HDL styles. The more specific, concise, and abstract the specification of the model function, the faster the simulation of the function will be. The following section (Section 5.5) will use an even more restricted HDL style that can yield radically better simulation speed.

The other option to improve simulation speed is *parallelization*. There has been significant research into parallel algorithms for hardware simulation over the years. Even though the results have shown performance improvements, no break-through has occurred. Event-driven simulation seems to be inherently hard to parallelize, and there currently is no commercially successful parallel event-driven simulation engine available.

Another important reason for the lack of commercial interest in parallelized simulation engines is that there are two powerful alternatives competing with this approach. The first is the utilization of pools of compute workstations all running independent simulations. The second is the most radical approach to speed up a single simulation job, the direct implementation of a simulation engine in hardware, as used in hardware accelerators and emulators. Hardware simulation engines are discussed in Chapter 10.

We call the most simple and straightforward way to improve simulation throughput *trivial parallelization*: running independent simulation jobs on a pool of workstations. For large design and verification projects, it is common to use hundreds, or even thousands, of workstations in parallel, all running simulation. The industry refers to this arrangement as the *simulation farm*. Instead of running one single model partitioned and parallelized across several computers, the workstations in the simulation farm all run their own independent simulation job. The attraction of this simple way to boost simulation throughput is evident: if the project has to run 1 million test cases of roughly equal length, the verification team can optimally use a farm of 1000 workstations by running a sequence of 1000 test cases on each machine. The improvement of throughput is nearly ideal (1000 times) in this case. In addition, it is simple to upgrade the simulation farm with additional machines if the project needs to scale up the simulation throughput. The result of such an additional capital investment is predictable because the throughput improvement remains linear with number of additional computers bought. The application of simulation farms is discussed further in Chapter 13.

5.5 CYCLE-BASED SIMULATION

Cycle-based simulation is a specialized technique to improve simulation efficiency. It has a long history of development and successful application on the largest design and verification projects [10]. The reason for the superior performance of cycle-based simulation engines compared with event-driven simulation is the simplicity of the algorithm and the total optimization toward a specific hardware design style-synchronous design. Therefore, as always, a tremendous speedup comes with the disadvantage of trading off general-purpose applicability.

On designs and projects in which cycle-based simulation applies, the speedup can be large. A speedup of 10 to 20 times and a DUV model size compression of more than 10 times are typically quoted; some sources even put the speedup at 100 times that of traditional event-simulation [11].

The downside of cycle-based simulation is that it puts severe constraints on the HDL style of the DUV. Pure cycle-based simulation engines do not support or ignore delay controls, limit sequential constructs significantly, and do not allow most test bench-specific features of the HDLs. Projects with large synchronous designs, however, can productively use cycle-based engines to speed up the DUV simulation, while leaving the test bench writing to the use of special-purpose test bench languages outside the realm of HDLs (see Chapter 6).

Most EDA vendors attempted to market pure cycle-based simulation engines during the second half of the 1990s. The significant methodology restrictions associated with this technology severely limited a broad market acceptance. This leaves pure cycle-based simulation mostly in the domain of microprocessor and server development houses, which typically run the largest simulation models. However, the EDA vendors integrated most techniques of cycle-based optimizations that are described below into the commercial simulation engines. There, they automatically optimize the simulation speed of those parts of a DUV model, in which the design restrictions hold. The fastest event-driven simulation engines today are in fact hybrids between pure event-driven engines and cycle-based technology.

5.5.1 Synchronous Design

The foundation of cycle-based simulation rests on a fundamental methodology restriction that applies to many modern designs, the synchronous design principle. If we separate the state-holding elements (latches, flip-flops, memory arrays) of a design from the combinational logic, it becomes clear that the function of the combinational portion is identical to the state transition and output generation function of a FSM.

The clock signal used to update the state-holding elements synchronizes the FSM update and the progression of the design through the state space. In a first approximation, we consider a clock signal that is central and occurs at the same time for all state-holding elements, which we simply call *latches*. We refer to such a clock signal as a *synchronous clock*.

On a historical note [10], even though it is easier to correctly design and verify synchronous designs than asynchronous designs, this design method originates from requirements for the manufacturing test of chips and not from functional verification. Manufacturing test uses test patterns that are able to isolate fabrication problems on a chip. For this procedure, it is necessary to be able to stop the clock on the chip at any time, supply a new state initialization, *clock* the design, and subsequently read out the new state of the chip. This approach prompted the demand for a synchronous clock and a design that is largely functionally independent from the actual frequency at which the clock updates the latches.

The longest delay along *any* update path through the combinational logic of a design defines the maximum frequency for the clock signal of a synchronous design (Figure 5.31). We call the calculation of this maximum frequency under which the design still functions correctly *timing verification*. The *critical delay path* is the longest delay path allowed from latch to latch. Any path with a longer delay leads to incorrect functioning of the circuit because the combinational result will not arrive in time to update the target latch correctly. The scheme also implies that combinational feedback loops are not possible.

Given that manufacturing test potentially applies any possible pattern to the combinational logic, it is no longer possible to use only functional patterns (only those patterns possible within the legal state space of the design), but all Boolean possibilities must be accounted for in timing

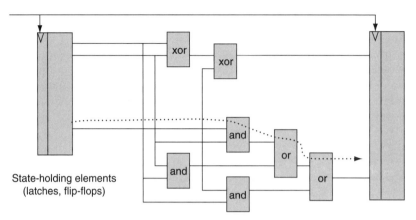

State-holding elements
(latches, flip-flops)

State-holding elements
(latches, flip-flops)

▪ **FIGURE 5.31**

Fragment of the network model of a synchronous design. The combinational logic between the state-holding elements must be able to propagate updates faster than the clock frequency of the latches or flip-flops. The dashed arrow shows the path with the longest delay–the critical delay path of this part of the design.

verification. In addition, the exact delays on the chip are unknown until a physical netlist is available with the exact placement and wiring data.

Therefore, rather than using dynamic techniques that would have to apply all possible combinational input patterns, timing verification is done with static, pattern-independent techniques. Timing verification tools process the physical netlist topologically as a graph and do not apply Boolean patterns at all. Thus, this process can be separated completely from the discipline of functional verification. Timing verification guarantees that the maximum clock frequency is low enough to enable correct electrical function of the circuit, whereas functional verification can focus exclusively on the functional content of the design.

This separation of physical from functional concerns is the foundation for the extreme performance optimization and simplification that cycle-based simulation engines offer.

5.5.2 The Cycle-Based Simulation Algorithm

The separation of timing and functional verification allows the HDL specification to be purely functional. This means that the HDL of a synchronous design needs to specify timing only for the clock signal. Even for this signal, the delay time, or *cycle time*, is rather arbitrary because the real cycle time can change with any iteration in the physical design process. In fact, for functional simulation all that is needed is the separation from a time at cycle "*n*" to the time at cycle "*n + 1*." Therefore,

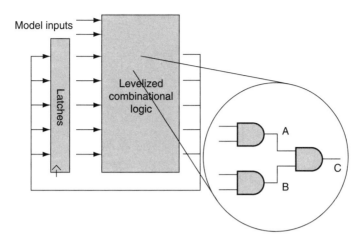

■ **FIGURE 5.32**

Model network for a cycle-based simulation. Starting from the network model of design under verification, the model ordering process combines all state-holding elements (marked latches) and levelizes the combinational logic blocks. Levelization starts at level 1 with all blocks that connect to model inputs or latches only. Any subsequent level n contains only blocks whose inputs connect to outputs from blocks of prior levels (maximally level n − 1). This results in an ordered directed acyclic graph as illustrated in magnifying glass view.

many cycle-based simulation engines do not reference physical time measures but simply an integer that denotes the current cycle.

It is evident that this abstract view of the DUV has a close affinity to *Algorithm 1* in Table 5.1. A possible cycle-based algorithm can take the *cycle* as the finest time granularity and simply update the model once per cycle.

The combinational logic description of a cycle-based model is devoid of timing control statements. It is a zero-delay specification and free of combinational feedback loops. By using the primary inputs and the current values of the state-holding elements as the starting points, as well as the primary outputs and the next values of the state-holding elements as the end points, it is possible to strictly order, or *levelize*, all blocks of the model network. Technically speaking the model is a *directed acyclic graph* (DAG). Figure 5.32 illustrates the basic view of this graph. By using simple gates as an example for combinational function, the magnifying glass cut-out in Figure 5.32 shows the ordering of the graph, which illustrates that if signals A and B are evaluated first, signal C needs to be evaluated once only per evaluation of the state machine function.

The cycle-based simulation engine proceeds from cycle to cycle by evaluating the combinational function graph and calculating the new latch and primary output values.

In comparison to the event-driven algorithm, the cycle-based engine does not need to schedule blocks because it is clear from their position in the graph when their evaluation is necessary. Although it is possible to use an event-driven scheme within the combinational function evaluation, most cycle-based simulation engines have implemented what the literature calls the *oblivious simulation algorithm* [12]. The oblivious scheme calculates all the combinational function at every simulation cycle and thus foregoes any dynamic event scheduling whatsoever. The algorithm trades off the redundant work of evaluating those parts of the model that do not change from cycle to cycle for the omission of complicated management of the to-do lists and time wheel management that are key to event-driven simulation (Section 5.3.4). The oblivious algorithm is extremely simple and, most importantly, a good basis for further optimization.

Another positive effect of the separation of timing from functional verification is the diminishing need of multi-value data representation for signals. With the exception of multiply sourced bus signals (discussed below), we can simulate most signals in the DUV with a binary value domain without loss of verification quality. This is a result of making the circuits synchronous, which eliminates glitches and hazards as a functional verification problem. It allows the dramatic simplification and simulation speed-up using a binary value set for the overwhelming majority of signals.

Figure 5.33 shows the power of the simplicity and capacity for simulation efficiency of this basic flavor of cycle-based simulation. The

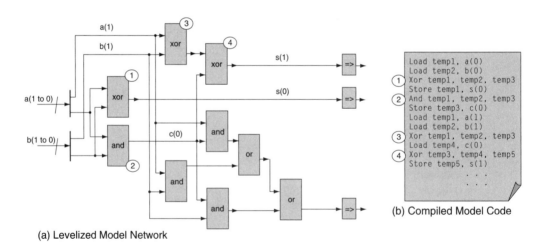

(a) Levelized Model Network

(b) Compiled Model Code

■ **FIGURE 5.33**

Cycle-based model of 2-bit adder design. (a) The levelized model network for the adder design with four model blocks marked by circled numbers. (b) The first section of compiled microprocessor machine code that represents the design under verification for a cycle-based simulation model. The logical instructions in the code are marked with numbered circles, cross-referencing the gates in Figure 5.33a that the instructions simulate.

example illustrates one possible extreme compilation of the zero-delay version of the 2-bit adder into a pseudo instruction set of a workstation microprocessor. The simulation model actually becomes a piece of executable machine code, a program.

The pseudo-code in Figure 5.33b uses symbolic names for the storage locations at which the simulation engine stores the representation of the original VHDL signals. The code follows the ordered graph of the model network. For every block in this example model, there is a corresponding Boolean logic instruction in the code. This scheme also applies to blocks that are more complicated by expanding the simple AND/OR/XOR functions, which happen to have single microprocessor instruction equivalents, to more complicated code sequences. For Figure 5.33, we can now translate every Boolean block function that has a single corresponding instruction in the pseudo instruction set into a series of approximately four instructions: two load instructions for the input operands, one logical instruction for the block function, and a store instruction for the resulting value. This example makes clear how extremely compact the cycle-based translation can become, especially when compared with an algorithm, which needs to traverse and maintain lists of scheduled blocks and to traverse a data structure that represents the model topology.

The following, very crude calculation illustrates the performance and size compression potential of cycle-based simulation. If a cycle-based simulation engine translates a DUV of one million gates into code for a 1-GHz microprocessor with the above instruction set, the approximate code size of the model would be 4 MB. If we assume a processor performance of one instruction per clock cycle, it is possible to run the cycle-based simulation of this model at a speed of 250 clock cycles per second.

Especially with larger models, the assumption of one instruction per clock cycle does not hold with the approach shown, because the generated code is linear. Rather than using the processor caches, the simulation engine program reads the model code from main memory every simulation cycle. On the other hand, it is possible to push the average instructions per model block well below the assumed four. It is visible in the small example of Figure 5.33 that the code does not need to store every intermediate result to a named signal and therefore does not need to store it into model memory. This optimization can eliminate many store instructions.

Overall, typical comparisons show improvements of cycle-based simulation engines by 10 to 20 times in speed and 3 to 10 times in capacity depending on what types of cycle-based simulation and event-driven simulation we compare. The capacity improvement often has a much bigger impact because it allows the simulation of designs that otherwise would not fit into the address space of the workstation on which the simulation needs to run.

Further optimizations are possible but beyond this discussion. Increased capacity of the model representation, even at model build time, as well as the fact that the model build process can statically order the model network graph, opens a variety of optimizations that originate in the disciplines of programming language compilation and logic synthesis. These optimizations reach from simple operations, such as forward constant propagation, to complex ones, such as elimination of redundant logic in the model. The simplicity of the basic graph-oriented ordering makes such optimizations affordable while still allowing reasonable model build times of minutes per one million gates.

5.5.3 Extensions to Basic Cycle-Based Simulation Engines

The basic cycle-based simulation scheme considered so far severely limits the style of HDL that the simulation engine can support. It is a very narrow slice of the HDL LRMs: some excluded because the design methodology allows us to (separation of timing verification from functional verification), and some constructs are not supported for the sake of performance optimization. The main purpose of extending the basic cycle-based simulation algorithm is to bring back some of the missing HDL features that improve the quality of verification even if that means lowering the efficiency of the simulation engine.

Multiv-alued Signal Support

The first example for the extensions to cycle-based simulation discussed here is the support for multi-valued signals. As mentioned above, multi-sourced buses (data type *std_logic* for signals in VHDL) require a more accurate value domain. With the simple, brute-force binary encoding of signal values, it is impossible to detect a driving conflict on a bus signal that has multiple drivers. It must be possible for the simulation engine to discern which one of multiple sources actually drives the bus actively. The VHDL value set for *std_logic* has nine logic values to make this differentiation possible. Multiple drivers on a bus with different driving strengths are not a problem for the DUV function as long as there is only one driver with the strongest driving strength. A cycle-based simulation engine should handle at least the condition of *"blue smoke"*–multiple drivers with opposing logic values that drive with the same strength. This extension requires a more sophisticated encoding of the logic values for bus signals, more than simple binary encoding, as well as a more elaborate handling of bus updates in the combinational logic. This extension has no big performance impact because only a minority of the signals in a standard design is buses.

An extension of all signals and state-holding elements to a multi-value set is much more expensive. This means that all signals need a multi-bit value encoding. All Boolean expressions are now more expensive as well because of the more complicated multi-value operation. However, only specialized tasks in verification need a cycle-based model of this flavor. An example of such a task is power-on reset (POR) simulation, which verifies that a design can initialize itself cleanly (for more discussion about these aspects of the verification task, see Chapter 9).

Experience shows that it is possible to extend binary cycle-based simulation to support Verilog-style four value simulation (0,1,X,Z) with a performance degradation factor of two to three compared with the basic algorithms. Hence, even with such an extension, it is possible to keep the performance and capacity advantage of the cycle-based simulation technology. Also, verification methodology can select this more expensive model only for the specific tasks it is needed for.

Multiple Clock Domains in Cycle-Based Simulation

There is a widely held prejudice against cycle-based simulation, implying that cycle-based simulation engines cannot accurately verify designs with state-holding elements clocked by clock signals at different frequency. However, this is not the case.

We can divide a design that has independent clock signals into partitions, which each have a single uniform clock. We call such partitions *clock domains*. We break the problem into two categories based on fundamentally different relationships between two clock domains. The first category is *synchronous clock domains*, in which the clock domains have an integer ratio relationship to each other. The second category is for cases in which the clock domains have a non-integer ratio. The non-integer ratio leads to a more complicated situation, and this category is called *pseudo-asynchronous* because the clock-edge relationships are constantly changing over time.

Figure 5.34a shows an example of a 2:1 integer ratio synchronous clock domain relationship. This example is used to explain how to support multiple clock domain simulation with cycle-based simulation engines. Assuming the rising edge of a model clock is the time when latches update to their new state, the fastest clock of the DUV is taken to synchronize model evaluations. The model update, the call of the *clock* command of a cycle-based simulation engine, can be considered a *clock tick* of some base simulator clock. Clocking the model at the rate of the fastest design clock will make sure that the verification will not miss a rising edge of any clock in the DUV. This scheme simply *over-clocks* the slower clock domains. Sampling the design at the frequency of the faster clock domain with the simulation engine allows visibility of all combinational updates from the faster clock domain to the slower domain, even though the state holding elements of the slower domain will not update during their off-times.

Figure 5.34b is an example of pseudo-asynchronous clock domains (3:2 ratio). The time when *clock2* rises coincides with the rising of *clock1*

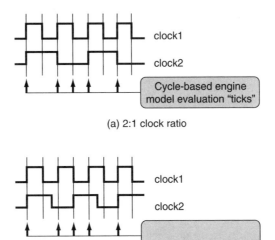

(a) 2:1 clock ratio

(b) 3:2 clock ratio

▪ **FIGURE 5.34**

Multiclock domains simulation with a cycle-base simulation engine. (a) A simple integer $2:1$ clock domain relationship; (b) a more complex non-integer $3:2$ mode. Both indicate where the simulation engine's model evaluation must occur to synchronize the simulation with the rising edge of every clock in the design under verification.

in some cases but also with the fall of *clock1* in some other cases, which illustrates the nature of this shifting clock relationship. Again, the figure indicates that the simulation engine's model evaluation tick occurs at all times when any clock of the DUV is rising. Because of the non-integer clock ratio, these calls to the simulation engine are not equidistant but follow a more complex pattern over model time.

In the most general case, the evaluation tick of a cycle-based simulation engine clock marks the time when it is necessary to *sample* the DUV because interesting events occur in the model. The verification of truly asynchronous clock domains is also possible using cycle-based simulation engines but is beyond the scope of this chapter.

The approach discussed here successfully fulfills the needs of multiple clock domain verification. It is clear, however, that it causes a performance penalty because each additional simulator clock causes a full evaluation of the model even of those clock domains, where no design clock is currently active. In Figure 5.34a, for example, the simulation engine has to evaluate the logic of the slower clock domain (*clock2*) twice as many times, as it would be necessary without the faster clock domain. Modern cycle-based simulation engines have built-in support for multiple clock domains that minimizes the performance penalty by not evaluating the logic of a currently quiet clock domain. This requires the simulation engine to have insight into clock domains and events on the clock signals. It is evident that the more clock domains exist in a design, the more cycle-based simulation engines need to embrace features of their event-driven counterparts.

Hybrid Simulation Algorithms

As mentioned in the introduction of cycle-based simulation, the methodology and HDL style restrictions imposed by this technology are not acceptable to many design and verification projects. Therefore, the EDA vendors and academia have developed hybrid algorithms that combine event-driven and cycle-based simulation into a new class of hybrid engines.

There are two basic approaches to a hybrid simulation engine: an event-driven engine inside a cycle-based simulation engine, or a cycle-based algorithm inside an event-driven simulation engine.

The first variant, event-driven updates inside a cycle-based engine, is quite commonly used and known research work in this area has been documented [13, 14]. The above example of multi-clock domain simulation explains the benefits.

The more popular approach is to combine a general event-driven algorithm with a core engine that speeds up simulation of designs, which contain islands for which cycle-based simulation applies. An important variant of this situation is the case in which the design itself is completely synchronous while the test bench heavily relies on event-driven constructs.

However, the success of such an approach is limited unless overwhelming parts of the model are compliant with the cycle-based scheme. Even if we assume cycle-based evaluation applies to 50% of a design, we will still only see a moderate speed improvement as the following thought experiment shows: if it were possible to simulate the synchronous 50% part of the model in zero time, the speed-up would only be a factor of two.

5.6 WAVEFORM VIEWERS

We return now to the user interface of the simulation system (Figure 5.1). The most important GUI component in a simulation system is certainly the waveform viewer. Usually, a simulation engine comes with its own waveform viewer tool. Some companies have specialized in this area, and they offer waveform viewers that work with many simulation engines. The purpose of this following discussion is to give an overview of what

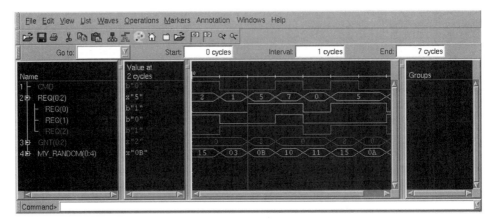

▪ FIGURE 5.35

A simple waveform window.

features a user can typically expect. However, we will not go into many details describing bells-and-whistle features.

All simulation engines are able to produce trace files during simulation runs to support debug. The files need to contain enough information to allow a user to look at the values of the HDL signals and variables after simulation. At minimum, a trace file has to contain the symbol name and signal value information.

Different EDA vendors have come up with different formats (e.g., value change dump, or VCD) that their simulation engines and waveform viewer tools support. A differentiator between trace file formats is how compressed this information is because for long simulation runs these files can obviously become rather large.

Figure 5.35 shows a first simple waveform window in an example tool, representative of the many available commercial offerings. Vendors have converged on standard look-and-feel features of such GUIs, so it is not surprising to see many common elements in this illustration. The menu and status bars show the standard control elements such as File/Edit/View, menu bars that can dock and undock and similarly standard GUI features.

The main part of the viewer shows four different panes. Leftmost is a list of signals currently selected for display. The signals have attributes such as their name and whether they are composites like vector or record types in the HDL. For the vectors it is possible to select a combined representation of the value in the value panes, for example, *REQ(0:2)*, or a representation of each signal bit by itself. There are two value panes in this example: a waveform that shows the signal values over a period of time, and values at a specific time. The user selects the specific time

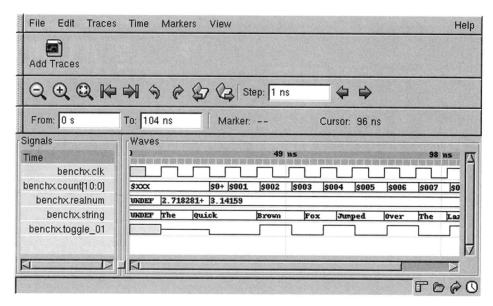

■ FIGURE 5.36

Example screen of the GTK Wave viewer.

using a cursor (vertical red line in the waveform pane) positioned inside the waveforms to easily align all signal values at that given model time.

In the example, the time base is *cycles*. This reveals that this tool belongs to a cycle-based simulation environment. For an event-driven simulation engine trace, the time-base would be a measure of time, such as pico-seconds or nano-seconds. This does not change the nature of the displayed waveform or the controls available to the user. Changes are still step functions at discrete time intervals. Only in analog simulation would a waveform view display smooth signal curves over time.

Figure 5.36 shows an open source waveform viewer that is compatible with the trace formats of many commercial simulation engines [15]. It demonstrates a time-base of nano-seconds and displays signals of other data types than just bit or integers (string data for benchx.string, real numbers for benchx.realnum).

Of course, an essential functionality is the movement of the waveform pane forward and backward in time over the waveform. This can occur by simply moving scroll bars or explicit directives in a menu of the cycle or time boundaries to be displayed. A more interesting way to move across time is a search for certain signal values or specific value transitions. Even just a search for the next value change on a signal that is flat over a long interval can be extremely useful. Consider, for example, an

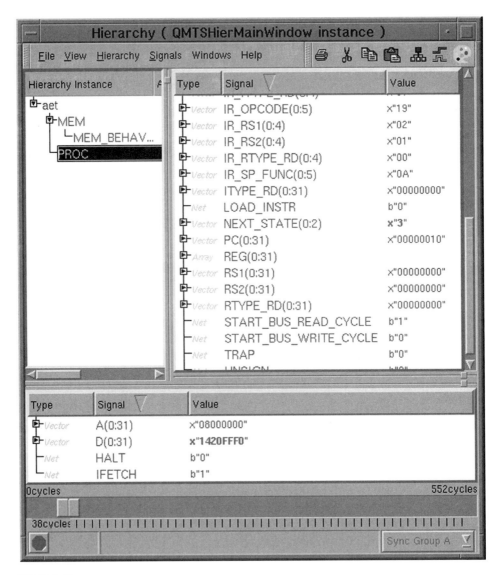

Hierarchy browser.

asserted error signal that usually stays inactive during most simulation runs. A user can load the trace file of a failing simulation test case into the viewer and quickly center the viewer to the time at which the error occurs by using the pull-down menu to search for the first value change of the error signal.

Typical viewer tools offer more than signal waveforms alone. Figure 5.37 shows a capability to traverse through the model's design hierarchy. The left-most sub-window shows a model with the instances *mem* and *proc*, with *proc* selected. This tree traversal widget lets the user expand and collapse sub-hierarchies. For a selected node in the hierarchy, the tree view displays all signals. In the sub-window with the signal list, the view shows the value for the current time (cycle) selected with the time slider widget at the bottom of the window. The additional signal area directly above the time slider is a grab bag for selected signals from across the hierarchy.

If the previous example has moved the debug view to the model source, Figure 5.38 extends this paradigm by putting all signal values into a display of the original source file (marked by brackets). Such a view is especially productive for the original author of the source HDL.

It is easy to see how a viewer with all the above capabilities evolves quickly to a full IDE (integrated development environment). Such tools resemble the C/C++/Java development environments that software developers have learned to depend on. Many modern simulation tools integrate such debuggers, addressing one of the bottlenecks of hardware verification: logic debug.

5.7 SUMMARY

Hardware description languages cover a variety of possible abstraction levels and specification styles. Designers today mostly use RTL or gate-level HDL to define the functionality of a DUV. Inherent in an HDL specification is the structure of a model network with behavioral blocks interconnected by signals. The simulation semantics of VHDL and Verilog imply event-driven simulation semantics.

Modern HDLs also provide features that support the writing of simulation test benches. In fact, the further development of both VHDL [16] and Verilog [8] emphasizes adding verification-related constructs. Chapter 6 focuses on test bench development.

A simulation engine compiles an HDL specification to the equivalent model network as the first step to build a simulation model. Event-driven simulation is a simple and efficient technology that scales across the full scope of the features that HDLs provide. It uses the model network to propagate signal changes during simulation runtime. An event-driven

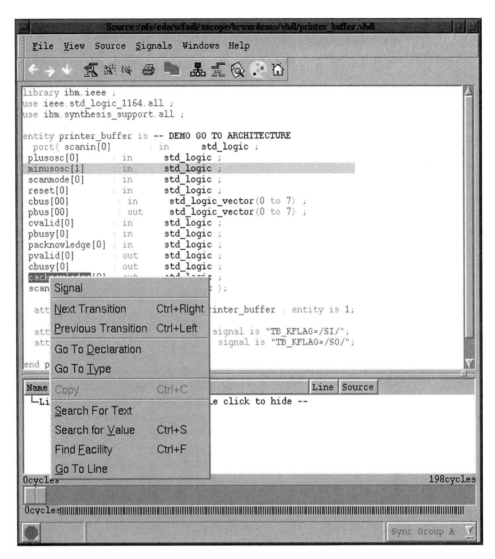

Source file browser.

simulation engine activates only those parts of a DUV model whose input signals change and skips all model regions that experience no input changes, thus avoiding unnecessary work.

Different simulation execution algorithms are possible for the restricted HDL style used to specify synchronous RTL or gate-level designs. A cycle-based simulation engine can transform this finite state-machine view of the HDL model into a levelized network. Where the event-driven engine leaves the execution order of the simulated model network to the dynamic signal flow, the cycle-based engine orders the network statically at model compile time. This opens a range of optimizations at build time that improves performance and size of the model at runtime.

Most of this chapter focused on discussing event-driven and cycle-based simulation technology in their purest form. However, the commercially offered high-end simulation engines today incorporate elements of both technologies in hybrid engines to support maximum speed and full support of all HDL features.

Aside from understanding simulation engines and their optimization, the discussion of cycle-based simulation is an important introduction to other technologies that we discuss in later chapters. Many hardware accelerators (Chapter 10) and the core algorithms of formal verification (Chapters 11, 12) all rely on the cycle-based or FSM semantics of model evaluation.

5.8 EXERCISES

1. Finish the sequence of event-driven simulation steps of Figure 5.27 until the model is in steady state, which means no more signal updates are scheduled.

2. The *xor* gate that drives the delayed assignment to signal $s(1)$ switches its output value from "*1*" to "*0*" (Figure 5.26, compare panels c and d). Explain the reason for this change.

3. Consider the following change of the model network in the figures underlying Exercise 2: assume that there is no delayed assignment but a zero-delay connection between the *xor* gate and $s(1)$. How does that change the model behavior from the step in Figure 5.26c onward?

4. Implement four different HDL models for a 32-bit adder using the HDL style used in Table 5.7. Run performance comparisons of the different styles by using an available simulation engine and enough test patterns to make the comparison worthwhile. Convert the VHDL of Table 5.7 to the equivalent Verilog if only a Verilog engine is available. For the VHDL case, compare the three HDL styles to a fourth variant using integer signal types.

5. Complete the pseudo-code of Figure 5.33b until it captures the complete logic of Figure 5.33a.

6. Summarize the main performance advantages of cycle-base simulation versus event-driven simulation.

7. Summarize the drawbacks of cycle-based simulation.

CHAPTER 6

CREATING ENVIRONMENTS

This second part of the overview of tools for simulation-based verification focuses on the simulation environment. A walk through the landscape of test bench writing serves two purposes. First, there is a general overview of the requirements for tools in this area. The main goal is to understand the principles of how languages and libraries can support well-structured test benches and higher productivity of verification teams. Second, interleaved with this discussion is a walkthrough of several available test bench writing tools and languages. We cover test bench aspects of hardware description languages, the *e* language, OpenVera, and SystemC.

Because there are a multitude of tools available, there is no room to cover every single one in detail. Instead, as the different areas of test bench writing are discussed, the chapter switches between different tools and highlights some of their specific properties. However, the goal of this section, and thus the thread of the discussion, is to gain an understanding of the challenges and the common features of these tools. Although the chapter looks at some of the distinguishing features of the tools discussed, the focus is on this *class* of tools as a group and not on detailed specifics of a single one of them. This is still an emerging, ever-changing field of technology, and it is more important to have a framework of the key concepts than a reference manual on specifics, which will be outdated quickly.

The ultimate measure for quality of a verification effort is the number of bugs found in the DUV specification. However, an assertion of this metric is only possible after the fact, at the end of the verification cycle. The bug detection rate is one indicator and feedback mechanism about the relative progress *during* verification (Chapter 13). *Verification coverage analysis* is the real systematic approach to generate insight into the quality of the verification done while the project is ongoing. The second part of this chapter completes the discussion of the simulation environment with an overview of different approaches available to assess verification coverage. The various coverage metrics, which industry and research have developed during the last few years, are classified into the areas of structural coverage and functional coverage. *Structural coverage* metrics instrument the design under verification (DUV) model with data collection capability tied to the organizational structure of the implementation or the hardware description language (HDL) specification of the DUV. Based on the collected data, coverage analysis is able to point to areas of the design that the verification driver components were not able to exercise. Instead of looking at structural features of the DUV, the *functional coverage* approach measures the verification progress based on an assessment of the design functionality covered by the verification work. The overview of coverage analysis is finished with a few of the data management challenges posed by the collection of coverage data across many simulation runs in large industrial verification projects.

6.1   TEST BENCH WRITING TOOLS

Chapter 3 introduced the base concepts of test benches and the principles to structure them so that the resulting simulation environment is flexible and productive. This section discusses the tools that are at the disposal of the verification engineer to accomplish this task.

Figure 6.1 highlights again the relationship between the simulation engine, containing the model of the DUV, and the different forms of test benches. In the discussion of features of HDLs in Chapter 5, their structural features were introduced, including easy connection of HDL test benches to the DUV and the management of replicated design units.

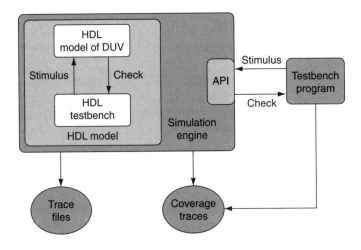

▪ **FIGURE 6.1**

The relationship between the test bench and the simulation engine. A hardware description language test bench is integrated with the model of the DUV, while an external test bench uses the simulation engine's programming interface to interact with the model.

This overview of the test bench tools looks more closely at VHDL and Verilog features that support the actual coding of driver and checker components.

The chapter then turns to test bench writing external to HDLs and simulation engines. There are technical foundations and challenges that any test bench library or tool has to address. Instead of introducing special-purpose test bench languages immediately, this chapter starts with the application of a general programming language as the foundation because test bench coding is also programming, using C++ as an example and designing the base architecture of an example test bench library as an educational thought experiment. Although a passing familiarity with C++ certainly helps the reader follow this description, more important are the general features incorporated into this example library design. The interesting parts of a C++ test bench library are those constructs that general programming languages cannot offer, and their discussion highlights the specific requirements that test bench coding creates. After the experiment of creating our own test bench library from the ground up, we are better prepared to appreciate the features of the custom-built languages and libraries offered by the industry today.

During the past few years, several special-purpose languages gained widespread usage. This chapter highlights some example features of the *e* language, OpenVera, and the SystemC C++ environment, the most popular high-level verification languages (HVLs) today.

6.1.1 HDL Languages as Test Bench Tool

From the beginning, the creators of HDLs conceived them as simulation languages to support both design and test bench writing. Verilog and VHDL are both very large languages, and at least half of the language definition is devoted to test bench writing. The following discussion does intend to introduce some of the fundamental concepts. There are complete books that cover the details of these languages and their use as test bench tools [1, 2]. The reader who is interested in a more detailed view of HDL test bench coding is encouraged to study one of the HDLs more thoroughly. In the following, we again assume the reader to be somewhat familiar with the HDLs used.

In an HDL environment, all test bench components—stimulus generators, monitors, checkers, and scoreboards—connect to the DUV structurally via signals (VHDL) or wires (Verilog). The explicit specification of the structural connection certainly is a basic capability of any HDL. Returning to the cache design example from Chapter 2 (see Figure 2.20), Figure 6.2 shows the implementation of the top level of a Verilog test bench.

In addition to the three instances—DUV, monitor, stimulus component, and their interconnecting signals (*wires* in Verilog)—the test bench code also contains the control of a central clock. The *initial* block keeps

```
// Testbench
module cache_test;

  `define CYCLE_TIME 100

  wire CMD_VLD, [0:3]CMD, [0:31]DATA_IN, [0:7]CMD_TAG_IN, [0:31]CMD_ADDR;
  wire RSP_VLD, [0:2]RSP, [0:31]DATA_OUT, [0:7]CMD_TAG_OUT;

  reg CLK;

  // instances of testbench components

  stim STIM (CLK, CMD_VLD, CMD, DATA_IN, CMD_TAG_IN, CMD_ADDR);

  mon MON (CLK, RSP_VLD, RSP, DATA_OUT, CMD_TAG_OUT);

  // instance of cache design

  cache CACHE (CLK, CMD_VLD, CMD, DATA_IN, CMD_TAG_IN, CMD_ADDR,
               RSP_VLD, RSP, DATA_OUT, CMD_TAG_OUT);

  // clock control
  initial begin
    forever begin
      CLK = 0;
      #CYCLE_TIME/2;       // this is where the time progress is controlled
      CLK = 1;
      #CYCLE_TIME/2;
    end
  end
endmodule
```

▪ FIGURE 6.2

Verilog test bench with stimulus and monitor component. This top level of a hardware description language model instantiates the DUV CACHE, a stimulus component STIM, and a monitor component MON. There is also an initial block that serves as the clock generator for the DUV, as well as time control component for the whole model.

the clock signal toggling every 50 ticks of the simulation engine's base clock, thus defining the base cycle of this simulation with a resolution of 100 time steps. The use of a symbolically defined constant for the cycle time is a simple example of how to create parameters in the HDL with a single point of control for change.

Figure 6.3 implements a simple *generator* component in Verilog. At simulation start time, the *initial*-block of *generator* loads the contents of a text file into a pattern array. *$readmemh()* is a *task* (similar to a *procedure* in other languages) that is part of the Verilog standard language environment. It allows the loading of hexadecimal data in textual format into Verilog arrays. Hence, the file *cache.patterns* is the real test case. The file can contain a regression set of golden test vectors, manually written tests, or a test pattern that a generation program creates. The *generator*

```
// Stimulus Component
module generator(CLK, REQUEST, CMD, DATA, ADDR, TAG)
  input CLK, REQUEST;
  output [0:3]CMD, [0:63]DATA, [0:31]ADDR, [0:7]TAG;
  reg    [0:3]CMD, [0:63]DATA, [0:31]ADDR, [0:7]TAG;
  reg    [0:107] patterns[0:1023], [0:10]ptr;
  reg    [0:107] n_patt;
  intial begin
    $readmemh("cache.patterns", patterns); ptr = 0; ready = 1;
  end
  always @(posedge CLK)
  begin
    if (REQUEST)
      if(ptr < 1024) begin
        n_patt = patterns[ptr]; ptr = ptr + 1;
        CMD = n_patt[0:3]; DATA=n_patt[4:67]; ADDR=n_patt[68:99]; TAG=n_patt[100:107];
      end
      else begin
        #1000;
        $display("Simulation Done!");
        $finish();
      end
  end
endmodule
```

■ **FIGURE 6.3**

Simple generator component in Verilog. At simulation initialization, the component reads a file of test patterns into the array patterns. The component input REQUEST triggers the generator to read out one new test pattern to its output ports at a time. After reaching the capacity of the test pattern array, the generator stops the simulation.

component is prepared to read 1,024 commands and supply them to the stimulus component.

After processing all patterns, the generator waits for 1,000 time steps and shuts down the simulation run. This certainly is a very crude form of hard-coded control. What happens if it takes more than these time steps to process commands that might be pending in the DUV? A real production test bench must implement a more appropriate test case control, most likely in the checker component.

Figure 6.4 instantiates this *generator* inside the stimulus component. We explained that it is important to separate the generator and the protocol components. Such a structure reflects the different areas of concern addressed by these components. If the generation process needs to be changed radically, the protocol component should remain untouched and vice versa.

Although Figure 6.3 encapsulated the generator in a *module*, for the example of the stimulus component *stim* in Figure 6.4, another structuring construct available in Verilog is highlighted. A *task* combines a series of sequential statements together and makes it callable as one atomic unit. The specialty of a Verilog task is that the user can suspend simulation execution inside the body of a task and can pass input parameters to a task and can return outputs at the end of the task execution.

```
module stim (CLK, CMD_VLD, CMD, DATA_IN, CMD_TAG_IN, CMD_ADDR) ;

  input CLK;
  output CMD_VLD, [0:3]CMD, [0:31]DATA_IN, [0:7]CMD_TAG_IN, [0:31]CMD_ADDR;

  reg CMD_VLD, [0:3]CMD, [0:31]DATA_IN, [0:7]CMD_TAG_IN, [0:31]CMD_ADDR;

  reg [0:3]N_CMD, [0:63]N_DATA_IN, [0:31]N_ADDR, [0:7]N_TAG_IN;

  reg REQUEST;

  // instantiate generator
  generator GENERATOR(REQUEST, N_CMD, N_DATA_IN, N_ADDR, N_TAG_IN);

  task write_command;    // protocol component
    begin
      @(posedge CLK);
      CMD_VLD = 1; CMD = N_CMD;
      DATA_IN = N_DATA_IN[0:31]; CMD_ADDR = N_ADDR;  CMD_TAG_IN = N_TAG_IN;
      REQUEST = 0;
      @(posedge CLK);
      CMD_VLD = 0; CMD = 0;
      DATA_IN = N_DATA_IN[32:63]; CMD_ADDR = 0; CMD_TAG_IN = N_TAG_IN;
      REQUEST = 1;
    end
  endtask

  initial begin
    CMD_VLD = 0; CMD = 0; DATA_IN = 0; CMD_TAG_IN = 0; CMD_ADDR = 0;
    N_CMD = 0; N_DATA_IN = 0; N_ADDR = 0; N_TAG_IN = 0; REQUEST = 1;
    forever begin
      write_command();                    // apply command using correct protocol
    end
  end
endmodule
```

■ **FIGURE 6.4**

Stimulus component for the cache DUV in Verilog. Module stim instantiates the generator component and contains the protocol component *write_command*, which translates every newly generated test pattern, supplied by generator, to the two cycle cache command required by the DUV. After completing the command protocol, the protocol component initiates the generation of the next test pattern by turning signal REQUEST back on.

The protocol component inside *stim* implements the protocol component with the task *write_command*. Every call of *write_command* will take a test pattern or command, newly delivered by *generator,* and apply it to the output of the stimulus component using the two model cycles that the input protocol of the *cache* DUV requires.

The example code in Figure 6.4 illustrates a bare skeleton of a real stimulus test bench component. The following are descriptions of the additional considerations a verification engineer would include to make this example robust and usable in a production environment.

Parameterization

Separating central decisions from actual code and encoding them as parameters is always helpful to make the test bench easily adaptable to different usage situations. For example, it would be much better to read in the name of the test case file *cache* the *patterns* from outside the test bench. This way a team can keep many different test case files in a single directory of a file system at the same time. We call such a collection of test cases a test case bucket.

Debug Trace File Generation

Verilog has a number of facilities to write out debug information. For example, the *$display()* call lets a user write text and signal values to the console; *$fdisplay()* routes this information to a file. If the test bench calls the pair *$monitor/$fmonitor* with a list of signals, the simulation prints out formatted name/value information at the end of every time step at which any of the referenced signals did change. Using such directed debug trace mechanisms allows a focused diagnosis of test bench problems. Of course, the verification can always use the trace file data that the simulation engine supports natively (Figure 6.1).

Randomization

The stimulus generation shown is completely deterministic. To fulfill any reasonably complete test plan, the actual tests must vary over a number of properties of the cache design interface

- Different commands, different sequences of commands
- Different temporal spacing between the command, i.e., up to eight commands back-to-back in sequence, different dead cycles between back-to-back commands
- Different and colliding target addresses
- A wide variation of the data values is probably not important

With the given test bench, the verification team can only accomplish this variation by creating many different *cache patterns* files, which cover these cases. It is possible to move some of the variability into the test bench code itself. Verilog offers a number of system tasks that support randomization. The most obvious is *$random()*, which returns a 32-bit random integer value. However, there are several additional tasks—for example, *$dist_normal()*, *$dist_exponential()*, and *$dist_poisson()*—that let the test bench writer control the statistical distribution of the randomized selections. All these functions support a "seed" parameter whose importance we explain below.

Verification engineers can use randomization either to pregenerate deterministic tests or during the runtime of a test bench-driven simulation (for further details, see Chapter 7). In either case, it is important, for the completion of the verification plan, that the project tracks which of the cases the stimulus component actually applied. The methods and techniques of this verification coverage tracking will be discussed in the second half of this chapter.

It is important that test bench writers understand the statistical characteristics of the random distribution they select in their stimulus components. This is even more important if there are holes suspected in the coverage tracking done by the project. HDL test bench implementations whose random distributions are deficient can leave dangerous coverage holes if a project relies on a specific distribution.

Another aspect of working with randomized testing is that the verification must be able to repeat any simulation run. If a simulation reveals a design error (or test bench error) it is necessary to rerun the simulation, perhaps many times, to support debug and later the validation of a fix. For the difficult bugs, it is also desirable to package the conditions that lead to the problem and be able to rerun the exact scenario for regression purposes. Repeatability is trivial for pregenerated tests if the test files are stored in a file system. However, if runtime randomization is used, it is vital to supply seeds to the random number generation functions. Using the same seed will guarantee that the simulation engine will repeat the generation of a sequence of random numbers in exactly the same way.

If a test bench uses runtime randomization in many different places, explicit random seed management is advisable. This means that the code should collect and set all seeds at one or only a few central places. Such an organization will make it easier to support a controlled exact rerun of a simulation test for debug or regression.

This section uses exclusively Verilog to demonstrate some HDL test bench concerns. This discussion is only an introduction to provide a flavor for the techniques available in this area, and, of course, VHDL would provide an equally good platform to illustrate these points. Although VHDL has no built-in randomization constructs, the power of the language supports many different ways to define random number generators. For an example of an elaborate package for random number generation, refer to *VHDL Random Number Generation Package* [4].

Many aspects of the test bench support constructs of HDLs very similar to general programming languages. In fact, advances in software engineering and general-purpose programming languages have heavily influenced the development of HDLs over the years. After all, the ADA language formed the base for VHDL, and the Verilog developers certainly took a serious look at the C language. As general software engineering embraced modern programming techniques such as object-orientation and function overloading, the HDLs followed suit, for example, object-oriented proposals for VHDL [4] or the object-oriented features of SystemVerilog [5]. In some ways, the test bench subset of HDLs has taken the hardware specifics of the HDLs and augmented them with general programming constructs such as tasks, procedures, functions, and all control structures available in a typical programming language.

6.1.2 C/C++ Libraries

Given the obvious need of programming capabilities in test bench writing, many have approached this area from the opposite direction: rather than extend HDLs, determine what extensions to a programming language are necessary to cast it productively as a test bench writing tool.

Certainly, C and C++ are widely popular programming languages available on any computer platform that possibly hosts a simulator tool. These languages have turned into a basic requirement of most computer or electrical engineering curricula, creating a large skill base from which verification teams can draw. In addition, as discussed in Chapter 5, most simulation engines offer a programming language interface through which a C or C++ program can control and interact with the DUV and the engine.

In the following, the basic elements necessary for a library that extends C++ to support test bench writing will be discussed. The following description is only an educational vehicle and does not refer to a library that really exists. We can only sketch out the implementation, with a focus on the principal requirements. The software organization described in the following section is only one possibility among many. Many projects in the industry have created their own environments, sometimes project specific and at other times carrying the libraries over from one project to the next, always refining and generalizing the approach.

Overall, this discussion will lay the groundwork to better understand and appreciate the productivity and usability features of the three commercial test bench writing environments (Vera, *e*, and SystemC) that we cover afterward.

Figure 6.5 shows our C++ library built stepwise from several different layers. Table 6.1 gives an overview of the tasks covered by the different library layers shown in Figure 6.5. The following discussion of the different C++ library features follows the list of service layers.

The Simulation Engine Abstraction Layer

The simulation engine abstraction layer allows test bench code to be portable between different simulation engines. With the multitude of commercial simulation engines available, this part of the library seems to be a daunting task. However, the standardization process has led to the program-language interface (PLI), the VPI for Verilog [6] and the

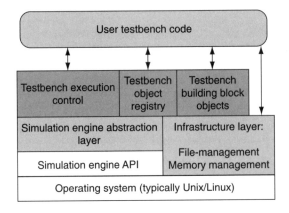

▪ **FIGURE 6.5**

Example C++ test bench library architecture. The top layers of the library are accessible by the user's test bench code and support an object-oriented structure. Test bench components are built as class instances and registered with the library, which takes over the control of test bench execution and offers predefined building blocks to improve test bench coding productivity.

TABLE 6.1 ▪ The five mayor layers of the C++ test bench library

Simulation engine abstraction layer	Abstract interface to simulation engine application programming interfaces that provides the rest of the library easy portability to any available simulation engine because all engine-specific code is concentrated in this layer.
Basic infrastructure layer	A centralized set of utilities providing a portable interface to operating system services like files, console inputs/outputs and memory management.
Test bench object registry	The library supports test benches built from user-defined classes that register themselves with this layer. Once registered, the library can call the user objects at appropriate times to perform their work.
Test bench building block objects	The library offers predefined building blocks as productivity aid for test bench writers.
Test bench execution control	The library controls when to call the different user test bench components in what sequence from this central library service layer.

foreign language interface (FLI) [7] and VHPI [8] for VHDL, which simplifies this task because most commercial simulation engines offer one of these interfaces. The following uses simple examples of PLI and FLI mechanisms to illustrate the capabilities of such interfaces. Common to this list of programming interfaces with their confusing set of acronyms is the functionality that allows a C/C++ program access to any named

HDL object in the DUV model. One of the most basic sets of portable functions the C++ test bench library has to provide is the ability to *get* and *set* model objects such as signals, wires, registers, and variables. For any given simulation engine, the *get* and *set* functions map to the appropriate interface offered by the engine, and they provide one single common interface to the rest of the C++ test bench library.

A most important design decision for the C++ library is the control flow mechanism between the simulation engine and the test bench. It is possible to differentiate between two basic approaches, the *integrated test bench* and the *separated test bench*. In the first alternative, the simulation engine always calls the test bench components. Even though the test bench components use a separate programming language, the engine application programming interface (API) treats them as natural extensions of the HDL supported. The separated test bench approach views the test bench as an independent program with its own internal control flow. In the overall process, simulation engine and test bench program hand control to each other in alternating fashion. When the simulation engine finds the model in steady state for a given model time, it hands control over to the test bench. Once the test bench components finish their work, the library hands control back to the engine to advance the simulation of the model. In the following, we discuss the integrated and separated test bench alternatives with advantages and disadvantages.

Integrated C/C++ Test Bench

The original intention of the Verilog PLI was to enable the calling of customized C functions from within Verilog. For example, the user could write a task (such as the *write_command()* task in Figure 6.4) in the C language and, if linked correctly with the executable program of the simulation engine, could call this task seamlessly from within the Verilog source code. Staying with the *write_command()* example task of Figure 6.4, the caller would refer to it as *$write_command()*, the "$" indicating an externally linked task.

Another common approach to integrate C/C++ test bench routines is to use a wrapper block in the source HDL. Figure 6.6 illustrates this with the *monitor* component of the cache test bench, using the FLI of a given simulation engine. The base mechanism is to define an empty VHDL entity annotated with a special *foreign* attribute, which tells the model build process that a specific C program is to be dynamically loaded at simulation startup time (elaboration time in VHDL) and an initialization function, *monitor_init()*, is to be called with certain parameters (string value *parms*).

The initialization routine has to establish addressability of the input/output signals inside the C program. In addition, the C code can establish *callback routines*. These routines are C functions, which the simulation engine must call at specific points in time. Examples of such

```
entity monitor is
  port (
    clk          : in std_ulogic;   -- Clock
    rsp_valid    : in std_ulogic;
    rsp          : in std_logic_vector(0 to 2);
    data_out     : in std_logic_vector(0 to 31);
    cmd_tag_out  : in std_logic_vector(0 to 7);
    cmd_tag_in   : in std_logic_vector(0 to 7)
    );
end monitor;

architecture c_code of monitor is
   attribute foreign of c_code : architecture is "monitor_init monitor.so; parms";
end c_code;
```

■ **FIGURE 6.6**

Wrapping a C code version of the cache monitor to a foreign language interface routine.

callbacks are the process code of the entity, simulator exit or checkpoint, and restart. Figure 6.7 illustrates the relationships between the foreign program *monitor.so* of the example used in Figure 6.6 and the simulation engine. The VHDL attribute provides the engine with enough information to load and call the initialization function of the *monitor* component. The *monitor_init()* function finishes the connection between the *monitor* component and the HDL model and simulation engine by calling a variety of FLI functions. A main task for *monitor_init()* is to register the function *monitor_proc()* with the engine using the mti_CreateProcess() FLI function. The registered function is a callback for the model evaluation that the simulation will call whenever the event-driven algorithm defines a necessary update of the *monitor* component. Via this callback, the engine treats the external C code similar to any other VHDL process in the HDL model—the model extension with C routines is complete and ready for execution.

Similar to PLI, the FLI also supports foreign subprograms, which are subroutines callable from VHDL but written in C/C++. PLI, on the other hand, also has mechanisms that support the embedding of C routines as modules inside a Verilog hierarchy, similar to the example shown in Figures 6.6 and Figure 6.7.

The idea of wrapping every test bench component behind an HDL façade takes advantage of keeping the HDL environment as the *master* environment. This has clear advantages for the test bench coder. There is no need to write a test bench execution component because the control flow stays with the host simulation engine; the simulation engine calls the test bench routines whenever the HDL semantics require the activation of a module/entity (e.g., when input signals change). Another advantage is that the connection of the test bench components to the HDL model occurs with the standard HDL structural connection mechanisms, component instantiation.

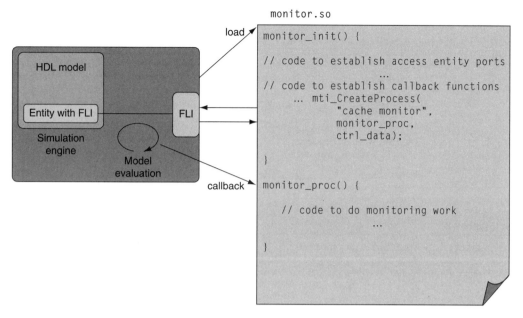

An entity with a foreign language interface causes the simulation to load a specified external program monitor.so at model initialization time. The main entry point of the program, specified in the VHDL attribute in Figure 6.6 (*monitor_init*), establishes data structures and other callback functions that the engine calls at the appropriate times. *monitor_proc()* is an example callback function. It acts similarly to a VHDL process inside a VHDL architecture of the corresponding entity. The callback is reactivated whenever the model evaluation algorithm deems necessary.

However, there are also some disadvantages. Because the host simulation engine calls the C/C++ code, calling and linking conventions of the host environment have to be satisfied by the C/C++ coder of the test bench. This tends to create a number of cryptic rules and a need to call a significant number of rather arcane C functions, which transport control and data back and forth between the C language and the HDL environment. PLI and FLI each encompass hundreds of functions. In addition, verification engineers often require structural changes in the test bench, such as the access to different signals or the need to instantiate additional test bench components. Every time there is a structural change in the test bench environment, HDL source changes occur as a result.

Embedding more and more test bench components in the HDL source becomes very hard to manage when a project evolves from unit-level verification to chip and system level.

A checker written for a unit simulation environment can be instantiated in a simulation HDL wrapper around the unit. However, when this unit is integrated into the chip-level HDL test bench, the question arises

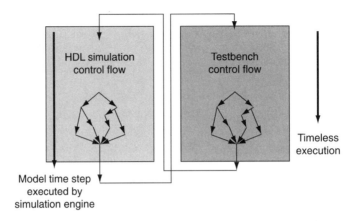

A separated C/C++ test bench and its control flow interaction with the hardware description language (HDL) model. The branching of arrows inside the execution flowchart of both the HDL model and the test bench indicate that inside each domain, control of execution is fully independent of the control flow in the other domain. Whenever the simulation engine finishes a model time step, control passes to the test bench. The engine only gets runtime control back after the test bench has finished all its work for the current model time. Simulation model time advances only during the activity of the HDL simulation from whose perspective the test bench execution is timeless.

as to where the checker instance should go. This dilemma was discussed in Chapter 5 when the characteristics of the HDLs were examined. Clearly, VHDL has no good solution. Verilog allows cross-hierarchy connections, which means the unit checker instance could be instantiated in simulation HDL wrapper around the chip. However, it becomes clear from this discussion that the amount of maintenance of simulation-only HDL wrappers on different levels of the simulation hierarchy quickly becomes excessive, which is the reason why the approach of the integrated C++ test bench does not scale well with larger projects.

Separated C/C++ Test Bench

A radically different approach is the total separation of the C/C++ test bench domain from the HDL context. The basic idea is to let the test bench library control the instantiation and the control flow of all test bench components itself, in a separate context from the HDL domain.

Figure 6.8 conceptualizes the control flow between the two domains. The HDL simulation proceeds to a predefined point in time at which the HDL model is in a steady state. At this time, the simulation engine passes control to the test bench. Now the test bench execution control takes over, calls whichever test bench components need to run next, and eventually returns control back to the HDL simulation engine. All the test bench activity between HDL simulation time steps is called a *test bench cycle*.

Several key observations about this scheme are notable. First, there is only one point in the test bench code at which control transfers back and forth between the test bench and the simulation engine. The simulation engine abstraction layer (Figure 6.5) of the test bench library should completely encapsulate this piece of code, thus freeing all verification engineers from dealing with arcane calling conventions and PLI function parameters. In addition, this scheme hides all the complexity of the back-and-forth control flow and the verification engineers can focus on their real job—creating effective stimulus and checking components. Second, tracking of model time stays with the HDL model. Model time passes only when HDL components are active. As a result, from the viewpoint of the test bench, time stands still. Once the simulation engine hands control to the test bench, all changes made by the test bench to the model signals and variables happen at the same time, in parallel. Time can advance only when control returns to the model; it is then that the actions of the test bench become observable in the model.

This strict separation of model and test bench domain dramatically simplifies the infrastructure and the communication between the two domains. It can also be argued that any other control flow would lead to the extreme complications of a *spaghetti flow* if any of the test bench component writers had to concern their code with execution control.

To drive that point further, consider Figure 6.9, which shows how data flows between test bench and HDL model. Although the test bench can read model variables and signals at any time during the execution of test bench code, the test bench library buffers all updates that go from the test bench to the model. The obvious place for this buffering is in the simulation abstraction layer of the test bench library. The buffered model update ensures that all changes from the test bench to the model occur at the exact time and all test bench components access the same consistent model state. If test bench components were able to change model state immediately, some components, when activated, would observe a different model state than do others. Under such conditions, the execution order of the test bench components would become very important, which would complicate the writing of the test bench dramatically, especially in a large project in which many verification engineers have to work in parallel.

Consider, for example, the test bench sets the two inputs of a two-way and gate to "1." If this action would propagate into the model immediately, there are two ways to handle this update. In the first scenario, the test bench library activates the simulation engine immediately and lets it propagate the changes, starting with the possible change of the signal on the output of the two-way and gate. The second alternative is to allow the change of the model signals but not let the simulation engine update the model with the subsequent changes.

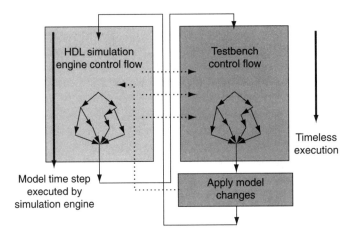

FIGURE 6.9

Control and dataflow between test bench and hardware description language (HDL) model. The dashed arrows show when the test bench code has access to the state of the HDL model (signals, variables, registers, etc.). Test bench components can inspect model state at any point during their execution. All changes to the model are buffered by the test bench library and applied only at the end of the test bench cycle. This algorithm ensures that all test bench components have access to the same unaltered, consistent model state.

The latter case is clearly illegal, as it would possibly show wrong simulation results (such as a two-way and gate with both inputs set to "1" and "0" output). The former case, updating the model in real time while the test bench code is active, has two problems. First, different test bench components observe a different model state. It now becomes the user's problem to manage which parts of the test bench run before others, clearly a complexity explosion and recipe for unmanageable spaghetti code. Second, if the test bench propagated every signal change through the model, the simulation engine must iterate through the model a large number of times, every time there is a model update from the test bench, causing a major degradation in simulation performance.

Given this simplified scheme of control and dataflow between test bench library and simulation engine (Figure 6.9), we can now list the principal interface, which the simulation engine abstraction layer presents to the rest of the test bench library (Table 6.2). Example usage code for this interface is introduced below.

The Base Infrastructure Layer

The basic infrastructure layer (see Figure 6.5) centralizes services that all components of a test bench use. Most of these services are concerned about resources owned by the underlying operating system, such as memory and files.

TABLE 6.2 ■ The base interface of the simulation engine abstraction layer for the C++ test bench library

	The user instantiates a signal object specifying the name of the model signal or variable (facility). Test bench components can access model signals only through such objects.
Signal_Object	*get_value()*: function of *Signal_Object* that returns the current state of the corresponding model facility.
	set_value(): function of *Signal_Object* that writes a new value into the corresponding model facility at the end of the test case cycle.
	For simplicity of the discussion, we assume integer facility values.
	The test bench library provides one instance of this class. It encapsulates all engine control functions of the different supported simulation engines and provides one portable interface to the other layers of the test bench library.
Simulation _Control	*clock()*: function that turns control over to the simulation engine for the duration of one simulation engine *clock tick*. A base clock tick can be one simulation cycle for a cycle-based engine or a discrete time interval for an event-driven engine.
	checkpoint()/restart() functions to suspend/resume simulation model.
	simulation_exit(): end HDL simulation end exit simulation engine.

Memory Management

Many components of a test bench allocate memory dynamically. For example, the scoreboard of the cache design (Chapter 3) needs to keep track of all outstanding commands. If our knowledge of the internal microarchitecture of the cache DUV guarantees that a maximum of eight fetch or store commands can be outstanding at a given time, the scoreboard component could just allocate a fixed buffer of eight entries at the beginning of the simulation. Under the fixed microarchitecture conditions, this is the most robust and least error-prone solution, and it provides the best runtime performance. However, if the design specification does not indicate a maximum number of in-flight transactions, the test bench needs to allocate buffer memory dynamically every time the stimulus component sends a command into the DUV and must unallocate it again when the DUV finishes servicing the command.

Dynamic memory allocation should be centrally controlled in a test bench, for example, by overloading the new() and delete() operators in C++. A well-written memory manager will increase test bench performance and make it easier to debug memory problems in the test bench code. A typical memory problem encountered with C++ programs is called a *memory leak*: parts of a test bench continuously allocate memory but never release it before the end of simulation. Memory leaks can create huge debug problems, especially in long-running simulations, when the jobs fail when they run out of memory. This can be horrendously difficult to debug if the test bench code does not have a central point of control for memory allocation.

File Management

A file manager has the important job of tracking all files that the test bench reads or writes during a simulation run. The more complex a DUV and the corresponding test bench become, the higher the number of files created by different test bench components rises. A file manager can keep track of location and time-date information of all input files and write out a bill-of-materials list at the end of a simulation run. This list is important when it comes time to rerun the exact simulation for debug or regression purposes.

Output files will be either status or debug and track files. Usually a project will standardize the layout of such files. A librarywide file manager will make a standardized layout of output files easy.

Test Bench Building Block Objects: Test Bench Components

The verification team organizes a test bench along the structural principles defined in Chapter 3. There will be stimuli generators, monitors, checkers, and scoreboards. In the following, these elements are called *test bench components*.

In a C++ environment, the library can map the test bench components to appropriate C++ classes. The class member variables hold the current status of a component, and the member functions define the operations available for the component. If a component class has member variables of the type *Signal_Object*, these objects give the component access to the corresponding facilities, signal, registers, and arrays, in the HDL model via their connection through the simulation engine abstraction layer. If the component writes a new value to a *Signal_Object*, using the *set_value()* function, the test bench library will update the corresponding model facility at the end of the test case cycle.

It is a good idea for the C++ library to provide a base class *Testbench-Component* (similar to the one shown in Figure 6.10). The test bench writer must derive any user component from this base class, which defines a common interface and services for all test bench components in the system. The interface includes common debug and trace functions, as well as imposing a fixed set of member functions that a user component must implement in its own way. C++ calls this type of a base class an *abstract base class*. Only derive user classes, which define the yet-undefined function of the abstract base class, can be instantiated in a test bench.

With this base class any components will have a function called *trace()*, which prints out the component's name. The function *execute()* is not defined for the base class, but this abstract declaration enforces that any derived user component class defines such a function. The intended use of *execute()* is that this function contains the actual execution code, the behavior of the test bench component. Because the base

```
class TestbenchComponent {

public:
  TestbenchComponent(string name);

  void trace() { cout << "Name of component" << mName << endl };

  void execute() = 0;

private:
  string mName;
}
```

■ **FIGURE 6.10**

Abstract base class *TestbenchComponent*. The class provides a *trace()* function, which is the same for all test bench components and requires any user-derived class to implement an *execute()* function. *TestbenchComponents* are named when instantiated to allow the library to communicate via component names with the user during debug.

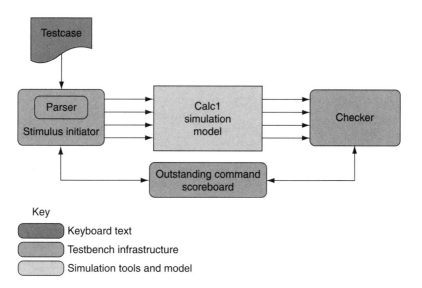

■ **FIGURE 6.11**

The Calc1 simulation environment with its three test bench components.

class *TestbenchComponent* enforces that every component has this function, it is easy for the test bench execution control layer (described below) to activate any component when necessary, just by calling its *execute()* function.

The test bench requirements for Calc1 (discussed in Chapter 4) are used as the basis for a more detailed example of the C++ test bench library. Figure 6.11 repeats the relevant parts of the structure of the

```
struct Operation {
  int cmd; int op1, op2, expResult, expResponse;
}

class ScoreBoard : TestbenchComponent {
 public:
  ScoreBoard(string name);

  void execute() {}; // ScoreBoard is passive
  void postOperation(int portNum, Operation &op); // log operation, set port not ready
  bool popOperation(int portNum);                 // un-log operation, set port ready

  bool port1Ready, port2Ready, port3Ready, port4Ready;

 private:
  Operation pendingOp[4];
}

class StimulusInitiator : TestbenchComponent {
 public:
  StimulusInitiator(string name, string filename);

  void execute(); // per port: if port ready apply next operation to
                  // model and post to scoreboard

  void registerScoreBoard(ScoreBoard &s);

 private:
  ScoreBoard *mScoreBoard;
  Signal_Object *req_1_cmd_in, *req_1_data_in, … ; // input interface of Calc1 DUV
}

class Checker : TestbenchComponent {
 public:
  Checker(string name);

  void execute(); // receive result, call scoreboard popOperation() and check

  void registerScoreBoard(ScoreBoard &s);

 private:
  ScoreBoard *mScoreBoard;
  Signal_Object *out_resp1, *out_data1, … ; // output interface of Calc1 DUV

}
```

■ **FIGURE 6.12**

Class declarations for the test bench components of the Calc1 simulation environment.

simulation environment for the Calc1 design. The test bench consists of three components that are mapped into C++ classes as shown in Figure 6.12.

The struct *Operation* in Figure 6.12 is a data structure that captures all data of a single Calc1 operation, including the expected response and result. The *ScoreBoard* component class captures one Operation per port. *ScoreBoard* does not necessarily need to be a *TestbenchComponent* because it is a passive component and its *execute()* function is empty.

This means that the *ScoreBoard* functions will be called by other test bench components directly, whereas the call of the test bench execution control is of no consequence. The methods *postOperation()* and *popOperation()* cover all operations of *ScoreBoard* and are called by other components. Every *postOperation()*, with the port number as an argument to the call, sets the *ready* field of the corresponding port in *ScoreBoard* (*port1Ready,...*), every *popOperation()* clears it. A *postOperation()* call carries a reference to an Operation data structure, which allows the *ScoreBoard* to copy the currently pending operation to its internal data buffer for the port.

The active components of this test bench are *StimulusInitiator* and *Checker*.

StimulusInitiator's constructor creates the *Signal_Object*'s, which corresponds to the four ports of Calc1 by using the correct model signal names. The other task of the constructor is to open and parse the test file. The execution control layer of the test bench library calls the *execute()* every test bench cycle. For every port of Calc1, *StimulusInitiator* checks whether the port is ready (using *ScoreBoard*) to accept the next operation. If true, the *execute()* function applies the operation to the model and posts it to *ScoreBoard*. If no more operations are available from the test file, *execute()* simply returns whenever it is called; at that point *StimulusInitiator* becomes inactive.

The constructor of the *Checker* class connects its *Signal_Object*'s on the output interface of Calc1. *Checker*'s *execute()* function monitors this interface, and once the model posts a results, *Checker* pops the corresponding Operation from the *ScoreBoard* to perform the check. Because the *popOperation()* call clears the *ready* field for the port in *ScoreBoard*, the SimulusInitiator is free to issue the next operation.

Both active components, *StimulusInitiator* and *Checker*, need access to the *ScoreBoard* of the test bench to be able call *ScoreBoard*'s data access functions. To give these components access to *ScoreBoard*, they both have the function *registerScoreBoard()*. The assumption behind this architecture is that the code, which instantiates the three components, will call *registerScoreBoard()* and pass in the reference to the *ScoreBoard* component.

As shown in Figure 6.13, the top level of the test bench instantiates the *Simulator_Control* infrastructure interface block and all three test bench components. This is also where the calls to the *registerScoreBoard()* function give the driver and the checker access to the scoreboard component.

The test loop iterates for 1,000 steps, calling each component's *execute()* function before telling *Simulator_Control* to simulate the HDL model for the next time interval (typically a model clock cycle). With the top-level test bench code, the overall structure and interlock of the different test bench library services that have been discussed up to this point can be seen.

```
main (int argc, char *argv[]) {

  Simulation_Control control;
  StimulusInitiator driver("Calc1Driver", "mytest");
  Checker checker("Calc1Checker");
  ScoreBoard score("Calc1ScoreBoard");

  driver.registerScoreBoard(score);
  checker.registerScoreBoard(score);

  for (int i = 0; i < 1000; i++)  {  // testcase execution loop
    driver.execute();
    checker.execute();
    control.clock();
  }
  control.simulation_exit();
}
```

▪ **FIGURE 6.13**

Top-level C++ test bench code for Calc1.

There are several obvious problems with the test bench of Figure 6.13. The most severe problem is the fact that the code calls the *driver* before the *checker*.

After the *driver* returns control to the test bench, there is no call to the simulation engine to update the model. This only occurs when the test bench calls *control.clock()*. Therefore, the results of the *driver* updates for the current cycle are not visible to *checker*. In addition, the *driver* cannot react to results that the *checker* will collect from the previous model update, *control.clock()* call last time through the loop. Remember, whenever the Calc1 design delivers results on the output interface, the *checker* calls the *ScoreBoard* to pop the registered, pending operation. This is the prerequisite for the clearance of the ready status of the corresponding port.

Because the program in Figure 6.13 calls the *checker* last, the *driver* will only be able to issue a new operation at the beginning of the next test bench cycle. As a result, this test bench is unable to issue back-to-back operations on a single port, a scenario that the functional specification of Calc1 clearly supports. Simply calling the *checker* before the *driver* will fix this problem. Now, directly after the update of the model by the simulation engine, the *checker* will observe a finished Operation, pop it from the *ScoreBoard*, and check its results. The *driver* component gets control right afterward and can issue the next Operation if the test case requires it to do so.

Another problem with Figure 6.13 is the hard-coded test file name. The top-level test bench accepts runtime parameters via the *main()* function interface. The test bench can parse the argv, argc parameter pair to extract a test file name provided by the user on the keyboard.

The hard-coded number of test bench cycles in Figure 6.10 is the final problem that needs discussion. To support different test files with varying number of test bench cycles, the driver needs to be able to communicate the fact that it has applied the last operation to Calc1, but this is not enough to determine the end of a simulation. Operations can take an undetermined number of cycles in the DUV. Only when the *checker* receives the results of the last operation from the outputs can test bench terminate the simulation run. To support this *end-of-test condition* checking correctly, the *driver* must signal the last operation to the scoreboard. For every operation that the *checker* pops from the scoreboard, the *checker* must now query the scoreboard for end-of-test and return that status back to the top-level test bench loop. In addition, the *checker* should verify at this point that the scoreboard has no more pending operations that the *checker* has not yet accounted for. We leave these changes of the C++ test bench as exercises for the reader at the end of the chapter.

Test Bench Execution Control

It is the main purpose of the library architecture in Figure 6.5 to encapsulate common functionality in a central place rather than letting the test bench writer replicate it, perhaps redundantly, across the user test bench code. There are two sources for common functionality that the library author can factor out and move into the library.

The first source is code that is typically part of *every* test bench. It would be a very repetitive, nonrewarding task for the verification team to include such code in every test bench, for example, the simulation engine abstraction layer, the file, and memory infrastructure layer.

Second, if certain control and communication flow mechanisms are available in the library, the test bench components can use those instead of personalizing such flows in special ways for every new test bench.

A good example for the second source of functionality is the test bench execution control. *Execution control* is the coordination of when to call the test bench components, in which sequence to call them, and when to finish the test.

As an example, Figure 6.14a shows the flow of the end-of-test control status for the environment of Calc1 as designed above. The *driver* detects the end-of-test condition first. The status flows from there to the scoreboard, to the checker, and finally to the top-level test bench loop.

Figure 6.14b shows a scheme, where *all* test bench components report status back to the library. The biggest advantage of this architecture is that the top-level test bench loop can now become generic. This scheme turns the *for* loop of Figure 6.13 into a *while* loop whose terminating condition is the overall end-of-test status.

Furthermore, it is now very useful to enhance the status to include more than only the condition that there are no more tests (operations)

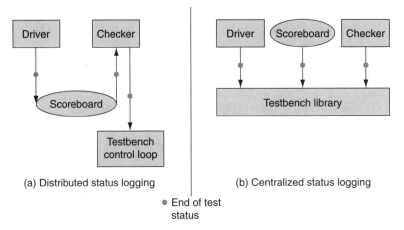

(a) Distributed status logging   (b) Centralized status logging

● End of test
   status

■ **FIGURE 6.14**

Distributed versus centralized status logging. All test bench components have to pass end-of-test status information to each other, via a predefined protocol when status logging is managed in a distributed way (a). The advantage of centralized status logging (b) is that the status is a first-class object supported by the test bench library, and there is no more code necessary that passes it between individual test bench components at specific times.

available for the current simulation run. If the status includes additional conditions, such as test error conditions, the structure in Figure 6.14b allows moving the test case termination check to the top-level test bench loop instead of hiding it in some test bench component (such as *StimulusInitiator*). The test bench top level now becomes the one place where the program makes *all* execution control decisions. This results in a single point of control for the test bench execution and therefore greatly improves the long-term maintainability of the test bench code.

Figure 6.15 shows the new interface for all test bench components in a changed class declaration for *TestbenchComponent*. Now every component returns its status to the caller of the *execute()* function. To let the library be the central place where the sum of all component status is accumulated it is necessary to let the library call the *execute()* functions of every component.

The *test bench execution control* layer in the library architecture in Figure 6.5 is the place where the calling of the *execute()* functions occurs. However, this layer can only accomplish this function only if

1. It has access to all test bench components and their *execute()* functions, and

2. It knows the correct calling sequence for these functions

This is the purpose of the *test bench object registry* in Figure 6.5. The object registry records every instance of a test bench component. Because every component class is a subclass of the base class

```
enum ExecuteStatus { done, error, continue };

class TestbenchComponent {

 public:
  TestbenchComponent(string name);

  void trace() { cout << "Name of component" << mName << endl;

  ExecuteStatus execute() = 0;

 private:
  string mName;
}
```

■ **FIGURE 6.15**

New *TestbenchComponent* class declaration including the status logging mechanism. Every test bench component's *execute()* function now returns status information. The test bench execution control layer accumulates this status and makes it available to the top-level of the test bench to make runtime control decisions.

TestbenchComponent, which enforces the existence of an *execute()* function, the base class constructor can register the component in a class *ObjectRegistry* behind the scenes of the library and the *execute()* function with the *execution control* layer.

Now that the library calls the *execute()* functions, there is a need for a mechanism that lets the user specify the calling sequence of the components to the library. For this example, the sequence of the component constructor calls was chosen for this, meaning that the *execute()* function for a component is called first if its constructor is called first.

As a result of all these changes concerning execution control, Figure 6.16 shows the new test bench top-level code, including the now simplified and completely generic test execution loop.

The library for Figure 6.16 was also changed to move the call to all *execute()* functions inside the library service *control.clock()*. This function now lets the library call all *execute()* functions in the defined sequence before the HDL simulation proceeds.

As a welcome side effect, moving this sequencing control to the library also opens opportunities to enhance performance of the test bench. Whenever a particular component indicates that it is *done* for the rest of the simulation of a test, the library can simply skip the call to its *execute()* function from then on.

Adding Additional Components

With the centralized execution control layer, it is now very easy to include additional test bench components or remove components without any need to touch the code of the test bench loop again. All a verification

```
main (int argc, char *argv[]) {

  Simulation_Control control;
  StimulusInitiator driver("Calc1Driver", "mytest");
  Checker checker("Calc1Checker");
  ScoreBoard score("Calc1ScoreBoard");

  driver.registerScoreBoard(score);
  checker.registerScoreBoard(score);

  do {
    control.clock();
  } while (control.status == busy);

  if (control.status == error) {
    … // error handling
  }

  control.simulation_exit();
}
```

■ **FIGURE 6.16**

Top-level C++ test bench code for Calc1, revised, with the test bench library now managing execution and status control.

engineer needs to do is add or delete the component's constructor call. Obviously, the new control structure has improved code maintainability greatly, which stems from the fact that the different components have become more modular and their code is more independent from each other.

Clearly, modularity becomes more and more important as DUVs and their test benches grow in complexity. This is also referred to as *scaling*. The more modular a test bench is, the better it scales as design and simulation environments grow.

Multiple Tests

The next step in improved versatility of our test bench is the addition of support for multiple tests. We can achieve the capability to run several tests in a sequence by calling the simulation engine and the test bench multiple times in a row. However, the start-up phase of the simulation, including initialization of the test bench, can become quite costly for large DUVs. To avoid this start-up overhead, it should be possible to support the execution of multiple tests in one run of simulation engine and test bench. This is accomplished by changing the test bench input parameter to be the name of a file, which contains a list of test files. There will be a main loop around the test case loop in Figure 6.16, which processes the list of tests. In addition, it is now necessary to reset the DUV between tests, which has the advantage that once a single test ends with a simulation error, the verification team is able to rerun just this test without having to rerun the previous tests of the original test list.

Execution Phases

With more complex DUVs it is not realistic to expect the verification engineer to group all the active test bench code in just one function: *execute()*. Typically, the work a component does during a simulation has different phases. For example, the test bench might need to initialize the checker when the DUV is reset at the beginning of a test (*init phase*). It then typically accumulates checking information during the runtime of the test (*execution phase*). Finally, at the end of the test there is a sweep over the accumulated information (*end-of-test phase*).

It would be possible to keep state information about which phase the test case is in, inside every component and have the *execute()* functions switch to the appropriate phase based on the current state. However, the test bench library can directly support this concept of finer modularization into separate functions. Figure 6.17 illustrates how such a scheme leads to a flow of execution control that lets the user position components into the different phases of a test bench run.

Test Bench Modularity

Centralizing infrastructure functionality can improve the modularity of a test bench. There are other ways to modularize complex test benches to improve their maintainability. As stated earlier, test bench development is software development, and therefore, all techniques of software engineering apply here. A major advantage of using C/C++ for test bench development is that many of these techniques apply directly.

The test bench components themselves do not need to have a monolithic structure similar to the one discussed so far in the examples. They can utilize other classes, and the member functions can call other functions.

As an example for the further application of modularization, consider the repetitive structure of the input and output ports of Calc1. There are four identical ports on both the input and output side. It would be possible to split out a common subcomponent for each of the three test bench components (*StimulusInitiator*, *Checker*, *ScoreBoard*). For example, there could be a *driver port* class that applies to a generic input port and is instantiated four times inside *StimulusInitiator*. Each instantiation takes a parameter that indicates to which of the four physical ports this particular port object connects. The common port class does eliminate the replicated code that processes four ports in the original test bench. However, reduction of tedious and error prone replication is not the only advantage. In addition, it is now very simple to add or remove ports in Calc1 and adjust the test bench easily. Good software engineering greatly improves this type of maintenance and scaling work.

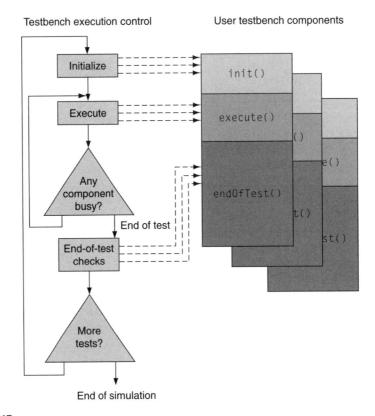

▪ **FIGURE 6.17**

Test bench execution control with separated execution phases. Instead of the single *execute()* function, every test bench component now has three separate functions—*init()*, *execute()*, and *endOfTest()*—that are called during the three respective phases of test execution.

For the design and development of C/C++ test benches, the verification team can use all common software modeling techniques available, as well as software development tools such as integrated development environments (IDEs) and debuggers that are available for all C/C++ programmers.

Test Bench Building Block Objects: *Params*

The last part of the test bench library architecture of Figure 6.5 that needs discussion are additional test bench common building block objects. This library layer contains an open-ended set of utility classes whose main purpose is productivity improvement for the test bench writer.

As an example of an important type of utility class, we introduce the class *Param*. As the name indicates, a *Param* object is a parameter for a

```
class Param {
 public:
  Param (string name);

  string getValue();
  void   setValue();
}
```

■ **FIGURE 6.18**

Definition of the utility class *Param*. An instance of this class is a named parameter usable anywhere inside test bench code. The constructor of *Param* requires a unique name for the object to enable the test bench to assign values to the object at runtime.

```
main (int argc, char *argv[]) {
  Param testcase("testfile");
  Simulation_Control control;
  ….
  control.initParams("my_paramfile");

  …
}
```

■ **FIGURE 6.19**

Instance of a *Param* object in the top-level C++ test bench program. The *Param* named *testfile* will be used in the program as a parameter that holds the name of a test case list file. *Simulation_Control*'s function *initParams()* reads a file (similar to the one in Figure 6.20) and assigns values to the *Param* objects listed.

test bench or one of its components. It is the nature of a parameter that it has no fixed value at compile time. The versatility of a *Param* comes from the fact that its value can be assigned at runtime. With a *Param* object, it is possible to set values of test bench variables at runtime and therefore influence certain behaviors of the test bench dynamically.

Figure 6.18 shows a simple *Param* class and Figure 6.19 shows an instance of a *Param* at the start of our example test bench. Every *Param* instance gets its own unique name, by which the test bench library can identify it unambiguously. The *Simulation_Control* class now needs the capability to parse a file (*Param* file). This file supports a simple assignment syntax, which names a *Param* on the left-hand side and assigns it a value on the right-hand side.

The *initParams* function of *Simulation_Control* parses the file specified as an argument and assigns the string values found in the *Param* file to the corresponding *Param* object found in the test bench.

In the example shown in Figures 6.18 through 6.20, the application of a *Param* simplifies the passing of a test case file name into the test bench. The verification team does this now through the *Param* file *my_paramfile*. The team changes the name of the test case file by changing the value of the *testfile Param* assignment inside *my_paramfile*. It is easy to see

```
testfile = "my_tests" ;
```

▪ **FIGURE 6.20**

Example of *Param* file *my_paramfile*. A *Param* file contains assignments of values to named *Param* objects in the test bench. *Simulation_Control*'s function *initParams()* reads such a file and assigns the values to the corresponding *Params*.

```
class RandomIntParam {
 public:
  Param (string name);

  int drawValue();
 private:

  ...

}
```

▪ **FIGURE 6.21**

Random integer *Param* class definition. *RandomIntParam* is a named *Param* that is able to provide a randomly generated integer through its interface function *drawValue()*. The class contains private data structures to manage a seed and random value range information such as the one shown in the examples in Figure 6.22.

how this scheme can simplify the management of many runtime parameters.

An important extension of the *Param* idea is the support of randomization tasks in the test bench.

Figure 6.21 shows the class *RandomIntParam*, which holds a named parameter with value type integer. Instead of reading the value of such a parameter once with a *getValue()* function, the intention of this parameter is for the test bench code to *draw* a value multiple times, whenever it needs a new random integer value. The name of the access function *drawValue()* indicates this usage.

Initializing a *RandomIntParam* with a fixed value from a *Param* file, as in the case of the basic *Param* above, does not appear useful. Figure 6.22 shows two examples for a possible use of file-supplied initial value. The first example shows a range definition. A possible implementation of *RandomIntParam* could use this value to limit the range of possible *drawValue()* results to be between 0 and 99. Although the probability for all numbers within the range of *my_random_param* is the same, the syntax for *my_other_random_param* is more elaborate, showing a possibility to specify multiple ranges and associate a weight specification with each range. The example forces the *drawValue()* function to return a value between "0" and "99" 90% of the time, the value "100" 1% of the time, and the value "101" 9% of the time.

Utility classes such as the *Param* classes show how the architects of the test bench library can easily extend it with additional functionality

```
my_random_param = 0 - 99;

my_other_random_param = { { 0 - 99, 90 }, { 100, 1 }, { 101, 9 } };
```

■ **FIGURE 6.22**

Example syntax for range and weighted range definitions for class *RandomIntParam*. The function *drawValue()* for *my_random_param* will return an integer between 0 and 99 with uniform distribution. *drawValue()* for *my_other_random_param* will return an integer in the range "0 to 99" 90% of the time, the value "100" 1%, and "101" 9% of the time.

that makes the test bench writers more productive because they can rely on already implemented utilities instead of rewriting them all the time.

Test Bench Performance

As test benches scale up in size and complexity with their corresponding DUVs, it is important to monitor their performance.

Chapter 5 showed how the industry puts into technology that improves simulation engine performance. It would be a waste of all this technology if the verification team did not regularly monitor the simulation test bench for its performance characteristics.

The runtime of a simulation job splits between time spent in the HDL model (the DUV) and time spent in the test bench. Efficient test benches utilize 20% to 40% of the total runtime. Obviously, such a number is just a rule of thumb. The key is to balance driver and checker robustness with efficiency, while avoiding test bench redundancy. A very efficient test bench measured by this performance ratio might be one that checks very little and does not capture all of the DUV internal bugs. On the other hand, a test bench, which checks and uncovers many internal bugs, might be very performance invasive to the overall simulation execution.

However, the following reasoning should illustrate how important it is to keep an eye on performance to optimize the vast resources that verification projects consume. If we assume a utilization of 50% of the simulation time by the test bench, it is not possible to speed up the overall simulation efficiency by more than two times with a faster simulation engine. Even if the verification team would buy the impossible, very expensive, *infinitely fast* simulation engine, capable of executing the HDL model in zero time, the overall performance improvement would just be a factor of two.

The verification team can measure the performance of a C/C++-based test bench with standard system utilities available to all programmers. Usually, the C/C++ compiler has a parameter that lets the programmer instrument the output code for performance measurement. After the run of a typical simulation job, it is then possible to inspect the data generated by the instrumentation with a profiler tool such as *gprof*. This tool prints out the details of time spent in each section of the test bench program. An advantage of C++ is to have such tools readily available. The reader can find usage information for gprof in various places on the Internet and as part of the Unix operating system reference information.

6.1.3 High-Level Verification Languages

During the past few years, special purpose languages for test bench writing have gained much focus and popularity. These HVLs are a variety of *domain-specific* languages. Such languages have built-in functionality targeted for one specific application domain. The idea is that if the vocabulary of such a language is built directly in terms of the application area, users will learn more easily how to use the language and will be instantly more productive compared with using a general-purpose programming language.

The following discusses some of the features all of the available HVLs share. The discussion of important features for test bench writers continues by turning to several example HVLs and highlighting some of their unique features. This is not an attempt to give the reader detailed usage information because this discussion should provide an overall map of the field of HVLs, a skeleton that makes further, more detailed study of an individual HVL easier.

Features of HVLs

All HVLs usually provide the following basic functionality.

- *Simulation independence* is fundamental for any such language. This allows the verification engineer to write a test bench that is portable between simulation engines from different vendors.

- *Full visibility* to all HDL model objects (signal, registers, arrays, etc.) is necessary to control all aspects of the DUV. It must be possible to read and write these model facilities.

- *High-level programming language features* such as complex data types, object-oriented class definitions, and modularity are another requirement that all popular HVLs share.

In addition to this list of features, modern HVLs include a few new features.

Temporal Expressions

The specification of sequences of events over time is at the heart of complex assertion checking (see Chapter 3). The HVLs have built-in constructs to express such temporal expression concisely.

Constrained Random Generation

Random generation of stimulus is one of the core capabilities of an efficient test bench. Thus far, the discussion of randomization has been limited to the probabilistic selection of a single value. Interfaces of real-life DUVs will not allow the free randomization of input signals and busses. Interfaces follow specific protocols. The purpose of a protocol is, of course, the limitation of the possible input values to a specific domain. There are two dimensions for *constraints* on input interfaces.

First is the value dependency of between different signals at the same time. For example, if the driver currently pushes a new operation into the Calc1 design, the reset bus should remain all zeroes during the two cycles it takes to launch the request.

Second are value dependencies over time. This constraint specifies value sequences.

Such dependencies can exist between different signals, or they can be necessary for the same signal. For example, once initiated, the reset of Calc1 should stay on for seven cycles. These are sequential constraints.

HVLs offer built-in features to express constraints, thus making the authors of driver code more productive.

Coverage Collection

One important measure of the quality of the verification cycle is the quantification of how much of the design functionality the simulation process has covered. HVLs offer built-in mechanisms to express which coverage information to collect over time. These data supply the verification team with information about which goals the test bench has hit during simulation.

Automatic Garbage Collection

One of the features the custom HVLs typically offer addresses test bench complexity and programming safety: the user does not (have to) directly control dynamic memory management. The runtime system of the language handles allocation and deallocation of dynamic memory automatically. The system tracks references to dynamically allocated memory and destroys data structures that are not referenced anymore from anywhere in the test bench. This circumvents completely the problem with memory leaks discussed in the context of C/C++ test benches above.

Interpretation Versus Compilation

Similar to any programming language, HVLs need their own compilers, debuggers, and runtime system. Some of these languages offer an interpreted runtime environment, which gives the HVL a script-like appeal in that there is no need to compile and link the test bench. To be able to achieve sufficient performance scaling capabilities, it is a requirement that the HVL environment also provides a compilation environment to support optimized runtime code.

A Flavor of OpenVera

OpenVera is an HVL marketed by Synopsys [9]. Synopsys donated the language definition to a consortium of several electronic design automation (EDA) vendors to create an environment in which multiple vendors support the language.

This is an object-oriented programming language that supports complex data types, classes, and inheritance. The syntax of the language is similar to C++ or Java for the programming language features.

OpenVera has a built-in data type that matches the four-value signal type provided by the Verilog HDL ("0," "1," "x," "z"). The connection to the HDL model in OpenVera uses the concept of test case *ports*, *interfaces*, and *bindings*. A *port* declares inputs to the test bench coming from the model. An *interface* specifies attributes of these inputs, such as signal widths, and the clock signal, which is used to synchronize the collection of the signal values from the model. OpenVera connects interface/port signals to the HDL signals via *bindings* by using hierarchical path names. The bindings unambiguously specify the location of the HDL signals in the model hierarchy.

The foundation for random generation in OpenVera is the concept of random variables (for an example, see Figure 6.23). The test bench declares the randomization domain and its boundaries at variable declaration time. OpenVera also supports the specification of weights to subdomains similar to the functionality discussed in Figure 6.22.

```
variable my_random_param in { 1:99, 101, 200:299 };

class foo {

  rand int rand1, rand2, rand3;

  constraint cons {
    rand1 > rand2 + rand3;
  }
}
```

▪ **FIGURE 6.23**

Random value support in OpenVera. At the creation of the variable *my_random_param*, its value is drawn from the range definition. The constraint block cons defines dependencies between random values of several variables.

In addition, it is possible to express constraints via named *constraint blocks* (*cons* in Figure 6.23), which limit the randomization of separate but related variables. Constraint blocks are declarative expressions, which express relationships between variables that are supposed to hold true throughout any randomization of the variables referenced. OpenVera enforces the constraints and the resulting values assigned to the random variables by a call to a function called *randomize()*; this would be *foo.randomize()* for the example above.

Driving randomized values into a DUV by using a mix of programmed code and declarative constraints expressed as value relationships is a powerful and productive method to design a test bench. OpenVera and other HVLs create random constrained variable values with a software component called *constraint solver* in the runtime system of the language. Constraint solving will be discussed in further detail in Chapter 7.

It is possible to specify constraints that the solver can *never* satisfy because the specification is contradictory. We call this a *constraint error*. If the OpenVera runtime environment detects this situation, it halts the simulation. The detection is only possible if the relations used to express constraints do not refer to other random variables. If the set of constraint expressions connects several random variables, the *randomize()* will return an error. It is the responsibility of the user test bench code to react appropriately to such constraint errors.

OpenVera has a unique feature to generate sequences of randomized variable values with its *stream generator* capability. A stream generator is similar to a grammar definition in *Backus-Naur Form* (BNF) format, which specifies how to generate a series of tokens [10]. BNF is a general scheme to specify derivation rules. A derivation starts with a complex, compound symbol that we replace by successively applying derivation rules until no more replacements are possible with the given set of rules. The derivation process stops at leafs for which no further replacement is available. Figure 6.24 shows an example for an OpenVera stream generator that defines the derivation rules to generate Calc1 test operations.

Figure 6.24 starts the specification of the Calc1 test format with the top-level rule *Operation*. It is possible to read this notation like a

```
Operation : Port Delay Command Operand1 Operand2 ;

Port      : Port1 | Port2 | Port3 | Port4 ;

Command   : Nop | Add | Subtract | ShiftLeft | ShiftRight | Invalid ;

.... .
```

■ **FIGURE 6.24**

OpenVera stream generator scheme to generate Calc1 tests.

```
Port      :   &(2) Port1 {printf("Port1\n");}
             | &(1) Port2 {printf("Port2\n");}
             | &(1) Port3 {printf("Port3\n");}
             | &(1) Port4 {printf("Port4\n");} ;
```

■ **FIGURE 6.25**

OpenVera stream generator with executable statements and weights.

generation scheme that always starts at Operation and ends with a complete compound value of a Calc1 operation.

The line in Figure 6.24 that has Operation on the right-hand side of the colon is the first replacement rule. The application of such a rule replaces the left-hand side with the right-hand side. If a component on the right-hand side has its own replacement rule, the generation scheme continues with the application of that rule. The scheme traverses depth-first recursively to resolve every component with its replacement. After the successful replacement of a component, the next component is resolved until all top-level components have been fully replaced recursively using the rules of the grammar.

Starting at the top of Figure 6.24, the generator specifies how five components replace Operation, thus effectively constructing an Operation from these components. The generator then replaces each component in turn with its replacement components until it has assembled a complete Operation as specified by the grammar.

Replacement rules often contain choices. For example, Figure 6.24 allows the replacement of *Command* by one of six different components. The logical *or* operator symbol "|" expresses the set of choices available at such decision points. Unless specified otherwise, OpenVera stream generators will make a random choice. However, it is possible to annotate the choices with weights. Such weights enable the user to constrain the generation in a certain direction.

As it visits grammar components sequentially, quite naturally OpenVera allows executable statements to be interspersed with grammar components. As OpenVera unrolls a grammar scheme, at every point it encounters a statement in the grammar specification, it executes the statement.

Figure 6.25 combines these two capabilities. *Port*'s replacement rule has to pick one of four alternatives. After making a choice, the rule instructs OpenVera to print a message. The random selection between the four possibilities is constrained by the designation of a weight expression at each alternative, &() expression). OpenVera allows any expression as weight specification. References to test bench variables in weight expressions allow verification engineers to specify very sophisticated stream generators.

In this example, OpenVera will choose Port1 40% of the time, leaving a 20% probability for each of the other ports.

```
struct BaseOperation {
  cmd  : [noop=0b0000, add=0b0001, sub=0b0010, shl=0b0101, shr=0b0110] (bits:4);
  op1  : uint (bits:32);
  op2  : uint (bits:32);
};
```

■ **FIGURE 6.26**

e base struct type declaration.

```
struct Calc1Operation like BaseOperation {
  port : [port1, port2, port3, port4];
};
```

■ **FIGURE 6.27**

e subtype declaration and extending a subtype.

OpenVera is a complete HVL that supports a number of features and requirements. More detailed overviews of OpenVera's features are available [9, 11]. The temporal assertion portion of the language is also available in the new, emerging HDL SystemVerilog [5].

A Flavor of *e*

The EDA vendor Verisity (now under Synopsys) develops and markets an HVL called *e*, which is the center of the test bench authoring and debug tool Specman [12]. Verisity has donated the definition of the *e* language to an IEEE standardization workgroup [13]. Similar to OpenVera, *e* is a fully featured HVL, which offers all the functionality described in the overview of HVLs. The following discusses only a few selected highlights of *e*.

e supports all common concepts of object-oriented programming languages such as data abstraction and inheritance. The basic language concept is a *struct*, which declares a class or a derived class. Similar to C++, *e* classes contain declarations of member objects such as data structures, functions, and procedures. A subtype class derives from a base *struct* type in the usual object-oriented inheritance relation.

Figures 6.26, 6.27, and 6.28 demonstrate some of the data structuring features of *e* by using *struct* declarations. Figure 6.26 defines a base *struct* called *BaseOperation* for the Calc1 operations data members command (cmd) and the two operands (op1, op2). In Figure 6.27 the subtype Calc1Operation derives from *BaseOperation* and adds the *port* member.

Figure 6.28 shows two examples how *e* allows the user to add additional declarations to an already existing struct using the *extend* clause. The first declaration simply adds the *delay* member data. The second declaration adds constraints to all Calc1Operation structs that a test bench

```
extend Calc1Operation {
  delay : uint [1..10];
};

extend port1 Calc1Operation {
  keep delay >= 2;
  keep cmd == add;
  keep op1 + op2 < 16;
};
```

▪ **FIGURE 6.28**

e extend declaration.

will create. However, the constraints apply only to those Calc1Operation structs whose *port* member has a value *port1*. The constraints guide the *e* runtime environment to generate only add operations for port 1, keep the sum of the operands below 16, and furthermore limit the delay until the next operation to a value between 2 and 10. The *port1* extension keeps the lower limit of delay to 2, and the first extension in Figure 6.28 limits all delay values to a maximum of 10.

With the *extend* clause, the *e* language provides a post object-oriented programming technique to test bench coding called *aspect-oriented* programming [14]. The main method object-oriented languages offer to decompose large software systems is the tree structure of class inheritance. If the programmer wants to add additional members to a class already compiled into the software, the natural approach is to derive a subclass and add the members there. However, the *extend* feature of *e* allows the user to "open up" already existing class definitions, add member data or functions, and change attributes of existing members. Adding constraints to the members of Calc1Operation in Figure 6.28 is such an example.

Extensions in *e* are not limited to the same source file that contains the original class definition. This opens the possibility of a powerfully layered approach to test bench writing. First, the verification team creates a base test bench with class declarations that cover the full range of possibilities allowed by the DUV specification. Figure 6.29 indicates this by placing the Calc1Operation class into the file *Calc1.e*. Calc1.e contains the full specification of an operation that applies to all ports of Calc1 and is part of the base test bench that is used in all simulations. The file *test_port1_adds.e* in Figure 6.29 defines constraints for some *aspects* of the base test bench, like port1 operations. The constraints are contained in a separate file that is loaded on demand, when the verification team decides to subset the behavior of the test bench. It is very practical to keep different constraint sets in different such add-on test bench files.

```
test_port1_adds.e:
extend port1 Calc1Operation {
 keep delay <= 2;.....
};
    Calc1.e:
    struct Calc1Operation {
     port : ..
     op1  : ..
     op2  : ..
     };
```

■ **FIGURE 6.29**

Creating tests in *e* by extending base classes and using aspect-oriented programming.

The verification team can use add-on files, or sets of related add-on files, as a template for the generation of biased random tests that target a certain aspect of the DUV functionality. This approach is much more powerful than storing many static, directed tests in separate test case files.

The *e* language allows the *extend* feature to change much more than the generation of random data values. For example, it is possible to append additional code at the beginning or the end of class member functions, allowing the verification engineer to add, dynamically at runtime, additional common functionality such as logging and debug tracing to a set of base test bench classes without the need to change the original class definitions.

The verification team must use this powerful flexibility of on-the-fly extensions carefully. On larger projects, in which the test bench can easily consist of thousands of source files, it is quickly possible to lose track of all the files and team members who define extensions to classes. A well-defined test bench architecture and rules that govern who can override base class behavior guarantee that a large test bench team does not lose control of their *e* code structure.

The *e* language offers *units* as special types of *structs*. A *unit* can only exist once in a test bench. It carries user-defined data structs inside and is itself typically connected to the DUV via an *HDL path*. This path gives all model facility references, which are inside a unit, a common prefix, and thus creates a context of hierarchy for the unit.

All user-defined units are rooted inside a unit called *sys*, which provides a common runtime context similar to the *main()* function is C. Other runtime functionality, such as file inputs/outputs (I/O), the simulation engine interface, and current session information are also encapsulated global units.

```
struct StimulusInitiator {
  event port1Ready, port2Ready, port3Ready, port4Ready;

  on port1Ready {// port 1 code //};
  on port2Ready {// port 2 code //};
  ...
};
```

▪ **FIGURE 6.30**

Sketch of an *e* *StimulusInitiator*.

Key structural elements of the *e* language are *events*, which synchronize the behavior between the HDL model and the test bench and among test bench components. Events allow specification of behavior over time.

Figure 6.30 shows how the use of events lets the *StimulusInitiator* for Calc1 synchronize itself with other test bench components. The struct for this test bench component connects the generation and transfer of an operation to the Calc1 inputs with the readiness of the corresponding port via the *on* clause. Whenever the test bench signals a port's ready event, it subsequently activates the connected member function.

Test bench code either *emits* events explicitly or associates the definition of the event to a *temporal expression*, which specifies a sequence of events over time. If the *e* runtime environment detects the occurrence of this sequence, it will emit the signal and broadcast it to all receiving test bench components. The reader is referred to a Web site [13] to find the details of the *e* event and temporal expression constructs.

Temporal expressions play an important role in the specification of properties for formal verification, and their importance and use in the context of formal verification will be discussed in detail in Chapter 10.

So far, all member methods discussed here were truly functions, meaning that once called, program control returns only at the end of a function. The *e* language also supports *time-consuming methods (TCM)*. These are functions that suspend their execution to either *wait* for or synchronize (*sync*) with the signaling of an event. A TCM is code whose sequential flow does not start and end during the same HDL model time but covers several simulation time steps.

The reader interested in a more thorough overview of *e* is referred to a Web site that contains a full reference manual [13]. There is also a book that covers the *e* language in depth [15].

A Flavor of SystemC

SystemC is a large C++ library that supports high-level hardware design, modeling, simulation, and verification. At this point, the Open SystemC Initiative (OSCI) drives the development of the library and provides the source code of the library free for download on the Internet [16].

SystemC originally targeted mostly the simulation and specification of designs in C++ as its main goal. The synthesis of subset of SystemC to register transfer level (RTL) logic is actually supported by several EDA vendors. This chapter will not discuss these aspects of SystemC; important here is one part of the SystemC library called the SystemC Verification Library (SCV). OSCI added SCV more recently, and its origin was the open-source project TestBuilder [17].

In the following, we review some aspects of SCV's large functionality.

The major EDA vendors support SystemC at this point, which guarantees test bench portability between *different simulation engines*. However, the library does not yet have a fully elaborated API, which would allow an easy, uniform implementation of the simulation engine abstraction layer for an arbitrary simulator. This is one of the still evolving areas of SCV.

SCV supports a range of built-in data types, all of which are also part of the design and modeling portion of SystemC. There are *sc_int* and *sc_uint* with fixed widths (64 or less), as well as the corresponding *sc_bigint* and *sc_biguint* types, with the latter providing arbitrary precision integers. The type *sc_bv* handles arbitrary length bit-vectors with bit-wise and range-wise access. sc_logic is a vector with a four-value data domain (Verilog-style: "0,1,x,z").

The library offers a number of services based on the built-in data types. The main areas are as follows:

- Randomization and seed management

- Constrained randomization

- Weighted randomization

- Support for transactions; transaction monitoring, and recording

- Sparse array support

Figure 6.31 shows some examples of the randomization support using built-in C++ types. The data type of the random variable functions as a C++ template parameter in its declaration.

The class *scv_smart_ptr* is what the C++ literature calls a *smart pointer* because it has the same look and feel as a data pointer. With a uniform

```
scv_smart_ptr<int> delay;
delay->keep_out(7);
delay->keep_only(0,10);
delay->next();          // --> generate new random value
```

■ **FIGURE 6.31**

Randomization for simple data types in SystemC Verification Library.

```
class Calc1Operands {
  sc_uint<32> op1;
  sc_uint<32> op2;
}

scv_smart_ptr<Calc1Operands> op;

op->next();    // completely randomized operands
```

▪ **FIGURE 6.32**

Randomization for user-defined data types in SystemC Verification Library.

distribution, SCV's constraint solver assigns the variable *delay* in Figure 6.31 a random value between "0" and "10," excluding the value "7" at all times.

A remarkable feature of SCV is the capability to declare user-defined data types to the system in such a way that constrained, randomized value assignments are available to these types exactly as for built-in types.

Figure 6.32 demonstrates how to pass the user-defined type Calc1Operands as a template parameter into the declaration of an *scv_smart_ptr*. As a result, every call to the member function *next()* will return a fully randomized value.

Obviously, a completely random selection is usually not what is needed in a test bench. Figure 6.33 shows the declaration of constraints used in SCV test benches. Because the library has to stay within the confines of C++, the constraint declarations are not quite as elegant and concise compared with those of OpenVera or *e*. However, the advantage with SCV is that the verification team can easily integrate any existing C++ class library into a test bench and have test bench functions available for those imported classes as well.

Figure 6.33 also illustrates the definition of derived constraints. *Small-IntConstraint* limits the sum of the two operands just as in Figure 6.28 for *e*, MyConstraint eliminates the case of equal operand values in addition to the first constraint. The test bench example instantiates a random variable, whose value SCV will generate following the associated constraint specifications.

Test benches use the *transaction-recording* feature, which SCV offers, typically in the implementation of a stimulus initiator. The generation component creates new transactions, which the protocol component translates into applied signal changes on the concrete DUV input interface.

Similar to the technique used by *scv_smart_ptr*, SCV also offers a class *scv_tr_generation*, which allows the user to declare a custom transaction with its data content to the library. The user then declares the beginning and end of individual transactions in the test bench code. These calls

```
class SmallIntConstraint: public scv_constraint_base { // basic constraint
 public:
  scv_smart_ptr<Calc1Operands> data;
  SCV_CONSTRAINT_CTOR(SmallIntConstraint) {
    SCV_CONSTRAINT(data->op1+data->op2 < 16);
  }
}

class MyConstraint: public SmallIntConstraint {
 public:
  SCV_CONSTRAINT_CTOR(MyConstraint) {
    SCV_CONSTRAINT(data->op1 != data->op2);
  }
}

MyConstraint m("constraint");

m.data->next();  // <-- constrained randomized value generation
```

■ **FIGURE 6.33**

Constrained randomization for user-defined data types in SystemC Verification Library.

records transactions in an external database and are accessible by external debug tools after the simulation is finished. To maximize the use of transactions in the debug process, it is also possible to record causal relationships between transactions. External viewer tools can visualize these relationships when they display a trace from a previous simulation run.

As was mentioned above, SCV is a library that is still evolving. Important areas that still need further definition and development are *temporal and nontemporal assertions, temporal constraints,* and support for *functional coverage*.

6.1.4 Other Test Bench Tools

To complete the discussion on test bench writing tools, this short section mentions a number of other approaches that have been popular with verification teams.

Scripting Languages

Before EDA companies focused on verification as a bottleneck for hardware design projects and developed HVLs as productivity aid, verification teams made use of scripting languages to write test benches and generate tests.

In the open source domain, there is a number of *scripting languages* that support rapid development of software [18–20]. The advantages of a scripting language are usually

- Interpreted execution: no compile and link cycle

- Weak type system: no tedious type declarations for data variables

- High-level data types: lists, dictionaries, hash-arrays

- Strong support of text processing

- Easy access to operating system services: files, directories, data management systems

Interestingly, there is no common, popular library for any of the scripting languages in the context of verification. All their uses have been more or less ad hoc. Undoubtedly, the ease of using scripting languages has led to their wide popularity.

However, there is typically a 5 to 10 times performance gap between an interpreted scripting language and a compiled programming language. This strong disadvantage severely limited the success of scripting languages as test bench authoring tools. If we assume a 50/50 split between the time spent in the HDL model versus the C/C++ test bench, the use of a scripting language would shift this relation dramatically. Assuming a 10 times worse execution speed of a scripting language, 90% of the simulation time would be spent in the test bench. This is clearly not an acceptable balance and use of large simulation resources.

Simulation runs are usually not standalone activities. There is a need to maintain the HDL and test bench code in source code libraries. Setting up a simulation run is preceded by a checkout of source code, compile, model build, and job distribution to a host simulation machine, and in the end the collection and triage of simulation results. Many of these data management and preparation activities can greatly benefit from the use of the flexible, highly productive scripting languages. Therefore, a verification engineer should be fluent in at least one or two of them.

Waveform Editors

There have been many attempts to use a graphical language to specify test bench behavior. Waveforms or timing diagrams are a very popular method to convey expected or generated signal changes in documentation of hardware interfaces. Consequently, waveform editors have been promising approaches for graphical test bench authoring [21–23].

One of the limitations of strictly graphical waveforms is that they only specify one scenario. To express the variations or alternatives in a waveform that is expected or to be generated on the interface of the DUV, these graphical tools need other graphic user interface (GUI) elements that allow the user to specify classes of possible waveforms.

These constructs lead to a need to connect individual waveforms and pages of waveforms together with property sheets. For realistically complex interfaces, the graphical model does not scale well, and the amount of necessary waveforms and property sheets become excessive.

In addition to the complexity of the specification medium itself, waveforms share one disadvantage with all other graphical specification methods. Once a more complex specification is finished, the daily maintenance of updates, such as signal name and property changes, requires typically more work in a graphical than a textual representation.

Consequently, timing diagrams and waveform editors have been limited to small design block simulation.

On the other hand, timing diagrams are a powerful and efficient communication medium between designers and verification engineers. Because of the popularity of waveforms in their informal use with paper and pencil, there remains hope that at some point an effective user interface technology will open timing diagram specification to a wider verification audience.

6.2 VERIFICATION COVERAGE

The verification team needs metrics for the quality and completeness of their work as the project proceeds over time.

There are obvious completeness criteria the verification team can derive from the discussions of the verification plan in Chapter 4. Keeping track of the status of different verification tasks is a fundamental piece of information about how well a project is progressing. Knowledge about which tests the verification engineers have indeed exercised from the test plan provides a necessary metric. Watching the bug rate is certainly a key piece of scorekeeping that guides a project.

Still, the central question for the verification team remains: "When is verification complete?"

Once the team has finished all planned verification tasks, run all tests, and the bug rate has dropped to zero, is it time to declare success? Kantrowitz and Noack provide a very insightful case study, which discusses this question from the perspective of a large industry project [24].

As discussed in the DVD video chip example from Chapter 1, exhaustive simulation of even small designs is not possible. The following example recalls the combinatorial explosion that makes verification such a daunting task.

Let the DUV be a 16-bit adder. Simulating all combinatorial possibilities of the adder takes 4 billion simulation cycles, assuming that this circuit does not have state-holding elements. If the project uses a simulation engine that is able to run 1,000 cycles per second, the team still needs around 50 days to simulate this trivial DUV exhaustively. When does the verification team stop simulation? Is it good enough to continue until the simulation has been bug-free for 3 days? How do they know that another day of simulation would not yield yet another bug?

Furthermore, is it truly necessary to simulate the adder DUV exhaustively to make a convincing case of verification completeness?

It is the task of *verification coverage analysis* to convince the verification team that they have done *sufficient* verification, not exhaustive verification, to satisfy defined quality criteria.

The following overview of coverage, its many facets and techniques, provides the reader with a conceptual framework for verification quality measurement. It also reminds that some of the metrics, which are easy to implement, are not necessarily good ones. Good coverage analysis relies on insightful instrumentation of the verification environment by using a variety of methods and metrics, most of them not automatically generated.

6.2.1   Overview

Verification coverage is the measurement of state space that simulation-based verification has touched in the entire environment. Coverage can measure DUV internal states, queues, and activities, as well as DUV inputs and even states of the verification environment components. Fundamentally, coverage is a measurement of how *well* the stimulus components have exercised the DUV. Coverage cannot make a statement on the quality or robustness of the checking components.

There are two completely complementary sides of the verification coverage task. First, there is coverage of the verification environment. Here, the objective is to measure how well the verification stimulus environment covers the *specification* of the design. This coverage aspect is called functional *verification test coverage*. Second, there is coverage of the function implemented in the DUV. This metric seeks to measure how well the verification stimulus activates or exercises the *implementation* of the specification in the concrete design. This coverage task is called functional *implementation coverage*. Figure 6.34 shows the two areas of coverage analysis side by side.

The base activity that precedes any type of coverage analysis is the collection of coverage measurements. The verification team collects the measures for functional test coverage from the stimulus initiator component, the test case, or the interface into the DUV. Implementation coverage analysis relies on measurements of activities inside the DUV by inspection into the HDL model during simulation.

Throughout the measurement and analysis activity, the verification team must never forget that the ultimate goal of coverage analysis is to *guide* the verification process, and not to prove its completeness. Completeness is an elusive goal that is unreachable anyway.

A seemingly simple coverage goal would be the combinatorial space spanned by the enumeration of all possible patterns on the DUV inputs, all possible states internal to the DUV, and all possible output patterns on the outputs of the DUV. Although this coverage metric is trivial to

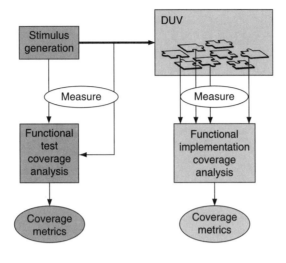

Verification test coverage versus implementation coverage.

define, it is also completely useless to guide the verification process, because it is unachievable.

Then, toward which targets should coverage analysis drive the verification process?

Dill and Tasiran define coverage analysis as the task to maximize the *probability of stimulating and detecting bugs*, at minimum cost (in time, labor, and computation) [25]. In the end, not very surprisingly, detection of hidden bugs is the main objective.

Figure 6.35 illustrates how coverage information can guide the simulation through the state space of a DUV to find the hidden bugs.

The generated stimulus drives the simulation through the state space in a meandering path. The task of coverage guidance is to influence the direction of the traversal to hit areas that are prone to hidden bugs. Coverage measurement is not productive for all the areas of the DUV that do not have any hidden bugs.

In summary, the amount of hidden bugs found measures the quality of the coverage analysis effort.

Coverage is a tool that helps the verification team to find bugs, and it is only a means to an end. A coverage measure that the verification team meets without finding bugs has only a limited value.

Several times it has been said that it is impossible to cover all parts of a design with simulation. Therefore, coverage must focus on error prone areas. In this sense, a good coverage metric needs to have a predictive component; it needs to be able to measure *bug coverage* [25].

Figure 6.34 distinguishes coverage efforts by their target areas—test coverage versus implementation coverage. Developers and researchers

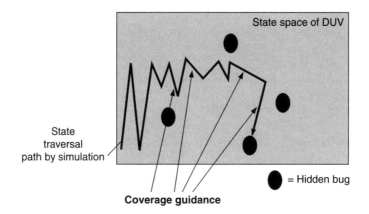

Functional coverage guidance to the hidden bugs. The overall rectangle represents the state space of a design under verification (DUV). Simulation traverses through this state space along a zig-zag trajectory. The hidden bugs in the DUV are shown as shaded circles. Influence of coverage guidance is shown by arrows that cause the simulation traversal to change in a different direction, hopefully closer to a hidden bug.

have evolved different successful schemes to specify coverage metrics for both applications. These schemes are referred to as coverage models.

It is possible to classify coverage models as either structural or functional. Both classes apply to verification test coverage or implementation coverage. *Functional coverage models* focus on the *semantics* of either the test or the design implementation. For example, did the test cover all possible commands or did the simulation ever trigger a first in, first out (FIFO) buffer overflow? *Structural coverage* models, on the other hand, tie into the representation of the domain to be covered. A good example for a structural coverage model is *line coverage*, a measure of whether all source lines in the stimulus generator program or the DUV HDL have been visited during simulation.

Before structural and functional coverage are discussed in more detail, we want to clarify the difference between functional test coverage and manufacturing test coverage because new students of the field easily confuse both areas.

6.2.2   Functional Verification Test Coverage Versus Manufacturing Test Coverage

It is important not to confuse functional verification test coverage with the problem of manufacturing test coverage [26]. We can compare and contrast manufacturing test coverage with aspects of functional test coverage to gain additional insights.

Manufacturing tests apply test patterns to a chip on a tester device to expose manufacturing flaws. It is typical for projects to speak of test coverage for these patterns to be in the high 90% range. This is a coverage metric measured against a *fault model*. Manufacturing tests do assume that a uniform model of faults can represent all relevant fabrication flaws. The test pattern generation has the task to select patterns that expose these faults at the output of the circuit. The predominant and successful fault model has been the *stuck-at* model, which assumes that the test patterns should expose signals in the circuit that are permanently stuck to a certain logic value.

The fault model for manufacturing tests has indeed a predictive component. Manufacturing coverage measures bug coverage.

There have been many attempts in research to create the equivalent of a fault model for functional verification. An example is a model that assumes that the designer accidentally switched the outputs of two HDL statements. The corresponding coverage metric measures the tests run in simulation by their ability to find such a switch. This fault model does not capture a large range of typical design bugs and therefore has not been successful in practice.

6.2.3 Structural Coverage

The application for structural coverage models is largely implementation coverage analysis. These models always tie into a structural aspect of the implementation of the test generation, the DUV, or the representation of the design HDL. Below are the typical structural models, presented in a sequence of increasing complexity.

Toggle Coverage

Toggle coverage measures how many times the signals and latches (facilities) in the HDL model have changed their logic value during simulation. The absence of signal change activity in an area of the DUV indicates that the stimuli did not target this area at all.

The advantage of toggle coverage is that it is a very simple, easy-to-understand model. Its drawback is, however, that it yields massive amounts of data, and the statement that 100% of all signals in a DUV have toggled does not yield any insight into the functional significance of the testing done.

Statement Coverage

Statement coverage or *line coverage* takes the syntactical structure of the HDL specification and measures which HDL lines were executed by the simulation run.

Similar to toggle coverage, this coverage model is easy to comprehend, and the absence of activity in areas of the HDL model highlights omissions in the tests. One of the problems with this model is that it only applies to HDL that is written as a sequential statement. Concurrent VHDL, for example, does not have a structure consistent with this model. The other limitation of line coverage is the missing semantic insight; the fact that an HDL statement has been executed results in no knowledge about the correctness of the content of the statement.

Branch Coverage

Branch coverage or *conditional coverage* looks at conditional statements in the HDL and keeps track of which conditions the simulation encounters and which it does not.

This model assumes that there is semantic meaning in the condition that the designer expressed in HDL. Decision points in the HDL specification are typically representative of different conditions to which the design needs to react. Therefore, the lack of exercising a decision in all possible, anticipated ways clearly indicates a lack of testing. The main limitation of this model is that conditional constructs are not the only way to implement decision in a design. For example, it is possible to specify a multiplexer as a *case* statement or as a set of *and/or* expressions. The former construct would lead to a coverage measurement point; the latter form would hide the branch condition.

Path Coverage

Path coverage is a refinement of branch coverage. Rather than looking at single conditional decisions in isolation, path coverage does an execution flow analysis of the HDL and identifies combinations of subsequent decisions into execution paths.

Figure 6.36 shows the automatic inference of two possible execution paths on a given HDL with if/then/else structure. If simulation had taken path2, branch coverage would have indicated that at some point the cond1-else branch and at some point the cond2-if path were active. Only the combination of the decision points into paths would have uncovered that the simulation hit the second nested cond2-if statement and not the first.

Although path coverage raises the functional semantic level higher than simple branch coverage, the drawback of branch coverage is more relevant here as well. This coverage metric does completely rely on the presence of certain constructs in the HDL. If the design team can use these constructs, the HDL style and the coverage analysis goals are in accord. However, many times the design team has good reasons to structure the logic of Figure 6.36 in other ways (e.g., high-frequency design constraints). This results in a goal conflict for the HDL structure. In these cases, it is typically coverage analysis that loses out.

path1 = cond1 & cond2   path2 = not (cond1) & cond2

```
if (cond1='1') then
  ...
  if (cond2='1') then
  ...
  else
  ...
  end if;
else
  ...
  if (cond2='1') then
  ...
  end if;
end if;
```

■ **FIGURE 6.36**

Definition of execution paths for coverage analysis.

Finite State Machine Coverage

Finite state machine (FSM) coverage associates a state-machine structure with HDL design and measures various aspects of the resulting model. There is *state coverage*, which measures which states of the FSM the simulation visited, and there is *arc coverage*, which accounts for the possible state-transitions and whether simulation traversed them or not. Similar to path coverage above, it is possible to combine states and arcs taken in the FSM structure and construct paths.

There are two variants of FSM coverage: the constructive and the inferred approach.

The constructive FSM coverage approach assumes that the FSM structure is clearly visible in the HDL syntax. The traffic light HDL in Chapter 3 is an example of this HDL style. The FSM HDL defines the state-holding elements all together in one signal declaration, and all the state-transitions are contained in one *process* statement (*always* block for the Verilog version). This approach works well if the design intent is explicitly visible in the HDL. If the HDL representation does not syntactically delineate the FSM, the constructive FSM coverage model does not apply.

Inferred FSM coverage does an analysis of the logic represented by the HDL model and assembles separate state-holding elements together into the inferred FSM state vector. Further automatic analysis yields the possible state values and the state transitions, as they are present in the model. The limitation of the inferred FSM approach is that the state machine, which the automatic analysis finds, may not be recognizable by the design team as an intended, designed state machine. The coverage reports will then refer to states and state-transitions, which simulation has not encountered, and these structures have no semantic meaning to the designer. Subsequently, it will be very hard for both the design and verification teams to reason about the missing scenarios that the coverage analysis highlighted.

Multiple State Machine

Multiple state machine coverage combines several state machines together into one coverage model and measure events that focus on relationships between them. Complex events such as interlocked and synchronized state-transitions are the target of this analysis. This area is still mostly in research and progress is limited by the ability of the analysis to identify the groups of FSMs.

Discussion of Structural Coverage Models

So far, we discussed structural coverage only in the context of the design and its HDL representation. Structural coverage plays a lesser role for the verification environment. Of course, it is possible to apply line, branch, and path coverage to any type of sequential code. Why would this not work for verification code?

Indeed, it is possible to instrument the code of checkers or monitor component. A checker or monitor has to inspect the HDL model over time and compare these observations against the specification. As the verification follows events in the model, it naturally assembles scenarios and transactions. All these abstractions are relevant to coverage analysis, and in some cases, the environment code might be the source of more effective coverage models. It is very practical to measure which conditions a checker or monitor had to compare against the specification and which scenarios it never encountered.

Structural coverage, especially the more sophisticated forms, can clearly improve the verification quality. The strength of structural coverage analysis, aside from its easy implementation, is its ability to point out holes of uncovered areas in the design.

However, as discussed above, it is clear that for any nontrivial design there will be areas that simulation will not cover. The real problem is deciding which areas are *safe* for the verification team to leave uncovered.

This is the common drawback of structural coverage. The indication of *absence of coverage* is its value. However, that is only the start of a reasoning process, which decides whether this result is relevant or not for the verification of the design. Structural coverage models have no ability to predict bugs; bug coverage model they are not.

Most EDA companies have embraced structural coverage measurement with vigor. This should not be a surprise, because it is straightforward to add and integrate most of the data collection for the structural models into the HDL processing tools that the vendors already provide. It is also much more runtime-efficient to evaluate the instrumentation embedded inside the HDL simulation compared with retrieving this data out of the model and processing them in the test bench.

All these advantages of embedded structural instrumentation have made structural coverage an important feature of HDL simulation engines.

6.2.4 Functional Coverage

Unlike structural coverage, there is no automated way to create functional coverage models. Functional coverage targets semantic aspects of the test generation or design implementation. Underlying all functional coverage activities there is the acknowledgement that it is necessary to choose which functional areas of the design need to be tested. Insight into the design semantics drives these choices, and they must come from the designer or the verification engineer.

A very important component of this insight is the knowledge of design complexity, of areas that are prone to bugs. The predictive bug coverage component of functional coverage models must come from the experience of the engineers.

There is no set of complex automation tools available to define functional coverage models. The tool support focuses mostly on the implementation of the coverage model and the efficient collection of the data during runtime. After the data are collected, the tools provide GUI support to help in the traversal of the results.

The most basic functional coverage model is the *coverage event (or coverage task)* [27]. A coverage event specifies an event in the model or the test bench, which is important enough that the verification environment must note and log its occurrence.

Functional coverage based on events has much similarity and synergy with assertion-based verification as discussed in Chapter 3. The event classification there applies to coverage events as well. Coverage events can be simple, static events and temporal event sequences; finally, it is possible to have a library of prebuilt coverage event building blocks. For example, a FIFO structure with its assertions such as *buffer overflow* is also a good target for coverage events such as *buffer full*.

As a result, event-based functional coverage models can use the same mechanisms as assertions for specification and evaluation during simulation. Temporal expressions, such as those that PSL supports, can drive event detection in a simulation engine [28]. PSL assertions and coverage are detailed in Chapter 12. Only after the simulation engine detects the event is there a need for differentiation between assertion and coverage event. The assertion violation leads to an error message and possibly the halt of simulation, whereas the simulation process just logs the coverage event information and stores it in a database.

The analysis of functional event coverage is simple. Besides the presence or absence of an event, the coverage results show additional information associated with the event. This could be a *count*, which specifies how many times simulation encountered the event and the name of the test case that triggered the event occurrence.

In addition, it is a good idea to collect events into *event groups*. The basis for the group can be, for example, the HDL entity or module. Other grouping criteria can be functional area, the association of the events to the same FSM, or the same dataflow structure. Once the database logs events under groups, a GUI that supports analysis of the coverage data will allow access to coverage results based on group selection.

A very popular structuring principle for groups of coverage events is the notion of *cross-product coverage*. The motivation behind cross-product analysis is the interest in the occurrence of a group of events in relation to each other.

Figure 6.31 shows a simple example of a cross-product that captures what the stimulus initiator drives into Calc1. The analysis of interest for this cross-product is the command distribution over all four ports. The goal to cover all cells of the cross-product is equivalent to the statement that the driver generated all commands, including illegal ones, at least once for every port.

The example in Figure 6.31 has only two dimensions because it combines only two variables into the cross-product. Models that are more complex will cover a multidimensional space. The reason cross-products are popular, especially when investigating the quality of stimulus generation, is that they organize the possibility of complex codependent enumerations into an easy-to-understand scheme.

It is possible to analyze the cross-product data per test case. Alternatively, the coverage collection tool can tabulate many test case results into

Port/command	1	2	3	4
No-op				
Add				
Subtract				
Shift left				
Shift right				
Illegal				

▪ FIGURE 6.37

Cross-product coverage analysis for Calc1 stimulus. The two dimensions of the cross-product are operations and ports. The coverage model gives insight into which operation/port combinations were not simulated versus which ones were and how many times they were simulated.

Port/command	1	2	3	4
No-op	X			
Add			X	
Subtract	X	X		
Shift left			X	
Shift right		X		
Illegal				X

(a)   Status report

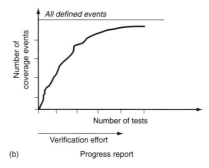

(b)   Progress report

■ **FIGURE 6.38**

Cross-product coverage reports. (a), Status report showing the summary of all coverage data up to a point in time. (b), Coverage results tabulated over time.

one result cross-product. Coverage tools typically provide two types of reports: status reports and progress reports [29].

The status report (Figure 6.38a) shows the current overall encountered coverage events in a snapshot diagram, whereas the progress reports (Figure 6.38b) display a curve of the increasing sum of encountered events over the process of test case simulation. The typical shape of the progress is asymptotical toward the goal of reaching all events, with a sharp increase in the beginning of the process. The early events are typically the easy ones to hit, whereas the events encountered later need much more effort from the verification team, tuning the stimulus generation.

Cross-product coverage event matrices are so easy to define that it is a typical phenomenon to see meaningless events defined. Nonmeaningful events are either *illegal* by their definition or are *impossible* to occur.

The verification team should turn illegal events into assertions, which once again demonstrates the synergy between coverage analysis and assertion verification. Impossible events are harder to identify. It can take a fair amount of reasoning over the design specification to understand which event combinations cannot occur. However, this effort is not lost because it goes hand in hand with the verification engineer's deeper understanding of the DUV.

It is useful to extend the cross-product of Figure 6.37 with another dimension. We add the response value from the output ports of Calc1. Now the cross-product spans the space of all commands, on all ports and with all possible response values. These combinations, however, are not all reachable, as with the shift commands and the overflow response. If the events are kept in the cross-product, there will forever be events that will not be covered.

It is important in the upfront analysis of the coverage model, to exclude illegal and unreachable events from the cross-product.

Currently, test bench environments support cross-product coverage analysis. In some cases, there is a separate library available for model definition and instrumentation functions, as well as the transport of the result to a centralized repository. The modern HVLs (OpenVera, *e*) have built-in support for coverage definition and data collection. The reader is encouraged to download the HVL manuals and study the verification coverage sections.

6.2.5 Coverage Bulk Data Collection and Management

Many commercial coverage tools are a great productivity help for the verification team. Often, their functionality supports the whole process from coverage model definition to data collection and analysis after the simulation has ended with easy-to-use interactive GUIs.

Any evaluation of such a tool set should ask questions about the support of more than a single simulation. In other words, evaluate how the coverage methodology scales for the case in which the verification environment runs a large number of simulations (bulk simulation).

The two most important aspects that influence scaling to support bulk simulation are as follows:

- How are the coverage results stored when the simulation is finished?

- How does the coverage analysis function access the stored coverage results?

Figure 6.39 illustrates the topology of a large verification project and one possible solution for a scalable coverage strategy.

The idea is that all compute servers, which run simulation, ship a result file at the end of the simulation job to a central coverage data server. This server has enough disk storage and compute power to handle large data volumes and compute intensive analysis algorithms over the coverage data. The user client machines send their requests for analysis to the coverage data server, which in turn sends results back to the user clients.

It is clear that the network capacity needs to be available to support large amounts of network traffic that results from this topology. In addition, it is very important that the size of the data sets that are sent via network is kept as compact as possible. One of the options for rebalancing the compute work is to let the user client machines do more of the algorithmic work to analyze the coverage status. The counterbalance to this approach could be an increased need for network bandwidth to give the user client machines access to the necessary data.

Verification coverage provides very important feedback that keeps the verification team informed about the quality of the simulation jobs.

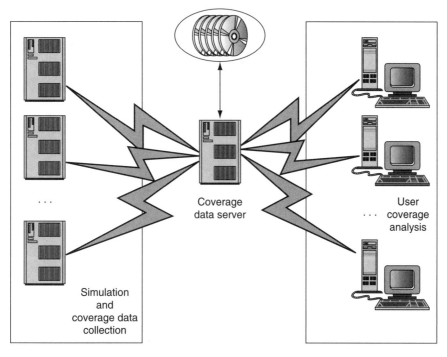

Bulk coverage data collection.

Coverage, the bugs found and the bug rate are the "eyes and ears" of the verification project.

6.2.6   The Right Coverage Analysis Strategy

The overall discussion in this section should highlight that coverage analysis is one of the harder problems for a verification team. Although there are many automatic tools that promise a quick fix for the coverage quandary, all of them have significant drawbacks. On the other hand, neither industry nor academia has so far found coverage metrics with the right necessary *predictive* capability to guide simulation into those areas of the state space where the hidden bugs are.

This leaves a verification team with a range of necessary incomplete alternatives to select the right coverage strategy for their specific project. However, the discussion above leaves us with useful guidelines that will result in a better use of coverage technologies and an overall better verification methodology. Table 6.3 attempts to collect some of these.

TABLE 6.3 ▪ Guidelines for the use of coverage analysis

- Use coverage analysis. Especially with random-biased stimulus generation, the verification is *blind* without the coverage feedback.
- Use coverage as a method that provides insight into verification progress, not as a tool that provides a set of absolute numbers. The verification team should not confuse reaching 100% of the coverage with a guaranteed bug-free design under verification (DUV). Coverage numbers are only useful with careful interpretation.
- The more insight it takes to create a coverage model, the more insightful the coverage feedback information will be.
- Use automatically generated coverage feedback mainly as an indicator for holes in the simulation coverage. Because automatic metrics take not much insight, the value of their positive feedback (events have been hit) is limited. Missing events, however, provide unambiguous feedback of missing verification in the areas specific to the metric used.
- Limit automatically generated coverage feedback to the amount of data the simulation infrastructure can support. Low-level automatic coverage collection often easily overwhelms a project.
- Use as much manually instrumented coverage data collection as possible. Manual instrumentation of the simulation process requires insight and effort. The insight provides useful coverage information; the effort limits the instrumentation to mostly useful coverage information.
- Instrument corner conditions in the DUV for coverage analysis. Corner conditions are naturally more error-prone. Examples of corner conditions are maximum and minimum resource allocations or rare collisions of events that need special treatment in the DUV implementation.
- Combine assertion checking as much as possible with coverage instrumentation and vice versa. Both activities are related, and insight in one usually provides insight in the other.
- Select the dimensions of coverage cross-products carefully. A cross-product that is too large likely provides not enough insight. Similar to the DUV state space, cross-products tend to blow up easily in size and simulation cannot cover all the events specified.
- Use broad coverage analysis at the level of functional unit simulation. Prioritize and review coverage goals at the higher level of the hierarchy. The unit-level simulation provides the broadest amount of functional coverage. Levels above unit simulation by intent will not reach all coverage measures that are in place for a unit. A selection of prioritized measures from the units and new measures should constitute the coverage goals for a higher verification level (e.g., *chip level*).

6.3 SUMMARY

The training of airplane pilots includes a lot of technical background on airplanes and the physics of flying because it creates better pilots. In the same way, a verification team has to gain a conceptual understanding of the verification technologies they use, to be better verification engineers. For this reason, this chapter took a detailed look "under the hood" of the technologies that are essential for building simulation environments.

Test benches are the primary vehicle of the verification work. On a large industrial project, it is common to have possibly dozens of engineers work on the development of test bench components. These components work on functional units at first, but as verification moves to the higher levels of chip and system verification, the team assembles many components from the lower levels, for example, checkers and monitors, to build the more complex test bench environment. Several chapters of this book discuss content and strategy of these test benches. In addition, the verification team needs to have a clear plan, up front, of the structure and architecture of the test bench at the highest level of the hierarchy. There, many pieces, reused from the lower levels, must build a robust larger piece of software. Therefore, it is necessary for the verification team to have a broad understanding of different test bench architecture and features.

This chapter covered a large landscape of applicable test bench technologies. Starting from the use of HDLs for test benches, we embarked on the experiment to design our own from-scratch C++ test bench library and then used that experience to survey a selection of available HVLs, namely, OpenVera, the *e* language, and SystemC. By using this overview of many issues with simulation engine interfaces and HVLs, the focus always was to provide the conceptual background of what are the common and unique characteristics a user can expect from these environments. This exercise of compare-and-contrast should help a further study of any one of these options available to the verification team.

Staying with the airplane analogy, airplane engine and cockpit can be compared to the role of the test bench in verification. From this view, coverage analysis is similar to the radar of the airplane. Coverage gives the verification team vital insight into the progress of their efforts and a direction to focus verification next to uncover the hidden bugs of the DUV. Functional test coverage analysis tracks test bench activity, whereas functional implementation coverage reports DUV state space visited during simulation. For both classes of coverage, the user can decide to use structural or functional coverage methods. Structural methods attempt to track coverage based on inherent structural properties of the test bench or the DUV specification and are therefore well suited for automatic coverage instrumentation via tools. The advantages and disadvantages of structural versus functional coverage, which relies mostly on manual model instrumentation was discussed.

While the field of coverage analysis is still evolving in the industry, it is nevertheless possible to specify a number of guidelines for a practical coverage strategy, which uses a combination of the available coverage analysis techniques that is optimal for a given verification project.

6.4 EXERCISES

1. Change the classes in Figures 6.12 and 6.13 such that the end-of-test reporting status flows from the driver to the scoreboard and then the checker and finally returns to the top-level test bench loop.

2. Change the test bench components from Exercise 1 to enable a check for pending, unfinished operations at the end of the simulation.

3. Change the test bench from Exercise 2 to support the name of a test case file as a command line parameter, function *main()*.

4. Sketch out how to add the hardware reset of the DUV to the top-level test bench loop in Figure 6.13.

5. Add control for the execution of several test cases to the top-level test bench loop in Figure 6.16. Change the test bench from Exercise 2 to accept a name of a test case list file as a parameter. The test case list contains the name of a test case file per line. Between test cases, reset the Calc1 DUV using the specification from Chapter 4.

6. Show how the test bench library architecture has to change such that test bench components can have a separate function for different phases of execution (hardware initialization, execution, end-of-test checking), not just a single *execute()* function (as a reference, see Figure 6.17).

7. The test bench of Figures 6.12 and 6.13 has replicated declarations and code concerning the four input and output ports of Calc1. Create a new port class for the driver and a similar one for the checker and replace the originally replicated code with four instances of the port objects.

8. Instrument the stimulus generator developed for the exercises of Chapter 4 (Calc1) with coverage collection code. Run the test case suite developed for Chapter 4 and inspect and discuss the coverage results.

9. Instrument the test bench of Calc1, developed for the exercises of Chapter 4, with code that captures coverage events in the HDL model. Run the test cases developed for Chapter 4 against this model and inspect and discuss the coverage results.

10. Using the Web site references and freely available reference material from the Internet, compare and contrast the coverage support built in to the HVLs OpenVera, and *e*.

CHAPTER 7

STRATEGIES FOR SIMULATION-BASED STIMULUS GENERATION

Complex designs require robust stimulus generation components. Together with the checking components, stimulus generation is critical for discovering design problems. This chapter describes methods for creating simulation-based stimulus generation in complex designs.

Earlier chapters used simpler example designs to illustrate deterministic test cases and introduce the building blocks of a simulation environment. The Calc1 design was used as an example of a relatively simple design under verification (DUV). To illustrate more complex stimulus generation techniques, this chapter launches the Calc2 design, which builds on Calc1.

This chapter introduces four corners of stimulus generation, which range from deterministic to random generation and from predetermined to on-the-fly verification environments. Each has strengths and weaknesses, which the verification team must evaluate using their insight into the function of the DUV. This chapter should enable the reader to plan a stimulus environment that appropriately matches the requirements of the design under verification.

When devising a stimulus environment, the verification engineer must understand the interrelationship of events and interface activity on the DUV. Often, the design places restrictions on the inputs, requiring intelligence in creating stimulus components. This is called *constraint solving* and is an integral part of complex stimulus generation. Insight into design constraints contributes greatly to the quality of the stimulus generation components. This chapter describes the process for evaluating design constraints and the methods for properly tuning the stimulus components to exploit these constraints.

No stimulus component is complete without coverage feedback, which provides invaluable insight into the quality of the stimulus components by highlighting areas of the design that the components have not exercised. Without coverage, the verification team can only speculate on the scenarios the stimulus components create. With coverage, they know for sure. We previously defined the types of coverage and coverage tools. This chapter demonstrates coverage's use to tune stimulus generation.

7.1 CALC2 OVERVIEW

The Calc2 design builds on the Calc1 example detailed in Chapter 4. On the surface, Calc2 has just a single, relatively simple specification change over Calc1. However, the change adds substantial complexity to the design.

The Calc1 design allowed only one command from each of the four port requestors at a time. All ports needed to wait until the calculator completed execution of the current command before sending another command. In the new design, the port requestor can send up to four commands into Calc2 from each of the four ports. Hence, this calculator could (theoretically) work on up to 16 commands at a single time.

This single design change has major implications to the system. Because there are two internal arithmetic pipelines in the calculator (one for *add/sub* and one for *shifts*), it is possible for commands sent from a single port to be executed out of order. For example, if all four ports send in three add commands followed by a shift command, the calculator is likely to execute the shift commands before the older add commands. However, the specification dictates that commands from the same port that use the same pipeline (add/sub or shift) must return in order.

To correlate the responses to the correct commands, the specification calls for adding a 2-bit tag to the input and output protocols. This tag shall be a unique identifier for each of the commands from each port. (Inside the calculator design, the hardware description language (HDL) maintains another pair of "internal" tag bits to correlate the command back to the correct port.) Therefore, each port requestor must keep track of the outstanding tags it has sent to the DUV to ensure that it never allows duplicate tags.

Figure 7.1 shows the input and output description of Calc2. Table 7.1 describes each of the input and output busses.

In Calc1, the HDL design merely had to latch the single incoming command from a given port and hold it until the priority logic forwarded the command to the adder or shifter ALU. The Calc2 design requires a more complicated structure. Now, the HDL design must implement a pair of queues to hold multiple commands. Rather than creating four individual queues for each port, the HDL implementation uses two queues, one for each ALU. As the port requestors issue commands, the Calc2 logic places the commands and data into either the add/sub queue or the shift queue. This guarantees the integrity of the order of operations because the HDL design places new commands directly into the queues as it receives them.

Although a port can now send up to four commands without receiving a response, the port requestor cannot send these commands in four consecutive cycles. This is because each command still requires two cycles to send both data operands. Figure 7.2 shows the timing of a single

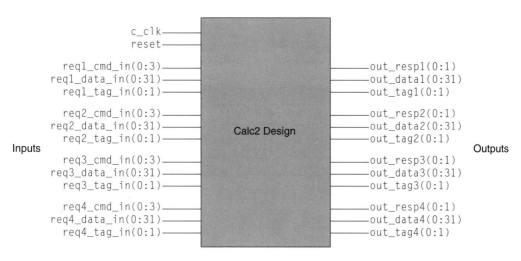

■ **FIGURE 7.1**

The input and output signals for Calc2, grouped by ports. Each port has the same basic signals and protocols.

TABLE 7.1 ■ Input and output descriptions

Input/output	Description
c_clk	c_clk is the main clock. Drive c_clk the same as in the Calc1 design.
reset	Hold reset high for seven cycles at the start of the test case. This signal must remain low during functional testing. Similarly, all input ports need to be driven low ("O"b, not "X" or "U") from the start of simulation.
reqX_cmd_in(0:3)	The command bus has the same definitions as Calc1: *Add* ("0001"b), *Subtract* ("0010"b), *Shift_left* ("0101"b), and *Shift_right* ("0110"b).
reqX_data_in(0:31)	The data bus has the same definitions as Calc1. The requesting port sends the operand data on back-to-back cycles. Operand1 data accompanies the command, and Operand2 data follows.
reqX_tag_in(0:1)	The tag bus is the 2-bit identifier for each command from the port. The port requestor can reuse the tag as soon as the Calc2 HDL responds to the command.
out_respX(0:1)	The output response bus has the same definition as Calc1: Good response ("01"b); invalid command or overflow/underflow ("10"b); and internal error ("11"b; never happens). "00"b on the response line indicates there is no response from that port on that cycle.
out_dataX(0:31)	The output data bus has the same definition as Calc1. This data accompanies a good response.
out_tagX(0:1)	The output tag bus corresponds to the command tag sent by the requester. It is used to correlate the response to the original command.

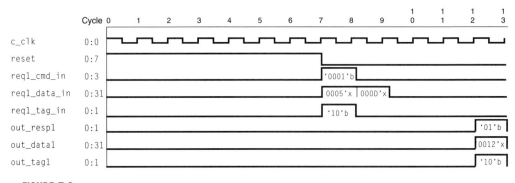

■ **FIGURE 7.2**

Timing diagram showing the protocol of a single add command for port1 in Calc2.

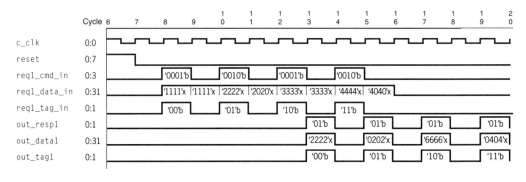

■ **FIGURE 7.3**

Calc2 timing diagram showing multiple add and subtract commands from the same port, each using different tag values.

add command on port 1, and Figure 7.3 shows multiple add and sub commands from port 1. Note that in Figure 7.3, each command uses a different tag value.

Because all of the commands in Figure 7.3 are adds and subtracts, this sequence only uses one of the two ALUs. As a result, the commands return in the same order that they were initiated. If other ports were to send commands, it would be possible for a single port to receive responses on back-to-back cycles. This would give a far less predictable response timing compared with in Figure 7.3, where the responses come every-other cycle.

Finally, there are some nonobvious implications of the changes to the design. Often, these implications are not in the specification, and the verification engineer realizes interesting cases only after simulation starts. A good example of this occurs in Calc2. The combination of parallelization of commands across two execution pipelines and multiple commands from a single port creates the potential for very interesting special cases, also called *window conditions*. Given the right state of the queues when commands arrive from a single port, it is now possible that the next command in both the *add* and *shift* queues is from the same port requestor. If the priority logic dispatched both commands simultaneously, the results from the adder ALU and the shifter ALU would collide at the output driver. To avoid this bug, either the priority logic must prevent the simultaneous dispatch of commands from the same port, or the output driver logic must be able to serialize the responses. In any case, the verification engineer must ensure that the stimulus component creates this special case during simulation and should document this in the verification plan.

The potential for this type of problem exists in most of today's designs. During the test plan development phase, the verification engineer must hunt for these scenarios. The key characteristic in these cases is resources shared across multiple paths.

7.1.1 Calc2 Verification Plan

Calc2 presents a greater verification challenge than does Calc1. Multiple outstanding commands, which can complete out of order, require a more sophisticated environment than do the deterministic driving and checking mechanisms used in Calc1. Because each port can send four commands, the variability on the interface timings increases such that the verification engineer needs to build an automated, programmed environment. With all the possible timings between four commands and four operations across four ports, the state space explodes to a point that the verification engineer cannot conjure up all of the necessary permutations manually.

The following section documents the verification plan for Calc2, following the test plan template introduced in Chapter 4.

Description of Verification Levels

Full verification of Calc2 requires two levels of verification. We will focus this verification plan on the top level. However, in a real project, the verification work would include unit-level plans for the priority logic, which is substantially more complicated than in Calc1.[1]

The verification team might consider unit-level verification for the two ALU units. However, in this case, Calc2 reuses both the add and shift ALUs from the Calc1 design. It is common in the design world to carry

---

[1] Verification of the priority unit requires a unit level specification including the input and output definitions.

forward design blocks from previous projects. This makes both the design and verification job easier.

Required Tools

Calc2 has the same simulation engine and license requirements as does Calc1. However, the added complexity of Calc2 requires a programming or high-level verification language (HVL) infrastructure. If multiple people share the verification effort, this infrastructure must include a code revision tool (RCS, CVS, Clear Case, etc). This allows the verification team to control the data management of the environment code via *check-in* and *check-out* from a centrally shared repository.

Risks and Dependencies

As this is a textbook exercise, there are none of the risks associated with normal industry products. In industry, this project might have risks such as not obtaining the required verification staffing or the lack of on-time delivery of HDL. Similarly, most of the dependencies inherent in industry designs do not enter into this exercise. Under normal conditions, the verification plan would explicitly state the following dependencies:

- Verification of the unit-level priority logic depends on the delivery of its specification

- Chip-level verification depends on the completion of the unit-level verification

- Tool and license availability

Functions To Be Verified

The verification engineer must verify the following functions in addition to those listed for the Calc1 exercise. This verification listing builds on the tests listed in Chapter 4 (4.4.2). Therefore, the tests in Tables 4.5, 4.6, and 4.7 serve as the foundation for the Calc2 test matrix.

Table 7.2 lists the first set of expanded test cases required for Calc2. The test case reference numbers begin with the number 4 because the Calc1 set of tests (tests 1 through 3) serve as the base for Calc2.

In addition, there are interesting corner cases that the verification environment must create. Table 7.3 describes these cases.

Note that this test plan calls for verifying all lengths of shift operations, but not all different add or subtract operands. This is because there are just 32 different possible shift operand2 values, whereas there are 2^{32} different add/sub operands.

TABLE 7.2 ■ Calc2 expansion test cases

Test reference number	Test description
4.1	Send multiple commands with variable timing between commands from the same port
4.2	Send commands using variable tags for each command
4.3	Send multiple invalid commands

TABLE 7.3 ■ Calc2 corner case tests cases

Test reference number	Test description
5.1	Send only a mix of *add* and *subtract* commands to fill the add queue
5.2	Send only a mix of *shift* commands to fill the shift queue
5.3	Verify mixes of overflow, underflow, and good response cases across back-to-back port commands
5.4	Verify all lengths of shift cases across back-to-back port commands
5.5	Verify the design under verification does not allow output collisions from both pipelines sending results to the same port simultaneously

The checking for Calc2 must verify that the design handles multiple interesting cases, along with the basic command-data-response checking. Table 7.4 shows some of the required checks.

Specific Tests and Methods: Environment

The Calc2 verification environment will take a grey box approach. All stimulus generation will occur at the top-level interface, driving the specified Calc2 inputs. Although most checkers and monitors will also be at the top level, some verification code will peek inside the DUV. Specifically, we have already stated in the test plan the desire to fill the queues, indicating a case for monitoring the internal state of the queues.

The Calc2 design goes beyond the limits of the capability of deterministic verification. Although formal verification is feasible, we choose a random-based environment for this design.

Construction of the stimulus initiators for any random environment should allow a bypass for deterministic verification. For Calc2, early simulations should be restricted to simple scenarios to verify the most basic functions of the DUV. The random controls will allow deterministic scenarios.

TABLE 7.4 ▪ Specific checks for Calc2 verification environment

Check reference number	Check description
1.1	Check that response value matches expected response based on command and data
1.2	Check that every command gets a response
1.3	Check for unmatched tags on the response port
1.4	Check that result data matches expected result based on command and data
1.5	Check for correctness of out-of-order responses across command pipeline types but never across the same command type
1.6	Verify in-order execution of all *adds/subtracts* or *shifts*, no matter which port sent the command
1.7	Check that the response tag matches the data for the command that was sent (tags do not get swapped)
1.8	Check that there are no unexpected or stray values on the outputs.

Randomization controls will enable the test case automation to choose command and data values rather than placing the burden on the test case writer. This provides a level of abstraction and a broader range of data and control stimulus. However, the environment needs the ability to limit, or *constrain*, the randomization, so that the verification engineer can steer the test case into interesting cases. The following inputs to Calc2 must allow for constrained random values:

- Operand data

- Command types

- Tag values

- Delay between commands

The environment duplicates these randomization controls for each port, allowing for independence across the requestors. Furthermore, the mechanism to choose the values must have a bias control (parameterized-random) to give the verification engineer influence over the statistical distribution of the values. This will allow control over such cases as the percentage of invalid commands sent in a particular test case.

The need for constrained random input values (versus pure random) is required on the tag values. The stimulus initiator may pick any tag value for a given port as long as that value is not already in use. Therefore, the stimulus initiator must have access to the record of outstanding tags, and must constrain itself to choosing unused tags.

The Calc2 environment will use the packet level of abstraction. The stimulus initiator for Calc2 will consist of two parts. The first is a random, packet-level stimulus generator. The "brains" of the stimulus initiator, the stimulus generator creates the packets, keeps track of port and tag availability, and posts inputs to the scoreboard. The second part is the interface protocol driver. This routine is the slave to the packet generator and converts the packets into the bit-level interface protocols. The verification environment will instantiate the stimulus initiator four times, once for each port.

The verification environment for Calc2 will use the transaction-based approach to checking. The transactions correspond to the packet-driven stimulus. Each transaction is a single command, tag, and data operation sent by the stimulus initiator. This method was chosen over a cycle accurate reference model approach because the cycle accurate reference model approach would require *cycle accurate* output predictions, which complicates the verification code beyond the requirements. Predicting the exact cycle of each Calc2 response is a cumbersome task that requires constant tuning with each change in the HDL. Our transaction-based approach verifies the correct answers for all operands, as well as the correct ordering of responses. Initially, the transaction approach might provide less accurate checking capability than does the cycle accurate reference model. However, the verification engineer can easily bolster the transaction-based approach by maintaining latency statistics (measurements of how many cycles each operation took). These statistics verify that the Calc2 pipeline has no unexpected stalls or delays, while bypassing the coding overhead of a cycle accurate reference model.

As with the stimulus, the environment will perform checking at the packet level. The checking component on each port follows a simpler, but similar model to the stimulus generator. One routine will package the response and data coming out of the DUV, and the second routine checks that the values are correct according to the data in the scoreboard.

The output-checking component must verify all of the checks outlined in Table 7.4.

In addition, the checking routine must inform the stimulus initiator (via the scoreboard) when tags are made available.

Finally, a monitor must track the state of the two queues. The verification team will use this information for coverage feedback, as well as checking that the queue does not overflow.

Test Scenarios: Matrix

Early verification of Calc2 should constrain the environment's randomization parameters such that it drives the basic functions identified in the test plan. Table 7.5 shows a test matrix for the basic functions.

The verification team checks off each box of the matrix as test cases complete. The team runs most of the basic tests (except those denoted) on a port-by-port basis.

TABLE 7.5 ▪ Calc2 basic test matrix

Function	Port 1	Port 2	Port 3	Port 4
Basic *Add* command				
Basic *Subtract* command				
Basic *Shift_left*				
Basic *Shift_right*				
All four tags				
Variable timing between commands				
Fill add queue (all four ports involved)				
Fill shift queue (all four ports involved)				
Invalid commands				
Overflow and underflow cases				
Various lengths of *shift* values				

As a few deterministic test cases complete successfully, the verification team starts to remove constraints from the environment's randomization controls. This allows the stimulus components to create a wider variance of cases simultaneously across all four ports. In practice, a verification team will migrate from the deterministic tests to an unconstrained environment. As the test cases become less constrained, the team uses coverage statistics to track the test matrix as well as other interesting scenarios. The following section of the test plan documents the tracking of the interesting cases performed under this method.

Coverage Requirements

The preceding test matrix articulates the most basic set of test case scenarios for Calc2. This is not enough to guarantee that the verification team fully exercises the HDL. Because of the many permutations of interesting events, Calc2 requires tracking functional coverage. This section of the test plan suggests only a few of the many functional coverage models for Calc2. The creation of further functional coverage models, including those dealing with tags, ports, command sequencing, and data ranges, are given as reader exercises.

Model 1: Number of commands in each queue. This model has an initial set of combinations of $17 \times 17 = 289$. This space is based on the total number of commands that each queue can hold (0 to 16). However, 136 of the permutations are illegal—those in which the total number of outstanding commands is greater than 16. Hence, the legal set of combinations for this model is 153.

Model 2: Number of concurrent invalid commands. The verification plan dedicates most of the Calc2 stimulus to valid commands. However, it would be interesting to track that the stimulus components send multiple invalid commands concurrently across all four ports. This model has a theoretical size limit of 17 (0 to 16 concurrent invalid commands).

But because the Calc2 DUV responds quickly to invalid commands (they bypass the ALUs), it is unlikely that it is possible to have a large number of concurrent invalid commands.

Model 3: Permutations of ports at the top of each queue. This model tracks which port sent the commands on the top of the two internal queues. The model size is $5 \times 2 = 10$, based on the five possible port values (four ports plus the case of an empty queue) on the top of two queues. All cases are legal. Of particular interest are the cases in which both commands at the top of the queues are from the same port.

Resource Requirements

For the Calc2 exercise, the resource requirements call for either one or two verification engineers. If two people work on the exercise, one should construct the stimulus components while the other writes the checking components. Because both components require access to the scoreboard, either engineer can write the scoreboard function.

The compute resources call for a single workstation on which the simulation engine runs. The exercise also requires other basic simulation-based tools, such as the debugger, a compiler (for either the programming language or the HVL), and a simulation engine.

Schedule Details

Depending on the experience level of the verification engineer, the Calc2 exercise will take between 15 and 40 hours of work by a single person. Existence of an initial code skeleton can significantly reduce the work.

This schedule is derived by breaking the work into its parts. The verification engineers will dedicate significant time to environment development and to DUV debug. We can break the environment debug down into individual components, consisting of the stimulus, checking, and scoreboard components. The scoreboard component is the simplest of these because it is a table driven by the stimulus and checking routines. The stimulus and checking components will take from 5 to 10 hours of coding each. Here, the verification engineer will focus on a single port and copy most of the code for the other three ports.

The debug schedule for Calc2 will vary based on the quality of the stimulus, checking, and error messages within the environment. With a quality environment in place, a verification engineer should be able to identify and debug Calc2 within 5 hours.

7.1.2 Calc2 and the Strategies for Stimulus Generation

The Calc2 test plan specifically calls for a random-based environment and a grey box approach. However, to illustrate the multiple strategies for stimulus generation, the Calc2 design will be used as a sample for each stimulus paradigm. Although a random-based environment is indeed the best fit for Calc2, it is feasible to verify portions of the DUV by using the various strategies described in the next section.

7.2   STRATEGIES FOR STIMULUS GENERATION

Verification can never compete with the number of cycles that the real hardware will encounter. In just a few seconds of runtime, the real hardware will exceed the aggregate number of simulation cycles run under verification. Yet the customer expects the verification "warrantee" to last the life of the machine. Therefore, from a practical standpoint, every verification effort is handicapped by a limited number of simulation cycles across a short delivery schedule.

To battle these odds, the verification team needs a robust strategy for creating stimulus for the relatively small number of available simulation cycles. The fundamental mantra behind the strategy is to stress the hardware more vigorously during every simulation test than it will ever be stressed again. This mantra holds when comparing stimulus stress across different simulation levels or during the lifetime of the part. The verification suite must contain more permutations, drive more interactions, and create more extraordinary cases over a short period of cycles than will be encountered in normal program or application activity. The ability to drive intricate scenarios is more acute at the lowest levels of simulation. When dealing with smaller portions of HDL, the verification engineer can control more of the internals via the input signals. Furthermore, at the lower levels of verification, the test suite is more likely to exercise a higher percentage of the entire HDL state space, as the total size of the state space is comparatively small. As the size of the design grows to the system level, it becomes more challenging for the verification engineer to overstress internals of the design and hit odd permutations.

Therefore, the verification team must take this approach to heart at each level. The lower levels of verification must create more stress on the smaller pieces of the design than the next levels will create on the aggregate of the smaller pieces. If this holds true, then each higher level of verification should uncover only those bugs caused by stitching logic together. The verification team should find bugs internal to a single portion of logic at the lowest level that contains that portion.

We have stated that finding these bugs requires a coordinated effort between stimulus creation and checking. This section describes methods and strategies for creating robust stimulus generation. Chapter 8 will focus on checking approaches to complement these stimulus strategies.

7.2.1   Types of Stimulus Generation

The verification test plan articulates the proposed verification environment for each level in the hierarchy. During that planning phase, the verification leaders make basic choices on stimulus generation. Two of the most fundamental decisions are

- Deterministic versus random stimulus generation
- Pregenerated test cases versus on-the-fly test case generation

Deterministic Versus Random Stimulus Generation

Chapter 3 highlighted deterministic testing. Deterministic tests create specific scenarios that the verification engineer wants to see. The scenarios are "determined" before running the simulation.

Random environments contain stimulus generation components that use pseudorandom number generators and probability tables to make decisions on input stimulus. The verification team programs intelligence about the DUV protocols into the stimulus components to limit the input scenarios to legal scenarios. The probability tables, which the verification engineer may adjust before runtime, bias the components' decisions on what inputs to send and how often to send them.

Most verification environments avoid completely random stimulus generation. In most cases, completely random stimulus does not adhere to the DUV's input protocols, rendering illegal scenarios. Therefore, random environments generally use constraints to limit scenarios to the legal subset of the input space.[2]

Although this chapter focuses on stimulus, it is important to note that random environments tend to use automated checking. Even though the verification engineer can hand-code specific checks on a deterministic sequence, it is prudent to use programmed scoreboard and checking components that allow for the wide range of possible input scenarios in random-based environments.

There is a broad range of possibilities between deterministic and completely random input stimulus. Even in deterministic environments, verification engineers routinely use pseudorandom number generation to create data. Conversely, verification engineers can tightly constrain random environments to create specific, nearly deterministic sequences. Figure 7.4 shows the range of stimulus generation between deterministic and random.

Most verification plans initially call for deterministic test cases. After the basic scenario test cases pass successfully on complex DUVs, the verification team will enable random generation to hit more of the state space. Therefore, testing tends to go from left to right on the axis shown in Figure 7.4.

---

[2] The verification plan may call for some deviations from the legal subset of input protocols. This is called error injection verification or bad path testing, and is covered in Chapter 9.

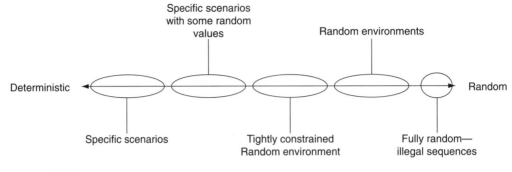

▪ **FIGURE 7.4**

The range of stimulus generation goes from deterministic or specific scenarios on the left to fully random sequences on the right. Verification engineers choose a mix of the extremes for their specific environment, depending on the test plan and design under verification requirements.

The verification team defines the deterministic tests based on scenarios they can conceive. However, there are too many cases beyond the bounds of the team's imagination and time constraints to verify without the use of automated, programmed environments. This is where random environments help. Random environments with constraint directives are effective at hitting a wide range of stimulus, which tends to find many bugs in areas that the engineer did not consider. The key is to have programmable constraints and enough compute resources for the random environment to explore the interesting state space.

In the early stages of verification, when the DUV and the test environment are relatively unstable and incomplete, the team will use the biasing parameters to constrain the environment so that the simulation is effectively a directed test. Later, when the design is more stable, the team relaxes those constraints.

Any time the stimulus components use random approaches, coverage metrics guide the team to search in untouched corners of the design. After all the simulation cycles, the coverage data may point to specific corners of the design's state space that the test suite has not exercised. Here again, it may be necessary for the team to write deterministic test cases to cover the holes.

Across each level of the verification hierarchy, the verification team needs to decide their strategy on deterministic versus random stimulus generation. At the lowest levels, deterministic test cases may cover the entire interesting state space. As the design size grows, the team will need to incorporate more and more randomization controls to hit the broad spectrum of input possibilities.

Pregenerated Test Cases Versus On-The-Fly Test Case Generation

Pregenerated test cases are those in which the input stimulus and output checking exist before running the simulation job. The verification engineer can read the test case and know exactly what it will do. These tests drive very specific scenarios. The stimulus creates unambiguous cases in the DUV such that the verification engineer can pregenerate the checking as well.

The alternative to predetermined test cases are those created *on-the-fly*, or while the simulation job is running. On-the-fly test cases use input constraint directives to create stimulus and make decisions on a cycle-by-cycle basis. These environments require a high amount of programmed intelligence in the stimulus components. Each cycle, the stimulus component makes decisions about what stimulus it will send for this cycle. The programmed intelligence within the stimulus component knows the legal input choices for a given cycle. The stimulus component will continue to send multicycle commands or data initiated on previous cycles and decide whether to initiate new commands. The constraint directives guide these decisions, allowing the verification engineer to control each test case to the desired level. The verification team uses the scoreboard or a cycle accurate reference model to communicate the generated stimulus to the checking components. A later section ("General Algorithms for Stimulus Components") describes general algorithms for making these decisions.

At first glance, there appears to be a one-to-one relationship between predetermined test cases and deterministic test generation. Similarly, random stimulus generation appears to have a tightly coupled relationship with on-the-fly generation. However, this is not the case. Predetermined and on-the-fly define *when* the verification team creates the test case with respect to the simulation run. Alternatively, deterministic and random define *how* the verification team creates the test case. It is common to generate predetermined, yet random test cases. For example, there are complex programs, called *test case generators*, that use bias-control input parameters and random number generators to create predetermined test cases. Good test case generators may create hundreds of different predetermined test cases from a single *template* (a single set of bias parameters). Each of these test cases differs, depending on the parameters and the initial value used to seed the random number generator. On the other end of the spectrum, deterministic tests can use some on-the-fly generation to drive inputs less critical to the test case intent. For example, a test case written to verify control logic may use on-the-fly generation for data packets. This style uses the same scoreboard checking techniques as a randomly generated, on-the-fly test case.

The previous section described the range of possibilities between deterministic and random test cases. Figure 7.4 showed that many test cases have both deterministic and random stimulus generation elements. For this discussion, *deterministic-leaning test cases* is defined as those written to test a specific scenario but may have randomization on some data or timings. *Random-leaning test cases* are defined as those with the freedom to create differing scenarios based on the pseudorandom numbers in the generation programs. By using those definitions, Figure

How the test is created

	Deterministic-leaning (written for a specific scenario)	Random-leaning (created using bias controls)
Pre-generated (prior to simulation)	Single scenario testbenches, usually written by hand to verify the specific scenario. Most often used early in the design schedule.	Test case generators using random parameters to bias the stimulus. Architecturally correct test cases are created, then run on the simulation engine.
On-the-fly (during simulation)	Single scenario test cases with some random generation of peripheral inputs. Random generation is used for inputs not critical to the test case intent.	Stimulus generated each cycle using parameter biasing to determine that cycle's inputs. The environment must have the knowledge of legal and illegal scenarios.

When the test is created

■ **FIGURE 7.5**

The type of test case stimulus combines deterministic or random with pregeneration or on-the-fly generation.

7.5 describes the four paradigms of input generation controls that result from the cross between pregeneration versus on-the-fly generation and deterministic-leaning versus random-leaning test cases.

There are appropriate times to use each of these four paradigms, as there are pros and cons to each. Pregenerated, deterministic tests are appropriate for designs with very few input signals or a small internal state space. This style of test case provides exact scenarios and precise control. Pregeneration (either deterministic or random) provides the verification team with a library of tests with a known set of input scenarios—what you see is what you get. However, pregeneration does have drawbacks with its inability to use the current state of the design to tailor the input stimulus. Pregenerated tests often use the most conservative input timing to control sequences in order to avoid creating illegal input scenarios. To avoid these overconstraint cases, verification engineers couple pregeneration with some on-the-fly capabilities. Pregeneration also requires maintenance over the life of the test case library as the design and specification changes. For these reasons, verification teams continue to migrate toward on-the-fly generated test cases, as evidenced by the growing popularity of HVLs that provide these capabilities.

Although the functional capability of the test case generation is the most important factor when choosing a test case type, the verification team must consider two other factors: memory usage and simulation performance. Both of these factors contribute to the verification team's ability to run test cases on their simulation engines. Simulation engines run on general-purpose computers (e.g., workstations), which have large but finite memory. On-the-fly generation techniques tend to use more memory as the test case environment must save the generated input (usually in the scoreboard or in a cycle accurate reference model) during simulation until the transaction or command completes. Pregeneration does not have this problem as the generation program and simulation run at different times.

The throughput (performance) of their verification suite is also a concern for the verification team. Here, the choice is between when the generation work occurs—either before the simulation job (pregeneration) or during the simulation (on-the-fly). A pregenerated test case will complete slightly faster than an on-the-fly test case running the same number of cycles against the same design because on-the-fly test case generation takes additional runtime workstation horsepower. However, verification teams often accept this trade-off because of the abundance of workstations and the additional capabilities of on-the-fly generation.

7.2.2 General Algorithms for Stimulus Components

No matter which stimulus generation paradigm the verification team chooses, the stimulus components, and especially the protocol component, use a similar algorithm for basic input transactions. The differences occur in step 3, listed below, when the environment initiates a new transaction or input sequence.

Stimulus generation programs follow this general decision-making order:

1. Check for global environment changes such as resets.

2. Continue required stimulus initiated on previous cycles.

3. Check if DUV can accept new stimulus and, if so, initiate based on generation paradigm.

Figure 7.6 shows a flow chart of this generalized decision-making algorithm. The flow chart shows only a single action on any given cycle. However, some DUV protocols may allow multiple actions in a single cycle. In that case, the order still holds, but the program may jump to the next decision after performing an action block.

If the environment takes the "Y" branch of the "new action allowed" decision block, the source of the "generate new stimulus" block in Figure 7.6 is the test case in a pregenerated paradigm, or a randomly chosen command in an on-the-fly paradigm. In both cases, the protocol

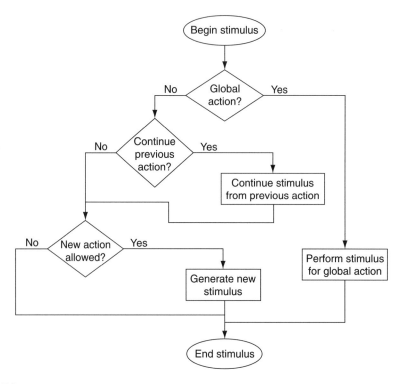

▪ **FIGURE 7.6**

A stimulus generation component's general decision-making algorithm for the beginning of each cycle.

component drives the inputs based on the new stimulus, applying the correct transaction protocols.

Stimulus responder components follow a slightly different algorithm, as these routines never initiate an action. Instead, the stimulus responder reacts to actions from the DUV. Stimulus responders follow this general decision-making order:

1. Check for global environment changes such as resets.

2. Continue response sequences for previous activity/requests from the DUV.

3. Initiate new response sequence for activity/requests that just occurred from the DUV.

Again, step 3 for stimulus responder components depends on the generation paradigm. In pregenerated tests, the stimulus responder sequence's source is the test case. In on-the-fly generation, the stimulus responder component may randomly choose a response based on the test case constraints or parameters.

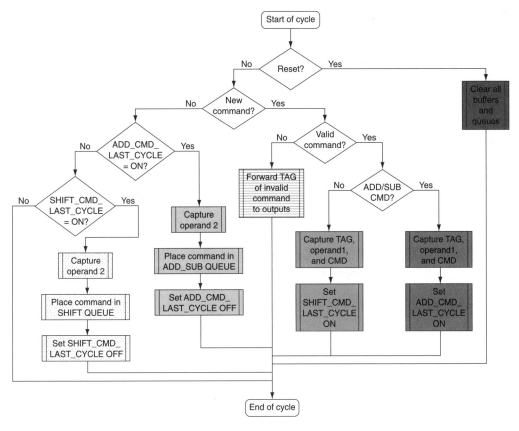

■ **FIGURE 7.7**

The stimulus generation algorithm for a single port on Calc2. The stimulus component uses this algorithm at the start of each cycle. The shading within the decision tree corresponds to the shading in Figures 7.8 and 7.9.

7.2.3   Applying the Four Types of Stimulus Generation to Calc2

The Calc2 test plan called for the verification effort to use a random environment. Nevertheless, for illustration purposes, we will step through an implementation of each of the generation paradigms using the Calc2 design as an example. Rather than look at the entire design, the focus will be on a single port and the logic sequence and state transitions for that port. In all cases, the verification team must replicate the stimulus generation for a single port across the other three.

Figure 7.7 shows the flow control for a single Calc2 input port. Each port's input flow feeds the Calc2 priority logic via the ADD_SUB queue and the SHIFT queue. Inputs to the port logic include the command, operand data, and tag lines. Outputs include the controls to write to the shift and add queues (which are located in the neighboring priority logic design). Other outputs are the signals that bypass the priority logic in the case of invalid commands. There are also environmental internal state machine controls that indicate that the stimulus component sent an *add* or *shift* command during the previous cycle. These controls allow the stimulus component to send the second operand data.

The different shading after major decisions indicates a state that the stimulus generation component enters. Consistent shading across the figures is used in this section to indicate the choice of shift commands, add commands, illegal commands, idle cycles, resets, and the second cycles for sending both add/sub and shift commands.

A major decision in Figure 7.7 is the "new command?" choice. This decision first requires knowledge of whether or not the stimulus component sent a command on the previous cycle and if there are already four outstanding commands from this port. If either is true, then the "N" branch of "new command?" must be taken. If both cases are false, there is still the decision of whether or not to send a new command on this cycle. If we choose not to send a new command, the stimulus component will drive idle values on the inputs. Otherwise, the stimulus component will take the "Y" side of the "new command?" decision block and initiate a new command.

The flow control shown in Figure 7.7 translates to the state machine diagram shown in Figure 7.8. This diagram indicates the legal transitions across six state machines in addition to the reset state machine.

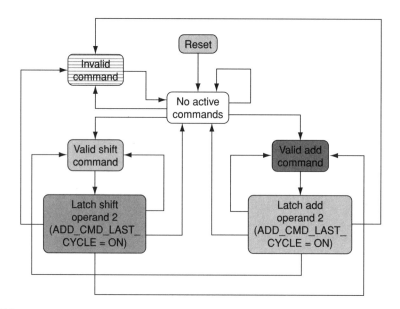

▪ **FIGURE 7.8**

The Calc2 single port stimulus generation algorithm's state machine diagram. The shading corresponds to the shading in Figures 7.7 and 7.9.

Because the design can enter the reset state at any time, all states have an implied (not pictured) transition back to the reset state machine. All other transitions not explicitly shown are illegal input sequences. For example, no valid command can follow an invalid command, as the protocols require that the cycle that follows a command (valid or illegal) be a null command. Therefore, it would break the protocol to follow an illegal command with another command the next cycle. This is interesting to note because the Calc2 DUV explicitly handles cases in which the input command is not a legal add, subtract, or shift command; however, the DUV does not handle cases in which the input stimulus sends commands on consecutive cycles. In the latter case, the Calc2 behavior is undefined. Therefore, it is appropriate for the Calc2 designer to place an assertion in the design to capture any case of consecutive commands.

The state machine diagram shows the two-cycle input sequence required for all *add*, *subtract*, *shift left*, or *shift right* commands. After receiving the second operand, the DUV internal logic ships the complete command packet (data, command, and tag) to the priority logic's ADD_SUB queue or SHIFT queue. On the following cycle, the logic can then accept a new command from the port inputs as long as there are available tags (less than four outstanding port requests). The inputs may also be idle, entering the logic into the "no active commands" state.

Figure 7.9 shows an exploded view of the state machine diagram. This figure shows how the possible execution state space explodes rather quickly. It depicts a portion of the legal transitions as defined in Figure 7.8 for seven cycles.

The dashed line shows a single path taken during simulation. Any type of stimulus generation (random or deterministic, pregenerated or on-the-fly) can create this path. However, each uses different methods to create the stimulus for the test case.

With an understanding of the Calc2 input port implementation algorithm, we can now examine the effects of the different stimulus types on simulation. Each of the four paradigms is described using Calc2 as the DUV.

Deterministic Test Cases

This exploded state machine view of Figure 7.9 repeats for all four Calc2 ports, although each port will follow different paths along the tree. For the following deterministic test case example, Port1 is assumed. Figure 7.10 shows a predetermined, deterministic test case for the dashed line path in Figure 7.9.

As with Calc1, the verification environment handles the reset sequence at the start of each test case. The DelayN field is also the same as with Calc1, in which this field indicates the number of cycles to wait until initiating the command.

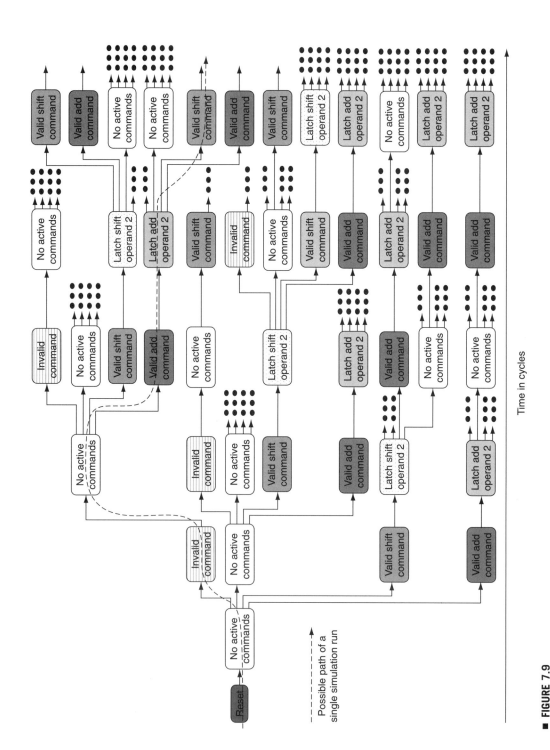

■ **FIGURE 7.9**

An exploded view of the state machine from Figure 7.8. This diagram shows all of the possible paths that a test case may take. The shading of each block corresponds to the shading in Figures 7.7 and 7.8.

```
/*  Port.tag  DelayN  Cmd    Operand1      Operand2      Result        Response*/
    Port1.0   0       "111"B "DEADBEEF"X   "BEADCAFE"X   "00000000"X   Illegal
    Port1.0   0       ADD    "00012345"X   "00054321"X   "00066666"X   Good
    Port1.2   0       SHL    "22222222"X   "00000002"X   "88888888"X   Good
```

■ **FIGURE 7.10**

Example predetermined, deterministic test case for Calc2 Port1.

A deterministic test case may continue beyond the sequence in Figure 7.10. It may also contain simultaneous commands from other ports. It is the job of the test case writer to define explicitly the sequences and expected results desired for each test case.

This paradigm gives complete control to the test case writer. There is no automation beyond the parsing of the command and bit-level stimulus translation. The test case writer makes all decisions on input values, including commands, timings, tag values, and data. This is an excellent method for testing specific short scenarios but becomes cumbersome for verifying a wide assortment of possible input scenarios. For example, test cases with more than four commands from a single port may cause headaches when trying to get hard-coded tags correct. Hard-coded tags require predicting the timing on responses in out-of-order cases. This requires trial-and-error, along with maintenance whenever the internals of the Calc2 priority logic changes.

Deterministic Test Cases with On-The-Fly Generation

It is easy for the verification engineer to generate a short test case by hand. However, writing a long, deterministic test case becomes quite tiresome. Imagine typing the syntax of Figure 7.10 for 100 commands. Creating the data and hand calculating the results is a time-consuming and monotonous job for long, deterministic tests. This is where the power of on-the-fly generation helps, even when coupled with deterministic testing. Rather than generating data and tags by hand, the stimulus component can do it. The following test case keeps the verification engineer's deterministic intent, while freeing the writer to focus on the sequence, not the data.

Figure 7.11 shows an example deterministic test case with randomization for Calc2 Port1. Figure 7.12 shows the verification environment that utilizes the test case in Figure 7.11. In this environment, the port protocol component replaces the "x" tag values and the stimulus generation component replaces the "rand" keyword operands. In few cases, the writer uses hard-coded values ("Port1.2" and "00000000"X data) in which the intent of the test case requires specific values. When this test case runs, the environment generates tags based on their availability. Because the DUV may return commands out of order, predicting the

```
/*  Port.tag      DelayN      Cmd         Operand1        Response*/
    Port1.x       0           "111"B      rand            Illegal
    Port1.x       0           ADD         rand            Good
    Port1.x       2           SHL         rand            Good
    Port1.2       0           "011"B      rand            Illegal
    Port1.x       1           SUB         rand            Good
    Port1.x       0           SHR         "00000000"X     Good
    Port1.x       3           SHL         rand            Good
    Port1.x       1           SUB         rand            Underflow
```

▪ **FIGURE 7.11**

Example deterministic test case with randomization for Calc2 Port1.

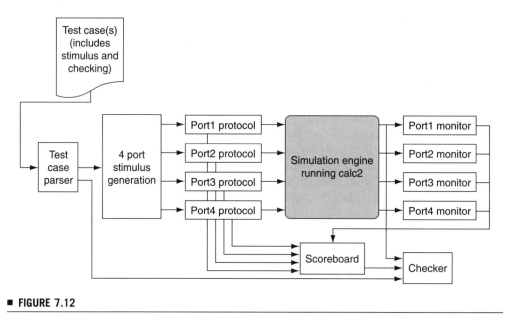

▪ **FIGURE 7.12**

The Calc2 verification environment for deterministic test cases.

sequence of returning tags on a long test case is a waste of time, requiring extensive trial and error simulation jobs. Furthermore, the test case would need ongoing maintenance each time internal DUV changes altered the response timings. Instead, the verification team builds the intelligence into the environment with a simple table that tracks outstanding command tags. If no tags are available, the environment cannot send in a new command until the DUV completes one. Otherwise, the protocol component simply uses an available tag to replace the "x" value in the test case. This is an elegant and efficient method that avoids duplicating the DUV priority and control logic, which would have to predict the ordering of the responses. Implementation of this algorithm involves communication between the protocol component and the monitor com-

Write by
port1 stimulus

Reset by
port1 monitor

Read by
port1 stimulus

Used by
port1 checker

Verified by
port1 checker

Port number	Tag	In use	Command	Operand 1	Operand 2
Port 1	00	0			
Port 1	01	0			
Port 1	10	1	SHL	"6F3C6870"X	"00000005"X
Port 1	11	0			
Port 2	00	0			
Port 2	01	1	SUB	"A318F792"X	"884429BC"X
Port 2	10	1	ADD	"AC7DCC59"X	"B6623D76"X
Port 2	11	0			
Port 3	00	1	SHR	"E3E99D88"X	"00000001"X
Port 3	01	0			
Port 3	10	1	SHR	"E6FE24F4"X	"0000001A"X
Port 3	11	0			
Port 4	00	1	ADD	"793F8731"X	"2F849275"X
Port 4	01	0			
Port 4	10	0			
Port 4	11	1	SUB	"A3BA1751"X	"2F849275"X

■ **FIGURE 7.13**

The format of the Calc2 scoreboard allows for quick indexing using the port and tag value (shaded fields). The verification components read and write to the other fields.

ponent. Therefore, the environment requires that the tag table be in a global area that both components can update. The stimulus component must write to the table to remove tag availability each time it sends a new command. The monitor component must free the tag in the table when the response comes from the DUV. This is a common approach used in many verification environments, with the scoreboard serving as a fine choice for placing the tag table (see Figure 7.13).

The stimulus component needs to be intelligent when it creates data values as well. The "good" or "Overflow/Underflow" keywords in the response column imply constraints on the operands. In the case of a *good* response for an *add* command, the environment must generate two operands whose sum is less than "FFFFFFFF"X (unsigned). The straight-forward approach to this is to first pick a number between zero and "FFFFFFFF"X and assign this value to Operand1. The algorithm then calculates Operand2's value by choosing a random number between zero and "FFFFFFFF"X – Operand1. The environment calculates operands for a "good" response for the *sub* command using an even simpler algorithm. After choosing Operand1, Operand2 must be less than or equal to Operand1. Overflow or underflow responses require breaking the above constraints. In the *add* case, operand1 may be between 1 and "FFFFFFFF"X, and Operand2 must be a number greater than "FFFFFFFF"X – Operand1. For the underflow case on the *sub* command, Operand2 must be greater than Operand1 (therefore, Operand1 cannot be "FFFFFFFF"X). The verification team builds these algorithms into the environment.

Because the environment generates the operands, there is no "Result" value column in the test case. The environment must perform the result value check based on the operand values created by the stimulus component. This check is simple enough to code into the environment. The stimulus component needs to post the tag, command, and operands to the scoreboard so that the checker component can calculate the expected value when the DUV returns a response.

The scoreboard is simply a data structure used by multiple verification components to communicate with each other. It is required whenever stimulus components create values on-the-fly. Figure 7.13 shows a scoreboard for Calc2, implemented as a table. Each row of the table corresponds to a tag from a particular port. The verification components read and write to the fields: "tag in use," "command," "Operand1," and "Operand2". This setup allows quick indexing into the scoreboard by the stimulus, checker, and monitor components.

The stimulus component reads the tag "in use" value to check for availability. If available, it sets the value to "in use" and writes the command and operand values when it sends the command. When the DUV completes the command, the monitor resets the "in-use" value, and the checker reads the command and operand values to perform the check.

This static table method works well for small, densely populated values such as this. In larger, sparsely populated scoreboard spaces, the scoreboard implementation requires a linked list or hash table with a search algorithm to find the desired value. Verification of designs such as caches requires this, as the simulation does not use the entire array but rather randomly chosen portions. Implementing the cache scoreboard as a static table might exhaust the workstation memory while utilizing very little of the reserved memory space.

Figures 7.10 and 7.11 demonstrate deterministic test case approaches to verifying Calc2. The first test case is fully predetermined. The second test case used some on-the-fly generation to ease the burden of writing long tests. Although the second test case contained some use of randomly created values, it is still deterministic because the test case writer dictated the specific scenario. We now move to the cases of random test cases.

Pregenerated Random Test Cases

Random stimulus generation uses an entirely different approach. The verification team automates the generation of the command and associated result values into either a test case generator (predetermined) or the stimulus components (on-the-fly). A test case generator program runs separately from the simulation environment, whereas an on-the-fly generation style integrates into the simulation environment.

Random-based test case generation requires programming the stimulus and checking algorithm intelligence into stand-alone software. There are generally two types of inputs to a test case generator: a template, or map of the desired test case, and a more general set of parameter inputs used to bias certain randomizations. Depending on the DUV, the team may choose to embed the parameter in the template input file. In the examples for Calc2, the parameter bias controls are separate from the template. The output of the test case generator is a test case (or test cases) that contains all the stimulus and checking information required for the simulation environment. The test cases created by the generator use the same style of verification environment components as deterministic test cases (shown in Figure 7.12). The test case parser will change to match the different format, but the concepts of the environment remain the same. The test case generator includes an internal, or reference, model of the DUV. The generator uses this model to precalculate the expected results given the inputs it creates. Depending on the complexity of the design, these models may be quite complex. Figure 7.14 shows the inputs and outputs of the test case generator.

Verification engineers commonly use test case generation to verify microprocessors or embedded controllers. Although microprocessors have a far more complex instruction set than do the few used in Calc2, Calc2 serves as a good demonstration of the test case generation technique.

Figure 7.15 shows three example template files for a test case generator for Calc2. The first template, called "most constrained," uses the test case generator to create a deterministic test case. The second template, "add queue intensive," is an example of the most common mode used in test case generation. The third template, "least constrained," allows the test case generator's randomization capabilities to dictate most of the resulting test case.

Templates provide a roadmap for the test case generator. The result is one or more test cases that follow the roadmap. The test cases run

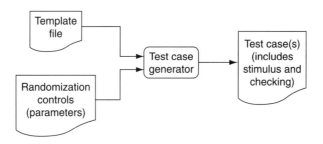

■ **FIGURE 7.14**

The test case generation environment uses a template file and randomization controls as input. The test case generator's output is a test case, complete with stimulus and checking.

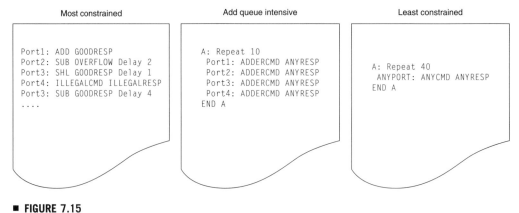

■ **FIGURE 7.15**

Three possible template files for a Calc2 test case generator.

```
/* Port.tag      DelayN    Cmd      Operand1        Operand2        Result          Response*/
   Port1.x       0         ADD      "396A29EF"X     "670B5C23"X     "A0758612"X     Good
   Port2.x       2         SUB      "7C2D3E49"X     "82C37526"X     "00000000"X     Underflow
   Port3.x       1         SHL      "2048BE96"X     "00000003"X     "0245F4B0"X     Good
   Port4.2       0         "A"X     "218BC572"X     "23C01864"X     "00000000"X     Illegal
   Port3.x       4         SUB      "B5610EF3"X     "37AD48E0"X     "7DB3C613"X     Good
```

■ **FIGURE 7.16**

A "most constrained" test case from generator.

separately against the Calc2 DUV, using the verification environment to parse the port commands, drive stimulus, and check results. The actual test case format, shown in Figure 7.16, is a variation of the format shown in Figure 7.10.

The test case generator in this example defers control of the tag specification to the verification environment. The test case specifies all other values, including the delays between commands. Some of these values originate from the template file (ports, command, delays, and responses). The test case generator creates the rest of the values (operands and results).

The second template, "add queue intensive," is a more interesting and common use of test case generation. Here, the template calls for the use of groups and randomizations in test case construction. Figure 7.17 shows the definitions of the groups cited in this test case, ADDERCMD and ANYRESP, along with other groupings that verification might use.

The first definition, ANYCMD, includes a second-level grouping, ANY-GOODCMD, which encompasses the four defined CALC2 commands. ANYCMD also includes illegal command types.

The command grouping used in the "add queue intensive" template, ADDERCMD, lists the *add* and *sub* commands. This group is interesting

```
ANYCMD: ANYGOODCMD, ILLEGALCMD
ANYGOODCMD: ADD, SUB, SHL, SHR
ADDERCMD: ADD, SUB
SHIFTERCMD: SHL, SHR
ANYRESP: GOODRESP, OVERFLOW, ILLEGALRESP
ANYPORT: Port1, Port2, Port3, Port4
```

■ **FIGURE 7.17**

The Calc2 test case generation list creates shorthand keywords for the template writer. Each keyword contains a list of possible values.

because the DUV directs these commands toward the adder ALU, whereas the commands in **SHIFTERCMD** use the shift ALU. Therefore, the intent of this template is to stress the adder ALU and the priority paths that lead to it. A resulting test case creates interesting scenarios that not only will keep the adder ALU busy but also because it forces all of the command traffic into a single control and data path, ensuring that intense corner cases occur.

Finally, the "add queue intensive" template uses the ANYRESP group, which encompasses all command response types. The test case generator uses the **GOODRESP** and **OVERFLOW** response types to guide the selection of operand data. The ILLEGALRESP is used only when the test case generator calls for an illegal command.

The final input file, randomization controls, defines the biasing between the selections that the test case generator makes. Figure 7.18 shows a sample randomization control file.

The randomization controls dictate the average ratio between the choices. Together with a pseudorandom number generator, the test case generator uses these bias controls to choose specific values each time it creates a command. Therefore, on average, a template using the ANYCMD keyword will choose legal commands 90% of the time and illegal commands in the remaining 10%. Of the 90% legal commands, the *add* command is selected 30% of the time, and so forth.

Figure 7.19 shows a possible test case created using the "add queue intensive" template. Note that after the reset, all commands must be *add* or *sub* as defined in the template. The delay values, as defined in the randomization control file, range from zero to five. The data selections appear to be random across a 32-bit range. However, closer inspection reveals that the response type constrains the operand values.

```
ANYCMD:      ANYGOODCMD 90
             ILLEGAL 10
ANYGOODCMD:  ADD 30
             SUB 30
             SHL 20
             SHR 20
ADDERCMD:    ADD 40
             SUB 60
SHIFTERCMD:  SHL 50
             SHR 50
DELAY Range:0 30
             1 25
             2 20
             3 15
             4 5
             5 5
RESPONSE:    GOOD 80
             OVERFLOW 20
ANYPORT:     Port1 25
             Port2 25
             Port3 25
             Port4 25
 . . .
```

■ **FIGURE 7.18**

The test case randomization controls defines the probabilities of each choice within a generation list.

The template calls for 40 commands (Figure 7.19 lists only the first 12). Note the regularity of the port command ordering (1, 2, 3, 4, 1, 2, 3, 4 . . .). The template dictated this ordering. The user could use another randomization control, called "ANYPORT" in the "least constrained" template, which would leave the port number selection to the test case generator under random biasing controls.

A single template file such as "add queue intensive" can spawn hundreds of unique test cases. Although Figure 7.19 shows a single example, the generator can re-run, using a different initial seed, creating a different test case that still follows the template. This capability enhances the verification team's ability to hit corner conditions in the design. In this example, the template will focus test cases on DUV controls such as filling the add queue and interactions between ALU data and control under stressful, back-to-back conditions. This is less valuable with the "most constrained" test case example, in which the only deviation would be in the data value randomizations.

```
/* Port.tag    DelayN    Cmd    Operand1        Operand2        Result          Response*/
   Port1.x     1         SUB    "CFAA6E5D"X     "BC18080A"X     "13926653"X     Good
   Port2.x     0         SUB    "9A1B0AC9"X     "E50F3803"X     "00000000"X     Underflow
   Port3.x     0         ADD    "CFB6FEC8"X     "28F188CC"X     "F8A88794"X     Good
   Port4.x     2         SUB    "3385D066"X     "2BC9B810"X     "07BC1856"X     Good
   Port1.x     1         ADD    "993C398E"X     "3CC2059F"X     "D5FE3F2D"X     Good
   Port2.x     5         SUB    "E58C0B0B"X     "2FF2F492"X     "B5991679"X     Good
   Port3.x     0         ADD    "76BA4E2A"X     "578E5BF5"X     "CE48AA1F"X     Good
   Port4.x     3         ADD    "57AFC991"X     "F954D4C4"X     "00000000"X     Overflow
   Port1.x     0         SUB    "D84EC9C7"X     "4612AEEE"X     "923C1AD9"X     Good
   Port2.x     1         SUB    "AABB1BFE"X     "2DFC9460"X     "7CBE879E"X     Good
   Port3.x     1         SUB    "91782416"X     "7D49CF59"X     "142E54BD"X     Good
   Port4.x     0         ADD    "3B60DBF6"X     "15F8F2F1"X     "5159CEE7"X     Good
   ...
```

■ **FIGURE 7.19**

An "add queue intensive" test case from generator.

```
/* Port.tag    DelayN    Cmd    Operand1        Operand2        Result          Response*/
   Port4.x     0         SHR    "6F3C6870"X     "00000005"X     "0379E343"X     Good
   Port3.x     3         SUB    "A318F792"X     "884429BC"X     "1AD4CDD6"X     Good
   Port1.x     0         ADD    "AC7DCC59"X     "B6623D76"X     "00000000"X     Overflow
   Port3.x     1         SHR    "E3E99D88"X     "00000001"X     "71F4CEC4"X     Good
   Port3.x     1         SHR    "E6FE24F4"X     "0000001A"X     "00000039"X     Good
   Port1.x     1         ADD    "793F8731"X     "2F849275"X     "A8C419A6"X     Good
   Port3.x     3         "C"X   "A3BA1751"X     "2F849275"X     "00000000"X     Illegal
   Port2.x     0         SHR    "C494A384"X     "00000007"X     "01892947"X     Good
   Port4.x     0         SHL    "D0D75B46"X     "0000000A"X     "5D6D1800"X     Good
   Port2.x     2         SUB    "65931FF4"X     "0F467BB9"X     "564CA43B"X     Good
   ...
```

■ **FIGURE 7.20**

A "least constrained" test case from generator.

The "least constrained" template in Figure 7.15 gives few constraints to the test case generator. The generator will create a test case with 40 commands of any type, with any possible response, from any combination of ports. Figure 7.20 shows the first 10 commands from a single test case created using this template. However, the random control biasing shown in Figure 7.18 still hold.

Even in this randomly generated test case, the stimulus components still must ensure that the inputs adhere to the DUV protocols. The timing between port commands is a prime example of this. The port stimulus component cannot send Calc2 a new command if no tags are available, regardless of the "DelayN" value dictated by the test case. Here, the definition of the DelayN field changes. It now indicates a minimum number of cycles between commands from the same port. After waiting DelayN cycles, the port stimulus component sends the new command if there is an available tag. Otherwise, the port stimulus component continues to hold the command until there is an available tag.

The test case generation software for Calc2 is relatively simple. More complex microprocessor test case generation falls into a category known as *knowledge-based test case generation* (KBTG) [1, 2]. Under KBTG lies a database pertaining to the specific architecture and design of the DUV, which contains all of the information needed to create interesting input stimulus and to predict the behavior of the microprocessor. Today's complex microprocessor cores require the database to have a deep knowledge of the architecture. This software handles the result prediction for any synchronous instruction stream for the given microprocessor.

Although it is likely that the Calc2 verification engineers could tuck the stimulus generation and result prediction logic into a single program as shown in Figure 7.14, complex microprocessors require the separation of these routines. Furthermore, the KBTG programmers personalize the stimulus generation for each new microprocessor core design, which is required to create stimulus that attacks the nuances of the new design point. Every time the design point changes for a new release of the processor, the test case stimulus generation requires updates in order to exercise any new microarchitecture design features, such as superscalar instruction grouping or pipeline depth adjustments.

On the other hand, the result prediction routines under KBTG only require updates when the design implements new architectural features. For example, if the latest version of the microprocessor supports binary floating-point operations, the KBTG programmers enhance the prediction logic for this support. However, the result prediction for legacy (previous) instructions remains unchanged.

On-the-Fly Random Test Cases

The final type of stimulus generation is on-the-fly generated random. This is the paradigm chosen in our verification plan and is the best fit for Calc2. On-the-fly generated random test cases have similarities to test case generation in that it uses constraint directives to make stimulus decisions. However, on-the-fly random generation makes these decisions while running simulation, rather than before the simulation, requiring the verification team to build generation intelligence into the stimulus components. The main advantage of on-the-fly generation is that the verification environment can create stimulus in reaction to the state of the DUV.

In the test case generation environment, the test case parser reads the predetermined test case and forwards the port commands to the stimulus component. In the on-the-fly random generation environment, the stimulus component receives biasing parameters as input and makes the stimulus decisions each cycle. The output prediction programming moves from the test case generation program into the stimulus, scoreboard, and checking components as well.

In the on-the-fly paradigm, the verification environment calls the stimulus component programs at the beginning of each simulation cycle. The stimulus generation components must track the state of the DUV and decide whether to send new stimulus, send complete stimulus that started on a previous cycle, or not send any stimulus. This is the same algorithm shown in Figure 7.6. Some of these generation choices may be limited based on how busy the DUV is (e.g., four outstanding port commands from a single port in Calc2) or on stimulus sent on previous cycles (e.g., the Calc2 requirement to send the second operand data on the cycle after the initial command and data). The protocol components translate the transaction-level decisions of the generation component into bit-level stimulus, maintaining good parity and protocols no matter what choices the generation component made.

Calc2 does not require stimulus responder components, but it does require stimulus generation components for each of the four ports. Figure 7.21 shows the algorithm for generating commands on-the-fly for Calc2. The flowchart represents a single port's stimulus. The verification team duplicates this for each port.

Each port has individualized constraint directives. These bias controls affect the outcome of the "send new command?" block, the "choose command" block, the "choose response type" block, and the "choose operand" block. In addition, the constraint directives may control the usage of specific tags by a port. The constraints may differ from port to port, altering the biasing of each instance.

The algorithm first checks to see if the stimulus component initiated a command on the previous cycle (2nd_Cmd_Cycle is ON). If so, it must complete the operation by sending the second operand. In this state, the stimulus component also uses the randomization controls to choose a Delay_Count, which indicates the between-command cycle gap on the port. Figure 7.22 shows a randomization control file. This sample indicates the bias controls for the Delay_Count.

To choose a value based on the randomization controls, the stimulus component first uses a pseudorandom number generation to pick a number between 1 and the sum of the individual weights (30 + 25 + 20 + 15 + 5 + 5 = 100 in the case of Delay_Count). The stimulus component uses the chosen number to index to the particular Delay_Count value. In our example, a random number between 1 and 30 would give a 0 delay, between 31 and 55 would give a 1-cycle delay; between 56 and 75 would give a 2-cycle delay, and so forth. Note that the sum of the weights need not total 100 as in the case of RESPONSE. This method of choosing a value for a variable works for any bias control table.

If 2nd_Cmd_Cycle is OFF, the stimulus component checks the scoreboard to see if there is an available tag. If no tag is available, then the stimulus component's work is complete for this cycle. If a tag is available, it checks to see if the Delay_Count is zero. A zero count indicates that the between-command cycle gap has been met. If the delay count is

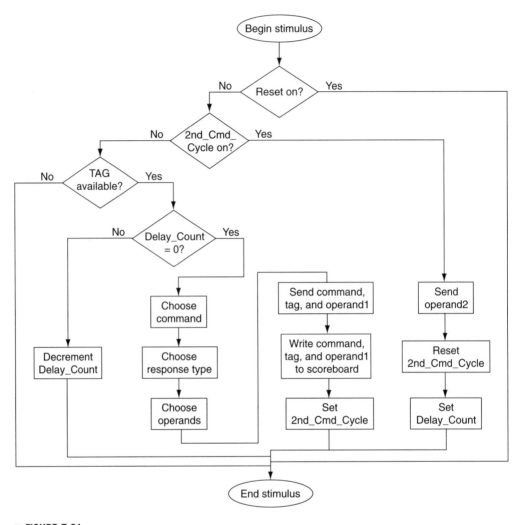

■ **FIGURE 7.21**

An on-the-fly generation algorithm for a stimulus generation on a single Calc2 port.

not zero, then it is decremented. Otherwise, the stimulus component chooses a command based on the randomization controls. In our example, there is a 10% chance that the stimulus component chooses to send an illegal command, a 30% chance of an *add* command, and so on. After choosing a command value, the stimulus component chooses a response value unless the command was an illegal value—in that case, the response must be "illegal." Finally, by using the response value ("good" or "overflow/underflow"), the stimulus component chooses operands using the same algorithm described for the "rand" operands in Figure 7.11. The order of decisions, in which the algorithm chooses the

```
/* Format is....              */
/* VAR NAME: Value1 Weight1   */
/*           ValueN WeightN   */
CMDS:         ILLEGAL 10
              ADD 30
              SUB 25
              SHL 20
              SHR 15
DELAYCount:   0 30
              1 25
              2 20
              3 15
              4 5
              5 5
RESPONSE:     GOOD 75
              OVERFLOW 15
SHIFTOP2:     0 25
              31 15
              OTHER
```

■ **FIGURE 7.22**

The randomization controls for the Calc2 on-the-fly stimulus generation component.

response type before the operand data, may seem odd. However, there is good reason for this ordering, as choosing data first will lock in a response type (e.g., *overflow/underflow* for *add/sub*). The verification engineer's intent is to have control over the average probability of *good* responses versus *overflow/underflow* responses, so the algorithm makes that decision first. The effect of one decision on others falls under constraint solving, described in a later section ("Constraint Solving in Random Environments").

After choosing all of the values, the stimulus component's protocol driver sends the command, tag, and first operand. It also sets 2nd_Cmd_Cycle to ON, indicating that the stimulus component must complete the command send sequence the following cycle.

The SHIFTOP2 values are of particular interest in the randomization control file. Here, the verification engineer indicates that there are special values within the range of Operand2 values for *shift* commands. Instead of an even distribution of numbers between 0 and 31, the two endpoints have a higher probability than the values in-between.

In an on-the-fly generation environment, the stimulus component continues to send commands until one of two events occur:

- The checker or monitor components encounter an unexpected DUV value.

- The environment hits its predetermined limit based on either the number of cycles or the number of transactions.

When one of these events occurs, the stimulus component will not initiate any new commands. If the stimulus component is in the middle of sending a command, it will complete the transaction as dictated by the protocols, and then *quiesce*. A quiesced stimulus component will not initiate any new commands but may complete any transactions started on previous cycles.

In the case of an error, the test case will complete a few cycles after detection of the error. It is good practice to allow the test case to run for a nominal number of cycles (10 or so) before stopping the simulation. This practice assists in debugging, as a designer or verification engineer can view traces of the HDL's behavior just after the environment detects the error. The reason this is important is that the HDL could arrive in a particular state from multiple paths. Allowing the test case to run beyond the error condition may assist in pointing to the exact path and cause of the bug.

In the case of the predetermined cycle or transaction limit, the test case completes when the DUV completes all commands. The environment relies on the scoreboard to indicate when the DUV has completed all commands or transactions. Either method of ending a successful test case is acceptable. Verification environments with cycle-based limits run until a predetermined number of cycles have passed. This is called the *quiesce cycle*. Alternatively, verification environments with transaction limits send a predetermined number of transactions before the environment quiesces.

7.2.4 Seeding Random Test Cases

Random test cases, similar to all verification jobs, must be repeatable. Repeatability is required because it is necessary to reproduce failures both for analysis and for fix verification.

Re-running a deterministic, predetermined test case is not a concern. The test case exists before the simulation run, so the verification team can save it for later use when the designer makes the required updates. However, in on-the-fly random, in which stimulus components make decisions during the course of simulation, there is no predetermined test case to "save."

To meet the repeatability requirement, a single initial seed value must be the root for all of the random number generators used by all environment components. Using an initial seed guarantees that the random number generators produce the same sequence of values when re-running the test case. Rather than saving a test case, the verification team saves the seed that generates the test case.

In addition, the verification team must save the randomization control file along with the seed. Using the same seed with the same randomization control file against the same simulation model will produce an identical test case. Conversely, a change in randomization control parameters will likely change the entire test case, even if the initial seed is the same.

Seeding each stimulus component requires careful planning and an understanding of random number generators' behavior. Given the same initial seed, a random number generator will produce the same sequence of numbers. Each time the stimulus component calls the random number generation function, it uses the previous random number to seed the next call. This gives a repeatable, but pseudorandom sequence of numbers. The good side of this is that it allows the verification engineer to reproduce a test case; however, each stimulus component must use different seeds or the components will act in concert. Using Calc2 as an example, Figure 7.23 shows three possible methods for seeding the individual port stimulus generators.

Method 1 in Figure 7.23 uses the initial test case seed directly for each of the four port stimulus generators. In this case, all four ports will initially send identical commands rather than make personalized decisions. Because all four ports use the same random number generation function, they will continually produce the same sequence of decisions. Rather than acting independently, the stimulus components are harmonic. This is not the verification engineer's intent. Method 1 will significantly handicap the verification environment's ability to drive interesting scenarios.

Method 2 appears to avoid Method 1's problem. The environment uses the initial test case seed to create different initial seeds for each stimulus component. Therefore, each stimulus component starts with its own seed. However, this method also has undesirable side effects. Because the random number generator uses the previous seed to generate the next number, all of the stimulus components under Method 2 create a similar set of random numbers, just offset by one, two, or three calls to the routine. Given the initial seed value of "a," the random number generator will produce values "b," "c," "d," "e," "f," "g," etc, in that order. Therefore, the initial test case seed, a, will seed port1 with seed b, port2 with seed c, port3 with seed d, and port4 with seed e. On the surface, this seems okay. However, port1's sequence of random numbers will be c, d, e, f, g, etc. Port2 will be offset only slightly: d, e, f, g, h. . . . This may lead to less than desired randomization across the ports.

Method 3 fixes the problem by introducing a second random number generator. The second random number generator produces an entirely different sequence of numbers than does the first, even when seeded with the same value as the other generator. By using the first generator to seed

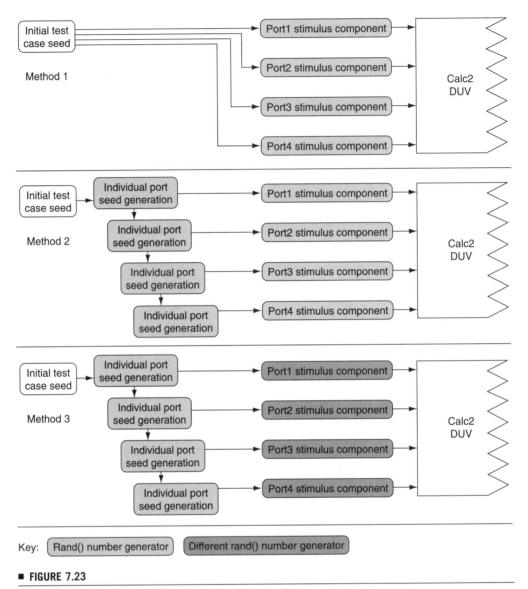

▪ FIGURE 7.23

Three methods for seeding duplicate stimulus components. Method 3 is the most effective algorithm for avoiding harmonic stimulus component activity.

the individual ports with different values and the second generator to make on-the-fly random biasing decisions, Method 3 achieves the verification engineer's intent of independent, randomly driven ports.

When re-running test cases for complex DUVs, any variation from the original simulation sequence quickly sends the new test case down a divergent path. Even the slightest of changes in DUV or stimulus component timing will result in a different test case from the original. Occasionally, this presents a hole in the on-the-fly random paradigm. When the fix for a design error changes the timing on the DUV outputs, it likely changes the cycle sequence for the stimulus component, forever altering the sequence of on-the-fly generated inputs. In this case, it is best to add coverage monitors to snoop for a recurrence of the error condition to assure that the stimulus component creates the error scenario and the design update fixed the flaw.

7.2.5 Constraint Solving in Random Environments

Every time a stimulus component chooses a value to drive into the DUV, there are restrictions on the possible choices. The most basic restriction is the number of input bits for that value. However, most input lines have further restrictions on the content of the control or data signals. These restrictions are based on the content and context of the input. These restrictions are called *constraints*.

Most verification environments have some sort of constraint solving challenge. A constraint solving challenge, as defined by Eyal Bin et al. "consists of a finite set of variables and a set of constraints" [3]. There is a range of possible values for each variable; however, choosing a particular value for one variable may restrict the realm of possible values for another variable. These implications are constraints. A constraint solving challenge occurs when a relationship exists between multiple input values.

In verification, there are two categories of constraint solving engines. The first is a general-purpose constraint solver. HVLs (Specman, Vera as discussed in Chapter 6) use powerful, general-purpose constraint solvers to aid in the attack of the exploding state space challenges faced by test bench authors. General-purpose constraint solving engines require a deep background and are beyond the realm of this book.

The second approach is to embed constraint-solving mechanisms in the test bench code. This category includes code written by verification engineers to solve constraints on the DUV. To this end, we offer approaches and examples.

In the course of creating verification environments for specific DUVs, engineers constantly deal with input constraints, which may restrict the value of a single variable or restrict other variables based on a relationship between them. Constraints may also exist over time, restricting inputs for a period of cycles or requiring responses with a number of cycles. Ignoring constraints in stimulus generation leads to illegal conditions and protocol violations. The most basic constraint on most designs is the set of legal decode values. The Calc2 design constrains the 4-bit command bus to five legal inputs: zero (no op) and the four command codes for *add*, *subtract*, *shift left*, and *shift right*. All other values are illegal commands. A more complex constraint in Calc2 is the restriction that each port may have no more than four commands outstanding at a given time. This is a temporal constraint, to which the verification environment must constantly abide. However, this is still a relatively simple constraint.

In Calc2, the case in which the operand data generation requires intelligence is our first venture into constraint solving between multiple variables. Here, the possible Operand2 values had to be tailored based on the type of response already chosen. The operands both have a large set of possible values (2^{32}), whereas there are two possible values for the responses for *add* and *subtract* commands: *good* and *overflow/underflow*. However, once the stimulus component makes a choice for one variable, it limits the other variable's legal solution space. For example, a "good" response for the *subtract* command constrains the second operand to be less than the first operand.

Importance of the Sequence of Solving Variable Constraints

When creating random environments, the order that the stimulus component assigns values to variables is a key decision made by the verification engineer. Choosing variable values in the wrong sequence may unduly limit the input stimulus. Such a limitation can handicap a verification environment so that certain areas of the DUV remain unexercised. It is therefore imperative that the verification engineer understand the constraint relationships between variables.

The data and response variables in Calc2 are a simple, yet powerful example of the implication of the sequence in which the stimulus component assigns values to constrained variables. The randomization table in Figure 7.22 shows that for *add* and *subtract* commands, it is the verification engineer's intent that the stimulus component creates "good" responses for 80% of the commands and "overflow/underflow" responses on the remaining 20% of the commands. Consider the two possible sequences: choose the operand data first, or choose the response first. If the stimulus component chooses the operand data first, then there is a 50% probability that the operands would produce an overflow or underflow response. Randomly chosen operand values in the range of 0 to $2^{32} - 1$ automatically constrain the response value; that is, once the stimulus component chooses operands without constraints, the response value is determined. Therefore, the correct sequence to implement the verification engineer's intent is first to choose the value for the response variable. Then, the stimulus component uses a constrained algorithm for choosing operands shown in Figure 7.11. The flowchart in Figure 7.21 indicates the correct sequence.

Constraint Solving in Stimulus Components

Constraint solving for specific DUV applications requires a three-step process:

1. Understand the interdependencies.

2. Prioritize the variables.

3. Analyze the implications.

The first step is to map all of the interdependencies of the input variables. This entails understanding which variables are closely coupled, loosely coupled, or unrelated. Closely coupled variables imply that when the stimulus component selects the value of one variable, another variable's (or variables') value is restricted to a small range. Loosely coupled variables imply fewer restrictions on the second variable's value. Choices between unrelated variables have no effect on the other.

Generally, the best method for understanding interdependencies on a particular DUV is to first group related input signals. A DUV may have dozens of input signals, but many of these are unrelated to each other. Group together those that are related. Stimulus components may act independently on these groups. These stimulus components may even be in separate modules. The four ports on Calc2 are an example of grouping related inputs. Within each port, input signals (data, command, and tag) values are coupled. However, across each port, these input signals are unrelated. Port1's signals imply no constraints on any other port.

Continuing down the path of understanding the interdependencies, the verification engineer should now map the closely coupled variables to each other. The loosely coupled variables follow. For every set of variables that constrain each other, test that the constraints are reciprocal; that is, validate that all of the same constraints apply regardless of which variable value is chosen first. Closely coupled constraints are generally reciprocal. For loosely coupled constraints, the order in which variable values are chosen matters.

On Calc2, the specifications imply coupling the signals on each port. Looking closer at the relationships within a port, we see a relationship between the response values and the commands. There is a 1-to-1 relationship between the *shift* operation and the *good* response (a *shift* command only gets a *good* response). The *add* and *subtract* commands have a looser coupling to the response codes, as the data and response values are coupled. We have already discussed the loosely coupled constraint relationship between the *add/subtract* operand values and the *good/overflow/underflow* responses.

Prioritization of the variables dictates the order in which the verification environment assigns values to variables. Understanding the implications of the sequencing of value choices is the heart of the prioritization process. Three factors dictate priority:

- Intent of the test

- The relationship between groups of coupled variables

- The relationship within variables in a group

The most important factor in sequencing variables is the intent of the test case. If the intent is very specific, the constraints on variable values are tight. Conversely, if the verification engineer's intent is to hit a broad range of the DUV space, then the variable values tend to be constrained only by the DUV specification. An example of a tightly constrained test case for Calc2 would be one written to verify a Shift_left of zero places from Port1. Here, only the tag and Operand1 values are unconstrained. The port, command (Shift_left), and Operand2 data ("00000000"x) are tightly constrained. On the other hand, the "least constrained" test case in Figure 7.15 is a template for a test case constrained only by the Calc2 specification. However, even that template can run tightly constrained, depending on the values in the randomization control file. In either case, the intent of the test case dictates a sequence of choices for variable values.

The relationship between groups of coupled variables and the relationship within variables in a group have equal priority when sequencing constraint solving. In many DUV specifications, there may be only weak constraints between groups of variables. This is the case on Calc2, in which the only constraining values that exist between the four ports are the reset line and the clock signal. Fundamentally, these two signals have little impact on Calc2 test cases except when the intent is to verify the reset or the clock.

Although there may not be constraints across groups of coupled variables, there are always constraints between variables in a group (otherwise, the variables would not be grouped together). Here, the order that the verification environment assigns values to variables is key in assuring the proper stimulus generation. The rule of thumb (after accounting for test case intent) is to sequence the variables by first choosing values for the variables that least constrain the other variables. This method leaves the largest available state space for choosing values for variables late in the sequence.

For a general-purpose Calc2 test case, this rule dictates the following sequence for choosing variable values within a single port. First, choose the tag value. Its value has no implication on the other values. (If there is no available tag, then the stimulus is tightly constrained to no new commands.) Next, choose the command, which will place constraints on the possible response values. The choice of response value follows. Finally, based on the chosen response value, choose the values for the two operand variables. Although the intent of the test case may alter this general-purpose sequence, this order of variable choices follows the rule of choosing the least constraining variables first.

After mapping the constraints and sequencing the variables, the final step is to analyze the implications of the sequence. This step searches for overconstrained variables, as well as constraints that unintentionally restrict the stimulus components from exploring states within the DUV. There are two types of overconstrained variables: those groups whose valid state space is null, and those groups with an unintentionally limited state space. Groups whose constraints unintentionally limit the state space are actually more dangerous for the verification engineer than those groups with unsolvable constraints, because the stimulus component's constraint solver will flag the unsolvable constraints but not the unintentionally limited constraints.

There are cases in which the intent of the test case overconstrains the variables. In these cases, no set of variable values exists that meets the intent of the test case. This occurs most often when the constraints on any single variable seem reasonable but the mix of constraint values unexpectedly creates an unsolvable state space. In other cases, the design rules or implementation make certain constraint solving tasks difficult or impossible. Here are three examples from Calc2:

Overconstrained Owing To Architecture Specification

(1) The case of a *SHL* or *SHR* command with an *overflow/underflow* response is invalid, and (2) The design specifies that an illegal command will only get an "illegal command" response not a good response.

Tightly Constrained Owing To Intent (Small State Space of Values that Solve Constraints)

A Shift test with a result of zero having nonzero Operand1 values and low Operand2 values (less than four). The intent of this test case is to verify the shift logic across a range of input values that produce a zero result. This requires choosing Operand1 values with zeros in the low-order n bits for SHL and high-order n bits for SHR, where n is the Operand2 value.

Overconstrained Owing To Microarchitecture

The verification plan calls for filling the add queue and shift queue. However, it turns out that no matter what constraints the verification engineer places on the stimulus component, it is impossible to fill the 16-deep internal queue! This is because the Calc2 priority logic continuously dispatches the top entry in the queue. Given the case in which all four ports have sent four commands and all of these commands are the same type (*add/sub* or *shift*), one command will be in the adder, one command will be entering the response output logic, and one will be on the Calc2 output signals. This leaves a maximum of 13 commands in the queue. No matter how fast the stimulus component sends commands, it can never fill the queue.

7.2.6 Coverage Techniques in Random Environments

Although analyzing the implications of the constraints is an important step, it is not foolproof. Therefore, the verification team needs back-up

TABLE 7.6 ▪ Coverage results for single Calc2 port across multiple simulation runs

Cross-product num	Tag	Command	Response	Count
30	10	ILLEGAL	Illegal	0
16	01	ADD	Overflow	3
17	01	SUB	Underflow	7
40	11	ILLEGAL	Illegal	127
10	00	ILLEGAL	Illegal	139
20	01	ILLEGAL	Illegal	147
7	00	SUB	Underflow	255
26	10	ADD	Overflow	258
36	11	ADD	Overflow	266
37	11	SUB	Underflow	270
6	00	ADD	Overflow	272
27	10	SUB	Underflow	272
11	01	ADD	Good	802
31	11	ADD	Good	823
2	00	SUB	Good	829
1	00	ADD	Good	846
22	10	SUB	Good	873
12	01	SUB	Good	881
21	10	ADD	Good	893
32	11	SUB	Good	914
33	11	SHL	Good	1136
24	10	SHR	Good	1162
3	00	SHL	Good	1189
34	11	SHR	Good	1201
23	10	SHL	Good	1211
14	01	SHR	Good	1230
4	00	SHR	Good	1236
13	01	SHL	Good	1242

in the form of runtime coverage techniques used to track the stimulus and DUV internal states. The ideal target of the coverage mechanisms in this realm is the cross-product of the grouped variables. Verification engineers should look for unexpected holes in the cross-product matrix.

The need for coverage in verification environments cannot be overstated. Verification engineers use coverage data to point to holes in their environments, test matrix, random bias controls, or constraint solvers. Errors in program coding, oversights in constraint solving, or typographical errors in bias controls can all lead to missed test scenarios. Coverage results allow the verification team to compare what simulations actually ran versus what the team expected to run.

Table 7.6 displays the coverage results from a set of Calc2 simulation runs. The results track the number of occurrences of each of the 40 possible cross-product variable values on a single port. This coverage model tracks only control values, not data values. Therefore, the coverage table

TABLE 7.7 ■ Illegal cross-product coverage combinations for coverage model shown in Table 7.6

Cross-product num	Tag	Command	Response	Count
5	00	ILLEGAL	Good	0
8	00	SHL	Underflow	0
9	00	SHR	Underflow	0
15	01	ILLEGAL	Good	0
18	01	SHL	Underflow	0
19	01	SHR	Underflow	0
25	10	ILLEGAL	Good	0
28	10	SHL	Underflow	0
29	10	SHR	Underflow	0
35	11	ILLEGAL	Good	0
38	11	SHL	Underflow	0
39	11	SHR	Underflow	0

derives the 40 values from the cross-product of the four tags, five commands, and two responses ($4 \times 5 \times 2 = 40$).

The cross-product number field shows the number assigned to each of the 40 cross-products. Note that Table 7.6 only shows 28 of the 40 possible cross-products. The other 12 cases are illegal cases, shown in Table 7.7. These cross-products are illegal because the result value cannot occur with the given command (illegal command with good response, or a *shift* command with an overflow response). A nonzero count field for any of the illegal cases in Table 7.7 would indicate a problem in the DUV.

The coverage results in Table 7.6 are ordered by the count field. This directs the verification engineer to unexpected count values.

The intent of the coverage model is to identify holes in the stimulus component that may have come about because of unintentionally limited constraints. Analysis of these coverage results does show three anomalies. Cross-product number 30 (tag "10"b, Illegal command, and Illegal response) has a zero-count value, whereas the illegal command and illegal response counts for the other three tags (cross-product numbers 10, 20, and 40) all have totals in the 100s. The verification engineer must investigate why the stimulus component is not creating this combination. The other two anomalies also require investigation. The results for cross-product numbers 16 and 17 show abnormally low count values compared with the other *add* and *sub* commands with overflow/underflow responses. These anomalies often indicate a constraint solving error in the stimulus component.

7.2.7 Making Rare Events Occur

Coverage counts such as those shown in Table 7.6 serve many purposes beyond the search for overconstrained values. Coverage data also provides insight into the workings of the environment's randomization controls. Over a long period of simulation cycles, coverage data should echo the probability ranges dictated by the randomization control files. Any significant deviation from the values of the randomization control file requires investigation.

Therefore, the data shown in Table 7.6 indicates an approximate 3:1 ratio of good responses to overflow/underflow responses for *add* and *subtract* commands. The data also indicates about a 1:1 ratio between *add/subtract* commands and *shift* commands. If the coverage data and the probability tables do not correlate, then the verification engineers must examine the stimulus component.

Many simulation runs ought to be dedicated to running the DUV in a "normal mode" of operation, which is characterized by a ratio of stimulus that reflects the expected load on the DUV when running an average workload. However, verification must take advantage of its ability to deviate into the unexpected, making normally rare events occur at a heightened pace. As stated in the introduction to this section, the verification suite must contain more permutations, drive more interactions, and create more extraordinary cases over a short period of time when compared to normal program or application activity. This indicates the desire to make rare events occur often in verification.

The fundamental reason to increase the rate of occurrence of rare events is that this is where nasty bugs lurk. As the designer writes the initial specification and proceeds with the HDL, the focus is on the normal mode of operation. Designers center their performance optimizations (bandwidth, throughput, latency) on the normal cases. Good designers also consider the odd cases, but it is difficult for a designer to think of all possible cases in a complex system. These rare occurrences are also known as *corner cases* and *window conditions*.

The verification team must allocate a substantial amount of effort toward driving corner cases. There are three prongs to this effort: probes of the design for special cases; examinations of coverage data; and automations that modify the randomization controls.

The most powerful lead in the search for corner case bugs is the design itself. The verification engineer must probe and investigate the DUV's microarchitecture and understand all of the various stimulus events. The microarchitecture includes queues, buffers, state machines, data paths, and controls. Stimulus events include all of the separate input commands and response codes, as well as interrupts and service support (resets, clocking, and initialization). Each of these items requires attention not only at the single event level ("has the buffer been filled?") but also at a cross-product level ("what happens when we take an interrupt when the buffer is filled?").

From a microarchitecture standpoint, rare events occur when independent single events align, there are data or control path collisions, or there are unusually busy conditions. These three areas require the attention of the verification team.

Although early verification efforts ensure the proper behavior during single events such as interrupts or buffer full cases, the verification engineer must focus simulation cycles toward alignment of multiple single conditions across a short period of cycles. This might entail busying the traffic into multiple queues simultaneously, or initiating external interrupt stimulus at such a pace that the interrupts inhibit forward progress of the DUV's function. These cases, rare as they may be, push the design into unusual conditions that tend to uncover unintended DUV behavior.

Collisions occur when multiple requestors vie for a shared resource simultaneously. Well-architected designs intentionally minimize the rate of collisions by providing enough resources for more than the average amount of activity. However, any time there is a shared resource, the potential for collisions exist, and the design must be able to handle these cases. A cache controller in a multiprocessor environment provides a good example. The design architects specify a cache size as large as the chip allows—large enough to provide low latency to multiple processors' data requests. Because of the relatively large cache size, the processors will usually access completely different addresses in the cache. However, the most interesting verification cases occur when multiple processors request the same data address at the same time. The cache must follow the architecture rules, only granting requests that maintain coherency and rejecting those that would allow access to old data or simultaneous writes. For this reason, verification's stimulus components should do the unusual—step up the pace of requests to the same address, effectively utilizing only a small portion of the cache for the duration of the test case. This forces collisions to occur at a much-heightened rate.

Bus busyness is another form of collision, in which the bus is the shared resource. Architects design busses to satisfy latency requirements, which necessitate a low utilization rate. Therefore, the hardware may average a 30% utilization rate on a bus, with peaks and lulls depending on the applications running on the system. Verification, though, needs to drive beyond the peaks, hitting the obscure conditions of near-total utilization. Verification engineers often find bugs based on the effects of constant retry actions, low bus availability, and high traffic rates.

The probability of the simultaneous occurrence of multiple corner cases may be quite low—maybe one in a trillion—but a trillion cycles at today's frequencies translates to merely a handful of minutes on the hardware. If verification mirrored the hardware applications' level of activity, many bugs would go undetected until hardware fabrication because of the limited throughput of simulation cycles. Therefore, it is the verification team's job to make all sorts of rare events occur frequently in simulation.

This requirement on verification highlights the need for stimulus components to run in modes that are independent of the hardware's base applications and programs. Although it is good to run some simulation with application-like mix of stimulus, this mode must be restricted to a minority of the verification effort. The specialized stimulus components that we have described act on the rules of the microarchitecture, which are different from the profile of the average application. Continuously changing the bias controls and stimulus parameters drives further divergence in stimulus profile, allowing the environment to create a wide range of internal DUV cases.

The Calc2 design contains multiple corner conditions that the verification team must stimulate. Under normal conditions, these cases are rare events that could contain DUV bugs. We now examine a few of these cases.

In the category of alignment of independent single events, the verification team would want to create the case in which the next command in both internal queues contain an *add* and a *shift* command from the same port. This will verify that the priority logic does not dispatch both commands simultaneously, causing a collision on the output bus. Similarly, the verification team should create the case in which the DUV forwards an invalid command (which the DUV should not place in either queue) directly to the output at the same time it completes an *add* or *shift* command from the same port. This is another potential data collision case caused by two independent commands.

Other Calc2 rare events, as documented in the verification plan, occur under unusually busy conditions. It is important to try to fill the add queue and, in a second test case, the shift queue. These test cases are independent because the stimulus can only focus on filling one queue at a time.

7.2.8 Stimulus Generation of Deadlocks and Livelocks

If there is one Achilles' heel to on-the-fly random environments, it is their inability to create *deadlock* and *livelock* conditions, which occur when the logic design cannot make forward progress when running an application and are usually the result of a resource conflict when two different components of the system vie for a shared resource. A deadlock condition is one in which processing completely halts waiting for access to a shared resource; a livelock condition occurs when processing appears to move forward, but irresolvable contention for a shared resource continually causes processing to retry or loop back to an earlier state.

Deadlocks and livelocks are most common in a multiprocessor system where a common storage controller provides memory and input/output (IO) access for many processors. A main role of the storage controller is to give each processor the appearance that it has the entire system's resources to itself, even though there are multiple processors connected to the controller. As a result, the controller contains many shared resources which, when not apportioned correctly, can cause deadlocks and livelocks.

The verification team must ensure that the design does not allow deadlocks or livelocks. This is not easy, as locking conditions often occur under rare circumstances because of separate repetitive and synchronized stimulus patterns. The "separate repetitive and synchronized" element is what makes it difficult for generic on-the-fly random environments to find locking cases. Verification engineers design random environments to make stimulus choices each cycle without regard to previous system activity. The randomness of the stimulus choices opposes the "repetitive and synchronized" locking conditions.

However, there are mechanisms that verification engineers can build into stimulus components to assist in the search of locking conditions in the hardware. Fundamentally, these mechanisms "derandomize" the random environment. These mechanisms bring persistent or repetitive stimulus to the environment in a search for locking conditions in the DUV.

To understand the verification techniques used to find locking conditions, first look at an example deadlock condition. Figure 7.24 shows a storage controller in a four-processor system. The memory controller must provide each processor with memory access to main memory while maintaining *coherency* across the system. Coherency means that there is a single value for every byte of memory within the system, or the storage controller may never allow two different processors to write the same byte of data simultaneously. Furthermore, if a processor holds data in its local cache (L1) with the intent to write to it, no other processor may have a copy of the data. However, all processors may have a copy of a specific byte of data if none intends to modify the data. Therefore, the storage controller maintains a directory that keeps track of the data within all processors. Whenever a processor requests new data, the storage controller looks in the directory to see if any other processors have the data.

Consider a case in which microprocessor 1 owns a modified copy of the data from address X, and microprocessor 2 owns a modified copy of the data in address Y. The instruction stream running on microprocessor 1 next looks to operate on the address X data based on the value of the data in address Y. Microprocessor 1 must request the data in address Y from the storage controller. Simultaneously, microprocessor 2 tries to access the data in address X. Both requests arrive at the look-up and invalidate logic in the storage controller. The storage controller checks the directory and tries to invalidate both processors' copy of their updated data. However, both processors await the return of their requested data before processing the invalidate request. At this point, the processors deadlock, as neither can make forward progress.

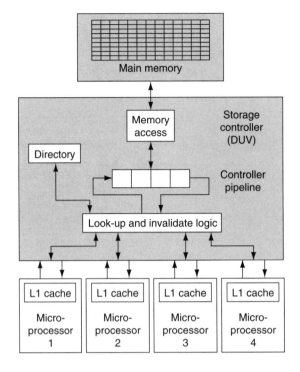

■ **FIGURE 7.24**

Microprocessor 1 holds the data needed by microprocessor 2 and vice versa. The system memory coherency protocols do not allow either processor to access old copies of the data. This can result in a deadlock.

This scenario represents a simple deadlock condition. Even so, a random environment needs special mechanisms to uncover this condition because the timing of the dual requests from the processors, the specific address dependencies, and the likelihood that a third processor's request could break the deadlock makes this an intricate scenario. Actually, this scenario is ripe for a deterministic test case that ought to be included in the verification plan. However, the verification team must look for other, more complex locking scenarios beyond this simple example. These cases require an automated mechanism.

Figure 7.25 shows the stimulus generation components for creating locking conditions within the storage controller environment. The dotted area indicates the additional automated mechanisms. The new mechanisms are in addition to the normal random stimulus environment. A mode switch enables normal random or "lock sniffing" mode.

The lock sniffing mode allows the verification team to input a hand-generated deterministic scenario, or enables an automated, highly constrained biasing mechanism. In both cases, the environment forwards a short, looping set of commands to two or more of the microprocessor

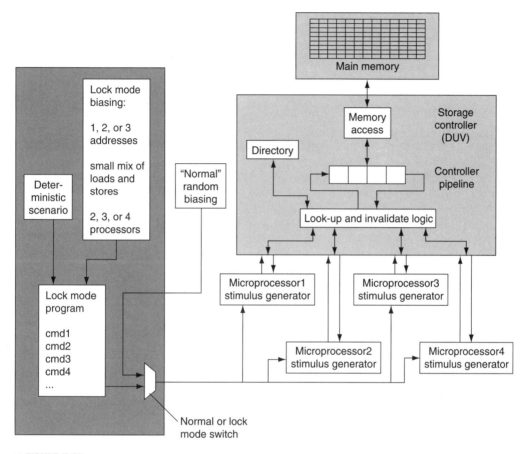

To create locking conditions in the storage controller, the verification team adds additional lock "sniffing" programming modes to the normal random environment. When in lock sniffing mode, the microprocessor stimulus generators loop on either hand-generated small programs or highly constrained automatically generated scenarios.

stimulus generators. The automated biasing mechanism's loop focuses on a small number of addresses to cause contention between the microprocessors. The verification team tunes the mix of instructions in the loop to cause thrashing in the storage controller pipeline. Adjustments to the number of stores and loads and the length of the command loop will have differing effects on the storage controller and can uncover locking situations. The verification team does not need to update the scoreboard or checking components (not shown in Figure 7.25) as the stimulus generation components still interface with the rest of the environment the same as in the normal mode.

Most DUVs that are susceptible to locking conditions have multiple stimulus interfaces. The storage controller in our example likely has additional ports for IO devices such as Peripheral Component Interconnect (PCI) or Ethernet. The verification team can add micro modes to these interfaces as well, because locking conditions may occur across different types of stimulus input. Some of the most complex locking conditions occur when an IO device locks out a processor, involving multiple shared resources across the system.

In attempting to find lock conditions, the verification team should always limit the number of active stimulus generators, as overstimulus can prevent livelocks and deadlocks from occurring. Too much stimulus is not conducive to creating lock scenarios because additional commands can bump the resource out of a deadlock or change the timing in a livelock. Two stimulus components may create a lock scenario that the team needs to uncover; however, another stimulus component could "unlock" the DUV before the checking components detect that the lock situation occurred. To prevent this, the loop mode program should contain gaps in which the environment sends no new stimulus until it detects the DUV continuing to make forward progress.

Deadlocks and livelocks are difficult to uncover in simulation-based verification. The verification plan should contain a healthy dose of deterministic test cases any time a DUV contains shared resources. The addition of automated, highly constrained lock sniffing modes will also help uncover these flaws. The verification team should augment their simulation-based verification effort with formal verification of DUVs with shared resources. Formal verification (Chapters 11, 12) can uncover some "pathological" locking conditions across the controls of DUVs with shared resources.

7.3 SUMMARY

Verification engineers have an array of choices for personalizing stimulus components to the DUV. These choices range across two axes: determinism versus randomness and pregeneration versus on-the-fly generation.

Traditional stimulus components were deterministic, relying on specific choices made by the verification engineer. Deterministic test cases drive precise scenarios onto the inputs of the design. Alternatively, the verification team can build their knowledge of the input protocols into the stimulus components and use constraint directives and biasing to control the range of input stimulus. Stimulus strategies may use a combination of both styles.

The second axis describes when the environment makes the stimulus decisions. Here, the choices are before running the simulation (predetermined) or during the simulation job (on-the-fly). In the predetermined paradigm, the verification engineer can look at the test case before running simulation. The verification team may use automation in the construction of predetermined test cases, allowing for a wide range of random choices during test case generation. Alternatively, the verification engineer can choose determinism, meticulously constructing the test case by hand. In the on-the-fly paradigm, the verification team defers creation of the test case until runtime, in which the stimulus components react to the current state of the DUV. Here again, the verification team may alter the amount of determinism or randomness in the choices that the stimulus components make.

No matter which paradigm the verification team chooses, it is imperative that they understand the constraints on the inputs of the design. Constraints describe the interrelationship between input signals and the limitations across a period of cycles. This chapter describes a method for solving constraints in the least restrictive fashion, which allows the stimulus component to generate the broadest set of input scenarios.

Finally, this chapter describes the use of coverage feedback to evaluate the quality of the stimulus components. Robust coverage metrics point to weaknesses in the verification environments stimulus generation controls. This feedback allows the verification team to update their stimulus components no matter which generation paradigm they choose.

7.4 EXERCISES

1. What other coverage models should the verification team document in the Calc2 test plan?

2. Explain the differences between the four types of test case stimulus.

3. Why do verification teams need to create both random and deterministic test cases?

4. What pitfalls must the verification team avoid when using random number generators for seeding stimulus components?

5. What is significant about the order that random drivers choose values for input signals?

6. What is the process for solving constraints in a random stimulus environment?

7. How does coverage feedback assist in evaluating the stimulus component? How does it help with evaluating constraint-solving algorithms?

8. Describe rare events. Why is it important to focus on creating these cases during simulation?

CHAPTER 8

STRATEGIES FOR RESULTS CHECKING IN SIMULATION-BASED VERIFICATION

A customer expects the verification "warranty" to last the life of the system. At the same time, the limited number of simulation cycles (compared to the life of the system) handicaps the verification effort. To combat this, the verification team needs a robust strategy for creating stressful stimulus during the relatively small number of available simulation cycles. However, the additional challenge beyond creating the stimulus is that the environment must identify all the bugs triggered by this stress. Driving the stimulus is only half of the equation. Remember the yin and yang of verification: not only must the stimulus aggravate the DUV, the checking components also must recognize when a bug exists in the design.

After creating the stimulus and checking components, the verification team can begin to debug the hardware description language (HDL) and the verification components. When the results of the design under verification (DUV) and the checking component disagree, the verification engineer must investigate the miscompare. This investigation is the debug phase, and during this phase, the verification team reaps the fruits of their component-building labor.

This chapter describes methods for checking complex designs using simulation. The Calc2 design is used to demonstrate multiple verification techniques that were introduced in Chapter 3 for results checking. The chapter then introduces the debug process and how choices in the verification strategy effect debug.

8.1 TYPES OF RESULT CHECKING

During the planning phase of the verification test bench, verification leaders must make the basic choices on stimulus generation. These choices, such as when the generation occurs, affect the results checking portion of the test bench. In addition, there is another aspect of results checking—when the verification environment performs the checking. The two choices are (1) throughout the life of the test case (*on-the-fly checking*) or (2) at the end of the test (*end-of-test checking*). The verification leaders need to consider both stimulus generation and results checking before making a decision on the overall test bench.

Remember there are three different types of self-checking test benches (see Section 3.4.2):

- *Golden vectors:* A test bench in which some knowledge base of valid output vectors is stored in the scoreboard. The checking component compares the DUV results to this knowledge base by calling the scoreboard and requesting the expected vectors. The checker does this either every cycle or every transaction.

- *Cycle accurate reference models:* A test bench in which the reference model calculates all expected outputs based on the input stimulus. The reference model re-implements the function of the DUV, usually in a high-level programming language (HVL). The checking component compares the outputs of both the DUV and the reference model.

- *Transaction based:* A test bench in which the DUV has identifiable transactions. The test bench uses a scoreboard to track commands and data driven on the inputs of the DUV. The scoreboard component performs the transformation from inputs to outputs, and the checking component then performs a callback to the scoreboard to retrieve a transaction to check.

Later sections discuss how the type of checking (either end-of-test case or on-the-fly) and test case generation affect the three different types of test benches.

8.1.1   On-the-Fly Checking Versus End-of-Test Case Checking

An important aspect of the test bench is when to perform the checking—either on-the-fly or at the end of the test case. In the on-the-fly paradigm, the verification environment performs checking during the simulation. The stimulus components initiate transactions, and as these transactions complete, the checking components immediately verify the correctness of the transaction. If the checking component detects any type of error, it records the time, transaction, and any other useful information for debug. End-of-test case checking performs at the completion of the simulation test, either within the simulation (end of simulation checking) or in a separate job (postanalysis checking).

On-the-Fly Checking

On-the-fly checking is most applicable to a DUV that operates on transactions and performs some type of data transformation on that transaction. Figure 8.1 illustrates this type of paradigm.

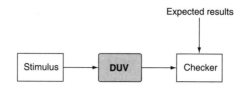

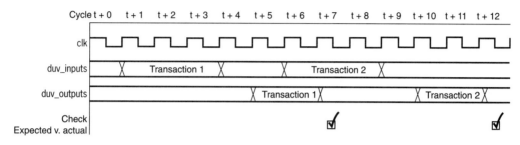

■ **FIGURE 8.1**

On-the-fly checking. The stimulus component initiates a transaction that lasts for three cycles on cycle t + 1 and t + 6. Each transaction completes on the outputs of the design under verification (DUV) in one cycle after the end of the transaction. The checking component senses the end of the output transaction and at that time compares the actual outputs versus the expected outputs. These expected outputs could be pre-calculated by using golden vectors, calculated from a scoreboard as in a transaction-based test bench, or generated in a cycle accurate reference model.

There are multiple benefits of on-the-fly checking that lead to this paradigm's common usage. These types of test benches are easier to debug and require less memory for simulation; as a result, they run faster than a pure end-of-test case checking paradigm. The addition of verification languages and verification aspects to traditional languages (Verilog, System C) tend to make on-the-fly checking easier to implement, allowing the verification engineer to easily create a transaction-based test bench. Debug is also easier with on-the-fly checking because the simulation stops when the checker detects an error during the simulation, rather than at the end. This assists in debug, which is discussed in more detail later in this chapter. The overall simulation requires less memory with on-the-fly checking because the checking component does not need to keep the expected data until the end of simulation: as soon as the checker finishes with a transaction, the checker releases that memory. Because less memory is required, the simulation tends to run faster. Moreover, with the performances of event-based simulators improving and the creation of cycle-based simulators (another performance increase), on-the-fly checks are more affordable.

End-of-Test Case Checking

End-of-test case checking applies when the checking components need to check the state of the test bench after the test completes. One scenario is to compare the contents of a cycle accurate reference model to the contents within the DUV. Another scenario is to check when the scoreboard and DUV queues to ensure that they are empty and no transactions are pending. This completeness check will find bugs if at some point during the test case data were incorrectly stored and never again accessed. End-of-test case checking tends to be used when any of the following conditions exist:

- The results remain persistent within the DUV's memory until the end of the test.

- Signal access is limited (e.g., acceleration or emulation).

- Check of the ending state of the test bench and/or DUV (queues being empty, reference model comparison, etc.) is required.

- Functions have system aspects (e.g., arbitration, latency, performance).

When using the end of simulation checking paradigm, the verification environment calls an end-of-test case checking routine when all the checking components have finished. This end of test routine will then perform any user-defined checks on the test bench and DUV. Figure 8.2 illustrates this paradigm.

In addition to the monitor observing the DUV outputs in Figure 8.2, the monitor may also capture internal DUV data for end of test case results checking. This allows the checking component to compare internal DUV resources (such as general-purpose registers) to the expected results. The environment predicts the expected results based on the type of test bench: golden vectors, transaction based, or cycle accurate reference model.

A different method of performing end-of-test case checking is to perform the checks outside of the simulation engine. It is similar to the end-of-test case checking within the simulation engine, except the simulation engine and verification environment programs complete before a separate program performs the checking. Figure 8.3 illustrates end-of-test case checking using a postanalysis program.

As with the end of simulation method, a monitor collects the transactions on the output of the DUV, but instead of writing it to memory, it writes to a file. Once the simulation completes, the simulation program exits (note that in Figure 8.3 the checking is not performed in the simulation wave window). Now a post-processing routine, independent from the simulation environment, invokes checking by using the expected results file and actual results file as inputs. This program checks for correctness of the results. As with the end of simulation method, the monitor can also probe into the DUV at the end of simulation to add any necessary states or conditions that it may need to check. Once again, the

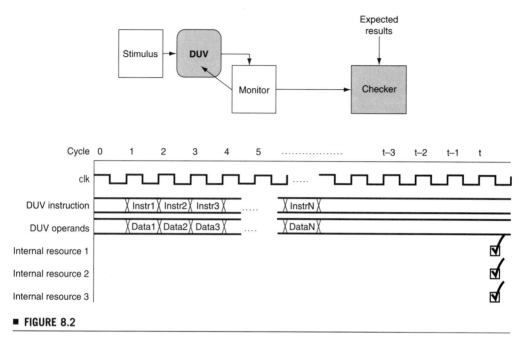

End-of-test checking: end of simulation. The stimulus component sends instructions and data to the design under verification (DUV) throughout the simulation. The monitor observes the DUV outputs throughout the simulation. Whenever the monitor sees a transaction on the outputs of the DUV, it captures the transaction and saves it to memory. (The monitor must capture the pertinent data for this transaction and cycle number.) On completion of the simulation, the environment calls the checking component. The checking component validates the transactions captured by the monitor throughout the test case.

source of the expected results depends on the checking paradigm: golden vectors, transaction based, or cycle accurate reference model.

End-of-test case checking applies well to functions having system aspects, for example, performance verification. Performance has different meanings depending on the application. In a data transmission system, the environment typically measures performance in both bandwidth and latency. Bandwidth is the amount of data successfully moved across the bus over a given timeframe, and latency is the amount of time the DUV takes to process each transaction. In a processor system, performance is the amount of work that the processor can perform in a given amount of time. This work may mean the number of instructions or the number of useful operations.

The common point between both a data transmission system and a processor system is that the measure of performance is over time. In calculating performance, monitors compute the average time of every transaction during the steady state of the system. Monitors typically ignore the simulation ramp-up and ramp-down times. If the calculation uses the

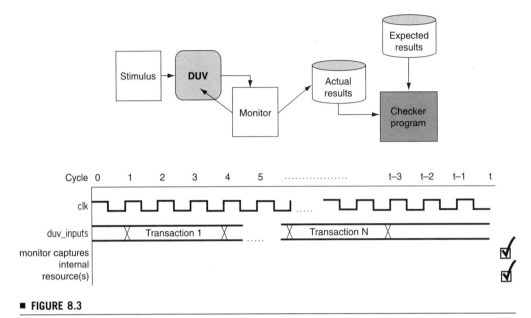

▪ **FIGURE 8.3**

End-of-test checking: postanalysis program. Some of the results checking is performed by an external program that is invoked after the simulation engine has finished and terminated.

ramp-up and ramp-down times, it skews the overall average to be less optimal. Because the performance goal is an average, it only makes sense for the verification engineer to apply this same strategy to the checking. That is, either post-process all the transactions response times to calculate the average, or compute the average of the transactions response times during the simulation and at the end of the test and compare this to the performance target. Because the verification environment must look at the average performance for the entire simulation, this is end-of-test case checking.

Another example is with processor test cases. For processor DUVs, the test case will often use end-of-test case checking to validate the state of the DUV at the end of the test. A test case selects specific registers for each operation and will either (1) not overwrite a calculated value or (2) store calculated values to memory before overwriting. Therefore, the test case preserves all results processed by the DUV during simulation, allowing for an end-of-test case checking. Referring back to Figure 8.2, the DUV inputs consist of a stream of instructions and operand data. The instructions perform precise manipulation of the operand data, using internal registers as resources (e.g., an ALU status register or general-purpose registers). At the end of the test, the checking routine compares the contents of the registers to the expected contents. These internal registers are not visible to the test bench without the monitor component.

This monitor component's main purpose is to capture the contents of the internal registers within the DUV for end-of-test case checking.

Combining On-the-Fly and End-of-Test Case Checking

It is more likely that a test bench will require a combination of on-the-fly and end-of-test case checking. The key is that the test bench contains the services to be able to perform these types of checks. Recall that the three types of test benches are golden vectors, transaction based, and cycle accurate reference models. Let us look at what facilities need to exist to perform on-the-fly and/or end-of-test case checking within these test benches.

Golden Vector Test Bench

In a golden vector approach, the environment calculates expected results by an external test case generation program or by hand (regardless of on-the-fly or end-of-test case paradigm). The environment loads the golden vectors into a scoreboard and/or the checker. As the DUV drives its outputs, the checker detects a transaction on the outputs of the DUV and captures it. The checker then calls a scoreboard function that returns the next expected data. The scoreboard will need to provide the expected data to the checker in the correct order. The environment can match the scoreboard transaction to the DUV output by implicit ordering of transactions within the golden vectors, by numbering each transaction, or by attaching an absolute time to each transaction. If the transformation allows for out of order data, then the scoreboard may require a search algorithm that correlates the transaction. Once the scoreboard returns the correct expected data to the checker, it then releases the memory that it had allocated for this data. The checker then compares the expected data to the actual data. In the case of a miscompare (expected is different from actual), the checker logs pertinent information for debug. This continues until the stimulus component does not initiate any more transactions.

At this point, the test case is over and any end-of-test case checking occurs. For end-of-test case checking, the scoreboard will, at a minimum, need to contain a method that ensures that the scoreboard is empty and no outstanding transactions exist. If any outstanding transactions exist, the scoreboard should flag an error.

Transaction-Based Test Bench

A transaction-based test bench is very similar to that of a golden vector test bench when a scoreboard is used. The main difference is how the expected data is calculated. In a transaction-based test bench, the environment gathers the expected results on-the-fly. Instead of loading the scoreboard with the expected data, it monitors the inputs to the DUV. The environment then performs the necessary transformation on the transaction sent by the stimulus component. This becomes the expected data for what the DUV will output. The scoreboard continues collecting and transforming the inputs to the DUV and will need to hand the correct expected data to the checker. The environment also needs to contain an end-of-test case checking method similar to the golden vector approach.

Cycle Accurate Reference Model Test Bench

When using a cycle accurate reference model test bench, the reference model receives the same inputs as the DUV. The reference model then produces the expected results at the same time as the DUV. The checker does not request any expected data; the checker simply compares the outputs of the DUV to the outputs of the reference model every cycle. If at any time they do not match, the checker indicates an error.

At the end of the test, a method should exist to compare any function specific contents of the reference model to the DUV. This depends on the contents of the reference model. Reference models can be deep or shallow in function. A deep function cycle accurate reference model will be a pure white box approach, closely mimicking the DUVs activities. A shallow function cycle accurate reference model abstracts as much as possible, verifying the intent over the DUV implementation.

For example, take another look at Calc1, which has two internal pipelines. Data are captured in consecutive cycles and then placed into an internal buffer (one buffer per port). The priority logic arbitrates across the buffers to determine which port gets access to these internal pipelines. On deciding on a winner, the priority logic then dispatches that *cmd*/data pair to the appropriate pipeline. Each pipeline executes, and the results are then placed onto the appropriate output ports to be driven out of the DUV (Figure 8.4).

A deep function model would contain each stage from the DUV and mimic its function (Figure 8.4a), thus verifying the DUV via implementation. A shallow function model performs the arbitration at the same time as the design, and performs the calculation of the result data in a behavioral fashion, thus verifying the DUV via intent and not implementation (Figure 8.4b).

The deep function reference model has an advantage in that an end-of-test case checking can be created to validate the contents of the DUV for each of the stages.

As can be seen in Figure 8.5, the implementation of a reference model spans from a pure white box approach to a grey box approach. The deeper knowledge put into the reference model creates a "whiter" box. The less knowledge placed into the reference model, the more abstraction and allowance for a grey box approach of verification.

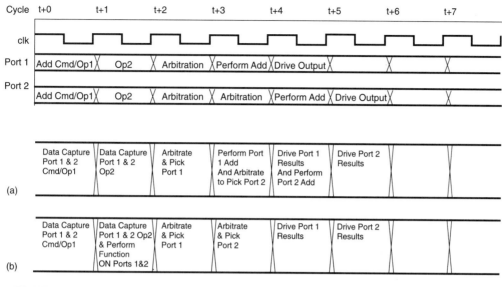

■ **FIGURE 8.4**

Calc1 Pipeline. (a) The deep function reference model mimics each stage. (b) The shallow function reference model performs the arbitration on the exact cycle that the logic does.

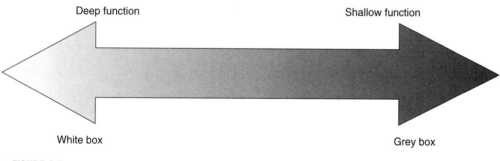

■ **FIGURE 8.5**

The deep function reference model is a pure white box approach that is required to change as the logic changes. The shallow function reference model abstracts what it can, thus becoming a grey box approach.

8.1.2 Pregenerated Test Cases Versus On-the-Fly Generated Test Cases

Checking does not depend on the type of test case generation—it can be deterministic or random—but it does depend on when the generation occurs, whether pregeneration or on-the-fly. The dependency on when generation occurs limits what type of checking may be applied.

Golden vectors are restricted to pre-generated test cases. On-the-fly generation does not apply to golden vectors, as the expected results are not available before running the test cases. The last two types of checking environments, transaction-based and cycle accurate reference models, can be applied to either pre-generated or on-the-fly generation test cases.

Another factor that limits golden vectors are situations in which the stimulus component requires feedback from the design. A verification engineer could treat this type of stimulus as "reactive." In these types of environments, pre-generation is not a good choice because of the false constraints (see Section 7.2.5). Because pre-generation is not a good choice, neither are golden vectors.

Either a transaction-based or cycle accurate reference model test bench can be applied to pre-generated or on-the-fly generated test cases. This is because both of these checking environments capture the transactions on-the-fly and do not require anything before the test case starting. The major difference between these two types of environments is that a transaction-based test bench has a higher level of abstraction (black box application), whereas a cycle accurate reference model environment contains precise DUV implementation details (white box approach). The cycle accurate reference model implies that the verification environment encodes quite a bit of the implementation (e.g., queue depths, pipeline stages). Verification teams should limit their choice of cycle accurate reference models to stable DUVs in which the implementation does not constantly change.

8.1.3   Applying the Checking Strategies to Calc2

As already stated, a transaction-based test bench would be the preferred test bench for Calc2, but, for completeness, this chapter also discusses the implementation of a golden vector and a cycle accurate reference model test bench. In the same way as was covered in the section on stimulus generation, the verification engineer must fully understand the design intent in order to create robust checkers.

When writing checking components, it is necessary to understand the verification requirements as specified in the verification plan. Table 8.1 recaps the Calc2 functions that were created when the verification plan was created (see Section 7.1.2) and highlights which component is responsible for that item.

Any function that lists the checker as the responsible component assumes that the stimulus component will make that scenario occur. However, if the stimulus component creates the scenario and if the test bench does not contain the proper checks, then it will not find any errors.

TABLE 8.1 ■ Calc2 functions

Calc2 function	Component responsible	Explanation
All four command types	Checker	Checker needs to ensure that all four commands actually work
All four ports	Checker	Checker needs to ensure that each port operates correctly
Variable timing between commands	Stimulus	Stimulus controls the input commands and when to send each one
Variable tags for each command	Stimulus	Stimulus controls the generation of the tags to send in for each command
Invalid commands	Checker	Checker responsible that invalid commands work as described
Filling of the add and shift queues	Stimulus	Stimulus controls the variable timing, thus it is in control of filling up the add and shift queues
Overflow cases for adds	Checker	Checker must ensure that add with overflows work properly
Underflow cases subtracts	Checker	Checker must ensure that subtracts with underflows work properly
All lengths of shift operations	Stimulus	Stimulus controls the operand 2 data for shift operations
Out-of-order responses across command pipelines	Checker	Checker must ensure that out-of-order responses occur properly
In-order execution within the pipeline	Checker	Checker must ensure that in-order execution occurs properly
Verify tags do not get swapped	Checker	Checker must ensure that tags and commands match up

The verification team must elaborate on each checking component responsibility function so that the team can specify the actual checking requirements. The elaboration of "all four command types" and "all four ports" indicates that the environment must check that

- The data and response is correct for a non-overflow *add* operation on each port.

- The response is correct for an overflow *add* operation on each port.

- The data and response is correct for a non-underflow *subtract* operation on each port.

- The response is correct for an underflow *subtract* operation on each port.

- The data and response is correct for a *Shift* left operation on each port.

▪ The data and response is correct for a *Shift* right operation on each port.

Continuing down the list, the checking component must validate that invalid commands are handled correctly. The component must verify that the DUV returns the "illegal command" response code any invalid command.

The checking component must validate that responses across command pipelines are performed either in order or out-of-order, depending on the command streams across all four ports. It must also validate that all responses from a command stream to the two pipelines are always in-order.

The last item to verify is that the DUV correctly processes every command/tag pair across all ports, meaning that the design does not give any superfluous response/tags pairs and that every command receives a response. If the checking component receives an unrecognized tag, then it must indicate an error. Similarly, if the design ever drops a tag, then the checking component must indicate that the DUV lost the command.

Golden Vectors Test Bench

Recall the pre-determined, deterministic test case for Calc2 Port1, as shown in Figure 8.6.

Notice the last two columns in the test case format: "Result" and "Response." This implies that in addition to the stimulus, this pre-determined test case generated the expected results for data and response. Because the expected results exist before the simulation runs, a golden vector test bench becomes a prime candidate to create for this type of test case. Figure 8.7 shows the verification environment that the verification team would create to support this pre-determined, deterministic test case for port 1.

As shown in the flow of Figure 8.7, the test case parser loads information into the scoreboard. This path contains various fields and expected data for each command. This information comes directly from

```
/* Port.tag   DelayN   Cmd    Operand1        Operand2        Result          Response*/
Port1.0       0        "111"B  "DEADBEEF"X    "BEADCAFE"X    "00000000"X    Illegal
Port1.1       0        ADD     "00012345"X    "00054321"X    "00066666"X    Good
Port1.2       0        SHL     "22222222"X    "00000002"X    "88888888"X    Good
```

▪ **FIGURE 8.6**

Pre-determined, deterministic example for Calc2 Port1.

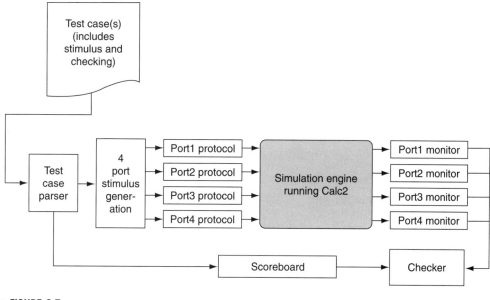

■ **FIGURE 8.7**

Calc2 verification environment using golden vectors test bench.

the test case. The scoreboard also requires the DelayN field so it can order the expected data for the checker. When the command emerges from the DUV on the outputs, the checker component requires information on the port number, tag, expected response, and expected results to determine if the outputs are correct for a particular command. The only information that the checker does not require is the command, Operand1, and Operand2 fields because the test case has already calculated the expected data.

As the test case runs, the port monitors observe the outputs. They capture the actual OUT_TAG, OUT_RESP, and OUT_DATA. The monitors pass this data, in addition to the time (cycle number), to the checker. The checker uses the data from the monitor to request that port's next expected data from the scoreboard. The checker then compares the expected data to the actual data. This continues until the end of the test.

Once the test is complete, the checking component calls the scoreboard's end-of-test case checking routines. In addition, the checker queries the number of transactions outstanding in the DUV's arithmetic, shift, and invalid queues; these should all be zero. If any queue contains unresolved transactions, then the checker indicates an error. In this type of test bench, all of the end-of-test case checking is within the components.

The approach described above meets the functional requirements because the checks for all the combinations exist (given that all combinations of stimulus occur). For any given command, data, and tag combination, the checking components verify the correct response, results, and tag combination on the outputs. This ensures that the checking components verify the following functional requests:

- All four command types
- All four ports
- Invalid commands
- Overflow cases for adds
- Underflow cases subtracts
- Tags do not get swapped

It is worth mentioning the algorithm the Calc2 verification environment uses to maintain order within each queue. This is required to verify two items: out-of-order responses across command pipelines and in-order execution within the pipeline. The plan must detail a specialized function that verifies that Calc2 DUV completes commands in the appropriate order. The simplest method for performing this check (remember, do not re-implement the design) is to track in the scoreboard, via a time stamp, the cycle number that the stimulus component initiates each command. This is the *sent cycle* for a given command. By ensuring that the time stamps complete in order within a queue, the checking component verifies the order within a queue. The checking component merely needs to confirm that, for each response, the sent cycle value is never less than the sent cycle from this queue's previous response. That is, as commands complete, the sent cycle time stamps always are higher than the previous.

However, in the golden vector paradigm, the scoreboard has no direct method of sampling the sent cycle. Instead of using the sent cycle, the scoreboard utilizes the fact that within a port, the commands must complete in order (with respect to the queues). So the scoreboard creates three first in, first out (FIFO) queues for each port—one for adds and subtracts (arithmetic FIFO), one for the shift lefts and rights (logical FIFO), and the last for any other command (invalid FIFO). The checking component then requests from the scoreboard the next expected data for a particular port/tag pair. The scoreboard compares this with the heads of the three FIFOs to decide what to return to the checking component. This method works because for a particular port, only one outstanding tag can be in use.

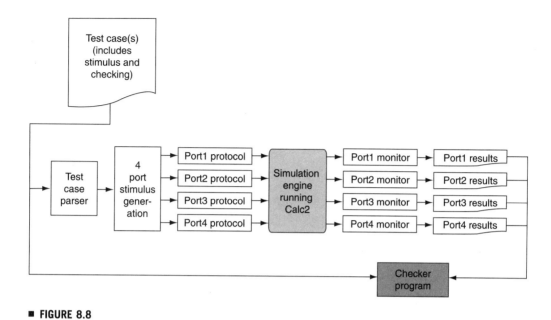

■ **FIGURE 8.8**

Calc2 verification environment using golden vectors and end-of-test checking.

To create these FIFOs, the scoreboard sorts the test case file from top to bottom: first by port number and then by command type. This needs to be done because the scoreboard only knows the delay from one command to the next (DelayN), it does not know anything about absolute time due to the pre-generation of the test case. Thus, it cannot predict the sent cycle. This scheme will validate the functional requirement for the in-order execution within the pipelines.

Another golden vector test bench approach exists that does not use a scoreboard. In this approach, it does the checking at the end of the test case within an external checking program. Figure 8.8 shows the test bench.

The verification environment uses a separate post-processing program to perform the checking. In this paradigm, the flow commences when the test parser reads in the test case and then loads the stimulus components (identical to the previous approach). The test begins and the stimulus components initiate transactions. The monitors observe the outputs (again, identical to the above approach) for any activity. When the monitors detect activity (a change in the OUT_TAG or OUT_RESP signals), they record the port information into a file. The content of the file is similar to the data captured earlier. For a given port, the monitor might record the data shown in Figure 8.9.

The monitors continue to capture the outputs until the end of the test case. At this time, the simulation ends and invokes the external

```
/* Port Tag    Time    Result          Response*/
Port1.0          8     "00000000"X     None
Port1.0         10     "00000000"X     Illegal
Port1.1         12     "00066666"X     Good
Port1.2         14     "88888888"X     Good
```

▪ **FIGURE 8.9**

Port 1 monitor output. Each line indicates when a transaction occurred on the outputs of the particular port.

checking program. The program uses the information from the test case and the results that the port monitors collected to validate that the results were correct.

By looking at the test case format, many of the required checking functions are easy to formulate. To check for responses, the checking program uses the tags to correlate the *cmd* field from the test case input file (see Figure 8.6) and response field from what the monitors captured. The test case shows that the checker can determine if the actual result and responses for the various commands across the ports match the expected results by correlating the port and tag. This validates everything but the in-order and out-of-order functionality. To validate this, the checking program uses the time stamps. It calculates the time stamps from the DelayN field in the test case. The results file already has the time stamp in the file. The checker must process all the ports' outputs to determine if the order is correct. To check the ordering within a queue, the program would first sort the output file results into buckets based on queue type (adds or subtracts go in order into the arithmetic bucket, shifts go into the shift bucket, and all other commands go into the invalid bucket). Then the program would sort each of these buckets based on the time stamp. The checker would perform this same type of sort for the test case. Now it compares the three buckets from the test case and output file from top to bottom. This verifies the ordering of the commands.

In both approaches, the checking component has satisfied all the functional requirements in the golden vector test bench.

Transaction-Based Test Bench

A golden vector test bench is only applicable when the expected data is available before simulation begins using pre-generation. If the verification team chooses to implement an on-the-fly generation scheme, then the team must utilize a different style of checking component.

On-the-fly generated test cases as in Figure 8.10 (taken from Chapter 7), no longer define the tag as a specific value. Instead, they specify the tag value per port as an "X," which means use the next available tag. In

```
/*Port.tag    DelayN      Cmd      Operand1     Operand2      Response*/
Port1.x       0          "111"B    rand         rand          Illegal
Port1.x       0          ADD       rand         rand          Good
Port1.x       2          SHL       rand         rand          Good
Port1.2       0          "011"B    rand         rand          Illegal
Port1.x       1          SUB       rand         rand          Good
Port1.x       0          SHR       rand         "00000000"X   Good
Port1.x       3          SHL       rand         rand          Good
Port1.x       1          SUB       rand         rand          Underflow
```

■ **FIGURE 8.10**

Deterministic with randomization example for Calc2 Port 1.

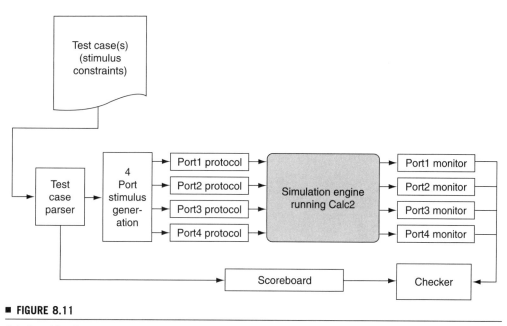

■ **FIGURE 8.11**

Calc2 verification environment using transaction-based test bench.

the golden vector test bench, the tag was important in correlating input commands to output responses. Now that the stimulus model chooses the tag during simulation, the test case cannot supply this information to the scoreboard and to the checking component. Now the scoreboard must collect the tags during the simulation. Figure 8.11 shows this test bench.

The flow shown in Figure 8.11 is similar to the golden vector test bench except that instead of the test case parser loading the scoreboard with all the data, now the scoreboard collects the information on-the-fly. During simulation, as the stimulus component initiates a transaction to the DUV, it also informs the scoreboard of this transaction.

This scheme simplifies the major complexity that existed under the golden vector paradigm: the scoreboard's inability to calculate the sent cycle. As detailed above, the scoreboard had to maintain multiple FIFOs per port and sort the information from the test case into these FIFOs. By having the scoreboard receive all of its information from the stimulus component and not from the test case loader, the scoreboard can calculate the expected data. Now that the verification environment captures the *sent cycle*, the checking component can now perform its checks as described previously.

In addition, this change also allows the verification environment to be robust enough to handle pre-generated or on-the-fly test cases (it becomes independent on the type of generation). To do this, the scoreboard must analyze each transaction sent into the DUV and create the expected data on-the-fly. With this change, the test case is now just a set of stimulus constraints.

Under the golden vectors paradigm, the verification environment did not perform priority checking across queues. The change to a full, on-the-fly checking paradigm enables this checking. The verification engineer could look at the problem using a statistical approach. If the verification team performs a statistical analysis across the ports, it should show that for a given set of fair inputs (on average, the two queues have the same number of transactions), the logic should give equal priority to the two queues because the two queues have an equal number of entries. This means that the latency from command to response across the two queues should be about equal over the life of the simulation. The use of time stamps assist in verifying this property. A modification to the scoreboard could allow it to track the latency for each port within the queues and analyze the data at the end of the test case. The checker can call an additional end-of-test case checking routine to determine that it fairly serviced each port. The only caveat to this approach is that the distribution of queue type (number of *add/sub* and *shift* commands) must be fair across ports. If the stimulus component sends all of one queue type, then this check will fail. Hence, a dependency on the generation constraint exists for the checking component. The checking component should only perform this latency verification routine when the stimulus component has sent an even distribution of traffic.

If the verification team really prefers the golden vector approach with a post-processing program, the above transaction-based environment supports this method. This environment deviates from the strict golden vector paradigm in that the scoreboard creates the transaction stream sent into the DUV instead of the test case. The post-processing program remains the same. Figure 8.12 shows this test bench.

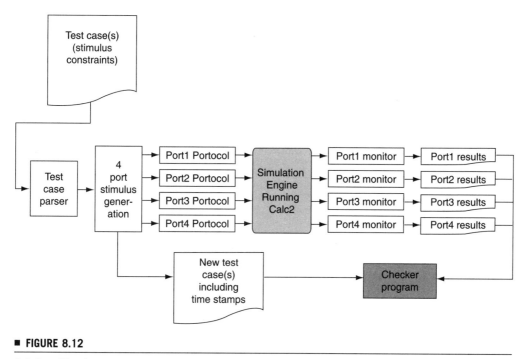

■ **FIGURE 8.12**

Calc2 verification environment using a transaction-based test bench with a postprocessing program.

Cycle Accurate Reference Model Test Bench

In the cycle accurate reference model type of environment, the reference model receives all inputs that the DUV receives and determines what the outputs should be on a cycle-by-cycle basis. Figure 8.13 shows the test bench that uses a cycle accurate reference model instead of a scoreboard.

In the reference model paradigm, the checker is simple—it only compares all outputs of the DUV with the outputs of the reference model. If there is a mismatch, the checker indicates an error. However, the reference model can be extremely complex. This approach is advantageous for a certain class of checking, in particular if the verification plan calls for regimented checking on the exact timing of outputs. If the DUV is out of step with the reference model for any reason (it may not be a critical bug), the cross-check with the reference model will catch it. Take, for example, the Calc2 single command timing diagram in Figure 8.14.

The stimulus generation component sends a command on port 1 at time 7. The DUV outputs its response six cycles later at time 13 as opposed to 12 (originally, the output was described to be on cycle 12 as denoted by the dashed lines in Figure 8.14); the reference model would

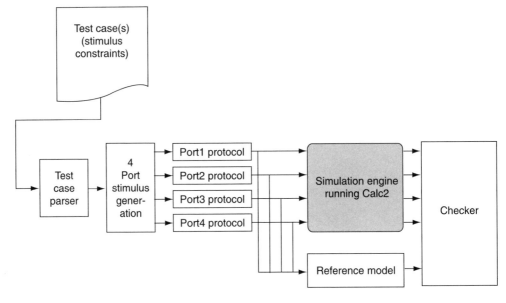

Calc2 verification environment using a reference model.

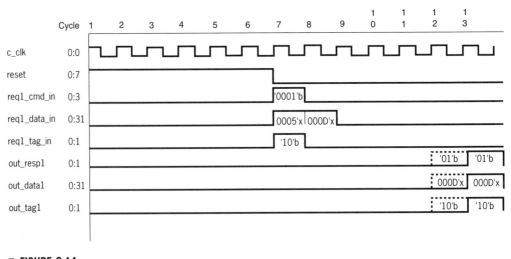

▪ **FIGURE 8.14**

Calc2 single command timing diagram.

issue an error that at time 12 a command response was expected but none was received. In the transaction approach, the scoreboard-based checker would not verify the exact latency and would allow the response at time 13.

The latency check seems easy as long as a single command is considered on a single port. However, the complexity can explode: what would the latency be of port 1 given an example in which there are 12 shift commands in one queue and 7 add commands in the other. If the environment has to calculate the latency for all commands all the time, the reference model complexity converges on that of the DUV.

With a reference model approach, the environment checks all functions within the design (including the algorithm Calc2 uses for maintaining order within each queue) inherently owing to the timely prediction of all outputs. Given the level of detail required in the reference model, it is extremely important to remember to implement the reference model differently than the design!

Coverage for Calc2

Chapter 7 discussed coverage requirements with respect to stimulus. However, some aspects of coverage are pertinent to checking. For instance, it is important to guarantee that for an *add* command with overflow, the overflow response actually occurred. It takes both stimulus and checking to ensure the design, as well as the coverage, is correct.

Verification engineers can fall prey to environment implementation errors as equally often as designers can on the DUV. For example, the verification engineer may make a change to the test bench that effectively disables a check. This could occur when the verification engineer needs to make a modification to a check and include some other condition. The original code might look like this:

```
. . .
If condition_a then {
# Check to ensure data is correct for condition A
} else {
. . .
}
. . .
```

A change is required to perform the check when either condition_a or condition_b (these conditions are mutually exclusive) occurs. However, the verification engineer inadvertently codes the following:

```
. . .
If condition_a and condition_b then {
# Check to ensure data is correct for condition A
```

```
} else {
  . . .
}
  . . .
```

Without manually validating the change, the verification engineer runs a complete regression thinking that if anything goes wrong, the test cases will catch the error. However, in actuality, the new code disables the check altogether.

A way to prevent this from happening is to put coverage on the checks within the test bench. Applying this to Calc2, the verification team needs to add the following event coverage recording to the checking component:

Output data of an *add, subtract, shift left* or *shift right* command is correct for non-overflow cases per port

- Output response for all commands are correct

- Tag correlation for all commands

- Priority checking within a queue

- Priority checking across queues

These are specific coverage checks on the checker code, not on the DUV outputs. For this to occur, the coverage event indicates that during runtime, the program reached the block of code in the checking component. If the verification engineer ensures that the simulation utilizes all checks, he or she also ensures that all the checks in the environment are functioning. This type of coverage check may also indicate a stimulus error in which the environment does not create the intended input stimulus. As any other coverage hole, the verification team needs to investigate and apply fixes to fill in these holes. The team could determine that these coverage items are incorrect or that they need to write more tests to fill in these holes.

Applying checking coverage to the test bench gives greater confidence to the overall environment.

8.2 DEBUG

Debug is the process of locating and correcting problems in the DUV or test bench. Debug is important because a swift and effective debug process saves time and schedule. Because quick debug saves schedule time, the measure is how fast the verification team determines the cause of the failure. Thus far this chapter has presented different checking component algorithms that lead to failure reporting. This section discusses what happens after that.

A failure could be from any of the existing environments. Once a test fails, the verification team must analyze the failure to find the cause of the problem. When a test fails, a bug could exist in one (or more) of the following areas:

- Design
- Environment
- Specification
- Tools

The area listed last, tools, is a rare source of bugs, so this is usually the last place to investigate. An example of a tool bug is when the simulation engine does not correctly calculate the proper value of a latch or signal in the design. This type of bug is rare because of the broad use of verification tools and is usually confined to beta or new releases of tools. A bug in the tools reveals itself when a calculated value in the DUV or environment does not match the input values of the HDL or program.

A verification engineer's job is to find the bugs in the HDL and report only these to the designer. In most cases, the verification team is best suited to differentiate between HDL bugs and environment bugs. Designers own plenty of tasks, but deciding what is a design bug versus a test bench problem is typically not one of them. If the verification team were to report all failures to the design team, they would soon lose credibility. Therefore, a verification engineer is responsible for sorting out the failures and determining what are design bugs versus test bench bugs. Only when a design bug exists does the verification engineer report it to the designer for repair. When a test bench bug exists, the verification team performs the fix. Because the verification engineer must have intimate knowledge of the function in order to create appropriate stimulus and checking, it makes sense for him or her to "dig-in" and assist the designer in locating the proximity of the bug.

In some cases, the source of the bug is owing to an ambiguous specification. In these cases, the architect must provide a more precise definition of the intent in the specification.

A good debug process is also important because the sooner the verification engineer locates and fixes the bugs, the more schedule time exists to run random simulations. The more simulations run in a random environment, the higher the overall quality of the design. The better the design, the smaller chance of hard-to-detect bugs that escape to the lab. Therefore, to reduce overall verification time and increase overall

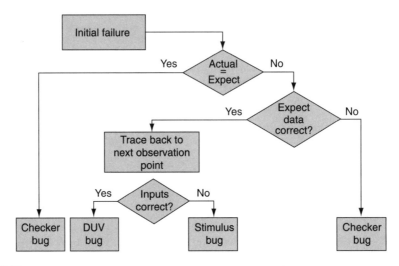

▪ FIGURE 8.15

Debug process.

verification productivity, the verification engineer should concentrate on ways to improve debug.

8.2.1 Debug Process

The basic debug process flow starts at the point of failure and traces back to the origin of what caused the failure. Figure 8.15 illustrates the process.

The main philosophy behind debug is the following question: why did a test fail? This will determine what to fix—the HDL, the verification components, the specification, or, in rare instances, the tools. Although this flow seems straightforward, the complexity of the debug process lies in determining which branch of the flow to take in the "Expected Data Correct?" and "Inputs Correct?" blocks.

When debugging a test case, it is common to see multiple checkers flagging a problem. Typically, the verification engineer can assume that all failures after the first one are side effects of the initial failure. This is primarily because of the difficulty in re-synchronizing the reference model/scoreboard once it differs from the DUV. Therefore, the verification team only needs to focus on the first failure reported from the test case. If subsequent failures exist, they will remain in the DUV, and the same test case will encounter them after re-running the simulation to test the initial fix.

Following the diagram flow in Figure 8.15, a checker indicates an initial failure. The first step for the verification engineer is to compare manually the actual and expected data by using the simulation trace output. These data can be from a single point in time or gathered over many simulation cycles. If the actual data equal the expected data, then the verification environment requires updating as the check that indicated the error is incorrect. If the actual data do not equal the expected data, then the verification engineer must determine which is correct: the DUV data or the verification environment's expected data.

The heart of the debug process lies in the validation of which results are correct. To determine if the DUV's or verification environment's results are correct, the verification engineer must trace the failure back to the input stimulus values. For example, to determine if the Calc2 DUV calculated a shift operation correctly, the verification engineer must match the result's tag to the initial stimulus to ascertain the actual command and data values. From there, the verification engineer must independently calculate the result and compare it to the DUV's and environment's values. If the expected data are wrong again, the checking component contains the bug. However, if the actual data are incorrect, this does not immediately indicate a design bug. It is still possible that an incorrect stimulus condition affected the design. An example of this in Calc2 could be if the stimulus component initiated two commands with the same tag, an illegal case with indeterminate results. In that case, the verification team must fix the stimulus component. In the end, the verification engineer must determine why the actual data are incorrect.

To do this, the verification engineer starts at the observation point determined by the failure. In black box verification, this is a DUV output. In white or grey box verification, the observation point could be internal to the design or a DUV output. In any case, the verification engineer must find the logic that feeds the observation point. In the best of cases, the verification engineer can correlate the observation point to a particular stimulus value or sequence; in the worst of cases, there may be a large convergence across the logic, meaning many paths might feed a single observation point. The verification engineer then spends time determining if the logic that feeds the observation point is correct. If that logic is correct, then the engineer must go back even further. The engineer must validate that all of these are correct (or incorrect). This continues until the verification engineer encounters a previous observation point in the test bench or the input stimulus. If the verification engineer reaches a previous observation point at which a checking component did not fire, then the area of the failure must be between the two observation points. The bug exists after this point (because this check did not fail) and before the area at which the check failed. However, the verification engineer must determine if the previous observation point is faulty. This trace-back process continues until the verification engineer finds the point in which the DUV or the verification environment miscalculated a value. This is the source of the bug.

In some instances, the specification is ambiguous, and both the checker and the design can be correct from an interpretation standpoint. In these scenarios, the specification is the source of the bug, and the verification engineer must consult the architect to fix the ambiguity in the specification.

However, having a good verification plan can reduce these situations. The specification authors need to be present during the verification plan review to address any misinterpretation of the specification. This will save time and avoid wasted efforts because there will be no waiting until a test fails because of a misinterpretation.

The debug process determines the specific failure by tracing a miscompare or unexpected value back to the point of origin. Therefore, the identification of the *failure point* (point of origin) is a critical step. The closer the specific failure is to the *observation point* (the checker at which the environment detected the miscompare value), the faster the debug process proceeds. Therefore, the verification team could streamline the process by adding more observation points to isolate the failure point quickly. To take this to an extreme, every node in the circuit could have a check on it. These checks would always be on so that when a check failed, no trace back would be needed because the team would know exactly what failed. However, this extreme case creates difficulties on multiple fronts. First, if the verification team imbeds internal checks throughout the design, the team tips the scales too far toward verifying the design's implementation rather than the design's intent. Second, maintenance of the extensive checkers becomes difficult, as the verification team must update internal checkers with every change in the design.

The other extreme is black box, in which no observation points exist within the design. This approach would just check the outputs. However, unless the design is small, it is likely that the failure point is logically distant from the observation point. Thus, the trace back is through a good portion of the design, lengthening the debug time.

Therefore, the verification team must strike a balance between the quantity of checkers and debug efficiency. The "meeting point" of these two approaches is the gray box paradigm. A verification engineer needs to decide where to place monitors or checkers within the design. This will allow some observation into the DUV and still cut down on the trace back. This "divide and conquer" approach assists in identifying the failure points quickly.

Let us take Calc2 as an example. The previous approaches of checking using golden vectors, transaction based, and reference model all assume use of a black box. To illustrate the importance of observation points, as well as shed some light into the black box, more details of implementation are required. The Calc2 design captures the command and data in two consecutive cycles and then enqueues this data into one of two internal buffers: one handles the addition/subtraction pipeline; the

other, the shift pipeline. A priority block exists inside the DUV to dispatch commands from the buffers to the pipelines.

Previously we discussed mechanisms to check the in-order and out-
of-order functional requirements. Now that the box is gray, observation
points (monitors) can be placed on the input of the priority block, as well
as a checker on the output of the priority block. By doing this, the previous discussion on the methods of checking the in-order and out-of-
order function in the various checking paradigms becomes much
simpler. The output checking of the DUV (versus the priority block) can
concentrate on the correctness of commands because the internal checks
will now validate the order of execution is correct. The other advantage
is that if and when the priority checks fail, the verification engineer
knows exactly where the bug exists.

Here are some general guidelines for deciding where to place
observation points in the design to aid in debug and provide additional
checking:

- Aim for mechanisms defined in the design's architecture.
  Observation points on these structures are stable and require less
  maintenance.

- Space observation points evenly throughout the design.

- Use observation points to augment the design team's assertions.
  Do not create redundant observation points for logic that already
  contains assertions.

The last of the above guidelines highlights an additional benefit of
assertion-based verification as discussed in Chapter 3 ("Assertion-Based
Verification: An Overview"). Assertions can have a very positive influence
on debug time. Using an ABV approach reduces verification time because
it pinpoints the failure immediately, and in addition, it does not require
a complete white box approach.

Previously, this chapter described the construction of effective checkers relative to a basic verification environment. There are additional
aspects of checking component construction that assist in debugging.
This includes how and when a checking component reports a failure,
which is critical in assisting the verification engineer during debug. The
more information that the checking component provides, the faster the
verification engineer can debug the failure. Just indicating that a failure
exists is not enough. When a verification component reports the failure
is equally important because the debug process goes faster when a
checker reports a failure when the failure occurred. Conversely, if the
failure occurred early in the simulation but the checking component indicated a failure near the end, the tracing back through time (i.e., many
transactions) is time-consuming and wastes simulation cycles that the

verification team could use for other test cases. This indicates an inherent disadvantage for end-of-test case checking.

For example, a test case ends and reports the following:

```
Simulation completed:
100 transactions sent
100 transactions received
1 error
```

This reporting style does not assist the verification engineer in debugging with respect to how and when the checker encountered a failure. These messages do not even point the verification engineer to the observation point. In this case, the verification engineer must debug the failure by viewing the trace file with no indication of what the error was or when it occurred.

Instead, the checker should log complete data about the failure. This should include many of the following items: the current cycle, the verification model, a failure message, the design hierarchy in which the checker encountered the failure, the nets involved in the check, the actual DUV values, and the expected values. For example

```
ERROR (Time 50): Checker: Port 1 — Wrong response
ERROR (Time 50): Checker: Port 1 — Expected Response: Good
ERROR (Time 50): Checker: Port 1 — Actual Response: Overflow
ERROR (Time 50): Checker: Port 1 — Expected Result: "0F12023F"X
ERROR (Time 50): Checker: Port 1 — Actual Result: "0F12023E"X
```

The information on the "how and when" of the error cuts down on debug time. This message style gives much more detail and steers the initiation of the debug process. The verification engineer knows to start debugging at cycle 50. The engineer also knows that the checking component found the error on port 1 and exactly what signal values did not match the expected values. This level of messaging speeds the initial portion of the debug process, quickly directing the verification engineer to the miscompare and assisting in localizing the failure point.

There are multiple tools in the arsenal that assist the verification engineer in discovering the "how and when" of a miscompare. These tools exist as mechanisms to reduce debug time and range from basic messaging to more advanced tools that allow for graphical debug of the test bench. The following are a set of debug tools:

- Print

- Assertions

- Waveform viewers

- Memory viewers

Print

The most basic reporting mechanism is *print*. To implement this mechanism for debug, the verification engineer simply adds print statements into the environment components to log test bench activity. This is a common debug mechanism for software designers. The print statements echo the values of the verification components at different times via some logging mechanism. This logging mechanism captures the information and directs it to a simulation log file or a dedicated log file. Verification engineers use dedicated log files for individual verification components (rather than a global log file that captures all components' messages), giving them the ability to sort through many messages quickly. This is especially useful during early component debug. Verification teams may also choose to use dedicated log files to sort logically separate data streams. In Calc2, for example, there are four independent requestors on four different ports. The team could choose to create the environment such that each of the four stimulus components logs every transaction into separate files. This way, if a failure occurs on port 2, debugging commences on the log file for port 2, bypassing potentially extraneous data from other ports. However, the verification engineer cannot discount the potential that other ports' inputs may affect each other. Therefore, the potential exists that while debugging a port 2 failure, the verification engineer traces commands from other ports' log files.

The down side to logging messages is that they tend to be very verbose. Components can generate thousands of lines of messages in a log file. This can also negatively affect the simulation engine's performance owing to the file input/output (I/O) throughout the test case.

A solution to this is to include programmed debug levels in the environment code, a technique the software industry has used for years. When running a test case in the default mode, the components use the lowest message level at which checkers only report errors—no other pertinent information. However, when an error occurs, the verification engineer reruns the simulation, applying a higher level of debug messaging. Now the components print detailed information to the log files, aiding the debug process. All units throughout the environment can use debug levels—not just checkers. This may include stimulus, scoreboards, checkers, and/or monitors. However, a global messaging method can easily lead to information overload with all the verification components logging information for the test case. Instead, the verification team may consider a more granular message logging paradigm in which parameters enable debug messages only for a subset of the verification components. This may assist in controlling the amount of information written to the log file while also avoiding the performance problem.

It is important to note that the verification team needs to plan this fine-grained control of debug message levels before writing the actual test bench code. It is very time-consuming to add such debug message control into already released code.

Although print statements work well for directly debugging verification components, verification engineers must rely on different means for debugging the DUV. Therefore, verification engineers add white box monitors (with print statements) to the environment or ask the designer to add assertions to the logic. If using monitors, the verification team creates them with the same type of controls as the other portions of the environment. This will allow fine control of the debug messages during simulation, which will help to maximize performance of the simulation engine and minimize information overload on the debugger. On the other hand, assertions will always "fire" based on the content of the assertion.

Assertions for Debug

Section 3.3 provided an overview of assertions. This overview only mentioned why assertions were good for debug. This section now discusses assertions in more detail and how they assist in debug.

Assertions can be used in two ways—embedded within the HDL (HDL assertions) and external to the HDL (non-HDL assertions).

Designers make assumptions when implementing the intentions of the specification. These assumptions include the designer's understanding of the input rules, as well as postulations for the internal structures of the design. By embedding assertions within the design, designers guard against violations of these assumptions. Coding the RTL in this fashion is a defensive HDL coding style. It helps to document the assumptions of the design for others, including cases in which another designer inherits the logic. Although commenting the design performs the same task, this is passive and violations will not result in simulation errors. Because HDL assertions are active, they perform the documentation of the assumptions and provide run-time checks. Now, when a simulation scenario violates an assumption, the assertions indicate when and where the violation occurred. This helps the debug process by immediately isolating the problem.

An example of this with the Calc2 design might be to have an assertion on the input *cmd* bus to assure that no two commands occur on successive cycles. If the stimulus component ever violates this assertion, the simulation engine would immediately raise an error within the test. This error makes for swift debug, as it would indicate that the problem was within stimulus component.

Non-HDL assertions are those that the verification team applies to the design. Unlike the HDL assertions in the DUV, these assertions are external to the design and coded as a check on an interface—similar to an interface monitor that is just checking for protocol compliance. Non-HDL assertions are useful when the verification team would like to provide additional observation points within a design. The benefit of writing an assertion rather than a protocol checker is that assertions are easier to write and maintain.

Assertions (either HDL or non-HDL) come in two flavors: concurrent and temporal. Concurrent assertions are those that must always hold true. Every cycle of simulation checks these assertions; for example, a cache design might assert that the read and write commands must not be active at the same time. Temporal assertions are those that are only true for a given time period under specific circumstances. The Calc2 *cmd* assertion mentioned above is temporal because it states that a command may not be sent the cycle after sending a command. The assertion will not activate again until another command is sent.

Most designers code using concurrent assertions. However, the temporal assertions are very useful, and thus the verification team utilizes them. This may change as designers become fluent in property specification language (*PSL*) or other temporal languages. These assertions guard against any violation of the rules. The violator could be from a stimulus component in a unit test bench, or it could be from a neighboring design block at a chip-level test bench.

Whether the assertions are HDL-based or non-HDL-based, they are beneficial because an assertion will guard the logic from any incorrect assumptions and guarantee that the downstream logic sees only legal stimulus. For debug, this accelerates the determination of the problem. Figure 8.16 shows the assumptions and guarantees encapsulated by internal assertions. The assert statements check input assumptions, raising an error when a violation occurs and guarantee specific output checks and flagging problems before they propagate to downstream logic.

Assertions also benefit reuse of the design. Once implemented, anyone who uses this DUV and its set of assertions gets the benefit for debug— the indication of a violation at the source of the problem.

Waveform Viewers

Often it is necessary to get more details when a test case goes awry. Many times when debugging, the verification engineer needs to view signals within the design and their values at different times within the simulation. To accomplish this, the verification engineer can use a visual tool and view the DUV's internal values in a waveform. A waveform viewer is now a mainstream tool packaged with every simulation engine. Electronic design automation (EDA) companies provide waveform viewers mainly because they are the most common type of debugger. For more details on waveform viewers, see Section 5.6.

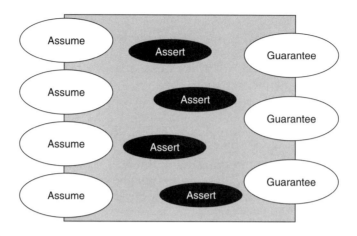

▪ **FIGURE 8.16**

Assertion guarding and guarantee.

Waveform viewers within the debug process display the signals and latches that are of interest after a test fails and, when tracing back through the logic, help determine the correctness of the actual outputs. Once it captures these signals and latches, the engineer compares these values to the ones that the checking component indicated was an error.

Another use of a waveform viewer during the debug process is to view the internals of the verification components. Stimulus components, monitor components, and checking components may have internal state machines just as a design might. A waveform viewer is a useful debug tool for a designer (to look at the HDL); it can be just as useful for the verification engineers to look at their code. By using a waveform viewer to show internal variables/states of the verification components over time, the verification engineer can identify bugs (just as a designer would) within the environment. This ability is very powerful and may show the source of a problem much more quickly than just using print statements.

Some EDA companies have focused on the debug issue and have added function to their waveform viewers beyond the functions covered in Chapter 5. Verification directly influenced one of these added features—abstraction. In some waveform viewers, the verification engineer can create or specify a user defined transaction based on abstraction principles. This is a powerful debug mechanism. Consider the case in which a verification engineer abstracts Peripheral Component Interconnect (PCI) read and write commands. Figures 8.17 and 8.18 show examples of PCI read and write commands. Notice how each utilizes the same set of signals; it is the temporal behavior of the signals over time that indicates whether the transaction is a read or a write.

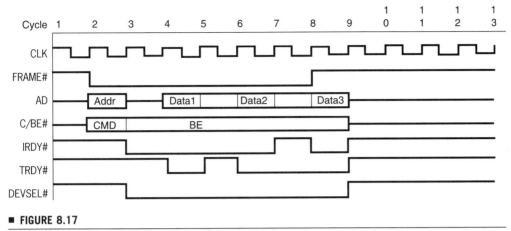

■ **FIGURE 8.17**

PCI read transaction.

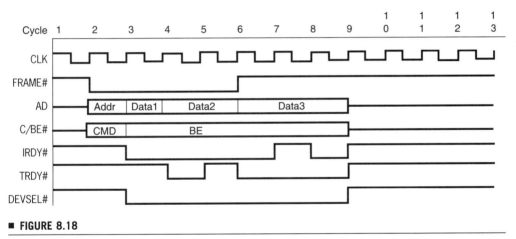

■ **FIGURE 8.18**

PCI write transaction.

A test fails with the checking component indicating incorrect data at a specific address. The verification engineer knows that the only way the DUV could corrupt this address is via a write transaction on the PCI bus. The engineer now needs to find which write transaction in the waveform was the culprit, but the waveform could contain hundreds of reads and writes. In a typical waveform, the engineer would have to analyze the individual set of PCI signals to determine whether the PCI transaction was a read or a write; however, in an abstracted waveform, the tool differentiates the read and write transactions and their cycles. Figure 8.19 illustrates the difference between a transaction abstracted waveform and a grouped waveform. The verification team created a group within the

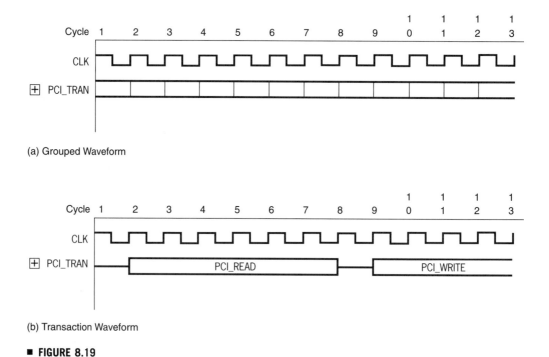

(a) Grouped Waveform

(b) Transaction Waveform

▪ **FIGURE 8.19**

Transaction abstracted waveform versus regular grouping waveform. (a) The view of when the grouped PCI signals are collapsed. (b) The same grouping of PCI bus signals, but they are abstracted based on their temporal aspects.[1]

waveform called PCI_TRAN that contains all the PCI signals. In the grouped method, the verification engineer observes that on every cycle some signals within the grouping have changed. When the verification engineer looks at the abstracted waveform, he or she sees exactly when each transaction occurred and how long it lasted. To see the details of the transactions, the engineer zooms into a transaction of interest, and then expands the group to see the individual signals. To look for the faulty write, the verification engineer need only search for the last PCI_WRITE to the failing address. This is simple using the abstracted waveform viewing technique.

Memory Debuggers

Another class of debugging tools deals with memories (physical HDL type memory such as caches, DIMMs, DDR, SRAM, etc.). These tools

---

[1] Signal grouping is shown in this figure. Grouping is when multiple signals are combined and shown as a combination of all the signals. A simple example is an array. It is a grouping of individual bits. This is extended so that a user can define their own groups.

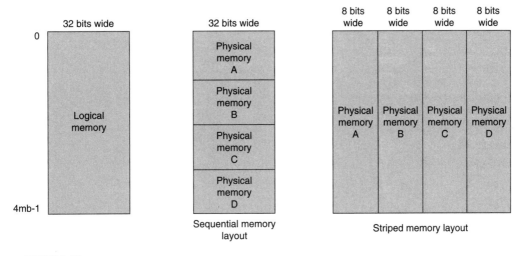

Logical to physical memory map.

assist the verification team in debugging memory controllers and any design that has extensive use of memory (either internal or external to the chip). Memory debuggers are important because the memory controllers implement the logical memory space differently than the physical memory layout.

Figure 8.20 illustrates two logical to physical memory maps. The chip has a logical memory of 4 MB, but the designer could implement this in different ways. This figure shows two different mapping techniques. The first technique uses four different smaller memories of the same data width (32 bits), each $\frac{1}{4}$ of the total addressable memory space. They are cascaded to represent the logical memory. A second technique uses memories that are $\frac{1}{4}$ of the data width but are the same total addressable memory space. Factors such as availability of memory, bandwidth requirements, and latency affect the choice of techniques. Many systems combine the two above techniques. A system could use 16 smaller memories that are $\frac{1}{4}$ of the data width and $\frac{1}{4}$ the total addressable memory space.

The problem with this is that when a verification engineer tries to debug a failing test, it takes time to look into the various memories and decipher the content. Data may be scattered throughout the physical memories in the system, even though from a logical standpoint, all the data are together. This consumes a lot of engineering time paging up and down in a waveform viewer, or doing the translation on paper or a white board. This is where memory debuggers assist the engineer. Their basic function allows the engineer to define the translation from logical to

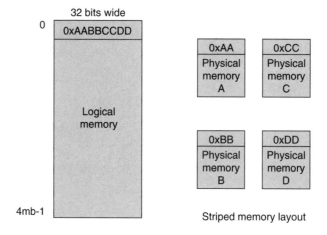

■ **FIGURE 8.21**

Striped memory layout example.

physical. Thus during debug, the verification team spends their time dealing with the logical format (typically the more intuitive view); and when the problem is found, they "switch" to the physical format by switching views. This enables the engineer to find the offending memory location quickly.

For example, consider a system using the striping memory layout. A transaction performs a write of data 0xAABBCCDD at address 0x0. Because of the physical layout of the memory, one memory does not contain all the data. The DUV scatters the data across the four physical memories: physical memory A contains data 0xAA, physical memory B contains data 0xBB, physical memory C contains data 0xCC, and physical memory D contains data 0xDD. Each memory stores the data at address 0x0. Figure 8.21 illustrates this.

Another aspect deals with buffer management such as linked lists. Many ASICs contain functions that deal with data packets. The designs store these data packets as linked lists within system memory, and the ASIC contains some internal structures to manage the lists (refer to Figure 8.22).

Memory debug tools give a verification engineer some extra functionality to traverse these buffers quickly and then go to that memory (either in a physical or logical view). The engineer can then backtrack through the logic that wrote this memory. Some of the tools go even further, enabling the verification engineer to define the buffer structure and then at end-of-test case checking time, make a single program call to the memory tool to validate that no buffers were lost. The tool performs the traversal of the memory structures to validate that the count contained

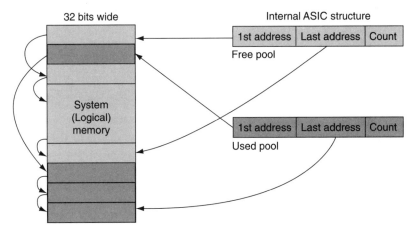

32 bits wide   Internal ASIC structure

■ **FIGURE 8.22**

Linked lists in memory. The free pool manages the available free buffers in the system, and the used pool maintains the buffers that contain valid data. In many environments, the verification team must verify this buffer management function. The team must ensure that the design never loses a buffer because if any buffers get lost, data is lost. This is similar to a software memory leak. If a hardware memory leak exists, then over time it cannot reclaim these data buffers. The only means of reclaiming this lost memory is to perform a reset of the device or system. In many applications, this is unacceptable.

inside the design matches the expected count contained within the tool. This saves the verification team from having to implement these checks themselves.

Overall, these debugging tools are a productivity aid. The verification engineer can survive without them. However, as mentioned previously, verification is the biggest lever the whole team has to reduce time to market. These debugging tools assist the verification productivity in reducing the overall time it takes to determine what caused a test to fail. Table 8.2 compares the different debug methods.

8.2.2 How Different Types of Test Benches Affect Debug

The stimulus and checking paradigms affect the debug process. Although all environment types require similar DUV approaches, the different stimulus and checking techniques require different approaches when debugging the verification components themselves. Specifically, the type of generation (pre-generation versus on-the-fly generation) and type of checking (on-the-fly versus end-of-test case checking) drive different internal debug strategies based on the information provided by the test case. When using a pre-generation strategy, all the facilities and

TABLE 8.2 ▪ Debug method comparison

Debug method	Pros	Cons
Print	▪ Applied anywhere	▪ Degradation of simulation performance ▪ Create lots of information ▪ Must architect into verification components
Assertions	▪ Applied anywhere ▪ Always active	▪ Rely on designer
Abstracted waveform	▪ Allows identification of different transactions quickly	▪ Applicable to transaction based environments ▪ Defined by user
Memory	▪ Allows different views of memory ▪ Allows viewing memory as used by design (linked lists, etc)	▪ Applicable to memory designs

stimulus are available before running any simulation cycles. On the other hand, on-the-fly generation components must run simulation cycles in order to decide if the stimulus is correct. The following sections provide details and insight on the differences between debugging pre-generation test cases, on-the-fly generation, and checking.

Debugging Pre-Generated Test Cases

Determining if stimulus is correct with a pre-generation stimulus component is the easier and less time-consuming than on-the-fly generation. Before running any simulation cycles, the verification engineer can observe the transactions that the stimulus component will send into the DUV. The verification engineer expects the stimulus component to send these specific scenarios in a legal format. If, through debugging, the verification engineer finds that the test case contains an error, then the generator (or writer) needs to fix the generation problem. If the test case is correct but the inputs to the DUV are not, then the verification engineer must fix the stimulus component.

However, debugging pre-generated test benches is often not so simple. Complexities arise in environments in which stimulus components require feedback from the design. In these cases, the stimulus component cannot send in the next transaction until it receives an acknowledgement from the DUV. Because of the timing and interaction between the stimulus component and the DUV, the verification engineer must determine if the pacing is correct at simulation runtime. Therefore, in these situations, pre-generation debug may only get the verification team part way. The verification engineer must debug the test case stimulus through run-time debugging methods.

Debugging On-the-Fly Generated Test Cases

Debugging on-the-fly stimulus component is not as quick as pre-generation. The reason is turn-around time. Because the verification engineer must run simulation in order to debug the stimulus component, there is an upfront wait time to determine if the stimulus is correct. In addition, the verification engineer must wait until after re-running the test case to the same point to determine if the fix was actually good.

For example, a test case that fails after 3 hours is determined to have a stimulus component bug. The verification engineer fixes the component and re-runs the simulation—another 3 hours—to determine the success of the fix. At this pace, the verification engineer can only perform one fix a day. Moreover, this does not even account for the debug time to determine that the stimulus component contained the issue.

However, the verification engineer is not limited to just using print messaging and waveform viewers. In on-the-fly generation, the verification engineer can also perform source code debug by using standard programming or HVL interactive debuggers. In very complex stimulus components, this may outweigh the turn-around time.

Debugging On-the-Fly and End-of-Test Case Checking

Debugging end-of-test case and on-the-fly checking require similar methods. Both require tracing back to the origin of failure. Thus, it is advisable to use debug tools, such as print statements, within the verification environment. These tools allow the verification team to trace a transaction from its conception (generation) through the environment to the checker. Many times, the verification team will add special fields to the data structures used within the verification environment. The sole purpose of these special fields is to assist in tracing back to the origin of the failure.

The verification team uses different mechanisms to perform this trace. One mechanism is to direct all the transactions to one log file. In this scheme, the verification team parses through this file looking for port transactions relative to the failure based on addresses, transaction types, or other events related to the failure. A different method is to correlate similar functions and direct each one to its own trace file. For example, in Calc2, the verification components could direct the printing of transaction information (i.e., trace information) to a log file on an individual port basis. At the end of simulation, four trace files exist, one for each port. If the verification team needs to perform debug on port 1, all the transactions that port 1 performed are contained in a single file. The trace file would contain pertinent information for every transaction such as cycle transaction was sent into the design, cycle at which the scoreboard performed its dispatch, cycle at which the checking component received its response, and cycle at which the check was performed. However, this scheme makes it more difficult to debug failures with roots in multiple port operations.

It is imperative that all the verification component authors stay "on the same page" when creating the print statements for these trace files. If the stimulus component creates four separate trace files (one per port) but the checking components log everything to one file, then additional burden is placed on the verification team to correlate everything.

8.3 SUMMARY

Results checking is affected by the stimulus generation choices and the type of checking required to validate the functional intent of the DUV. On-the-fly checking is one paradigm, and end-of-test case checking is another. In most situations, the verification team will require both paradigms of checking. On-the-fly checking is applicable to test benches in which a transaction-based approach is being used. End-of-test case checking is typically useful when results remain persistent within the DUV's memory until the end of the test, when signal access is limited, when checking the ending state of the test bench and/or DUV, or when checking any function that has system aspects.

In many situations, on-the-fly and end-of-test case checking are combined to obtain the best of both worlds. To achieve this, the verification environment must be architected properly (as was described when the different results checking methods were applied to Calc2).

Debug is important (and crucial) in the verification cycle. A good debug approach can cut down the time it takes to verify a design. Then engineers spend less time doing debug and more time writing and running tests, thus gaining functional coverage and completing the criteria for the verification task much faster. Many tools exist to assist the verification team in the area of debug. These tools are all productivity boosters, and they allow the verification engineer to spend less time debugging.

Having good debug mechanisms in the environment will also cut down on the time required to decide whether a bug is in the design or in the verification environment. To create an effective debug strategy, the verification engineer must consider the effects of the different types of stimulus generation and results checking have on debug. Once the verification engineer understands these items, he or she can formulate an effective debug strategy for the verification environment. A good debug strategy allows the verification engineer to navigate quickly the design and verification environment to find the source of the failure.

8.4 EXERCISES

1. Explain the differences between the four types of results checking.

2. When should on-the-fly checking be done? What about end-of-test case checking?

3. How can coverage assist in checking?

4. Define the debug process.

5. When a failure occurs, can a test bench and design both be correct? If so, how can this be avoided?

6. Discuss the impacts of the different types of stimulus generation and results checking on debug.

7. For Calc2, what type of end-of-test case checking should be in place?

8. Give an example for assume type assertions for Calc2.

9. Give an example for guarantee type assertions for Calc2.

10. Define at least two assertions that could catch a bug before it is caught by a checker on the output ports for Calc2.

11. Using the verification plan and strategies for stimulus as outlined in Chapter 7 and the strategies for checking from this chapter, create a verification environment using your choice of an HVL. The environment should use on-the-fly generation, coverage metrics, and a combination of on-the-fly and end-of-test case checking techniques. You will need to download the Calc2 HDL (download from the companion Web site for this book)—and create a simulation model using your vendor's engine. Describe any more bugs and indicate the test scenarios that uncovered them.

CHAPTER 9

PERVASIVE FUNCTION VERIFICATION

When starting a design effort, it is natural for the verification and design teams to focus initially on the main function of the design. In this chapter the normal chip operations are called *mainline* functions. Much thought goes into the stimulus and checking components required to verify the architectural compliance and the microarchitectural features of the chip's mainline function. Amazingly, verifying hardware functionality under normal operations is only half of the verification battle, because the end users' expectations are much greater than basic system functionality. Verification teams must also create tests for functions beyond the normal stream of operations.

Pervasive functions are those operations beyond the normal chip or system operations. These functions support the chip infrastructure, allowing the end user to get the system into a good state, to manage it while running mainline operations, to administer maintenance operations, and to diagnose any problems. These functions are globally woven into the chip design and orthogonal to the mainline functions. Pervasive functions include the resetting of the hardware, built-in self test (automated, hardware-driven diagnostics), recovery scenarios, chip level testability, low-power modes, and all hardware debug mechanisms. This chapter discusses the basic strategies required for success in pervasive verification.

The amount of pervasive function required for the hardware depends on the customers' expectations and the usage of the hardware. Some hardware may have little or no recovery mechanisms, leaving the consumer to perform recovery by switching off the power and rebooting. On the other hand, robust designs have intensive error detection and recovery schemes, allowing the system to maintain functionality by disabling bad hardware until replacement parts become available. These systems have complex software interfaces and can pinpoint failing components, divert traffic to alternative resources, and inform the consumer and field engineers of the required maintenance. In these systems, designers set aside a substantial amount of the silicon real estate for pervasive function—all of which the verification team must test.

Pervasive verification requires as much early attention and planning as mainline functional verification. The verification team includes the pervasive verification work in the verification plan, sizing the schedule, and the effort along with the rest of the labor. The design and verification teams must avoid the impulse of forging ahead with main function design and verification while leaving pervasive design until the latter stages of the project. Early pervasive planning saves design and verification rework later.

In large servers or other robust systems, a separate *service element* controls initialization and other pervasive functions. Service elements run specialized software, called *firmware*, that performs initialization, diagnostic, and recovery actions on the hardware. Many of the pervasive functions described in this chapter require the guidance of a service element. Although the service element itself requires verification, this chapter restricts the pervasive verification discussions to the effects of the service element (and its software) on the hardware function it drives and the implications for the stimulus and checking components.

The amount of design verification investment into pervasive function is surprisingly large. Although designers tend to deliberately contemplate and document mainline functions for all scenarios, they are more apt to overlook pervasive function. However, pervasive function is inherently complex. In some pervasive areas such as error recovery, the number of illegal conditions that hardware needs to handle is orders of magnitude larger than that of the legal conditions. Experienced design and verification teams know that although pervasive function implementation may seem straightforward, the amount of time and resources needed for proper execution of all pervasive functions often overshadows that of mainline function.

9.1 SYSTEM RESET AND BRING-UP

Of all the verification tasks, the most important is ensuring that the product reset works correctly. When engineers power-on early silicon parts, the first hurdle is getting the hardware initialized to a state in which it can run functional operations. An outstanding verification effort on these main functional operations is rendered irrelevant if the engineers cannot get the hardware into a state in which it can run basic operations. Therefore, all verification plans must include full reset and system bring-up testing.

When engineers initially apply power to real hardware, the internal latches and arrays are in an undetermined state. Most likely, the initial state of the hardware is different every time the engineers bring it online. From a functional perspective, the initial state is probably not a legal state—it may have bad parity, illegal or incompatible values in the state machines, and conflicting signals. Therefore, the design team imple-

TABLE 9.1 ■ Comparison of initialization via reset signal and scan reset methodologies

	Reset Signal	Scan Reset
Speed of initialization	Faster	Slower
Repair flexibility in fabricated hardware	Low	High
Ease of verification effort	Simple	Medium
Ease of hardware design language	Simple	Simple
Ease of synthesis and physical design	Simple	Medium

ments a standard method for returning the hardware to a known-good, initial state.

There are two basic methods for initializing the hardware. The intent of both cases is to place the hardware into a consistent, operational state. The first method uses a single input line, called a reset signal, to initiate a hardware reset. The second uses the scan rings to propagate the correct values to each latch. In either case, verification of hardware reset entails two parts. The first is verifying the initialization of each latch in the system to a determined state. The second part requires verifying that the initialized state enables the hardware to run normal main functional operations.

Table 9.1 compares reset signal initialization to scan reset initialization. The main reason for using the scan reset methodology is for its ability to fix defective hardware through alterations in the initial values. Designers can repair the hardware by scanning alternative values into special registers. Designers can also fix faulty initial values, although with proper verification these cases can be avoided. The repair flexibility comes at the cost of initialization speed and ease of physical design effort and verification effort. However, there are tools available to automate the wiring process during synthesis and physical design.

In complex computer systems, the initialization routine may be under the control of a software supervisor or service element. In this case, the software still uses one of the two hardware initialization methods. Additionally, the software also performs diagnostics, array initializations, and other start-up functions.

9.1.1 Reset Line Initialization

Many hardware devices receive an external reset signal intended to initiate the hardware to a known-good, idle state. The input signal propagates to each latch/flip-flop often through re-drive buffers, used to re-power the input signal across the chip. Upon receiving the signal along with a normal clock, each latch sets itself to either a zero or one value. Figure 9.1 shows the general layout for reset-line hardware. Figure 9.1 does not show the clock tree, which accompanies the reset line.

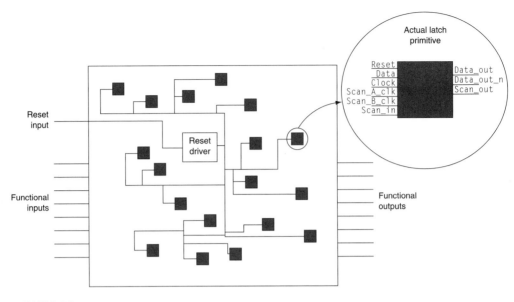

▪ **FIGURE 9.1**

Each latch contains a reset input that when activated by a centralized reset driver, sets the value of the latch to a known-good state (usually "0").

The latch primitive shown in Figure 9.1 shows all the latch inputs and outputs. This includes three scan-related input signals, Scan_A_clk, Scan_B_clk, and Scan_in, as well as one scan-related output signal, Scan_out. In a system that utilizes a reset initialization scheme, the function of the scan ports is for chip testability. During normal operations, the clock signal, Clock, gates functional data into the latch. The latch has both normal and inverted output ports.

Verification of Reset Line Initialization

As previously stated, the verification team first ensures that the reset line sets all latches to a determined state. The team can perform this using either simulation techniques or formal verification. Under simulation, the test case must start with all latches in an undetermined state. Most simulation engines provide a multi-value capability that includes an undetermined or unknown state called "X" or "u" (see Section 5.1.1). With the clocks toggling normally, the test case drives the input reset signal for a predetermined number of cycles. During that period, the test case and verification environment must ignore any error signals or illegal states. The test case then drops the reset signal. At this point, the test case or verification environment should dump the value of all latches and flag an error for any latches that still have an undetermined state value.

For simulation engines that allow only zero and one values for latches, the verification engineer must still run this task. Instead of initializing the latches to the undetermined state, the test case should put random values in all of the latches. After the reset sequence, the test case dumps all of the latch values and compares those values with previous reset simulation jobs. If the hardware reset works properly, these initial values will always match from test case to test case, no matter what initial random values the reset test case assigns to the latches. Additionally, the verification team should use this reset state as the starting state of the design for all mainline test cases. This shows that the reset leaves the design under verification (DUV) in a good state.

Formal verification of indeterminate initial values mirrors the simulation process. The test environment initializes all latches to the X state and then runs the reset. The final rule check verifies no remaining X states exist in the model.

The second part of the reset verification process ensures that the initial values enable proper running of the hardware. First, the verification environment should check that no errors or illegal states are present in the hardware after reset. Then, starting from the reset state, the environment runs multiple mainline functional test cases. These tests should run successfully, showing a clean reset state.

Depending on how many cycles the reset sequence takes, the verification team must choose one of two paradigms. For short reset sequences, they can run the reset sequence before every mainline test. In hardware with extended reset sequences, the team can run the sequence once, take a snapshot of all the values, and then initialize all the latches to these values at the start of the individual mainline test cases. In either case, the mainline functional test case should run successfully.

The Calc1 and Calc2 designs use a reset line for initialization. All of our sample environments have held the reset line for seven cycles before starting mainline function. The verification team can verify the reset of both Calc designs by raising the reset line for seven cycles and then dumping the latch values. In a multiple-value simulation engine, no X state latches should exist. In a two-value simulation engine, the verification team should randomize the starting latch values before each run and then check for consistent values after each test case's reset completes.

In complex systems with multiple hardware chips, a particular chip may require specialized latches to accomplish a reset. These latches reside on the chip inputs and outputs and protect the chip or other chips from invalid states during the reset sequence. Latches that protect the chip from invalid inputs during the system reset sequence are called fencing latches. Latches that protect other chips from invalid inputs are called boundary latches. Boundary latches drive the outputs of a chip. A particular chip may have any mix of boundary and fencing latches: none, one type, or both types (Figure 9.2).

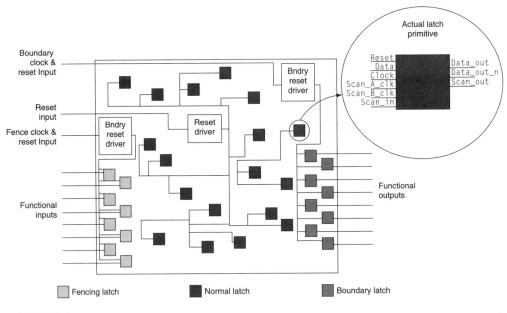

▪ **FIGURE 9.2**

Chips may have fencing and boundary latches. This allows the system to reset without having its multiple chips affect each other with "stray" values. The internal, fence, and boundary types each have their own reset controls.

Systems require these specialized latch types because chips may not reach their initialized state simultaneously. If a chip that has already been reset receives raw input signals from an uninitialized chip, the chip in the reset state will likely go into an error state because the inputs are illegal.

Fencing latches provide a protective wall around the chip to protect it from invalid inputs. Fencing latches receive separate reset and clock signals than the internal latches, as shown in Figure 9.2. These clocks turn on after the system initializes the driving chip(s) and the incoming signals are valid. Boundary latches, shown driving the output signals in the chip in Figure 9.2, receive a separate reset and clock signals. These signals initialize the chip's output drivers to valid states so that other chips receive good inputs.

The system initializes boundary latches first but blocks their data clocks until the system resets the entire chip. This prevents the output signals from receiving and then driving bad inputs after initialization. The system activates the fencing latches' clocks only after it resets the chips that drive incoming signals. This protects the chip from receiving invalid inputs.

Verification of boundary and fencing latches requires appropriate sequencing of the input signals. This sequence matches the system reset sequence. The system architects must define and document this sequence. Verification should proceed as described above, first verifying that after the reset sequence the chip has no X states and then verifying that the initial state allows test cases to run successfully.

9.1.2 Scan Initialization

Scan initialization is the alternative to reset line initialization. Rather than using a centralized reset control, scan initialization propagates values from one latch to the next in a ring structure. The designers place each latch into the ring based on physical proximity, minimizing the wiring required to go from latch to latch. This is called a scan ring. Scan rings serve multiple purposes, including initialization and chip debugging. However, the original and most used function of the scan ring is for physical chip testability. Scan initialization takes advantage of the scan ring structure already in place for testability purposes. Section 9.1.3 focuses on the design and verification of testability features.

The ring loops from a scan driver through all the latches on the chip and back into the scan driver. Rather than have the scan ring traverse the entire chip before returning to the scan driver, the wiring returns back to the scan driver multiple times. This breaks the chip scan ring into stumps. The stumps do not assist in the scan initialization process but are integral for high-speed chip testability. Each stump may contain hundreds of latches, but, again, for testability purposes, the design team aims to keep the length of each stump approximately equal to all other stumps. Figure 9.3 shows a scan ring and stump structure. The design team also breaks the fence and boundary latches into separate stumps.

As with the reset line initialization, there are multiple types of latches. Figure 9.3 shows three stumps of normal, functional latches plus a boundary stump. A typical chip may have dozens of stumps, each with hundreds of latches.

Although the chip's physical implementation breaks the scan ring into stumps, the logical scan initialization routine links all stumps into one long scan ring. When in initialization mode, the DUV's scan driver connects the returning scan data from one stump to the outgoing scan data for the next stump.

The inputs to the DUV's scan driver include scan clocks, a scan enable, scan mode, and a scan input. When the scan mode is set to reset and the scan enable line is high, the software system reset driver sends a new scan input value with each toggle of the scan clocks. A single toggle of the scan clock includes raising the scan_a_clk signal, dropping it, and then raising the scan_b_clk and dropping it. A single toggle of the scan clocks allows a value on the scan_in to propagate through a latch. For example, using the chip shown in Figure 9.3, it takes 18 scan clock toggles to reset the normal latches—one for each normal latch. The first

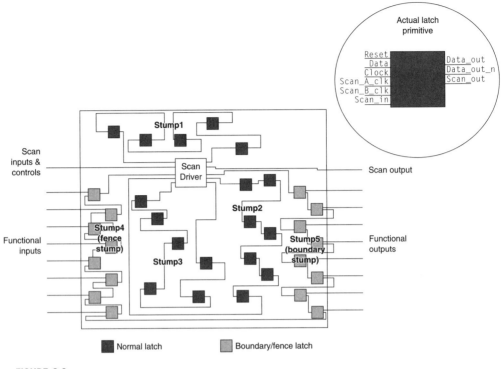

Actual latch
primitive

Reset
Data
Clock
Scan_A_clk
Scan_B_clk
Scan_in

Data_out
Data_out_n
Scan_out

Stump1

Scan inputs & controls

Scan Driver

Scan output

Stump2

Functional inputs

Stump4 (fence stump)

Stump5 (boundary stump)

Functional outputs

Stump3

■ Normal latch   ■ Boundary/fence latch

■ **FIGURE 9.3**

Under scan ring initialization, the designer links all latches, boundary, fence, or internal, into individually shifting stumps. A single stump contains only one type of latch.

scan input value propagates further through the ring with each clock toggle. After the 18th toggle, the first value is in the last latch in the third stump, whereas the newest value is in the first latch in the first stump. The boundary and fence stumps reset uses a separate scan enable but the same method.

The scan rings also assist with hardware debug. During initial scan ring reset, the chip level scan output contains garbage and the system ignores these data. However, once initialized, system test engineers can use the scan output line during debug to view the values of every latch on the chip. The service element shifts the entire ring, reading the scan_out value while also feeding it back into the scan input. The entire scan operation allows the service element to capture each latch's value while also ensuring that it leaves the chip in the same state as before the scan operation. This function is so vital to system debug that it exists in chips that use both the scan and the reset line initialization schemes. Further details on the use of scan rings for debug are provided in section 9.3 of this chapter.

In some chips or systems, the system controller can only drive zeros onto the scan_in pin during initialization. This allows faster initialization and may not require a controller. However, this loses some of the flexibility of scan reset repair in the fabricated hardware. In these cases, the designers insert inverters into the scan ring path before (and after) each latch that requires initialization to a '1'b value. Although this simplifies the system controller operation, it adds verification complexity to the DUV. One of the most common bugs found in this scheme is that the scan ring contains an odd number of inverters. This indicates that the designer inserted an inverter before a latch that needs a '1'b initial value but failed to insert an inverter after the latch. This, in turn, initializes latches further down in the ring to the opposite value as intended.

Verification of Scan Ring Reset

Verification of scan ring resets is similar to reset line initialization verification. On multiple-value simulation engines, the chip should start with all latches in an undetermined state. With the appropriate scan_enable inputs high, the scan reset test case toggles the scan clocks and drives initial values, one-by-one, on the chip's scan_in signal. This method requires that the verification engineer knows the exact order of all the latches in the scan ring. Zero and one values propagate through the chip until the test case stops the scan clock toggling. This occurs when the first value reaches the last bit in the logical scan ring (the last bit on the last stump). On an average chip, this sequence takes hundreds of thousands of cycles to complete.

When the test case completes the initialization, the checking occurs. Special checking should be in place to verify that every latch's scan_out wire drives one and only one scan in value. All latch values are dumped and initial values checked (no X states should be present). Any latches not on a scan ring still have an X state. There are specific cases where this is the intended behavior, and the verification engineer must investigate each of these incidents.

The test case should repeat the process for the boundary rings as well. Because this type of initialization takes an enormous number of cycles, the test case must save the state of all latches after initialization. The verification team uses these values to initialize main functional test cases to show that the chip can run from the reset state.

9.1.3 Testability and Built-In Self-Test

Although scan initialization uses the scan ring structure, its original purpose is for physical chip testability. Testability is a final step of the manufacturing process when technicians screen individual chips for defects, using expensive test machines that probe the chip's input and output pins. The technicians apply test vectors to each chip's pins using the scan ring stumps to propagate test data patterns throughout the latches of the chip. After loading the vectors, the chip test tool toggles the functional clocks for a few cycles, activating the transistors throughout the chip. The speed of the clocks is dictated by the speed of the test machine, which is slower than most of today's chip frequencies.

The initial test vector is not a legal functional state. Instead, test-engineering tools select specific vectors that maximize chip-wide circuit activity. After running a few cycles, the chip test tool again uses the scan ring structure to read the new state of the chip's latches. The new state is a function of the initial test vector and the circuit flow between latches. The new pattern is a signature of the initial test vector. Separately, software tools predict the correct value of the signature based on the gate-level design model, using the same initial test vector. The signature is distinctive for each initial test vector on a given chip design. If the new state, as seen by the chip test tool, matches the predicted signature, then the chip passes the manufacturing screening process. If the signature does not match, it is an indication of one or more ill-formed or defective circuits or wires.

The test patterns only uncover physical circuit defects and do not confirm that a chip meets its functional or architectural requirements. Testability only shows equivalence between a manufactured chip's physical constructs and the gate-level design model. In fact, random test patterns are not suited for functional verification mainline testing because the test patterns reflect illegal values in the functional machine states and run for only a few cycles. Similarly, patterns generated by functional verification's stimulus components are not suited for testability because functional verification patterns tend not to exercise an adequate number of circuits in a short number of cycles. As chip complexity and frequency increases, testability becomes a bigger challenge. Test machines cannot keep pace with the chip frequencies, meaning that the chip's circuits do not run at the intended chip frequency during test. Furthermore, the overhead and cost of loading, dumping, and re-loading new test vectors become unwieldy. As a result, test engineers are turning to on-chip test solutions known as built-in self-test (BIST). BIST uses one or more automated engines (state machine designs inside of the chip) to drive patterns through logic or arrays. Because the BIST engines are part of the chip circuitry, they run more vectors and gain higher test coverage in less time than standard test processes. Additionally, BIST enables test vectors to run at the chip's intended frequency rather than at the speed of the external test tool.

Traditionally, software tools automatically insert scan ring logic for testability. Engineers consider these tools reliable enough that no functional verification is required. However, this only holds true if the intent of the scan logic is for testability only. Dual usage of a chip's scan rings for initialization or for debugging through scan ring dumping (as described in Section 9.3.1) requires functional verification.

Engineers use BIST for dual purposes. First, BIST runs automated test patterns as part of the manufacturing process. The second usage of BIST is to initialize specific parts of the chip. During physical testing of the chip, the logic BIST (LBIST) patterns result in a specific signature as discussed above. During initializations, array BIST (ABIST) engines quickly clean and reset large arrays with good parity or initial values. Verification teams contribute to both BIST purposes before manufacturing.

LBIST Engine

The LBIST engine, using the scan ring stumps discussed in Section 9.1.2, drives pre-determined patterns into all the latches. This engine is part of the scan driver DUV shown in Figure 9.3. Unlike the single logical scan chain mechanism used for scan initialization, the LBIST engine uses each stump simultaneously to quickly propagate the pattern. The engine then toggles the normal system clocks for a few cycles, engaging the chip circuitry, which transforms the original patterns into new signatures. The testability tools measure the amount of physical gates that the patterns drive while also predicting the signature. The LBIST engine still requires a test machine, but the test machine does not toggle the functional clocks. Instead, it must only enable LBIST controls and collect signatures for comparison.

Figure 9.4 shows the connections between the scan driver logic and an LBIST engine. The LBIST on-off controls enable the engine to select the appropriate multiplexer inputs (mux1 . . . muxN) used to drive either a continuous scan ring or the LBIST test patterns. In test pattern mode, the LBIST engine drives unique patterns into each stump simultaneously. Then, the LBIST engine enables the chip's functional clocks, running the circuits at the intended frequency. Finally, the LBIST engine again scans the stumps, shifting-in a new pattern while reading the current stump signature based on the previous pattern and the functional clocking. The LBIST engine collects each stump signature and forwards it to the test machine for comparison against expected values. In continuous scan mode, the multiplexers simply connect the output of the previous stump to the input of the next. This allows the engineering team to scan the chip for initialization and debug.

Verification of the LBIST Engine

Verification of LBIST has dual purposes. The first purpose verifies the LBIST engine functionality and connections to the chip. The second purpose verifies that the signature in simulation matches the signature created by the predictive testability tools.

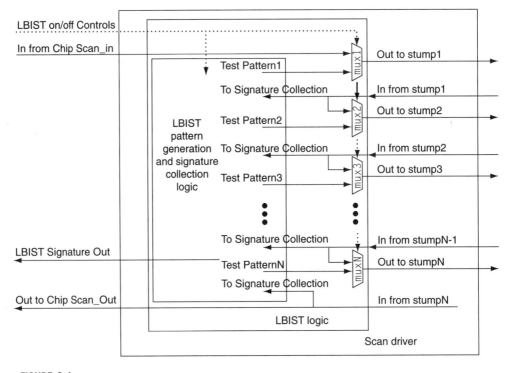

The LBIST control logic inside the scan driver creates test patterns into the chip and collects signatures, enabling at-speed testability.

The verification team must check multiple modes to ensure LBIST functionality. With the additional multiplexers, the verification team must make sure that the chip can both scan for initialization and run LBIST and that both modes are mutually exclusive. Additionally, verification must check that LBIST does not interfere with vital clocks and phase lock loops (PLLs), which allow the chip to run at the intended frequency. Scanning testability patterns while using the on-chip clocks cannot interfere with these clocks.

Checking that the predicted signature from the testability tool matches the signature collected during simulation proves that the LBIST connections are correct. To run this test, the verification team should drive chip level inputs (black box testing) and collect the signatures via chip outputs. This ensures that the LBIST engine works via the chip test machine. The stimulus for this test is straightforward—it corresponds to the stimulus that the test machine applies on the fabricated hardware. The checking is simply a matter of comparing the signatures to those predicted by the test tools. This may seem like a double check on the test tool's signature creation capability. In part, this is true and worthwhile, because chip complexity also produces tool complexity. This is also a good check that the simulation model accurately reflects the complex clocking functions of the DUV. In the end, matching signatures from the simulation model and the test tools gives high confidence in the signatures delivered to the fabrication facility for hardware testability.

ABIST Engine

As with LBIST, the verification team runs the ABIST engines to verify the patterns as well as to check the initializations. When a chip first receives power, the arrays are in an undetermined state. The ABIST engine tests large arrays, searching for faults by writing patterns and reading them back out of the array. The ABIST engine then writes all good patterns into the array. The good patterns are often zeros with good parity or all zeros if the array has a "valid bit" for each entry. The verification test cases step through this process to ensure that the ABIST engine correctly identifies bad array sectors and initializes the array.

Verifying that the ABIST engine can identify bad sectors requires the simulation test case to emulate a bad array cell. This means using the simulation engine to inject an error in a single bit (or multiple bits) across the array to zero or one. Injecting an error in a simulation engine overrides the value of the bit(s), simulating the effects of a bad circuit. No matter what value the ABIST engine writes, the injection, or stuck value, overrides the ABIST value. This appears as a physical fault to the ABIST engine on approximately half of the patterns it reads. On the other half of the patterns, the stuck value matches the ABIST written value, causing no mismatch. The test case must verify that the ABIST engine flags the correct array sector.

Verifying the ABIST initialization sequence is simple. The test case should start in an undetermined state (X or random values) and apply the control signals that initiate the ABIST initialization. When the ABIST initialization completes, the test case should verify that the DUV has set all rows in the array to the correct, initialized value.

The importance of verifying BIST functions cannot be underestimated. Before powering on a system, all chips must go through manufacturing screening. Verification of the LBIST patterns provides confidence in the patterns, speeding the manufacturing test process and ensuring that the chips that make it through the screening process are good. Verification of ABIST provides critical assurance that the chip's array reset process works correctly.

There is one final task on verifying all BIST engines. The verification team must check the reset of the BIST engine itself. It is feasible to use either a scan reset or reset signal initialization scheme for BIST. In any case, the verification team has to include BIST engines in the reset verification plan.

9.2   ERROR AND DEGRADED MODE HANDLING

Many of today's chips work in systems that require some level of reliability. At a minimum, this translates to the need for self-diagnostics. Each chip must be able to detect when invalid conditions occur in its circuitry. In the most robust systems, chips not only need to self-diagnose failures and errors but also need to perform self-healing functions. Verification must ensure that these functions work properly.

In the following sections, verifying error detection and self-healing hardware are discussed. The vital element to remember when verifying all of this function is that the verification environment must reproduce the conditions that occur because of physical errors. These error conditions come in two classifications: hard errors and soft errors. Hard errors occur when the hardware is physically broken. These errors are persistent. To simulate hard errors, the test case must over-ride the simulation model values with a persistent stuck value. Remember that the simulation engine is a software model, not a physical model—it is the verification engineer's job to make the software model act like the physical model (the Line Delete Case Study in the Case Studies chapter describes exactly this verification failure). Soft errors, on the other hand, are not persistent. These errors occur when cosmic rays or alpha particles strike latches or memory cells, causing them to change value once. The particle does not damage the physical hardware, but the current value in the latch or array is incorrect. To simulate soft errors, the verification engineer must stick a bit for a short period (often just for one cycle).

Whether the design can recover from a hard or soft error depends on a combination of factors. These factors include the state of the design when the error occurred; the criticality of the data in the affected signal, latch, or array; and the ability of the system to recover the changed or lost data. A recoverable error is one that the DUV can correct while guaranteeing the operation results. Alternatively, a non-recoverable error is one where the system cannot guarantee the integrity of the application results. Verification must differentiate between these cases and test that the system never allows the DUV to permute a non-recoverable error condition into a recoverable condition. Conversely, the verification team wants to ensure that the DUV does not classify recoverable errors as non-recoverable cases.

9.2.1   Verifying Error Detection

All error and degraded mode handling starts with the detection of an error. The amount of error detection capability within a chip differs with the required level of reliability. The most robust systems have parity on control signals and on data paths, with error correction codes (ECC) on vectored data busses such as arrays and buffers [54]. ECC gives the system the ability to detect and correct errors across a broad number of bits. Depending on the implementation, designers can use ECC to correct one or more bits and detect errors across even more bits. A common implementation of ECC uses an 8-bit encoding appended to a 64-bit vector to correct any single-bit error and detect dual errors.

Designers must add extra logic to the DUV to manage errors. This logic includes monitor signals to read parity signals and detect whether a soft or hard error has flipped a bit. Other monitor logic watches the functional logic for illegal states in the state machines or invalid command values. This is the internal error checking logic.

Verification of hardware error detection follows a three-step process: check the hardware's monitoring logic, verify that the hardware correctly reports the error, and verify that the hardware correctly isolates the source of the error. The three steps are detailed below.

Step 1: Verifying the Hardware's Monitoring Logic

Verification's first task is to check that the hardware's built-in monitoring systems are correct. This verification occurs on all test cases, including those not intended to test error conditions. In the least, all test cases must monitor the hardware for unexpected activation of internal error checkers. When the test case does not inject an error, the internal error checkers should remain inactive.

The more challenging verification task is to verify that each internal error checker turns on appropriately. The test case or environment does this through error injection. Error injection under simulation precisely sticks bit values at specific times. Error injection may emulate a hard error or a soft error, depending on the test case intent. In either case, the injection should either trigger an internal error checker or the test case must complete error free. The difference between these two cases is based on the actual timing of the error injection and the ongoing internal activity. If the error injection occurs on a bit that remains unused during the test case, then an internal error checker will not turn on. What makes the verification task more challenging is the notion that at a given time, most of a chip's logic may be idle. To cause an error condition, the injection must occur on an active bit. This is simpler on hard errors because eventually the hardware is likely to use a bit. The appropriate verification technique for soft errors is to hold a value stuck until the hardware uses that bit and then turn off the injection mechanism. However, there are many subtleties in error injection, including the soft error injection mechanism. If the verification engineer intends to create a soft error, the test case should not simply inject until the hardware detects the error and triggers the internal error checker. This approach overlooks the case where there is an error in the internal error checking logic. Instead, the test case or environment must monitor for when the DUV uses the injected bit and then turn off the soft error. If this occurs,

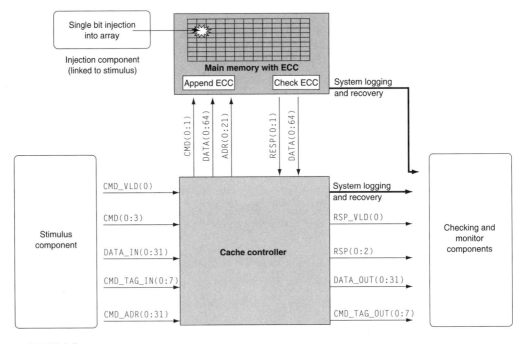

■ **FIGURE 9.5**

During simulation, a single-bit error injection into an ECC protected array should have no effect on the test case, because the ECC logic should repair the bit.

the DUV either correctly flags the error or the test case does not pass, citing the DUV for failing to flag the injection. The key is that the test case should not rely on the DUV's error checking but on the usage of the injected bit.

Test cases must intelligently manage error injection into arrays. Most arrays are too large to expect the test case to utilize the entire space. Therefore, the test case must align injections into the parts of the array exercised by the test case. Test cases that inject single-bit errors (either hard or soft) into arrays protected by ECC should expect the injection to have no effect on the test case results because the ECC logic corrects the single-bit error. Therefore, single-bit error injection into ECC protected arrays can (and should) be done by the test case environment during mainline functional tests, not just during pervasive function verification. However, pervasive test cases must verify the logic correctly handles dual bit error injection into ECC protected arrays. In these cases, the DUV cannot use the data because it is unable to isolate the flipped bits. The DUV must discard the entire line of data.

Figure 9.5 shows the verification environment and DUV design for a cache controller and main memory. The main memory contains ECC append and checking logic that enables correction of single-bit errors. In this figure, an error injection stimulus component continually sticks a single bit in the array, whereas a normal mainline test case runs through the stimulus, monitor, and checking components. The injection should have no effect on the test case because the ECC correction logic fixes any flipped bits. The verification engineer should design the injection component such that it zaps different locations in the array in different test cases, with the sole constraint that it chooses locations in the array used by the particular test case.

Step 2: Verify Error Reporting

The next step in verifying error detection logic is ensuring that the hardware correctly flags detected errors to the system level. For this activity, error reporting falls into two fundamental categories: cases where the system must take recovery action and cases where the hardware just needs to log the occurrence of an error. Robust systems require logging all errors, including those from which the hardware recovers and corrects (e.g., using single-bit ECC). This enables the system to detect trends in faulty hardware or even request preventative maintenance on parts that have higher than usual recoverable errors.

Because there are two categories of error reporting, verification must ensure each error flags the appropriate level to the system. Significant errors must request recovery actions, whereas errors from which the hardware has recovered should just present the log to the system. The verification team builds this intelligence into the checking and monitor components.

Step 3: Verify the Hardware Correctly Pinpoints the Erroneous Source Logic

The final step in error detection is making sure the DUV correctly pinpoints the source of the error. This may not be trivial, because a single error condition may quickly spread to other parts of the logic, causing multiple internal error checkers to activate. Because errors tend to cascade, it is important that the system identify the original failure. The DUV must perform first error data capture, and the verification suite must make sure this logic works correctly. Chips with this level of recovery have central error logging DUV, with inputs from all internal error checkers. The latency from each error checker to this central logging repository must be the same. This allows the logic to identify which checker activated first.

Verification of first error data capture is straightforward. The error captured by the central logging DUV should correspond to the error injected by the test case or environment. The first error data capture logic should lock out all cascading error checkers or flag these as secondary errors.

9.2.2   Verifying Self-Healing Hardware

In robust systems, the hardware must heal itself after an error condition. Designers have used many different mechanisms to handle error conditions. Aside from in-line adjustments such as single-bit error correction using ECC, these mechanisms fall into four categories:

- Hardware reject
- Hardware retry
- Software-assisted recovery
- Hardware degradation

Hardware Reject

Hardware reject is the simplest form of action that the DUV takes. Reject conditions occur when a portion of logic identifies an error on its inputs. The logic refuses to accept the input, preventing the error from propagating by shielding itself from the incorrect control or data. Designers often create a control path back to the initiator, indicating that a reject occurred. This informs the initiating logic that the receiving logic dropped the input because of an error. In some cases, the receiving logic does not provide a response, requiring the initiator to time-out and retry the request later.

The Calc1 and Calc2 examples both use hardware reject functions for illegal commands. The Calc2 design, which correctly implements the reject, has bypass logic specifically for cases of unknown commands. The logic returns an "invalid command" response. Our Calc2 test plans contain multiple scenarios for verifying that the design properly handles invalid commands.

Figure 9.6 shows a second example using the cache controller. Here, the error injection stimulus component sticks a bit on the incoming command (or the command parity) signals. The cache control logic detects bad parity on the input lines. The input cannot be trusted, so the logic bypasses the command queue and returns a reject response.

Verification of these cases requires specialized test case checking. Because the error injection changes the expected result of the input stimulus, the environment must inform the checker and monitor components of the reject condition. Verification engineers implement this feature via the scoreboard with an additional "reject" field. This field communicates the injection to the checking and monitor components. It is up to the test case writer to decide whether the stimulus component retries the operation. In a real system environment, the initiating logic would likely resend the command after a reject, but that is not required in a test case whose intent is to verify the reject action.

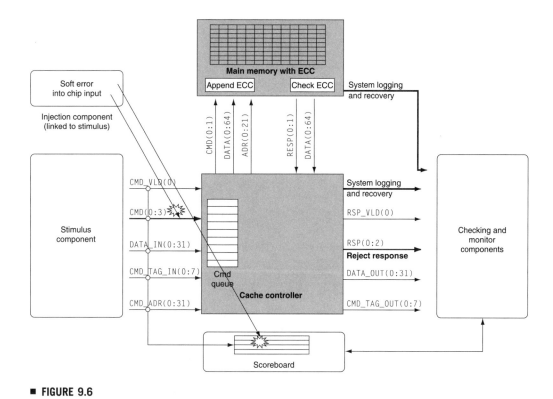

■ FIGURE 9.6

Injecting an error on a control input requires a coordinated environment where the scoreboard communicates the injection to the monitor and checking components.

For retry cases, the verification environment should turn off the interface error injection to simulate a soft error. If there were truly a broken input wire to the cache controller (a hard error), the cache controller would continually reject the command. In robust systems, the initiator would retry the command (maybe a few times) before reporting the problem to the system controller and system software.

Hardware Retry

Hardware retry occurs when the DUV detects an error on which it can take action without affecting other parts of the system. Hardware retry attempts to fix a failed operation by repeating it. Retry operations work well on soft error conditions where the problem is transient. Retry conditions require that the hardware contains the error to a small portion of the system. Errors that cascade beyond logic affected by the retry algorithm must go through software-assisted recovery. In the containable case, the hardware should first attempt to repeat the operation. If the error checking logic does not detect the error after repeating the operation, the retry is successful and hardware requires no further action. However, if the error checking logic detects an error upon retry, software-assisted recovery or hardware degradation is required.

Verification of hardware retry does not require much overhead. The verification team can utilize mainline test cases that exercise the DUV target of the retry action. The test cases need only add the transient injection to the environment, causing the retry action to occur. When successful, the DUV contains the error and repeats the hardware operation. The test case should complete with the same results as the case without the injection—only taking more cycles because of the retry action. The test case environment must also make sure that despite the successful retry action, the DUV logs the error to the system. Verification engineers must pay special attention to the coding of the checking components for hardware retry. The checking component must be able to identify the case where the hardware fails to clear the injected error. The code must detect latent errors in stored data or incorrect machine states that otherwise might go undetected in normal mainline testing.

Figure 9.7 shows the cache controller and main memory verification environment with an error injection into the controller's pipeline. The

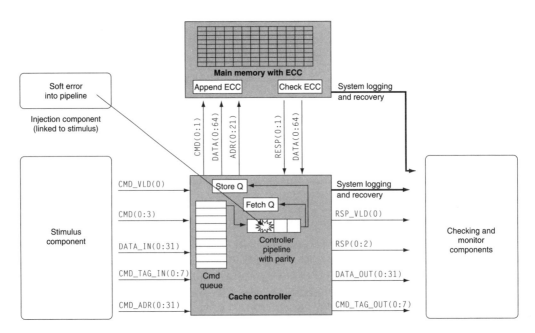

■ **FIGURE 9.7**

A soft error injected into parity-protected control logic causes the logic to initiate an internal retry. The test case should succeed; however, the logic requires additional cycles to execute the retry.

pipeline DUV, protected by parity, should detect the flipped bit and call for hardware retry. In this case, the DUV should flush the pipeline after all commands ahead of the detected error complete. Then the command queue can re-initiate the failed command. If the error is a transient (soft) error, the verification environment turns off the injection and the retry succeeds. A hard error in the pipeline, simulated by a continuous injection, requires software-assisted recovery, likely followed by hardware degradation. In the case of a transient error, the stimulus, monitor, and checker components run a mainline test case to completion. Without the error injection, the test case completes in fewer cycles than with the injection due to the extra cycles for the retry action. In addition, the monitor and checker components should expect to see the cache controller log the retry action.

The Calc2 designs contain no logic for hardware retry or for managing any type of internal hardware failures. If, for example, a failure occurred on a valid bit in either of the Calc2 queues, the hardware would not detect the error and would either lose a command (if the valid bit turned off) or contain an illegal command (if the valid bit turned on). Either case leads to architectural violations. To protect against such failures, the Calc2 design would require detection logic throughout the control and data flows to handle hard or soft errors.

Software-Assisted Recovery

Software-assisted recovery is necessary when the hardware detects an error in which there is no reject or retry action. The software that assists in the recovery action resides on the service element. Because service elements exist only in the most robust systems (usually highly reliable servers), software-assisted recovery is limited to high-end machines.

Hardware may request service element intervention due to many different error scenarios. The hardware should limit these cases to errors that it cannot resolve through retry or reject actions. Three main causes of software-assisted recovery are for recurring errors, errors where data may be lost, or for cases where the error may propagate to other parts of the system. Generally, the service element attempts to repair the hardware by resetting it. Failing that, the service element removes the failing hardware from the system configuration (degraded hardware mode). Degraded modes require alternate paths through the system or alternate, less efficient use of system resources. If there are no alternate paths, then the service element must take the system off-line for repairs.

Software-assisted recovery slows the throughput of the system while the recovery action occurs. The hardware first informs the service element of a failure through an interrupt. At that point, if available, the service element contains the error by fencing the recovering hardware from the neighboring, unaffected hardware. Fencing effectively puts a wall around the failing hardware, preventing other hardware from driving inputs and using outputs. Hence, the throughput of the system slows while the recovery action occurs.

The next step in the recovery action resets the hardware. The service element initiates the reset, which clears the state of the hardware. This cleans any soft errors in the hardware but does not have an effect on hard errors (broken circuits). Hard errors cause software-assisted recovery again, which, after reaching a threshold, invokes an action to degrade the system. In the case of a soft error, the recovery action effectively repairs the hardware and allows it to continue to function. After the reset, the service element may need to restore certain machine states to their pre-error values or back to the last known-good state. Finally, the service element brings the hardware back on-line and lowers the fences to the neighboring hardware.

Verification of software-assisted recovery requires specialized function in the stimulus, monitors, and checking components. These functions are in addition to the normal operations of a mainline test case. Any error injection and recovery actions must occur during the course of normal operations. The point in time when the injection occurs should vary from test case to test case.

The additional functions in the stimulus components required for software-assisted recovery are the error injection function, step-by-step recovery actions, and fence test probes.

Error Injection Function

The error injection function of the stimulus component sticks internal signals, latches, or array elements until the hardware flags an interrupt. Stimulus components can inject into either data paths or control logic. In either case, the error injection function requires some finesse because of the temporal nature of the hardware. At any given time, only a subset of the hardware is valid or in-use. The challenge for the verification engineer is to flip a signal or latch in the hardware that is in use by the test case. Feedback for a successful injection comes in one of two ways: either the hardware raises an interrupt or the monitor or checking components flag an unexpected value on the outputs of the DUV. The latter indicates a bug in the logic where the hardware failed to detect an internal error. If neither of these actions occurs, the injection failed and the stimulus component must try again. To raise the probability of a successful injection, the stimulus component can operate in a white box paradigm, observing the control signals inside the design and triggering the injection when the target logic is in-use.

Step-by-Step Recovery Actions

After the hardware raises an interrupt, the stimulus component invokes the next phase of the recovery action. Up to this point, the stimulus com-

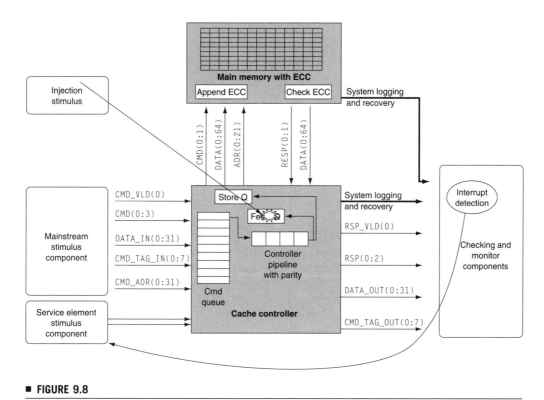

■ **FIGURE 9.8**

Software-assisted recovery requires coordination between the checking and monitor components and the service element stimulus component.

ponent has been driving normal stimulus into the hardware. Now, the specialized stimulus functions gain control.

The step-by-step recovery actions of the stimulus component mirror the function of the service element from the time the hardware flags the interrupt. These actions vary depending on the hardware but usually start with the fencing function. After that, the stimulus component walks the hardware through the recovery and reset sequence, raising the input signals as the service element would. Figure 9.8 shows the cache controller example with the additional components. The monitor and checking components contain the usual mainline checks along with an error and interrupt detection collection point. This portion of the checking component provides a feedback path to the service element stimulus component used to initiate the recovery action.

Fence Test Probes

During the recovery actions, the mainline stimulus component should conduct fence test probes. This action verifies that the DUV's internal fence logic prevents the DUV from acting on stimulus during recovery. The real neighboring hardware (the logic that drives inputs into the DUV) could occasionally drive signals into the DUV while the DUV is undergoing recovery. To cover these cases, the stimulus component should have modes to drive normal stimulus or random "garbage" on the interface. Because of the fences, the checker components must ensure that the DUV ignores all fence probe stimulus.

Another example of software-assisted recovery occurs when a system must work around a failure on a high-speed link between chips. To enable this recovery scenario, the design team includes an extra link bit, or spare bit, between the chips. A 32-bit interface might contain a 33rd spare bit just in case a driver or wire takes a hard error. The logic on both sides of the interface may detect the corrupted bit using parity or ECC codes and send an interrupt to the service element code. A simpler retry action cannot fix this failure, because both chips need to shut down the interface for the repair action. During the recovery action, the high-speed drivers perform calibrations on the new bit and cease usage on the failing bit path. During the repair action, no data traffic may pass on the link.

Verification of this scenario requires four steps.

- **Step 1: Continuous Injection.** Unlike retry or reject cases, the error injection component must perform a continuous injection to simulate a hard error on the link. With mainline traffic running across the chip-to-chip interface, both chips in the DUV detect link errors via the ECC logic as shown in Figure 9.9. As the link errors continue, the link error counters ("counters" in Figure 9.9) reach their threshold and raise an interrupt. During this time, the monitor and checking components should see no indications that there are errors on the link as the ECC logic corrects the corrupted packets continuously driven by the stimulus component.

- **Step 2: Monitoring for the Link Failure Threshold.** The verification environment can accurately predict when the counters reach the threshold using white box monitors on the link. The environment keeps its own counter to verify the threshold comparator. This allows the checking component to expect the interrupt at the appropriate time.

- **Step 3: Service Element Intervention Performing the Bit Sparing.** When the interrupt occurs, the service element raises the fences in the two chips. It then commences the bit-sparing sequence and brings the link back on-line. During this time, the stimulus components should continue to drive patterns, probing the interfaces for fencing failures. The stimulus component does not write these patterns to the scoreboard, because the proper DUV behavior is to ignore the inputs while fenced. If the DUV failed to fence all the inputs, the failure would manifest itself as unknown data or as responses on the DUV outputs.

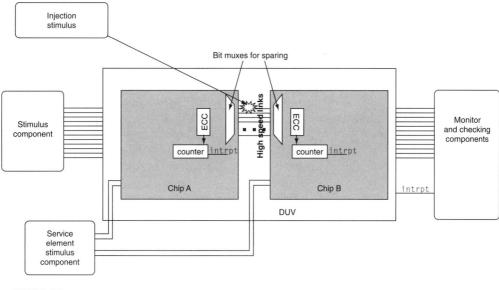

■ **FIGURE 9.9**

A recurring error on a high-speed link requires the service element's intervention to spare out the bad link. Throughout the test case, ECC logic maintains data integrity for single-bit errors.

- ■ Step 4: Verification That the Hardware No Longer Uses the Bad Link. After the recovery and sequence completes, the service element component lowers the fences, bringing the chips back online. The stimulus components restart mainline scenarios, now expecting the DUV to accept and process the commands and data. It is critical that the injections on the bad link continue after sparing. The bad bit on the link is still bad, and the hardware should not use it. The verification environment must ensure that the DUV never uses the bit again on either side of the link. There are multiple ways to accomplish this in verification. One method is through white box monitoring of the bit, making sure it remains inactive. A second method would be to inject soft errors on other bits on the link. Even though this method injects two errors on the link simultaneously, the DUV should only observe the soft error, because the hard error is on the bit that has been retired. The ECC logic cleans the soft error and the mainline test flow continues without errors.

Hardware Degradation

The final mechanism in verifying self-healing systems is hardware degradation. Hardware degradation is a form of software-assisted recovery where the system detects that a portion of the hardware no longer functions properly. Degradation can only occur when there is an alternate path through the system. The system must be able to survive without the failing hardware.

System architects who specialize in self-healing systems spend a great deal of their time creating back-up mechanisms in case of hardware failures. The goal is to remove all single points of failure that could bring down the system. This raises the reliability and the availability of the system.

Hardware degradation requires service element and firmware interaction. Unlike the cases of software-assisted recovery described above, hardware degradation occurs when the hard error prohibits successful recovery or reset. Furthermore, a hardware degrade action permanently lowers the efficiency or throughput of the system, at least until installation of a replacement part. The service element firmware may invoke hardware degradation based on the severity of the interrupt code, or if the same interrupt has occurred frequently enough, the firmware identifies the problem as a hard error.

Examples of degradable hardware include systems with extra power supplies, back-up service elements (for code or hardware failures), or even spare processors. The Line Delete example in Chapter 15.1 (Line Delete Escape) is an example of a hardware degradation operation, where the system deactivates a line of memory.

The verification process for degraded hardware is similar to that of software-assisted recovery. The verification team must first ensure that the hardware identifies the error and raises an interrupt to the service element. At this point, the service element permanently disables the failing hardware and enables any bypass paths. The final verification step checks that the failing hardware remains off-line and unused.

This section described cases where the verification components performed the function of the service element. The components implemented the service element algorithms, avoiding the need to include the actual service element hardware and firmware in the environment. However, at a system level of verification, it is desirable to include the firmware in the verification environment. This allows the design team a chance to debug the firmware code before running it on the fabricated hardware. Verifying the hardware and firmware together is known as hardware/software co-verification (see Chapter 10).

9.3   VERIFYING HARDWARE DEBUG ASSISTS

Much of this book focuses on the first half of the verification cycle described in Chapter 1. Verification teams spend most of their effort creating environments that remove bugs in the DUV before hardware fabrication. They use software tools and models of the hardware logic that ease the debug of the DUV without the cost of fabrication. Software tools such as waveform viewers give simulation a huge productivity boost not available to the team once they move to the fabricated hardware.

Testing and debugging fabricated hardware presents major challenges compared with the comfort of simulation environments. The simulation environment's ability to probe all the internal signals all the time is a huge advantage. When a test case fails in simulation, the simulation engine can capture a complete trace and can re-run the same test case until the team completely understands the bug and verifies the fix. Testing on fabricated hardware is quite different. Here, test cases are often programmed applications running on the system and may take days to complete. When a test case fails on the fabricated hardware, the design and verification teams require information about the failure. Yet most of the required debug information is unavailable unless the design contains specific mechanisms for hardware-assisted debug.

Two main challenges in debugging fabricated hardware are isolating the point when the error occurred and capturing enough internal information to discover the root of the problem.[1] Because tests may run for billions of cycles, isolating the point in the test case when the error occurs may be a bit like finding a needle in a haystack. Of course, this is not a problem when hardware error detection logic flags a problem. On the other hand, if the failure shows itself as wrong data on the system output, the incorrect data could have been residing in storage for millions of cycles. This not only masks the root error, it also makes it difficult to pinpoint the cycle when the logic error occurred.

Chip and system architects allocate silicon area to assist in hardware debug. These functions provide a small but critical window into the inner workings of the fabricated chip design. The goal of these functions is to ease the difficult task of debugging the fabricated hardware, slashing the amount of time it takes to understand a failure from weeks down to hours. However, the verification team must allocate significant resources toward verifying the hardware debug functions. As with any other hardware feature, the verification team will uncover flaws in the initial DUV implementations of these debug features. Without a solid verification effort, the hardware debug functions will not work when needed in the fabricated hardware environment. Then the team would need to debug the debug features.

9.3.1 Verifying Scan Ring Dumps

Scan rings (described above under Scan Initialization) provide a powerful debug function as well as the aforementioned test, reset, and

---

[1] This text assumes that the problem found in the fabricated hardware is a design logic error. However, it is also possible that a failure occurs because of other reasons, such as a faulty circuit or a timing issue. Engineers can spend hours (or days) isolating the failure to faulty circuits, timing issues, or design source if the chip does not contain automated mechanisms such as BIST.

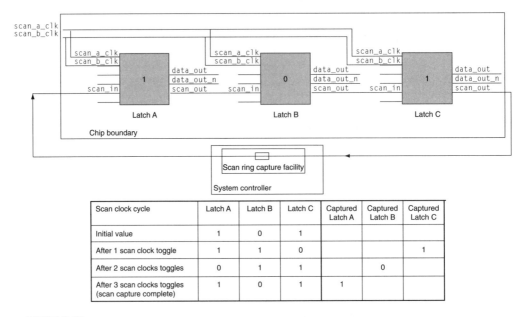

Scan clock cycle	Latch A	Latch B	Latch C	Captured Latch A	Captured Latch B	Captured Latch C
Initial value	1	0	1			
After 1 scan clock toggle	1	1	0			1
After 2 scan clocks toggles	0	1	1		0	
After 3 scan clocks toggles (scan capture complete)	1	0	1	1		

▪ **FIGURE 9.10**

The scan ring dump example operation shows just three latches in the chip. As the System Controller toggles the scan clocks, the latch values propagate through the scan ring.

initialization tasks. Because the scan rings indirectly connect every functional latch to a scan_out chip pin, the engineering team can read latch values as well as initialize them. This function takes the scan ring usage well beyond traditional testability and the correct-by-construction tools that insert the scan rings.

The procedure for reading the scan rings first requires that the system stop the functional clocks. Then, the system controller follows a similar procedure to initialization, where the system toggles the scan_a_clk and scan_b_clk to move data through the ring. The difference between debug operations and initialization is that during initialization, the data driven on the scan_in pin are the ring initialization data, whereas during debug operations the system captures the scan_out data and also drives it directly back into the scan_in pin. This allows the system to acquire the entire ring data and, after scanning the entire ring, leave the chip in the same state as before the scan started. Figure 9.10 shows an abbreviated block diagram of this process, using only three latches in the design. At any given time, *Latch C's* current value appears on the chip's scan_out line and the System Controller captures that value. As the System Controller toggles the scan clocks again, it feeds the current *Latch C* value into the chip scan_in, driving that value into *Latch A*. After three scan clock toggles, the System Controller has captured the values of all the latches and has rotated the proper values back to each of the latches.

The scan ring dump procedure is a powerful debug utility for the team that tests the fabricated hardware. When a failure occurs, the scan ring dump provides insight into the state of the chip. However, as with all functions, the verification team must run the scan ring dump procedure in simulation to ensure that the chip or system works correctly.

For scan ring dump verification, the verification team needs to combine test case structures from the mainline test suite with the test case used for initialization verification (from System Reset and Bring-Up, above). The mainline test case provides a good DUV state, whereas the initialization test case provides the scan clock-toggling infrastructure. The scan ring dump test case requires the following differences compared with the scan ring initialization test:

- Initialization of the DUV to a good state

- Connection of the scan_out pin into the scan_in pin

- Capturing the scan_out values for checking

- Upon completion, verification that the chip is back in the same state as before the operation.

For scan ring dump verification, the DUV must be in a known-good state. The easiest way to do this is to run a mainline test case before starting the scan ring dump. The best mainline test case is one that puts the DUV into a very busy state, varying the latch values throughout the DUV. For the scan ring dump operation, the test case stops the functional clocks at the height of the mainline test's activity—not after the mainline test completes. This leaves the DUV's latches in a good, but not idle, state. With the functional clocks stopped, the scan ring dump operation begins by enabling the scan operation and toggling the scan clocks. Because the verification team uses the mainline test case infrastructure, they must program an additional mode into the drivers and checkers. The drivers must enable the scan operation (scan clock toggling, connection of scan_out to scan_in, etc). All mainline monitors must disable checking during the scan, because the scan operation drives the DUV into unexpected states while shifting the scan rings.

Unlike the initialization test case, the scan ring dump test case must hook the scan_out pin back to the scan_in pin. The test case accomplishes this by reading the scan_out value and driving that value back into the scan_in pin. Feeding these values back into the DUV ensures that the scan ring dump is non-destructive to the DUV, meaning that when the dump completes, the DUV is in the same state as before the dump.

This operation rotates the ring one time such that the latch values return to their original position.

As the latch values appear on the scan_out pin and the test case drives these values into the scan_in pin, the test case must also capture each scan_out value and maintain that value for checking. After the scan dump operation, each captured value must be equivalent to the corresponding latch values from before the scan dump operation started. This checking ensures that the system controller sees the correct latch values.

The final step in the verification of the scan ring dump operation is to check that the chip or system returns to the state it was in before the operation. Because the scan ring dump operation is non-destructive, all latches must end up with the same values as just before the scan ring shifts began. An initial check for this is to perform a three-way comparison for each latch. All three of the following values for each latch should be equal: the value of the latch before the scan, the value captured by the system controller during the scan, and the value of the latch after the scan.

However, just verifying that the latches return to their original state may not be sufficient. Scanning could be unintentionally destructive to other elements of the chip or system. To detect that the scan operation preserved the entire state of the DUV, the verification team should leverage the mainline test case used initially to put the DUV into a busy state. Recall that the scan ring dump operation requires stopping the functional clocks in the middle of running the mainline test. This leaves the DUV in a good, but not idle, state. The scan ring dump operation should leave the DUV in that exact same state. Therefore, the verification engineer should be able to continue running the mainline test case by simply de-asserting the scan dump inputs, restarting the functional clocks, and re-enabling the mainline drivers, monitors, and checkers. With the exception of the number of cycles that the test case takes, the mainline test case should complete normally. The verification team often finds that any unexpected values flagged by the monitors or checkers can be traced back to changed states in the DUV after the scan ring dump operation. These changes are bugs.

9.4 LOW-POWER MODE VERIFICATION

Extended battery life, circuit leakage, and heat dissipation are three of the biggest challenges faced by today's chip design teams. Many chips run in portable electronic devices where consumers base their buying decisions on product functional capabilities and average battery life. The best products balance leading edge features with a smart power savings strategy. In fixed location devices, limiting the chips' power consumption not only saves the customer in their utility bills but also requires less aggressive heat dissipation solutions. Chips that draw more power often need elaborate and expensive cooling infrastructures, including fans, heat sinks, and even refrigerants. Therefore, there is a strong business incentive for designers to limit the power that a chip draws.

Power saving strategies fall into two categories: turn off unused portions of the chip and slow down the cycle time of the chip. Both strategies can yield significant power savings. Moreover, both strategies require specialized verification environments.

In all power savings modes, the verification task falls into three steps. First, in any dynamically controlled power savings mode, the verification team must prove that the design correctly enters into the power savings mode. Second, the verification team ensures that the design always gives the architecturally correct result under power savings modes. Third, the verification team must check that when a unit enters power savings mode, the logic behaves as expected—usually by verifying that the clocks shut off and the unit has no activity.

9.4.1 Power Savings Through Disabling Functional Units

Chips contain functional units that, at certain times, the software applications do not exercise. Examples of units include specific acceleration engines such as floating-point units or broad connectivity devices where the user does not utilize all ports. These units are all candidates for power savings modes. Candidates for unit-level power savings fall into two categories. First, sub-units such as acceleration engines derive power savings in a dynamic fashion, shutting down under specific applications and reactivating only when the chip requires utilization of the unit. Dynamic power savings are application dependent, where the disabling and re-enabling of the unit depends on the chip activity. The second category is static power savings where the customer's configuration dictates power savings. In static power savings, the machine settings disable units for prolonged periods or even permanently. Figure 9.11 shows examples of both types.

It is important to note that idle sub-units still draw significant power. To stop power leakage in idle portions of the design, the chip must shut off the clocks to that unit. This actually makes verification of power savings easier.

Verification of Power Savings Through Disabling Functional Units

Verification of dynamically controlled power savings is more complex than the static type, because the verification team must create tests to show that the chip correctly enters and exits power savings modes. Static power savings only requires verifying idle clocks to the sub-unit through the length of the test.

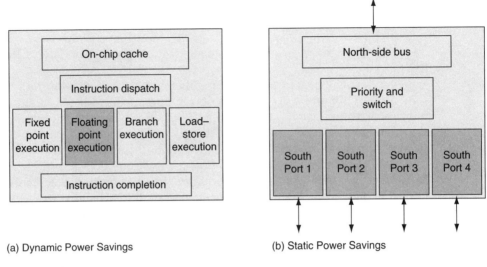

(a) Dynamic Power Savings   (b) Static Power Savings

▪ **FIGURE 9.11**

(a) A sample superscalar microprocessor with four parallel execution units. Certain applications may not require the floating-point unit (shaded area), making it a candidate for power savings. (b) An input/output bridge chip, which contains four parallel south ports (shaded). Because the customer may not configure all four ports simultaneously, each of the port units is a candidate for static power savings.

The verification team follows a four-step process for verifying power savings modes. The first step requires that the verification team test that the DUV correctly enters and exits the power savings mode. The challenge for the verification team lies in the creation of dynamic power savings test cases. Here, the verification team must understand the exact mechanism that initiates the unit's disablement in the DUV. In the case of the floating-point example, that mechanism might be a certain threshold of cycles passes without encountering a floating-point operation.

First, the verification team must update both the stimulus and checking components to verify that the DUV enters and exits the power savings mode. The stimulus components must create the conditions for the power savings mode. For dynamic power savings, those conditions may be that the stimulus component must prevent certain operations—whatever the exact mechanism is as described by the specification. For static power savings, the stimulus component may just need to initialize internal registers to the power savings state. For checking components, the verification team must enhance the code to detect that the DUV has entered the power savings mode. This includes verifying that the DUV updates pertinent system status register values and takes all appropriate power savings actions. Similarly, when the power-saving condition no longer exists, the test case must verify that the DUV detects that it must move back into full-power mode.

The second part in verifying power savings modes is to validate that the system operations complete with the correct architectural results. This implies that the stimulus and checking components continue to run normally. Power savings modes cannot alter the architectural results of a test case when compared with running the same test case without power savings. In some cases, power savings may degrade system performance, and the verification team needs to adjust checking components to compensate for these differences only.

The third step in verifying power savings modes is to show that the power savings mechanisms work as planned and to provide feedback to the designers and architects. To perform this check, the verification team must directly monitor the internals of the DUV for true indications of power savings. In most cases, this means that the monitor components spy on the functional clocks that feed the disabled unit to ensure they remain inactive for the duration of the power savings mode. The verification team cannot rely on the stimulus component and architectural correctness alone, because the only way to know that the design reaps the benefit of power savings is to monitor the internal signals directly. Any activity on clocks, latches, or arrays during power savings modes indicates the DUV may not have put the unit to sleep.

The final step is similar to step two. Instead of verifying that the system operations complete correctly during power savings mode, the test case must check compliance when the DUV returns to full-power mode. As part of the architectural checking, the test case should closely monitor the DUV during transitions into and out of low-power mode. When the DUV switches modes, it still must maintain good machine states and cannot miss interrupts.

The verification team cannot directly measure power savings, because the simulation engine does not have physical current, leakage, and power draw information. However, the verification team can provide inputs for estimations of power savings by comparing identical test cases run with and without power savings. A common metric used in such a comparison is the number of latches and arrays affected by the power savings mode as well as the duration of the idle clocks.

9.4.2 Power Savings Through Cycle-Time Degradation

Reducing the chip or system cycle time lowers power consumption. Whereas chip architects may prescribe this mechanism directly for power savings, design teams also use it to prevent a catastrophic overheating scenario. High-frequency chip speeds, which burn power at a higher rate than the same chip at lower frequencies, also place the chip in physical danger if the power consumption exceeds the thermal dissipation capabilities.

Fabrication processes prescribe specific thermal tolerances based on rules customized for the manufacturing process. Exceeding these thresholds can cause damage to the chip. Although the architects must design the chip to maintain its target cycle time under most conditions, there may be certain applications that use a broad range of chip resources simultaneously, causing a larger than usual power draw. To prevent this disastrous situation, designers add on-chip temperature sensors to the chip. These sensors provide a warning when the chip is reaching a critical temperature. The logic then dynamically adjusts the chip's cycle time.

A second usage of cycle-time degradation for power savings occurs during prolonged idle periods of the system. Again, certain applications may under-utilize system resources, providing the opportunity for power savings when the user does not require high frequencies. No matter what the end goal, more and more design teams use frequency degradation as a tool for achieving power savings.

Verification of Power Savings Through Cycle-Time Degradation

Although functional verification does not play directly into the physical timing aspects of cycle-time degradation, there are implications to the verification environment. Affected areas include verification of the appropriate cycle-time degradation triggers and checking that the design updates the correct logical state registers. Additionally, the verification environment must support reinstating the cycle-time to higher frequencies as required.

Any cycle-time degradation trigger uses a state machine or register value to invoke the action. A thermal sensor, for example, sets a state machine latch that must trigger the cycle-time degradation. Although the verification team cannot create a thermal crisis in a simulation environment, the stimulus component can overwrite the value of the thermal sensor's state machine latch, which in turn should invoke the appropriate degradation of cycle-time. This requires the verification team to update their stimulus and checking components to simulate the thermal crisis.

Mainline test cases that create lots of DUV activity are best suited for verifying cycle-time degradation features. While at the peak of the test case activity, the stimulus component overwrites the degradation state machine trigger in the DUV. The checking components must verify that all appropriate DUV actions occur as the specification dictates. This would include checking that the DUV writes the control values that slow down the clock frequencies, reset the state machine register that initially called for the degradation activity, and set any required logging registers. Additionally, the verification environment must turn off the state machine sensor some time later. This simulates the condition where the chip has cooled sufficiently to regain full speed. The stimulus component resets the register and informs the checking component. The checking component must verify that the hardware resets the frequency controls that allow the chip to run at full speed.

9.5 SUMMARY

Verification of pervasive functions requires much of the same ingenuity and concepts used for mainline function verification. As with any verification activity, the stimulus components must create the appropriate scenarios and the checking components must always be able to detect incorrect DUV activity. Most pervasive function verification requires a level of integration with the mainline environment components, allowing "normal" test cases to run as the background to the pervasive function test. This interoperability necessitates early planning for pervasive function so that the verification team need not overhaul the components for pervasive tests.

Pervasive functions provide critical services to the system, including initialization and debug capabilities. After fabrication, many of these functions are the first portions of the hardware exercised. Other pervasive functions, such as error recovery, require huge amounts of verification team effort as well as simulation cycles. For all the legal cases verified in mainline tests, there are orders of magnitude more illegal scenarios where hard or soft errors affect the hardware. Complete verification of these capabilities requires the imagination and focus of the verification team. Without this effort, the hardware could be dead on arrival.

9.6 EXERCISES

1. How do verification engineers utilize the X state capabilities of most simulation engines creating initialization test cases? Without the X state capability, how would the verification team simulate initialization?

2. Verification of recovery functions requires injecting hard or soft errors into the DUV. What are the implications of hard errors on the verification environment components compared with soft errors?

3. What must checking components verify if an error injection goes undetected?

4. Hardware designs may use fencing to temporarily prevent other chips from affecting the logic during initialization and recovery

activity. What should the stimulus components do with the chip input lines during this time?

5. When debugging an error during simulation, why might it be beneficial for the verification engineer to provide a trace of only a single cycle rather than the usual trace of hundreds of cycles? What process does this mirror?

6. Why is it important to verify that clock and latches do not toggle in units that are in power savings modes? What do the verification engineers need to customize in their environment to check this adequately?

CHAPTER 10

RE-USE STRATEGIES AND
SYSTEM SIMULATION

System simulation is the first time the verification team brings all the logic together into one simulation environment. Previous levels of verification focus on all the functions contained within one unit or chip, whereas system-level verification concentrates on the connectivity and interaction of all the units and chips. System simulation focuses on how the customer uses the system as an end application of all the chips. Still, system can mean many different things. The application of the chip or chips defines the system. For example, a system for a server might include the processor, an oscillator, memory, a chip that bridges transactions to and from the processor to a memory subsystem (called a *north bridge*), a chip that bridges transactions to and from the input and output (*I/O*) subsystem (called a *south bridge*), a graphics controller, and the board that connects them all together. For a networking processor chip, the system includes an oscillator, memory, physical interface (PHY) modules (gigabit Ethernet PHY, Asynchronous Transfer Mode (ATM) PHY, etc.), switch fabric, and the network processor. An embedded system would contain an embedded processor, memory, Ethernet PHY, universal serial bus (USB) port, and application specific logic. Many times this embedded system is self-contained within one chip, which is called a *system on a chip* (SoC).

Regardless of what kind of system it is, the verification environment for that system contains stimulus components (both initiators and responders), monitor components, scoreboard components, and checking components. To leverage the verification work done previously at the lower levels, verification components may be re-used. In addition to these components, the system verification team may be responsible for other verification components. These other components are written by the system verification team, purchased from a vendor (a third-party model), or acquired from another group.

Because re-using chip and unit verification components is a significant portion of system simulation, this chapter initially details re-use strategies. It then covers the methods for verifying a system in functional simulation and issues associated with SoCs or, more generically,

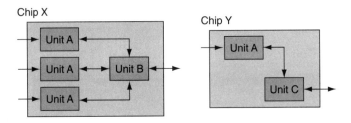

▪ **FIGURE 10.1**

Design re-use. Multiple usage of a single unit (many instances) within a chip or within multiple chips.

issues associated with verifying *re-usable IP* (intellectual property) in a system.

The chapter also discusses advanced simulation techniques that address the unique challenges of system simulation. Hardware acceleration and emulation are covered, which address the radically increased need for simulation performance. The last topic that is covered is simulation between several simulation engines, called *co-simulation*. Co-simulation is necessary in some system-level verification efforts because of the need to integrate different types of verification IP into one cohesive verification environment.

10.1 RE-USE STRATEGIES

Re-use allows the verification team to leverage verification components and design blocks across a chip or across multiple chips in a system. As it does for design, the concept of "create once, use in many places" applies to verification components as well. The result is improved time to market and reduced resource requirements. Figure 10.1 illustrates an example of design re-use (verification aspects of re-use follow).

In this example, unit A is used across the two chips, X and Y, and many times within a single chip, X. The re-use of unit A allows for better resource utilization. The development team for chip X only needs to design two units: A and B. The development team for chip Y only needs to design one unit, C, because it re-uses unit A from chip X. This type of design re-use is called *horizontal re-use*, because the team uses the design blocks across a single chip (as in unit A within chip X) and across multiple chips (unit A used in both chip X and Y).

Because verification is a large part of the design effort, it makes sense that the same concepts for design re-use apply. Applying re-use concepts to verification reduces the duration of a project. So, in general, horizontal re-use occurs when a team uses a design unit or verification compo-

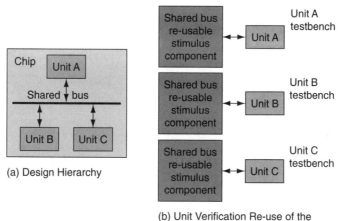

(a) Design Hierarchy

(b) Unit Verification Re-use of the
shared bus stimulus component

■ FIGURE 10.2

Horizontal verification re-use: using verification components across a level of verification. (a) A chip in
which three units, A, B, and C, interface to a shared bus. (b) The interface to this shared bus is identical, so the verification team creates a re-usable stimulus component for the three unit verification
environments.

nent multiple times at the same level of the hierarchy. Figure 10.2 is an
example of horizontal re-use within verification.

In this example, units A, B, and C all connect to a common shared
bus. Because the units have a common shared bus, there is no need for
each verification team to develop its own stimulus component. Instead,
a verification team can create a re-usable stimulus component for each
unit test bench. This concept can expand to include other common verification components such as interface monitors and checkers. This is an
example of horizontal re-use because the team utilizes a set of verification components across the same level of the verification hierarchy (in
this case, unit test benches). More details of how to achieve horizontal
re-use are discussed later in this chapter.

Another form of re-use, *vertical re-use*, is unique to verification. Vertical verification component re-use is the usage of verification components
up the levels of hierarchy. Vertical re-use is important to system simulation because it allows for the verification team to leverage what has
already been implemented. This, as in horizontal re-use, allows for optimization of resources. Figure 10.3 shows a simple example of vertical
verification re-use.

As shown in Figure 10.3, unit A's test bench has two verification components associated with it: a stimulus component and an interface
monitor/checker. This design unit is at the periphery of the chip. This
means that the chip level verification team can re-use the stimulus component from the unit test bench in their test bench. In addition to the

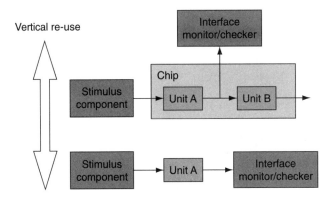

▪ FIGURE 10.3

Vertical verification re-use: using verification components up the levels of hierarchy (from unit up to system).

stimulus component, the chip level verification team also utilizes the interface monitor/checker to assist in their debug activities. Therefore, vertical re-use occurs when a higher verification level utilizes verification components from a lower level. More details of how to achieve vertical re-use are discussed later in this chapter.

Verification components that can be re-used both horizontally and vertically are referred to as *re-usable verification IP*. Re-usable verification IP allows companies to maximize the verification work. This may occur when a company develops multiple chips that use an industry standard interface such as peripheral component interconnect (PCI) and share the stimulus and checking components across projects. Alternatively, if many groups within a company develop the same verification components, resources are wasted. As inefficient as it may seem, many reasons exist for why multiple groups may develop similar verification components independently. It could be that the different groups utilize different hardware description language (HDL) and/or verification languages or that the different groups require different functionality from the verification components. However, if one group concentrates on developing re-usable verification IP, then all groups within the company can leverage that expertise and reduce overall resources. To go one step further, a company can purchase re-usable verification IP from vendors. This IP may seem expensive at first, but usually in the end it saves money. These companies have a magnitude of uses for these components (thus enhancing their function), more than a local team would ever get. With this broader use, the quality of their product increases. Additionally, purchased verification IP is most likely to follow the interface specification, because many different verification teams test it against their different design implementations. There is a level of safety in the higher number of users.

One last aspect of re-use is the ability to bridge the gap from functional simulation to and from formal verification. The use of assertions helps to accomplish this. The reason is that most formal tools accept industry standard assertions as the checks.

10.1.1   Guidelines for Re-Use

Re-use may seem very easy, because the concepts are simple. In reality, few companies and groups achieve a high degree of re-usability because they fail to put guidelines in place. The following guidelines allow test bench components to be re-usable:

- Independent stimulus components

- Configurable logging of messages

- Generic scoreboard components

- Dynamic mapping of signals into verification components

- Packaging verification components

- Documentation

Independent Stimulus Components

Stimulus components need to be independent of all other verification components. They should not communicate with any other component nor should any other component communicate with the stimulus component. Figure 10.4 shows an example of why independent stimulus components are critical for re-use.

In Figure 10.4a, unit B's test bench contains a stimulus component that directly communicates to the scoreboard. This works well at the unit level and also has advantages because the developer of the stimulus component already knows much information of what is to be driven into the design under verification (DUV). However, looking at Figure 10.4b shows the usage of unit B at the next higher level of verification. At this level, internal checking is desired for debug. It can be seen that the ability to re-use the scoreboard at this level now has issues. The chip level cannot re-use the scoreboard because it requires the stimulus component, which is now replaced with the design, to communicate with the scoreboard.

Adhering to this guideline allows for vertical re-use of any verification component. Many verification engineers are tempted to provide the data sent into the DUV to the scoreboard component directly from the stimulus component. Their reasoning is valid: Why create another verification component to monitor the inputs when the stimulus component already contains the data sent into the DUV and can directly inform the

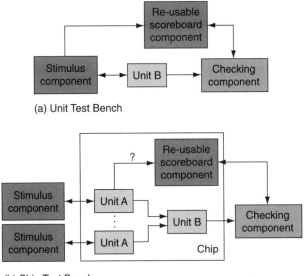

(a) Unit Test Bench

(b) Chip Test Bench

▪ **FIGURE 10.4**

Independent stimulus components. (a) A stimulus component for unit B that communicates directly to a scoreboard. (b) The usage of unit B at a higher level (where some intermediate checking is desired for debug); the scoreboard is now nonfunctional.

stimulus component of new data? However, if the verification team wishes to re-use the scoreboard or checker components at a higher level where the real HDL design replaces the stimulus component in the test bench, then the scoreboard component will not receive any data. Therefore, the best solution for re-use maximization is to add a monitor component to the interface between the stimulus component and the DUV. The monitor component spies the data on the interface and informs the scoreboard. The verification team then re-uses the monitor component at the higher hierarchical level to drive the scoreboard, even in the absence of the stimulus component.

Configurable Logging of Messages

When re-using verification components, the requirement of debugging and informational messages exists as with any other environment. However, there are additional issues to consider. The first issue is that the components need the ability to have configurable and controllable messaging (including debug level and filters). This helps prevent information overload of debug messages (see Chapter 8). Another issue, from the developer's standpoint, is that the verification component needs to have debug messages for when it is determined that there is a bug in the component. For this, the component needs a debug level to give detailed messages that are useful to the developers of the component. The end user will not care about any internally specific messages that the component might produce. The last issue to consider is the ability to customize how the messaging occurs. The developer of the verification component does not know the end environment or how it will be utilized. It may be that one particular user wishes to capture all the debug messages from the various components into a single simulation log file, whereas another user requires each verification component to log its information into its own separate file. This ability requires the developer of the verification components to create a message handler that can handle configurable debug levels as well as different logging mechanisms.

Generic Scoreboard Components

To achieve a high degree of re-use, scoreboard components must be generic and not specific to the particular input protocol or the checking function. The verification team may use a scoreboard in different manners, depending on their implementation of horizontal or vertical re-use. The scoreboard should be generic in the sense that it contains the abstract data that the DUV receives on its inputs. The interface to the scoreboard should be via an application-programming interface (API) as opposed to direct monitoring of the input interface. An API should exist for the checking component to get the expected data from the scoreboard as well. The scoreboard's checking API must be extendable or overridden because the functions within the API may be different within the different test benches that utilize the scoreboard.

Vertical re-use drives the requirement for having the API, instead of the scoreboard, monitoring the DUV inputs. Figure 10.5 shows two test benches, one for unit level and one for chip level.

Unit A buffers inputs before passing the data off to unit B. Unit A is a simple first in, first out (FIFO) buffer. Unit B processes the data and sends it out of the chip. Because there are multiple instances of unit A and unit B processes the outputs of these, data can be received out of order on the outputs of the chip.

The verification team uses a scoreboard in the unit test bench. This scoreboard contains an API to enqueue data into the scoreboard. The same scoreboard can be re-used vertically in the chip level test bench. The chip test bench has multiple instances of the stimulus and interface components. Each interface component uses the same API to enqueue data to the scoreboard. If the scoreboard contained the interface monitor directly, instead of an API, when the team re-used the scoreboard at the chip level, the scoreboard would need to be modified to accommodate the multiple buses. Creating and using the API alleviates this.

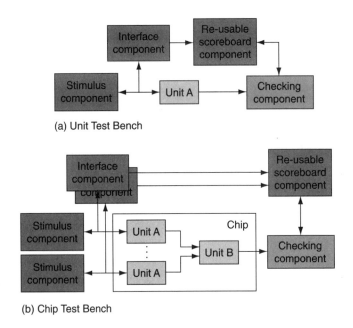

(a) Unit Test Bench

(b) Chip Test Bench

■ **FIGURE 10.5**

Re-using a scoreboard. (a) The usage of a scoreboard for a unit test bench. (b) The usage of the same scoreboard from a chip test bench.

Vertical and horizontal re-use both drives the requirement for the checking API to be overridden or modified. Figure 10.4, in addition to illustrating the need for an API on the stimulus side, also illustrates the need for a checking API. Because the scoreboard is being re-used, the function within the scoreboard is different at the unit versus the chip level. At the unit level, the scoreboard acts like a simple FIFO. The unit test bench checking component uses the API to "request" the next data to check for from the scoreboard. However, at the chip level this is not the case. At the chip level, the function is not a simple FIFO, as out of order data packets can arrive, so now the scoreboard must be able to handle this. Two different methods exist for managing this. The first method is to have the unit verification team (the scoreboard authors) handle the chip verification needs. This requires the unit verification team to create the scoreboard with the chip team in mind and maintain it as bugs are found in the scoreboard. The second option is to use an extendable API (using object-oriented principles) that allows the chip verification team to enhance the API as needed. The unit verification team creates a scoreboard that contains the data structures and an API to get at those data structures, whereas the chip verification team extends the base function of the scoreboard to accommodate their needs.

Both cases require the same amount of effort-enhancement of the scoreboard to support the different uses. However, if the unit verification

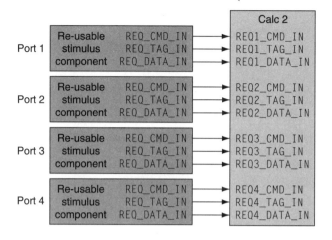

■ **FIGURE 10.6**

Horizontal naming issues. By keeping names generic, the same component can attach to many units or to the same unit many times to help facilitate horizontal re-use.

team is responsible for creating and supporting the scoreboard, they must understand all the re-use environments. This may not be practical if the verification team re-uses this scoreboard across projects. On the other hand, when the verification team provides an extendable API, they split the work across teams. This allows the unit team to focus on unit simulation and the other verification team, wherever that team may exist, to focus on their own specifics. Third-party models utilize this extendable method with their IP.

Dynamic Mapping of Signals Into Verification Components

The names of the interface signals in which the monitors, checkers, and stimulus components interact must be configurable to allow for re-use either horizontally or vertically. In a horizontal scope, a single verification component may be instantiated numerous times within an environment, or a single verification component may connect to different units where each unit may have different signal names. In either case, the connections to the verification component are different.

Calc 2 (see Chapter 7) is a good example of this, as shown in Figure 10.6. Each port has a different set of names (REQX_CMD_IN, REQX_TAG_IN, REQX_DATA_IN, where X is the port number), but a single stimulus component could be created to attach to each port. The stimulus component outputs must map to each of the four different ports on the DUV. By allowing for dynamic mapping, the end-user would only need to "configure" the component for its specific mapping. Without this mapping, the end-user would need to copy and paste individual

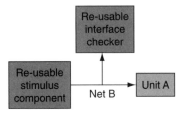

(a) Unit Level of Verification

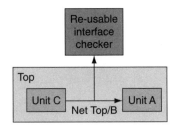

(b) Higher Level of Verification

▪ **FIGURE 10.7**

Vertical naming issues. By keeping names generic, the same model can attach up the levels of verification to help facilitate horizontal re-use. (a) A unit level verification environment where the interface checker is monitoring net B. (b) The same interface checker is re-used but now it needs to monitor Net Top/B.

components and modify each one. This leads to higher maintenance and reduces the overall benefit of re-use.

For vertical re-use, most unit environments' top level is the unit itself. However, when this unit is within the chip, extra levels of hierarchy exist. Thus, verification components need to be "attached" to the different levels. Figure 10.7 shows an example of the vertical naming issue.

In this example, the signal name to which the common interface checker attaches changes its name because of hierarchy prefixes. If the verification components have a static interface (i.e., directly connects to specific design signals), then it would be difficult to re-use the verification components up the hierarchy.

The ability to have a dynamic mapping mechanism is crucial for re-use. This way, the component can attach to any of the necessary signals at any level, either horizontally or vertically.

Packaging Verification Components

Packaging a verification component gives the end-user the ability to instantiate and easily use the component. Packaging includes all the structures and documentation that the verification team requires to bring the verification component into production seamlessly. If it is not easy to use the components, the likelihood is that the verification team writes their own. Packaging verification components allows the end-user to apply them more efficiently and instantiate the verification components into different environments easily.

The package should be a self-contained structure for the components. If the component has dependencies on any specific environment, then the verification team must carry these dependencies to any environment that will contain this component. If not, then the component will not work.

Two different packaging approaches exist. One method is to encapsulate the re-usable components (stimulus, monitor, scoreboard, and checker) into one package that behaves differently based on constraints. In this scheme, the verification team would create the components with the packaging method in mind. For instance, the dynamic mapping structure mentioned above is re-used across all the components. This also means that the verification team also needs to add "mode" switches that operate differently based on the package constraints. These switches turn different parts of the components on and off. The verification team could create a mode for the stimulus component. This mode would control the enabling of the stimulus component. By doing this, it allows the end user to activate the stimulus component based on the environment. A unit test bench would require an active stimulus model, but within the chip level test bench the stimulus model is passive because the real logic drives the interface. However, the other components of the package (monitors and/or checkers) remain active. Taking the "modes" one-step further, the verification team can include constraint-controllable levels of checking and monitoring in the package.

The other method is to package each verification component separately. This allows the end user to select the exact components to put in the test bench. This provides the greatest flexibility to the end user. Unlike the previous model, this only uses necessary components. Hence, some of the above-mentioned modes are not required. A verification team would not need to turn on or off the stimulus model. If the test bench at the next higher level does not require the stimulus component (because the real logic exists), then the verification team would not instantiate it. A disadvantage to this paradigm is that the end user must now create and configure all the separate components individually. This may be inefficient when components share similar interfaces.

The basic difference between the two methods is the placement of the work emphasis. Re-use requires a little more planning and work for implementation. The complete package paradigm requires the developer(s) to perform more work (including more modes) and to solve any intercomponent dependency issues. The independent component package paradigm shifts this responsibility to the end user. In many cases, it makes sense for the developer to perform this work because they are the most familiar with the individual components. It may take the end-user more time in using the components because they are not familiar with any inter-dependencies between them.

The advantage to having the developer do the work and having a more integrated package is that the end-user only has to worry about configuring one big component. All inter-dependencies of the inner components are in the packaging (if any cross-constraints exist). The disadvantage is that the developers creating these components need to do more work. However, the more times that verification teams re-use the components, the more worthwhile the pre-packaged method becomes.

In addition to deciding on a packaging mechanism, the verification team must also reflect upon and document the scope in which they will use the verification IP. The verification team must take into consideration any dependencies, such as simulation engines, high-level verification language (HVL)/HDL, operating system, and compiler. Any of these aspects may limit the usage of the verification IP. These limitations may be acceptable depending on the targeted user audience, but the users need to know about them.

Documentation

Documentation is advantageous to any design and verification endeavor, but it is necessary for re-usable verification components. The end user must be aware of what constraints and controls they have over the components. Documentation is a fundamental requirement for re-use. If the end user does not know how the components behave or how to control their behavior, then the user will not trust the verification IP. Documentation is also important in informing the end user on any limitations or configuration options that are available. The following is a list of features that, at a minimum, should be documented:

- Basic function
- Usage notes and limitations
- Modes and constraints
- Release notes

Documentation of the basic function of the verification component should exist so that the end user knows what the verification component is intended to do. If developing a verification IP for sale, then this basic function can exist in some "glossy" that marketing and sales use to promote the IP. However, if this IP is used only for internal purposes, then the documentation could simply be text file (a "README" file) that explains the basic concepts and purpose of the IP.

In addition to the function, usage notes and any known limitations need to be listed so the end user does not try to use the verification IP in the wrong way. The usage notes explain how to use the verification IP. It describes how to instantiate the component into a test bench, how to compile it (if applicable), and how to link it into any specific simulation engines. Any limitations should also be noted here, such as limitations on what operating systems are supported. The end user can use the verification IP more effectively once they know the limitations.

The documentation needs to explain any modes and constraints that are available to the end user. The end user needs to know how to control the verification IP, what variations are available in the parameters, and what they do when changed. This allows the end user to direct the verification IP for their specific implementation and purposes.

Release notes are important because they allow the end user to know what is new in a particular release. It could be that an end user has an issue with a particular release of a verification component and will upgrade once a new feature has been included in the component. An easy way to convey this information is to put it into a set of release notes that indicate the reasons for this release and how it differs from previous releases.

Documentation gives more credibility to the verification components and removes some of the support burden from the developers of the verification IP. It allows the end user to instantiate and use the verification IP easily by explaining the purpose of the switches and constraints. In addition, the documentation explains any limitations and new features that are included in the verification IP.

10.1.2 Horizontal Re-Use

As mentioned previously, horizontal re-use is defined by the use of the same verification components across the same level of verification hierarchy. Horizontal re-use occurs when multiple units exploit a single verification component in the same hierarchical level (Figure 10.2). In this section the additional complexities that exist when developing verification components for horizontal re-use are discussed.

Different scopes of horizontal re-use exist and, depending on the scope of re-use, different complexities exist. Verification engineers apply horizontal re-use within the following scopes:

- Re-use across units (within a chip)

- Re-use across chips (within a company)

- Re-use across companies (realm of electronic design automation (EDA) IP developers–third-party IP)

Re-use across units has the narrowest scope. This means that a single team understands the functionality that the verification components must support. At a minimum, the teams all fall under the same project scope.

The scope of function that the components must support broadens when re-using components across chips (but within a company). Here, the teams may not fall under the same project, leading to conflicts due to prioritization of function requirements, resources, and schedule. This paradigm requires communications and a unified decision-making process that maximizes company effectiveness.

The broadest scope is a verification component that is fully re-usable. This is where the component supports all the capabilities of the protocol and interface (it is fully compliant in that it follows and supports the complete specification). This scope focuses on third-party verification IP. Many EDA companies have created a business model around writing verification IP. Because their customers demand high-quality IP (verification engineers expect a high degree of quality from what they purchase!), these companies not only focus on the protocol and checks of the verification IP they are developing, but also in documentation and packaging. They know that the easier it is for their customers to use their IP, the broader use it receives. If the verification IP is hard to use and control, then customers will not purchase the IP and the company will lose market share.

Horizontal re-use has its own complexities because many times the components are not all encompassing in terms of functions supported. For example, a verification team working on chip A that contains a PCI interface is going to create re-usable verification PCI components for their company. Chip A's function specifies support for single beat reads and writes only (this is a certain type of PCI bus transaction). Thus, this team concentrates on this function for the verification components. Somewhere else in the company, a team is designing chip B that also contains a PCI interface. Chip B's verification team heard of this common verification component and now depends on it to meet their schedule. However, chip B, in addition to single beat reads and writes, also supports burst length reads and writes. To make the component re-usable, chip A's PCI verification team must now add additional function because of chip B's requirements. If they were to leave this out of the verification components, then chip B could not use it and would have to create their own component, thus creating additional work. Alternatively, chip B's verification team could copy the components and add their functionality to it—which in the end may be the faster approach.

10.1.3 Vertical Re-Use

As mentioned earlier, using the same verification components up the levels of verification hierarchy is vertical re-use. This can occur when the chip level team uses internal checks and monitors from the unit levels or exploits a stimulus component from a unit (Figure 10.3). Here, the challenges associated with implementing vertical re-use are described.

The difficulty in vertical re-use is that the requirements for a stimulus component at the unit level are typically different from the top level, especially for stimulus components that must initiate transactions (as opposed to reactors). Most unit environments want a highly randomized stimulus component with a small set of directed tests to achieve high functional verification coverage. However, at a chip and system level, the verification teams desire randomization "on a higher level." This means that within a unit test bench, stimulus components tend to focus randomization at individual transactions and generate these transactions randomly across the DUV interface. At the next level, the stimulus components require more control in generating specific sequences. The randomization at this level is across transaction sequences, not on the transactions themselves. Or the desire is to create random sequences involving more than one type of stimulus component (hence needing the ability to coordinate different stimulus components to create a desired higher level sequence). This requires the verification team to produce a stimulus component capable of either type of randomization control.

Vertical re-use of components in a unit test bench that have no external interfaces at the next higher verification level are typically limited to monitors and checkers. This is because in the next level of hierarchy, the DUV replaces the stimulus components with the real design. However, checkers and monitors remain valid if the verification team follows the re-use guidelines in the construction of the verification components. The verification team doing the next level of verification simply includes these components into the test bench. The desire to do this is to try to reduce the debug time for the system level of verification (see Chapter 8).

Another aspect of vertical re-use is the use of assertions (either internal or external). Internal assertions carry up the hierarchy automatically because the designers embedded them in the HDL. The verification team treats external assertions the same way as monitors and checkers. They are contained as part of the package of code that the unit verification team delivers to the next level of verification.

10.1.4 Applying Re-Use to Calc2

Calc2 is used, as described in Chapters 7 and 8, as an example of applying the re-use guidelines to a verification environment. In this example, Calc2 is a unit within a chip. Figure 10.8 shows the next level of hierarchy that uses the Calc2 unit.

Calc2, along with three other units, forms a processing engine. This basic flow of the processing engine is that attached to the memory controller unit is some memory. The dispatcher units fetch the "next" transaction by issuing a series of reads from different addresses from the memory controller unit. The memory controller unit responds by

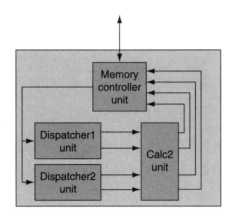

▪ **FIGURE 10.8**

Calc2 processing engine. The potential usage is shown of the Calc2 design at a higher level where the designers architected it to have two dispatch units. Each can dispatch two items at a time. The memory controller unit interfaces with the dispatch and Calc2 unit.

providing the data for each read. Once the dispatcher units acquire all the necessary data, they initiate transactions to the Calc2 unit, and upon these transactions being finished, the memory controller unit updates its memory.

The verification team performing this level of verification wishes to re-use the checkers from the unit level of Calc2 within their verification environment. They choose to do this because of debug time. They believe that by re-using the checkers, they reduce their coding and debugging time considerably.

To do this, the original verification environment first described in Chapter 8 needs to change because of the challenges of vertical re-use. Figure 10.9 shows the original Calc2 verification environment.

The original verification environment for Calc2 using a transaction-based test bench had the following verification components: one stimulus generation component and four port protocol components, a scoreboard, a checker, and four output port monitors.

The original Calc2 verification environment does not support re-use. The stimulus component is dependent on other verification components—the output port monitors. Remember that the output port monitors sent the completed command's tag back to the stimulus component so that the stimulus component could recycle the tag. In addition, the scoreboard component depended on the scoreboard. It received its transactions directly from the stimulus components; thus, in our new environment when the real logic (the dispatcher units) drives transactions, the scoreboard will not receive any. Another re-use rule violation is that the unit team hard-coded the port monitors to observe the signals at the

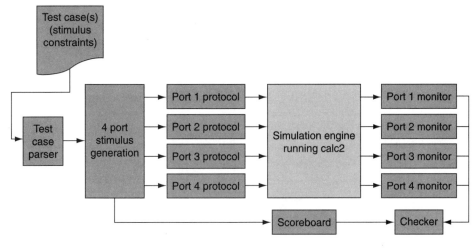

■ **FIGURE 10.9**

The original Calc2 verification environment (transaction based) from Chapter 8 where the stimulus, scoreboard, and checking components are all dependent on one another.

unit level. This violates re-use, because at the next level of verification the signal names are different.

The unit team must revamp the Calc2 unit environment to support re-use. From a verification architectural level, these changes create an environment as shown in Figure 10.10. This figure shows the new re-use friendly Calc2 unit environment.

To fix the independent stimulus component violation of re-use, the team adds two new verification components per port: an input port monitor (Port iMonitor) and an output port monitor for the stimulus component (Port Stim Monitor). The reason for the input port monitor is to disconnect the direct communication between the scoreboard and the stimulus component. Now, the input port monitors observe the input buses directly and then interact with the scoreboard. At the next higher level, when the stimulus component does not exist, the input port monitors still capture the inputs to the Calc2 portion of the DUV and pass those transactions to the scoreboard. The new output port monitors for the stimulus components removes the stimulus and output port monitor dependency. At the new level of verification where the stimulus components do not exist, the output port monitor is not able to communicate with the removed stimulus component.

The hard-coded paths to the inputs and outputs of the DUV need to be removed as well. This is accomplished using a dynamic mapping mechanism whereby an input file supplies the monitor with a virtual (the name that the component uses) to real (the signal name within the test bench) signal mapping. Then, the next level of verification only needs to

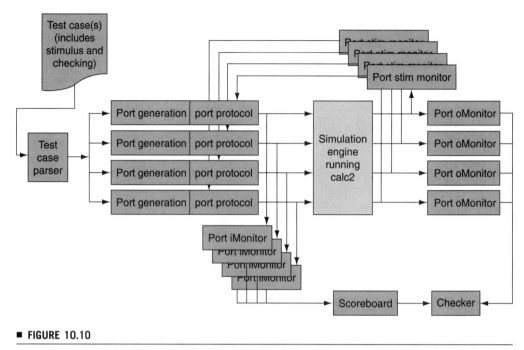

■ **FIGURE 10.10**

Calc2 re-use friendly verification environment.

specify a new mapping within a file that would be specific to the components and the hierarchical level. This same change is made to the input port monitors and the stimulus protocol components (the reason for the latter will be seen momentarily).

One additional change splits the port stimulus generation component into four separate components—one for each port. Now each port contains a stimulus model (which has a generation and protocol component), input port monitor (Port iMonitor), output port stimulus monitor (Port Stim Monitor), and output port monitor (Port oMonitor). The I/O port monitors communicate with the scoreboard and checker and does not interact with the stimulus components. Now the stimulus components are not specific to any port.

Because of the changes (including the change to the stimulus protocol component for dynamic signal mapping), the verification engineers for the unit can concentrate on one set of components and instantiate them as many times as required—in this case, four. If in the future the design were to change to support more ports, the environment scales quickly. The verification team concentrates on making changes to functional portions of the environment–scoreboard and checker—and then simply changes the number of port component instantiations within the test bench. The stimulus components themselves do not need changes.

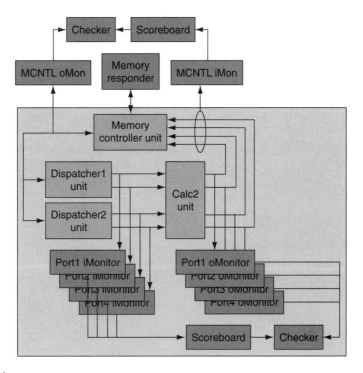

Calc2 processing engine and verification environment with re-use of unit level monitors and checkers.

The next level of verification now exploits the appropriate verification components as shown in Figure 10.11.

The next level of verification utilizes the port I/O monitors in conjunction with the scoreboard and checker. The monitors and checkers flag any failure within this area immediately and reduce the overall debug time. This method is similar to assertions—the verification team has implanted the checks within the larger DUV. Now, as with assertions, the test bench has internal checking components that guard against inputs and guarantee the outputs. In addition to the Calc2 unit, the next level test bench also has other components it is re-using. In this case, the memory controller unit's verification components are also being re-used for the same purpose as the Calc2 unit. With these components being reused, the only component this team must provide is the memory responder verification component. By utilizing these internal monitors and checkers, this verification team leverages existing verification components that allow them to reduce overall verification time because the debug time is reduced. This can further be expanded upon to include the monitors and checkers from the dispatcher units.

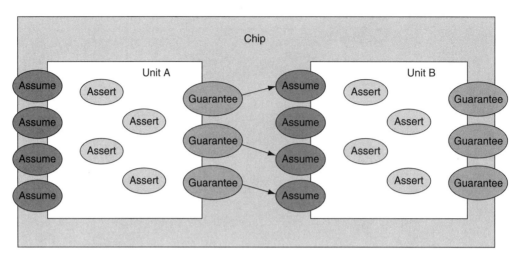

▪ **FIGURE 10.12**

Cascading of assertions shows how assertions hold true throughout the hierarchy.

10.1.5 Assertion Re-Use

Assertions express properties of the logic that hold true regardless of where the logic is used. Therefore, regardless of where the designers instantiate the logic (in a unit environment or in a system environment), the assertion is always valid. This is a form of vertical re-use. If multiple units have assertions and these units merge at the chip level, then all the assertions, from all units, must still hold true. Figure 10.12 illustrates the cascading of assertions and how the assertions protect against any assumptions on the inputs and guarantee the outputs of their particular unit. When the designers cascade the units together with these assertions at the next higher level (re-using the assertions vertically), then the verification team benefits from the assertion safeguards that assist in debugging when a test fails.

Figure 10.12 shows that both unit A and B contain assertions inside the logic. If, during a test, an assertion fails within B (but not within A), the verification team quickly pinpoints the unit with the failure. Unit A's assertions guarantee that the stimulus component is behaving properly. Therefore, because unit B's assertions flagged the problem, the issue resides between the assertions in unit A and the assertion in unit B that indicated the problem. This isolates the problem area very quickly.

Let us make a slight change and say that unit A has assertions (acting as protocol monitors) on its outputs (versus internally) and unit B has assertions on its inputs. Again, during a test an assertion fails within unit B, whereas unit A reports no errors. This indicates conflicting information between the two units. Unit A's assertions should guarantee that unit

B only receives valid stimulus. Unit B's assertions are guarding against any violation of its assumptions. Because an assertion within unit B failed, this indicates an inconsistency of interface protocol assumptions between the two units. Without the re-use principal, finding this discrepancy tends to consume a lot of time. Instead, this method reduces the debug time dramatically.

The problem is that the two units of this interface are not following the same set of protocol assumptions. While the engineering team fixes the logic and the assertions, the verification team needs to review and update the unit verification environments to correspond to the design change. At least one component, if not both, must correct the problem, because there was a verification team failure in allowing conflicting interface protocols to exist in side-by-side units. Furthermore, the whole test bench needs to be regressed (including coverage analysis) with the updates. To catch this problem earlier, the verification team can perform horizontal re-use with unit A's output monitors. Unit B's verification test bench would re-use some of unit A's verification components.

The theory of assertion properties holding true wherever they are used also applies to formal methods (refer to Chapter 11 for more details on formal verification). The verification team creates these properties using a language supported by the formal verification tool such as property specification language. Now the verification team gets the benefit of these assertions, whether they use a formal method tool or a functional simulation based environment. Figure 10.13 shows the dual usage.

Formal methods verify the unit on the left side of Figure 10.13. The verification team may then include the assertions in the simulation-based environment on the right side of Figure 10.13. Because both types of technology require different environment assumption formats, a problem might exist if the separate assumptions are not equivalent. The re-use of the same assertions ties the two environments together and

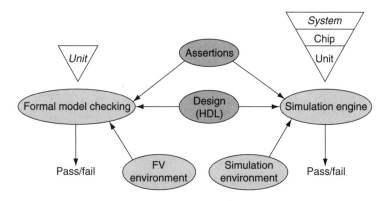

■ **FIGURE 10.13**

Assertion re-use from formal verification to functional simulation-based verification.

allows the validation of these assumptions. This is in addition to the debug advantages of vertical re-use with assertions.

10.2 SYSTEM SIMULATION

As verification moves up the hierarchy, the test bench must evolve to ensure that all the units work together correctly. Units, verified separately, must now work as a system. The system level validates any assumptions made within the lower level environments, both in the design and in the verification components. The purpose of system simulation is to ensure that the separate units work together to perform the intended applications. System-level test benches must exercise broad functionality because they bring together all the design units for the first time.

In this section the question of how the system verification team builds its test benches is dealt with. Just as in a unit environment, a test bench exists to portray the universe for this system. At the system level, there are different mechanisms for creating this test bench. The system verification team can utilize existing verification components from the unit verification environments or create its own verification components. In many cases, multiple test benches exist (which is similar to a unit environment); however, the system level may be too large to re-use them. This leads to a common system-level challenge in obtaining the performance required on the test benches. In many cases, a day or more to run a single test is typical. As a result, system-level verification often requires higher speed simulation engines to process the volumes of cycles on large DUVs.

Once the system-level verification team creates the test benches, the team uses them to ensure that all connectivity is correct and that all the units and chips interact properly to obtain the intended functionality. This requires that the system verification team run tests that target interaction of units and not the functions that are completely self-contained within a chip or unit. This section looks at how the system simulation team has to deal with the same issues as the unit levels, and in addition, they must deal with the multitude of test benches, modes to be run (configurations), overall simulation performance, and potentially integrating a multitude of verification IP.

Re-using design IP, whether it is to create an SoC or just to assist in reducing overall development time, contains its own set of complications at the system level. These complexities are also addressed.

10.2.1 Systems Test Bench

As mentioned earlier, a test bench models the universe for the DUV. At the system level, the test bench drives the application level. This is where the total function of the system comes together in a final environment.

System-level test benches must exercise the end-to-end functionality of the system.

The verification team usually requires numerous test benches for a single system-level model. Some test benches verify different system-level modes of operations such as specific configurations. Others may use stimulus components from lower levels of the verification hierarchy to ensure that basic chip-to-chip or unit-to-unit assumptions hold. The system-level verification team may need to create their own test benches that exercise application-level functionality, such as I/O requests traveling through the system to the microprocessor and then back to the requesting I/O.

Regardless of how many test benches exist, each test bench requires the same types of verification components as a unit environment—stimulus components, scoreboard components, and checking components. However, the system faces the decision of how to acquire these components. In many cases, the system verification team can re-use what the units have already created. In an ideal situation, the system verification team should only need to create stimulus components for application-level functions. For these test benches, the verification team may use the application itself for stimulus creation or write their own stimulus component that mimics system-level function. In either case, they re-use the checking components from the lower levels.

However, system simulation requires a different tact than lower levels. At lower levels, especially at unit levels, the verification team attempts to hit all cases across the DUV. At the system level, the state space is too big. Instead, the verification team must count on the lower levels for hitting the detailed scenarios while they focus on a higher level of abstraction–the system functionality. The focus must be on commands and stimulus making it through the system end-to-end and for applications to run to completion. Because of the scope of the system-level tests being different from the units, the unit verification components may not have the required function. This is especially true for stimulus components. If a verification engineer did not write a stimulus component with system-level functionality in mind, then it cannot be re-used. System simulation targets very specific function within the DUV—interaction and connectivity of the units. Devising tests to focus on these application-level areas typically requires very specific sequences of transactions to occur or for sequences of transactions between different stimulus components to be coordinated. For example, a systems test to ensure that a certain type of PCI transaction is aborted properly when an external interrupt becomes active during that transaction requires coordination from the PCI stimulus components and from the external interrupt stimulus component. If these two stimulus components do not support the control necessary to cause this event, then the verification team must make a decision: Do they write their own model or have the unit team add this functionality to the component? Depending on the specific needs, either option may be viable. This must be decided on a case-by-case basis.

Re-using monitors and checkers at the system level is easy if the unit verification teams follow the re-use guidelines. Vertical re-use is as simple as including the verification components in the test bench. One thing to keep in mind is that for every verification component added, system simulation performance is going to decrease.

One way to help alleviate performance issues is to use only the bare minimum set of verification components. The trade-off is that when a test fails, it may take longer to debug because observability within the DUV decreases. A solution is to create a *layered environment*. A layered environment has the ability to enable or disable portions of verification components as needed. This way, initial tests are run with the bare minimum components, maximizing performance and throughput. When a test fails, the team enables other components (or portions of existing components) to give better debug information.

In some cases, the verification team may not have a defined system environment. If a team creates an application specific integrated circuit (ASIC) to sell to various customers, then the customer, not the ASIC team, defines the system "universe." However, the ASIC verification team must create a superset of the possible system configurations based on the ASIC's intended usage. This information comes from the architects and product teams.

However, for most, the specific usage has already been defined for the particular product and they set off to re-use lower level components and create end-to-end stimulus. Here, the verification team goes beyond the chips and includes inter-chip packaging such as cards and boards. The verification team and package design teams coordinate efforts to use a common set of schematics to build the systems test bench. In these scenarios, interconnect of the product is verified before getting silicon back in the lab.

10.2.2 Connectivity and Interaction of Units

In most ASIC flows, the top level of the chip looks like a black box schematic containing multiple instantiations of lower level units. The designers place any logic required to "glue" the units together into its own separate unit and instantiate it parallel to the others. Therefore, the top chip level just connects all the units to each other and to the chip I/O pins. At this level, it is critical to verify this interconnection.

Verifying connectivity goes one-step further at the system level if multiple chips come together to form the system. Here, the verification team performs system simulation of the target environment to validate the connectivity between all the chips in the system. This assists the product team with validating their schematics.

To validate this interconnection, the system verification team creates test cases that provide a broad range of system-level interaction trying to exercise all interconnections. Skill and knowledge is required to create those tests because the system verification team must understand lower level functionality, the internal interfaces between units, and the interaction between the units. Once understood, then the team constructs the system-level tests to target the connectivity.

As with the lower levels of verification, coverage remains a key topic. Knowing what the DUV actually did in system level compared with the intent of the test benches is as important as ever. For connectivity at the system level, toggle coverage can be used to assist in deciding whether the test cases have exercised all the connections within system. Toggle coverage measures what signals have switched—from a logic zero to logic one and from logic one to logic zero. Thus, if any facilities have not toggled, then some interconnections have not been exercised. This type of coverage is typically a "freebie" that requires no additional work from the verification team. Most commercial simulation engines have an option to enable toggle coverage. All the verification team must do is to enable the option, run the test cases, and then analyze the results.

The tests that focus on connectivity also cause interaction between the units. This brings us to the next purpose of system simulation: verifying functions that span units. These functions are prime candidates for system-level verification. At lower levels of the hierarchy, the verification teams created each environment with stimulus components intended to behave as the real portions of the design. Because the verification components are behavioral models and not the real logic, they may not act as the real logic does (and probably does not intentionally). Therefore, when the design sub-components interact with one another at system level, the verification team may find bugs.

Any functions that spans multiple portions of the DUV are items that the system-level verification team should target. Below are some typical functions that are prime candidates for system-level verification. These may not be the only functions, but these are very common among any system:

- Interrupts
- Power-on-reset (POR) and configuration
- Changing of chip modes on-the-fly
- End-to-end data and command flow
- Code loads to exercise system or processor functions

Internal or external interrupts drive interaction between many units. Interrupts cause an exception in the machine or they request the system to stop and handle special work. This requires a change in what all the units are doing. This disruption from mainline function to exception or handling routines necessitates many units to save their current state and then change their operation. Once the system handles the interrupt, the units restore the state of the machine and continue running as they did before the interrupt. For example, when a split write transaction is on a PCI bus and the chip receives an interrupt from somewhere in the system (either internally or externally), the chip must terminate the transaction. This requires the PCI unit to respond appropriately onto the PCI bus to abort the transaction. The memory controller must finish its current memory cycle and flush its buffers, and some control flow is required to reallocate that memory into a free pool so that it can be used by some other resource.

POR and configuration cycles are interesting because this is what brings the system "on-line". These tests require that all units in the system are connected properly and that they are initialized to the correct state. The very nature of initializing all of the units requires interaction. Chapter 9 covered specific POR verification methods.

Changing modes on-the-fly may require portions of the system to be quiescent. Typically, when a unit changes modes, it has a requirement that all interactions with it cease until it completes the change of mode. This requires interaction of the units. First, the unit changing its mode indicates a quiescent request to all units interfacing with it. These units then indicate they have suspended interactions to the requesting unit. The unit then changes mode and indicates to all other units they may resume operations. This entails a lot of interaction. Derivatives to this interaction exist where a system controller oversees and directs the change in modes.

End-to-end data and command flow, by nature, focus on interaction. Because the focus is on the application, many design components get involved. An example of this is in networking chips. FIFOs (queues) exist to perform buffering. In many cases, these buffers fill up. When they fill up, the desired action applies a pacing scheme to allow the buffers to empty. In this situation, the logic writing to the buffer must stop. If this does not occur, data packets may be corrupted or lost if the buffer over-flows. Therefore, the system team may have specific tests that target filling up the FIFO. This also validates the normal buffering functional-ity within the system because this normal mode must take place before the buffer can be filled.

Within a processor system (either it is embedded, general purpose, or network), some level of microcode runs to perform functionality. Loading this code and running it requires many units to interact. The loading of the code requires interaction of the microprocessor with memory. As the code runs, its instructions fetch and move data to and from various parts of the system.

As with lower level environments, the verification team runs the tests while applying constraints to the stimulus components. These con-straints indicate how these components should stimulate the DUV (in this case the system). Meanwhile, the test bench re-uses the lower level monitor and checking components to validate the operations. From this standpoint, the system-level simulation environment is just like the lower level environments.

Now that the team has identified, written, and run the test benches, how do they know that the test bench exercised the intended function? As with the lower levels, functional coverage can help identify what the verification environment has not exercised and directs the team to put more effort into untested areas. As the test cases run, verification components watch for the test to exercise pre-determined coverage points. When exercised, the verification components (typically monitors) collect and log the coverage event. What makes system-level coverage more difficult is the fact that re-use is limited for functional coverage. Typically, the units only contain coverage events that are for within that unit. They do not contain coverage events that span units, a far more interesting subject for system simulation because the system verification team's focus is on the interaction. The system team must either re-use lower level coverage events and make cross products with other units or write specific verification components (monitors) to capture these higher-level coverage points.

Tests that focus on interaction also exercise connectivity. The two go hand-in-hand. However, coverage for connectivity and interaction is different. Code coverage tools can gather coverage for connectivity, whereas functional coverage is required for interaction.

After creating the tests, a suite of test benches and test cases exist. The system team now must intelligently cross these two items for performance issues at the system level. A single test case may take hours or even days to run. If the verification team simply ran every test against every applicable configuration, it would require an overwhelming amount of computing power and memory. Special purpose simulation machines, discussed in Section 10.3, address this requirement. However, a small set of these machines typically exists, and they are in high demand across the different verification teams. The system team can apply some strategy to reduce the overall requirements for these machines.

One strategy is to align the tests and configurations, only running tests against the applicable configurations. For example, a PCI and interrupt test case was mentioned where the test ensured that a PCI transaction was aborted properly because of an interrupt. Also mentioned was that the chip's memory controller unit supports three different memory configurations. This test is not required to run in all three configurations. The purpose of this test is to ensure the interaction of the PCI unit with the interrupt unit. One test bench needs to be chosen to run this test in, not all three.

Another strategy is to use a random technique where the test randomly chooses which configuration to run against. Over time, as the test runs multiple times, it exercises all the configurations. The verification team can also apply this method to the above PCI/interrupt example. The memory configuration could be randomized, so that over time all three of the memory configurations are exercised.

One additional strategy is to create new test benches that have certain functions "stubbed" out. If a test targets only certain units to interact, then any units that are not participating can be removed. This creates a smaller memory footprint for the system simulation environment and decreases overall run time of the tests. An example of this is within a multiprocessor system. A test could focus on a single processor doing memory reads and writes. Because this test only focuses on one of the many processors, the verification team can remove the other processors from the model. This removal not only saves on memory footprint, but also improves simulation speed because the model is smaller.

However, doing this adds to the total number of test benches that must be maintained by the system verification team. The team must know when to use each test bench. If the wrong test bench is used, the simulation may indicate a false failure. This wastes both compute resource and time of the verification engineer to debug the test.

10.2.3 Verification Challenges in a Re-Usable IP World

Another system-level aspect of verification evolves from including IP from other groups or vendors into the system simulation environment. Including this IP creates challenges for the system verification team. The verification team must solve issues surrounding the re-use of this IP. These issues are re-using verification components of these IP blocks and debug of logic that includes this IP.

These issues abound in SoC designs as well. As already mentioned, a SoC contains an embedded processor, memory, and any functions that make the ASIC unique. In a SoC, the architect chooses some of the components of the system from a library of pre-existing design blocks and then adds their own units to differentiate their product in the market. What sets a SoC apart from a normal system is that the components within a SoC have rigid interfaces that cannot be changed (unlike a normal chip where the designers may collaborate and change the interface protocols as they see fit). The other item that sets SoCs apart is the fact that the impact to finding a bug after fabrication is costly. In systems that have multiple chips mounted on a board, there exists room to implement patch logic to get around bugs discovered after fabrication. This is not the case with a SoC. If any bugs are found after fabrication, then a re-spin of the complete chip is required.

Re-Use of Verification Components

In many situations, re-usable IP designs do not come with verification components. These re-usable IP blocks do have verification environments, but often the providers do not include the verification components to their customers. Shipping verification components with IP blocks require the IP provider to support the mainstream verification environments, including the simulation engines and HVLs from all major vendors. For the IP blocks that do include verification components, many issues may surround re-using these components. Merging multiple source environments from different vendors can be a trying task, especially if the source environments use different engines or HVLs. One IP block may have used Synopsys' Vera language to implement the verification components, whereas another used SystemC, another used Verisity's *e*, and yet another used Verilog. The environment requires work to utilize the verification components within one environment (if it can be done at all). Additionally, there may be additional costs due to licensing of the tools.

Depending on the situation, the verification team may choose to explore the use of a third-party source that would provide a cohesive set of verification components to ensure compatibility. Again, there may be costs associated with this. This is along the lines of the system team writing their verification components for system.

The last aspect of re-use with IP occurs when the design team adds logic to differentiate their system from a competitor's product (especially in a SoC). Ideally, the verification team creates a unit environment to verify the new function. However, the unit verification team must interpret various data books regarding how the different interfaces work. As already discussed, this interpretation can lead to incorrect assumptions. Based on this, re-use becomes important—ideally, the unit team should be able to re-use verification components from other units to verify interface protocols. Again, tool compatibility issues can further complicate environment creation. If any verification components exist, they may not work in the end-user environment, and this new unit's verification team will be required to create new verification components.

In all cases, the verification team must work with the design architects in evaluating what IP units are available. The design team must take into account verification requirements when making decisions on which external IP to purchase.

Debug

Debug is typically harder and more time consuming in an environment where the IP logic may not be visible, verification components may not exist, and access to the IP teams may not be an option. Because of these issues, it may take longer to debug failures.

In many cases, the chip design teams may not have access to the HDL; the logic is in gate-level form or the unit uses some encryption technology so the internals are not available to debug at all. In this situation, the IP is a black box—with reduced visibility that increases debug time.

If the IP providers do not follow re-use guidelines, a limited number of verification components may exist at the next level of verification hierarchy. This reduces the ability to observe the design and flag problems as they occur. Furthermore, in cases where a gate-level model exists for IP, the process of creating the IP removes any verification components. Gate-level IP went through synthesis, which eliminates any internal assertions.

In a traditional system verification environment, the design and verification teams are available to consult with the unit teams when issues arise. The unit teams develop most units specifically for this particular system; thus, they are on the same program. In this case, when the team encounters issues, a simple path exists to gain assistance from the individuals that authored this unit (either the verification team and/or the design team). When re-using design IP, this is not the case. Often, the original team is not available because they have moved onto a completely different project. In this situation, no simple path exists to the original team. The system verification team must debug the environment with little or no assistance from the original team. This can be a very lengthy and tedious process. Furthermore, this may uncover a situation that the original owners never documented in the re-usable IP specification. When this occurs, it may mean a change in the architecture to get around this problem. This highlights the requirement of performing system simulation with re-usable IP.

10.3 BEYOND GENERAL-PURPOSE LOGIC SIMULATION

System simulation moves the focus of verification for the hardware components toward their real application space. This results in unique challenges driven by the need for radically higher simulation speed, the desire to verify the components in their real target system, the increasing role of software in the system implementation, and the import of design components (IP) that require their own simulation environments. Table 10.1 lists the approaches to the challenges of system simulation. The need for simulation compute power increases rapidly as verification proceeds from chip to system level. One strategy to counter the growing need for performance is to use specialized hardware for logic simulation. Such *simulation accelerators* have a long successful history in verification.

Logic *emulation* became feasible in the early 1990s as programmable hardware structures became available. The idea of loading a register transfer level (RTL) model of a chip into a piece of programmable hardware that is directly connected, or literally *plugged-in*, to the target system has a powerful attraction to any verification project.

In addition, at the system level of the implementation hierarchy, software is likely to be part of the system implementation. *Hardware/soft-*

TABLE 10.1 ■ Approaches to the challenges of system simulation

Approach	Purpose
Simulation accelerator	Address need for more simulation compute power
Logic emulation	Address need for more simulation compute power
	Debug chip or system in target environment
Hardware/software coverification	Address need for more simulation compute power to be able to debug software
Co-simulation	Address problems with system component having unique requirements on a simulation technology

ware co-verification is the task to simulate at least those layers of the software on the RTL model that interact closely with the hardware. Logic acceleration and emulation engines provide enough RTL simulation performance to allow software debug in real time. Alternate techniques like cycle-accurate, abstract models are viable alternatives for the higher levels of the software stack.

Co-simulation is used wherever the need exists to import a system component that has its own unique requirements for its simulation environment that a single logic simulation engine cannot support. Although such a runtime coupling of several simulators always has simulator-specific challenges, which go beyond the scope of this section, there are general principles that are common to all such IP-import scenarios.

10.3.1 Acceleration

Hardware acceleration has been tried in many compute-intense areas, among them database engines, Lisp engines for artificial intelligence applications, and logic simulation. In most areas, general-purpose computers have eventually proven to be the superior solution. Their advantage is based on the breakneck pace of the 2x/18 months performance improvements of processor speed and the cost-performance leverage of chips that are manufactured by the millions versus a few thousand expensive special-purpose chips.

Hardware-accelerated logic simulation is an exception to this observation. The need for radically increased simulation performance, especially for system simulation, has motivated hardware design engineers since the 1980s to develop accelerators and has yielded many successful solutions [55, 56].

Two different implementation approaches can be differentiated for simulation accelerators (Figure 10.14). The first approach uses an *indirect implementation*: The base premise here is that a simulation engine is implemented in hardware. The second approach utilizes programmable hardware elements to achieve a *direct implementation*, a direct mapping of the RTL specification into hardware structures.

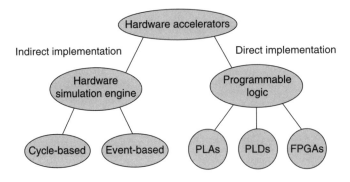

▪ **FIGURE 10.14**

Classification of different hardware acceleration approaches. The direct implementation maps the RTL model directly into logic structures in hardware. The indirect implementation creates a hardware version of a logic simulator. Programmable logic arrays (PLAs), programmable logic devices (PLDs), and field programmable gate arrays (FPGAs) are different types of programmable logic structures discussed in the text.

Indirect Implementation–Hardware Simulator

Both basic simulation algorithms, cycle-based and event-based, have successfully built the basis for hardware accelerators. As an example, the conceptually simpler cycle-based approach is briefly discussed.

The grandfather of all cycle-based accelerators is the EVE machine, which consists of a vast network of primitive *logic processors* (*LP*) [55]. Every LP is a simple processor whose instruction set consists of a Boolean function and the input values for a four-input logic gate (Figure 10.15a). LPs continuously loop through a sequence of such instructions. Every pass through a complete sequence constitutes a simulation cycle. Figure 10.15c shows several LPs interconnected to a cluster where different LPs can cross-communicate gate input values between each other through a multiplexor (MUX) interconnect structure.

The more LPs are available, the more Boolean functions the accelerator can evaluate in parallel. On counterbalance, the communication between LPs takes extra time. The art of mapping a DUV to such an accelerator, model build, is to find the right trade-off between more parallelization, which yields faster simulation, and sequential execution to avoid cross-LP communication. Overall, the base performance of an accelerated model is determined by the longest chain of sequential gate instructions on any of the LPs.

Figure 10.16 uses the example of the adder DUV from Chapter 5 to illustrate the scheduling problem that is at the core of the model build process for many hardware accelerators and emulators. Figure 10.16a shows a schematic view of the DUV and gives every block a numbered label. In Figure 10.16b, the gates are scheduled, attempting to keep as

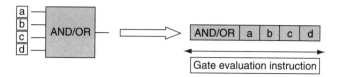

(a) Logic Gate Primitive

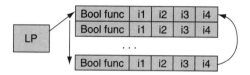

(b) Logic Processor Element

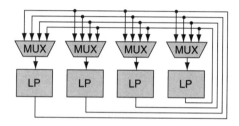

(c) Logic Processor Cluster

■ **FIGURE 10.15**

Building blocks for a cycle-based hardware accelerator. (a) An example of how a four-input logic gate corresponds to a single instruction for a logic processor (LP). (b) An example of how an LP executes a sequence of gate instructions. (c) Four LPs are put together to a cluster of LPs that are able to exchange gate input values among each other via a multiplexor (MUX) interconnect structure.

many of the four LPs busy as possible. This is somewhat successful because overall we need six LP time steps for one simulation cycle of the 12 gate DUV.

Of course, a hardware accelerator needs to support more functionality than Boolean function blocks. Hardware elements for RAM arrays and register/latches are also needed, and their access needs to be scheduled into the flow of logic evaluations. It should be obvious that the software that synthesizes HDLs into the accelerator primitives and schedules the execution of the evaluation over time is as critical a part for an accelerator as the hardware engine itself.

The two main parameters that define the base speed of a cycle-based hardware accelerator are the *number of LPs*, the *instruction depth* of a single LP, and the LP instruction cycle time. If the model of a DUV does not fill all instruction slots of all LPs, which would mark 100%

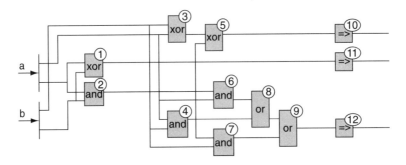

(a) Adder Example Design

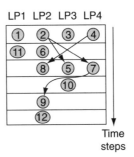

LP1 LP2 LP3 LP4

Time
steps

(b) Adder Design scheduled across 4 LPs

▪ **FIGURE 10.16**

Adder example design mapped to primitive logic gates (a) and scheduled for partially parallelized execution on an accelerator that consists of four LPs (b). The arrows in b symbolize cross-LP communication. It is assumed that the time necessary to transport a signal value from one LP to another is the same as the time an LP needs to evaluate one gate instruction (which is overly optimistic).

utilization of the hardware, the model build software can trade-off parallelism with scheduling depth to achieve the highest performance.

The model evaluation speed, which can be calculated by the longest LP instruction sequence, is called the *raw accelerator performance*. The *actual accelerator performance* is lower in practice and depends highly on the structure of the total accelerator-test bench interaction. Different approaches of this interaction are shown for the control flow of the setup in Figure 10.17a and 10.17b, whereas different alternatives for the data flow are illustrated in Figure 10.17c and 10.17d.

The overall objective of an optimized test bench/accelerator setup is to maximize the time spent in the DUV versus in the test bench. All time spent in the comparatively slow test bench while the accelerator sits idle wastes a valuable resource. A cycle-by-cycle setup, like in Figure 10.17a, might be tolerable for a software simulator. If a hardware accelerator is driven this way, however, the overall simulation speed does not increase

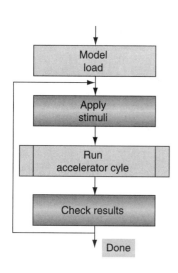

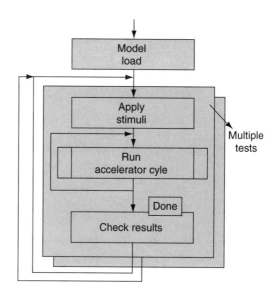

(a) Tightly Couple Testbench/
     Accelerator Control Flow

(b) Optimized Testbench/
     Accelerator Control
     FLow

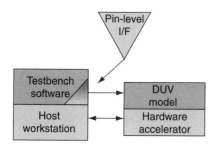

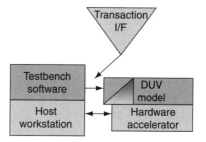

(c) Signal Pin-Level Testbench/
     Accelerator interface

(d) Transaction-Level Testbench/Accelerator
     Interface w/*Virtual Logic*

■ **FIGURE 10.17**

Different test bench/accelerator integration scenarios. (a) This setup applies stimuli and checks before and after every accelerator cycle and is therefore most intrusive. (b) This scenario optimizes the time spent actually simulating the DUV. (c) The case where the test bench interacts with the DUV in the accelerator on the level of individual signal pins is illustrated. The test bench part that maps transactions to signal interactions is shown as a triangle. (d) This setup shows this code mapped to virtual logic and loaded into the accelerator to minimize the overhead of the test bench/accelerator interface, moving it to the transaction level.

because the stimulus/check loop dominates performance completely. Figure 10.17b pushes the stimulus/check application outside the loop that runs cycles on the DUV and therefore minimizes the time spent waiting for the software on the workstation. In addition, several tests are run in a row, thus amortizing the time spent to load the model into the accelerator over several test cases of a *bucket* of test cases.

The data flow interaction scenarios of Figure 10.17c and 10.17d illustrate how the interaction between test bench and DUV can be abstracted to the transaction level, thereby enabling the transfer of work (shown as a shaded triangle) from the test bench to the DUV. This creation of so-called *virtual logic* is a key principle to optimize the utilization of a hardware accelerator.

Direct Implementation–Programmable Hardware

Programmable logic arrays (*PLAs*) were the first hardware structures whose Boolean function was definable after chip manufacturing. Figure 10.18a shows an example of a typical PLA. The input signals (*i1, i2, i3*) are fed into a programmable AND/OR structure, the *AND* and *OR* planes. The personalization of this flexible combinational logic block occurs by blowing fuses that connect the inputs of *and* or *or* gates, respectively.

Whereas PLAs can only implement combinational logic, complex programmable logic devices (CPLDs; Figure 10.18b) are the next step in the evolution of more complex programmable logic because they support the implementation of combinational logic as well as registers and arrays. The disadvantage of more complex building blocks is the increased complexity of the model build software that has to map HDL logic to these complex structures and use the switch interconnect matrix to combine them to build up a complete implementation of the DUV.

Field programmable gate arrays (FPGAs; Figure 10.18c and 10.18d) take a more structured building block approach. The base element typically uses a MUX, which allows universal programmability of the combinational logic component, and a flip-flop, which allows the integration of state-holding elements to implement the state of the DUV state machine function. The FPGA chip supports a programmable interconnect of many of these basic building blocks. Very soon, FPGAs will reach a capacity of 10 million gates. Already today there are families of FPGAs that embed a general-purpose micro-controller on the same chip to allow even more programmability of the chip.

Accelerators that use FPGAs (or simpler forms of programmable logic) as their base building blocks have one clear advantage over the accelerators, which use indirect implementation of the DUV: FPGA implementations can be much faster than hardware simulation engines. The two main disadvantages, however, are the higher price and the higher complexity of model build, which raises the model build times considerably.

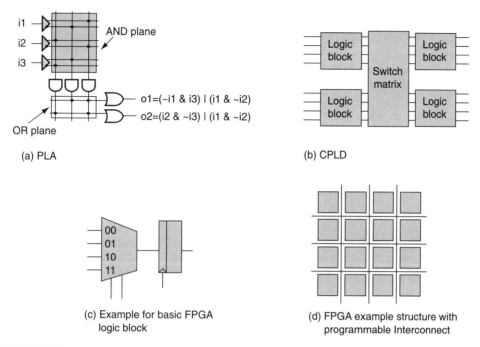

i1 — AND plane

o1=(~i1 & i3) | (i1 & ~i2)
o2=(i2 & ~i3) | (i1 & ~i2)

OR plane

(a) PLA

(b) CPLD

(c) Example for basic FPGA
logic block

(d) FPGA example structure with
programmable Interconnect

■ **FIGURE 10.18**

Programmable logic as it evolved over time. (a) A simple example of a programmable logic array (PLA) with the characteristic AND and OR planes. (b) More complex logic blocks of a CPLD (complex programmable logic device) are connected via a programmable switch matrix. (c) The basic building block for a typical FPGA (field programmable gate array). Model build maps all DUV logic to this universal building block. (d) The FPGA example of many such building blocks in a checkerboard pattern with a programmable interconnect structure.

If simulation speed is of prime concern, an FPGA-based accelerator is preferred. If price and model build turn-around time are more important, a hardware simulation engine is the better solution.

10.3.2 Emulation

The main differences between high-end accelerators and emulator engines are the speed requirements and the support to connect the emulator to real hardware, the *target hardware*.

Emulators can operate at a raw speed of 100 kHz to 1 MHz. At these performance levels, it is realistic to model parts of a system in the emulator, whereas the rest of the system, which exists as real hardware already, connects directly to the emulation machine. Even at these speeds, it is typical that the target hardware has to operate at a slower frequency to match the clock rate that the emulated model is able to achieve. This is an extra requirement for the target hardware and the interface between the DUV model and the target hardware. I/O or bus interfaces between DUV and target hardware are a typical example for a productive setup for emulation. For example, PCI's lowest bus frequency is 33 MHz. To perform emulation with a system utilizing PCI, the PCI bus in the target system must be lowered to match the PCI speed in the emulator.

Although the emulator connects to the target hardware on one side, it also needs a workstation server interface. The server provides the capability to load the DUV model, control the execution over time, and give the verification team a debugging interface into the DUV model on the emulator. Even more than for the accelerator case, it is critical to keep the server-emulator interaction to a bare minimum so that the emulator can run uninterrupted most of the time. Otherwise, the workstation server performance will severely limit the speed of the overall setup.

Originally, only CPLD or FPGA implementations yielded a platform fast enough to support the speed requirements for emulation. The higher speeds achieved did offset the higher price and higher complexity of the model build. However, in the last few years, indirect implementations similar to the ones discussed above improved in performance enough to make emulation engines viable. The basic operational principle of these engines is the same as for the cycle-based accelerator in Figure 10.15. The difference in the design is a much higher number of LPs with a much reduced program stack depth. This results in much higher parallel execution of the DUV logic per cycle.

Figure 10.19 puts performance and capacity of the software simulation, acceleration, and emulation platforms in perspective. Typical high-end engines were chosen for each category, because they are available in the EDA market.

A higher range of capacity over performance is shown for the software simulator because it is used more typically over these ranges and the performance scaling is more interesting in that case. For a smaller practical range, model size and performance can be traded in the application of an accelerator. It is necessary to achieve a certain minimum performance with the emulator to support the already slowed-down target hardware. This leaves no room to trade model size and performance.

10.3.3 Hardware/Software Co-verification

Hardware/software co-verification is used when there is a requirement to simulate together a DUV and (some of) the software that interacts with the hardware under design. There is an increasing importance of hardware/software co-verification in today's verification methodologies.

The main driver has been the occurrence of more and more programmable controllers as building blocks for designs (such as embedded processors and micro-controllers). This leaves the design engineer with the option to implement some of the specified function of the DUV in

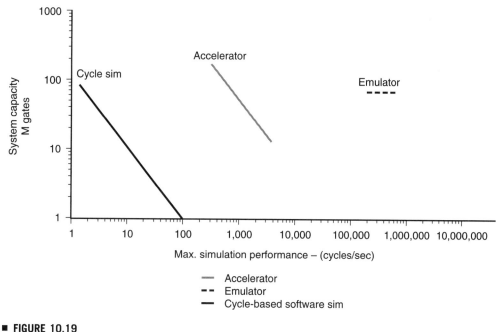

■ **FIGURE 10.19**

The performance and capacity comparison between software simulation, three different accelerator machines, and an emulation engine shows the scalability of the different platforms.

software and only part of it directly in hardware. Hardware/software *co-design* is concerned with the optimized partitioning between the hardware partition and the part of the design that is implemented as a program for a micro-controller. The optimization step usually has to consider performance versus cost. Of course, it is possible to repair bugs in the software after manufacturing of the part. However, such problems are very expensive if they prevent progress during the bring-up phase of the chip in the lab, which makes hardware/software co-verification a necessity.

There are two methods to support the verification of software with the DUV hardware, a *layered verification* and the brute-force *total system simulation approach*, both of which are characterized briefly.

Layered Verification

The layered approach separates different levels of software that run on the embedded processor. Layer 1 is the part of the code that interacts most closely with the hardware features of the processor. It typically initializes the processor and interacts with features like interrupt control and diagnostic registers. Layer 2 is the application layer that assumes the processor implements the instruction set architecture correctly.

It is most productive to simulate only layer 1 together with the RTL model of the hardware. The amount of code is very limited, and it is possible to cover the more limited scenarios of this layer with RTL simulation. If necessary, acceleration or even emulation engines (for performance reasons, not to connect target hardware) provide a performance boost to run enough of the low-level code to prevent wasted lab bring-up time.

For layer 2 of the code, the application layer, a high-level model of the processor is used for debug. This high-level model implements the instruction set architecture in abstract form and thus provides the code an execution and debug platform. Such a model is usually called an *instruction set simulator* (ISS). An ISS model can easily run at a speed of 50 to 100 kHz on a workstation. Besides the excellent cost/performance of the ISS model, it also provides the software team with the advantage of starting the debug process of the code much earlier than what the availability of the RTL would allow. Parallel development opportunity translates directly into faster time to market of the overall project.

Total System Simulation

The brute-force alternative to the layered approach usually requires the investment in accelerator or emulator hardware. It is possible that there is no significant advantage to partition the software to support the layered verification approach. Here, all software needs to be loaded into the DUV on the accelerator/emulator and simulate both RTL and software together, with all the apparent disadvantages.

One reason for the need to keep all code together and simulate it with the DUV hardware can be the high interaction of the code-driven microcontroller with *surrounding* DUV. In this scenario, the software debug aspect is not the main reason to run the software on the DUV model. It is even possible that the software debug still occurs on an ISS model. However, the hardware verification needs to run enough of the application code to hit a sufficient number of scenarios where the software of the embedded processor drives features in the surrounding hardware.

It is possible for this case to replace the RTL of the embedded processor with the ISS and resort to a co-simulation scenario. All parts of DUV are simulated on the RTL—except the processor. The combination of code plus ISS model is separated and acts as a special driver for the remaining RTL model.

This alternative to hardware/software co-verification leads us naturally to a brief overview of the challenges of co-simulation.

10.3.4 Co-simulation

Co-simulation is necessary whenever integration of two independent simulations into one larger system-level simulation is needed. The normal approach of model integration on the system level is the inclusion of all model parts into one single simulation model.

There are several possible reasons why this might not be feasible. It is possible that different model partitions require simulation engines with different simulation paradigms. Examples are RTL model partitions that need to simulate with an ISS model or an analog simulation model.

Alternatively, the system model might need to integrate a piece of design IP, which the supplier does not deliver in source form but only as a completely assembled simulation model. In this case, it may be necessary to couple multiple simulations using the *same* simulator for each model partition.

Finally, it can be necessary to cut a large system simulation model into several partitions to minimize the memory requirement of each partition by itself or to optimize performance of the overall simulation by distributing the partitions across multiple simulation servers.

In all these cases, co-simulation means a coordinated run of several simulations. Figure 10.20 illustrates the two main alternatives to achieve the coupling of two simulations.

Figure 10.20a shows a centralized coordination program that exists independently of each individual simulation *A* and *B*. Neither simulator is aware of the coordination. The *co-simulation control* program interacts at the test bench level with either simulation engine. The access to either simulation model or its signals is left to the API of either simulation engine, which the test benches use anyway. The tasks of the co-simulation control program are

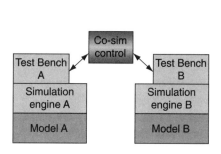

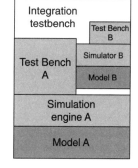

(a) Centralized co-simulation control

(b) Simulation Engine A is the master process

■ FIGURE 10.20

Different approaches to co-simulation. (a) This scenario treats the two simulation engines (A and B) as independent and connects them via a central co-simulation control program. (b) This scenario uses simulation engine A as the master process and links both simulation engine B and test bench B into test bench A, resulting in one single process overall.

- Synchronizing the start of both simulation engines

- Transfer of the signal values crossing model *A* and *B*

- Maintaining the central simulation time and synchronizing the advancement of time in either simulation

It is possible that at least one of the simulation engines involved in the co-simulation does not require running as its own separate program (process). For example, if the integration involves an ISS model that can by linked-in as a library, the scenario of Figure 10.20b might by appropriate, where the test bench for *model A* just links in the simulator and *model B*. For simulator *A* the coupled simulator is just an extension of test bench *A*.

The co-simulation control program of Figure 10.20a and its tasks still exist in the scenario in Figure 10.20b. However, this functionality is now totally integrated into the two test bench programs.

A couple of challenges that typically exist for the synchronization of multiple simulation engines across the signal interface that connect the model partitions need to be highlighted. They are illustrated in Figure 10.21.

The co-simulation control program is active after completion of each time step of the co-simulation. At this point, it has to transfer the signal

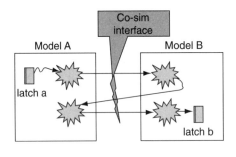

(a) Co-simulation across
combinational logic boundaries

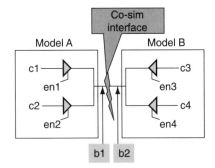

(b) Co-simulation across a multi-source
bus interface

 represents combinational zero-delay logic

▪ **FIGURE 10.21**

Recurring interface challenges for co-simulation. (a) A path through combinational logic that connects *latch a* in *model 1* with *latch b* in *model 2*. (b) The challenge of running co-simulation across an interface that consists of a multisource bus signal. Each model (A and B) drives two bus contributors onto their respective half of the bus signal (b1 and b2).

values of the partition-crossing signals to the simulation engine of the adjacent partition. Ideally, the simulation can proceed with the next time step after all values have been exchanged.

However, it is possible that the logic across an interface requires update and value propagation within the *same* time step. Such an example is shown in Figure 10.21a. Here a signal update that originates from *latch a*, crosses into *model B*, runs through zero-delay logic, crosses back into *model A*, and after more model partition crossing ends up as an input signal to *latch b*. Because this signal change needs to propagate with zero delay back and forth between *model A* and *B*, co-simulation control needs to call the simulation engines *A* and *B* multiple times for the *same* simulation time.

The exact amount of times each partition needs to be updated for the current time depends entirely on the topology of the interface between the partitions. The co-simulation control program needs to contain mechanisms that continue updates that bounce between partitions until the model is stable for the current simulation time. Obviously, the multiple re-simulations of the same partition have a negative performance impact for the overall system simulation but are unavoidable to ensure correct co-simulation results.

System hardware components typically connect with multiple-source buses with each other. For co-simulation this can easily lead to interface scenarios like the one shown in Figure 10.21b, where the co-simulation interface cuts through a bus signal.

The challenge of this scenario is that neither simulation engine (*A* or *B*) has access to all contributors of the bus. *Model A* only has contributor *c1* and *c2*, which connect to partial bus *b1*. Partial bus *b2* only has the contributor *c3* and *c4* from *model B*. Only an algorithm that has access to each individual contribution value can maintain the fully resolved value of bus b. It is not correct if co-simulation control just transfers the partially resolved values *b1* and *b2* to either partition. A further evaluation of this example is left as an exercise to the reader.

It is possible to create a custom co-simulation harness for every concrete project situation as it occurs. Typically, verification teams have a library of co-simulation-related functions they can draw from.

Further factoring out of co-simulation control code can occur to support concept in more generic ways. For example, it is possible to write a co-simulation control program that works generically for a large class of commercial simulators and deals directly with their programming APIs. There have been attempts to place such EDA products in the market under the name *simulation backplane*, which suggests a generic plug-and-play capability for co-simulation. So far, the technical value-add achieved over the ad-hoc solutions has not made these products economically viable.

10.4 SUMMARY

System simulation adds a variety of challenges to the verification task. These challenges have created the motivation for a number of unique approaches and tools.

As with design re-use, verification re-use leverages work done by various teams throughout the entire company, thus reducing overall schedules. However, to capitalize on each other's work, the teams must follow specific re-use guidelines. The basic guidelines to assist a verification team in writing components that obtain a high degree of re-use were described. By following these guidelines, the verification team reduces the set of re-use complexities, whether for vertical, horizontal, or both paradigms.

System-level verification requires many of the same aspects of a unit verification environment. System verification environments contain verification components that drive the test benches. These components may be acquired in various ways. Options include re-use of the unit verification components, acquiring the verification components from another group, or writing specific verification components for the system level.

Numerous test benches exist for a system-level environment, and because of performance reasons, the verification team must optimize the tests across these numerous test benches. In addition to managing tests across test benches, the system verification team must also take into consideration the performance of the tests at the system level. The system verification team may choose to build the test benches using a layered approach. This layered approach does not contain all the monitors and checkers—only the required ones. Then if a test fails, the verification team re-runs the test with other verification components enabled to provide better observability for debug.

Regardless of how the test bench comes together, tests verify the connectivity of all the chips, units, and IP blocks as well as their interactions. As with lower level simulation environments, the team must apply coverage to the system-level environment to assist in determining what has been exercised and what is still left to be done.

For systems that contain re-usable IP, verification tool incompatibilities may create challenges in capitalizing on pre-existing verification components. In addition, debug of these systems become harder without the assistance of the original authors or HDL code.

Hardware acceleration engines address the exploding need for fast simulation cycles for the larger system models. Emulators bring the speed of the simulated DUV to a level where it can be integrated into its target system, using real hardware for already existing system components.

The increasing use of embedded processor cores drives the need for better methods in hardware/software co-verification. In some cases, this goal is achieved using our faster accelerator and emulator engines. In other situations, hardware/software co-verification better uses co-simulation where the embedded software runs on a higher level ISS model, which runs coupled with an RTL simulation of the rest of the DUV.

Co-simulation is a general scheme to run multiple simulation partitions together as one system. The main challenges of co-simulation occur in the context of synchronization and signal value transfer between the different partitions. There is no general-purpose co-simulation framework readily available for a verification project, but there is a body of experience and recurring problems that need to be addressed up-front to allow a faster set-up of a co-simulation scenario.

10.5 EXERCISES

1. List and discuss the different types of re-use.

2. Discuss the two types of packaging techniques that are used for re-usable verification components and discuss the pros and cons.

3. Discuss the purpose of system-level simulation.

4. Describe the differences between a directly and an indirectly implemented simulation accelerator.

5. Experiment with different scheduling schemes for Figure 10.16b. Try to minimize the number of steps needed.

6. Evaluate why it is wrong to run co-simulation in Figure 10.21b with a scheme that transfers the partially resolved bus values $b1$ and $b2$ between *model A* and *B*.

7. Using the verification plan and strategies for stimulus as outlined in Chapter 7 and the strategies for checking from Chapter 8, create a verification environment in which the verification components are re-usable (use your choice of HVLs). You will need to download the Calc2 HDL from the companion Web site for this book and create a simulation model using your vendor's engine. Describe any more bugs and indicate the test scenarios that uncovered them.

PART III

Functional
Specification

CHECKPOINT
Plan
Review

CHECKPOINT
Lessons
Learned

Create
Verification
Plan

Perform
Escape
Analysis

Stimulus, Checkers,
Formal Verification
Develop
Verification
Environment

Debug
Fabricated
Hardware

Systems
Test

Verification
Cycle

Run
Regression
Tests

Debug
HDL and
Environment

CHECKPOINT
Tape Out
Readiness

HDL

Designer
Implements
Functional
Specification

FORMAL VERIFICATION

Part 3 continues to focus on the portion of the Verification Cycle that focusses on the development of the Verification Environment. While simulation-based verification is the most widely used method of functional verification, formal verification continues to grow and meld with mainstream design efforts. In the past, formal verification was hampered by size constraints and language complexity, but advances on both fronts have opened the gates to widespread usage of formal techniques in functional verification.

Chapters 11 and 12 introduce formal verification, discuss the algorithms behind the methodology, and describe the Property Specification Language (PSL/Sugar). Major portions of the text are devoted to *Boolean Equivalency Checking* and *Property Checking*, the most widely used formal methodologies. Chapter 12 also includes a description of semi-formal verification, a leading method that melds formal techniques with simulation based methodologies.

CHAPTER 11

INTRODUCTION TO FORMAL VERIFICATION

In simulation, the verification environment visits one state of the design under verification (DUV) at a time. This process can be viewed as *state traversal*. The set of all possible states for a DUV is called its *reachable state space*. The overwhelming size of the DUV's state space is the biggest verification challenge (Section 1.1). Throughout this book, the main technique underlying all verification tasks is simulation of the DUV. However, there are severe limitations of this approach that will be discussed now.

At every state visited during simulation, checkers and monitors are active to test whether the state itself is legal and whether the DUV generates correct output results. Fast simulation engines and environment code enable a more efficient and faster state traversal. A key metric for the quality of the verification cycle is the amount of the DUV's reachable state space *visited and checked*. Simulation stimulus components of high-quality and coverage feedback ensure that the state traversal visits different and interesting states within the reachable state space, which again increases the efficiency of this process.

However, the size of the reachable state space does not allow an exhaustive, simulation-based state traversal for any interesting, real-life DUV. Therefore, simulation-based verification is fundamentally limited to checking correctness of the design in a case-by-case fashion. For any case not checked or design state not visited, the simulation-based approach cannot give any assurance that the design behaves correctly. This means that functional simulation in reality is *testing* and not really *verification* of the DUV. This is, for hardware design, the direct equivalent of what the pioneer computer scientist, E.W. Dijkstra, described with respect to program testing versus true software verification: "Program testing can be used to show the presence of bugs, but never to show their absence!" [57].

The promise of *formal verification (FV)* is to achieve stronger, true verification of the DUV instead of merely testing with simulation-based methods. FV can provide full verification for at least part of a DUV, full checking of properties for all DUV states, in contrast to the limited.

During the last decade, FV has established itself as a productive additional weapon in the arsenal of the verification team. This chapter discusses some basic principles of FV and introduces different methods and application areas. Many engineers still misunderstand FV as an academic approach. However, rapid improvements and much practical use of formal methods yielded advances in areas like specification and assertion languages. These advances not only improved productivity of verification methods in the formal field, but also have influenced simulation methods.

It is not the goal of this chapter to dive into the theoretical foundations of FV. Many texts contain these foundations, and they are recommended to the interested reader [58, 59]. In contrast, this chapter shows where FV fits into the overall verification cycle to give the verification engineer a more intuitive understanding of its strengths and weaknesses. The concepts behind FV are developed in this chapter. The discussion then follows the historic path of the successful application of FV technology to formal equivalence checking of two DUVs. Afterward, the goal of formal proofs from the simple property of equivalence to general properties of design correctness is generalized. Using the example of a simple bus arbiter as a backdrop, the basics of temporal property specification are introduced. Properties are one part of the FV environment, which is very similar in concept to the simulation environment introduced in Chapter 3. FV technologies process the model of the DUV and the FV environment together, using the paradigm of state exploration to prove that a property is valid or provide a counterexample. We end with an overview of the principles of property verification, which is the key application of FV techniques today. In Chapter 12 we apply these insights to the application of the practical tools available to verification teams.

11.1 FOUNDATIONS

The central focus of FV is the attempt to *prove* with mathematical certainty the correctness of a design. Proof means that the verification is exhaustive and therefore the checking is valid *for all cases*. This implies a mathematical rigor to FV. The advantage of the strong reliance on formal, mathematically sound methods is that the application of FV leads to true verification (as opposed to just testing) where completed successfully.

Because formal methods grew out of the field of theoretical computer science, the vocabulary and presentation of FV often uses mathematical terminology. This reliance on theoretical terminology can be intimidating and may even obstruct the view of the merits and difficulties of the application of FV in hardware verification. However, it is also true that as the field of FV matures rapidly, verification teams today can draw on many software tools that have formal methods at their core but do not require a detailed knowledge of the inner, theory-heavy mechanisms to apply them successfully.

In this way, the development of FV is very similar to the way simulation technology itself matured. For example, it is hardly necessary to understand the theoretical details of constraint solving algorithms to apply constraint directives in a simulation driver. However, a general understanding of constraint language constructs and the limitations of their applicability make the verification engineer more successful.

In this chapter, a structural rather than a detailed mechanical understanding of formal methods is provided. A few basic concepts are defined first, which are the foundation of the following discussion of formal methods for hardware verification.

11.1.1 Design Correctness and Specifications

The focus of the earlier chapters is on simulation of the hardware design language (HDL) representation of a DUV. Often we call the HDL the *implementation* of the design. It is important to remember that the correctness of a design is never just a statement about one particular representation of the DUV [60]. We can only postulate correctness of a design relative to a *specification*. A specification makes statements about properties an implementation of the DUV should realize.

Figure 11.1 shows an example of a hierarchy of specifications. The lowest two levels of the hierarchy are familiar from previous chapters. The gate-level representation implements the register transfer level (RTL) specification, which in turn is an implementation of a high-level specification of the DUV. The high-level specification could be, for example, the requirements specification for the DUV from a customer standpoint.

There are two types of specifications: *high-level models* and *properties* [58]. Both types specify what encompasses the correct behavior of an implementation.

First, a higher-level model is a complete operational or behavioral specification of the design implementation. The RTL model is an example

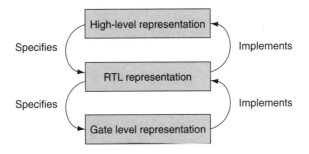

■ **FIGURE 11.1**

Example for three levels of design representations. The high-level design representation is the specification for the register transfer level (RTL); the RTL representation is the specification of the gate level. Every lower level representation is an implementation of the higher level specification.

of a high-level model specification for the gate-level implementation. The implementation realizes all functional aspects that the high-level model specifies operationally. We call the correctness of a DUV relative to an operational model *equivalence*. Equivalence checking verifies that the design implements all operations or behaviors of the specification. Equivalence checking was the first FV approach successful in the domain of industrial application and has been the most successfully applied FV technology to date.

The second type is the specification of properties. Properties are attributes of behavior that the implementation should always honor. By their very nature, properties do not provide a complete specification of the implementation but make a statement about functional *aspects* of the DUV. The description of the Calc1 design in Section 4.4.1 provides many properties. For example, a basic property of the design is the description of which output results to expect based on which input commands. The statement that the design services commands on a first-come, first-serve basis is another property of Calc1.

Properties can be *static* or *dynamic*. This classification is similar to the one we used in the introduction of assertions in Section 3.3. A static property is a condition that holds true in the design at one particular time or at all times. A simple example of the condition expressed for a specific point in time is the property that after power-on-reset, all latches of the DUV are initialized to "0." A static property example for all times is the condition that the parity bit on a data bus always indicates odd parity.

Dynamic properties are *temporal properties*. This is the more general, more powerful case of property specification. In fact, static properties are a subset of temporal properties. The typical example for a temporal property is resource management of data buses: A bus arbiter that receives a *bus_request* input signal issues the *bus_grant* output signal after a maximum number of cycles. The general form of such temporal properties states a series of events as pre-conditions and then postulates a sequence of events as post-conditions to be verified.

The specification of temporal properties is the most important, most successful specification mechanism used in modern FV approaches. The pre-dominant use of *property specification* in FV also makes the term *property checking* often synonymous with FV.

A design implementation, or DUV, is *correct* if all properties of its specification hold true. There are different ways to reach a correct design from a specification (Figure 11.2). The simulation-based approach translates the specification into drivers and checkers. The automatic synthesis method uses algorithms to create an implementation that is correct-by-construction. FV relies on a formal specification and proves that all properties of the specification hold true in the implementation.

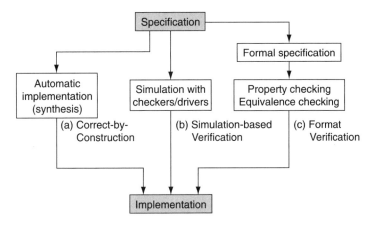

Three different paths to achieve a correct implementation from a specification. (a) Automatic tools are used to synthesize the implementation. (b) A simulation environment is derived from the specification for a traditional simulation-based verification methodology. (c) The formal verification (FV) approach that requires a formalized specification before the verification team can drive the FV flow.

11.1.2 Computational Complexity

This chapter began by stating again that the core verification problem is the exponential nature of the DUV's reachable state space. The exponential nature of the reachable state space exists independently of whether verification uses simulation-based or formal methods. The promise of FV, to offer a more complete verification than simulation, means that formal methods must address the state space traversal and checking in different ways from simulation. A quick side discussion about complexity introduces metrics helpful to appreciate the nature and size of the problem that we attempt to solve with FV. Complexity theory classifies problems based on the difficulty of their solution.

Computational complexity [61] is a sub-field of theoretical computer science that addresses the resources required to solve a computing problem. The most important resources are the time and memory (or space) required to run all the steps of an algorithm.

The *time complexity* to solve a problem is typically dependent on the size of the input to be processed. If we denote the size of the input with the number n, the time it takes to process the n inputs is a function of n. An abstract measure of time complexity does not account for the exact function, only how n factors into the function. Computer science has come up with the *Big-O* notation. If the time needed to process the input grows linearly with the size of the input, we say that the time complexity is $O(n)$ (called "order n"), whereas if the time grows quadratic with the input size, we say complexity is $O(n^2)$ (called "order n-square").

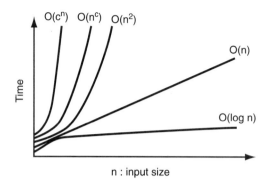

▪ **FIGURE 11.3**

Survey of time complexity classes drawn as graphs of time over the size of input that needs to be processed.

For example, the time complexity to simulate the scan ring dump procedure (Section 9.3.1) is $O(n)$: The time required to shift the scan ring grows proportionally with the number n of latches in the scan chain. If the designer creates double the amount of chains with half the number of latches, simulation only needs to run half the amount of cycles to scan all chains. If the simulation engine is a pure cycle-based engine (oblivious evaluation; see Section 5.5.2), half the amount of cycles means half the amount of time for the procedure. In any case, given the DUV does not change with the exception of the scan chain order, the time complexity of the procedure is linearly dependent on the length of the chains.

As a second example, the steps required to simulate all possible input patterns through a block of combinational logic with n inputs has a complexity of $O(2^n)$, which is exponential growth. Even with a modest increase in the number of inputs, the number of simulation steps grows rapidly, quickly making exhaustive simulation impossible for real-life designs. Figure 11.3 shows several classes of complexity functions as a graph of time over input size n.

The fastest growing are the quadratic, the polynomial ($O(n^c)$), and the exponential ($O(c^n)$) functions (where c is a constant selected such that it bounds the complexity with an upper limit). Complexity theory calls problems *intractable* whose algorithmic solution requires exponential time (or space/memory) in the worst case. There is much research to classify which verification problem has exactly which order of complexity.

For our purposes, it is sufficient to say that both the input space and the state space of a DUV grow exponentially ($O(2^n)$) with the number of inputs and the number of state bits. The problem of processing every element of a DUV's input and state space is intractable, and the exponential nature of this expansion is often called the *state space explosion problem* [62]. The complexity is exponential for either dimension: time and space/memory. Explicit state space traversal takes exponential time to visit all states, and storing information about every state explicitly takes an exponential amount of memory. The memory to store one byte of information explicitly per state of a DUV with 100 state holding elements (flip-flops, latches, RAM cells) would need 2^{100} bytes, clearly more than exhausting the address space of even a 64-bit workstation.

Simulation-based methods tackle the state space explosion with the attempt to verify only the *relevant* state space, guided by the verification plan and coverage feedback. Even though FV promises to provide proof or exhaustive verification, formal methods face the same state space complexity. In the remainder of this chapter, we explore the different ways in which FV technology addresses the state explosion problem.

11.1.3 The Myth of Linear Scaling of Simulation

What makes simulation so compelling as a verification algorithm is that the growth of the model and the decline of simulation speed are linear functions of the increase of DUV size, measured in number of RTL statements or gates. This behavior has kept simulation the main workhorse of verification while design sizes grew ever larger.

As we have seen, however, the verification problem grows exponentially. Verification teams must not fool themselves into the false sense of security when design growth goes parallel with only proportionally slower simulations (Figure 11.4).

The complexity of the verification problem does not disappear for the simulation approach. It is present in the fact that the overall simulation

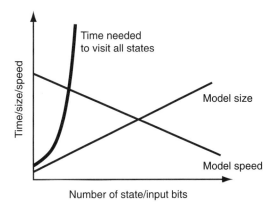

■ **FIGURE 11.4**

Simulation speed and model size scale linearly with increasing design under verification (DUV) sizes. The time needed to simulate the state space of the DUV, however, increases exponentially.

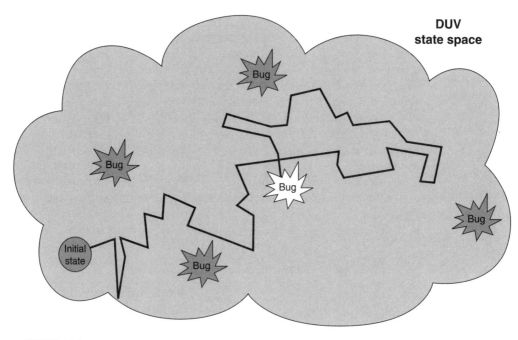

**DUV
state space**

■ FIGURE 11.5

Path of one simulation from an initial state through the reachable state space of a design under verification (DUV) to a design bug.

time needed to traverse the full state space grows exponentially. In the face of this exponential growth, a linear speed increase by faster simulators, parallel simulations in workstation farms, or hardware accelerators provides only some relief but brings simulation nowhere close to a possible exhaustive verification.

Figure 11.5 illustrates how a single simulation is akin to a random walk through the reachable state space of the DUV. Simulation proceeds one state at a time through the reachable state space. Smart drivers and coverage feedback guide the walk at every point until we hit, hopefully, a design bug.

Simulation is able to process state spaces of gigantic sizes (greater than 1 billion gates) but at the expense of state space coverage. This makes simulation-based methods very practical in the verification team's endeavor to find bugs. Simulation is not a strong method to confirm the absence of bugs.

11.1.4 Mathematical Proof Methods in FV

The use of mathematical transformations using symbolic logic is one form of FV. For combinational logic, the Boolean algebra and its axioms

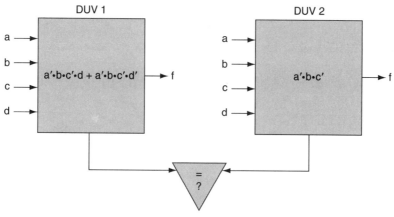

$a' {\cdot} b {\cdot} c' {\cdot} d + a' {\cdot} b {\cdot} c' {\cdot} d' = a' {\cdot} b {\cdot} c' {\cdot} (d + d')$: distributive law

$a' {\cdot} b {\cdot} c' {\cdot} (d + d') = a' {\cdot} b {\cdot} c'$: complementary theorem

■ **FIGURE 11.6**

The application of Boolean algebra to prove equivalence between two designs.

are the foundation for correctness proofs. Applying the axioms of the algebra and theorems, derived from the axioms, we can transform Boolean equations symbolically without changing their logic value. Figure 11.6 shows a simple example using algebraic transformations to show the equivalence between two Boolean circuits.

Automatic theorem provers are programs that let the user specify a statement (a *conjecture*) in symbolic form to prove it is a consequence of axioms and theorems, which the user loaded into the prover beforehand. The language for the axioms, the theorems, and the conjecture is usually mathematical logic. Theorem provers play an important role in the FV of some types of hardware, for example, floating-point units in microprocessors. Typically, these are areas where the direct application of mathematical theorems is very natural because the target design is the immediate implementation of a mathematical concept. A typical example is the verification of floating arithmetic units as described in Russinof [63].

However, their application requires a deep knowledge in mathematical logic, and the prover tool usually requires that an expert user closely guide the program through the mathematical proof steps. This, so far, prevents a wide application of theorem proving in industrial projects, with the exception of a few niche areas. For this reason, we do not discuss theorem provers any further. For the reader who wants to explore the capabilities theorem proving more deeply, we recommend the Web sites on ACL2 Language, HOL System, or PVS Specification and Verification System as starting points [64–66].

For the remainder of this chapter, we focus on the two most successful, automated methods of FV, equivalence checking and property verification.

11.2 FORMAL BOOLEAN EQUIVALENCE CHECKING

We start the deeper exploration of FV with a discussion of Boolean equivalence checking (BEC), where FV had the most successful application to date. Because the specification of the verification task is extremely simple, the equivalence of two different representations of the same Boolean function, we can use equivalence checking as a good introductory discussion to exhibit some of the algorithms and concepts that find use in many other FV applications.

The task of equivalence checking is a primary target for the application of formal methods for two reasons. First, it supports the important assurance that no design transformations, many of which occur in a VLSI design flow, harm the correctness of the design. Equivalence checking proves, which means it verifies exhaustively, that a design representation is functionally equivalent to its specification even after many manual or automated design transformations (Section 11.2.1). With this application, equivalence checking supports an implementation refinement flow that is correct by construction.

The second important application area for BEC is the proof of a DUV implementation against a higher-level model specification. The constraint is that high-level specification and implementation can only differ in the way they specify their combinational Boolean functionality because, as we see in the following sections, BEC only works if the states and state holding elements of the models compared are identical. Nevertheless, this allows the verification team to use the most abstract, concise, and implementation independent model of the DUV for the bulk of the functional verification work. With this second application of equivalence checking, the design and verification teams can use the higher-level model purely as a specification, not to drive a synthesis-based automatic implementation process.

For example, the design team might have to specify the actual design implementation as custom transistor circuits. If and only if formal equivalence checking can prove that the transistor netlist is functionally identical to the RTL specification can the verification rely on RTL simulation for the majority of the functional simulation work.

The alternative to the equivalence proof is simulation of a finite set of tests on both models with comparison of the results. As shown in above, this method is limited to a fraction of the actual DUV state space and, in addition, severely cuts into the precious simulation cycles available for the functional RTL simulation.

11.2.1 The Role of Equivalence Checking in the VLSI Design Flow

The modern VLSI design flow uses a number of manual and automatic design transformations between the RTL specification and the *physical netlist*, a design representation that is the input to the manufacturing process of the VLSI chip.

Figure 11.7 shows two alternative paths from the RTL specification to the physical netlist, the automated, tools-driven, and the custom circuit implementation. The automatic flow (Figure 11.7a) starts with logic synthesis, a program that maps the RTL specification into a pre-defined library of Boolean logic gates for the given, fabrication-specific, silicon technology. Pre-placement and wiring is the first *physical design* step.

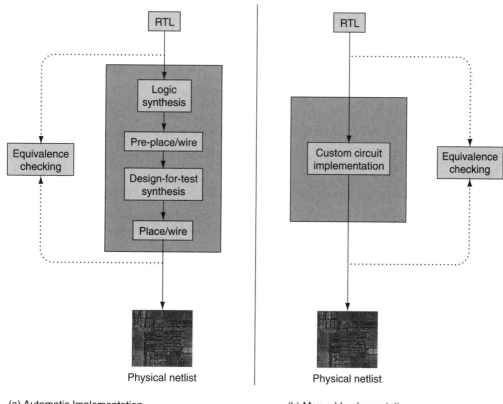

(a) Automatic Implementation   (b) Manual Implementation

■ **FIGURE 11.7**

The position of formal equivalence checking in a typical VLSI design flow. (a) The automatic implementation flow. (b) The alternate flow where a custom designer manually implements the circuit.

This step positions the gates into their approximate geometric location on the chip, using optimization criteria such as shortest wire length, wire noise-reduction, and timing as its primary constraints. *Design-for-test* synthesis supports the automated insertion of testability logic (scan ring and built-in self test, as discussed in Chapter 9, Testability and Built-In Self Test). The final placement and wiring step finishes the physical design of both the mainline and pervasive function.

BEC is vital to verify that all these tools in the automatic implementation flow operate without changing the function of the DUV. Figure 11.7a shows two inputs to BEC in the automated flow, the RTL and the physical netlist. This guarantees the checking occurs as closely as possible to the original specification and the final physical implementation and therefore covers all steps of the flow. However, it might be more practical for ease of debug to check the output of every step (e.g., logic synthesis) separately by comparing input and output data of each tool. Whereas the automated flow can be considered *correct-by-construction*, the use of BEC gives a guarantee that no tool bugs or tool application errors interfere with the correctness of the implementation. Automatic logic synthesis provides a great productivity advantage for the implementation of RTL designs into gate-level, whereas at the same time the tools-driven flow is much less error prone than a manual implementation. However, these tools are large software systems and possibly introduce errors during the transformation of the logic. BEC provides the necessary safety net to catch such tool errors.

The main reason for custom circuit implementation (Figure 11.7b) is the need for extreme physical optimization for speed or compactness of the design. Experienced circuit designers take the RTL specification and implement its function manually on the transistor level. The role of BEC in this scenario is even more vital than in the automated flow, because it checks against human errors inserted into the implementation.

11.2.2 Main Elements of an Equivalence Checker Tool

Figure 11.8 shows the breakout of the main components of a BEC tool. Because of the position of equivalence checking in the design flow, the checker needs to support the import of different input formats, which each have their own challenges. The import of the RTL specification requires a full HDL compiler. Various netlist formats used in the automated design implementation flow, including the gate-level netlist shown in Figure 11.8, need their specific input parsing function. The third class of import components is the circuit functional abstraction block. It reads the transistor-level netlist coming out of the custom design process and translates it into a switch-level specification. Using circuit pattern matching and switch-level simulation techniques, the functional abstractor then calculates the Boolean behavior of the switch-level netlist [67]. The abstraction has to map all dynamic circuit behavior to a static

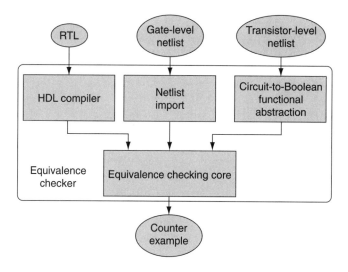

■ **FIGURE 11.8**

The main components of a Boolean equivalence checker tool. The core of the checker relies on import from the various input formats that exist in the design flow of Figure 11.7.

Boolean network that the BEC core can compare with the other input formats.

The result of all input processing is a design representation internal to the BEC tool that is uniform for all classes of inputs and is well suited for the tool's core equivalence checking algorithms. If the comparison shows any discrepancies between the design representations, the equivalence checker reports these in the form of at least one counterexample.

The most user-friendly presentation of a counterexample shows the differences of the compared DUV representations in the form of Boolean values back annotated into the two original design representations. With all signal values visible in the context of the original design specification, the designers productively debug the equivalence failure using the counterexample like a failing test pattern.

11.2.3 Sequential and Combinational BEC

The BEC core, shown in Figure 11.8, uses a common model to represent the design after the import into the equivalence checker. The model format is a data structure that represents the finite state machine (FSM) view of the design. Because the task is the comparison of two models, the tool reads in two different design representations and converts both to the FSM view.

Figure 11.9 shows the general scheme that connects two FSM with the input vector and connects the out vectors via a bit-wise XOR function

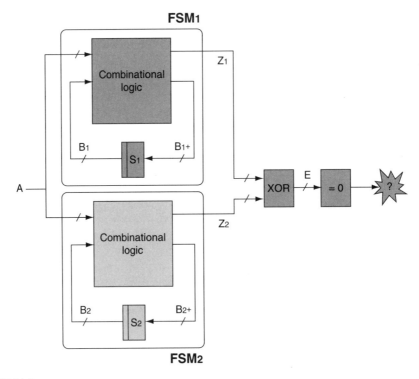

▪ **FIGURE 11.9**

The general setup for the proof of equivalence between state machines FSM_1 and FSM_2. Both machines are connected to the same input stimulus, whereas the outputs feed an XOR check condition. The checker proves equivalence by showing that vector E has a constant 0 value at all times.

condition. The state of both machines is stored in state-vectors S_1 and S_2, which are both initialized to their initial value set. The two state machines are equivalent exactly if the vector E on the output has a constant value of 0 at all times.

We know from the discussion of complexity (Section 11.1, Foundations) that the equivalence problem suffers from the exponential state space explosion. Even for small DUVs we have no way to use exhaustive simulation to prove equivalence.

The first step to a practical solution of the equivalence problem is a simplification of what we want to achieve. Figure 11.10 recasts the general problem to just a BEC problem by asserting that the state vectors of both machines are the same at all times. This means we drive the vectors B_1 and B_2 with the same value B and feed the next state vectors via an XOR-condition to a second output vector E_2. These changes assert that the state vectors of both FSMs are the same at all times, starting with the same initialization.

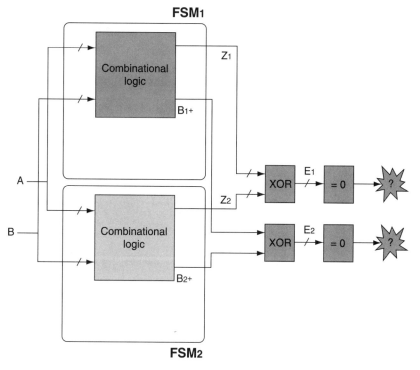

■ **FIGURE 11.10**

Simplification of the general equivalence checking problem to combinational Boolean equivalence. In addition to the inputs, now the state vectors are held to the exact same value at all times. With a second XOR condition, the next-state vectors B_1^+ and B_2^+ are checked for equality at all times as well.

The checker tool proves *combinational Boolean equivalence* if E_1 and E_2 are 0 at all times. Even after this drastic simplification of the original problem, BEC is still of significant practical use. It allows the exhaustive comparison of two state machines with the same set of states and the same initial state. The application in terms of the methodology flow, described above, means that the state vectors and the state encoding of the DUV stay constant after the definition of the RTL. This restriction is reasonable for most practical applications because many tool-driven design transformations and optimizations change the combinational part of the DUV only. We call the more general problem of FSM equivalence *sequential equivalence checking*.

A combinational Boolean equivalence checker does not have to explore the state space of the DUV, which makes the problem much more tractable. The reader should note, however, that exhaustive simulation still cannot solve the problem of combinational equivalence checking for practical DUV sizes. The amount of simulation steps necessary to step through each possible input value of the DUV grows exponentially with the number of inputs. Other methods and algorithms are necessary to address this complexity.

11.2.4 Core Algorithms for Combinational Equivalence Checking

The core task of BEC is a well-known research topic that has yielded several different strategies, which can lead to a successful equivalence proof. However, every single strategy has a worst-case behavior that leads to either exponential memory or time requirements. This is not surprising, because the base problem has exponential complexity. It turns out that many times the algorithms show their worst-case behavior under different conditions dependent on the structure of the DUV. Where one algorithm shows exponential behavior, another approach can still yield practical results and vice versa. A usable equivalence checker therefore requires the application of several different algorithms combined into one tool.

The most established techniques to BEC are the use of canonical representations and automatic test pattern generation (ATPG) or satisfiability testing (SAT) solvers. We start with a discussion of canonical forms followed by a description of the other techniques. Kuehlmann et al. first introduced a generalized hybrid approach of putting all these different techniques together into a hybrid approach as a multiple *solution engine* [67].

Canonical Forms

It is the main property of a *canonical form* that it represents every unique Boolean function in one unique way, independent of its original implementation or representation. One way to perform BEC is to translate two representations of the combinational logic of a DUV into a canonical form and check for identical results.

An example for a very simple canonical form is the truth table. Figure 11.11 shows two implementations of a DUV and the single corresponding truth table. As long as we order the input signal columns exactly in the same sequence (a, b, c), the truth table derived from any different gate-level implementation is identical. Once the BEC tool converts the implementations to their corresponding truth table, the equivalence proof turns to a simple comparison of all rows of f.

It is immediately clear that the truth table is not a practical canonical form for a BEC tool. The table grows $O(2^n)$, and therefore DUVs with more than 32 or 64 inputs overflow the virtual address space of any computer on which the tool could run. In addition, the comparison of the results column f also has a $O(2^n)$ complexity, meaning the time needed to do the actual, albeit computationally simple, comparison grows expo-

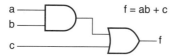

(a) Implementation 1 of Function *f*

a	b	c	f
0	0	0	1
0	0	1	0
0	1	0	1
0	1	1	0
1	0	0	1
1	0	1	1
1	1	0	1
1	1	1	1

(c) Truth Table for Function *f*

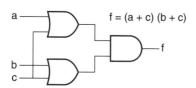

(b) Implementation 2 of Function *f*

■ **FIGURE 11.11**

(a) A gate-level implementation of a Boolean function "f." (b) An alternate, equally valid one. (c) The truth table for function "f" as canonical form that is the same regardless of the implementation.

nentially. The cost of the conversion from gate-level to truth table is also part of the total complexity of this algorithm.

From the truth table example we can derive four complexity criteria that all need to be considered when selecting a canonical form for a practical BEC tool.

1. Efficiency of the conversion into the canonical form

2. Memory requirement

3. Efficiency of the comparison of two representations of the canonical form

4. Efficiency to generate a counterexample in case of a miscompare

The last criterion is of trivial complexity for the truth table approach because the program can simply print out the values for *a*, *b*, and *c* for the first row of *f* that is not identical between the truth table of both DUV representations.

Another set of popular representations of Boolean functions are the *disjunctive normal form (DNF)* and the *conjunctive normal form (CNF)* (also called *sum-of-products* and *product-of-sums*) [68]. Figure 11.12a shows the two functions for the sum and carry signals of a multi-bit adder. The $c(i)$ function is already in DNF format. The function for $s(i)$ uses the *xor* operator and is therefore not a DNF. Figures 11.12b and 11.12c show the transformation of this function to DNF.

The main problem of using a DNF for equivalence checking is that a sum-of-products specification is not a canonical form unless it is a

```
s(i) = a(i) xor b(i) xor c(i-1)
c(i) = a(i)b(i) + a(i)c(i-1) + b(i)c(i-1)
```

(a) Multi Adder Logic for Adder Output Stage *i*

```
x = a xor b xor c
  = a'bc' + ab'c' + a'b'c + abc
```

(b) XOR function between 3 variables

```
s(i) = a(i)'b(i)c(i-1)' + a(i)b(i)'c(i-1)' +
       a(i)'b(i)'c(i-1) + a(i)b(i)c(i-1)
```

(c) DNF (sum-of-product) Specification of Adder Sum

▪ **FIGURE 11.12**

(a) The generalized combinational function for a multi-bit adder. (b) The XOR function for three variables are specified. (c) The equation of the adder sum into a sum-of-products notation is expanded.

minimized DNF. Many different DNFs for the same logic function exist (another example is Figure 11.11). Minimization of Boolean functions is a well-known exponential problem itself. This violates criterion 1 for a usable canonical form; the transformation is extremely inefficient. In addition, in the worst case, the DNF of combinational functions grows exponentially in size.

Figure 11.12a shows how the equation for the ith bit of an adder carry generator is recursively dependent on the $(i - 1)^{th}$ bit. Successive replacement of $c(i - 1)$ with the carry logic of the previous stage explodes the number of terms. The equation of a three-input XOR function is transformed into its DNF in Figure 11.12b to illustrate the exponential expansion during the translation of the XOR. Because the sum for stage i of the adder in Figure 11.12a is exactly such a three-input XOR, the sum of n-bit adder recursively expands into an exponential set of DNF terms, which makes the DNF unusable according to criterion 2 for canonical forms; the size of the DNF can become intractable.

The most popular canonical form is the *binary decision diagram (BDD)*, which is a graphic representation of Boolean functions. The currently common form of BDDs first appeared in Bryant [69]. A BDD is a directed graph with nodes labeled by the variables used in the Boolean function. Each node has two outgoing arcs, which are labeled with *0* or *1* and represent the value of the node's variable. The graph has a tree format like a decision diagram. We start with a randomly chosen variable as the root node and connect its outgoing 0/1 arcs. At the end of each arc, we connect the next variable node. This procedure continues until all variables are used. All outgoing arcs connected to the nodes for the last variable end at constant nodes for the values of 0 or 1. The leaf constants are chosen such that every path from the root to a leaf ends with

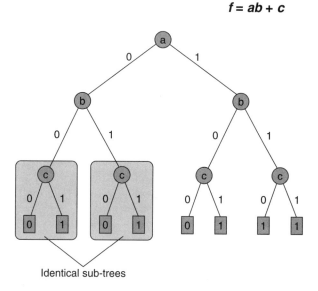

f = ab + c

Identical sub-trees

■ **FIGURE 11.13**

Binary decision diagram for the function $f = ab + c$. The diagram has a tree format starting with one arbitrarily chosen variable. For each Boolean value, the diagram branches to a subtree with the next chosen variable of function f as anchor. The two marked identical subtrees indicate that the value of variable b does not control the resulting value of f, which leads to the first simplification of the BDD in Figure 11.14, where we skip variable b altogether for this subtree of the diagram.

the function's result value for the valuation of its variables represented by the arcs chosen during the traversal.

Figure 11.13 shows such a BDD for the function used in Figure 11.11. At every level of the tree diagram, we use the same variable to label the next node (e.g., variable b on level 2 of the tree). Because this variable ordering is constant, we call this type of BDD an *ordered BDD*.

Figure 11.14a shows a simplification of the BDD in Figure 11.13. We have eliminated those nodes where the 0 and the 1 arc arrive at the same sub-tree, which means that this node does not contribute to the value of the function at all. The BDD of Figure 11.14b shows the same Boolean function but with a different sort order for the input variables. Clearly, the selection of this sort order affects the structure of the diagram and the amount of nodes and edges needed to represent the given Boolean function.

Finally, Figure 11.15 shows a *reduced ordered BDD* (ROBDD). In addition to the reduction achieved with Figure 11.14a, the ROBDD also merges *all* identical sub-trees to achieve this minimized form. The ROBDD for any given Boolean function is unique and therefore canonical, regardless of the original representation of the function.

f = ab + c

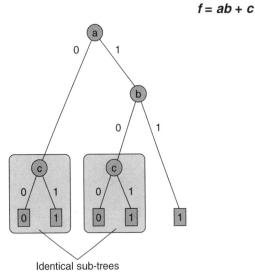

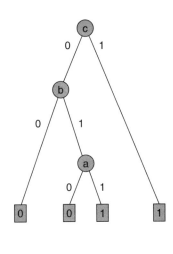

(a) BDD with variable sort order [a, b, c]

(b) BDD with variable sort order [c, b, a]

▪ **FIGURE 11.14**

Binary decision diagrams (BDDs) for the same function but with different sort orders have a different size, measured by the number of nodes and edges. Figure 11.14a marks the two instances of identical sub-trees that the ROBDD diagram in Figure 11.15 combines into one instance, thus reducing the size of the diagram even more.

f = ab + c   **f = a xor b xor c xor d**

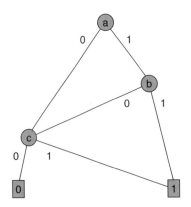

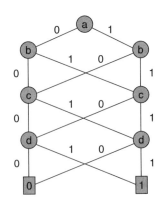

(a) ROBDD for **f = ab+c**

(b) ROBDD for XOR function with 4 variables

▪ **FIGURE 11.15**

Reduced ordered binary decision diagrams (ROBDDs) for two example functions. (a) The final ROBDD form of $f = ab + c$. (b) With the ROBDD of a four-input XOR function, how BDDs for this "hard" function grow only linearly with increasing number of inputs is illustrated.

One of the great practical advantages of BDDs is that they yield a compact representation of functions compared with other canonical forms. This is true even for some of the functions where the other representations explode in size when the number of inputs grows. For example, Figure 11.15b illustrates how the ROBDD for the multi-input XOR function grows only linearly with the number of inputs. In comparison, a truth-table representation for this function grows exponentially.

This does not mean BDDs circumvent the exponential complexity of the problem itself. There are classes of functions, for example, arithmetic functions like multiply or divide, whose BDD representation size grows exponentially with the number of input variable. In addition, in many situations BDD size is sensitive to the variable ordering. The growth in the number of BDD nodes per input variable for the same function can vary between linear and exponential depending on the choice variable ordering.

The problem to find the optimal variable ordering for minimal BDD size is again of exponential order. *This shows that complexity of the base problem never disappears completely; it just reveals itself in different aspects of the distinct algorithms.* Fortunately, research has found many good heuristic methods for variable ordering that BEC tools utilize when BDDs grow beyond a certain threshold.

However, BDDs behave well across a large class of Boolean functions, which cause problems for other canonical forms. The positive practical characteristics of BDDs discussed led to their popularity as the main canonical form for analysis of Boolean functions. This applies not only to equivalence checking but also to other applications in FV and logic synthesis.

ATPG and SAT Solving

ATPG is originally a domain of the field of manufacturing test (see Section 6.2.2). As shown in Figure 11.16a, the goal of ATPG is the generation of an input pattern that stimulates the combinational logic of the design in such a way that the outputs show a wrong result if the internal signal x is stuck-at-1 (or stuck-at-0).

ATPG algorithms can address equivalence checking if the search is directed toward patterns that show a *different* result on the equivalent outputs of the combined designs in Figure 11.9. In essence, BEC tools use ATPG to find counterexamples where the outputs Z_1 and Z_2 as well as B_1^+ and B_2^+ show a conflict.

The classic ATPG algorithms use implication and decision procedures [68] and work on a gate-level structural representation of the design. Starting from the stuck-at signal, ATPG uses forward and backward implication to find a pattern that reveals a wrong result.

In Figure 11.17, we see a simple example for the implication procedures used in ATPG. Figure 11.17a combines the two implementations

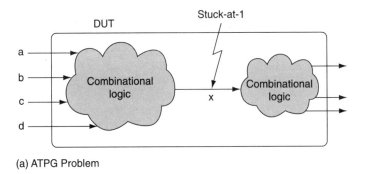

(a) ATPG Problem

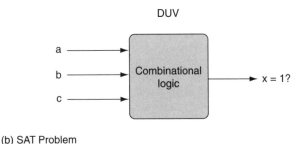

(b) SAT Problem

▪ **FIGURE 11.16**

Problem definitions for automatic test pattern generation (ATPG) and SAT. (a) A design-under-test (DUT). ATPG tools attempt to find a vector for inputs *a, b, c, d* such that a stuck-at-1 fault on the internal signal *x* is detected by a wrong result on the outputs of the DUT. (b) The general configuration for a SAT solver, whose goal it is to find an input pattern *a, b, c* that the value of output *x* is 1.

of the function used in Figures 11.11 into one combinational test design whose output *e* indicates whether the two implementations are equivalent. To make the example slightly more interesting, we inserted a problem into the second implementation with the inversion of signal *c* on the input of the gate *a OR c′* (marked with an inversion *dot*). In addition, we named internal signals in both design parts (*i1, i2, i3*) to be able to refer to them in the following.

The decision procedure (Figure 11.17b) starts at the output and postulates a miscompare. The following steps take this starting point and walk the design backward toward the inputs with the goal to either derive signal values by implication or choose signal values where a degree of freedom exists and the output conditions still hold.

Step (2) of Figure 11.17b executes a choice of values that satisfy the condition of step (1). This choice implies signal values in steps (3) and (4). Recursively working backward toward the design inputs, the procedure postulates implied values in steps (5) and (6). However, the implications do not completely force specific input values yet. Steps (5) and

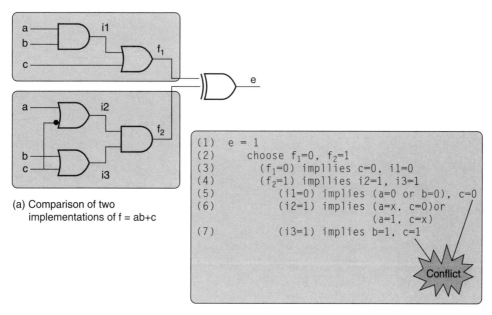

(a) Comparison of two
   implementations of f = ab+c

```
(1)   e = 1
(2)       choose f₁=0, f₂=1
(3)           (f₁=0) impllies c=0, i1=0
(4)           (f₂=1) impllies i2=1, i3=1
(5)              (i1=0) implies (a=0 or b=0), c=0
(6)              (i2=1) implies (a=x, c=0)or
                                (a=1, c=x)
(7)              (i3=1) implies b=1, c=1
```

Conflict

(b) Partial ATPG Implication Sequence

■ **FIGURE 11.17**

Example of a simple automatic test pattern generation (ATPG) procedure. (a) The two implementations of $f = ab + c$ as shown in Figure 11.11a/b combined by an XOR condition to show equivalence. Note the erroneously inserted inversion. (b) A snippet of a decision procedure that attempts to find an input pattern for *signals a, b, and c*, which reveals a miscompare and sets output e to 1.

(6) log the possible choices as *OR* conditions. Finally, step (7) concludes with an implication that contradicts an implication made in step (5).

Whenever the ATPG decision procedure finds conflict, it needs to backtrack to a decision (choose) point before the conflict. In the example, this *backtracking* step sets the procedure back to step (2) to start over with a different choice.

Full ATPG also must run implication forward from the stuck-at signal to the outputs to provide the expected fault results. In the worst case, the ATPG algorithm may require an exhaustive enumeration of all possible input patterns. This is clearly as intractable as exhaustive simulation. However, especially for cases where the two models are *not* equivalent, ATPG can efficiently reveal counterexamples. Even though ATPG becomes unusable under its worst-case behavior, it is a very practical tool for many real-life designs.

The SAT problem definition is similar to the starting point of ATPG. The difference is that a SAT solver attempts to find an input pattern that stimulates a single output signal to 1 (Figure 11.16b) as opposed to an internal stuck-at value propagated to the output. The SAT problem

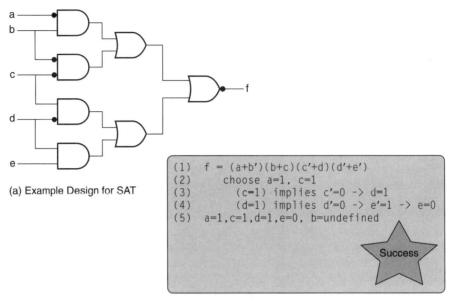

(a) Example Design for SAT

```
(1)  f = (a+b')(b+c)(c'+d)(d'+e')
(2)     choose a=1, c=1
(3)        (c=1) implies c'=0 -> d=1
(4)        (d=1) implies d'=0 -> e'=1 -> e=0
(5)  a=1,c=1,d=1,e=0, b=undefined
```

Success

(b) Example SAT sequence

▪ **FIGURE 11.18**

A simple example for the Putnam-Davis SAT procedure. The process converts the example design of a to a conjunctive normal form and applies the SAT solver algorithm in (b). Step (5) of the SAT procedure results in an input pattern for *a, b, c, d, e* that satisfies function *f*.

translates directly to equivalence checking, for example, in Figure 11.17a: If the SAT solver can prove that signal *e* cannot be satisfied (drive to 1), then it proves equivalence of the two implementations.

Figure 11.18 shows a simple example to introduce one of the popular SAT algorithms [70]. The gate-level design in Figure 11.18a implements function *f* from a DNF. The example shows a SAT process finding an input pattern that satisfies *f*, which is a simple Boolean function with no direct connection to equivalence checking.

The first step of this SAT algorithm is the conversion of the design into a CNF. This format is the basis for the Putnam-Davis SAT solver. The algorithm successively chooses a variable and replaces it with the value 0 or 1. At every such point, it recursively calls itself to choose the next variable value. If at the end of the recursion all variables either have defined values or are explicitly left undefined (variable *b* in Figure 11.18b), the assigned variable values satisfy the function. If at any point in the process the function cannot resolve to 1 because of a contradictory variable assignment, the algorithm backtracks to the last choice and takes the alternate assignment. If the program has chosen all alternate assignments and found no solution, the function cannot be satisfied (*UNSAT*).

There are many approaches to SAT solving. Kuehlmann et al. and Briere and Kunz are good starting points for an overview [71, 72]. Links to the newest research can be found in reference [73]. For insight into highly efficient SAT solver algorithms, we refer the reader to [74–76]. The improvements in SAT solvers during the last few years have made them a key component for hybrid multi-engine BEC tools.

Structural Analysis and DUV Partitioning

BDD analysis, ATPG, and SAT solvers all have a potential for exponential worst-case behavior requiring either intractable amounts of memory or time. Several heuristic techniques are available to cut down the size of the initial DUV representation to postpone the threshold where any of the actual equivalence algorithms exhaust the machine resources.

Structural analysis or optimization reduces the amount of redundancy in the DUV, whereas DUV partitioning attempts to divide the DUV into smaller pieces for which the BEC algorithms prove equivalence individually. Typically, DUV representations derived from HDL compilation show a redundancy rate of 30% to 50% [71]. The main sources of redundancies are replicated structures and signals tied to constants. Replicated structures originate either from timing optimization, where the designer parallelizes logic to lower the fan-out load, or from the repeated use of common library elements, which include the same equations inside. The use of common library elements is also the main source for tied signals: Universal building blocks offer more flexibility than needed in all instances, which is why in specific situations unused input signals are tied up or down to provide a default, don't-care function.

Heavy replication is also inherent to the task of equivalence checking. As shown in Figures 11.9, 11.10, and 11.17, the BEC tool receives an input model that connects two different representations of the DUV with XOR logic. Especially if both models are structurally similar, the DUV replications are a cheap target for simple redundancy reduction algorithms.

Structural optimization is, of course, by itself a problem with exponential cost. However, as we just discussed, the target for optimization is so large in practice that even simple, cheap heuristics have a chance to reduce the size of the model for BEC dramatically.

A selection of such simple heuristics contains

- Constant propagation
- Hash-based redundancy removal

Constant propagation works most effectively on a Boolean network model. The propagation algorithm takes constant inputs of Boolean

Model 1

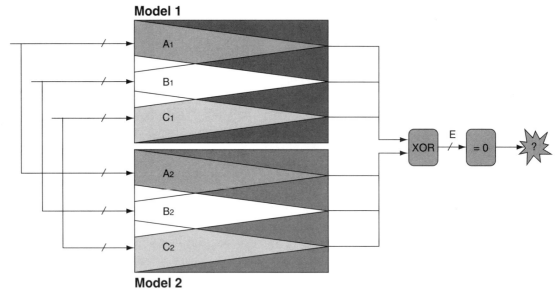

Model 2

▪ **FIGURE 11.19**

The horizontal partitioning approach to equivalence checking. The equivalence checkers take outputs from either model and compare only the logic that specifically drives these outputs. In this example, the comparison occurs between the pairs of logic partitions A_1, A_2, B_1, B_2, and C_1, C_2.

functions and attempts to *push them forward* to the sinks of the function. A constant *0* on an *AND* function propagates directly to its outputs. The same is true for a constant input on an *OR* function. In both cases the *AND* or *OR* can be eliminated. The hash-based redundancy removal records a unique hash-value for every block in a Boolean network model. The program derives the hash from the input signal names and the actual Boolean function of the block. Hash collisions quickly point to potentially redundant blocks that the optimizer can combine into one.

An even more powerful reduction approach for equivalence checking is *DUV partitioning*. We can differentiate between *horizontal* and *vertical* partitioning. Figure 11.19 illustrates the horizontal partitioning approach to equivalence checking.

The equivalence checker successively picks a pair of inputs, one per DUV model (*Model 1* and *Model 2* in Figure 11.19) for the check. It iterates over all DUV outputs. For each iteration step, the tool eliminates all the logic that does not directly drive the given outputs. This *cone-of-influence reduction* leaves only *logic cones*, cut out of the full DUV logic, for every comparison step. This transformation reduces the number of inputs into every compared cone and reduces the overall amount of logic per checking step. Modern BEC tools do this step automatically without user interaction.

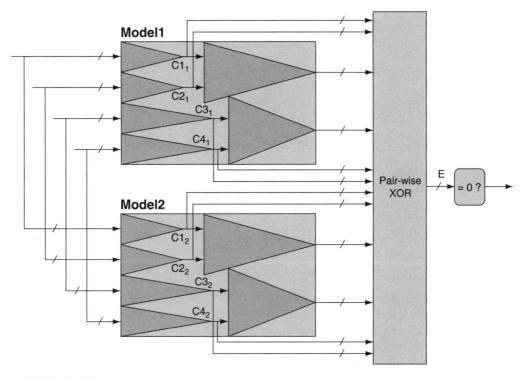

■ **FIGURE 11.20**

Vertical partitioning using cut points C1, C2, and C3 allows the comparison process to prove equivalence for smaller subcones with less number of inputs and logic. Horizontal partitioning only works if the equivalence checker can indeed prove that the cut points are Boolean equivalent. The XOR check now takes not only the model output to compare pair-wise but also the signals that represent the cut points in each model.

Vertical partitioning selects intermediate points inside the logic of either DUV model. This cuts the depth of the logic cones compared at each step as well as number of inputs and amount of logic covered by the cone. Figure 11.20 shows an illustration of this principle: C1, C2, C3 are the *cut points* for which the checker must prove equivalence for the partitioning to succeed. Either the user specifies the cut points manually or the BEC tool has built-in heuristics to find these automatically [77].

11.2.5 Blueprint of a Modern Equivalence Checking Tool

In this section, we want to put together all available elements and algorithms discussed into a single coherent design of a Boolean equivalence checker. Discussing the different algorithms at our disposal for this task, we learned that the fundamental exponential nature of the problem does not disappear using a single "magic" algorithm. However, the different

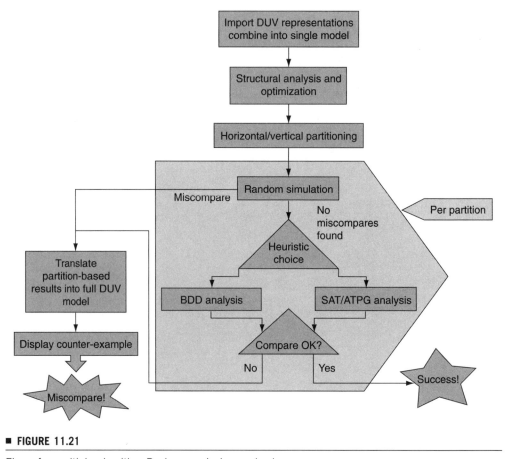

Flow of a multiple algorithm Boolean equivalence checker.

approaches have different strengths and weaknesses. This clearly leads to a desirable architecture that encompasses most of these algorithms and puts them together in a flow where heuristic choices select the appropriate times when a certain algorithm is most applicable.

Figure 11.21 shows a possible overall flow for such a hybrid, multiple algorithm, equivalence checker tool. After the import of both DUV representations, a structural analysis and optimization squeeze out as much redundancy of the combined model as possible, consistent with a reasonable turn-around time for the overall task. The partitioning algorithms follow afterward. Per partition, the BEC tool first uses simple random simulation, which cheaply filters out easy-to-find miscompares. Random simulation is an inexpensive filter, because it finds gross mismatches between the two models quickly. It is a heuristic choice of the tool how long to use random simulation before proceeding to the more expensive algorithms.

Heuristics are the basis for the choice between BDD-based or ATPG/SAT-based analysis. It is also possible to abort one algorithm in favor of the other, if it exceeds a certain time or memory threshold. Random simulation generally never concludes success; the BEC tool uses it only as a filter for easy-to-find fails. A non-fail result still is overall inconclusive with respect to equivalency. BDD or ATPG/SAT analysis can conclude either success or failure. Success means a proof of equivalence for the given partition. Failure means the result is inconclusive because the tool either exceeded resource limits or found a miscompare. In the latter case, the algorithm needs to generate a counterexample pattern, which it needs to enlarge from a partition-limited pattern to a DUV-wide pattern to allow efficient user debug. Only after all partitions prove to be equivalent can the tool signal the successful conclusion to the user.

Today's BEC tools have brought FV into the mainstream of verification. Without equivalence checking, the massive reliance of modern verification methodologies on fast RTL simulation would not be possible. BEC frees the verification team from most encounters with gate-level DUV implementations and certainly from the need to run massive simulation cycles on the switch-level implantation of aggressive custom circuit designs. All larger commercial electronic design automation vendors now include BEC tools in their offering, for example, Formality from Synopsys, Encounter Conformal from Cadence, or Formal Pro from Mentor Graphics, to name a few [78–80].

In addition, sequential equivalence checking, despite its increased complexity over combination equivalence checking, has made progress toward practical project application. The base technologies to prove sequential equivalence are the same as those used for functional property checking, which we discuss next.

11.3 FUNCTIONAL FV—PROPERTY CHECKING

We defined *property checking* above as the main focus for functional FV. As mentioned before, this limits the scope of our FV discussion to the subset of model-based formal methods and explicitly leaves theorem-proving methods aside. The reason is that property checking is overwhelmingly the most practically important technology in the industry today.

Central to property checking are of course the mechanisms to *specify properties* themselves. During the 1990s, a wide variety of property specification languages evolved. In the last few years, the electronic design automation industry organization Accellera has devoted considerable effort to standardize a common property specification language [81]. The result is the language PSL, which we discuss in detail in Chapter 12 [82]. In addition, assertion language concepts, to which property specification is closely related, have taken a hold in design language standards like

SystemVerilog as well [81]. In this section, we prepare the in-depth discussion of property specification tools in Chapter 12 with a close look at the basic principles underlying these tools. In this context, we introduce the FV environment, which consists of checker and driver components similar to the simulation-based environments. After the introduction of the principles of temporal logic, we conclude the section with an overview of a typical FV tools flow.

The target for model-based property checking is the FSM model of the DUV. To check formally that a design conforms to a property, it must be proven that for all states and all state transitions when the property is *relevant*, the FSM does not violate the conditions expressed in the property. The question is how to express in a systematic way when the property is relevant.

11.3.1   Property Checking Versus Sequential Equivalence Checking

Static properties are like assertions (Section 3.3): They are conditions that hold true for all possible states of a DUV. More general are temporal properties, which hold over a selected subset of the DUV's states. Static properties are merely the subset of temporal properties where that subset of states includes all states. Static properties can be expressed using Boolean logic expressions, for example, the *one-hot* value condition for a collection of enable signals of all drivers on a data bus. Temporal properties must in addition specify for which DUV states the checks need to hold.

Therefore, one practical way to specify temporal properties is the use of a state machine whose logic tracks the DUV state and applies the checking at the relevant states. The requirements for such a checker FSM are not different from those for a hardware specification, and therefore it is quite possible to implement a checker FSM with an HDL.

As Figure 11.22 shows, the checker FSM does need access to the inputs, outputs, and internal signals of the DUV. The checker tracks the DUV execution through its state space, keeps track of its own states, and generates a 1-bit signal for every property that it checks. These checker output signals indicate at every moment of time whether the DUV violates a particular property, and we name them appropriately *fail signals*.

We can recast the goal of functional FV. The task is to prove that there are no cycles with an active fail signal.

Properties that check DUV internal states are implementation-dependent assertions. Sometimes the access to internals is necessary, just as described in the gray, white, and black box discussion in Section 3.2.

Of course, this implementation of properties in Figure 11.22 is just a different view of an HDL test bench (see Chapter 5). It can be beneficial to use the HDL checker in simulation and FV. If the state space explo-

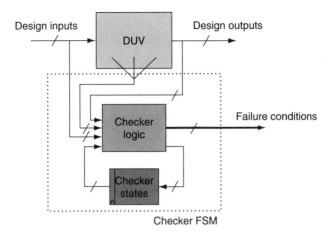

Design inputs   Design outputs

DUV

Failure conditions

Checker logic

Checker states

Checker FSM

■ **FIGURE 11.22**

A checker finite state machine (FSM) connects via inputs to the design under verification (DUV) (inputs, outputs, internal signals/state), keeps track of its own state, and generates a failure condition bit per property that it checks.

sion prevents the FV methods from proving that certain fail signals are always off, simulation can re-use the checker to verify those fails do not occur during all simulation cycles. This is a method to leverage the investment into the FV checker also if the FV problem turns out to be intractable. In general, the HDL checker needs access to DUV internal signals. As discussed in Chapter 5, this is possibly a problem when the RTL used is VHDL. HDL checker components need to be instantiated at the right levels of hierarchy to give the checker proper access to the DUV signals it needs to perform the verification.

The DUV is an FSM itself. A comparison of Figure 11.22 with Figure 11.9 shows that property checking is just a special case of the sequential equivalence check. If we assign the DUV to FSM_1 and the checker to FSM_2 and we make the checker observe and check all DUV outputs during all cycles, the setup of Figure 11.22 does check for sequential equivalence. The clock of the checker FSM is always the same as the DUV clock, as we discuss further in Chapter 12.

Sequential equivalence checking is a much more complete check of the DUV and is therefore harder than the checking of a collection of some functional properties. In fact, the more different the two representations are, the harder it becomes. Similar simplification techniques as were discussed above apply here to cut the equivalence-checking problem into smaller problems.

With the progress in practical FV algorithms during the last 5 years, sequential equivalence checking has made inroads into the methodology of real projects. Figure 11.23 shows one of the advanced schemes that have worked well for the verification of functional processing units.

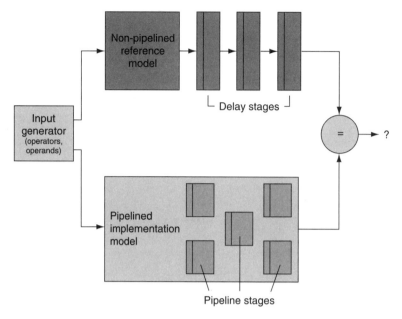

Application of sequential equivalence checking where the implementation of a pipelined execution unit is verified against a simplified, nonpipelined reference model. The delay stages of the reference model ensure that the time delay is the same for the outputs of the reference model and the implementation model.

In the example described in Jacobi et al., the verification team created an extremely simplified RTL reference model of a floating-point unit, which acts as a specification for the implementation model [83]. The reference RTL is less than 1/30th the size of the pipelined implementation and much easier to keep correct.

The verification team added a number of delay stages to the reference model to adjust the timing of its outputs to that of the implementation model, which pipelines its operations internally. In addition, the inputs of both models connect to an operand/operator input generator. This block creates all legal scenarios expected by the DUV. Leaving the model inputs open would be equivalent to allowing (and checking) all possible Boolean input values at all times, which is far more than the functional specification for the DUV prescribes. Jacobi et al. show in detail how they achieved a *complete* FV of the unit with this scheme [83].

11.3.2   The Myth of Complete Verification With FV

As usual for new technologies, exuberant proponents of formal methods accompanied the introduction of FV into the mainstream of verification with statements that created unrealistic expectations. A key promise associated with FV is that FV of a DUV is complete verification.

However, there are two main obstacles in the way of a complete verification with today's FV tools. First, the completeness of FV is equal to the completeness of the properties that the design and verification teams specify. Property verification, where the properties are short of a complete reference model, is bound to be incomplete. How many properties make a complete specification? The question of what defines completeness for a set of properties is still a topic of research [84]. It is important to distinguish clearly between the completeness of the FV of properties and complete verification. Successful FV means exhaustive verification of a property or set of properties. Only a complete set of properties, formally verified, means complete verification.

The second obstacle against complete verification with FV is the practical difficulty of proving properties against the state space explosion. To circumvent the problem of exhausted memory or unlimited runtime requirements, the FV team typically specifies constraints on the input values and sequences the tool should pursue. If the DUV inputs are unconstrained, the state exploration has to consider every possible input value at every state. Clearly, the user must constrain the inputs to the legal set of input sequences already to avoid false fails based on completely open inputs. This is the purpose of the FV input driver, which we discuss below. In many cases, the reachable state space of a real-life DUV is still too large for an exhaustive exploration even with the constrained inputs. Therefore, it is common practice to constrain the inputs even further and consider just a subset of the functionality per FV tool run. We call this technique *case splitting* and discuss it further in Section 12.3.4. Figure 11.24 shows how the DUV state space is limited per one FV tool run by input constraints. Eventually, the FV tool will run out of resources, which also limits the state space that the FV covers exhaustively even further.

In summary, simulation drives a single (possibly long) scenario and checks multiple properties (Figure 11.5). FV in practice drives all possible input scenarios while only checking a single property at a time. Where FV algorithms run freely over the reachable state space, checking is exhaustive. Typically, however, the team has to partition the exhaustive exploration into constrained subsets of the reachable state space within which the verification coverage is complete. As a result, FV has the strength of full exploration within a constrained state space, which is a powerful method to gain absolute confidence in the correctness portions of a design. It is the task of the verification team to select those portions where complete verification is possible and desirable.

11.3.3 Properties for an Example Design

In this section, a small example is studied, the design called *ARB* in Figure 11.25, to make the discussion of property checking more concrete. *ARB* is a simple design that arbitrates the access to an unspecified

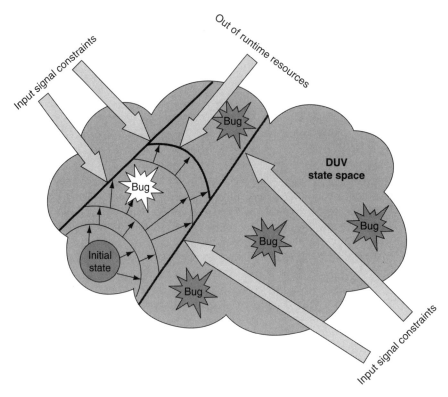

▪ **FIGURE** 11.24

Practical limitations against a complete state space traversal with formal verification (FV) technologies. The state space exploration starts with an initial state and proceeds from there through all reachable states while checking a property. The concentric rings starting at the initial state mark the consecutive exploration steps. To circumvent the problem of state space explosion, the scope of the traversal is constrained. Arrows illustrate how constraining the design under verification (DUV) inputs limits the state space considered by the traversal. The user specifies which input sequences should not be considered. The example shows the exploration to exhaust the available runtime resources after four steps. We highlight one property violation as a detected bug (white star).

resource between three requestors. The requestors apply for resource access by raising their assigned input bit of vector *req[0:2]*. Once *ARB* sees the input *cmd* asserted, it must grant the resource to one of the requestors by raising their corresponding bit on *ARB*'s output vector *gnt[0:2]* after a fixed amount of cycles. Figures 11.25a–d lay out the details of the specification for *ARB*.

In Figure 11.26 we translate the *ARB* input assumptions and behavior specification into the topology of a DUV connected to a protocol checker and a property checker. The purpose of the protocol checker is simply to watch over the environment of the DUV and raise an error if the actual signal interaction violates the input assumptions of Figure 11.25. The main focus is on the property checker with its various inputs and the

Input assumptions:

(1) cmd is an active-high pulse that can occur at most every two clock cycles.

(2) If cmd is active, req[0:2] is not "000".

(3) req[0:2] is valid only when cmd is active.

(4) If gnt[i]='1', req[0:2] must be '000'.

(b) ARB input Assumptions

ARB behavior specification:

(1) gnt[0:2] is valid (one-hot) two clock cycles after cmd was active and '000' at all other times.

(2) The valid gnt[0:2] must correspond to one of the req[0:2] signals that were active when cmd was active.

(3) The internal signals a and b cannot be on at the same time.

(d) ARB Behavior Specifications

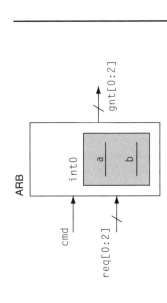

(a) ARB I/O's

(c) ARB Example Timing Diagram

■ **FIGURE 11.25**

Specification of the ARB example DUV. (a) The input/output pin specification. (b) The assumptions about the environment driving ARB on its inputs. (c) The behavior of ARB with an exemplary timing diagram. (d) The specification ARB's expected behavior both on the outputs as well as on some internal observation points.

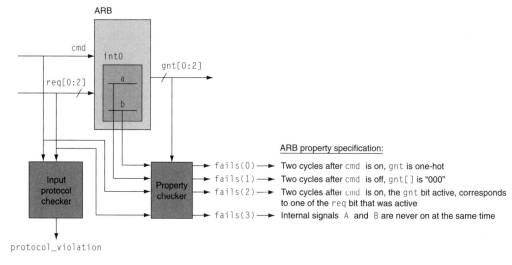

■ FIGURE 11.26

This model connects an input protocol and a property checker block to the DUV (ARB). The outputs of the property checker represent the four properties written out in English language and connected next to their corresponding fails() bits. The fails() bit turns on if the DUV violates the specification.

four *fails()* output signals. Every *fails()* bit represents one of the four properties that we check.

If verification finds any legal way to stimulate *ARB* such that one of the *fails()* bits turn active, a property violation and therefore a design bug is identified.

In Figure 11.27, we finally translate the property specification for *ARB* into an HDL checker. The module has two *always* blocks. The first *always* block tracks *cmd*'s presented at the inputs of *ARB* and counts the cycles after every such event. Two state bits indicate the significant intervals needed for the check of the property condition: two and four cycles after *cmd* was active. The second *always* block simply uses these interval marker bits to initiate the correct Boolean checks at the right time and raise the corresponding *fails()* bit if the check fails.

The first three properties are all *temporal* in nature. They depend on a specific state indication as provided by the first always block. The last property (*fails[3]*) is a static property because it is checked every cycle regardless of whether *ARB* is processing a *cmd* or not. The checker FSM encoded in the first *always* block captures the time boundaries for the activation of the temporal properties of *arb_property_checker*. In this example, the state machine is relatively simple because we can naturally encode the state in a cycle counter. For more complex output protocols, it is necessary to implement several FSMs, which might all be more elaborate.

```verilog
module arb_property_checker( clk, cmd, req, gnt, a, b, fails);
  output req [0:3] fails;
  input cmd; input [0:2] req; input [0:2] gnt;

  reg [0:2]counter; reg [0:2]save_req; reg cmd_pending;

  reg two_after_cmd; reg two_after_cmd_down;

  initial begin counter = 0; cmd_pending = 0; end;

  always @(posedge clk) begin

    if (cmd==1) begin
      cmd_pending = 1; save_req = req;
    end

    if (cmd_pending && (counter < 3)) counter = counter + 1;
    else begin
     counter = 0;
     cmd_pending = 0;
    end

    if (counter==2) two_after_cmd = 1; else two_after_cmd = 0;
    if (counter==3) two_after_cmd_down = 1; else two_after_cmd_down = 0;
end

always @(posedge clk) begin

  fails = 4'b0000;

  /* property 0 */
  if ((two_after_cmd) && (gnt != 3b'001) && (gnt != 3b'010) && (gnt != 3b'100)) begin
    fails[0] = 1;
  end

  /* property 1 */
  if ((two_after_cmd_down) && (gnt != 3b'000) begin
    fails[1] = 1;
  end

  /* property 2 */
  if ((two_after_cmd) && ((gnt & save_req) ==0) begin
    fails[2] = 1;
  end

  /* property 3 */
  if (a& b) fails[3] = 1;

end
endmodule
```

■ **FIGURE 11.27**

Verilog implementation of the ARB property checker.

It is an option for the verification team to drive an FV effort with *arb_property_checker* or to instantiate that module into a simulation model. Obviously, if the FV effort can *prove* that any or even all of the *fails[]* bit can never be on, we have a much stronger statement, one of true verification, compared with running many simulation cycles.

A closer study of the Verilog checker shows that the code clearly takes into account that the inputs of *ARB* follow a specific protocol correctly. For example, if *cmd* stays on for more than one cycle, the first *always* block in Figure 11.27 will not work correctly. This is a perfectly valid way to code the property checker, as long as either the environment guarantees conformant behavior by the driver or the protocol checker is in place. HDL assertions or an explicit input protocol checker, like the one shown in Figure 11.26, protects the checker from overly constrained assumptions on the DUV input interface.

This example, as simple as it is, should demonstrate that the specification of properties in an HDL could be quite tedious and error-prone. Four sentences in English turned into almost a page of Verilog code. This overhead is one of the reasons for the development of *property specification languages*. Such languages, because they are domain-specific, can be much more concise and therefore a real productivity boost for property specification tasks. Even more importantly, a concise specification in such a language can be easier to understand and maintain and therefore safer for the FV process overall. We discuss property specification languages in more detail in Chapter 12.

11.3.4 DUV Drivers for FV

Like simulation-based verification, FV needs a model for the environment of the DUV. If the inputs of the DUV are open, which means no source drives them, the FV process must assume any input value combination at any time is legal and possible. This is necessary because FV's goal is to *exhaustively* check or prove the properties. Open inputs imply that the customer could plug the DUV into any context with any temporal behavior. We say that in this case the inputs are *unconstrained*.

In practice, it is rare that a DUV can really function correctly in a totally unconstrained environment. As with in simulation, however, it is desirable to consider as few constraints on the DUV inputs as possible. The proof of a property for a DUV is stronger if fewer constraints are assumed on the inputs. For example, assume the DUV block of Figure 11.26 would still function correctly even if the environment supplied new requests every cycle. We would not encode into the property checking implementation the constraint that *cmd* can be on at most every other cycle. As a result, the FV team would have to prove all three temporal properties under fewer constraints, which would make the DUV itself more robust for diverse environments.

In Figure 11.26, we protect the FV environment from false input behavior with a protocol checker. This is only a passive function. In addition, just like in simulation, the FV effort needs the specification of an active *driver* that provides stimulus to the DUV inputs. The driver's role is to drive all possible input stimuli into the DUV but constrain the input values enough so that the property checker does not report *false fails*. A

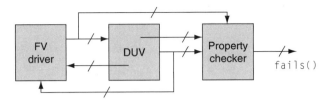

■ **FIGURE 11.28**

The complete functional formal verification (FV) environment creates a closed model. The FV driver supplies all possible input stimuli. The property checker traces inputs, internal states, and stimulus over time and asserts every cycle via the fails() signals, whether the DUV complies with the properties of the functional specification.

false fail is a DUV bug report created by an input stimulus that will never occur in the DUV's real target environment.

Figure 11.28 shows how the complete functional FV environment creates a closed model with a driver on the DUV inputs and the property checker connected to the outputs. The whole purpose of the FV effort is to prove that the *fails()* signals are always "*0.*"

If this exhaustive proof via FV is successful, we have 100% confidence that the DUV is without bugs for the properties specified. This is a verification result with the highest confidence possible. However, it is important to understand the caveats of this statement! As mentioned above, the completeness of the verification is dependent on the completeness of the set of properties. We also see it is dependent on the completeness of the FV driver. FV drivers must be as *complete* as possible in their specification of all legal inputs stimuli over time—otherwise the purpose of FV is defeated.

The most effective way to gain completeness for the input stimuli is to leave the value unspecified. An unspecified value for an input implies *all possible values.* For a bit-level signal, this means *both* 0 and 1 are specified, and an exhaustive method must use *both values.* Even though FV algorithms must explore simultaneously all possible values of an unspecified signal, we call such signal *non-deterministic.* A non-deterministic signal assumes all values in FV, whereas, if used in a simulation model, a simulation driver would chose a random value from the legal value set.

Non-determinism is a powerful means to specify FV drivers. A signal can be set to a non-deterministic value for all times or for a specific time. Figure 11.29 shows two different views of how to use non-determinism to specify all possible inputs to the *ARB* DUV in Figure 11.26. The flowchart specification (Figure 11.29a) makes the two random choices an operation of the driver. First, a random number 1 to *n* is chosen as the cycle delay before generating a new *cmd* signal value of 1. Second, there is a random selection of eight choices for all the possible bit-pattern for

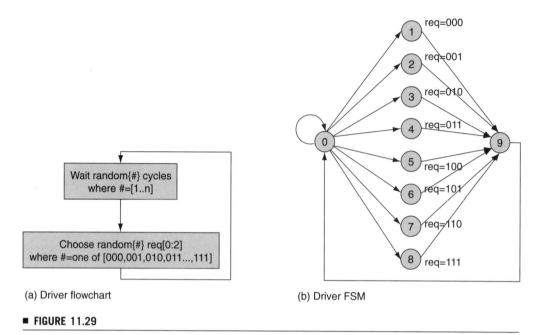

(a) Driver flowchart   (b) Driver FSM

▪ **FIGURE 11.29**

Two equivalent ways to specify the nondeterministic generation of all possible requests on the ARB (Figure 11.26) input interface. (a) Flowchart that uses random selection for the *req[]* input. (b) Non-deterministic state diagram.

the *req[]* vector. We can view Figure 11.29a as the *operational* specification of an *ARB* driver. The state-diagram (Figure 11.29b) specifies a non-deterministic state-machine for the *ARB* driver. States 1 through 8 supply all possible *req[]* patterns to the DUV input. The non-determinism means that the driver FSM is in all states 1 to 8 at the same time. When applied to our FV problem, the exhaustive state exploration will have to explore states 1 to 8 in conjunction with any legal state the *ARB* can be in at the same time.

In summary, we use non-determinism to express concisely all possible combinations of stimulus. A simulation run chooses one *random* value at a time; an FV tool exhaustively visits *all possible choices*.

Just as we used HDL to specify properties above, it is possible to specify an FV driver using HDL constructs. Mostly, the FV driver is a standard FSM. The only new construct needed is a function that selects non-deterministically from a range of possibilities. Such a function would allow operations similar to the ones described in Figure 11.29a. VHDL is sufficiently powerful to define such a function. The System Verilog extension of Verilog provides similar capabilities. The standard simulation semantics of either HDL indeed executes a random selection. If such a specification is the input to an FV tool, the tool applies the broader, all-choices-at-the-same-time interpretation.

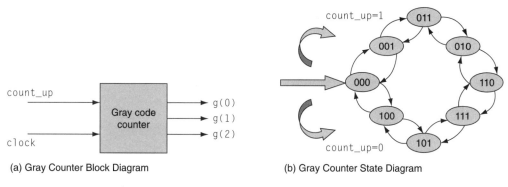

(a) Gray Counter Block Diagram   (b) Gray Counter State Diagram

■ **FIGURE 11.30**

A simple gray counter as a basis for the discussion of temporal logic. (a) The input/output signals of the counter. (b) The counter's state diagram. For simplicity, the state encoding is identical with the encoding of the output vector *g(0)* to *(2)*. The state transition in the counterclockwise direction occurs if the *"count_up"* input is 0 and *"count_up=1"* results in the clockwise direction. A thick arrow marks the initial power-on state "000." Again, for simplicity of the discussion, no reset line is specified on the gray counter's input side.

The property specification language PSL has a *modeling layer* that contains extensions to Verilog, which serve exactly the purpose to specify FV drivers as described here [81].

11.3.5 State Space Traversal and Temporal Logic

Temporal properties assert specific behavior to the DUV relative to the DUV's progression through its reachable state space. Temporal logic is a system of specification that allows the expression of relationships between assertions at different times. There are different versions of temporal logic, and there is much in-depth literature about the topic [58]. We start the discussion with a simple example DUV.

Figure 11.30 shows the state diagram and the input/output signal definitions. The encoding of the states, which is identical to the value of the output vector of the block, exhibits the behavior defined for Gray encoding: For every up- or down-count transition, only one bit of the state vector changes. From the initial starting state, the counter steps up or down one Gray encoding word at a time. If we draw out the progression of all states that the counter can possibly visit, we arrive at the unfolded, expanded state, transition diagram of Figure 11.31.

We defined temporal logic as a way to express assertions over time. The following bulleted list shows queries that are examples for such assertions, which can be answered using the unfolded state transition diagram of Figure 11.31.

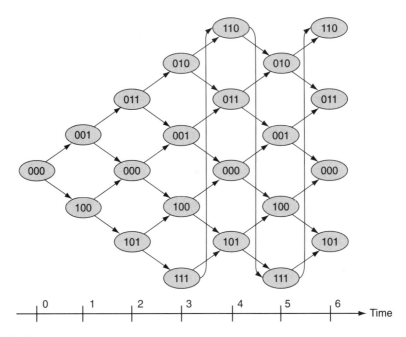

▪ **FIGURE 11.31**

Expansion of all possible state transitions of the gray counter from Figure 11.30 over time. Every time step represents a cycle (from left to right), starting with the initial state "000." Every arrow that leaves a state in the upward direction represents the state transition for "*count_up=1*"; every array going in the downward direction indicates "*count_up=0.*"

- Is there a path from the initial state that reaches the value **g()="111"**?

- Starting at state **g()="100"**, is it possible to return to that state in five cycles?

- For every state transition, does the value of the vector **g()** always change in one bit?

As the state space unfolds in Figure 11.31, it becomes apparent that we do not encounter any new states or state transitions after time step 5. A state exploration, which follows this expanded diagram, is said to have reached a *fix point* when it only continues to repeat transitions that were encountered before.

The graph in Figure 11.31 represents a tree (turned side-ways in this figure). In fact, we can represent every state exploration in this tree format. If the FSM has several possible initial states, all these states will be roots of the tree.

One variant of temporal logic, called *linear time logic (LTL)* has operators that let us specify properties based on sequences of time steps. If

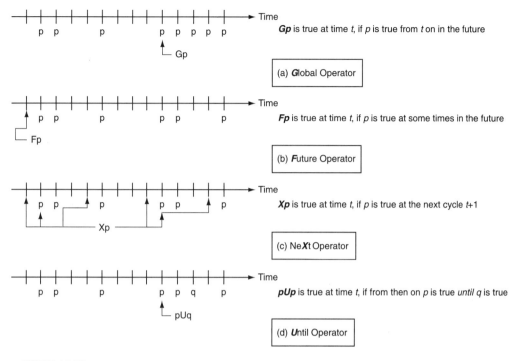

A selection of temporal operators of linear time logic (LTL). These operators allow specification of properties that bind the base property **p** to a relationship with events in the future. (a) The **G** (**G**lobal) operator that specifies a time from when **p** is true for all future times. (b) Example of **F** (**Future**), the operator that specifies a time from when **p** is true sometimes in the future. (c) Ne**X**t operator that specifies **p** is true during the next cycle. (d) Example of the **U**ntil operator.

p is a basic static property or assertion (e.g., "vector **v** is one-hot encoded"), then the formula "*Operator **p***" specifies a temporal property. Figure 11.32 illustrates several LTL operators [85]. **p** typically is a Boolean formula.

A more powerful type of temporal logic, called *computation tree logic (CTL)*, allows specification of properties based sets of paths through the exploration tree. CTL pairs the LTL operators from Figure 11.32 with operators that specify a set of paths. Figure 11.33 shows some CTL examples using a graphic notation. The set operators, or *path quantifiers* [62], that are part of CTL are

- A: for *all* future paths in tree
- E: there *exist some* future paths in the tree

The FV jargon includes a popular classification of types of properties that we discuss briefly here. We call properties based on *Fp* operator

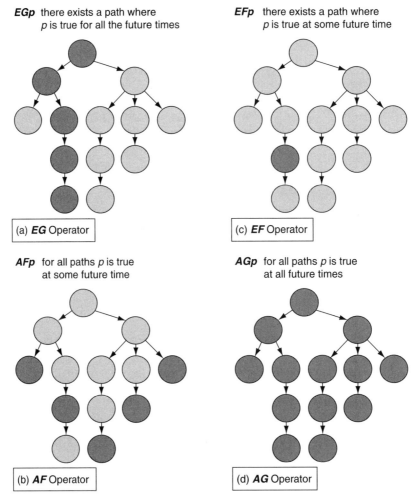

EGp there exists a path where
  p is true for all the future times

(a) **EG** Operator

EFp there exists a path where
  p is true at some future time

(c) **EF** Operator

AFp for all paths *p* is true
  at some future time

(b) **AF** Operator

AGp for all paths *p* is true
  at all future times

(d) **AG** Operator

▪ **FIGURE 11.33**

Computation tree logic operators specify properties for sets of paths in the state exploration tree. The dark shaded circles represent states for which the property **p** is true. (a) The existence of one path through the tree for which **p** is true at all times. (b) All paths have at least one time step were **p** is true. (c) The condition that there is at least one time step in one exploration step where **p** is true. (d) Application of the operator pair that requires **p** to be true all the time.

liveness properties. A liveness property expresses a desirable state that occurs eventually at some future time. *Safety properties, based on the **Gp** operator,* are those that specify that the DUV never violates the property.

These two classes are important because their computational complexity is dramatically different. The search space for a liveness property is potentially unbounded. A tool can prove a liveness property only if the algorithm used to traverse the reachable state space can actually find a

TABLE 11.1 ■ Two Properties of the Gray Counter Example of Figure 11.30

There is a path from the initial state that eventually reaches the value g() = "111"	EF (g() = "111")
Starting at state g() = "100," there is a path that returns to that same state in five cycles?	AG(g() = "100"→ EX(EX(EX(EX(EX(g() = '100'))))))

fix point, which indicates it can contain the full reachable state space in the computer's memory. For many DUVs in practice, a liveness property might not be solvable (or provable) because of the state space explosion. On the other hand, a tool can check a safety property at every state that it is able to explore. If the tool cannot explore all states, the proof is limited to those states that are containable within the computers memory or are reachable in a reasonable time. However, even if a full exploration is not possible, the tool produces results for all the explored states.

In practice, we often can transform liveness properties into safety properties by limiting the amount of cycles that the tool is supposed to explore into the future. For example, instead of specifying that *eventually a grant follows a request*, we can specify that *every grant follows a request after at most x cycles*. This limits the checking of the property to at most *x* cycles and makes the problem more tractable.

The practical use of these LTL and CTL notations is limited. In fact, the authors of *Sugar* chose the name for the PSL/Sugar property specification language to allude to the *syntactic sugaring* of CTL—deliberately done to make temporal expressions more intuitive and user friendly [82]. However, it is important to understand the underlying concepts of how property languages cast the specification of time systematically into the description of *paths* and *sets of paths* through the state space.

After a little experimentation with these operators, it becomes clear how the temporal logic can specify properties far more concisely than the manual implementation of the checker FSM as used, for example, in Figure 11.27. Table 11.1 applies CTL operators to express two properties of the Gray counter of Figure 11.30. In Chapter 12 we do not use CTL directly because it has lost most of its practical value in the field. For complex temporal properties, CTL formulas tend to become quite complex, which makes them hard to maintain and error-prone. The modern property specification languages apply a much more user-friendly, intuitive syntax. The principles of the temporal logic, introduced by LTL and CTL, however, remain the basic foundation of property specification.

11.3.6 Functional FV Tool Flow

Now we have all the ingredients necessary to discuss the nature of functional FV tools. An RTL model represents the DUV. We express

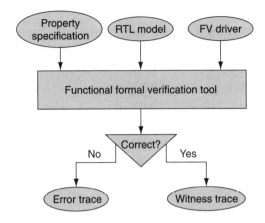

■ **FIGURE 11.34**

General flow for a functional formal verification (FV) tool.

properties in temporal logic. In addition, most DUVs require their inputs to follow a specific protocol and cannot tolerate the inputs to take on any possible value at all times. Therefore, the third input element necessary for functional FV is the input driver. Figure 11.34 shows the general flow for a functional FV tool.

The outputs of the FV tool are traces for the error and the success case. In the case of a property violation, the error trace shows one example of signal values and state space traversal that leads to the error. A welcome benefit of FV algorithms is that in most instances the algorithms produce the *shortest* possible trace that leads to the error.

Even in the case that the tool finds no property violation, the user will find a *witness trace* very helpful for analysis. A witness is a trace that shows one example where the property was true. The value of this trace is that it allows a user to see the actual effect and interpretation of the abstract property for the actual DUV. Temporal properties can be very compact, and therefore it is easy to overlook subtleties in the timing behavior of the property. The witness trace gives the user a different viewpoint on the property, showing it in a procedural behavior whereas the specification uses a declarative formula unless HDL checkers are used. The witness trace shows the user whether the tool interpreted the property in the intended fashion or not.

11.4 SUMMARY

In this chapter we introduce the reader to the basic concepts of FV. All previous chapters described verification methods that addressed the finite amount of state exploration that limits simulation. The generation of stimulus and the methods of functional coverage are all techniques that attempt to drive simulation into *interesting* areas of the design— areas thought to be complex and error prone.

FV starts with a bold premise that we can do much better than simulation. This premise states that we can use exhaustive state space exploration and mathematical methods to prove that a design is correct for all conditions.

The first part of this chapter introduced an important an imminently practical method of FV, equivalence checking, especially BEC. We learned about different classes of algorithms that all have a role in what is the fundamentally intractable problem of proving that two representations of the same DUV are equivalent. In the end, it is necessary to use a whole collection of these algorithms synergistically because no single one works in all cases.

Functional FV is an even harder problem. It entails either sequential equivalence checking or property checking. Using high-level specification and equivalence checking with the RTL implementation for pipelined execution units is an emerging promising field of FV.

We base property checking on a similar framework as in simulation. There is a need for an input driver to constrain the stimulus that the FV algorithms evaluate on the DUV inputs. We can implement the properties in basic form as checker FSMs in HDL. However, more powerful and concise methods are available to specify temporal properties.

In the next chapter, we discuss practical property specification languages and applicable algorithms that are the basis for functional FV tools. As with the equivalence-checking problem in this chapter, the key to success lies in the application of several algorithms together to prove properties. The algorithms used there are remarkably similar to the one we use for equivalence checking here.

11.5 EXERCISES

1. Assume one full simulation cycle for the *ARB* DUV of Figure 11.25 takes 1 msec. How long does it take to use simulation to drive *ARB* through all possible input patterns? If the number of requestors grows from 3 to 16, how much longer would a complete simulation take?

2. Implement the protocol checker of Figure 11.26 in HDL.

3. Re-write the property checker of Figure 11.27 in VIIDL. Implement the protocol checker of Figure 11.26 as VHDL assertions that are integrated into the VHDL checker code.

4. Implement a random stimulus generator for the *ARB* DUV of Figure 11.26 in VHDL.

5. One possible implementation of a Gray code counter (Section 11.3.4, DUV Drivers for FV) uses a binary counter and combinational logic, which translates binary code to gray code. Implement a Verilog version of such a Gray counter implementation. Implement an HDL checker with three *fail* signals that encodes the three example Gray code counter properties of Section 11.3.4.

6. Define the combinational function that transforms a 3-bit binary code into Gray code in two ways: first using a truth table and second using a Karnaugh-Veitch diagram. Translate both into a BDD and show the Boolean equivalence between the two equation sets developed using the two methods.

7. List additional Gray code counter properties that were omitted from the list of examples in Section 11.3.4.

USING FORMAL VERIFICATION

Chapter 11 introduced functional formal verification (FV) as a method that uses exhaustive state exploration to prove properties of a design under verification (DUV) and find bugs in the design. The mathematical rigor of Boolean and temporal logic is the basis for the specification of properties. A complete FV environment includes the model of the DUV itself, the formal specification as a set of properties, and an FV driver, which specifies all possible input stimuli for the DUV. Figure 11.28 shows a block diagram with all basic elements of a complete FV environment: the DUV, the property checker, and the FV driver.

The discussion now turns to the more practical side of FV. A design and verification team needs productive mechanisms to use the formal technology. This includes all components of the FV environment. For the DUV model, the focus is exclusively on the register transfer level (RTL) representation, because it plays the main role in the verification cycle. Chapter 14 introduces high-level modeling and its FV application for the pre-RTL phase of the design. The arrival of well-designed, intuitive, property specification languages makes the specification of property checkers accessible to verification teams as well as designers. Property specification has matured to the point where it is subject to industry standardization, and in the case of PSL it also covers the field of FV drivers.

Whereas the electronic design automation (EDA) industry converges on standardized languages for the FV environment, the FV tools and algorithms are still heavily evolving and the focus of much advanced research. Any practical FV tool has to address the main roadblock of this discipline, the state space explosion. There are two main goals of research and development addressing this problem. First, there is development of new algorithms to extend the frontier where the actual DUV state space exceeds a tool's capacity. Improvements in this area lead to an improved baseline of tools usable for FV. Second, there is focus on user-friendly ways to let the engineers specify which areas of the state space are more "relevant" to explore than other areas. This approach accepts the inevitable capacity limit and addresses ways to let the user guide the power of exhaustive state exploration into areas where the DUV has higher complexity and bug rates.

This chapter has three parts. First, a review of an approach to embed property specifications into the realm of hardware design languages (HDLs) by encapsulating classes of properties into HDL library blocks that the user can simply instantiate into the DUV where properties need to be checked. Then an overview of the property specification language PSL, which is the most developed stand-alone property specification language in the industry at this time. We do not expect the reader to be conversant in PSL after this introduction. It is more important to build a conceptual framework that positions PSL such that it is easy to study the wealth of further material that is available in specialized books and on the Web. In the third part, we discuss current FV algorithms and their strengths and weaknesses as well as the evolving discipline of semi-FV.

The focus on PSL in this chapter is a good example for a property specification language. At the time of this writing, PSL has moved further through the maturation and standardization process of the industry. The upcoming alternative to PSL is SystemVerilog, which has many attributes that parallel PSL [86]. We expect the reader will be able to project the discussion of PSL with relative ease to SystemVerilog, especially since the underlying FV technologies are the same.

12.1   PROPERTY SPECIFICATION USING AN HDL LIBRARY

Although it is possible to specify properties with pure HDL constructs, the approach is not very productive (see Figure 11.27). Coding of properties more complex than a simple Boolean assertion and especially temporal conditions is very error-prone because it is hard to decipher the original intent from a sequence of implemented HDL code.

On the other extreme, property specification with computation tree logic (CTL) or linear time logic (LTL) was standard practice for FV engineers in the 1990s. However, the very abstract mathematical character of these formalisms did prevent a broader use of FV techniques by design and verification teams. As the assertion-based methodology became more popular, it became important to have notations that are more productive to lower the entry barrier to these new technologies.

We demonstrate the middle ground between plain HDL coding and the use of mathematical formulas by discussing two projects whose goal it is to define a concise, easy-to-learn property specification method for designers and verification engineers. The two projects are the Open Verification Library (OVL) and the Property Specification Language (PSL), both of which are products of the EDA consortium Accellera [87]. We discuss OVL in the next section and reserve The Property Specification Language PSL completely for the overview of PSL.

12.1.1 The OVL

The OVL project groups classes of properties, which occur often in typical design situations, into a library of assertions that can be instantiated in standard HDLs (Verilog/ VHDL). The authors implemented OVL as a pure HDL library that is freely accessible on the Internet; it is usable by any project and all tools that support the host HDL can automatically work with this library. This means that OVL is useful both in a simulation and in an FV flow.

OVL contains a set of Verilog modules and VHDL entity/architectures, one for each property class. These OVL elements are assertion monitors marked with the name prefix *assert*. The engineer specifies a property by instantiating such a monitor in the HDL of the DUV or the test bench. Every monitor has a set of ports that probe the DUV and feed the DUV state to check logic inside the monitor.

Currently, OVL consists of 31 library elements. The standard uses a consistent interface for all these assertion monitors. Figure 12.1 shows the scheme OVL assertions are instantiated in both Verilog and VHDL. The *parameters* (*generics* in VHDL) personalize specific aspects of an instance of an assertion monitor, like the error message to be printed, a severity level to be associated with a violation of the assertion, and options for FV tools. Naturally, the ports are the means by which an assertion monitor connects to the logic of the design in which it is instantiated. Parameters are always constants passed into the monitor, whereas the ports provide the variable state of DUV that the assertion checks every cycle. Figure 12.3 shows a fully developed example of instantiated OVL assertions in Verilog.

Each OVL assertion has four main elements that define its functionality (Table 12.1). The first three elements use signals connected via the ports of the assertion instance. The parameters of the instantiation supply the reporting element.

The port name for the *triggering event* is *clk* to indicate that the primary intention is to synchronize assertion checking with a clock in the DUV. Most OVL monitors have the port *clk*. Assertion and event sampling always occurs with the positive edge of *clk*. Every monitor instance specifies a control signal, the *enabling condition*, which can enable or disable

```
VERILOG:  assertion_name #( parameters ) instance_name ( arguments );
VHDL:     instance_name : assertion_name generic map ( parameters ) port map ( arguments );
```

■ FIGURE 12.1

All Open Verification Library assertion monitors are instantiated using the same scheme. The assertion_name denotes the name of the specific assertion monitor in the library. The parameters specify severity level and assertion error message among other controls of the assertion behavior. The arguments are the signal ports of the assertion element that connect the checking logic to the DUV.

TABLE 12.1. ▪ Main defining elements of an OVL assertion

Triggering Event	A specific event like a clock synchronizes the checking of the assertion condition.
Enabling Condition	Assertions have an individual condition that enables/disables the monitoring.
Tested Condition	This is the asserted condition that is checked each time the triggering event occurs.
Reporting	Message and severity used to report an assertion violation.

the assertion at any time. The OVL documentation uses the port name *reset_n* for this signal. This name designate one intended use of this port is to indicate that an initial reset phase has finished during which the assertion check should not be active and assertion violations are expected and not an error. A zero value for *reset_n* implies the assertion is active. In addition, OVL provides a global variable that allows overall control of all assertions in the RTL model. This gives the model environment, for example, a test bench, global control over all assertions.

Table 12.2 lists all assertion monitors that the OVL standard currently defines, together with a short explanation of their function. Actual usage examples follow in Figure 12.3.

The simplest monitor types check combinational conditions (*assert_always, assert_never, assert_always_on_edge, assert_even/ odd_parity, assert_one_hot/cold assert_zero_one_hot*). They exist primarily to provide a base assertion infrastructure with the convenience of a packaged functionality that can be tedious to code directly in an HDL. An instance of *assert_one_hot* conveys the intent of the check more directly than a series of equations that implement the "one hot" condition.

All other OVL monitor types specify sequential properties. They sample and capture DUV states and express conditions expected to occur over time. The complexity of the specified sequential conditions ranges from checks for simple value transitions (*assert_transition, assert_increment/decrement, assert_no_underflow/overflow*) to the synchronization of two dependent events (*assert_implication, assert_handshake,* various window assertions) and finally to complex general event sequences (*assert_cycle_sequence*) that approach the generality of LTL properties as described in Chapter 11.

The OVL evolved from an assertion-based simulation methodology. The library's greatest strength is that it came from a real project environment with its features grounded in the needs of real design and verification engineers. The interface to the library elements is systematic. Ports and parameters with the same names have the same semantics and always occur in the same sequence.

A very clear strength of OVL is the support for infrastructure provisions concerning clocking and control of the assertions. When OVL

TABLE 12.2. ■ OVL assertion monitors

Name	Ports	Semantics
assert_always	clk, reset_n, test_expr	Continuously assert *test_expr*.
assert_always_on_edge	clk, reset_n, sampling_event, test_expr	Continuously monitor *test_expr* at every specified edge of *sampling_event* (edge type specified by parameter).
assert_change	clk, reset_n, start_event, test_expr	Continuously monitor *start_event*. Once *start_event* occurs, check for change in *test_expr* within specified number of *clk* edges (parameter).
assert_cycle_sequence	clk, reset_n, event_sequence (n:0)	*event_sequence* is a concatenated vector (n, . . . , 0). Monitor starting event (vector index n). Once starting signal is true, check for events (vector indices n-1 to 1) to occur in subsequent cycles of *clk*. If the starting signal occurs again, the sequence is re-started. A parameter defines whether the assertion checks (a) that all events must follow once monitoring starts or (b) that the last event (vector index 0) must occur once all previous events did occur.
assert_decrement	clk, reset_n, test_expr	Assert value of *test_expr* will never decrease more than parameter value.
assert_delta	clk, reset_n, test_expr	Assert *test_expr* will always change within the bounds of two parameter values.
assert_even_parity	clk, reset_n, test_expr	Assert *test_expr* always has an even number of bits asserted.
assert_fifo_index	clk, reset_n, push, pop	Monitor and accumulate number of *push* and *pop* values over time. Assert that the accumulated value stays within the range specified by a parameter value.
assert_frame	clk, reset_n, start_event, test_expr	When *start_event* is true, *test_expr* must be true within minimum and maximum cycle range specified by parameters.
assert_handshake	clk, reset_n, req, ack	Highly parameterized monitor for *req* and *ack* signal pair; asserting (a) no multiple *req's* without an *ack* (b) no *ack* without a *req* (c) no multiple *ack's* for one active *req*.
assert_implication	clk, reset_n, antecedent, consequene	If *antecedent* condition then assert *consequence* condition will occur.

TABLE 12.2. ■ *Continued*

Name	Ports	Semantics
assert_increment	clk, reset_n, test_expr	Assert *test_expr* never increases more than parameter value.
assert_never	clk, reset_n, test_expr	Assert *test_expr* is false.
assert_next	clk, reset_n, start_event, test_expr	Assert *test_expr* is true a parameterized number of cycles after *start_expr* is true. Supports overlapping sequences where a new start_event occurs before the previous sequence is finished.
assert_no_overflow	clk, reset_n, test_expr	Assert *test_expr* never changes from max value to a value greater than max or reach a value less than or equal to a min value. Max and min are parameters of the instance.
assert_no_transition	clk, reset_n, test_expr, start_state, next_state	Assert *test_expr* never changes value from *start_state* to *next_state*. Note the flexibility because *start_state* and *next_state* are variable expressions.
assert_no_underflow	clk, reset_n, test_expr	Assert *test_expr* never changes from min value to a value less than min or greater than a max value. Max and min are parameters of the instance.
assert_odd_parity	clk, reset_n, test_expr	Assert *test_expr* always has odd number of bits asserted.
assert_one_cold	clk, reset_n, test_expr	Assert *test_expr* has at most one bit off or inactive state with all zero bits or all one bits depending on parameter.
assert_one_hot	clk, reset_n, test_expr	Assert *test_expr* has always exactly one bit on.
assert_proposition	reset_n, test_expr	Assert *test_expr* at all times; there is no clock or triggering event for synchronization.
assert_quiescent_state	clk, reset_n, state_expr, check_value, sample_event	Assert that *state_expr* equals *check_value* when *sample_event* is true.
assert_range	clk, reset_n, test_expr	Assert *test_expr* never has a value outside a min/max range, inclusive. Min and max are parameters of the instance.
assert_time	clk, start_event, test_expr	Assert *test_expr* is true for at least a parameter-specified number of cycles after *start_expr* is true.

TABLE 12.2. ■ *Continued*

Name	Ports	Semantics
assert_transition	clk, reset_n, test_expr, start_state, next_state	Assert *test_expr*, once its value reaches *start_state*, always changes to *next_state*. Note the flexibility because *start_state* and *next_state* are variable expressions.
assert_unchange	clk, reset_n, start_event, test_expr	Assert *test_expr* stays unchanged once *start_event* occurred. Check that the value remains unchanged for the number of cycle specified by parameter.
assert_width	clk, reset_n, test_expr	Once enabled, assert *test_expr* holds between min and max number of cycles. Min and max are parameters of the instance.
assert_win_change	clk, reset_n, start_event, test_expr, end_event	Assert that once *start_event* occurs, *test_expr* changes its value at least once before or at the cycle when *end_event* becomes true.
assert_win_unchange	clk, reset_n, start_event, test_expr, end_event	Assert *test_expr* does not change between occurrence of *start_event* and *end_event*.
assert_window	clk. reset_n, start_event, test_expr, end_event	Assert *test_expr* holds between occurrence of *start_event* and *end_event*.
Assert_zero_one_hot	clk, reset_n, test_expr	Assert *test_expr* has always has at most one bit on.

emerged in public, typical FV property specification languages still simply assumed a single centralized clock in the DUV, which made the specification of a synchronizing clock unnecessary. However, many designs have multiple synchronous clock domains, which make the specification of a reference clock for sequential properties important. A simulation environment usually drives the DUV through phases where it initializes the DUV, at which time the checking of functional assertions (e.g., bus collisions) would trigger false assertion fails. Therefore, it is of great practical importance that assertions have a global enable/disable mechanism such as OVL provides.

Figure 12.2 illustrates how OVL assertions, which are instantiated in the DUV or in the test bench driving the DUV, can be used as targets for FV tools.

The example DUV in Figure 12.2 has two clock domains. It is necessary that each internal assertion have a provision to specify to which of the two clock domains it belongs. The assertions use their clocks for two purposes. First, the design clock domain itself updates its state machines with this clock and the assertion logic needs to sample the DUV logic synchronously. Second, this same clock updates the internal state monitoring machine, which implements the sequential assertion tracking. Figure 12.2 shows three instantiated assertions that are target for FV tools to prove. The assertion on the input signals is a *constraint*. The user specifies with an instantiation parameter whether an assertion is a constraint or not (Figure 12.3). Constraints on input signals specify behavior that the FV tool can assume to be illegal and therefore never to occur.

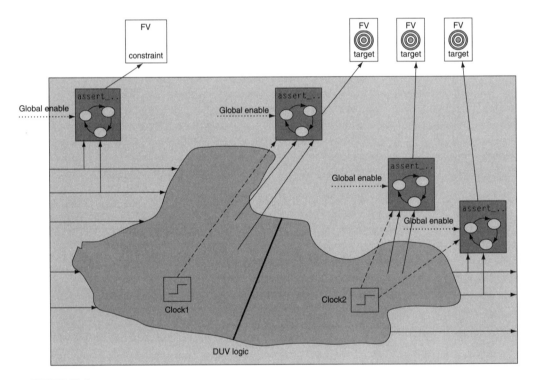

▪ **FIGURE 12.2**

Instantiation of OVL assertion monitors in a design under verification (DUV). The design has two separate clock domains driven by their own oscillators. Each of the three DUV internal assertions connects to their respective clocks (dashed arrows) for synchronization. The stylized state diagram inside the assertion boxes indicates that all assertions can be sequential and need to use the clock of their design target clock domain. A global enable signal controls when the assertions are active. The three internal assertions define target properties for formal verification (FV) tools. A supported OVL parameter declares the assertion on the DUV inputs as a constraint. FV tools use constraints as assumptions of behavior that does not occur.

TABLE 12.3. ■ Input Constraints and Properties of the ARB Design

Constraint 0	*cmd* is active high and can occur at most every two clock cycles
Constraint 1	If *cmd* is active, *req[0:2]* is not "000"
Constraint 2	*req[0:2]* is "000" when cmd is not active
Constraint 3	*req[i]* is "0" when *gnt[i]* is '1'
Assertion 0	*gnt[0:2]* is valid, one-hot, two cycles after *cmd* was active
Assertion 1	*gnt[0:2]* is "000" two cycles after cmd turns inactive
Assertion 2	the valid *gnt[i]* must correspond to one of the *req[i]* that were active when *cmd* was active
Assertion 3	The internal signals *a* and *b* are never on at the same time

12.1.2   Using OVL to Specify Properties

We now return to the example design of Chapter 11 (see Section 11.3.2) the arbiter ARB. For quick reference, we repeat the input assumptions (constraints) and properties specified in Figures 11.25 and 11.26 here in Table 12.3.

Again, we assume a Verilog implementation where we separate the DUV from the property checker code. Please note that this is not necessary if we can implement the assertions exclusively as instances of OVL assertion monitors. The OVL elements are internally marked "verification only" to be excluded from logic synthesis or Boolean equivalence checking and therefore do not pose a problem for the implementation process of the DUV because they are excluded there.

In Figure 11.26, we separated the input protocol checker from the property checker. Because all OVL assertion monitors have a parameter that lets the instance specify whether it is a real assertion or whether it is meant to be used as a constraint, we can group the four constraints that define the input protocol into the property checker for convenience. This grouping is useful for the case of the ARB design where the input protocol checker mostly needs the same input signals as the property checker.

Figure 12.3 shows the complete Verilog code for the combined input protocol and property checker *arb_property_checker*. We add another input signal, *reset_n*, which lets the environment that instantiates the checker decide when to arm the assertions. All other inputs are identical to the plain Verilog checker of Figure 11.27. We name the constraints and assertions after their entries in Table 12.3 and we use exclusively OVL assertion monitors to implement them. Constraint 3 actually multiplies out into three separate assertions, one for each bit of the *req* and *gnt* vectors.

Every assertion monitor instance has its associated parameter values as well as the port connections. We use comments to clarify the seman-

```verilog
module arb_property_checker( clk, reset_n, cmd, req, gnt, a, b);
    input cmd;   input [0:2] req; input [0:2] gnt; input reset_n;

  reg [0:2] savereq;

            // parm 1 = severity
            // parm 2 = number of cycles that test_expr must be true after start_expr
            // parm 3 = restart flag
            // parm 4 = assertion is constraint for FV tool
            // parm 5 = fail message
  assert_time #(30, 1, 0, 1, "cmd is active more than once cycle")
    constraint0 (clk, reset_n, cmd == 1, cmd == 0);

            // parm 1 = severity
            // parm 2 = assertion is constraint for FV tool
            // parm 3 = message

  assert_implication #(30, 1, "cmd active without valid request")
    constraint1 (clk, reset_n, cmd == 1, req != 3b'000);

  assert_implication #(30, 1, "request is on while cmd is off")
    constraint2 (clk, reset_n, cmd == 0, req == 3b'000);

  assert_implication #(30, 1, "req[0] is on when gnt[0] is on")
    constraint30 (clk, reset_n, gnt[0] == 1, req[0] == 0);
  assert_implication #(30, 1, "req[1] is on when gnt[1] is on")
    constraint31 (clk, reset_n, gnt[1] == 1, req[1] == 0);
  assert_implication #(30, 1, "req[2] is on when gnt[2] is on")
    constraint32 (clk, reset_n, gnt[2] == 1, req[2] == 0);

  // save the last request
  always @(posedge clk) begin
    if (cmd==1)begin
      savereq = req;
    end
  end

            // parm 1 = severity
            // parm 2 = number of events to be checked
            // parm 3 = check all events in sequence not just first and last
            // parm 4 = assertion is constraint for FV tool
  assert_cycle_sequence #(30, 3, 1, 0, "gnt not one-hot two cycles after cmd")
    assertion0 (clk, reset_n,
               { cmd==1, 1b'1, ((gnt==3b'100) || (gnt==3b'010) || (gnt==3b'001)) });

  assert_cycle_sequence #(30, 3, 1, 0, "gnt is non-zero during off time")
    assertion1 (clk, reset_n,
               { cmd==0, 1b'1, (gnt != 3b'000)});

  assert_cycle_sequence #(30, 3, 1, 0, "illegal gnt result")
    assertion2 (clk, reset_n, { cmd==1, 1b'1, (gnt & savereq) != 0 };

            // parm 1 = severity
            // parm 2 = option for FV
            // parm 3 = fail message
  assert_never #(30, 0, "a and b on at the same time!")
    assertion3 (clk, reset_n, a && b );

endmodule
```

■ **FIGURE 12.3**

Verilog version of *arb_property_checker* using the Open Verification Library. In addition to the property checks, this version of arb_checker includes all the input protocol checks, which ensure that the environment drives the design under verification with the correct stimuli.

tics of each parameter, because their positional specification in Verilog does obscure their meaning. It is certainly one of the disadvantages of Verilog OVL that the parameters and port connections do not indicate their intent easily. The named association of generic maps and port maps in VHDL allow a clearer specification of the intent.

We chose a severity level *30* for all assertions, assuming this value has a specific meaning for the simulation or FV tool that will process the DUV and the property checker. It certainly is a welcome flexibility that OVL lets the user specify the error message string and the severity code as part of the instance specification.

Whereas the input protocol constraints make heavy use of *assert_implication*, the main mechanism to specify the property checks is the *assert_cycle_sequence*. We need to use the sequence assertion construct because the ARB specification defines most properties using a timing relationship (two cycles) to the incoming ARB *cmd*.

The *arb_property_checker* of Figure 12.3 has no output signals like the plain Verilog version of Figure 11.27. The Verilog-only version needed a convention (signals of a *fails* output vector) to indicate which conditions are targets for FV tools. OVL assertions do not provide explicit output signals, and their result valuation over time is an implicit target for FV tools, as Figure 12.2 indicates.

The example in Figure 12.3 highlights the powerful conciseness that OVL provides in the specification of assertions, especially sequential ones. Even with the inclusion of all input protocol checks and heavy commenting to explain the instance parameters, the source text of Figure 12.3 is about the same size as the source text of Figure 11.27. More importantly, every check takes two lines only, is purely declarative, and is not dependent on another check. This makes maintenance of the property checker overall much easier. In the Verilog-only version, all checks depend on a sequence of code and variable assignments in an *always* block. Any change to this code sequence for one assertion can have unforeseen side effects for another assertion. This interdependency of pieces of sequential checking code makes the checker of Figure 11.27 hard to maintain. In contrast, it is possible to change or even delete any of the constraints or assertions in Figure 12.3 and the remaining code would still work correctly.

The OVL property checker of Figure 12.3 still needs one *always* block to store the original request vector at the time a *cmd* is issued. This value (*savereq*) is needed to enable the check of the *gnt[0:2]* result two cycles later. It is a simple example for the general case where assertions and property checks need access to scoreboard information. OVL has much stronger provisions to check sequences or windows of specific events than for the capture of data values and their correlation. If an assertion needs to access current data and correlate it with some prior data in any way, the user needs to create HDL helper *processes* or *always* blocks that capture or scoreboard this data. The FV literature sometimes calls such helper processes *satellites* [88].

The lack of score-boarding facilities is very common for current property specification languages because they focus more on the control flow aspects of a DUV.

The first two events of *assertion0* and *assertion2* in Figure 12.3 check for the same leading sequence (two cycles after *cmd*), which means that the logic implementing both assertions is similar and partially redundant. The trade-off here is whether to keep the two assertions separate to ease long-term maintenance or whether it is better to optimize the amount of logic inserted into the model for assertion checking purposes. There are good arguments for both sides, and a project should make a conscious decision which aspect is more important.

It is the clear contribution of OVL to enable assertion-based property checking for both simulation and FV within the bounds of the standard HDLs. Before OVL, property specification languages were only applicable to FV tool sets. This meant that FV engineers wrote properties in a formal language and the non-FV verification team wrote the test bench checkers in a simulation language, thus creating two camps and two separate activities. After the arrival of OVL, there is no question whether there are two separate property-checking activities that are legitimately redundant. The team writes specifications for properties and assertions only once for both simulation and FV. Only this synergy between the two verification disciplines makes the successful introduction of FV technology affordable and ultimately possible.

The restriction to encode all assertions as module instances in OVL also has clear disadvantages. Probably the biggest disadvantage is the necessity to use parameters and port maps to provide the necessary input to an assertion monitor. Unless the user knows the positional parameters and arguments extremely well, the instances of the assertion monitors appear cryptic and hard to maintain without a constant cross-reference with the OVL reference manual. It is certainly possible to envision a more user-friendly notation for the encoding of properties.

Another problem, which stems from the restriction to fit OVL fully compatibly into the host HDLs, is the restriction that it is not possible to nest OVL assertions. For example, *assertion0* in Figure 12.3 could be much more concise if it was possible to use *assert_one_hot* as the last event in the event sequence. However, Verilog does not allow nesting of a module instance in the port map of another module instance. The same restriction is true for VHDL.

We introduced OVL as a bridge between pure HDL methods and custom property specification languages. OVL exploits the capabilities of the existing HDLs to the limit. FV tools and property languages first developed separately from the rest of the verification tool set. For this technology to break out of its niche status in product verification methodologies, it was necessary to combine the practical value of OVL and its applicability to simulation as well as FV with the strong mathematical foundation and sense of completeness of the FV languages. The Accellera effort to standardize one property specification language for FV and simulation has the goal to accomplish this objective with one single property specification language.

12.2   THE PROPERTY SPECIFICATION LANGUAGE PSL

The property specification language PSL, also known as PSL/Sugar, is the result of a standardization effort by the industry consortium Accellera. Sugar originates from IBM Research, and FV projects have used it since 1994 as the main property specification language in an industrial setting inside and outside IBM. Initially, Sugar was very close to CTL and merely provided "syntactic sugar" to make CTL more user-friendly. The content of Sugar grew through practical use in several industry projects. Finally, Accellera selected Sugar as the basis for its property language standard. Through the standardization effort, which included a systematic collection of requirements for such a language, Sugar evolved into PSL in its current form [89].

Even though we discuss PSL as part of FV, most of the language is usable equally well in a simulation methodology. The part of PSL that only applies to FV is marked very explicitly by the language design team in the language reference manual *LRM* [89].

PSL belongs to the class of *domain specific languages*. It is independent of any other language or HDL and its single purpose is property specification. There are two modes to use PSL. First, it can be used *stand-alone*, which means that the user can group PSL specifications into their own files. Obviously, the user has to have a way to link or anchor the properties to the areas of the design they target and connect to. PSL provides such a mechanism, and we discuss it later in this section. The second mode to use PSL is the *embedded* mode. In embedded mode, designers write PSL properties and assertions directly into the HDL files of the DUV.

The intended user base for the embedded mode is obviously the designer community because they own the DUV HDL files. The embedded mode attempts to motivate an assertion-based design style, where the designers treat assertions and properties as constructs that are equally important as the DUV implementation and handle these specifications at the same time as they make design implementation decisions. Designers use embedded PSL constructs typically for simpler assertions. More complicated properties that take more space and more time to develop, especially if they need supporting HDL satellites, will likely be maintained external to the HDL files. The user base for the stand-alone PSL mode is both the design and the verification team. However, the verification team usually maintains the more complicated properties. We discuss both modes to use PSL below.

TABLE 12.4. ■ Bottoms-up specification of the four PSL layers

Modeling Layer	Use to model FV or simulation drivers, scoreboards, satellites
Verification Layer	Directives to direct the use of properties towards verification tasks like assertion or coverage. Directives to link standalone PSL properties to the target DUV areas.
Temporal Layer	The core of PSL: constructs to specify temporal, sequential properties. Any multi-cycle property uses the elements of this layer.
Boolean Layer	Boolean expressions are the building blocks for all the layers above this layer.

TABLE 12.5. ■ One-hot assertion in VHDL and Verilog

VHDL	Verilog
(gnt(0 to 2)="100") or (gnt(0 to 2)="010") or gnt(0 to 2)="001"))	((gnt[0:2]==3b'100) ‖ (gnt[0:2]==3b'010) ‖ (gnt[0:2]==3b'001))

12.2.1 Overview

PSL has four different parts that build on each other and that the LRM therefore calls layers. Table 12.4 shows this structure with the more basic layers at the bottom of the table.

Whether we embed PSL directly into the target HDL file or use the stand-alone mode, there is a strong motivation to use the same syntax for signal, vector, and signal-type references in Boolean expressions as we use in the HDL. For example, the Boolean equation to express the assertion that the *gnt* vector is one-hot appears very different in VHDL or Verilog (Table 12.5).

It is quite obvious from Table 12.5 that it would be very helpful if a PSL assertion would conform to the basic syntax style of the host (in case of embedded PSL) or target (in case of stand-alone PSL) HDL. With this motivation, it is understandable that the developers of PSL decided on a language that has different syntactic *flavors*.

PSL has four flavors at this point: VHDL, Verilog, SystemVerilog, and GDL (a language, which we will not discuss further here).[1] This means that some constructs of PSL borrow their syntax from the associated HDL, used for the DUV or the modeling layer, which we call the *host* HDL.

---

[1] GDL currently is a placeholder for a future version of EDL environment modeling language that is part of IBM's RuleBase system and is not yet specified in the PSL LRM [86].

The differences in the flavors are most apparent in the Boolean expression syntax: PSL uses the expression syntax of the host HDL. In the temporal and verification layer, the HDL language influence is less apparent and limited to some syntactic details, like the use of the specification *"is"* in the VHDL flavor. The host HDL colors the modeling layer of the chosen PSL flavor prominently.

The modeling layer provides the capability to specify FV and simulation test bench drivers, scoreboard modules, and satellites analogous to the *always* block in Figure 12.3. PSL uses the synthesizable subset of VHDL, Verilog, and SystemVerilog for the modeling layer with some extensions. These extensions are necessary to express non-determinism, as we describe in Chapter 3 (see Section 11.3.3).

PSL flavors make the language flexible and easy to use in the context of a particular HDL. On the other hand, PSL properties used in the context of one host HDL are not easily portable to another host HDL.

12.2.2 The Boolean Layer of PSL

Any property or assertion in PSL makes a statement about events and states in the DUV. It is necessary to reference signals, registers, and variables or, in general, HDL facilities in PSL statements. For this, regardless whether in its embedded or stand-alone form, PSL makes the host HDL expression language available to the user. This is the base layer of PSL flavoring.

Any valid Boolean expression of the host HDL is a valid Boolean expression of PSL. The expression operators of the PSL flavor as well as the syntax for the DUV facility references are the same as for the host HDL. For example, the one-hot property expressions in Table 12.5 directly show the VHDL (left) and Verilog (right) flavors of PSL.

In addition, PSL offers a number of its own constructs, operators, built-in functions, and declarations that go beyond what the host HDL has available for Boolean expressions. These additions exist either for convenience or to satisfy needs of the specific application field of PSL. Table 12.6 lists the added PSL operators and built-in functions.

Five built-in functions are labeled as *temporal* in Table 12.6. These functions evaluate over time the expression passed in as their argument. Any evaluation over time needs a reference clock as the basis for the sampling of expression values. If not specified otherwise, PSL leaves the time base for the temporal clock to the tool that evaluates the expressions. This applies not only to the temporal built-in functions but also to the properties of the temporal layer of PSL. On one hand, this keeps the granularity of the time resolution to the evaluating tool and therefore keeps PSL very flexible. In some situations, however, this default behavior does not deliver the desired results because it leads to ambiguities. The interpretation of the same PSL specification for a VHDL event-driven simulator is different from an FV tool, which uses a cycle-based evalua-

TABLE 12.6. ▪ PSL built-in functions and "union" operator

Built-in Function or Operator	Explanation
expr1 -> expr2	Implication: if expr1 is true, then expr2 is true.
prev(expr[,num])	Temporal: previous value of expression passed in. Optional num (constant) selects the expression value *num* number of cycles back.
next(expr)	Temporal: next cycle's value of expression passed in.
stable(expr)	Temporal: Boolean result, true if current value is the same of previous cycle value.
rose(expr)	Temporal: Boolean result, true of single bit input expression passed in changed from 0 to 1.
fell(expr)	Temporal: Boolean result, true of single bit input expression passed in changed from 1 to 0.
isunknown(expr)	Boolean result, true if bitvector expression passed in has any values other than 0 or 1.
countones(expr)	Return integer value for number of bits on in bitvector expression passed in.
onehot(expr)	Boolean result, true if bitvector expression passed in has exactly one bit on.
onehot0(expr)	Boolean result, true if bitvector expression passed in has exactly one bit on or is zero.
expr1 **union** expr2	Both input expression must be same type. Non-deterministically returns either expr1 or expr2.

tion of the DUV. For the example in Figure 12.4, the simulator evaluates the expression *stable(a)* using VHDL's delta-time approach, thus reacting to the sub-cycle changes of signal *a* in cycle 4. These changes are not visible for the cycle-based evaluation, which therefore returns a different result.

To give the user explicit control over the event and state sampling times, PSL provides a construct to specify a sampling clock for expression evaluation. Every property in PSL can be associated with an explicit *clock expression*. When the clock expression, which can be any Boolean expression usable as the *if* condition in the host HDL, returns true, the associated properties are evaluated. The clock expression is the sampling condition for PSL properties. We discuss associated clock expressions below as part of the temporal layer of PSL.

The Boolean layer contains a *default clock declaration* that defines a clock expression used by all properties and temporal expressions that appear in PSL directives (see Section 12.2.4), which do not have an explicit clock associated with themselves. For the example in Figure 12.4, we could use the default clock declaration of Table 12.7 that specifies explicitly that the sampling time for *stable(a)* should be the time when the signal *c_clk* has a rising edge. The default clock declaration applies to all properties that do not have an explicit clock expression.

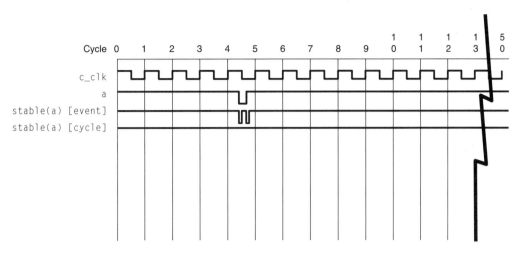

The same expression *stable(a)* returns different results when evaluated by different tools. Signal *a* is constantly on over time with the exception of a drop to 0 in cycle 4. The period of the clock signal *c_clk* defines the clock cycle. The cycle-based evaluation of *stable(a)* (marked [cycle]) returns a constant value of 1 during all cycles, whereas the event-driven evaluation (marked [event]) reacts to the two value changes during cycle 4.

TABLE 12.7. ■ Default clock declarations in VHDL and Verilog flavor of PSL that make the evaluation of the expression stable(a) independent from the interpretation of time of a given verification tool

PSL VHDL Flavor	PSL Verilog Flavor
default clock is (c_clk'event and c_clk = '1');	**default clock** = (posedge c_clk);

Two of the constructs in Table 12.6 are unique: *next()* and *union*. Both are only usable in the modeling layer of PSL because they can only occur on the right-hand side of an assignment statement. The *union* operator supports a non-deterministic assignment of a variable in a test bench driver. For a simulation test bench, the non-determinism can be interpreted as a random choice, whereas for the FV driver the assignment signifies true non-determinism. The random choice between the two operands of the operator satisfies the minimum requirement to express non-determinism. The built-in function *next()* allows access to the next state value of an expression, which is especially useful in the test bench environment in a situation where test bench code needs access to the next-state value randomly chosen of a variable driven by a *union* expression.

12.2.3   The Temporal Layer of PSL

The temporal layer of PSL defines how to construct properties that define behavior of the DUV over time. The key language element added here are *sequential expressions*, which, besides Boolean expressions, are the core constructs to specify properties. Where Boolean expressions evaluate the DUV state in a given single cycle, sequential expressions make a statement about DUV states across several cycles.

SEREs: Sequential Extended Regular Expressions

SEREs are the base building block to create sequential expressions. In its simplest form, a SERE is a sequence of Boolean expressions that specify the DUV state over a sequence of cycles.

Figure 12.5 shows an example of the simplest SERE with two elements, which describes a sequence of events where the values of two expressions turn true in subsequent time steps. The comma-separated list enumerates a sequence of events that the verification tools seek to match against actual events in the DUV. Such a sequence is a property by itself, and it can also be a building block to express more complex properties. There is a set of operators to combine two SEREs with each other. Table 12.8 shows two examples.

SEREs, like Boolean expressions, can have associated clock expressions and then become *clocked* SEREs. Table 12.9 shows the general syntax and simple examples for clocked SEREs.

SERE1 and SERE2 in Table 12.9 use the Boolean value *true*, which matches all DUV states trivially. The effect of *true* is simply to sequence to the next cycle.

Figure 12.6 illustrates the differences caused by different clock expressions using a set of example waveforms. We assume that the tool, which

TABLE 12.8. ▪ SEREs can be concatenated or fused together

Some operations on SEREs	
{ expr1; expr2 } ; { expr3; expr4}	Use ; for concatenation of sequence
{ expr1; expr2 } : { expr3; expr4}	Fusion - use : for overlapping Concatenation, such that expr2 and expr3 occur in the same cycle

```
{ expr1; expr2 }
```

▪ **FIGURE 12.5**

Simple sequential extended regular expression (SERE) that specifies a sequence of states where *expr2* follows *expr1* in the next cycle.

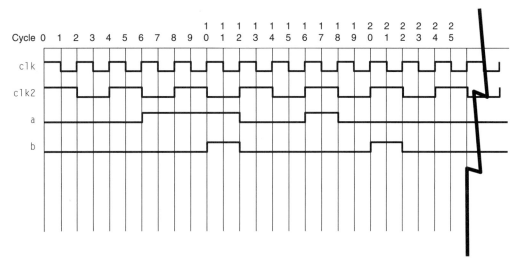

■ **FIGURE 12.6**

Waveform with two clocks (*clk* and *clk2*) and several configurations where signal *a* switches on, followed by an active signal *b*. In cycle 6 *a* turns on for six cycles, overlapping *b*, which turns active in cycle 10. The activity of *a* in cycle 16 does not overlap with *b*'s active state in cycle 20. We use this waveform trace to illustrate the matching rules for the clocked sequential regular extended expressions of Table 12.9.

TABLE 12.9. ■ SEREs or sub-elements of SEREs can have explicit clock expressions to control the sampling time of the events. When clock expressions are nested, the inner clock expression takes precedence over outer clock expressions. An outer clock expression applies to all non-clocked sub-elements. SERE1 uses the same clock for all parts of the SERE whereas SERE2 applies a different clock to sample signal a

Clocked SEREs	
{ SERE } @ clock_expr	General syntax used to associate an explicit clock expression with a SERE.
{ a; true; b} @clk	*b* follows *a* after one *clk* cycle delay (SERE1)
{a @ clk2; true, b} @clk	Sample *a* at *clk2* not *clk* like the rest of the SERE.(SERE2)

evaluates the two SEREs from Table 12.9 on this waveform, uses a cycle-based algorithm similar to a cycle-based simulation engine. SERE1, which synchronizes with *clk* in all its parts, does match twice, between cycles 6 and 10 and again between cycles 16 and 20. SERE2 yields only a single match. The first time *a* is active at the same time as *clk2* (cycle 8), *b* turns on in cycle 10 when *clk* is active. This matches the *true* expression in SERE2, but in cycle 12, where SERE2 tries to match *b*, *b* is off

{ a & !b; !a & !b; !a & b } @clk

▪ **FIGURE 12.7**

SERE3—a sequence specified to match exactly the waveform of *a* and *b* that starts at cycle 8 in Figure 12.6.

already, which makes the sequence fail. Starting in cycle 16, SERE2 does match exactly.

It is important to recognize that every step of a sequence evaluates only the signals referenced in the current cycle. Any signal not referenced has no influence on the matching progress and can therefore assume any of its possible values. This is illustrated by the application of SERE1 starting in cycle 3. SERE1 matches the waveform, even though signal *a* stays active for the next two cycles.

New users of PSL often make the wrong, intuitive assumption that SERE1 would only match the waveform for *a* and *b* that starts at cycle 8. Figure 12.7 shows a tightened sequence specification with SERE3 that does match only the sequence where *a* and *b* are turned on for a single cycle only.

The name SERE alludes to *regular expressions* as used in other languages [90]. Usually, programming languages or user interfaces use regular expressions to specify patterns to match an input stream. Here, the input stream for SEREs is the sequence of states and events in the DUV. The simple enumeration of fixed consecutive sequences used in the figures above is interesting but not flexible enough to express matching rules needed for designs in practice.

SERE Repetition Operators

Another set of constructs, which make SEREs more applicable to real-life designs, are the *repetition operators*. There are three different repetition operators. The *consecutive* repetition operator specifies that a SERE or a sub-sequence should repeat several times consecutively. The *non-consecutive* repetition operator allows the repeating sequence to occur with gaps in between. The *GOTO* repetition operator is similar to the non-consecutive operator but forces the sequence to end exactly with the last repetition of the sequence. Table 12.10 shows different applications of the three repetition operators. We use the simple model of a telephone call as the basis for the examples.The repetition operators allow the user to specify complex SEREs that are able to match whole classes of possible waveforms.

In addition to the full specification of a sequence as part of a property, PSL supports the concept of *named sequences*. Named sequences can be instantiated in multiple properties, thus supporting the concept of re-use.

TABLE 12.10. ■ SERE repetition operators introduced by example. The DUV has three signals named dial, ring and answer, which we use to represent the starting sequence of events for a telephone call

Consecutive repetition operator [*]	
{dial; ring[*]; answer}	*dial*, followed any number of *ring*s, until *answer*
{dial; ring[*1:4]; answer}	*dial*, followed by *ring* for at least 1, max 4 cycles (Verilog flavor range syntax) before *answer*
{dial; ring[+]; answer}	*dial*, followed by at least one, possible many *ring*s until *answer*
{dial; [*]; answer}	*dial*, followed by any number of cycles before *answer*; no specification for signal *ring*, therefore the SERE will match with or without any *ring* between *dial* and *answer*
Non-consecutive repetition operator [=]	
{dial; ring[=3]; answer}	*dial*, followed by three, possibly non-consecutive, *ring*s then *answer*, possibly non-consecutive
{dial; ring[=1 to 4]; answer}	*dial*, followed by between one and four, possibly non-consecutive *ring*s, *answer* possibly non-consecutive (VHDL flavor)
GOTO repetition operator [->]	
{dial; ring[->5]; answer}	*dial*, followed by five *ring*s, possibly non-consecutive, then *answer* in the very next cycle
{dial; ring[->1:3]; answer}	*dial*, followed *by* between one and three, possibly non-consecutive *ring*s, then answer in the very next cycle

Because named sequences can have parameters, it is possible to create general sequence patterns as building blocks that the user can adapt to a specific design configuration at instantiation time. A related concept is the *endpoint*. An endpoint is a Boolean variable that indicates when an associated sequence completes. Like a named sequence, the user declares an endpoint with possible parameters and instantiates it later inside property specifications. For further details on named sequences and endpoints, we refer to the PSL reference manual [89].

PSL Properties

The user specifies properties using the building blocks described so far, Boolean expressions and sequences, combining them with *temporal operators*.

Table 12.11 shows an overview of many temporal operators available to define properties. We refer again to the PSL reference manual for the complete definition of the many varieties of temporal operators supported by PSL [89].

As shown in Table 12.11, the user can declare properties using the keyword *property* followed by a name and optionally a set of parameters to personalize the property differently for every instance.

TABLE 12.11. ▪ Overview of temporal operators used to specify PSL properties. With the exception of property ortho2 all properties are declared using the Verilog flavor of PSL

Always	
property ortho1 = **always** (a!=b);	Sub-property *(a!=b)* holds at all times (Verilog flavor)
Never	
property ortho2 **is never** (a=b);	Sub-property *(a=b)* never occurs (VHDL flavor)
Next	
property call1 = **always**(dial -> **next** ring);	Property that holds in the *next* cycle
property call2=**always**(dial-> **next**[3]ring);	*next[i]* specifies *i* cycles later

property
  call3 = **always**(dial->
        next(!ring->
          next(ring->
            next ring)));
	Cascading implication and *next:* assert
	dial, followed by no *ring*, followed by
	two cycles of *ring*

sequence suffix implication |->, |=>	

property
  call4 = **always**(
    {dial} |-> ring[*1:3]; answer});
	If left-hand side (lhs) of |->,
	|=> holds, right-hand side (rhs) must
	   hold, too.
	|-> : last cycle of lhs = first cycle of
	   rhs (overlap)
	|=> : no overlap

property
  call5 = **never**({dial} |=> {ring;
    ring; ring});
	call4 : *dial* and first *ring* in same cycle.
	call5 : *ring* in next cycle after *dial*.

This discussion of PSL's temporal operators and their use in the context of property specification completes the survey of the temporal layer of PSL. As mentioned several times, PSL is a larger language than we have room to illustrate here. This is especially true in the area of temporal operators where PSL offers a plethora of different variations, all serving the goal to capture typical needs in practical designs with a set of concise constructs.

12.2.4   The Verification Layer of PSL

The verification layer of PSL provides constructs called *directives*, which specify the purpose of the properties that the user defined using the temporal layer of the language. From the larger set of directives, we just select a few typical ones for this discussion.

TABLE 12.12. ■ Two examples of the PSL assert directive

assert always (req -> **next** ack);	unnamed property, directly specified as part of assert
assert call1 **report** "no ring in the cycle after dial";	instantiation of named property (Table 12.11) with error message string

Assert

The *assert* directive instructs the verification tool to check that the property holds for the first cycle. It is up to the tool how much of the DUV state space it covers when it checks the assertion. FV is supposed to check the complete reachable state space, whereas simulation only checks those areas of the state space that the test bench stimuli reach.

The assert directive either instantiates a named property or specifies the property directly (Table 12.12). Optionally, an assertion includes a message to use for the reporting of an assertion violation.

Assume

The *assume* directive is useful to specify input constraints of the DUV; these are the input behaviors that the verification tool should exclude when it evaluates the design for the asserted properties. There is no obligation for the verification tool to prove the assumption. For simulation-based verification, *assume* possibly instructs the test generator to only create tests that agree with the assumed property.

For FV the assume directive is a filter that prevents the tool to navigate the DUV into states that cannot occur given these input constraints. A simulator can treat the *assume* directive exactly like an *assert* directive, thus flagging test bench behavior that violates the DUV's input constraints.

Assume_guarantee

The *assume_guarantee* directive is similar in intent to the *assume* directive: to communicate to the FV tool evaluating the DUV properties that certain input conditions are illegal and will therefore never happen. In addition, *assume_guarantee* instructs the verification tool to verify that the assumed property does indeed never happen, like an *assert*, for example, when the DUV is instantiated into an enclosing DUV.

Tables 12.13 and 12.14 use one of the input constraints defined for the ARB design as an example for the usage of the assume directive (refer to Figure 12.3 for the OVL version of this).

TABLE 12.13. ▪ Example of a PSL assume directive

property constraint0 **is always**
   ({cmd='1'} |=> {cmd='0'});
assume constraint0;
	Named property for constraint0 in ARB design
	   (Figure 12.3)
	Instantiation of constraint0

TABLE 12.14. ▪ Example of a PSL cover directive

cover {(cmd='1' **and** req(0)='1')}
   report "req bit 0 occurred";
	Coverage event for legal req(0) request
	   on ARB design

TABLE 12.15. ▪ Example *vunit* ARB_CHECKER for the ARB design

vunit ARB_CHECKER(ARB) {
   default clock = (**posedge** clk);
   property always ({cmd}|=> ...
   assert ...
 	
   ...
}
	Bound to module ARB
	
	clk, cmd are ARB internal signals; *vunit*
	   binding makes ARB the *vunit* scope

Cover

The *cover* directive instructs the verification tool to log the occurrence of a property as a coverage event. Like the assert directive, the cover directive has an optional message string associated that the tool can print out when coverage of the verification is reported.

Verification Units

The purpose of a *verification unit* is to group a set of properties and verification directives and link them to the associated DUV. Verification units are the PSL constructs that let the user define *stand-alone* PSL checkers. In addition to properties and directives, a verification unit can also contain statements and declarations that are part of the modeling layer.

PSL supports several types of verification units. We discuss only the *vunit* here, which is the most general verification unit available to the user.

A verification unit is explicitly bound to a module (or entity/architecture in VHDL) or to an instance of such. With this binding, the *vunit* has access to the scope of the module it refers to, which means that all signals visible in the module are visible and accessible to the *vunit*.

Table 12.15 shows an example of a *vunit* that refers to the ARB DUV module. We use the Verilog flavor of the PSL construct.

Embedded PSL

As discussed above, PSL supports stand-alone mode (using the *vunit* construct) and some commercial tools support an embedded mode. Putting PSL assertions right into the DUV HDL satisfies the desire to drive an assertion-based methodology where the designers specify as many assertions as possible when they write the HDL implementation.

The current PSL standard does not specify syntax for the embedded mode [89]. However, several EDA vendors have taken the lead and have implemented a mutually compatible pseudo-standard, which Table 12.16 shows in example form for Verilog and VHDL. The user places PSL statement into the source of the DUV HDL using formalized comments to hide the added PSL from the HDL compilers. This ensures that the DUV still uses the standard HDL and compiles correctly for an HDL tool set that does not support PSL yet. PSL-aware HDL compilers read the comments and parse everything between the keyword *psl* and the closing semicolon as a PSL construct.

The examples in Table 12.16 also highlight again the adaptive nature of PSL, always assuming the syntax flavor of the host HDL to blend in with the style of HDL coding around the embedded properties.

In the VHDL standard committee discussions have apparently begun with how to include PSL directly into the VHDL language, which shows the still somewhat fluid nature of property language development in the industry.

12.2.5 The Modeling Layer of PSL

PSL supports a modeling layer to allow the specification environment components: drivers and checkers. This comes from the realization that PSL constructs target mainly the specification of sequences of events over time. The data flow and correctness aspect of checking usually needs scoreboards to keep data over many cycles, data that later need to be correlated and checked to assess correctness of the DUV. Synthesizable

---

TABLE 12.16. ▪ Examples of embedded PSL for Verilog and VHDL. The PSL statements are comments in the host HDL. An embedded statement must start with the keyword psl and ends with the semicolon, possibly crossing several lines. Every facility (signal, variable, etc.) of the host module is accessible to the embedded PSL statements

Embedded PSL in Verilog	Embedded PSL in VHDL
// **psl assert always** (a & b) // @(**posedge** clk);	– **psl assert always** (a **and** b) – @(clk'**event and** clk='1');
// **psl property** p1 = // **never** ((opcode=='LOAD)-> // **next** (opcode=='LOAD)); // **psl assume** p1;	– **psl property** p1 **is** – **never** ((opcode=LOAD)-> – **next** (opcode=LOAD)); – **psl assume** p1;

HDLs are well suited to specify the behavior of all these functions. In addition, the hardware interpretation of synthesizable HDLs lets tools transform such drivers and checkers into a finite state machine (FSM) view, which is required to apply the FV algorithms (see Section 12.3).

PSL supports both synthesizable VHDL and Verilog on the modeling layer. In this context, wherever an HDL expression can appear in the HDL, any PSL Boolean expression can appear as well, extending the host HDL with PSL. In addition, PSL extends its Verilog flavor with higher-level constructs like integer ranges and *struct*. As mentioned previously, verification units support the use of modeling layer constructs.

12.2.6 Using PSL to Specify Properties

We now want to apply PSL to the ARB design example used in Chapter 11. The purpose of the repeated implementations of the checker for ARB is to compare and contrast the use of PSL with the other methods of property specification available, like the use of pure HDL or OVL checkers.

We return to the table of constraints and assertions for the ARB design (Table 12.3). Figure 12.8 shows a verification unit in PSL that encodes all the constraints and assertions specified in Table 12.3.

We define a default clock to avoid the syntactical clutter and redundancy that occurs when using the same clock expression everywhere. The first three constraints use implication much like the OVL constraints do in Figure 12.3. *constraint3* uses a construct of the temporal layer that was not introduced previously: the *forall* iteration operator. The use of *forall* is intuitive; it is a shorthand operator that defines a whole group of properties that all have the same structure using a syntax template like a macro. The obvious advantage of *forall* is the conciseness achieved by compressing a repetitive pattern into a single property declaration. It is notable that there are more efficient implementations of *forall* than a straight macro-like expansion with all its replication. Still, users should use *forall* cautiously, because the downside of this power is that it becomes easy to specify a large number of possibly redundant properties quickly. The verification team needs to make conscious trade-offs here.

We use the *assume_guarantee* directive for the input constraint checking that will instruct the verification tool about the input constraints, but will also check for violations of these from the test bench or if the DUV is instantiated into a larger DUV.

Three of the four assertions are sequential. *assertion0* uses implication and the *next* operator with the number argument to specify the required value of *gnt* two cycles after *cmd* is active. *assertion1* and *assertion2* use sequence suffix implication to specify the expected behavior of ARB two and three cycles after the *cmd* signal is active. If we needed to maximize conciseness, we could even merge these two assertions into a single one,

```
vunit arb_property_checker(arb) {

    default clock = (posedge clk);

    property constraint0 = always (cmd -> next !cmd);

    property constraint1 = always (cmd -> req != 3b'000);

    property constraint2 = always (!cmd -> req==3b'000);

    property constraint3 = forall i in 0:2 : always (gnt[i] -> !req[i]);

    property assertion0 = always (cmd -> next[2] (onehot(gnt)));

    property assertion1 = always ({cmd, !cmd} |=> {[1]; gnt==3b'000});

    property assertion2 = always ({cmd, !cmd} |=> {(gnt && prev(req,2))!=0 };

    property assertion3 = never (int0.a & int0.b);

    assume_guarantee constraint0 report "cmd is active more than once cycle";
    assume_guarantee constraint1 report "cmd active without valid request";
    assume_guarantee constraint2 report "request is on while cmd is off";
    assume_guarantee constraint3 report "req[i] is on when gnt[i] is on";

    assert assertion0 report "not one-hot two cycles after cmd";
    assert assertion1 report "gnt is non-zero during off time";
    assert assertion2 report "illegal gnt result";
    assert assertion3 report "a and b on at the same time!";
}
```

■ **FIGURE 12.8**

PSL version of the *arb_property_checker* with the same functional content as the OVL version of the checker in Figure 12.3.

because the sequences specified do overlap. However, the specification listed *assertion1* and *assertion2* as separate, both with their own error message. For maintenance and debug reasons it is also better to keep the two assertions separate. *assertion1* uses a constant repetition operator to specify a dead cycle for which there is no value evaluation. *assertion2* shows the power of the *prev* built-in function. Being able to capture the value of the *req* vector from two cycles *before* the value check occurs avoids the creation of a score board *always* block as we needed in the OVL and Verilog implementations.

Finally, *assertion3* illustrates the use of hierarchical signal references in Verilog. Because the *vunit* of Figure 12.8 binds to the *arb* module, all signals of the module are in the *vunit's* scope and directly accessible without explicit declaration. This includes access into instances nested inside *arb* (see Figure 11.25).

Overall, Figure 12.8 proves the value of PSL's dedicated role as a domain-specific language for property specification. Once through the initial investment to learn PSL, the user can specify properties very clearly and concisely, which has obvious advantages as a documentation vehicle as well as for the longer-term maintenance of the PSL code.

There is a large selection of introductory material and examples available [91]. Cohen et al. and Foster et al. are additional resources for further study [92, 93].

12.2.7 Advanced PSL Topics and Caveats

It is very possible to make good use of PSL even after a short learning effort. However, deeper study reveals that PSL is quite a complex language, and it is important to understand its semantics in more detail before it is possible to write complex, unambiguous properties. This section serves as an introduction into some of the advanced topics and attempts to create a sense of caution and a motivation to dig deeper into the complex areas of PSL before committing a larger project with only an intuitive understanding of the language.

Implicit Property Sampling

The importance of explicit clock expressions was expressed above. Unless a property has an associated explicit clock, the sampling and checking of the property is up to the verification tool used. Besides the problem of portability from tool to tool of properties without clock expressions, there is the deeper problem of incompletely defined semantics. For example, a simple *assert* with an unclocked Boolean expression will be evaluated by a simulator whenever it evaluates a change in one of the signals that participate in the expression. If the simulator detects glitches in these signal values, this can lead to an assertion violation. However, if the evaluation sequence of the simulator happens to leave the glitch undetected, no assertion violation occurs. The user can control the exact time when to evaluate a property only using explicit clock expressions.

First-Cycle Only Properties

New users easily overlook the problem of properties that inadvertently only check the DUV once during the very first cycle. Table 12.17 shows examples of such first-cycle only properties.

PSL semantics define that the verification tool checks a property whenever an implicit or explicit repetition requires it. The obvious operators that imply continuous repetition are *always* and *never*.

For the corrected *call6* in Table 12.17 (lower left), the explicit use of the infinite repetition operator *[*]* specifies that the sequence does not begin in the first cycle only. There can be a sequence of unlimited cycles before *dial* turns true. This requires PSL to check in every cycle whether the *[*]* repetition ended and the next step, *dial*, did occur. Obviously, the

TABLE 12.17. ■ First-cycle only properties ortho3 and call6, and two possible corrected versions

Accidental First-Cycle Only Properties	
property ortho3 ((a&b)!=0); **assert** ortho3;	*ortho3* has no repetition or *always/never* operator
property call6 {dial} |=> {ring; ring; answer }; **assert** call6;	*call6* has no *always/never* or [*]
Corrected Properties	Alternate Corrections
property ortho3 **always** ((a&b)!=0); **assert** ortho3;	**property** ortho3 **never** (a&b); **assert** ortho3;

property call6 {[*]; dial} |=>
   {ring; ring; answer };
assert call6;
	property call6 **always** ({dial} |=>
	   {ring; ring; answer });
	assert call6;

use of the *always* operator (lower right in Table 12.17) fixes this problem as well.

Overlapping Properties

For a new user the issue of *re-starting* or *overlapping* properties is very surprising. Because PSL must evaluate repeating properties at every sampling time, it can occur that a temporal property, whose evaluation started in a previous cycle already, re-starts its evaluation again. This does not mean that the previous evaluation stops, it merely means that *another instance* of the evaluation starts.

Although this feature of PSL allows the checking of overlapping or pipelined transactions, the user must take great care and fully understand all the implications of re-starting sequence properties. This is arguably the most complex area of PSL and the user needs to understand it well. Otherwise, surprising and confusion property checking results will be difficult to debug.

Figure 12.9 shows an example of the re-starting behavior of a PSL property. The sequence specified can have a maximum number of three parallel matches. Every match evaluates the full sequence by itself, and a lack of the correct event occurrences would lead to a failing property. It is easy to extrapolate the re-starting behavior of the re-starting sequence in this example because the sequence, once started, has a fixed length and there are no ambiguities in the interpretation of the events in the trace of the DUV.

Figure 12.10 uses a variable length sequence as the example property. This gives a glimpse of how difficult the assessment of even relatively simple sequences can get.

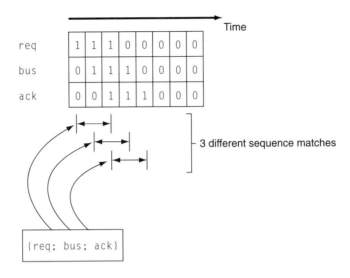

▪ **FIGURE 12.9**

An example of a restarting, overlapping sequence. The text box shows the example property as a PSL sequence definition. A trace of the three signals affecting the property over time is shown. The property implies that three overlapping matches of the specified sequence occur.

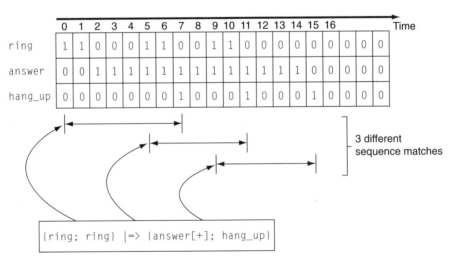

▪ **FIGURE 12.10**

Second example for a restarting, overlapping sequence. This example uses a variable length sequence.

We return to the class of telephone call examples. The property specified checks for sequences of calls on the receiver end. A normal sequence consists of two rings, an answering action over several cycles, and eventually the hang-up of the phone. Now, it is possible that another ring occurs before the hang-up completes the previous call (think of an advanced *call-waiting* feature with a depth of more than one). This is the situation where another match of the sequence property starts.

The matches drawn in Figure 12.10 are correct for very subtle reasons. The property, as written, expects *at least* one cycle with *answer* active after the two *ring*s and before *hang_up* can legally turn active. In cycle 7 this leads to the unambiguous interpretation that the *hang_up* signal closes the first call (= match of the sequence). The same happens again at cycle 11 where the second match of the sequence finishes. Clearly, the association of sequence elements, while overlapped, occurs on a first-in, first-out basis. Because the given trace in Figure 12.10 does not allow any other interpretation, the result of the property checking is unambiguous.

The trace in Figure 12.11 changes slightly compared with Figure 12.10, and this causes totally unexpected behavior of the property checks for the uninitiated user. The way the property is written, given the semantics of PSL, allow for sequence matches that might surprise the user. In cycle 8 the *hang_up* signal turns active. Both currently active matches of the property interpret this event as the closing event of their sequence. After this occurs, no uncompleted match of the property tracks the event

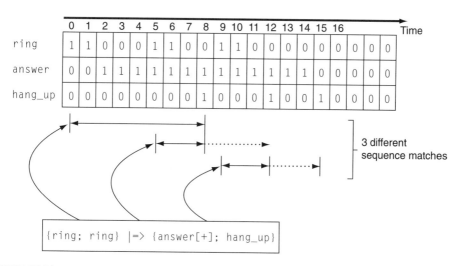

■ FIGURE 12.11

A different trace from the DUV with the same sequence property as Figure 12.10. The different timing of the *hang_up* signal in cycle 8 (versus 7) and cycle 15 (versus 11) creates ambiguity. Instead of interpreting the sequence as overlapping (dashed arrows) or even nested (not shown), the first active *hang_up* leads to a finish of both early matches of the sequence.

trace of the DUV. In the next cycle 94, another sequence starts. The set of ambiguities continues in cycle 12 when the third instance of the sequence finishes successfully, leaving the remaining cycles with *answer* active and the final *hang_up* in cycle 15 dangling and unchecked. If the complete set of properties for this example DUV checked for a sequence of non-requested *answer* and *hang_up* signals, the trace from cycle 13 to 15 would trigger a failing property.

There are two possible better interpretations for the trace in Figure 12.11. The one most similar to the interpretation of Figure 12.10 would finish the first sequence in cycle 8 but keep the second match going. The same would then have to occur in cycle 12, where only the second match would finish, whereas the final, third sequence would continue until cycle 15. The second alternate interpretation of the trace would allow for nested sequences in a LIFO scheme (last-in, first-out). Possibly, sequence instance 1 would start in cycle 1 and continue all the way until cycle 15. The second sequence would start with the double *ring* in cycle 5 and finish in cycle 8, whereas the third, and again nested, sequence would run from cycle 9 to cycle 12. Staying with the analogy of the *call-waiting* scheme, this would signify a long phone call, with two shorter ones that interrupt the first.

What is the real source of the problems with these properties in Figures 12.10 and 12.11? Clearly, these examples tell a cautionary tale, showing the new user that even simple sequences can bear surprising complications and surprises. The core of the problem, however, is that the properties, as written, do not have access to enough knowledge about the design to allow the correct interpretation. Besides the three DUV signals, there is need for more temporal information to be able to disambiguate the trace in the intended way. The simplest solution is to add information to the property that contains data about which instance of the sequence is active at any given point. The modeling layer of PSL can provide this added data. Figure 12.12 shows one possible implementation of a more complete checker.

The checker in Figure 12.12 hard-codes the interpretation of a LIFO scheme for incoming calls. Every new call will be finished first, before returning and ultimately finishing the previous call that was active when the current call started. A different, more complex, call-nesting scheme will need a more complex supporting model surrounding the property check. The core of the solution of Figure 12.12 does circumvent completely the notion of multiple instances of the same sequence by creating one unique sequence property per possible call sequence in the DUV. The disadvantage of this scheme is that there now is a fixed upper limit for the number of active sequences in the *vunit*.

False Positives

Properties that produce false negatives are a hassle but usually not a problem for the verification effort. False negatives are failing properties

```
vunit phone_checker(phone) {

  default clock = (posedge clk);

  reg call_count;
  initial call_count = 0;

  always @(posedge clk) begin
    if (posedge ring) call_count += 1;
    if (hang_up)      call_count -= 1;
  end

  assert

  forall COUNT in 0:15 :
    always ({ring && (call_count==COUNT); ring} |=>
              {answer[+]; hang_up && (call_count==COUNT)} );
}
```

■ **FIGURE 12.12**

A more elaborate version of the phone sequence checker. This *vunit* keeps track of the number of nested call sequences by updating the variable *call_count*. With a hard-coded limit of 16 possible nested call sequences, the *assert* construct uses a *forall* template to prepare for 16 different instances of the property sequence, each of which is distinguished by its associated value of *call_count*. Because a sequence only finishes when the *call_count* is still the same value compared with when the sequence started, this implementation enforces a last in, first out scheme.

that inadvertently flag an event in the design as wrong when there is actually no problem. The typical reason for false negatives is that a property defines allowable events too narrowly and does not account for window conditions that are actually legal in the DUV. The verification team has to clean up and correct false negatives to make sure only real DUV bugs lead to failing properties in FV or simulation.

False positives are a much more severe problem because they give the verification team a wrong sense of security. False positives are properties that do not fail on DUV errors because they are constructed wrongly and do not really check what their authors intended to check. We describe two typical classes of false positives with examples of assertions using implication: false positives where the pre-condition of the implication is not reachable and such properties where the postcondition is always trivially true. Figure 12.13 shows both classes.

The pre-condition of property *p1* in Figure 12.13 will never trigger, because the constraint in the *assume_guarantee* clause excludes exactly this condition. Obviously, the example is an extremely contrived one, using a blatant contradiction in two adjacent properties. However, in real projects with many properties and constraints, it is easy to overlook subtle contradictions, especially those of temporal nature. The literature calls this class of false positives *vacuous* properties. Interestingly, it is possible to apply the same algorithms used to explore the state space for

```
vunit checker(design) {

    assume_guarantee always (a!=b);

    property p1 = always (({(a==b)} |=> {blip; blip} );

    property p2 = always ({a} |=> {[*], done});

    assert p1;
    assert p2;
}
```

▪ **FIGURE 12.13**

PSL checker example for false positives. Both properties *p1* and *p2* never fail.

```
property p2 = always ({a} |=> {[*], done}!);
```

▪ **FIGURE 12.14**

Turning the sequence property from Figure 12.13 into a *strong* (operator !) sequence property requires PSL to guarantee the sequence finishes or fails otherwise.

property violations also to prove the absence of such contradictions or *vacuities*. Many available tools support vacuity checking.

The problem with property *p2* is that the infinite repetition operator *[*]* allows for the sequence to never finish. This means that in cases where the *done* signal never turns active, *p2* still never fails, and the post-condition sequence never finishes.

Figure 12.14 fixes the problem of *p2* with a different construct, the *strong sequence*, identified with the ! operator. PSL requires that a strong sequence finishes once started, thus avoiding the problem of a false positive. There is a whole set of the strong variety operators in PSL that we do not have the space to discuss here in detail but refer the interested reader again to the EDA Web site [89].

We now come to a close of our overview of PSL and the end of the discussion on property specification. As the discussion evolved from pure HDL through OVL and into the special-purpose language PSL, the goal stayed the same: to give the reader an overview of the main concepts relevant to property specification. Every one of these languages, including the property specification part of the newer and still emerging SystemVerilog, has different constructs on the syntactical surface to deal with the same essence of property specification: the specification of events and their relationship over time in the DUV [86]. The syntax and the lingo might be different for the different languages, but the base mechanisms are largely the same.

We now expect the reader to see through the outside packaging of these mechanisms in *any* of the above languages and have a grasp on their particular strengths and weaknesses. With the base concepts of property specification in mind, it should be possible to apply either language successfully after a moderate learning effort.

12.3 PROPERTY CHECKING USING FV

After the deep excursion into the topics of property specification, we now return to the discussion of using FV to prove the absence of property violations by the DUV implementation.

12.3.1 Property Re-Use Between Simulation and FV

It is important to keep in mind that for the languages and mechanisms of property specification that we surveyed, the principle of re-use is extremely important. Both simulation and FV are able to check these properties (see Figure 10.12). However, if FV tools are able to prove properties of the DUV, there might be the question why simulation needs to care about them. It was the original position of FV research and development that FV properties are for FV tools and have no place in simulation. At that early stage, the ultimate promise of proof with FV was so powerful that developers did not see a need to invest energy making their specification languages re-usable for simulation and FV. This led to a separation of disciplines and to the creation of the *special* verification subteam within the overall verification team.

The separation itself creates problems in an industrial project environment. The design team now faces two teams, using different lingo, each wanting to extract specifications from the designers for verification. In an environment of exploding design complexity and shrinking project schedules, this double load on the design team is very problematic and often not practical. This is the first reason why re-use of property specifications across simulation and FV is vital for the overall verification team to succeed.

The second reason to make property re-use a central requirement for verification is the fact that the big promise of FV overtaking property verification altogether remained unachieved. FV algorithms, like all other verification approaches, face the brick wall of the state-space explosion problem. FV tools cannot practically prove all properties that specify the behavior of an industrial-size DUV. It is certainly desirable to get the strongest possible assertion of properties that tools technology can achieve. A formal proof is the most desirable verification of a property. However, there is a strong need for a back-off strategy when state-space explosion makes the FV proof impossible. As far as the FV tools can drive the state space traversal successfully, they cover that portion of the state space completely and can identify bugs, even if the algorithms cannot complete a proof. If all else fails for the true verification of a property, simulation must be available to get at least some assurance about the validity of the properties.

12.3.2 Model Compilation

We know from Chapter 11 (Figure 11.22), that the FSM view is the ultimate representation needed to do FV on the combination of DUV, properties, and FV driver, which all together define the environment for property checking. Many but not all FV algorithms operate on the FSM view of the combined Formal Model. The tool flow for functional FV in Figure 12.15 shows that an FV tool needs to translate all three sources of specification into this view before the FV algorithms can then evaluate the overall model.

As Figure 12.15 also shows, the FSM logic that checks the properties ends up driving a set of *fails* signals. For this transformed and assembled Formal Model, correctness means that starting from any legal initial state, the model can never reach a state where a *fail* signal is active.

Although this translation is necessary for all discussed property specification mechanisms, the pure HDL and the OVL approach have the advantage that they rely on the HDL implementation of the properties.

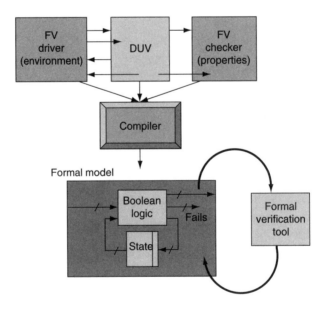

▪ FIGURE 12.15

The flow of model compilation for formal verification (FV). The compiler translates all three components, driver, DUV, and properties, into the finite state machine view. The resulting *Formal Model* is the representation on which the FV algorithms operate.

Therefore, for these we can re-use the HDL compilers/synthesizers, which exist for the DUV HDL already, and use them for the translation of the properties as well.

For property languages, which support CTL or LTL temporal logic constructs (like PSL), the translation is more complicated. There is much research work devoted to the problem of efficiently generating the FSM view of properties. Aberbanel et al. describes such an effort for the property language Sugar, the pre-cursor of PSL [94]. In fact, the paper discusses the tool FoCs (*formal checkers*), which now supports a subset of PSL and is available for download on the Internet [96]. FoCs not only generates an internal FSM view of the properties, but also even writes out the translated properties to VHDL and Verilog. The resulting HDL is usable in many HDL simulators and therefore makes PSL re-usable between FV and simulation.

The amount of reachable state of the DUV and the FV test bench in the generation of the Formal Model is the main measure of the translation efficiency because, as we know from the discussions in Chapter 11, the main limiting factor for FV is the size of the reachable state space. It is important to realize that this state space is not just dependent on the DUV alone, but also on the driver and checker logic, all of which the model compilation assembles.

It is the task of the FV tool to apply exhaustive verification algorithms effectively against the fully assembled model to prove that there are no states, where the property *fail* signals are active. We discuss some of the functional verification algorithms next.

12.3.3 Formal Functional Verification Algorithms

An FV algorithm that attempts to prove the absence of failing properties needs an internal representation of the state graph defined by the FSM of the Formal Model of Figure 12.15. In principle, we can think of the exhaustive proof as a process that walks the state graph from a defined set of initial states explicitly checking the properties at every state on the way. Of course, the capacity of FV tools and algorithms is limited. Typically, the user has to guide and control the tools very directly to apply the power of exhaustive verification in the critical areas of industrial-sized DUVs. To support the users in the effective application of this technology, we discuss some of the different approaches that implement this FSM traversal when checking of properties.

Model Checking

Key concepts for the state space traversal described above are *reachable states* and *reachability analysis*. A state is a reachable state when there is a legal input sequence that leads the model to it from an initial state.

Reachability analysis is the process that successively proceeds from every reached state to every state reachable in the next step.

Model checking is the established academic term for what we described as the FSM traversal and check for properties [95]. *Explicit* model checking uses a direct, explicit representation of the states as data in a graph. The checking process starts from the set of legal states and proceeds forward, always applying all legal inputs to the DUV. This reachability analysis progresses cycle by cycle, enumerates all reached states explicitly, and checks every state for property violations.

Figure 12.16 illustrates the reachability algorithm's progression from a set of legal initial states through the combined state space of the DUV and the FV environment (Formal Model). Cycle by cycle, there is a frontier of already reached states from which the algorithm proceeds to the set of next states, applying the logic of the FSM and all legal input combinations, thus defining the next frontier of states to be checked for property violations. By definition and baring any resource limitations, the algorithm eventually covers the complete state space and therefore uncovers all bugs.

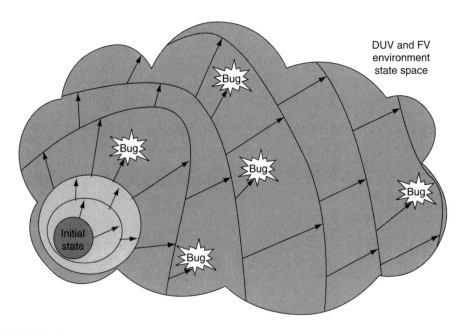

▪ FIGURE 12.16

Starting with the set of possible initial states, model checking proceeds in a breadth-first way through the reachable state space of the Formal Model. The arrows and the boundaries illustrate the progression from any given set of states to the frontier of the set of states reachable in the next cycle. Using the exhaustive breadth-first method, all five bugs are reachable within a maximum of seven cycles.

For small FSMs, explicit model checking is very runtime efficient, which makes it a favorite candidate for model checking of higher-level design representations with a smaller, abstracted state space. The biggest problem for this algorithm is the state-space explosion, which results in a corresponding explosion of the explicit state data the tool needs to manage. Explicit model checking scales well up to a state space of several million reachable states. Consider the fact that a DUV with 32 state bits already spans a potentially reachable state space of four billion. The explicit representation of such a small FSM already exhausts the virtual address of 32-bit workstations. This shows that the practical limits of explicit model checking are clearly in the smaller state space domain.

Symbolic Model Checking

During the early 1990s, FV research received a big boost by the invention and rapid development of *symbolic model checking* [97, 98]. The characteristics of the FSM are stored symbolically using binary decision diagrams (BDDs). As discussed in Chapter 11, BDDs are a compact representation of Boolean functions. Symbolic model checkers represent the next state functions and the property *fail* functions using BDDs. In addition, BDDs also encode the states symbolically. Rather than explicitly enumerating every single state, like in explicit model checkers, symbolic model checkers use BDDs to specify sets of states in the form of Boolean functions. With this help of BDDs, it is possible to create algorithms that perform reachability analysis and state machine traversal with much more memory efficiency than explicit model checking.

Most FV tools in practice today use a symbolic model checker at least as one component. Still, the practical limit of pure symbolic checking are DUVs with 100 to 300 state bits, which constrains the applicability of this technology to smaller designs.

Bounded Model Checking

The idea of *bounded model checking* (BMC) is to limit (bound) the length of the path taken during FSM traversal to an integer n [99]. If the verification tool finds a property violation, a bug, up to that point, the tool stops and reports a counter-example trace to the user. Otherwise, the tool increases n to a higher value, until the state space explosion prevents the tool from progressing. The BMC approach acknowledges the fact that in many practical cases model checking cannot complete a proof but can be extremely useful as a bug-finding tool.

Surprisingly, once researchers accepted the premise of BMC to limit the number of cycles over which to operate the model checking state traversal, they found much more efficient algorithms to implement it. The most popular solution reduces the sequential FSM traversal problem

Formal model

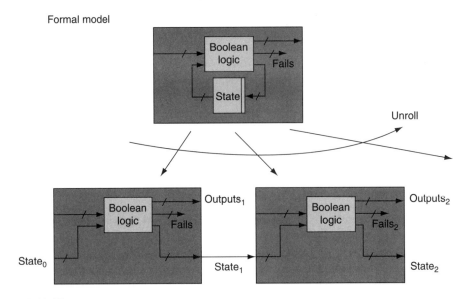

▪ **FIGURE 12.17**

Unrolling a sequential circuit for bounded model checking with SAT. Unrolling the finite state machine (FSM) into a combinational circuit reduces the sequential problem to a combinational problem. The example in this figure unrolls an FSM twice. For every cycle, we replicate the Boolean logic. Every replication represents the values of the FSM logic in a given cycle. The signal names carry a subscript to denote their respective cycle. We replace the state-holding elements with wires between the replicas. This makes the initial state $state_0$. The results of the cycle1 replication feed the cycle2 replication and so on.

down to a pure combinational problem, as we illustrate in Figure 12.17. The tool accomplishes this reduction by replicating the Boolean logic of the Formal Model once per cycle for which it needs to perform the property check. In the end, a chained combinational circuit replaces the FSM for n cycles. We call this transformation *unrolling*.

The goal of BMC remains to prove that the set of *fail* signals never turns active. Given the unrolled circuit's combinational structure, for some algorithms this problem is much simpler to solve than the original FSM verification problem. We can now apply many of the techniques that applied to equivalence checking as discussed in Chapter 11. In particular, the FV tool can use the satisfiability testing (SAT) and automatic test pattern generation (ATPG) algorithms to generate input sequences that activate a property fail. The unrolling of the FSM transforms the model checking problem, which is memory limited, into a problem that now is only time-limited. It is up to the tool and the user to limit the time spent attempting to create a counterexample for the asserted property.

Because of its good scalability and applicability on larger DUVs, BMC has evolved into one of the primary algorithms for FV tools. Clearly, BMC cannot prove the absence of bugs; it is useful mainly for bug hunting. Because BMC misses the attribute of guaranteed exhaustive verification, it is our first example of a class of approaches called *semi-formal* algorithms, which we discuss further below (see Section 12.3.5).

12.3.4 Solutions to Address the Problem of State Space Explosion

The primary element driving FV capacity limits is the size of the reachable state space in the Formal Model. Because, in the first approximation, the state space grows exponentially with the number of state bits, optimizing the number of state bits of the model is the most powerful lever to shrink the problem size down to make FV tool application feasible. The list of solutions to address the problem of state space explosion contains a number of techniques the verification engineer can use as well as optimizations that modern FV tools do automatically. The following list is by no means a complete enumeration of the state of the art in state-space reduction techniques but contains some of the more commonly known approaches.

Serial Application of Properties

Temporal properties translate into FSM logic that is part of the Formal Model in Figure 12.15. Typically, if the user only applies one property at the time, the combined state space of DUV and environment is smaller. Clearly, this is a trade-off between increased runtime and the need of multiple runs versus the number of state bits for the individual run. The overall process is more tedious, includes bookkeeping about which properties have passed the verification cycle already, and potentially implies an overall longer turn-around time. However, application of the properties one-by-one might be the only way to avoid the state space explosion, which results in inconclusive proofs.

Typically, the graphic user interface of modern FV tools contains selection and bookkeeping mechanisms that make the serial application of multiple properties for a DUV convenient.

Case-Splits: Constraining the DUV or the Environment

Case-splits are another technique to limit the state space of a single FV tool run, replacing the full proof with a series of less comprehensive partial proofs.

We explain the concept of case-splits using the example of a primary input vector that provides an op-code to an ALU. Assuming there are 256 possible op-codes, the design verification tool needs to account for 256 independent possibilities at every cycle where the environment of the DUV can apply a new op-code. In the case where DUV plus environment becomes unmanageable for the FV tool because of state space explosion, a possible alternate way to drive the tool is to run the verification with one op-code at a time. This constraint on the inputs cuts down the number of cases that the FV tool needs to consider in parallel and therefore limits the state space considered. However, the verification team has to select the constraints carefully, to not accidentally eliminate scenarios, and to keep hidden bugs undetected. For example, verifying one op-code at a time on the ALU above does eliminate any scenarios of sequential dependencies between the different cases from consideration.

Again, modern FV tools offer facilities to ensure correct bookkeeping of the selected constraints to avoid or highlight uncovered cases at the end of the verification cycle.

The application of selective constraints for case splitting does not only apply to primary inputs of the DUV. Another technique is the selective, iterative constraining of internal signals of the DUV to a subset of their possible values. This limits the DUV state space considered in a single run of the tool. It is critical for the user to ensure that iteratively the superset of all constraint runs equals the full set of possibilities the DUV implements.

Clearly, the techniques of sub-setting inputs or internal operations to manage the state space brings the verification with FV tools closer in style to simulation-based verification. We apply one set of case-split and overriding constraints per execution of the FV tool. Only the combination of all runs, covering all possible sets of constraints, provides complete verification. A single FV run appears analogous to a simulation test case. However, in simulation we always execute one single path or pattern at a time. FV-based verification, on the other hand, still considers all possibilities of DUV and FV test bench inside the space limited by the manual constraints and overrides. Therefore, the FV-based approach usually provides much better verification coverage per verified property even if manual constraints and serial verification were used to get around the state-space explosion problem.

Manual Reduction of Data Path Widths

The reduction of vectored data paths to a smaller vector size is a popular manual method to decrease state space of the DUV without significant loss of verification coverage.

Staying with the ALU example from above, assume that the ALU uses a 64-bit data path. This means internal registers typically have a vector width of 64 as well. It is obvious that very quickly, such a DUV accumulates a set of state variables of hundreds or thousands of bits, pushing the state space easily beyond the grasp of FV algorithms. It is possible to reduce the data path width drastically and therefore the associated state space with loss of significant control logic verification. This is especially easy to do if the designers prepare the HDL of the design for the reduction by using symbolic parameters instead of hard-coded vector sizes. The simple re-definition of the vector size parameter reduces the state space dramatically and improves the reach of FV algorithm for control logic properties.

Cone-of-Influence Reduction

The most powerful automatic technique to cut down the state space of the Formal Model is the *cone-of-influence reduction*. This reduction does a topological analysis to eliminate all logic, combinational or sequential, that does not contribute to a particular property under verification. Properties not influenced by sequential logic at all or influenced only by a narrow subset of the whole DUV benefit greatly from this optimization. The FV tool can prune all parts of the DUV and FV environment not directly connected with these properties from the model before the actual verification algorithms starts, thus possibly shrinking the state space of the verification dramatically. Very often, this optimization makes the difference between a manageable state space and the inconclusive run of the FV tool that exhausts all available memory.

The cone-of-influence reduction is particularly successful when applied to designs that make heavy use of the assertion-based design style. Many of the implementation assertions do not need a deep state traversal because their range into the surrounding logic is typically quite shallow (e.g., one-hot property).

Localization

Localization is one example of a class of model transformations that modern FV tools do automatically under the covers. The idea is to eliminate sequential logic that drives signals internal to the DUV and replace it with purely random drivers. Figure 12.18 shows the principle of this transformation.

With localization, the FV disconnects a part of the DUV logic that drives a property and replaces it with randomly driven signals. If the tool can prove that the property holds despite the unconstrained behavior on the artificial internal boundary, by inference the property holds for the real DUV as well. If the property fails, no result can be reported, because the unconstrained boundary signals may have behaved in illegal ways that the real DUV logic would not have allowed. Most likely, the error report would consist of false fails. Usually, the FV tools attempt a different localization operation after a failed attempt and proceed until it finds a boundary for which it can prove compliance of the DUV with the prop-

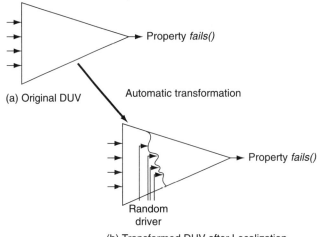

(a) Original DUV   Automatic transformation

Property *fails()*

Random
driver

(b) Transformed DUV after Localization

▪ **FIGURE 12.18**

Localization optimization for formal verification application. (a) The original DUV where a set of sequential logic drives a property *fails* signal. Localization selects a logic boundary inside the DUV where it replaces the original DUV logic driving the boundary signals with randomly driven signals. This transformation allows the disregard of all the driving logic and can disconnect that portion of the DUV before further verification. If the tool can prove that the *fails* signal cannot turn active under the completely unconstrained driving conditions using random stimulus, the proof for the property under the more constrained conditions of the real DUV logic is accomplished.

erty. If not successful after several iterations, the FV tool gives up localization and pursues other algorithms.

12.3.5 Semi-Formal Verification

Because of the exponential complexity of the FV problem, all modern FV tools provide a collection of the optimizations discussed above under their covers. In addition to the application of these transformations, these tools alternate the application of different bug-finding algorithms. Figure 12.19 shows the principles of this hybrid approach.

Previously we discussed the first algorithm that bridged the space between exhaustive FV and random simulation. BMC provides full FV-like coverage only for a subsection of the DUV state space. Semi-formal verification tools drive this concept much further. They alternate exhaustive state-space search algorithms with BMC, localization, and random simulation algorithms. The assumption is that the overall DUV state space is too large for exhaustive algorithms. Therefore, the semi-formal tool uses random simulation to drive the DUV into *interesting* portions of the state space where it then applies exhaustive search for property

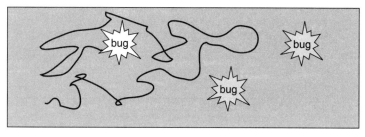

(a) Random Simulation

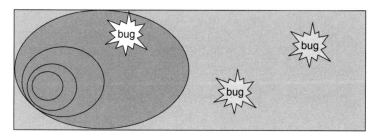

(b) Exhaustive Search

(c) Alternating between Exhaustive Search and Random Simulation

■ **FIGURE 12.19**

The advantages of hybrid semi-formal verification (FV) systems, which alternate between different approaches. (a) The verification coverage gained by the application of pure random simulation. (b) The exhaustive coverage of FV for a subset of the overall design under verification (DUV) state space. The state space of practical DUVs is too large for FV tools to cover it successfully in its completeness; therefore, FV in practice only covers a portion of the DUV state space. (c) The alternating application of random simulation and exhaustive search, which provides the largest verification coverage of all alternatives.

TABLE 12.18. ▪ Starting point for an exploration of the commercial Formal and Sem-Formal Verification space

Cadence: FormalCheck	Synopsys: Magellan
Mentor: 0-In Archer	Averant: Solidify
Real Intent: Verix	@HDL: @Verifier
IBM: RuleBase PE	

violations there. Once the tool reaches the limit of manageable state space, it turns again to random simulation.

One variant of the semi-formal paradigm uses actual traces provided by traditional random simulation to seed the semi-formal tools and drive the exhaustive application of FV from that starting point.

Semi-Formal verification attempts to combine the strengths of random simulation and FV in a synergistic, new way. This approach has high promise to improve the overall verification coverage dramatically but is still in heavy research and early application. This new approach is certainly the most exciting development in verification research at this time.

One important lesson already emerges very clearly out of the development of semi-formal technology. It will be vital in the future that the disciplines of traditional random simulation and semi-formal verification can share the mechanisms for property checking and input constraint declarations. The verification team of the future will need to apply either technology wherever appropriate, and it will be vital to have input specifications that are portable between the different technologies.

12.3.6 EDA Vendors Supplying Formal and Semi-Formal Verification Tools

Table 12.18 provides the names of several EDA vendors together with the name of the tools they provide in the FV and semi-formal verification space. Because this is a highly dynamic space of research and development, the list is by no means complete or representative and readers should use it merely as a starting point.

12.4 SUMMARY

In this chapter we extend the discussion of FV technology begun in Chapter 11 further to property specification and checking.

The center of the first half covers tools and languages for property specification. Besides the use of pure HDL, the OVL provides a library of HDL building blocks to make property specification easier.

PSL is a full-blown property specification language. It is the basis for an important industry standard in this space, and in this chapter we use it as the primary example to discuss all major aspects of property specification. Besides the productivity-enhancing concise surface of PSL, there is a coherent set of constructs that allow the concise definition of powerful temporal properties.

Functional FV today is enabled mostly by a variety of tools that use symbolic model checking at their core. In addition to the exhaustive verification by model checkers, practical FV tools use a number of optimizations that tackle the problem of state space explosion. The variety of different heuristics to enable FV in the mode of bug finding leads to new hybrid FV tools that allow the user to select many different approaches to apply FV.

The newest evolution of FV technology combines the scaling of random simulation with exhaustive coverage of FV in the new technology semi-formal verification.

Once considered applicable only in the academic domain, FV technology has been successful in many industry projects and continues to increase in importance in any modern verification methodology.

12.5 EXERCISES

1. Create the top-level model RTL for the ARB design of Using OVL to Specify Properties in a module called *top* that instantiates the *arb_property_checker* and the design *arb*. Use the *arb_checker* that implements the assertions using OVL.

2. Explain why exercise 1 cannot be implemented in VHDL with the same model hierarchy.

3. Specify properties for the Gray counter (Chapter 11, DUV Drivers for FV) using PSL.

4. Use the ARB design of exercise 1 and use the PSL properties of Using PSL to Specify Properties to gain experience with PSL in a commercial tool environment.

5. Use the ARB checker of Figure 12.12 and add coverage directives that ensure assertion coverage for the following events:

   (a) Ensure that all requests have been exercised
   (b) Ensure that all grants have been asserted
   (c) Ensure that arbiter corner cases have been exercised (e.g., two requests at the time)

6. Specify PSL properties for calc1 and exercise them using simulation and / or FV tools available

7. Modify the checker in Figure 12.12 to switch the checking from a LIFO sequence to a first in, first out sequence.

8. Use Table 12.18 as a starting point to assemble an up-to-date list of the main commercial FV and Semi_FV tools and their capabilities.

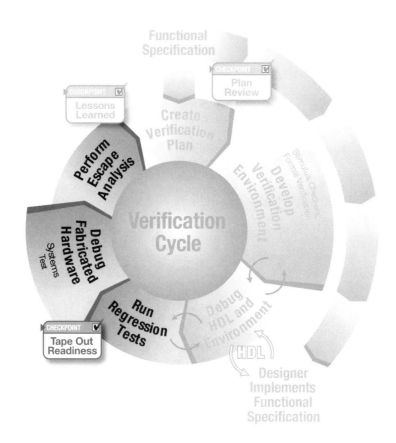

With a solid understanding of functional verification techniques for creating robust environments, the next steps in the Verification Cycle are the regression stage, the tape-out readiness checkpoint, debugging the fabricated hardware, and escape analysis. These stages provide a backdrop for the verification team to reflect upon the strengths and weaknesses of their environments, both before tape-out and after receiving hardware results. Chapter 13 focuses on these parts of the Verification Cycle.

The most complex designs require advanced functional verification techniques. These techniques include high-level model verification before register transfer level implementation, bootstrapping simulation efforts, and coverage directed stimulus generation. These are the topics of Chapter 14.

CHAPTER 13

COMPLETING THE VERIFICATION CYCLE

The verification team spends most of their effort in the first half of the verification cycle. Weeks of planning lead to a sound verification plan that, in turn, yields a robust verification environment. Building that environment and debugging the DUV take the lion's share of the verification effort. As the team completes the environment, they focus their efforts on sweeping the design of the last bugs before initial hardware fabrication. However, the verification cycle continues well beyond fabrication, as the design team tests the fabricated hardware and prepares for final manufacturing.

Before hardware tape-out, the verification team completes sections of their test plans as they verify the entire chip or system's functional specification. In most complex systems that require hierarchical verification, lower level test plans complete before system levels. In addition, across a single level of the hierarchy, functional testing proceeds in waves, with the verification team creating initial tests before moving on to more complex scenarios. As the bug rate declines on the initial tests and the lower levels of the hierarchy, cursory testing of these functions continues under *regression*, where the verification team ensures that new functions and features do not break previously verified functions.

The verification team considers bug rates when using the regression system and also for deciding when their work is nearing completion. To measure bug rates, the verification team must use a problem-tracking tool to monitor the uncovered bugs. These problems can be early in the process or late during regression. Either way, the problem-tracking tool allows the verification team to track the bug rates and status efficiently.

Before long, the bug rate falls for all functional verification, and the design enters the final stages of circuit layout, timing correction, and physical implementation. This is the time for the verification team to take stock in their work, analyze their environments, and study their coverage data. The team scrutinizes their work, proving to themselves that they have covered all the necessary functions and showing that the design is functionally ready for fabrication.

At some point, the design team must make a decision to commit the chip or system to fabrication. Part of this decision comes from the verification team. The verification team needs to know when to give their approval, signaling that the design is functionally correct. During the hiatus between tape-out and receiving fabricated hardware, the verification team continues to run regression cycles.

The entire design team eagerly awaits arrival of the first samples of hardware. Upon arrival, it is time to check the fabricated chips in a real operating environment. This is an intimidating point in time for the verification team, because the speed of the fabricated hardware outpaces the sum of all the simulation cycles in a matter of seconds. This is also the point at which the verification team gets their evaluation.

Despite all their efforts, verification teams working on complex chips and systems cannot detect all bugs before hardware fabrication. However, the team must meet certain expectations, such as flawless chip initialization (reset scenarios) and basic functionality. However, at gigahertz speeds running customer applications, it is all too likely that the hardware will come across dozens of scenarios never encountered during verification. When a functional flaw exists in any of these new scenarios, the verification team again jumps into action, performing the last stage of the verification cycle: *escape analysis*. Here, the team investigates the missed scenario, categorizes the design flaw, and updates the verification environment. This process ensures that the verification team learns from the "escaped" flaw and improves their capabilities for the next generation of hardware.

This chapter discusses these latter stages of the verification cycle, from regression to escape analysis. These activities provide key structures for a complete and robust verification effort.

13.1 REGRESSION

As the design project progresses from its preliminary phases, verification moves from initial, simple tests to the more complex scenarios. At the same time, verification that started at the lower levels of the design hierarchy continues up to units, chip, and system levels until all parts of the verification team are active at the same time.

On large engineering projects like chip design and verification, it is vital to enable work in parallel in most disciplines. A serialized progression would lead to unacceptably long project durations. Parallelism allows work downstream to start before a preceding process step is finished. Like an assembly-line operation, this pipeline process compresses the overall project schedule.

13.1.1 Regression in the Verification Flow

The verification team can start work on the level of functional units as soon as the design RTL has enough content and design level simulation

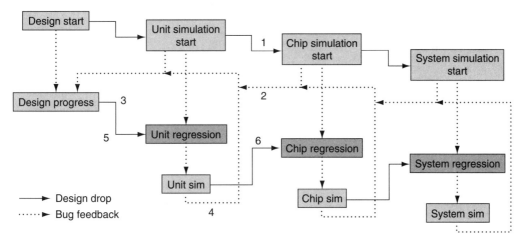

Design and verification cycles on different hierarchy levels proceed in parallel after the initial design drop from the design team. At various intervals, the design process and the bug feedback from verification leads to design changes and new design drops. On every verification level, an inserted regression step ensures previously reached verification maturity is retained in the new design drop.

is mature enough to make the unit work productive. The design team can hand off a new set of RTL design sources to the unit simulation team at this time. We call this repeated delivery of a packaged set of HDL that contains a certain level of functionality a *design drop*. As soon as all the units of a chip have reached a maturity level that allows the chip verification team to make enough forward progress, they receive the first design drop of the whole chip. Subsequently, the system simulation team can start their work in parallel when the chip-level teams assert a first health-level of the chip simulations.

Figure 13.1 illustrates the parallel progress between the design team and verification teams on three different verification levels: unit, chip, and system.

The "Chip Simulation Start" block in Figure 13.1 is the beginning of the chip level verification effort. The chip level verification team would receive a design drop from all the lower levels of verification (1 in Figure 13.1). This team would then perform their testing on that collection of design drops. During their initial testing they may encounter bugs that the lower levels did not find. When this occurs the design must be fixed; therefore, the simulation is handed over to the designer to look at (2 in Figure 13.1). Once the designer attempts a fix, it is handed to the unit level of simulation so they can regress the fix to ensure nothing else is affected by the fix (3 in Figure 13.1). The unit team then regresses this new design drop. If during the regression of this new design drop the unit verification team encounters other issues, they feed this back to the designer (4 in Figure 13.1). The designer again attempts another fix and does another drop to the unit verification team (5 in Figure 13.1). Eventually, the unit team validates the fix via the regression. At this point, the unit team then performs a drop to the chip verification team so they may progress (6 in Figure 13.1).

In general, after the first design drop has moved from units all the way to the system level, all parts of the verification team can work in parallel and feed bug reports back to the design team. As the design team releases new design drops to the verification team in return, it is necessary to merge the changed design into the running process without disrupting the already made progress. The worst case would be a reset of the process that requires a re-working of all previously completed verification.

The verification team performs a *regression simulation* on every verification hierarchy level to assess that previously asserted design correctness still applies to the new design drop. The regression ensures that the bug fixes work and that the fixes and newly added design functions do not break the DUV in unintended ways. If the regression completes successfully, the verification teams can proceed quickly to verify the new functional content and the overall process makes forward progress. In the more general case, we speak of a *regression verification*, which includes both simulation and formal verification. Regression verification prevents the functionality of new DUV drops to backslide to some earlier buggy state.

A *regression environment* is a set of HDL models, test bench configurations, test cases, and formal properties that have to run successfully to assert sufficient quality of a new design drop and let the verification team proceed productively forward. We call the execution of the regression environment a *regression run*. This regression environment could be the complete current environment meaning the regression run uses all existing tests.

There are two main concerns that a regression environment must address. First, there must be measurable quality criteria to ensure the effectiveness of a regression for the iterative verification cycle. Second, it is important to minimize the time it takes to complete a regression run (which is why you usually do not use the complete set of tests in the regression environment). Being able to turn around regressions quickly makes them a key tool to improve productivity in the parallel design and verification cycle. The following sections discuss each of these concerns.

13.1.2 Regression Quality

On any hierarchical verification level, regression runs must establish baseline quality criteria for every new design drop. Regression verification is selective re-testing of the DUV. The test selection must regard two main sources for the regression runs: tests that previously failed and tests that broadly cover the base functionality implemented thus far by the design team. Both classes of tests collected together form a *regression suite*.

A regression must re-run the specific tests that failed on the earlier design drop to ensure that the design team did indeed fix the problems. Initially, these tests can be very specific and deterministic to be able to hit the exact error scenario uncovered before. Afterward, it is very effective to remove the constraints on the randomization parameters and directives of these tests to cover the DUV state space around the previous specific error scenario. Such an extension of the static re-run scenario ensures that the bug fix was a real error resolution, not just a specific patch; in addition, it further stresses an obviously error-prone area of DUV.

The power of formal verification comes to play strongly if the required regression tests are actually property checks that previously failed using formal verification technology. The formal verification ensures the exhaustive proof of the property against all DUV inputs and behavior that the regression environment allows.

The second class of tests in a regression suite contains static and dynamic tests that cover as much as possible of the currently implemented functionality of the DUV. The team selects the tests based on functional content and coverage metrics that were measured during prior runs of the tests. For the static tests, the functional coverage remains stable from one design drop to the next. This is true as well for property checks applied with formal verification tools. For the dynamic tests, however, the coverage metric is a probabilistic measure because of the random nature of the environment.

Ultimately, the utility of a regression suite is determined by its success to identify low-quality design drops, thus preventing a backward slide in DUV quality between successive design drops.

The goal to reach comprehensive re-verification coverage with a regression suite is in direct conflict with the goal to run a regression very quickly over a new design drop and then return to the main process of the DUV verification. The verification team must find a pragmatic compromise between the two objectives to create a regression suite that is both comprehensive and fast enough.

13.1.3 Regression Efficiency

A regression suite can become a bottleneck of the verification cycle. This occurs when the verification team runs out of productive work on the current design drop and must wait for the regression run to complete on the next design drop. Switching to a new design drop becomes a necessity when bugs, which the design team fixed in the next drop, become the main obstacle to progress on the current drop.

There are two ways to improve the turn-around time for regression suites. The first approach, *test case harvesting*, optimizes the test selection such that tests with higher coverage are preferred. This minimizes the number of tests contained in the regression suite. Second, the team can split the overall suite into separate jobs and run them in parallel on several computers, typically referred to as a *workstation farm*.

Test Case Harvesting

Minimizing the size of the regression suite requires the use of functional coverage metrics. Every test case records its coverage using the same coverage criteria. Over the full sequence of tests, the regression environment checks whether a test has hit coverage points that prior tests did not visit before. Test by test, the environment accumulates the overall coverage high water mark. If a test does not hit a new coverage point, it does not contribute to the purpose of the regression, and therefore the verification team can eliminate the test from the regression suite.

Figure 13.2a illustrates this technique, which we call *simple harvesting*. There is a sequence of seven tests and a record of the coverage achieved by each test shown as a mark in the 4×4 matrix of a simple example coverage space. After each test completes, the newly hit coverage events accumulate to a total coverage score for all tests so far. Below each test case's coverage matrix, Figure 13.2a shows the accumulated coverage of the regression suite up to this test. In the end, the regression suite is not able to cover the whole coverage space. However, every new test hits a new coverage event. Using the simple harvesting scheme does not yield a reduction of this regression suite. The regression suite does yield high coverage of the overall space, but with simple harvesting we need to run all the tests to achieve this.

Simple harvesting has the advantage of very low runtime overhead on top of the coverage data collection. This technique can eliminate redundant tests efficiently when applied over large sets of tests and a limited coverage space, especially in cases where the individual tests trigger only few coverage events each.

However, the disadvantage of the method is the limited optimization potential governed by the simple incremental test-by-test analysis. The example in Figure 13.2 shows this drawback because a more complex method, shown in Figure 13.2b, can cut the number of tests almost in half while retaining the high overall coverage achieved by the now much shorter regression suite.

Complex test case harvesting is a process where the regression environment keeps the coverage results for each test case and does a global analysis over all tests of the regression suite. The goal of the analysis is to find the minimum number of tests required to hit all coverage points that the whole regression suite covers. Figure 13.2b shows that the example achieves this with four instead of seven tests.

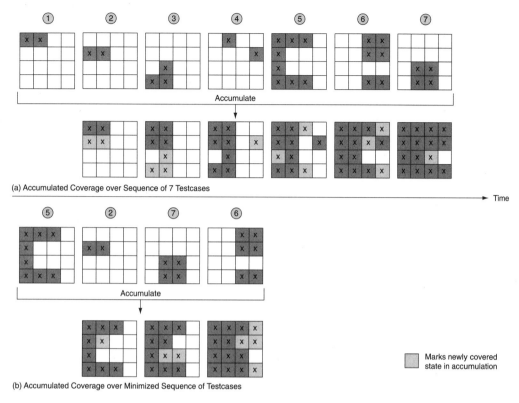

(a) Accumulated Coverage over Sequence of 7 Testcases

Time

(b) Accumulated Coverage over Minimized Sequence of Testcases

Marks newly covered state in accumulation

■ **FIGURE 13.2**

Example for efficient test case harvesting. The matrix of 16 coverage points is shown as a table. (a) A sequence of seven test cases, each represented by its table with the coverage points that it reached. Below that sequence is a set of matrices marked to show how the overall coverage of the regression suite accumulates. After each accumulation, the summary highlights the newly hit coverage points. (b) How a shorter sequence of tests selected from the original seven in a can accumulate the same set of coverage points.

The underlying optimization problem is the *set cover* problem in the academic literature, and its complexity is exponential with the number of tests [100]. The set cover problem is not verification specific. In its mathematical definition it is a set of sets whose union has all members of the union of all sets. For a regression suite with a large number of tests, complex test case harvesting requires the use of approximate algorithms because an attempt to do full optimization exceeds any reasonable time limits and defeats the purpose of the regression verification. Recently, the problem has attracted new research [101].

Whether using the simple or complex test case harvesting techniques, the reduction of tests in the regression suite will lead to higher regression quality as those tests that are running exercise the necessary function with little overlap.

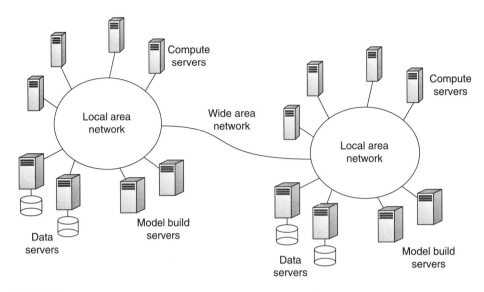

▪ **FIGURE 13.3**

Efficient regression suite processing uses a workstation farm to distribute the verification tests across a large number of computer servers. The farm can be spread across several local-area network clusters, which are connected via fast wide-area network. In addition to the compute servers, the farm uses dedicated high-performance machines to build simulation models or to run formal verification tasks. Data servers with large disk capacity host the simulation models, coverage data, and regression results.

Workstation Farm—Simulation Grid

The second way to optimize the runtime of a regression suite is the application of parallel processing. Splitting the suite into test cases that each can run on a different computer is trivial if the tests are independent of each other. A workstation farm is a set of workstations connected via a local-area network. A batch control environment allows the verification team to launch compute jobs into the workstation farm.

As Figure 13.3 shows, a workstation farm typically consists of a large number of compute servers, which process the individual regression simulation jobs. Model build and formal verification usually need faster, high-end machines with a large main memory footprint. Workstations with large disk capacity store the prepared simulation models that they ship to the compute servers over the network. The data servers are also the place to store coverage and regression result data.

A workstation farm that is used for regression runs is managed by batch control software that monitors which compute servers are available and transfers individual regression runs to them. At the completion of a single regression test, the compute server transfers the results back to one of the data servers. One popular solution package to manage workstation farms used by electronic design automation vendors is the *Load Sharing Facility* [102].

Because simulation is usually a processor-bound application with little input/output (I/O), the compute servers can easily be shared with an interactive user. This allows the population of desktop workstations of designers and verification engineers to be part of the pool of compute servers and typically extends the capacity of the workstation farm dramatically. Now, when the workforce is not utilizing the processors on the desktop (they go home for the day), the workstation farm kicks in and utilizes these processors.

During the last few years, the concept of *grid computing* has gained popularity and support with a groundswell of supporting software [103]. A computing grid is a distributed collection of computers, managed together as one large compute resource. It is possible at any time to commission applications into this combined resource. Simple applications can run on a single computer of the grid, whereas parallel, cooperating applications use the network to tie several machines dynamically together to form a parallel machine. The one application that pushed grid computing into the public consciousness was NASA's SETI@Home, an application that allows millions of personal computers on the Internet to participate in analyzing radio telescope data to find signs of extraterrestrial life.

This description shows the great similarity between verification workstation farms and on-demand computing grids. We expect that typical regression verifications will soon be grid-computing applications.

Long Tests Versus Short Tests

One basic requirement for effective use of workstation farms is a methodology that keeps regression tests to a relatively short duration.

If a complete regression contains 10 long test cases, the parallelization of the regression run can only use up to 10 compute servers. The turn-around time for the regression suite is as long as it takes to complete the slowest test. If that test is 10 hours long, no workstation farm can cut the regression time below 10 hours, even if the total time to run all tests in sequence is just 15 hours. However, if we can limit the length of the longest individual test to 1 hour, a workstation farm of 15 servers can take down the regression time to 1 hour, an order of magnitude faster than before. Over the course of a project, the accumulated acceleration of regression runtime has a strong, positive impact on product time-to-market.

Smaller tests also have the advantage that in case of an error that occurs late in the test, the re-run and debug will not require a long start-up time. On the other hand, how can short tests create enough stimuli to run the DUV deep into interesting corners of its state space? Common sense dictates that it takes a longer test to set up the interesting window conditions that reveal the bugs in the design.

The solution to this problem is to let the test case driver support an intelligent setting of the initial state of the DUV. Regression tests do not need to start with the power-on-reset simulation. A single, separate simulation can ensure that power-on-reset works (as described in Chapter 9). Instead, it is very productive to reset the DUV at the beginning of a regression test into a known legal state that is a snapshot of an *interesting state* at which point the DUV executes the test case stimulus under duress. Obviously, this scheme requires more work in defining interesting starting states for the test case driver (Chapter 14 contains more information on this). The payback in speedup of regression testing, however, is well worth the effort.

13.2   PROBLEM TRACKING

Any problem that is encountered throughout the project impacts the team. Every problem must be resolved. The problem areas might deal with HDL logic bugs, verification environment bugs, timing, synthesis, and tool problems. We focus on the first two—HDL logic bugs and verification environment bugs. Some of the most common problems related to these pertain to the specification, defects (either in the DUV and the verification environment), and enhancements to the verification environment.

One key to resolving all the problems is to track them. This ensures that no problem goes unresolved, because there is documentation of all problems that have occurred during the course of the project. In addition to ensuring that all problems are resolved, the tracking also allows the management team to stay informed on the progress of the overall project.

Many teams overlook tracking problems that deal with the specification. Because this is the source for the design and verification effort, any problem associated with the specification is worth tracking. Finding ambiguities within the specification is common. By tracking these ambiguities, it ensures a clear and concise specification. If they go unnoticed, it can lead to misinterpretation of the specification. In other cases, details are just missing from the specification. In either case, the verification team needs to ensure they correctly understand the intended behavior.

In Chapter 8 we discussed the debug of problems (within the DUV and the verification environment). What was not covered is the tracking of such problems. Logging and tracking of any problems then ensures resolution. The verification team should track any problem encountered within the verification environment (to include the DUV).

In addition to problems within the verification environment, the verification team should also track any type of enhancement request. These enhancements could be to the HDL or to the verification environment. By tracking these enhancements, the team creates a list of items to consider acting on if time permits. If time does not permit for the current release, then it becomes a list of items that need to be resolved for the next release of the chip. It can be something as simple as changing the arbitration scheme within the design or as drastic as rewriting a verification component for re-use.

Now that we know what to track, what has to be decided next is how to track the problems or enhancements (both referred to as *issues*). Chip design is a large hardware project that uses software concepts and constructs as a skeleton for creating the hardware. Many of the same project issues plaguing hardware engineers also plague software engineers. Problem tracking is one of those concepts that the hardware community needs to adopt from the software community. The software community has used formalized tools to perform the tracking of issues. There exist many commercially and freely available issue-tracking tools. (A search on "Problem Tracking" on the Web will result in hundreds of hits.) Some functions that are mandatory for these issue-tracking tools are subscription capability, query capability, and report generation.

Subscription capability gives users the ability to subscribe to categories or classes of issues. The tool notifies all subscribers when the status of these issues changes (see below on the life cycle of an issue). This relieves some of the burden of having to review each issue for any change manually. Manual checking for updates to issues when a verification engineer may have hundreds of open issues hinders productivity.

Query capability is another productivity booster. The query capability allows the verification engineer an efficient way to search the database based on different criteria. Because of the nature of chip design, the verification engineer may be working with levels of logic that are not the most current. Because of this fact, when the verification engineer finds a bug he or she needs to ensure that this is not an already known bug and subsequently fixed in another release of the logic. Without this capability on big projects, it may take a long time just to check to see whether this issue is a new issue.

The last mandatory function is report generation. When we discuss metrics, we will see that this is the mechanism of how to create the bug closure rates. Again, this is a productivity booster. If this function did not exist, a verification engineer would manually create the bug closure rates. In most cases, this is a waste of a valuable resource.

With the advent of these issue-tracking tools, the tracking of problems and enhancements becomes more manageable. These tools allow tracking of an issue throughout its life cycle. The *life cycle* of an issue is the phases a problem or enhancement goes through between when it is conceived and when the problem or enhancement is resolved. Most of the tools are configurable to meet the team's needs. Figure 13.4 shows the life cycle of an issue for a typical chip design project.

The life cycle of an issue determines how to track an issue. Every issue contains a status field as well as numerous other fields such as owner,

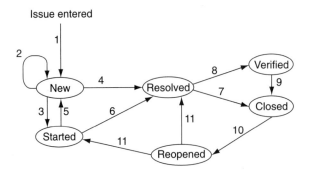

■ **FIGURE 13.4**

Issue life cycle from the creation to the closure of an issue.

issue number, description, date opened, date closed, unit, and issue type. These fields are just an example, and any given project is subject to creating their own that are pertinent to the project. However, the status field is an important feature because it defines where an issue is in its life cycle.

When a verification engineer opens an issue, its status is *new* (1 in Figure 13.4). At this point, the tool assigns an owner to the issue based on other fields defined within the project (such as unit or class). For specification issues, the tool assigns the author of the specification as the owner. For design issues, the tool assigns the issue based on the unit. The same would be true for verification. The owner then looks at it and reassigns it to another owner based on investigation of the issue (2 in Figure 13.4). In this case the status remains *new*. Or the owner changes the status to either *started* (3 in Figure 13.4) or *resolved* (4 in Figure 13.4). By classifying it as *started*, the owner acknowledges that it requires further study. However, by marking it *resolved*, the owner may already know the resolution of the issue (the problem may already be resolved in a newer version of the logic or verification component).

When an issue gets to the *started* state, it means that the tool assigned the issue to the proper person for resolution. The owner, on further investigation, may find that their piece (logic or verification component) does not cause the problem described by the issue. Some other upstream piece may be the cause of the problem. At this point, the owner would re-assign the issue to another person by changing the owner (and hence changing the status from *started* to *new*) (5 in Figure 13.4). If this is not the case and the owner determines the resolution, the issue is then changed to *resolved* (6 in Figure 13.4).

An issue in the *resolved* state indicates that the owner (designer for logic bugs, verification engineer for verification environment issues, architect or designer for specification issues) understands the problem or has decided on a course of action for resolution of the issue. The type of action the owner takes may be one of many. The following list shows some of the actions the owner may choose to take:

- Fixed: A fix for the problem is available.

- Defer: The fix to the problem or enhancement is not put into this version of the product.

- Duplicate: Someone else already found this issue. The owner should document the original issue number so that the originator can find the resolution to the issue.

- Not reproducible: The owner could not reproduce the problem. If this problem reappears, then reopen the issue.

In any case, the originator of the issue must validate that the resolution is satisfactory. The owner of this issue cannot close it until completing this step. If the resolution was not satisfactory, the originator would then re-open the issue. If the resolution is satisfactory, then the resolved issue is marked as either *verified* or *closed*. The determination of whether to mark the issue as *verified* or *closed* depends on the resolution action (as listed above). In all cases but "fixed", the issue becomes *closed* (7 in Figure 13.4). If the resolution is "fixed", then the issue must go to the *verified* state (8 in Figure 13.4).

Marking the issue as *verified* means the originator of the issue has viewed the resolution action and agrees with it. For issues that pertain to logic or verification components, the issue remains in this state until the originator receives the fix. Once the originator receives the fix, the issue is then marked *closed* (9 in Figure 13.4). In the case of a specification problem, the verification engineer would validate that the updated documentation matches the intended behavior.

When a user determines that a closed issue is not resolved, they reopen that issue. At this point, the tool marks the previously closed issue as *reopened* (10 in Figure 13.4), which indicates that the issue requires further action. The individual who marked it resolved (now the owner) must revisit the issue and decide what to do with it. The owner would then make a decision on how to proceed. Depending on the course of action, the issue may be marked as either *started* or *resolved* (the decision on what to do is similar to when an issue is in the *new* state) (11 in Figure 13.4).

The *closed* state indicates the end of the life cycle for the issue (meaning that the resolution action to the issue is correct). However, a previously closed issue can be reactivated by changing the status back to *reopened* (10 in Figure 13.4). This may occur because the original resolution was inappropriate. For example, a user may reopen an issue previously classified as "not reproducible" based on new information. This is also the case when a deferral resolution on an issue is no longer applicable, that is, management reprioritizes deferred functionality to the current release of the chip.

Now that we understand the life cycle of an issue, we need to determine what types of issues are worthy of tracking. Tracking all issues is ideal. Realistically, we should only track those items that are worth the effort. The rule of thumb is that an issue is not worth tracking if the effort involved in creating the issue is greater than the effort to resolve the issue. However, this is just the rule of thumb. Every project has different guidelines.

13.3 TAPE-OUT READINESS

To this point, we discussed most of the verification cycle—verification plans, verification environments, simulation based verification, debugging of the environment, formal based verification, and regressions. That brings us to the question of when is the design ready to commit to manufacturing. Before sending a design to manufacturing, the entire design team must meet the established *tape-out criteria*. Tape-out criteria is a series of checklists that indicate the completion of planned work for a chip before release to manufacturing. Tape-out criteria has many components, verification being one of them. In this section, we discuss verification-related completion criteria.

However, before getting to completion criteria, we need to discuss metrics. Keep in mind that every company has its own set of tape-out criteria and metrics. The purpose of this section is not to discuss every metric that is used, but to discuss some of the metrics and their relevance to tape-out readiness.

13.3.1 Metrics

Metrics allows the engineering team to assess the overall progress of the project. By keeping metrics, the project's managers can assist the development process by shifting resources and evenly distributing work among engineers and skill groups. They do these tasks based on the metrics and feedback from the team (including the verification teams).

The most common verification metrics are bug closure rates and coverage closure. These two metrics assess the progress of the verification effort and dovetail with common design metrics such as HDL completion and timing closure.

Bug Rates

The bug rate shows the pace at which the verification team discovers bugs and designers fix them. This is an indication of progress for the team. The verification team tracks two separate bug rates. The first is

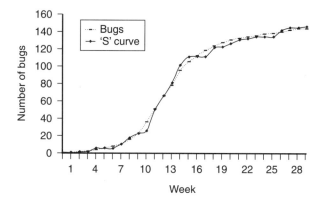

Bug discovery rate.

when the verification team logs a bug (*bug discovery rate*). This occurs when the verification team creates a new issue in the problem-tracking tool. The other is when the owner of the bugs fixes them (*bug closure rate*). This again is determined from the problem-tracking tool; it is when the issue has been closed by the originator. Both are important so that the team can tell if the designers are keeping up with the bugs. If the number of open issues each week remains constant (the number of new bugs equal the number of fixed bugs, but not necessarily the same ones), then the project is well balanced. If the number of open issues grows from week to week and the designers are not keeping up with them, then the team needs to take corrective actions. Figure 13.5 shows an example of bug discovery rates.

Notice that the bug discovery rate follows the shape of an "S." The team typically expects bug discovery rates to follow this path. In the beginning the environment is too unstable; thus, the verification team finds few bugs. As the environment matures and the verification team begins running valid test scenarios, the bug discovery rate rises sharply. Then near the end, the discovery rate levels off as the verification team finds fewer and fewer bugs [105].

Another metric to track when it comes to bug closure rates are the age of the open issues. The team does not want a series of old bugs hanging around. These bugs hold up testing until the designers release the fixes to the verification team. By not providing fixes in a timely fashion, the verification team cannot progress because they constantly are running into the same bug. Age issues can also be a sign that the design needs to be "re-micro-architected." It could be that the fix is so complex that it takes weeks to fix.

Bug discovery rates do not fall off overnight. The verification team can use this rate to predict the trend over the upcoming weeks. Figure 13.6 shows an example of bug discovery and closure rates.

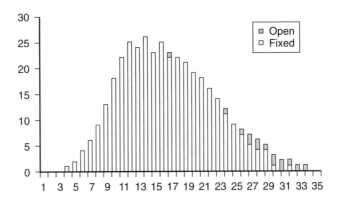

■ **FIGURE 13.6**

Example of bug discovery and closure rate.

For this example we assume the project is well balanced—the number of bugs found in a week is close to the number of bugs fixed. In the beginning of the verification effort the bug rate is zero, and the verification team finds no bugs because the environment is not yet functional (weeks 1 to 3). As the environment becomes stable, bugs are uncovered (in both the logic and the verification components). As the verification team progresses, the bug rate increases (weeks 4 to 11). Eventually, the bug rate flattens out as the design becomes more stable and mature (weeks 12 to 16). As verification progresses, the bug rate drops (weeks 17 to 29). As the end of the verification for a given unit nears, the team focuses on the last coverage items (corner case tests). During this time, the design team is feverishly closing the last remaining bugs (weeks 30 to 34). Note that in these weeks the last remaining bugs are not closed as fast as previously. Typically, these last remaining bugs are the corner case bugs that take more time to analyze and fix (as well as regress to ensure that nothing else is broke). Finally, every function is covered and all tests pass successfully in regression (week 35).

Another good item to track is the location (what logic piece) where the verification team finds the bugs. If a particular HDL unit has an inordinate share of the bugs (compared with other equally complex units), then this may indicate that the unit (or portions of the unit) needs to be re-designed.

Coverage Closure

Although the bug rate metric measures closure on problems found by the verification team, the *coverage closure rate* measures how the environment does against its functional testing criteria. Coverage closure means that the verification team has met their defined coverage goals. The closure on coverage is for both functional as well as structural (code

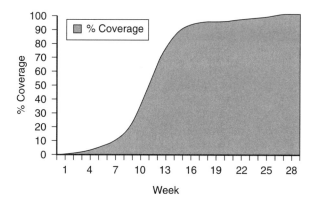

■ **FIGURE 13.7**

Example of functional coverage closure.

coverage). Functional and structural coverage closure measures the overall effectiveness of the test scenarios.

As mentioned in Section 6.2, functional coverage targets semantic aspects of the test generation or design implementation. Functional coverage metrics assists in determining whether the verification environment exercised all the identified coverage items. The key here is "identified," because the verification environment may not have exercised functions not identified in the coverage or test plans. If there is no coverage item for a function or logic condition, then no one can measure if it was exercised or not. If the stimulus component does not exercise certain function, then the checking components can not identify a failure within that function (remember the yin-yang). Figure 13.7 illustrates the closure of functional coverage over time (the verification effort).

When the environment is in its infancy and discovering basic environmental component and logic bugs, the team turns off coverage collection. Measuring coverage is a distraction; the most basic test scenario must first run successfully (weeks 1 to 4 in Figure 13.7). As the tests start exercising more logic function, coverage collection commences (weeks 5 to 19). The closure on coverage slows dramatically once the team has verified most mainstream function. At this point only the corner cases remain, and the verification team focuses on creating the stimulus conditions required for these difficult scenarios. Once these final tests pass, functional coverage reaches 100% (weeks 20 to 31).

The curve shown in Figure 13.7 shows a typical functional coverage graph for many projects. It illustrates the progression of functional coverage of the verification effort of a unit. Every week the verification team measures their functional coverage and charts that against their functional coverage goals (from the verification plan). Later we discuss how this is important to completion criteria.

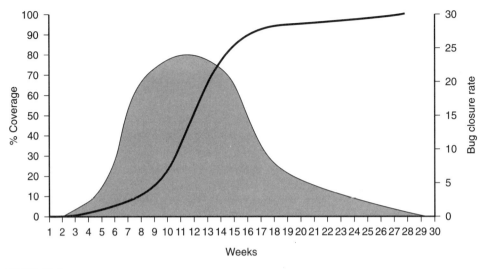

The relationship of bug closure rates to the percentage of functional coverage.

You may notice a correlation between bug rates and functional coverage closure. Figure 13.8 shows the correlation of bug rates to functional coverage closure.

Note at the apex of the bug rate curve is when coverage starts to increase dramatically. At this point (week 11), the design becomes more stable and the bug rate decreases from an increasing rate to a constant rate. Coverage continues to increase dramatically as the bug rate starts to decline (up to week 17). Now, as the bug rate starts to flatten out as the verification team finds fewer and fewer bugs week to week, the coverage flattens out as well. As mentioned previously, this is when the verification team is addressing the corner-cases. At the end of the verification effort, note how functional coverage becomes 100%, whereas the verification team discovers no new bugs.

It is unlikely that the bug rate will drop before the coverage curve approaches its final apex. If the bug rate drops off when functional coverage is only 50% complete, the team should investigate this strange anomaly immediately!

In addition to functional coverage, the verification team should also consider structural coverage metrics. Structural coverage analysis points out holes of uncovered areas in the design (see Chapter 6). The verification team gathers structural coverage metrics near the end (when functional coverage is nearly 100%). As already mentioned, the gathering of structural coverage is typically "for free" in that no additional work is necessary from the verification team except having to enable it in their tool sets. There are numerous types of structural coverage; most of them (excluding statement) are subjective to the logic implementation. Using structural coverage as a metric depends on the project and coding style of the RTL. For those projects where the coding style lends itself to structural coverage, using statement coverage is a minimum requirement. This is because any absence of activity in areas of the HDL model highlights omissions in the tests. The other limitation of statement coverage is the missing semantic insight; the fact that an HDL statement has been executed results in no knowledge about the correctness of the content of the statement. This is why structural *and* functional coverage go hand-in-hand.

13.3.2   Completion Criteria

A design team does not want to send the design to manufacturing until verification completes its validation of the logic. With deterministic tests, the verification team completes its criteria when all tests have completed successfully. However, random-based verification environments are different. Every test scenario with a new random seed might exercise different areas of design (which is exactly the reason why verification teams use it). With the large state space problem, how does the verification team ensure that their verification suite covers enough of this state space to ensure a quality design?

The metrics discussed earlier are all contributing factors to the answer of this question. Bug closure rates, functional coverage, structural coverage, and open issues are all factors that influence completion criteria. In addition to those metrics, two other items are crucial in determining the answer to the question. The first item is a verification review for each unit and level of hierarchy. The second is a pre-determined period of bug-free regression. Figure 13.9 shows the diagram that the verification team must follow when deciding when to ship the design to fabrication.

Functional coverage metrics are one of the first things the verification team must do when assessing how close to done the team is. If functional coverage is below 100%, then the verification team requires more effort (more work in front of them). The team must continue to regress and enhance the test scenarios to close out those last remaining coverage items.

Not only should the verification team look at functional coverage, they should also look at structural coverage. Structural coverage is a critical metric because it can indicate areas of logic that the test scenarios did not exercise (specifically statement coverage). Ideally, if the verification team defined functional coverage properly, statement coverage will be at 100%. However, in many circumstances statement coverage is less than 100%. If this is the case, then the verification team, together with the designer, must review the areas not covered. If the designer finds logic that the verification teams test scenarios should have exercised, then the verification team must enhance the functional coverage metrics to accommodate the new function within the area of the code that the testing suite did not exercise.

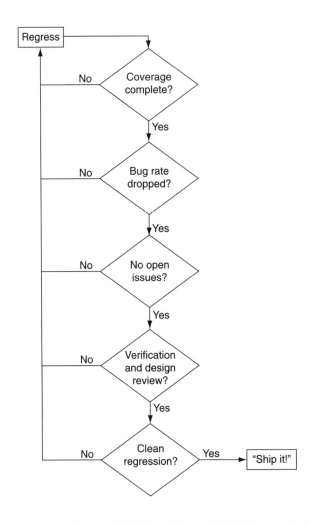

▪ **FIGURE 13.9**

Deciding when the verification team is done is a series of decision points that typically start with analyzing coverage.

If coverage is okay, then the verification team needs to scrutinize the bug discovery rate. The rate at which the verification team finds bugs gives an indication of how close to completion the verification team is. If the verification team finds bugs daily, it indicates that the logic is still in flux. Until the design stabilizes and the verification team does not find any bugs, it is not ready for fabrication.

If the team deems the bug discovery rates have dropped significantly and the coverage items are okay, then the verification team must review the open issues. Open issues indicate if any outstanding problems or enhancements exist (see Section 13.2). If any open issues are due to bugs, it indicates that the logic may change unless the resolution action is to defer. The owners of all open issues must close the issues before sending the chip to fabrication. This means that all issues have an acceptable resolution associated with them. The resolution may be to defer to the next release. Nevertheless, a resolution that the team agreed on exists.

If the verification team gets to the point where coverage, bug rates, and all issues have an acceptable resolution, then the next step is to have a verification review. This review scrutinizes the verification test bench and test plan. For every unit that contains a verification plan, the team holds a formal review of the plan and its associated test bench. The audience of review includes that unit's verification and logic design team, the verification and logic design teams of any unit it interfaces to, and the architecture team. The topics of the review are as follows:

- How the stimulus components work (especially random aspects)
- What functions the verification components check
- A review of what the functional coverage items are

This review is a quality statement. It allows the other team members to provide input on how the neighboring units really work and allows the architects to give input on the intent. At the conclusion of the review, any work items need to be logged and assessed for risk. Any high-risk items indicate more work for the verification team.

The last step in the completion criteria list is to have a clean regression suite of tests for a pre-determined period after the verification team achieves their coverage goal. This is a safety net. Because of the nature of random simulation, the verification team should continuously run the regression suite for a certain amount of time. This allows random simulation to explore other areas of the state space that the verification and design teams may have missed when creating the tests and coverage goals. There is no scientific formula for the duration of this time. However, if the verification team uncovers a bug at any time during this period, the bug is fixed and the regression time resets. The verification team should analyze the new defect, update the coverage goals, and test plan.

The metrics discussed above may show a false positive. Inevitably, the final answer to the question on whether the team sends the chip to manufacturing is a decision based on risk.

13.4 ESCAPE ANALYSIS

Escapes refer to problems not detected using the methods used in verification. Figure 13.1 illustrated that the higher levels of verification progress with their effort and bugs may be found. The lower level verification team, to ensure the bug fix is correct, re-creates these bugs within their verification environment. For the team to do this, they must analyze the bug and determine why their team did not find the bug first. The missing of the bug by the lower level verification team is classified as an escape; however, this type of escape is handled in the normal flow of the verification cycle before tape-out and is not discussed here.

The escapes that occur during *systems test*, where the DUV is the fabricated hardware, are the most costly because it may require a re-spin of the hardware. These logic bugs "escaped" detection on all levels of verification, from designer simulation through system simulation. Although the purpose of verification is to avoid escapes to fabrication, the reality is that today's chips and systems are too complex to uncover every bug in pre-silicon verification. In most cases, the verification team could have caught an escape to systems test using simulation or formal verification at one or more levels of the verification hierarchy.

Any escape indicates a blind spot somewhere in the verification environment. The blind spot is a hole in the stimulus or checking components—or both. The purpose of escape analysis is to pinpoint environment blind spots and fix them for future generations of hardware [106].

This stage of the verification cycle dictates that the verification team analyzes all verification escapes. This analysis includes a description of the current methodology (at all verification levels that could have found the bug), the changes made to the methodology to plug the hole, and a full bug classification. The purpose of this stage of verification is to learn from current problems and to ensure that the verification environments improve from generation to generation. Much like history, teams that fail to study the past are doomed to repeat it. The entire hardware design team's attitude is a key part of the escape analysis process. It might be easy to view escape analysis as a punishment or as finger pointing. It is not. Escapes occur on every complex product, and escape analysis is merely the means to understand and improve for the next generation. The design team and management must take a positive view of an introspective and direct analysis of the verification environment failures. The only unacceptable behavior is when the verification team allows an escape to occur a second time. Thorough escape analysis avoids this.

Escape analysis proceeds in two stages. The first stage occurs as the design team uncovers any bugs on the test floor hardware. At this time, the escape analysis process examines the individual bug, focusing on a real-time fix for the hardware and the verification environment. The second stage occurs later, as the hardware enters manufacturing and ships to customers. At this time, the process dictates that the team looks at all the bug escapes together, searching for trends and signatures in the escape data.

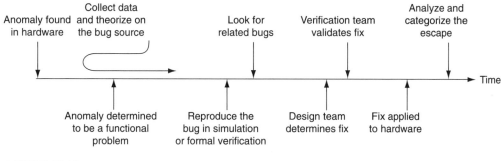

■ FIGURE 13.10

The order of activities for the individual bug analysis stage of escape analysis.

13.4.1 Individual Bug Analysis

The foundation of escape analysis lays in the study and investigation of individual escapes to systems test hardware. A major characteristic of the early part of this stage is the sense of urgency required to understand the bug and reproduce it in verification. Later, after the team applies the fix to the hardware, the individual bug analysis continues with an in-depth look at why the bug escaped.

Figure 13.10 shows the timeline for the individual bug analysis stage. The stage starts when the team finds an *anomaly* in the hardware. An anomaly occurs when the expected results from the application or systems test exerciser do not match the actual results. This could be data miscompare, a control signal mismatch, or an unexpected error condition. At first, the team must probe the hardware and associated data to discover the source of the miscompare. Failures in the hardware may be functional but may also come from physical flaws or circuit timing problems. As with functional verification, the failure could be a result of a test exerciser or application problem that expected the wrong result (and the hardware got it right!).

If the anomaly turns out to be a functional problem, the verification team kicks into action. Unfortunately, the next step in the process, finding the source of the bug, may be quite difficult and time consuming because these functional problems are complex in nature. Bugs found in the hardware are often due to multiple overlapping conditions and unusual data or control patterns. After all, if the problem was not a complex scenario, surely the verification team would have found it!

A key enabler to understanding the source of the bug is the collection of data about the failure. This entails dumping hardware logs, including latch states (see Section 9.3.1) and collecting information about what the application or test exerciser was doing when the bug occurred. Using this data about the failure extracted from the hardware, the design and verification teams theorize about the source of the bug. Often, initial theories on the bug source do not pan out.

In any case, the design and verification teams cannot prove any theory true until they create the failure in a verification environment. Here, the design team compares the data points from the systems test hardware to that of the verification environment. The design team can consider the failure understood only when the verification environment trace data exactly matches the hardware environment data. Again, collecting a large amount of data from the hardware is important in this step. Not only does the data assist the engineering team in theorizing the source of the bug, but also it is critical to have as much data as possible to confirm that the team correctly understands the failure. The more collaborating data on the bug, the more likely it is that the bug reproduction in verification points to the exact conditions.

Bug reproduction in verification is no simple task. The symptoms and the theories about the bug point to specific environmental settings for the verification components. Verification teams use both deterministic and random environments to reproduce the failure, depending on the theory. Initial attempts at bug reproduction often fail, requiring multiple revisions to the environmental settings, probability tables, stimulus generation, and checking. With each revision, the design and verification team hone in on the bug, learning more about the symptoms. Finally, when the verification test case matches the test floor scenario, the checker fires and the team has reproduced the bug.

In the quest for reproducing a bug in verification, there are cases where the verification environment finds a different bug than the one found on the systems test hardware. Verification teams call these *cousin bugs* because of the similarity to the bug found in the hardware. Cousin bugs have similar characteristics to the original flaw in that the environmental settings and the functional area are related. The team must take care not to declare success in reproducing the original bug when discovering a cousin bug. The only way to tell the original from a cousin is by matching the hardware data to the verification environment.

As part of the escape analysis process, the verification team may discover cousin bugs after reproducing the original bug. Escape analysis requires an introspective look on the verification plan and environment after reproducing each bug. The team may decide that a certain complex area of the design needs more verification. Systems test hardware escapes bring a different perspective—call it hindsight—to the verification team. This perspective leads the team to add interactions to their environments, changing the scenarios and possibly uncovering cousin bugs.

After reproducing the hardware bug in the verification environment, the design team gains full knowledge of the problem. They develop a fix for the bug and implement it in the HDL. The verification team, armed with a test case that reproduced the bug, re-runs the scenario using the updated design as the DUV to prove that the fix works. All checkers and monitors remain active in the environment, guarding against breakage in other areas of the design. Collateral damage to other parts of the design is, in fact, a major concern to the design and verification teams. A fix to a complex area of the design may plug one hole but open another. For this reason, the verification team runs a full regression against the entire design.

This fix, and any other fixes, goes through the entire design and verification process before the team releases it as an engineering change to the fabrication facility. Both the time and cost of re-spinning the hardware demonstrate the importance of quality verification. Initial quality in verification prevents drastic hardware redesigns, and robust escape analysis ensures that the applied change fixes the original bug as well as any cousin bugs.

The worst-case scenario is to fabricate an engineering change and find that the original flaw still exists. This possibility stresses the importance of robust data collection from the hardware systems test and attention to detail in the reproduction of the bug in the verification environment.

Having found, analyzed, reproduced, and re-verified the bug, the crisis phase passes, allowing the verification team to step back and complete the escape analysis. During this final phase, the verification team takes an in-depth look at why the verification environment missed the bug. Was a stimulus component incomplete? Did a checking component fail to detect certain flaws? It is even possible that both the stimulus and checking components have shortcomings that the verification team must fix. Finally, the team categorizes the failure and captures key metrics about the bug.

It is important for all leaders in design, verification, and especially management to guard against defensive behavior during the analysis phase of the design. Finger pointing and politics are detrimental to the entire process, causing the verification team to run for cover rather than performing an unbiased analysis. This is when true leaders rise to the occasion, maintaining their technical integrity during the most stressful of times. Verification leaders have a marvelous chance to show their strength, conviction, and leadership capabilities during escape analysis. The best verification leaders reflect on all hierarchical levels of the environment and then perform unbiased and thoughtful analysis. This leadership delivers insights into improvements required to maintain pace with the ever-increasing design complexity.

The final stage of individual bug escape analysis feeds the overall project-wide escape analysis, which occurs later when the product ships to customers. Aside from correcting the stimulus and checking components, the verification team categorizes the bug and then documents key metrics about the escape. These metrics classify the bug's characteristics from both the verification team's point of view and the designer's point of view.

For each individual escape, the verification team classifies and documents the following categories:

- Time-to-understanding
- Bug level of difficulty
- Area of bug
- Work-around capability
- Designer's classification

Time-to-Understanding

Time-to-understanding is a simple metric. For each bug, time-to-understanding is the number of elapsed days from the first encounter of the anomaly on the hardware to the reproduction of the problem in verification. Collecting this metric gives the design and verification teams insight into future improvements for bug isolation in the hardware. Prolonged time-to-understanding negatively affects time-to-market, one of the key project metrics. Engineering teams can add debug capability features to next generation hardware designs based on the information collected on the time-to-understanding. By collecting this data, the team can analyze the correlation between bug type, bug area, and time-to-understanding and then use this data to improve time-to-market on future systems.

Bug Level of Difficulty

The *bug level of difficulty* is an appraisal of the bug's complexity. Verification teams may struggle when documenting this metric. Initial thoughts may evoke an emotional reaction that "if the bug escaped the verification cycle, clearly it was difficult to find." A qualitative approach to assessing bug difficulty varies from verification engineer to verification engineer, depending on experience. Additionally, certain bugs are more difficult to find depending on the level of verification hierarchy. Therefore, evaluating a bug's level of difficulty requires a structured, quantitative approach.

The quantitative assessment process for evaluating the bug's level of difficulty starts by checking existing verification data: the verification plan and coverage results. The person doing the assessment should note whether the verification plan specified test cases or parameters that could have led to finding the bug in verification. If not, the bug analysis should call for a new section of the verification plan for future systems. Next, the assessor should note which levels of verification hierarchy could have encountered the bug in their environment.

Analysis of coverage results leads to a conclusion as to how close the verification environments came to encountering the bug. This conclusion only speaks to the stimulus generation capabilities of the environment, not to the checking. It is conceivable that the verification environment created the exact scenario, but the checking components failed to identify the design flaw. Other possibilities in analyzing the coverage data range from the verification environment having nearly hit the failing scenario to not having come close at all. Another possible conclusion from coverage data analysis could be that future systems require a new set of coverage metrics. This occurs when the current coverage metrics do not contain data necessary to assess how close the verification environment came to hitting the bug.

After analyzing the verification plan and coverage metrics, the quantitative assessment of the bug's level of difficulty continues. At this stage, the verification team assigns a rating to five separate categories. The five categories span the realm of possible reasons for a verification environment to miss finding a bug. The assessor assigns each category a number between 0 and 3, indicating the category's contribution to the verification environment missing the bug. A score of 0 indicates that this category has no bearing on creating the bug in simulation. A score of 3 indicates that this category greatly affects the creation of this bug in verification. Within the categories, the verification teams should set guidelines for the 0 to 3 scale to maintain consistency in the assessments of all the bugs. After scoring each category, the sum of the five categories indicates the bug's overall level of difficulty, with the more complex bugs having scores above 7 and 8 (out of 15) and the least complex having scores closer to 0. Many bugs require a combination of multiple categories to capture the bug.

The five categories are cache or memory set-up, configuration dependency, cycle dependency, sequence dependency, and expected results.

The category for *cache or memory set-up* indicates whether the bug required an obscure initialization of a DUV memory component. A high score in this category means that the memory needs to be in a strange state to reproduce the bug. Examples include the bug requires the memory data to equal the memory address and the bug requires uncorrectable errors in specific memory locations.

Configuration dependency denotes the DUV components needed for the bug to occur. If the bug occurs in normal DUV configurations, this category receives a 0 score. On the other hand, if the bug requires certain components to be off-line or disabled and this is not a normal configuration, then the analysis awards a higher score to this category. An example is when the bug occurs only when half of the cache is disabled.

Cycle dependency indicates that two or more events align in a small window of cycles. This category often scores high, because many escapes occur because of overlapping micro-architectural events. Another name for cycle dependency is *window condition*. An example is when the bug occurs when a specific interrupt reaches the DUV exactly one cycle before the in-buffer fills.

The *sequence complexity* category indicates that multiple events must occur in a specific order for the bug to occur. This category often correlates to the cycle dependency category, because many bugs require a specific sequence of events in a small window of cycles. An example is when the bug occurs in a microprocessor when an interrupt comes between a branch-on-zero instruction and a multiply instruction.

The *expected results* category indicates the difficulty in creating the checkers that flag the erroneous behavior. The other four categories speak to the stimulus generation. A high score in this category means that it is hard to identify when this bug occurs. An example is when the bug is a corruption in a queue's pointer such that the DUV remains functional but loses some performance.

Area of the Bug

Area of the bug describes the type of function under which the defect occurs. Traditional categories include mainline testing, resets, specification, and recovery or error injection. However, these categories are not fixed and vary based on the type of design under test. The team should add other design specific categories as appropriate.

The area of the bug classification is easy to record. Simply note the type of testing required to find the bug. However, even such a simple denotation yields insightful results when the overall escape analysis completes. Then, the team can see if a verification weakness exists in one of these categories, based simply on the number of escapes in the category. For example, the team would want to bolster their reset verification effort if 50% of the escapes were in this category.

Work-Around Capability

Designers often build "escape routes" for bypassing difficult areas of the design just in case they find a debilitating bug in the hardware. Complex systems often contain multiple disable and *work-around* paths just for this situation. Good work-around capability highlights the design's versatility and the system architect's foresight into the difficulties of getting a system to market on time. The design team can enable a hardware work-around in multiple fashions, including direct disablement of function or with a code work-around in a processor. Occasionally, a system may even ship to customers with a work-around path enabled. In any case, under escape analysis, the verification team documents how easy or difficult it is to make hardware testing progress by bypassing the bug once the team discovers it in the hardware.

Work-around capability falls into four categories. The first category, called *tolerate*, indicates that the bug occurs rarely. Additionally, to fall into the tolerate category, it must be easy for the design team to recognize that the flaw occurred. In this case, the bug does not hamper hardware test progress and requires no work-around. If the bug were to become more persistent, the design team would need to identify a work-around.

Designers use the second category, *direct and non-gating*, for cases where a work-around fixes the exact problem and does not hinder further hardware testing. In this case, the bug may occur often, but a work-around exists that completely avoids the failing scenario. This category requires that the work-around does not inhibit testing of any other area of the hardware.

The third category, *indirect or functional disable*, indicates that there is a work-around but enablement of the work-around turns off additional functions or scenarios. The granularity of the work-around is such that other cases beyond the bug may take the work-around path or that the work-around inhibits some other functional testing.

Design teams hope to avoid the final category, *none or major function disabled*. This category means either that the bug completely halts hardware testing progress or that the designers cannot exercise a major portion of the logic until new, fixed hardware reaches the test systems. This could take weeks and has a detrimental impact on time-to-market.

It is incredibly important to continue to make testing progress after a bug's discovery, yet it is not always easy to do. Often, a bug may inhibit further testing progress or hide other downstream bugs. Therefore, categorizing and tracking the work-around capability yields learning toward areas of the design that need enhancement for future systems to become "immune" to difficult bugs.

Designer's Classification

The *bug level of difficulty* classification views the escape from a verification engineer's perspective. It illustrates what type of updates the team needs to make to the drivers and checkers to plug the hole that allowed the escape. On the other hand, the *designer's classification* of the escape examines the bug from the design implementation point of view. This classification describes the specifics of the design bug.

Designer's classification has three categories: specification, high-level design, and HDL. Additionally, the HDL category, the most common of the three, has multiple sub-qualifiers to describe the type of HDL coding error.

A specification error occurs when the design documentation incorrectly describes the intended behavior of the chip or system. The result is that both the design and verification team create their code based on the specification's erroneous description. This case occurs infrequently because the number of people who review the specification is great enough to catch most specification errors.

A high-level design escape arises because of incorrect or, more commonly, overlooked assumptions about the design microarchitecture. Escapes occur in this category when the base design fails to account for all cases or when the microarchitecture cannot properly handle all scenarios.

The HDL category accounts for most escapes. These are implementation escapes where the designer's code did not perform correctly. There are many possible reasons for an HDL escape, leading to the need for sub-qualifiers to describe the escape. The sub-qualifiers are assignment, checking, data algorithm, control algorithm, synchronization, interface, and association.

The assignment qualifier signifies a failure to initialize or set correctly a latch or array value in the design. Designers may also use this qualifier to identify failures to tie input signals. An escape due to an assignment failure is often the result of a coding oversight. Examples include failures to reset latches to the appropriate value or, if during an assignment, the HDL loads invalid data into a register.

The second qualifier, checking failures, occurs when the HDL fails to appropriately validate control or data signals. Basic checking, such as parity or check-sum bits, falls into this category. Additionally, this category covers failures where the HDL omits checking an input error signal, causing the design to operate upon data that it should drop.

Designers qualify escapes as data algorithm failures when the HDL does not handle properly a scenario based on specific data. Often, certain input data signifies special cases to the control logic. If the design fails to identify the special data code, the designers classify the failure as a data algorithm escape. Simple examples might include cases of overflow or underflow in an arithmetic logic unit (ALU), where the data should signal specific control logic overrides.

The next qualifier, control algorithm escapes, signifies cases where the logic did not perform correctly on specific, non-data-related cases. These failures occur when a designer omits logic to handle special cases or groups cases together inappropriately.

Synchronization failures indicate that two portions of logic failed to manage resources together. This may occur when independent portions of the logic are required to operate simultaneously based on control or data inputs. Synchronization failures also include cases where logic vying for shared resources fails to operate under the set assumptions. Synchronization errors often lead to race conditions, premature resetting of data, or late resetting of data.

Designers use the interface qualifier to denote escapes based on communication or assumption differences between design units. These escapes occur when a design fails to utilize a signal in its intended manner or when the HDL fails to set an input to a specified value for the condition. Designers also use the interface qualifier for protocol violations between units. Because verification does focus on these areas, interface errors usually occur on esoteric cases.

The final qualifier, association, occurs when a control structure fails to maintain a relationship between itself and specific data. Association escapes occur most often when two different units use different assumptions about the same data.

The designer's classification is important to the escape analysis process because it helps hone future verification environments for the most common error types. The classification also assists designers in improving their coding styles, communication, and even future micro architectural designs.

13.4.2 Escape Examples

Finding good escape examples proved to be challenging. Access to hundreds of escape write-ups existed, but a few examples with the right level of complexity were needed. Too simple an escape and the reader would ask "How could this simple bug escape?" On the other hand, too complex a bug requires intimate knowledge of the chip structure and architecture. Four escape examples are described here.

Example: Microprocessor's Compression Engine

The first example is from a microprocessor's compression engine (Table 13.1). It is a corner case where an instruction stream fills a buffer in the hardware and the controls are set to a maximum value. This example has a substantial sequence complexity.

Example: Pack Instruction Gives Wrong Answer

The second example deals with a mainline microprocessor instruction sequence (Table 13.2). This case also has a high sequence complexity and introduces a cycle dependency complexity because the pack instruction must follow a specific instruction within one cycle. This escape shows how the verification team can plug the hole in the test case generation methodology by creating a new template that targets the symptoms of the failure.

Example: Extended Address Bits on I/O Adapter Interface Not Handled Correctly by Storage Controller

The third escape illustrates the importance of the verification team following the design specification rather than the designer's description of

TABLE 13.1 ▪ Microprocessor's compression engine

Escape Name	Compression Miscompare				
Description	Compression engine writes output-buffer shadow-register at the wrong time. This only happens if the data-buffer is completely full and the Expansion Character Entry Size is set to the max of 260 bytes but the operation only utilizes in the range of 2 to 20 bytes.				
Time-to-understanding	2 days				
Level of difficulty	Cache Setup	Cycle Dependency	Config Dependency	Sequence Complexity	Expected Results
	0	0	0	2	0
Area of bug	Mainline				
Work-around capability	Direct, non-gating				
Designer classification	HDL—control algorithm				
Current verification methodology	*Unit Simulation* There was no unit simulation test case that had the combination of Expansion Character Entry Sizes needed for creating this problem scenario.		*Chip Simulation* The test case generator can generate Expansion Character Entry Sizes from 0 to 260. It can be a fixed number, but then every Character Entry has the size of 260. Otherwise, the generator can randomly choose the size.		
Verification methodology change	*Unit Simulation* We created a unit test case out of the test case P1710.		*Chip Simulation* Improvement of the performance of generating compression test cases to get higher simulation coverage in this area. We now can request two ranges for the Expansion Character Entry.		

TABLE 13.2 ▪ Pack instruction gives wrong answer

Escape Name	Pack Instruction Gives Wrong Answer
Description	A pack instruction follows a MVC (move character) instruction. The pack instruction stored into its own instruction stream does not clean up properly and results in a wrong answer. The problem occurs if one pack instruction executes conditionally on a branch path and that branch is resolved wrong and a different pack instruction immediately executes on the resolved branch path. The HDL is not resetting a latch properly for the pack operation. The latch name is pack_hdw_zd_q and it represents that the high double word is zero. There are two things that can set it: 1) fxu_e2 cycle and aim_dw_zd and 2) pack and (not r2_fld(0)). The r2_fld holds the L2 field, and this indicates there is no second double word if the L2 field is less than 8. The hold path of this

TABLE 13.2 ■ *Continued*

Escape Name	Pack Instruction Gives Wrong Answer				

latch is the only part that is degated by kill (dly_kill_dec_q) or endop (dec_ctl_rst_q). So on a store in its instruction stream that modifies the R2 field, the pack first appears as though it needs only 1 double word of data, then it gets killed but this latch does not reset. Then the pack reissues with the true R2 field that indicates that it needs to store two double words. The failure is that only the first double word is stored.

The fix is to clear the latch completely, including hot setting paths and hold paths. Here is the logic:

OLD:

pack_hdw_zd ⇐ ((pack and aim_dw_zd and fxu_e2) and (not fxu_hold)) or

(pack and (not r2_fld(0))) or

(pack_hdw_zd_q and (not dly_kill_dec_q) and (not dec_ctl));

NEW:

pack_hdw_zd ⇐ (((pack and aim_dw_zd and fxu_e2) and (not fxu_hold)) or

(pack and (not r2_fld(0))) or

(pack_hdw_zd_q and (not dly_kill_dec_q) and (not dec_ctq))

) and (not dly_kill_dec_q);

Time-to-understanding	2 days				
Level of difficulty	Cache Setup 0	Cycle Dependency 1	Config Dependency 0	Sequence Complexity 3	Expected Results 0
Area of bug	Mainline				
Work-around capability	Tolerable				
Designer classification	HDL—logic hole				
Current verification methodology	*Unit Simulation* There was no unit simulation test case that created this problem scenario.		*Chip Simulation* At the chip simulation level, millions of test cases were run with the combination of pack and branch wrongs. We never hit the particular window (e.g., pack with a certain R2 field that gets executed conditionally or overlaid by its own store).		
Verification methodology change	*Unit Simulation* We have written new test case generation templates to stress the problem. The new templates produced test cases that reproduced the exact problem. All these test cases are now part of our regression.		*Chip Simulation* None		

the logic (Table 13.3). In this case, the verification engineer committed a fundamental transgression by not requiring an immediate specification update upon discovering the flaw in the documentation.

Example: Storage Controller Deadlock Caused by Synchronous Load Loop

The last escape is a complex deadlock condition that occurred in a multi-processor server system (Table 13.4). This escape illustrates the difficulty in creating deadlocks in random environments because deadlocks are often caused by repeating sequences of activity.

13.4.3 Escape Analysis Trends

During the individual escape analysis phase, the verification team focuses on verifying the bug fix and plugging holes in the environment related to the escape. In the best cases, few bugs escape and the product ships to customers ahead of schedule. However, any time there are more than a few escapes, the verification team must step back and look at all the escapes together, searching for escape trends. This is the overall escape analysis phase.

The key concept of the overall escape analysis is to search for areas of weakness in the environment. By identifying weaknesses, the verification team can improve the environment for future products. Individual escapes always point to very specific deficiencies in the verification environment or test case suite. By looking at all the escapes together, the team can observe signatures—strengths and weaknesses.

Verification teams should look for trends in two areas. First, they should look for hierarchical deficiencies. Second, the team analyzes the escapes for functional deficiencies. The individual escape classification work, described above in the *bug level of difficulty* section, steers the overall bug analysis activity.

Hierarchical deficiencies point to levels of the verification hierarchy that need strengthening. During the individual bug analysis phase, the verification team updated portions of the environment at one or more verification hierarchical levels. If a particular level required re-work for many escapes, the team should evaluate whether or not that level needs an overhaul in strategy.

A common outcome of the hierarchical analysis is the decision to change the environment from a deterministic strategy to an automated or random driven environment. This occurs when the volume and complexity of the escapes indicate that the verification team cannot create all the deterministic test cases required to cover the state space of the DUV at a particular level of the hierarchy. The environment needs rework to create a component strategy that utilizes parameters and automation, along with coverage metrics, to create the broad swathe of scenarios required by the DUV's complexity level.

TABLE 13.3 ■ Extended address bits on I/O adapter interface not handled correctly by storage controller

Escape Name	Extended Address Bits on IO Adapter Interface Not Handled Correctly by Storage Controller
Description	During Logical Partition testing on the system level hardware, we found that the HDL code picks up extended address bits from the wrong bits on the I/O adapter interface. The I/O adapter transfers 2 double words, bytes 0–3 and 4–7. The storage controller HDL picks up all extended address bits from byte 3, but the Storage Controller Workbook and the I/O adapter interface specification both show the least significant extended address bit coming from byte 4 bit 0. The storage controller does not obey the interface specification. This means I/O cannot address correctly above 2-GB storage.
Time-to-understanding	1 day

Level of difficulty	Cache Setup	Cycle Dependency	Config Dependency	Sequence Complexity	Expected Results
	0	0	1	0	1

Area of bug	Mainline
Work-around capability	Indirect with functional disable (cannot use addresses above 2 GB)
Designer classification	HDL—interface
Current verification methodology	The chip level verification environment extensively covers the address on the I/O adapter interface. However, in this case the checking component expected what the Storage Controller designer coded instead of what the interface documents specified. Because the storage controller design agreed with what the simulation was expecting, the checking component detected no error. The original I/O adapter interface specification contained an error showing too many address bits. For clarification, the verification team consulted the Storage Controller designer rather than the I/O adapter designers. This allowed the verification team to test to the incorrect interface description. The architects later updated the I/O adapter specification to correct the number of address bits, but the verification team missed the change.
Verification methodology change	The I/O macro and I/O interface checking code have been updated to check for the corrected interface description. This does not ensure that the description is correct only that the implementation follows the description. A system model with a real I/O bridge and Storeage Controller that was sensitive to the address bits being correct and executing I/O ops would be required to fully verify this in simulation. The designer has verified with the I/O bridge team that we have the address bits correctly identified now. The team also updated the system level simulation environment to include this adapter and all addresses, including those above 2GB.

TABLE 13.4 ▪ Storage controller deadlock caused by synchronous load loop

Escape Name	Storage Controller Deadlock Caused by Synchronous Load Loop
Description	Root cause is a synchronous loop in the Storage Controller pipeline, which is causing an I/O adapter operation to time out. The cause of the loop is multiple processor load requests trying to send cross-invalidate requests to another set of processors. However, the processor continually receives cross-invalidate reject responses. The reject responses are due to the other processors waiting for an entry in their respective Storage Controller Store Stack (the Storage Controller maintains a stack of outstanding store requests from each processor) to become available so that the processors can release stores in their L1 Cache's Store Buffers. The Storage Controller logic locks the Store Stack requests out of the pipeline due to a combination of selecting the higher priority loads ahead of them and cache interleave conflicts caused by these loads. We are much more likely to see this problem on two I/O adapter systems than in four I/O adapter systems because one pipe in each cluster is always available for stores each cycle. This makes it more difficult to fill the Store Stacks. It is also more likely to hit this bug on systems with large numbers of processors, which can more easily generate the load traffic needed to lock out the stores.
Time-to-understanding	1 day

Level of difficulty	Cache Setup	Cycle Dependency	Config Dependency	Sequence Complexity	Expected Results
	1	3	2	3	0

Area of bug	Mainline
Work-around capability	Tolerate
Designer classification	HDL—control algorithm
Current verification methodology	In the Storage Controller chip simulation environment, we never created a case where the processor sent a long stream of cross-interrogate reject responses. This is because of the random nature of the processor stimulus component's cross-invalidate response generation. The stimulus component periodically sends cross-invalidate reject responses based on a percentage probability. Normally, this percentage is in the range of 3–7%, which is not sufficient to create the hang condition.
Verification methodology change	We generated special configuration and program changes to cause infinite cross-invalidate reject response streams from processors. This change readily reproduced the deadlock in greater than 60% of the random test cases. We needed program changes to allow for the fact that processor load commands that require invalidates would never complete during the test case and the storage controller would never quiesce (still trying to send cross invalidates) by the end of the test case.

A second conclusion of hierarchical analysis may be that the environment's parameter structure or internal algorithms are ill suited for the DUV's function at a particular level of the hierarchy. In this case, escapes may have occurred because the constraint solving structure fails to hit key scenarios in the DUV inputs. Alternatively, escapes may have occurred because the parameter table needs expansion to hit all the scenarios.

The above cases point to deficiencies in the stimulus components. However, if the individual bug analysis work shows that multiple escapes occurred because of missed checks in the components, then the verification team must focus on the checking components. In this case, the environment may require the scoreboard and monitors to capture more information or new algorithms to create additional checks in the checking components.

After analyzing the environments for weak levels of the hierarchy, the verification team should look for trends in functions. If multiple escapes occurred in a specific functional area, then all levels of hierarchy need to upgrade their stimulus and checking capabilities with respect to this function.

Weak functional areas occur in complex functions. Again, the *bug level of difficulty* classifications steer the team toward these areas. If the individual escape analysis concludes that multiple escapes had high scores in the *cycle dependency* or *sequence complexity* areas and these escapes all pertained to a single function, then the verification environment requires enhancement for that function. In this case, multiple levels of the verification hierarchy require these enhancements.

13.5 SUMMARY

As the verification team nears its completion of its test plan, regression becomes important. A regression test suite allows for the verification teams at the different levels of the hierarchy to work in parallel. By utilizing the regression test suite, the verification team verifies a certain level of function for the next level of verification, and this level of function is stable for all future drops. This ensures that the verification team at the higher level are not impacted by any new function because the regression suite of tests provides quality assurance. Another aspect of regression is the ability to allow the verification team to be efficient in their testing. By performing test case harvesting, the verification team creates an optimized suite of tests to cover the targeted functions. By utilizing this new regression suite in a workstation farm, the verification utilizes a "grid computing" environment to cut down the overall time it takes to perform the regression.

However, the regression step in the overall verification cycle keys off a reduction in bug rate. The verification team calculates the bug rate by observing the problem-tracking tool where any issue that is found within the verification realm is logged. This same problem-tracking tool also assists in the decision of when to send the design to fabrication.

Before the team sends the design to fabrication, they must decide when enough functional simulation cycles have been run such that the chip performs flawlessly in the customers system. This requires an analysis of many different aspects of verification. The first thing that the verification team must analyze is coverage—both functional and structural. If the analysis determines that the verification team achieved its test plan goals, then the team must look at the bug rates. The bug rates assist in determining how stable the design is. If the bug rates are high, history tells us that it is unlikely for the rate to drop off suddenly. Bug rates drop off over time; thus, seeing high bug rates means that more verification is necessary. After looking at the bug rates, the team needs to look at any issues that still need to be resolved. By looking at the issues, the team has insight to what problems still exist. While the team looks at the open issues, they can prepare and host a review of all the verification environments. This peer review allows the whole team (designers, verifiers, and architects) to analyze the individual verification environments to ensure a cohesive and comprehensive test plan. Even after the verification team finishes the analysis of coverage and bug rates and reviews any open issues and verification environments, there still exists one last item. The verification team must ensure a clean regression due to the nature of random simulation.

Escape analysis is the final process in the verification cycle for a single system or product. The activity calls for a careful introspective view of the months or even years of work devoted to creating the components and test cases. The escape analysis activities occur in two phases. First, the frenzied phase of fixing an individual escape requires the verification team to participate in solving and understanding the bug found in the hardware. During this phase, the verification team evaluates the escape and environment deficiencies. Later, the verification team looks at the forest rather than the trees and searches for large-scale improvements required for future products.

By performing escape analysis, the verification team hones their skills and environments. If the team works on follow-on products, escape analysis provides direct feedback to the next generation of product. This improves time-to-market and saves re-fabrication costs. Even if the verification team disbands to other unrelated products, the insights and learning gained from escape analysis improves their work on components and strategies in these other areas.

13.6 EXERCISES

1. It is close to sending the design to fabrication, and the verification team has classified its work for a unit as "done." A designer then changes some HDL. The designer claims that the change was purely cosmetic—that is, it was to comment some of the logic for maintenance reasons. What course of action should you take in terms of verification?

2. What are the stages of individual escape analysis?

3. Why is it important to perform overall escape analysis based on the learning from the individual escape analysis?

4. What is the significance of searching for cousin bugs?

CHAPTER 14

ADVANCED VERIFICATION TECHNIQUES

So far, this book has focused in-depth on those mainstream topics in functional verification that are common for most industrial projects. During this detailed walk-through, a few evolving and less established areas for any modern methodology have been left out. This chapter returns to these areas, describes their relevance, gives a short overview of available solutions, and points out which direction the industrial practice is currently headed.

Given the inherent complexity of the verification task and the problem of state space explosion, the verification cycle relies on a lot of compute power. Many projects use whole farms of workstations that run simulation and formal verification (FV) 24 × 7. Although powerful workstations, fast simulation engines, and intelligent test benches have greatly improved the efficiency of simulation, the question of the quality of the verification cycles is always looming in the background. Chapter 6 discussed how coverage metrics and coverage data collection allow us to gauge the progress of the verification cycle with the goal to drive testing into yet uncovered areas of the DUV function. Chapter 13 introduced the techniques of test case harvesting that enable the verification to create the smallest set of regression tests that achieve the highest possible coverage. All these methods ensure fast traversal of as much of the *interesting* state space as possible. Even with all these general tools at hand, it is still very possible that subsequent tests in the verification of a DUV spend much time re-visiting the same part of the state space repeatedly before each one extends its activity into new domains. The first part of this chapter discusses verification techniques that skip such redundant cycles using directed methods that save precious verification cycles for the testing of unique scenarios.

The different abstraction levels usable to specify hardware function was discussed in Chapter 5. The predominant abstraction level used in today's real-life projects is the Register Transfer level (RTL). Most of the design community has a complete working and intuitive understanding of the properties and requirements of an RTL specification. The industry has assembled a large infrastructure of tools around this notion. However, RTL specification also originally developed as an abstraction, leaving behind the gate-level specifications that designers had used before. For the last few years, the quest for the next abstraction level has been under way. Again, the promise of more abstraction is the availability of a usable design specification earlier in the design cycle and an improved productivity for design and verification teams. The currently most prevalent ideas and approaches to high-level modeling are discussed in the second section of this chapter.

Coverage-directed test generation appears to be the next step in the development of simulation environment tools. There are two threads in the discussion of this topic in the third section of this chapter. One method is reactionary in nature, when the process adjusts the stimulus generation using coverage measurements collected after running test cases. New research investigates the use of automation in the feedback loop. Algorithms harvest the coverage data and then change the test case parameters to achieve higher coverage for the subsequent tests. For the second method, the stimulus component or test generator uses an abstract model during the process of test generation. Using this model, the generator is constantly able to analyze the effects of subsequent steps of a current test case, thus being able to generate the next test step with the coverage metrics in mind. This new breed of test generators is able to create tests with good coverage *by construction* rather than measuring coverage after the actual execution of the test on the DUV model.

Given the wide variety of these advanced techniques, the level of discussion is introductory with the intention to give the readers a basic framework of understanding, enough to continue a deeper study of these fields on their own.

14.1 SAVE VERIFICATION CYCLES—BOOTSTRAPPING THE VERIFICATION PROCESS

It is possible to gain dramatic improvements in verification efficiency using a technique called the *bootstrapping the verification process*. The idea is to short-cut verification cycles that normally would be part of many or even all tests. It is not necessary to iterate through the same redundant cycles repeatedly many times. Instead, the verification team performs such redundant testing only once and lets the verification environment skip over it for all other tests.

14.1.1 Separating Power-On-Reset and Mainline Verification

A good introductory example for the bootstrapping technique is the power-on-reset (POR) verification. As discussed for the *reset-line verification* in Section 9.1.1, the team does not have to perform the POR sequence of a DUV at the beginning of *every* mainline test. Instead, the team can run the sequence once, take a checkpoint snapshot of the reset

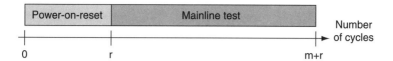

(a) POR for every mainline test

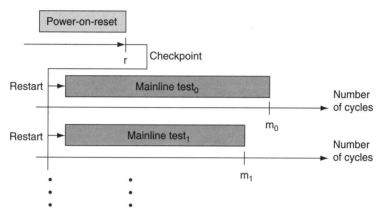

(b) POR once for many mainline tests

■ **FIGURE 14.1**

(a) If the DUV starts verification in a random initial state (or "x" state), power-on-reset (POR) cycles need to precede the mainline test to initialize the DUV correctly according to the design specification. (b) The smarter use of resources executes the POR sequence only once and uses a much faster check-point-restart scheme to load the DUV state after POR quickly at the beginning of every mainline test. For n mainline tests and r cycles needed to run through the POR sequence, the overall savings is n times r verification cycles. In reality, the POR verification occurs more than just once. Still, the accumulated savings of not verifying POR with every test can be tremendous.

state of the DUV, and use a checkpoint-restart shortcut at the beginning of every mainline test. Using this technique, the verification team saves the amount of time spent in the POR sequence for every mainline test case they run. Assuming this occurs many thousands of times and for most of the test cases run by the verification project, the savings by eliminating redundant cycles can be quite substantial.

Figure 14.1 illustrates this technique. Assuming that the loading of the DUV POR checkpoint state does take significantly less time than running the POR sequence, the savings in verification cycles is the number of test cases multiplied with the number of cycles needed to reset the DUV. This technique is not only applicable to simulation-based verification but also to FV. It is a significant shortcut for FV to be able to start from a single defined initial state after POR and pursue the state exploration from that point instead of doing the state exploration from a whole range of

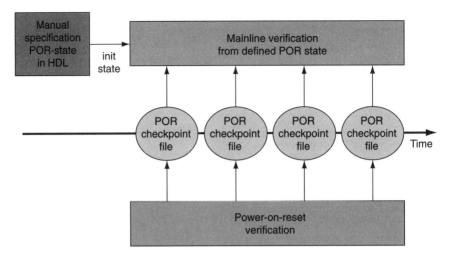

▪ **FIGURE 14.2**

Mainline verification at first takes the initial state of the design under verification from the HDL specification. In parallel, power-on-reset (POR) verification starts and, over time, provides verified POR checkpoints to mainline verification at regular intervals.

possibly undefined initial states. Given the exponential dependency of the FV algorithm on the number of states, the start from the defined POR state may be the deciding factor, making FV algorithms applicable to a given DUV.

The technique to de-couple POR reset verification from mainline verification has the additional advantages of separating tasks, which the verification teams can pursue in parallel. The time savings from this de-coupling become more important as the reset sequence of the DUV becomes more complicated. The two efforts can proceed in parallel with the mainline bug discovery and turn-around time rarely affecting POR verification progress as well as POR logic bugs never gating mainline verification.

Obviously, there is the question how it is possible to use a POR checkpoint while POR verification proceeds in parallel. Figure 14.2 shows how at first mainline verification uses the initial-value reset specification that the designers define in their hardware description language (HDL) code. In the Verilog HDL, initial values are typically defined in *initial* blocks; in VHDL, the designers achieve the same thing using initial value assignments.

Once the teams separate POR and mainline verification, they can optimize the methods of verification according to the special requirements of each discipline. For example, it is advisable to utilize multiple-value ("x"-state) simulation for the POR task to ensure that the POR cleanly affects all state elements of the DUV. As a result, mainline simulation can take advantage of a much faster two-value simulation for most of the logic, except special areas of concern like tristate buses.

14.1.2 Bootstrapping the DUV Into High-Potential States

It is possible to generalize this technique of starting the DUV in a POR checkpoint state to bootstrapping of the DUV into any *interesting* state. Such an interesting or *high-potential* state is a starting condition that is close to a stress situation for the DUV, one where subsequent verification runs the DUV likely into window conditions. The reasoning behind such a strategy is that DUVs typically contain more and more complicated bugs around window conditions. Furthermore, it is assumed it is non-trivial to reach such high-potential states during the normal verification cycle because they are *deep* inside the DUV's state space, far away from the POR state and typically defined by the occurrence of co-dependent corner conditions. A good example is the near-full condition of several resources inside the DUV.

Figure 14.3 shows an illustration of the bootstrapping function driven by an *initializer component* that is part of the verification environment. Similar to the discussed POR checkpoint-restart technique described above, the initializer component can apply a previously saved checkpoint file to force the DUV into the high-potential state. Of course, a previous verification run has to encounter the high-potential state and save it to a checkpoint file. The alternative to re-starting from a checkpoint is to use a piece of deterministic driver code that overrides all necessary state variables in the model of the DUV and sets them consistent with the high-potential state. Verification engineers can write such a specialized driver only if they have detailed knowledge about all the necessary state settings that constitute the high-potential state.

It is the advantage of this bootstrapping technique that the DUV can be fast-forwarded efficiently close to potential bugs rather than letting the environment's stimulus component drive the DUV over many cycles into such a high-potential state using a constrained random driver strategy with some relatively unknown probability.

The easiest method to obtain checkpoint files for high-potential states is to use the functional coverage instrumentation (see Chapter 6) of the DUV. Whenever the environment detects that the coverage instrumentation indicates reaching a high-potential state of the DUV, it checkpoints the DUV state to file for later re-load.

Although this method is very powerful in making verification more efficient and avoiding redundant verification cycles, there is a significant caveat. When the DUV is set directly into a high-potential state, the verification environment, all stimulus and checking components including the scoreboards, have to be able to tolerate and support this. Ideally, the whole test bench itself would be part of the checkpoint file. This would ensure that any transactions currently in flight inside the DUV would be

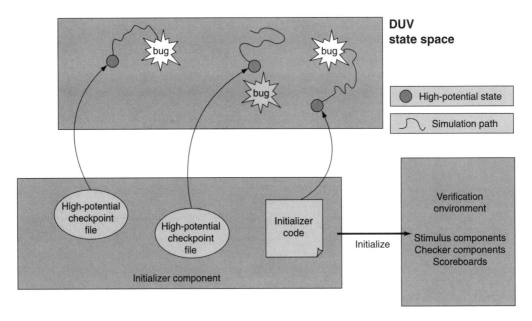

▪ **FIGURE** 14.3

An initializer component uses checkpoint files from previous verification runs or dedicated code to bootstrap the DUV into high-potential states. The main property of these states is that they put the DUV close to window conditions, which are likely to contain design bugs. Three different tests with three different starting conditions are shown. In this example, only one of the checkpoint file initializations results in a simulation path that hits a bug. The third simulation, starting from an initial state driven by dedicated driver code, also exposes a bug successfully. The initializer component also needs to initialize the verification environment consistently with the DUV's state.

contained in the test bench data structures and reinstated by the initializer component, to be in the correct context when the initialization component hands control to the test bench. This support for checkpoints of the whole test bench has to be part of its architecture from the start because it is impossible to retrofit it once the verification team has written large portions of the code. As an alternative, the team can provide special environment initializer code that puts the test bench into a state consistent with the DUV bootstrap state.

For an example of this bootstrap method, return to the cache design from Chapter 3. A very practical technique to fast-forward this design into a high-potential state is the technique called *cache warm loading*. As the name indicates, an initializer component pre-loads the cache quickly at the beginning of the verification to represent states that normally only occur after the cache has serviced many requests (Figure 14.4).

With a near-full cache, for example, the DUV will soon have to delete cache lines to accommodate new requests from main memory. Setting up the near-full condition is much more efficient than running through a series of requests that fill up the cache to such a state. This is also an

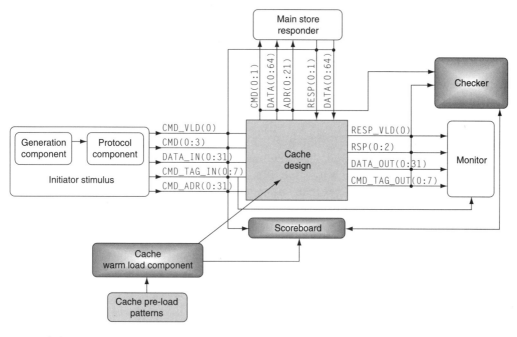

■ **FIGURE 14.4**

The cache warm load component is a special-purpose initializer component. It loads from a selection of predefined cache contents (preload patterns) directly into the DUV model to set the DUV into high-potential state. Examples are near-to-full cache or cache content that likely triggers specific corner case conditions given the underlying microarchitecture of the design under verificaiton. The warm load component also must set up the scoreboard to enable correct checking during the subsequent verification.

example how the initializer component must set the test bench into the corresponding correct state. The warm loader must synchronize the scoreboard with the cache contents it loads into the DUV. This is necessary to enable the scoreboard to provide correct content tracking information to the checker component during the subsequent verification cycles.

This bootstrapping technique is similar to the process outlined in Section 12.3.5, where semi-formal verification tools switch between different state-exploration algorithms. Taking a checkpoint from one verification run to another can be an effective method to seed the verification cycle very directly toward bug-prone areas.

14.1.3 Manipulating the DUV Specification Provoking States of Resource Conflict

An effective alternative to the bootstrapping techniques of the above section should be briefly mentioned. It is often possible to adjust the HDL specification artificially to limit the amount of resources a DUV provides. For example, it is possible to artificially lower buffer sizes in the DUV just for focused verification runs that should more likely encounter the condition where the buffers are full. Assuming that such a provocation of resource conflicts in the DUV generates more likely corner cases and error conditions, this method amounts to an effective directive for the verification effort.

This method works equally well for simulation and FV. In addition, there is again a similarity to the discussion explaining how FV efforts can artificially limit the state space for FV tools to circumvent the state explosion successfully. Manipulating resource sizes in the DUV is analogous to the artificial restriction of data path widths discussed in Section 12.3.4, Solutions to Address the Problem of State Space Explosion.

Obviously, the verification team must take the utmost care in manipulating the DUV HDL in this way to eliminate any possibility of an accidental change that changes the semantics of the design specification.

14.2   HIGH-LEVEL MODELING: CONCEPTS

High-level modeling is a concept only discussed in passing so far (see Chapter 11). A taxonomy of the hardware specification domain was defined in Chapter 5 but turned our attention quickly to the most prevalent specification levels used in the industry today: RTL- and gate-level. This is where 90% to 95% of the design and verification activities in the industry presently occur. All these DUV specifications are exact implementations down to the individual state elements (latches or flip-flops). One of the advantages of this level of abstraction as the main workhorse for verification is the ability to prove Boolean equivalence with the implementation down to a transistor-level netlist (see Chapter 11).

Chapter 1 and Figure 1.1 position high-level design (*HLD*) of chips in the overall project flow. It is during that first phase of the design, with no RTL model available yet, where a high-level model is useful to formalize early design decisions and make them available in the form of an executable model.

Given that there is no well-established definition of this field in academia or industry, it is almost easier to define high-level modeling by what it is not: an RTL specification of the DUV. The RTL requires too much detail and needs too much maintenance effort as the design team explores major design alternatives during HLD. The requirement to support easy adaptability to major design changes is one of the main reasons to use a higher abstraction level than RTL for a high-level model. What exactly constitutes that abstraction level is at the center of diverse approaches currently pursued by many in the field.

Before some of the more prominent approaches to high-level modeling are discussed, the different applications of a high-level model should be focussed on. Figure 14.5 defines its role in the design flow.

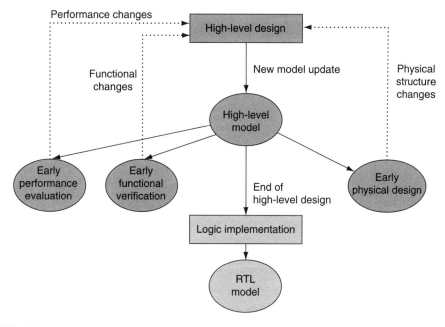

■ **FIGURE 14.5**

The high-level model formalizes design specifications and decisions made during the high-level design (HLD) phase. The model has three different applications during HLD. First, the team assesses the performance of the design to ensure the design point satisfies the customer's performance requirements. Second, the verification team takes advantage of the model by performing early verification. Third, the model drives early physical design decisions where the team uses structural model elements to perform early floor planning, placement, and wiring. The model analysis of each of these three activities can drive changes into the HLD process (dashed arrows), which result in changes in the high-level model. After all early analysis concludes with satisfying results, HLD ends and the implementation of the design under verification begins.

14.2.1 Applications of the High-Level Model

There are three main application areas for a high-level model. Each area has its own strong reasons to demand a model as the basis for early analysis.

Early Performance Evaluation

Besides the function that a DUV provides, the performance executing this function is a crucial property of a design. It is critical during HLD to ensure that the chosen design point satisfies the requirements. Therefore, performance evaluation is necessary during HLD. If a high-level model is available, the team can base the analysis of performance properties on this model. Typical performance properties are the amount of cycles necessary to complete a DUV transaction or the sustained peak execution of series of transactions. The associated metrics are *latency* and *bandwidth*.

Traditionally, the performance domain uses its own dedicated performance model as described in Mukherjee et al. [107]. Such models are normally extremely abstract models, which have performance analysis as their only objective. Popular approaches are abstract queuing or transaction models that represent the major DUV data flow elements as managed resources. On this basis, such models specify the operations of the DUV in form of transactions. Transactions define the execution of operations on data as it flows through the design. Performance analysis collects statistics about the flow of these transactions, individually and as an average over large numbers of them. A pure performance model usually does not need to implement the processing of the data that accompanies the transactions. It is important how many clock cycles the number crunching in a functional DUV unit takes but not what the calculated result is. Data processing results are only necessary where the control flow depends on decisions that stem from data content. This relative independence of data results allows pure performance models to abstract away the data processing implementation of large parts of a DUV.

A high-level model as defined in this section must be more detailed than a pure performance model. The analysis of the time spent by operations or transactions flowing through the DUV is the core task of performance prediction during HLD. However, the other two disciplines of the HLD analysis triad, functional verification and physical design (PD), require more detail in the high-level model.

A key requirement for performance analysis is a high-speed model. Projects use pure performance models early and sometimes in addition to a high-level specification model because of the need for the highest possible speed. Performance benchmarks for hardware designs usually require the performance model to run through a large number of operations. Because design parameters change during the course of HLD, these benchmarks have to be run many times, and it is vital to react and validate these changes quickly.

Thus, using a high-level model for early performance analysis creates two main requirements: high execution speed (100 to 1,000 faster than the speed of an RTL model) and model instrumentation or analysis that supports the collection of transaction timing information.

Early PD

PD uses the physical attributes expressed in a DUV specification. PD is the process that places partitions of the design, *placeable objects*, onto the rectangular area of the chip and routes the wire connections between these. During HLD, major functional partitions or units of the chip define the granularity of placeable objects known up to this point in the design process. It is the task of the design team to specify the estimated dimensions of these partitions and the positions of the signal interface pins on

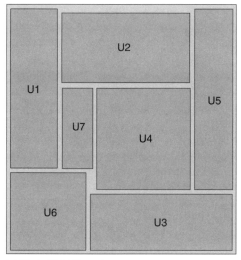

(a) Early DUV Floorplan

(b) Physical Chip Layout

■ **FIGURE 14.6**

Comparison of early partitioning of the DUV during high-level design (HLD) and the final chip layout. (a) The abstract partitions of the DUV as they are known during HLD (pins and wires are not shown). The design team splits the DUV into seven partitions with dimension estimates. Using the partitions' area and interconnect structure, the early physical design process can define a chip floor plan and run placement/wiring analysis to ensure the chip can be manufactured. (b) The final detailed layout of the chip implementation for comparison.

the partition shapes. Given the area and pin number estimates of the partitions and the partition interconnect structure, the PD process can start with early placement and wiring studies that ensure even during HLD that the DUV will fit the chip size and it is possible to route wires successfully for all partition-to-partition and partition-to-chip input/output (I/O) connections.

Figure 14.6 illustrates the early partitioning of a chip during HLD and compares it with the final chip layout.

If the high-level model for early PD is to be used, it is necessary that the partitions and their I/O interconnects can be extracted from the model. This requirement defines the need for the model to represent the partitions as explicit objects. Only then is it possible for the designer to attach area information to a partition. It is not necessary but very natural for the designers to also explicitly specify I/Os on partitions and specify how the partitions are interconnected. Alternatively, a partition can define its I/Os implicitly. For example, whenever a partition references a signal from another partition, an early PD analysis program could infer a partition I/O.

Regardless to which extent the designers specify partitions and inter-connects explicitly, the early PD analysis of the DUVs requires the high-level model to contain enough information about the *physical structure* of the implementation. This requirement imposes a structure on the high-level model itself. For this reason, a pure performance model does not satisfy our definition of a high-level model for HLD.

Early Functional Verification

The verification team is the one that probably has most to gain from the use of a high-level model as part of HLD. Rather than letting the design team work with informal documents, white-boards, and napkins, a high-level model forces an explicit specification of the DUV's functionality early.

The verification team can use the model for three important purposes. First and most obvious, the model can build a solid basis to learn the design itself. Many times, one of the critical bottlenecks in a project is the knowledge gap between the design and the verification team. Having an explicitly coded and, preferably, executable model usable in FV or simulation allows the verification team hands-on learning of the design specification. The second advantage is the ability of the team to use the high-level model to bring up the verification environment much earlier. Unlike a traditional flow, where stimulus and checker components are developed in parallel with the RTL implementation, an HLD phase with a high-level model allows this work to start much earlier. This gives the verification team a chance to have the basic environment ready for the very first RTL delivery from the design team. Of course, the third major goal is the verification of the high-level model itself. Because the high-level model encodes many design decisions, running the model with the first level of checkers and stimulus generators allows the team to verify the major aspects of the DUV's functionality in this early project phase. Results of this verification are important drivers into the change feed-back loop of the design during HLD.

Clearly, the high-level model is an abstraction of what the RTL design specification implements. It likely is not exact enough to encode many detailed window conditions, exceptions, and corner cases. However, it should specify the major mainline functional features of the DUV and can therefore be the target for an effective first approximation of a veri-fication environment.

14.2.2 High-Level Modeling Styles

The main goal of HLD is to define the major design decisions early. It is the phase of the project where it must be possible to discover major flaws in the concepts. The process must support major re-definitions of the DUV without much penalty and re-work. Some of the requirements and

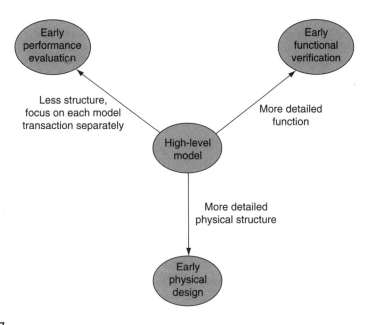

■ **FIGURE 14.7**

The three design disciplines have conflicting goals that drive the development of a high-level model. Although performance evaluation needs a fast model that focuses on model transactions separately to allow quick adjustments of the model, the areas of functional verification and physical design (PD) strive to have as much details about their domains in the model as possible. The more the model represents physical structure, the more accurate the early PD analysis. Similarly, early verification is more complete if the model contains more of the detailed function. A design project must set the rules for a productive compromise between these goals early on to be able to utilize the high-level model successfully.

principles that make a high-level model valuable for the three major design disciplines under consideration were outlined above.

It is important to keep in mind two bounding conditions for the development of such a model. First, it must support several of the disciplines equally well. As discussed, there are goal conflicts between the different areas, which means the team has to strike a *compromise* to make each area as successful as possible (Figure 14.7). Shaping the model for one of the design disciplines at the expense of the others diminishes the overall value of the model. Second, the teams have to keep in mind that the model is only a *first approximation* of the real DUV implementation and, as such, is incomplete and abstract. Only those design aspects contained in the model are the subject to HLD analysis. On the other hand, it is not affordable to encode *all* design implementation decisions into the high-level model, because that defeats the purpose of HLD, which is to evaluate and quickly change the design, and therefore the model, without major effort and penalty.

If a project decides to use a high-level model as the vehicle to drive HLD, it has to set the goals and their implication to these bounding conditions up front to be successful.

In the following, different possible approaches to high-level modeling are characterized. Many factors drive the decision about which of these approaches a project selects. Some of these factors are the available skills on the team and the actual balance the project places between the three early design analysis disciplines.

HLD Languages

As discussed in Chapter 3, the HDLs are designed to cover some of the needs of high-level modeling. In particular, VHDL and the newly developed SystemVerilog have capabilities to support abstract modeling [108].

The clear advantage of using VHDL or SystemVerilog for this task is the familiarity of the language to the design team. These languages are strong in expressing physical structure, supporting the specification of partitions and interconnect between those as first-class constructs of the language. Their behavioral modeling constructs allow the coding of abstract algorithms as opposed to a detailed logic implementation. In addition, at the end of high-level design, the team can seamlessly refine an HDL high-level model down to the implementation level. This approach is attractive because the team never changes the modeling language, just the abstraction level. Where an abstract behavioral algorithm defines a functional unit at first, a detailed structural implementation can replace it during the implementation phase. It is even possible to have the implementation of the different partitions proceed on different schedules. The full model analysis can then proceed with a *mixed-level model*, where some partitions use their high-level model specification, whereas other partitions, which are further in the implementation phase already, use the implementation HDL.

Unlike for models written in a programming language, it is possible to translate many behavioral constructs of the HDLs into an equivalent finite state machine representation, which support early FV on the high-level model. If a team carefully chooses the relevant subset of the HDL used for high-level modeling, FV can provide significant strength to the early verification cycle.

The main disadvantages of using an HDL for high-level modeling are the resulting difficulties for performance analysis with such models. HDL models tend to be slower than models written in a general-purpose programming language. The inherent overhead of the signal change protocol in an event-driven simulation engine (see Chapter 3) slows down the model execution in comparison with simple function calls to execute model operations in a pure performance model. Performance analysis also depends on the ability to instrument the model to measure the impact of design decisions. It is easier to add such instrumentation, which provides trace information over long model runtimes, into a model implemented in a programming language.

In addition, the familiarity of the design team with the HDLs has the inherent danger that the team adds *too much* detail *too early* in the design cycle. If there are no clear guidelines up front as to which function is part of the high-level model and which part to abstract out, the designers likely start implementing detailed logic. This defeats the goals of a fast high-level model and the ability to accommodate major re-design decisions efficiently during HLD.

Programming Languages

Many design projects, especially those where the DUV implements algorithmically intense function, use C/C++ language modeling as the strategy to drive HLD. This approach is very typical in the area of graphics processing chips [109].

Using C/C++ provides the team with much flexibility in the implementation of the high-level model. The execution speed of such models is typically very high. In addition, the integration of the model into other software components, like transaction stream generation and instrumentation for performance analysis, is easily accomplished. A main attraction of C/C++ modeling is that the model is extremely portable to a variety of compute platforms and there is no need to pay license fees for a special-purpose simulation engine during the early phase of the project.

Although supporting the performance analysis area well, the downside of C/C++-based modeling is the lack of structural insight that PD and functional verification can have into the model. This is most severe for PD, which depends on the specification of structural partitions and their interconnecting wires. If the C/C++ model just uses function calls to transfer data values from one partition to another, there are no good analysis tools to extract the structural interpretation out of the encoded model. The ability of the functional verification team to create early unit stimulus and checker components depends on the team's ability to use the C/C++ model's modular structure in the setup of the simulation environment. The more programming language modularity exists, the more the simulation team can tie their code into these structures with the expectation that the design team will preserve this structure as physical partitions when it switches to the HDL-based implementation later. There is no hope to utilize FV effectively on a pure C/C++ model.

SystemC

The biggest disadvantages of a pure C/C++ model are the missing explicit structure of partitions and the need to code a control flow algorithm (how does control pass from partition to partition at runtime?) for every new project.

TABLE 14.1. ▪ Selection of widely known alternate approaches to high-level modeling

SpecC	C/C++-based modeling framework focusing mostly on System-On-a-Chip high-level modeling [110].
Handel-C	C-based modeling, with proprietary extensions. Focus in synthesizable hardware modeling [111].
Bluespec	Proprietary high-level modeling language [112].
Murphi	High-level specification language using a concept called *guarded commands*, which specify the functional behavior of hardware. Highly focused on application in early formal verification. [113]

The popularity of C/C++ modeling and the need for a standardized simulation framework that is re-usable for many projects led to the development of the Open SystemC Initiative (OSCI) [114]. OSCI provides an open-source implementation of a simulation framework entirely based on C++. The framework offers the foundation for high-level modeling. SystemC supports the specification of modules and interfaces as well as the obvious capability to implement the behavioral function of a design partition in the C++ programming language using process constructs. Part of the framework is a simulation engine that supports the execution of a model written in SystemC.

SystemC encapsulates the structural aspects of the high-level model in C++ classes. More and more model analysis tools appear in the commercial electronic design automation vendor offerings that target SystemC, enabled by the standardized definition of the structural aspects of the framework.

Other Approaches and Languages

One sign that the field of high-level modeling is still emerging and no single methodology has convinced the industry up to this time shows in the wide variety of alternate approaches. In Table 14.1 some of the more well-known projects and offerings are listed. This list is by no mean complete as the area is still very much in flux.

Overall, with exploding design sizes and complexities and with industrial projects that had enough practical success with high-level modeling, this area of early design methodology gained increasing attention in research and development. It is clear that HLD as well as the related system-level design are areas of major promise and investment of the industry.

For further study of the different directions in high-level modeling, the reader is referred elsewhere [115–117].

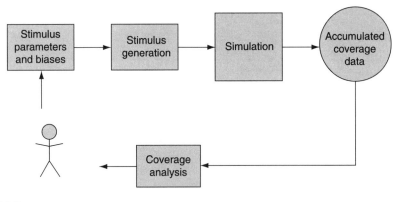

Feedback of coverage measurements taken during simulation runs lets the verification engineer tune the parameters and biases of the stimulus generation to reach so far unverified areas of the design.

14.3 COVERAGE-DIRECTED GENERATION

The collection of coverage information during simulation is a necessary activity to gauge the success of random-biased stimulus generation and to avoid that the verification team verifies areas of the DUV and its architecture insufficiently. Figure 14.8 illustrates the coverage feedback loop.

As is the purpose of any controlling feedback loop, coverage feedback improves the quality of verification. There are two main disadvantages to the scheme in Figure 14.8. First, the feedback involves human interaction, which makes the analysis and the tuning of the stimulus generation very labor intensive and therefore quite expensive. Second, the reaction of the overall verification flow occurs *after the fact*. We simulate first and then find out that the stimulus driver did not hit new interesting design aspect, and only then do we adjust the stimulus.

There has been much research in recent years to improve the effectiveness of this coverage feedback loop. All the different approaches can be subsumed under the title *coverage-directed generation (CDG)*. CDG comes in several different flavors. They can be categorized based on where they place the coverage feedback loop in a new, adjusted flow.

Dynamic Coverage-controlled Stimulus Generation

Modern high-level verification languages (HVLs) (see Chapter 6) support coverage collection constructs, which instruct the HVL runtime framework to collect coverage information [118, 119]. Usually, the verification cycle accumulates the coverage measurements from each individual run

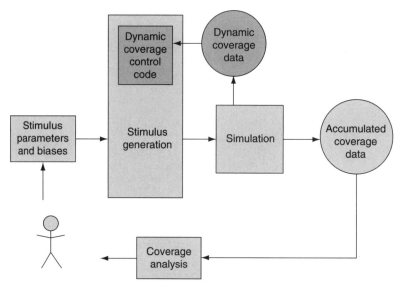

Dynamic coverage-controlled stimulus generation collects coverage data during an individual simulation run and makes it directly available to the stimulus generator (dark gray elements). It is the responsibility of the code in the stimulus generator to make the appropriate choices based on this feedback.

to external files and data structures. Subsequent simulations use the accumulated coverage information to improve their effectiveness.

Dynamic coverage-controlled stimulus components, however, use constructs that make the coverage data of the current simulation directly available to the HVL environment (Figure 14.9). The stimulus component can now use information about events that did occur during the current simulation and can make decisions about subsequent stimulus during the same simulation run.

The capability to access coverage information at runtime gives the verification engineer immediate feedback about the results of previous stimuli applied and enormous control over the next simulation steps. The downside of this very tight feedback loop is the limitation of the coverage insight to the current simulation run only.

Model-based Coverage-driven Test Generation

The model-based generation process is less applicable to biased-random stimulus generation but to the generation of biased-random test cases. Figure 14.10 shows the position of this technology in the simulation flow.

The verification team creates an abstract model of the DUV's microarchitecture, which enables the test generator to use micro-architecture conditions and constraints during the generation of test cases. The idea

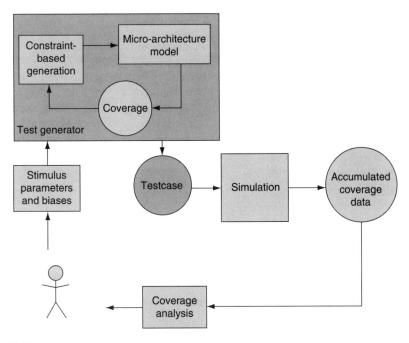

■ **FIGURE 14.10**

Model-based coverage-driven test generation. The test generator includes a model of the design under verification's microarchitecture. In addition to the stimulus parameters and biases from the verification engineer, the generator uses constraints coming from the internal microarchitecture model to generate test cases, which have a high coverage by construction.

behind this scheme is to generate test cases that have a known, high coverage *by construction*. Using the micro-architecture model to provide the coverage metric for the test cases during their generation lets the verification know how well the tests cover the DUV even without running the tests on the model at all.

There are a few examples of approaches in this emerging field [120–122]. At this time, there are no commercial tools available in this domain.

Automated Coverage-controlled Generation

This newest scheme attempts to address the human component in Figure 14.9 and replaces it with an automated component that uses machine-learning algorithms (Figure 14.11).

The base technologies applied in this area are Bayesian networks, which have proven very successful in other areas of machine learning and artificial intelligence [123, 124]. The idea is that over time and over many simulations, the coverage feedback program changes the stimulus parameters and biases slightly and collects the subsequent changes of

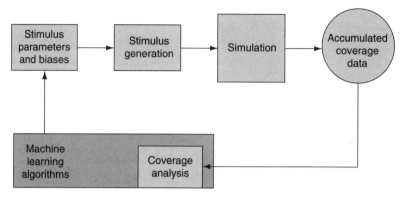

▪ **FIGURE** 14.11

Replacing the human analysis in Figure 14.9 with a machine-learning program addresses the costly component of the traditional coverage feedback loop with automation.

coverage during simulation. Based on the reactive behavior of the system, the machine-learning component of the feedback program accumulates probabilistic sensitivity information that lead to an ability to target so far uncovered areas of the DUV.

Applying machine learning to the coverage feedback loop certainly points to one of the frontiers and possible high productivity gain areas that verification research attacks currently.

14.4   SUMMARY

This chapter reviewed advanced techniques in verification that go beyond the standard verification curriculum.

Bootstrapping verification provides us with techniques to circumvent the redundant re-execution of the same verification cycles many times over again, thus making the verification cycle more efficient.

High-level modeling is an emerging practice that lets projects formalize design decisions during HLD and starts many design analysis processes earlier than the traditional paper-and-pencil HLD. It also accelerates the start of the verification cycle because it gives the verification team a chance to develop their infrastructure earlier and bootstrap the teams learning of the design.

CDG is the newest research frontier in the attempt to improve the efficiency of simulation. Three different approaches in different states of maturity were shown. Dynamic coverage-controlled stimulus generation is the technique available to many verification engineers today, because it uses coverage feedback inside a test bench where the stimulus generator can react directly to the activity seen in the simulation model.

Model-based CDG and automated CDG are still in the research phase but show promising results already.

This chapter discussed all the advanced topics in an introductory style to give the reader an entry-level understanding and enough preparation for further study as these technologies evolve further into the mainstream of verification practice.

14.5 EXERCISES

1. Using Calc2 as the example, how would you apply some of the bootstrapping techniques of Section 14.1?

2. For each of the sections 14.2 and 14.3 of this chapter, select one of the references listed under "Chapter 14" in the References sections at the end of the book, and explore and summarize the information.

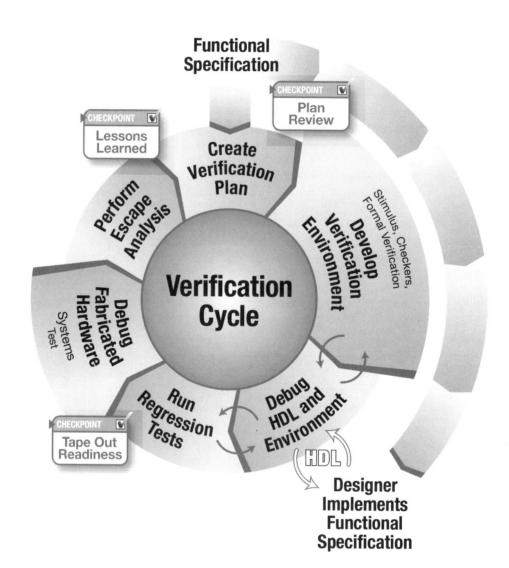

PART V

Functional
Specification

CHECKPOINT ☑
Plan
Review

CHECKPOINT ☑
Lessons
Learned

Create
Verification
Plan

Perform
Escape
Analysis

Develop
Verification
Environment

Stimulus, Checkers,
Formal Verification

Debug
Fabricated
Hardware

Systems
Test

Verification
Cycle

CHECKPOINT ☑
Tape Out
Readiness

Run
Regression
Tests

Debug
HDL and
Environment

HDL

Designer
Implements
Functional
Specification

CASE STUDIES

A major theme within the Verification Cycle is learning from previous verification efforts. Within the Verification Cycle, escape analysis and the feedback loop enable this learning. However, experience is also critical for success. Therefore, this chapter presents three case studies from our own verification efforts.

The Line Delete, Branch History Table (BHT), and Network Processor examples vary in approach and focus. However, together, these case studies provide valuable lessons on creating verification environments, following the Verification Cycle, providing robust drivers and checkers, hierarchical verification, and re-use techniques.

CHAPTER 15

CASE STUDIES

The verification cycle has been discussed in its entirety. Along the way, many examples were presented. In this chapter we discuss three industry case studies that illustrate the principles presented.

These case studies illustrate the yin and yang of stimulus and checking components from Chapter 2, coverage and its usage to bias test cases from Chapters 5 and 7, error-handling verification from Chapter 9, system verification and verification component re-use from Chapter 10, and finally regressions and escape analysis from Chapter 13.

15.1 THE LINE DELETE ESCAPE

This case study helps illustrate the strategies of verification as described in Chapter 2 as well as error-handling verification as described in Chapter 9. It shows how the marriage of drivers and checkers is required to perform verification successfully. Other references to Chapter 2 include the verification cycle and levels of verification hierarchy. It also demonstrates the ability to mimic real-world scenarios (hard errors as described in Chapter 9) in the simulation engine.

15.1.1 Background

In September 1990, IBM delivered the Enterprise System 9000 to customers as the latest in the family of bi-polar technology mainframe computers [125]. The system set new highs in performance, reliability, and serviceability. The microprocessor, storage controller, and input/output subsystem design features included multiple execution pipelines, out-of-order execution, and nearly 100% error detection and fault isolation, giving customers confidence that their data were correct and their system had negligible downtime.

IBM developed the technology used to fabricate the 3090 system in parallel with the design. With aggressive goals set for the technology, the engineers expected to exercise many of the system's reliability features as soon as the first hardware systems were manufactured for early systems test (on the fabricated hardware). A leading concern was the ability to manufacture and yield level 1 (L1) cache arrays with no imperfections. The expectation was that the early systems test hardware would have to contend with partial-good L1 arrays. Partial-good arrays are ones in which portions of the cache array do not contain physical defects and thus can be used.

To this end, the design team integrated the capability to work around physical defects from manufacturing in the array segments during normal system operation. The hardware could detect any of these bad array segments and mark the segment as defective, inhibiting any further use of that portion of the array. The smallest denomination of the L1 array that the design could remove from service was a line of data (128 bytes). Hence, this function was dubbed *line delete*.

To enable the line delete function, the designers built specialized features into the system. Later, the team utilized these features to increase total system reliability in the customers' environment. A key utility was the appending of error correction codes (ECCs) to each double word (64 bytes) of data in the cache. A single byte of ECC allows for single-bit error correction and double-bit error detection when coupled with each double word of data [126]. Data in the L1 cache were stored with appended ECCs, and the hardware checked the data upon retrieval from the cache. If a bit of data was corrupted during its time in the cache, due to either a bad array cell (*hard error*) or a transient particle (*soft error*), it would be corrected when it was fetched from the cache, maintaining data integrity. The hardware then trapped all data corrections, tracking and recording repetitive failures from a given line of the array. If failures from a particular location in the cache in the array exceeded a preset threshold, the hardware would raise a flag to the service code indicating that a line delete action was required.

The service code intervention served two purposes. First, it logged the line delete action so that failing hardware could be tracked. Second, it directed the hardware to perform the required line delete action by writing to the appropriate control register in the L1 cache control logic.

When the system took a line of data out of service, the hardware would read the data from the bad location, make corrections using ECCs, and mark the line as defective, preventing any future storage to that location in the array. Because the L1 cache was a four-way associative design, deactivating a single line resulted in only slight performance degradation. Figure 15.1 depicts the line delete scenario.

Verification of the line delete function required verification engineers to perform tests at different levels of the design hierarchy (verification hierarchy from Chapter 2). At the unit component level, full validation of the ECC logic and the threshold logic was essential (this included injecting errors as described in Chapter 9). At the chip level, the verification engineers validated the line delete action and retirement of the line. Finally, at the system level, the team verified the entire function,

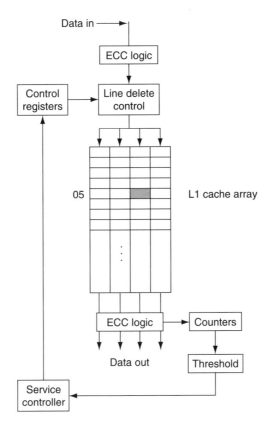

■ **FIGURE 15.1**

Line delete system level view. All the components used in the line delete case study are shown. The shaded area in the L1 cache array indicates a line of data where a double word has a double-bit error. The line delete function should take this sector of the array (address 05, congruence class C) out of service.

including the interaction with the service code (hardware/software co-verification from Chapter 10).

15.1.2 The Verification Environments

The first function that the team verified was the ECC generation and checking logic. Here, it was necessary to confirm that the hardware could detect and correct a flipped bit in every position of the double word, including the ECC bits (all 72 bits). The simulation environment included only the ECC generation logic at the input to the array, the array itself, and the ECC detection and correction logic at the output of the array. Test cases stored 72 double words of random data into each of the four congruence classes at various locations in the array. The ECC generation logic appended 8-bit codes to the 64 bits of random data and stored the data. The test cases methodically *injected* a single-bit error into the array location in each of the 72 double words in each congruence class. Injections were done on each of the 72 bits. Finally, the test case individually accessed the data locations from the array, verifying that the ECC logic on the output of the array corrected every injected error. The verification team repeated the unit level test with dual errors injected into the array, and the ECC logic correctly flagged that the data had uncorrectable, dual-bit errors.

At the next level of verification (in this case it was above unit but below chip—the verification team combined many units and called this element level), the team verified ECCs, threshold, and line delete action as part of the mainline program environment. The mainline environment consisted of running long instruction streams against the processor logic [127]. When merged with the line delete verification environment, the mainline instruction stream test was expected to run to successful completion whenever single-bit error injection was performed on the L1 array. The test validated that the ECC logic cleaned up the injected errors and the instruction stream ran as if there were no injections. The team added checkers to the mainline environment to monitor the threshold counters to ensure that the counters incremented when expected (based on knowledge of where the injections were made in the array). The tests also validated that the hardware raised the appropriate interrupt when it reached the threshold. However, the service code was not invoked until system-level simulation. Instead, at element level, the test case overwrote a value into the hardware control latch that orders a line delete (this was done in the same fashion as discussed in Section 14.1.2, "Bootstrapping the DUV Into High-Potential States). This was an approximate emulation of the service code function on the hardware.

To validate the double-bit error scenario, the team ran similar element level mainline tests with two injections into "bad lines" in the array. Once again, the test expected the instruction stream to run to successful completion. However, the test would take more simulation cycles because the line of data was required to be re-fetched from the L2 cache behavioral based on the uncorrectable errors detected on the output of the array. Until the threshold was met, the uncorrectable data were discarded by the logic, which caused this re-fetch action. Once again, when the threshold was met, the service code was emulated by writing the control register that invoked the line delete function.

At the system level, the verification team simulated the entire line delete action during functional tests in conjunction with the real service code. Longer instruction streams were run with the hardware model of the storage controller (including the L2 and main memory) and the processor. Single- and double-bit injections caused threshold detection and line delete actions. Re-fetches from the L2 or main memory occurred after appropriate detection of double-bit errors. The tests verified that the service code wrote the appropriate control registers back into the hardware after raising the threshold interrupts, and, in the end, the test instruction streams ran to successful completion.

15.1.3 The Escape

When the engineering team performed initial tests on the fabricated hardware, the L1 arrays were, as predicted, plagued by physical defects. The system enabled the line delete function to flag sectors of the array that had multiple instances of dual (uncorrectable) errors, and the service code trapped thresholds flagged by the ECC counters. Software traces of the service code showed that the system invoked the appropriate code and that it was initiating line delete actions upon the proper congruence class lines back in the hardware. Yet uncorrectable ECC errors persisted from the same bad lines despite the appearance that the system removed the bad lines from service. What had happened?

Escapes can occur whenever there is a deficiency in either a driver or a checker (the yin yang of verification from Chapter 2). In the case of the line delete, the drivers were initially creating the scenarios needed to verify the function. However, the drivers and checkers failed to close the loop on the key verification question "how will I know when the function is failing?"

The tests described above fully validated both the ECC logic and the threshold logic; there were no problems there. The service code was performing as expected, and it was writing the proper control registers back to the hardware, as confirmed by scan traces of the hardware. However, when the software updated the hardware's control registers, the L1 control logic continued to use bad array locations, causing tests to fail because of a continuous stream of uncorrectable ECC errors.

As the engineering team debugged the problem on the test floor, the team also initiated reviews of the simulation environments in a parallel effort to understand the problem. That effort paid off. The team found two flaws in the tests—one in the driver and one in the checker—either of which would have discovered the problem.

The flaw in the driver was at both the element and system levels. The error injections that the test case made to specific cells worked correctly, causing the hardware to meet the preset thresholds. However, once the threshold logic caused an interrupt, the test case ceased to inject into the set location in the L1 cache. This action by the test case driver did not correctly imitate the logic, because the bad cells in the real hardware would be persistent. The verification engineer stopped injecting errors, *assuming that the line delete action would disable the bad line* and that the program data would go to other lines in the congruence class.

The second flaw was in the checking code of the simulation environment. Here, the code did not ensure that the hardware never used a disabled line in the array. Appropriate checking would have put "garbage" data into the proper line in the array after the line delete action. This would ensure that any access to the bad line would result in a failing test case due to the hardware reading garbage data from the array. The verification engineer failed to cover the case of "how will I know if the bad array location ever gets used again?" It would also have been appropriate to add a second check at the end of the test case to make sure that the hardware never overwrote the garbage data in the bad section of the array.

The actual bug in the hardware was that the designer failed to wire the line delete controls to the line delete control register. This prevented the invocation of line delete logic at the array inputs, despite the threshold interrupts and the proper service code update of the control registers. After reproducing the bug in the simulation environment, the team created a fix in the next release of the hardware, verified it with updated test cases, and the line delete function worked correctly thereafter. This action of re-creating the failure in simulation and regressing the fix was discussed in Chapter 13.

15.2 BRANCH HISTORY TABLE

This case study helps illustrate the usage of verification levels as described in Chapter 2, stimulus components and test case generation described in Chapter 7, coverage usage as described in Chapters 5 and 7, and checking components as described in Chapter 8.

The unit was verified in its own environment because the higher levels of verification would not be sufficient. The case study also shows how in some situations a completely random, on-the-fly stimulus approach will not work. What is created is a unique combination of both pre-determined and on-the-fly paradigms to solve the conflicting requirements of broad coverage and repeatable instruction streams that is needed to validate the logic. It also illustrates how a cycle accurate reference model is used for checking the logic and how the stimulus must manipulate both the logic and the cycle accurate reference model to perform the verification. Finally, the case study illustrates how the verification team used coverage models to focus the biasing of the tests to hit cases not seen in the cumulative simulation jobs.

15.2.1 Background

The IBM CMOS S/390 Parallel Enterprise Server G5 System (G5) more than doubled the performance of the previous (G4) server. It was the first single system image to break the 1 billion-instructions-per-second barrier. One of the many performance enhancements incorporated into G5 was the addition of a branch history table (BHT). Because G5's performance improvement relied greatly on this addition to the micro-architecture, the verification team focused on the BHT's architectural compliance as well as its performance enhancements.

In the previous generation IBM CMOS S/390 Parallel Enterprise Server (G4), there were no hardware-specific mechanisms for branch performance. Instead, the logic used a static algorithm to "guess" which direction a branch would take. The algorithm simply states that all conditional branches are guessed not taken and "usually taken branches" are guessed taken. Branches such as Branch-on-Count are "usually taken" because the instruction is often used at the end of a loop to branch back to the top of the loop. In average workloads, the G4's static algorithm results in about two of three branches being guessed correct.

Verification of the BHT logic required a specialized effort. Aside from integration into the processor level of the verification hierarchy, the verification team created a stand-alone BHT unit-level verification environment (verification hierarchy as discussed in Chapter 2). This environment used unique stimulus components and test case generation techniques (as discussed in Chapter 7). The environment also used microarchitectural checkers for enhanced bug detection and performance verification (checking aspects as described in Chapter 8). Finally, the team exploited coverage models to direct the test case generation and to ensure the stimulus touched interesting portions of the design (discussed in Chapter 7).

15.2.2 BHT Purpose and Logic Design

The purpose of a BHT is to improve the performance of a microprocessor. A BHT accomplishes this in two major ways: pre-fetching the branch-target instruction stream and accurate prediction of branch direction.

Pre-Fetching the Branch-Target Instruction Stream

To keep a constant flow of instructions through the pipeline, microprocessors maintain multiple instruction buffers. Instruction buffers hold a contiguous set of instructions, as illustrated in Figure 15.2. In Figure 15.2, the microprocessor has eight instruction buffers. Each buffer holds eight contiguous single byte instructions. Normal instruction execution proceeds from one instruction to the next. As execution reaches the end of an instruction buffer, the microprocessor switches execution to a new instruction buffer that holds the next instruction. Each instruction buffer contains control information, including a valid bit and the starting address.

This ordered processing might be broken by a branch instruction. Before a branch executes, the branch-target instruction stream must be loaded into a new instruction buffer. Without a BHT, this operation

▪ **FIGURE 15.2**

Instruction buffers hold a contiguous set of instructions.

occurs after the decode of the branch instruction during the address resolution stage of the microprocessor pipe. This delays the execution of the branch (pipeline stall) until the microprocessor loads the branch target instruction stream into an available instruction buffer. But with a BHT, the microprocessor loads the target instruction stream before decode ("pre-fetch"), allowing the branch to immediately proceed and avoiding pipeline stalls.

For example, the microprocessor previously encountered address "012345684"X and identified it as a branch instruction. The next time the executing instruction address gets close to this address, the BHT identifies an upcoming branch. Using the target-address saved in the BHT, the microprocessor pre-fetches the previous targets of the branch at address "012345684"X. By the time instruction execution reaches the branch, the microprocessor has already loaded the target-address instruction stream into an available instruction buffer.

Accurate Prediction of Branch Direction

When a branch is decoded, the processor must choose a direction to continue decoding. The choice is between continuing to decode down the current instruction address path or jumping to the target of the branch. This guess will be proven correct or incorrect when the branch executes, a few cycles after decoding the instruction. If the processor guesses wrong, the microprocessor must flush the pipeline and restart at the correct instruction. The BHT increases the probability that the processor guesses the correct direction to decode after the branch by recording information about each branch that the microprocessor encounters.

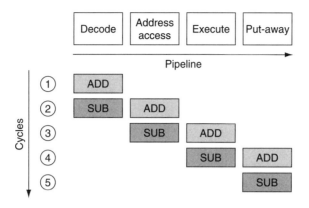

■ **FIGURE 15.3**

Two instructions in a simple microprocessor pipeline. Two contiguous instructions are shown, an ADD followed by a SUB, passing through a four-deep microprocessor pipeline. It takes the microprocessor five cycles to complete both instructions. This is optimal instruction throughput for this pipeline.

The G5 microprocessor's BHT records previously taken branches in the BHT array. This allows the BHT control logic to scan ahead in the instruction stream, searching for upcoming branches. The algorithm used by the logic improves the percentage of correctly guessed branches by about 7%. More importantly, the BHT enables the microprocessor to pre-fetch the target instruction stream, avoiding pipe stalls once the branch is decoded.

The BHT control logic scans the array ahead of the decoding instruction address searching for upcoming branches, initiates pre-fetches for upcoming branches found in the array, and informs the microprocessor's decode logic when a decoding branch has already been pre-fetched. Furthermore, the BHT control logic must write to the BHT array after a branch executes to maintain the branch's history.

Figures 15.3 through 15.5 demonstrate the effects of a pipeline stall and a guessed wrong direction on a branch.

Figure 15.3 shows the effect of the pipeline stall as the branch instruction completes the decode stage.

The SUB instruction could be the instruction that follows the branch or the first instruction at the target of the branch. In either case, Figure 15.4 shows the case where the microprocessor guessed the correct direction after the branch instruction. If the microprocessor guesses the wrong direction, the pipeline would purge the SUB instruction before it completes and then restart the pipeline with the correct instruction after the branch. Figure 15.5 shows the case of the "guessed wrong direction."

With an optimally functioning BHT, the microprocessor avoids the pipeline stall and pipeline purge. The BHT avoids the pipeline stall by pre-fetching the branch-target instruction stream many cycles before

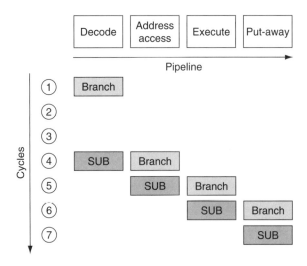

▪ **FIGURE** 15.4

Branch with no pre-fetch causes a pipeline stall. The pipeline stall occurs because the processor must calculate the branch target address and then fetch that instruction address into the instruction buffers. In a best-case situation, this takes just two cycles (as shown). The two instructions complete in seven cycles.

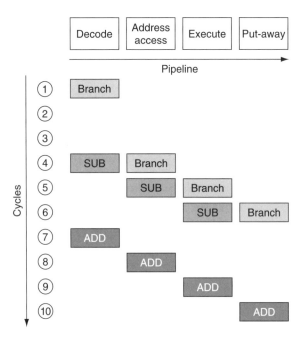

▪ **FIGURE** 15.5

Branch with no pre-fetch causes a pipeline stall and the branch direction to be wrong. In this case, the microprocessor takes 10 cycles to complete two instructions.

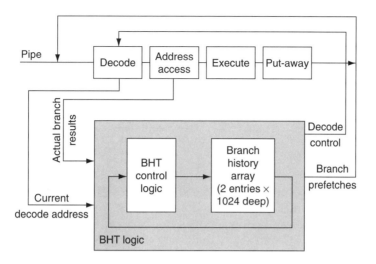

■ **FIGURE 15.6**

BHT logic design. The format of the BHT array is 1,024 entries deep and two partitions wide, allowing the microprocessor to store data for up to 2,048 branches. The main pieces of data held for each entry in the array is bits 8:30 of the branch target address, bits 12:17 and 28:30 of the branch instruction address, and control bits. Bits 18:27 of the instruction address are used to index into the 1,024 deep array.

decoding the branch. When the microprocessor decodes the branch, the BHT assists in choosing the correct direction to continue execution. In this case, the branch and following instruction complete in just five cycles, the optimal throughput shown in Figure 15.3.

The G5 BHT consists of the branch-history array logic and the surrounding control logic. Figure 15.6 shows the BHT's communication with other parts of the processor pipeline.

The BHT control logic receives multiple signals from other parts of the microprocessor. Those signals include the current decode address and actual branch results. The BHT uses the current decode address to direct the array search for upcoming branches. The control logic uses the actual branch results to update the contents of the array with new branch information or updates to the array control bits. The control bits include information on how often the branch has been taken and whether or not the branch target remains stable.

The BHT control logic drives signals to the microprocessor pipeline as well. Those signals include pre-fetch controls and decode alerts. The pre-fetch controls initiate instruction buffer fetches to the target of upcoming branches. The decode alerts occur when the pipeline decodes a branch instruction for which the BHT pre-fetched the target address. It informs the pipeline that the BHT already loaded the branch target address into the instruction buffers and that there is no need to stall the pipeline.

15.2.3 BHT Verification

Although chip and systems level testing verifies architectural compliance of the BHT, it does not catch problems where the BHT logic fails to perform as intended. This is because the architectural results of a test where a branch is initially guessed wrong are the same as the results of the same test where the branch is guessed correct. The guessed wrong test just takes longer to execute because the processor pipeline has to recover from decoding the wrong instruction path. Therefore, verifying the G5 BHT logic required a new unit-level approach that monitored performance and architectural compliance.

The unit-level design under verification (DUV) included just the BHT logic shown inside the box in Figure 15.6. Therefore, the verification environment abstractly modeled all other parts of the microprocessor to which the BHT interacts, including the pipeline. The checking components were required to independently model the BHT array and certain controls to catch performance related BHT bugs (a reference model approach as described in Chapter 8).

The requirements for the unit verification environment were as follows:

- The verification driver code must maintain run-time control of the instruction stream and the branch resolution to manipulate the BHT logic.

- Full independent checking of the control and array logic must occur to catch performance problems.

- Certain code portions, such as the BHT array pre-loader, must work at the unit level and at higher levels of verification.

One of the most interesting concepts in writing the stimulus components for the BHT is that a completely random, on-the-fly stimulus approach does not work. This is simply because the BHT works on "history," meaning that the stimulus must repeat previous instruction addresses to invoke action from the design. For the BHT array to have "a hit" and initiate a pre-fetch operation, the current instruction address, fed to the BHT environment by the stimulus component, must be a close predecessor to a previously established branch address. Choosing instruction addresses at random does not drive enough instruction stream repetition to exercise the BHT. Furthermore, the environment must recall where it previously established branch addresses and maintain those instruction addresses as branches (in some cases). Otherwise, the BHT predicts branches that the stimulus components later identify as non-branch instructions, continually causing the BHT to invoke pipeline flushes and resets. At the same time, a deterministic approach could never reach all the cases in such a complex function.

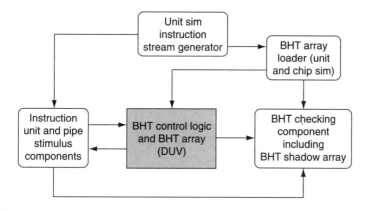

■ **FIGURE 15.7**

■ **FIGURE 15.7**

The BHT verification environment.

Therefore, the verification plan required constrained automation to hit a broad range of scenarios while maintaining the look and feel of repeatable instruction streams. The verification team chose a unique combination of both pre-determined and on-the-fly paradigms to solve the conflicting requirements of broad coverage and repeatable instruction streams.

Because of the requirement for repeatability of the instruction streams, the environment used pre-determined randomization to establish multiple instruction streams for a long-running test case. The verification team encapsulated this code in the environment's Instruction Stream Generator, shown in Figure 15.7. The verification environment called the instruction stream generator once at the start of each test case.

Although the environment used pre-determined instruction stream generation, the instruction unit and pipeline stimulus components (also shown in Figure 15.7) relied upon on-the-fly randomization to exercise the wide range of possible paths that a given instruction stream might take. On-the-fly randomization controls included decisions on

- Whether a branch was taken or not taken

- The accuracy (correct or incorrect) of the BHT predicted branch target address

- Whether a predicted branch turned out to be a branch instruction when the instruction address finally decodes

The stimulus components, modeling the processor pipeline, made all these decisions on-the-fly during the simulation test case.

Rather than start test cases with an empty BHT array, the verification environment used a BHT array loader to initialize the array. This allowed the test case to create interesting stimulus right from the start of simulation. The BHT array loader used the input from the instruction stream generator to intelligently generate data to stick in the array. The inputs to the loader were generic enough that other levels of verification could also preload the BHT array using the same code. The array loader simultaneously initialized the BHT array in the DUV as well as the shadow copy used by the environment for checking.

The BHT checking component maintained an independent copy of the contents of the BHT array. The checking component used this data to predict when the BHT logic should take action. Checking included verifying that

- The DUV made appropriate pre-fetch requests

- The DUV updated its array with correct data

- The BHT correctly interacted with the pipeline logic

Instruction Stream Generation

The instruction stream-generation for the BHT logic was one of the novel approaches used in the BHT verification. The following section describes the algorithm used to create the pre-determined instruction streams.

It is important to note that from the BHT logic's perspective, only two pieces of data are important for each instruction: the instruction address and whether the instruction at that address is a branch.

The unit simulation random instruction-stream generator used a pseudo-random number generator and a parameter table to create the instruction streams. The parameter table dictated the probabilities of certain key decisions that influence the characteristics of the instruction stream. The first action based on the parameter table is the decision on how many blocks of entries within the BHT array the instruction streams use. Figure 15.8a shows this.

A block is a set of contiguous entries in the array. The length of each of these blocks is variable and is based on another parameter. Because it is desirable to cause branches to overlay other branches in the BHT array during the test cases, the number of entries used by the instruction stream was restricted to only the blocks chosen. A small number of blocks cause the BHT to "thrash" or cast-out many BHT entries during the simulation. A larger number of blocks reduces the number of cast-outs and increases the efficiency of the BHT logic.

The next decision, shown in Figure 15.8b, was how many separate instruction streams to create. Each instruction stream can be of varying length and can have multiple branch instructions throughout the stream. Each of the streams is terminated with an always-taken branch to a restricted area (address 7FFFFFFCx), which is manipulated throughout

BHT array

Partition A   Partition B

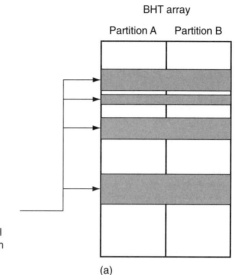

1.
Randomly choose congruence class blocks within the BHT to use for an individual testcase. Using few numbers of blocks will increase castouts and contention within the BHT.

(a)

2.
Choose the number of instruction streams and the length of each instruction stream.

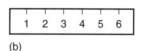

(b)

3.
Create each i-stream, using a random bias to decide if each instruction is a branch, and if it is, whether or not it's conditional and a loop. For each branch, recursively create the branch path i-stream. All i-streams end with a branch to address 7FFFFFFC.

I-stream N

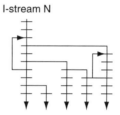

Each of the instructions in I-stream N are mapped from the chosen congruence classes in step 1. If the instruction were a branch, the BHT would record it into one of the shaded areas.

(c)

■ **FIGURE 15.8**

Instruction stream generation algorithm.

run-time to branch to the start of another instruction stream. Each instruction stream has a unique starting instruction address used to identify the instruction stream.

Finally, the instruction stream generator created each instruction. The generator used the parameter table to decide whether each individual instruction is a branch or not. Because the BHT logic was not privy to the actual opcodes, only instruction addresses needed to be generated. For instruction addresses that are designated as branch instructions, the generator created the type of branch (usually-taken or conditional) using the parameter table. If the generator chose an instruction to be a branch, it spawned a new stream starting at the target of the branch instruction. Figure 15.8c shows this activity. All these instructions addresses lie within the range of blocks chosen in the first step (Figure 15.8a).

It is important to note that once the generator designated an address as containing a branch instruction, it would not change for the duration of the test case. This allowed the BHT array to have a history of branch addresses. The exception to this rule was for rare, devious stimulus occasions, which resulted in the BHT predicting a branch, only to find out on decode that the address did not contain a branch instruction.

BHT Array Loader

When instruction stream generation completes, the BHT array loader uses this information to preload the DUV and the shadow array with a subset of the branch instruction addresses. The loader has various modes that affect the efficiency of the BHT control logic. The modes vary the correctness of the preloaded data with respect to the simulated instruction streams. The modes range from "loading all correct data for the upcoming instruction stream" to "loading random data" (nearly equivalent to not preloading the array at all). In between these two cases are modes that load partially good data. Partially good data might be a correct branch instruction address, but the branch target address is incorrect. Another variation would be to preload the array with branch information at an instruction address where there is no branch. The partially good data cases cause the BHT control logic to incorrectly predict branches during the test case, putting the processor pipe through appropriate recovery action. These types of devious cases are important to verify early in the design cycle.

On-the-Fly Stimulus Components

The stimulus component includes an instruction unit and pipeline behavioral. It is the main control code used to drive the BHT logic. The stimulus component provides the instruction stream to the BHT as it would be presented if the entire processor were in the model. It also provides execution completion data to the BHT control logic in the same manner as the execution unit. The execution completion data consists of "end-of-operation" pulses for all instructions as well as branch direction and guessed correct or incorrect data for branch instructions. Therefore, this code controls whether or not the BHT logic predictions are correct. Because the instruction stream is entirely under the control of the stimulus component (and is not checked for architectural correctness), it uses the parameter table to vary the probability of a correct or incorrect response from the execution unit.

This methodology is a very powerful way to stress the BHT logic. Because the BHT is not privy to the instructions opcodes (and therefore there is no need to create real instructions, only instruction addresses), the stimulus component can jump around these pseudo-instruction streams in whatever way the probabilities fall. Hence, the parameter table gives the stimulus component the ability to focus on corner conditions in the logic, allowing for better logic coverage in the test cases.

BHT Checking Component

With the stimulus component having full control over the instruction stream and the branch results, the most difficult task is checking for correctness. To perform the checking, the component uses the BHT shadow array as the cycle accurate reference model. Still, the verification programmed all the knowledge about the BHT function into the checking component, including appropriate actions in corner cases. The correct actions were verbally cross-checked with the other instruction unit and execution unit designers.

However, the checking component did not have to duplicate the entire BHT logic to verify the test cases. This is because the stimulus component is in control of the upcoming sequence of events and can therefore "cheat" to predict the proper BHT results. Because the components know whether or not a branch is going to be taken based on the probability table, the code has the advantage of being able to "see into the future" of the pipeline, avoiding the need for all the logic that the BHT controls must carry.

Example Test Case

The following example demonstrates the flow of a single test case. This test case was a typical successful simulation job, meaning that it ran to completion without flagging any errors.

Before the test case simulates cycles, the code invokes the instruction stream generator. As detailed in Figure 15.9(1), this test case started by choosing to restrict the BHT array addresses to just four blocks, each of varying length. This choice of a relatively small number of blocks affects the cast-out rate of the BHT array as the test case proceeds, because all the instructions generated have instruction address bits 18:27 in the range of 037x-03Dx, 0A2x-0A3x, 120x-132x, or 204x-22Ax. If a larger number of BHT blocks have been used, the average cast-out activity in the test case would likely decrease.

After choosing the BHT blocks, the instruction stream generator uses the parameter table probabilities to choose the number of instruction streams and their lengths (Figure 15.9[2]). In this case, seven instruction

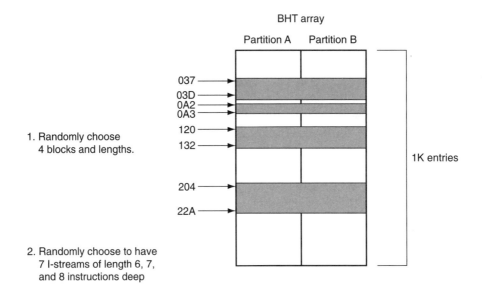

1. Randomly choose 4 blocks and lengths.

2. Randomly choose to have 7 I-streams of length 6, 7, and 8 instructions deep

3. Create 7 I-streams. The first one, 7 instructions deep, is shown here:

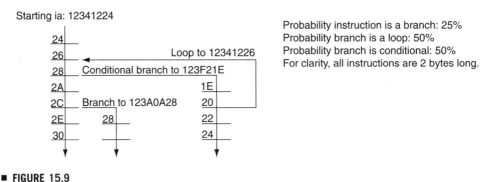

Probability instruction is a branch: 25%
Probability branch is a loop: 50%
Probability branch is conditional: 50%
For clarity, all instructions are 2 bytes long.

▪ **FIGURE 15.9**

Example of a test case flow.

streams are to be generated, each of length six, seven, or eight instructions deep. The depth refers to the number of instructions in the first path, which terminates with a branch to address 7FFFFFFCx. All instruction stream stubs created from each branch have less depth than the prior instruction stream.

Finally, the generator creates each instruction stream. The first one, shown in Figure 15.9(3), has a depth of seven instructions. In this example, the generator uses a probability of 25% to decide whether an instruction is a branch. Hence, 3 of the 12 instructions created for this stream were branches. Other probabilities, as shown in Figure 15.9(3), resulted in 1 of the 3 branches being a loop (the branch target is upward in the instruction stream) and 1 of 3 branches being a conditional branch. All instructions addresses (bits 18:27) reside in the blocks of the BHT chosen in Figure 15.9(1).

The generator creates six other instruction streams using the same process. Figure 15.9 does not show these other instruction streams.

The preloading of the BHT array and shadow array with data follows the instruction generator. The array loader chooses branches from the seven instruction streams to load into the array. If more than two branches have identical instruction address bits 18:27, then the array loader chooses only two to preload. The others make their way into the array when encountered during the normal execution of the test case. The array loader changes some of the target addresses to cause incorrect branch prediction early in the test case.

After preloading the arrays, the test case begins to clock cycles. The first action taken by the pipe stimulus component is to randomly choose one of the seven instruction streams as the initial instruction address. The component chooses the instruction stream shown in Figure 15.9c first and then drives the inputs to the BHT with a current instruction address of "12341224"x. The stimulus component proceeds to fill the decode-to-execute pipeline with the instruction addresses. In the meantime, the BHT logic looks ahead in the array and correctly identifies the first upcoming branch because it was preloaded into the array. That branch, located at address "12341228"x, has its target address, "123F21E"x, pre-fetched by the BHT logic. The pipe behavioral in the stimulus component responds to the BHT logic request for pre-fetch. As the stimulus component emulates the pipeline, it decodes the branch instruction. The BHT logic correctly signals that the branch target instruction address has already been pre-fetched and that pipeline decoding should continue down the branch target path (guess taken). As the stimulus component drives the BHT logic inputs to simulate the movement of the pipe, the branch instruction reaches execution. In this case, the behavioral chooses to respond with "guessed correct" in the execution cycle, and no pipeline recovery is required. In the meantime, the BHT logic has not pre-fetched the upcoming branch (loop back to "12341226"x) because it was not preloaded into the array. As the stimulus component's pipeline encounters this instruction, it imitates a pipe stall that fetches the target address. The branch is guess-taken as it is not a conditional branch, and the decoding continues back at the target of the loop.

Simulation continues in this fashion until reaching the last instruction in the stream. As stated, the last instruction in the stream is always a branch to address "7FFFFFFC"x. This address holds a second branch that has a target address of the initial instruction in one of the seven instruction streams. The stimulus component overwrites this address into the array with a new target after every encounter of the

"7FFFFFFC"x address. This mechanism allows the test case to complete one instruction stream and then jump to another randomly chosen instruction stream. The test case continues to run until a predetermined quiesce cycle. Upon reaching the quiesce cycle, the test case completes the current instruction stream and performs a final consistency check of the BHT array versus the shadow array.

This particular test case simulated 10,000 cycles, executing a combination of the seven instruction streams 191 times, each with differing permutations based on the contents of the array and the random numbers generated for probabilities. Had the checking code flagged an error, the environment would halt simulation and print the error message detailing the miscompare to the results file. An example of a miscompare might be the failure of the BHT logic to pre-fetch a target address that the checking component indicates should be pre-fetched.

Aside from collecting error data, the results file contains a cycle-by-cycle record of the activities of the BHT and pipe behavioral. This information is invaluable for quick problem determination. The verification team can also use the results file to collect coverage information, providing feedback for parameter table adjustments. These adjustments enable the stimulus components to exercise more logic function in the following test cases.

BHT Coverage

The verification team used functional coverage metrics (as described in Chapters 5 and 7) to assess the BHT environment and adjust the probability tables. The team defined six coverage models to track the amount of logic touched by the simulation environment. We detail two of these models here.

The simpler of the models indicated the usage of the control bit states in the BHT array. The verification team defined this model using four pieces of data:

Model: (WriteType, EvenOdd, OldControlBits, NewControlBits)

The environment collected data from the test cases after each write to the array. The first piece of data, WriteType, indicated one of three possible scenarios that initiated a write to the BHT array:

- A new write to the array over top of an invalid entry
- A new write to the array over top of a valid entry, or
- A write to the array that is updating an entry (write over itself)

The next piece of data collected for this model is whether the write was to the even or odd side of the array. The third and fourth pieces of data indicated the transition from the old control bits to the new control bits. The control bits (of length 2 bits) have values of 00, 01, 10, or 11. Control bits indicate information about the data in the particular array position.

The decoded values meant "invalid entry," "strongly taken branch," weakly taken branch," and "wrong target." Strongly taken versus weakly taken indicated the confidence level in the branch being taken the next time it was encountered.

The following cross product defines the size of the state space for this model:

$$(3 \times 2 \times 4 \times 4) = 96$$

However, the design placed restrictions on the actual number of legal cases. For example, because the control bit value of 00 indicates an invalid entry in the array, if the WriteType field is "a new write over an invalid entry," then the OldControlBits field must be 00. Restrictions such as this bring the number of legal combinations down to 30. Over the course of multiple simulations, the environment encountered all 30 cases (100%).

The second model is a far more complex example. It deals with all the possible permutations that can occur to a single branch. The model definition is

Model: (Bt, Tp, Tact, Pwtar, In, CC, SA, CB, K, C1-3, C3-5, C5-7, C7-9) where

Bt = Branch type (certain or always taken)

Tp = Taken prediction (predicted taken or not predicted)

Tact = Taken actual (not taken or taken)

Pwtar = Predicted wrong target (correct target or incorrect target predicted)

In = In array at decode (in array or not in array)

CC = Number of valid entries in the array congruence class at decode (0, 1, or 2)

SA = Branch came from system area (in system area or not)

CB = Control bits in array at decode (00, 01, 10, or 11)

K = Pipeline stage that branch was at when pipe recovery occurred (0 = no recovery, 1–9)

C1-3 through C7-9 = The number of cycles that the branch was in a stage of the pipe (0, 1, 2, or more cycles)

The cross product of this model yields 622080 possible coverage states.

$$(2 \times 2 \times 2 \times 2 \times 2 \times 2 \times 3 \times 4 \times 10 \times 3 \times 3 \times 3 \times 3) = 622080$$

However, less than one-third of these are legal states.

The verification team used these models to focus the biasing of the parameter table to hit cases not seen in the cumulative simulation jobs. For example, the branch permutation model might have originally shown that the stimulus components never created cases of Tact = 1 & Pwtar = 0 during simulation. This would indicate that every time a branch was actually taken, the BHT logic supplied the correct target address. To fix this deficiency, the verification engineer would adjust the biasing in parameter table item "Result of Branch." This item dictated the probability that a branch was taken, not taken, or taken but to a different target address. In this case, coverage results would indicate the need to raise the biasing on the different target address. This action would raise the probability that when the BHT logic identified a branch, the stimulus component's pipeline behavioral would return a "wrong target address" after executing the branch.

The verification team analyzed all models that did not hit 100% coverage for trends. In large models, the verification team does not expect 100% coverage. The team analyzes the data, searching for large gaps in the cross-product results.

15.2.4 Results

The BHT unit simulation effort was a success. The unit environment uncovered 18 BHT bugs before processor level verification. Of the 18 problems, 6 were architectural and 12 were performance problems. Although the architectural bugs would have been found at the processor level, finding the problems earlier in the design cycle was beneficial in that the problems were easier to debug and regress the fixes before getting to the next level of verification (as discussed in Chapter 8 and 13).

The focus on coverage directly attributed to finding 3 of the 18 problems. The verification team discovered these bugs after adjusting the parameter table due to holes shown by the coverage metrics.

The processor and system level verification efforts uncovered three additional BHT logic problems. These problems were all beyond the bounds of the unit verification effort, because they depended on microcode interactions.

The prototype hardware was a resounding success, because the hardware test uncovered no BHT related bugs in the CMOS chips. The BHT was fully functional on the first pass, assisting in the time-to-market concerns that surround releasing servers.

15.3   NETWORK PROCESSOR

This last case study illustrates the strategies involved at the chip and system level of verification. It is a look at how a network processor was verified at the chip and system levels. Specifically, it demonstrates the complexities of re-use as described in Chapter 10 and details how multiple test benches were created to handle chip level simulation performance issues.

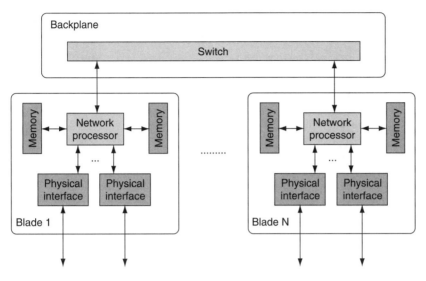

■ **FIGURE 15.10**

System-level example of a network processor verification environment.

15.3.1 System Overview

A network processor is a processor that has been customized for networking applications. A typical processor (like the Intel Pentium or the IBM PowerPC) is built to serve a general purpose: It allows its users to apply it to any number of things-word processing, transaction processing for banks, various internet applications, and so on. A network processor is a specialized processor that targets one specific application-routing network traffic efficiently. It might be to route traffic from one network type to another or to perform higher-level functions such as voice-over Internet protocol processing. The network processor is architected to handle the specific tasks associated with networking. Figure 15.10 illustrates a network processor system.

The system is composed of two main components-a backplane and a blade. The backplane contains the switching fabric that routes packets between the "N" blades. "N" varies depending on the configuration. A fully populated system has 64 blades. Each blade contains a network processor, memory, and the physical network interfaces (PNIs) such as Ethernet.

Figure 15.11 shows a high level diagram of the composition of a network processor.

The network processor has five subsystems comprised of many units-a PNI subsystem, a processing complex subsystem, an ingress control unit, an egress control unit, and a switch interface (SIF) subsystem. The network processor acts as two independent flows, ingress and egress. The

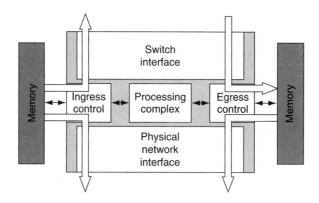

▪ **FIGURE 15.11**

Network processor internal composition.

two flows share the processing complex. The ingress flow is as follows: The PNI subsystem receives network traffic, strips off the cyclic redundancy check (CRC) from the packet, and places that data into memory via the ingress control. The ingress control subsystem notifies the processing complex that data are in memory to be processed. The processing complex then uses that data and performs many different operations on them. Once the processing complex has finished, it notifies ingress control subsystem that the data are ready to be sent out of the chip via the SIF subsystem. The SIF subsystem then segments that data into smaller packets, called cells, and sends those to the switch with the appropriate switch routing information.

The egress flow is similar except that the SIF and PNI subsystems reverse roles and the egress control subsystem replaces the ingress control subsystem. The SIF subsystem receives the cells from the switch and places them into memory; when it receives all the switch cells that comprise a complete data packet, it reassembles the cells into the data packet and then notifies the egress control subsystem that then notifies the processing complex. Once the processing complex finishes with a data packet, the egress control subsystem then notifies the PNI subsystem to send the data out of the chip onto the network. At this time the PNI overlays correct CRC at the end of the packet.

The PNI connects to different physical interface chips to support different protocols-up to ten 10/100 MB Ethernet, one 1 GB Ethernet, four OC-12 ATM, or one OC-48. Each PNI chip connects to the network processor differently. In a system, one blade may have five 10/100 MB Ethernet physical interface chips, and on another blade, an OC-48 ATM physical interface chip is used.

Within a system, one blade is dedicated as the control point. This control point blade is no different from any other blade except for some additional functionality-an embedded microprocessor (not shown in Figure 15.11). The network processor has a mode to enable the control point function (enabling the internal microprocessor). When the network processor is acting as a control point, the internal microprocessor is responsible for configuring (initializing) and maintaining the system. Regardless of whether the network processor is functioning as a control point or not, it is always processing network packets.

The network processor initialized itself in various ways. When the network processor was in a non-control point mode, a boot state machine loaded the processor complex with the code it will run to perform the processing of the packets. The boot components consisted of the processor complex and a boot state machine. The boot state machine simply read the contents of an attached electrically erasable programmable read only memory (EEPROM) via an inter-integrated circuit (I^2C) interface and loaded an internal instruction memory in the processor complex. Once the loading of the memory was complete, the boot code then signaled the processor complex to start executing the instructions.

When it was in a control point mode, the boot state machine loaded the embedded microprocessor with control point boot code instead of the processor complex. Upon completing the code load, the boot state machine then instructed the embedded processor complex to start executing. The code that was loaded in the microprocessor was required to load the processor complex with its instructions.

One additional function that the embedded processor could perform was to be able to create ingress packets that could be sent to the other network processors in the system to configure them as well.

15.3.2 Verification Effort

The overall verification effort on a network processor required unit level, chip level, and system level, all with dedicated simulation efforts (test benches, verification components, and re-use). The chip and system verification teams did not create any additional verification components because they re-used the appropriate components from the unit levels.

This added complexity as the unit level verification engineers had to consider both chip and system level functionality when creating some of the verification components.

PNI Unit Verification Test Bench

The PNI unit verification environment was very similar to what is presented in Chapters 2, 7, and 8. However, a good degree of re-use was accomplished because the whole system is designed around routing packets or frames depending on the network protocol. Because of this, most verification environments contained a frame formatter verification component that was responsible for generating frames.

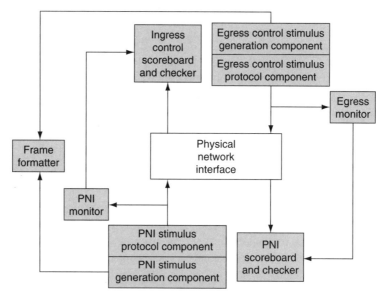

PNI unit verification test bench. The ingress flow and egress flow both use the frame formatter for generating data.

Figure 15.12 shows the unit verification environment for the PNI. Notice how both the ingress and egress flows utilize the frame formatter. As mentioned earlier, the ingress and egress flows are independent. For ingress test scenarios, the PNI stimulus component called on the frame formatter to get a list of frames that would be sent into the DUV. Depending on the protocol configured for the port (recall that the PNI supports multiple protocols), the PNI stimulus generation component would call the frame formatter to get different lists of frames to be sent into the DUV. For the ingress flow, the frame formatter had to support generating a packet that had a correct CRC as the last byte in the packet. One function that the PNI unit performed was discarding packets that had incorrect CRC appended. To simulate a packet being corrupted, the frame formatter would be called with an appropriate parameter indicating how many of the packets it was generating would contain invalid CRC. In these cases, the Ingress Control checker would validate that only the cells with correct CRC were indeed passed through the DUV.

On the egress side, the opposite occurred. The Egress Control stimulus component would call on the frame formatter, and it did not want correct CRC because it would be appended onto the packet by the DUV. The PNI checker would check that every packet was appended with correct CRC.

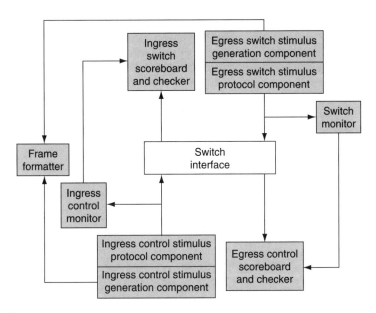

■ **FIGURE 15.13**

SIF unit verification test bench. The ingress flow would take a packet and segment it into 64 byte switch cells. The egress flow would capture the numerous switch cells into memory.

SIF Unit Verification Test Bench

The SIF unit verification was similar to the PNI, except it dealt with cells instead of packets. All the data that the SIF passed were in a cell format. A packet was comprised of numerous cells, and a cell was exactly 64 bytes. Six bytes of every cell contained switch routing information and cell integrity information.

The ingress side of the SIF would take a packet and split it into cells with the last cell being padded to 64 bytes. The SIF would insert the correct switch routing information and cell integrity (much like the egress PNI). As indicated in Figure 15.13, the Ingress Control stimulus generation component would call the frame formatter to receive a list of packets that would be sent into the DUV. The ingress control monitor passed the packets that are sent into the DUV to the Ingress Switch checking component, which would segment the packet into the appropriate cells and ensure the DUV sent the correct cells with the appropriate switch header information.

The egress flow was the reverse. It called the frame formatter to get a list of packets, and it would then segment the packet into cells and send those cells into the DUV. However, it did not include any switch routing information; in this case it was random. As with the PNI, it did insert

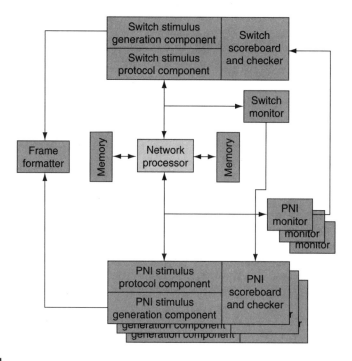

Network processor chip test bench.

both correct and incorrect switch integrity information to ensure the SIF would handle them correctly. The SIF did not perform the reassembly of the cells. That function was left up to the Egress Control unit. The SIF just stored the data into memory buffers that the egress control unit passed to the SIF. The Egress Control checking components validated that the correct data was received.

Chip Verification Test Bench

Figure 15.14 illustrates the chip level simulation test bench. Every dark gray box is a verification component (or set of them) re-used from the PNI and SIF unit verification environments.

Because the two unit teams were already using the frame formatter to obtain the correct packet information, the chip team just had to re-use the components from the unit levels. However, the frame formatter had to be enhanced to handle chip simulation. Because the core of the network processor had specialized hardware designed to handle different types of network protocols like Apple Talk, IEEE 802.3, and IEEE 802.5, the frame formatter now had to generate correct network packets for the different protocols, not only from the physical interface level but also from an encapsulation type. This was a different function than what the PNI and SIF unit verification teams needed. Each of these units only required data that met the physical protocol. However, the other functions relating to CRC and switch cell integrity was still required to ensure error recovery on these interfaces.

Another required change to the unit verification components was to change the monitor functions. At the unit levels, the PNI and SIF sent the expected data to different verification components than what was required at the chip level. At the chip level, the monitors and checking components now must communicate. Special hooks were implemented in the unit monitors to communicate to the correct scoreboard when the units were contained in the chip test bench.

Another change to the unit verification components was required in the scoreboard. Both the PNI and SIF units sent out the data as it was received (first in, first out). At a chip level, this paradigm breaks down because the core processing engine may send things in a different order from what was received. Because of the ability to receive things out of order, the scoreboard functions for both the PNI and SIF had to contain a mode.

This caused for churn at the unit levels when the chip verification team was trying to get tests to pass. The unit verification teams had to define a function in the scoreboard to handle the fact that at the chip level, packets may be received out-of-order.

Chip Test Bench Configurations

One issue to contend with was the numerous configurations that a blade supports. The PNI supports different networking chips from different vendors. The unit level verification team verified that the PNI works correctly with the various interface standards. Because of the sheer number of vendors that supply these interface chips, it was not feasible to create configurations for every existing network chip. Instead, the chip level verification environment focused on the differences in micro-architectural features for each of the configurations. For instance, one 1-GB Ethernet port fills up the memory buffers much faster than one 10/100-MB Ethernet port. Therefore, the verification team created various test bench configurations to mimic these scenarios.

The chip level simulation scenarios were categorized into five areas:

- Initialization

- Ingress

- Egress

- Control point

- Wrap

The verification team used the initialization tests to verify the micro-architecture and the connectivity of the boot components of the network processor. The boot components consisted of the processor complex and a boot state machine. The boot state machine simply reads the contents of an attached EEPROM via an I²C interface and loaded an internal instruction memory in the processor complex. Once the loading of the memory was complete, the boot state machine then signaled the processor complex to start executing the instructions.

The verification team created a test bench that was different from the one presented in Figure 15.14. For these tests, the verification team created a test bench that only contained the chip and an EEPROM model.

The verification team had created the EEPROM model such that it would provide an instruction set that would do a very specific task. The instructions loaded were to simply allow the processor to write an internal register. The verification team had an internal monitor that would observe this internal register. On seeing this register written with a specific value, the monitor would indicate the test was complete. Because of the nature of the I²C interface, the test took a long time in simulation to complete. The verification team performed this test only when the logic changed. It was a directed test and did not require any randomization because the software performs the rest of the initialization of the network processor.

In addition to the above initialization test for the processor complex, the verification team also created a similar test that used the embedded processor to load the internal instruction memory.

Ingress tests focused on the ingress flow-the flow of network packets to the switch. These tests validated the micro-architecture and the connectivity of the ingress components.

The tests constrained the PNI stimulus verification components to send in various network packets. As previously discussed, the PNI verification components used from the unit level verification environments required a mode to enable it to notify the switch scoreboard rather than communicate with the ingress PNI scoreboard. This was a simple hook for the unit verification team to add because the design funnels all network traffic to one switch. The PNI stimulus generation component did a function call to the frame formatter to generate a list of packets to be sent into the network processor. The frame formatter generated the list of packets based on constraints that the PNI stimulus generation component passed to it. Some of these constraints included the following: destination ports, packet type, and packet sizes. It also generated a unique signature for every packet. This ensured accountability for every packet within the system. The PNI stimulus generation component then sent the packet into the DUV via the PNI stimulus protocol component. The PNI stimulus protocol component interfaced differently to the DUV based on the packet type. When the packet was sent to the DUV, the PNI monitor inspected the packet, calculated the expect data, and then placed the packet into the switch scoreboard queue. The switch monitor verification component observed the DUV outputs. For every cell that came out of the DUV, the monitor stored it. Once receiving all the cells for a packet, the monitor then sent the received packet to the scoreboard for checking. The checker, on receiving a packet from the monitor, would search through its queues for a packet that matched the signature. If the expected match was received, the checker would remove the list from its queues. This would continue until the end of the test.

Once all packets were sent into the DUV, the test case would end after some latency time. This latency time was to ensure that all packets had a chance to be processed and sent to the switch. Once this time had expired, the checker would make one last check to ensure all packets sent into the DUV were received on the switch side.

There were two conditions where the number of packets sent into the DUV would not match the number of packets received at the switch. One was when a packet was to be discarded, and the other was when the processor was to inject a packet (create a packet and then send it as if it was received at the PNI). In these cases, the verification team had to monitor internal facilities of the DUV so that the verification environment could accurately predict the behavior.

Egress tests focused on the egress flow—the flow of switch cells to the network. These tests validated the interaction and connectivity of the egress components. The egress is similar to the ingress except the roles are reversed. Now the switch generation component called the frame formatter for a list of packets to send. Again, the frame formatter generated these with unique signatures. The switch protocol component then segmented the packets into cells and sent those into the DUV. At this time, the switch monitor notified the correct PNI scoreboard of the expected packet. The PNI monitor observed the outputs of the DUV and, on receiving a packet, checked it against what was in the PNI scoreboard. Again, the unit verification team added a mode to the switch verification component to allow it to transfer the expect packet to one of the "N" PNI scoreboards. An internal monitor also was used to predict when packets would be injected or discarded.

In addition to the ingress test scenarios, the verification team used the ingress test bench to verify the control point test scenarios. These test scenarios verified the ability of the processing complex to communicate with the microprocessor and vice versa. All these tasks are not in any mainline test and are considered both connectivity and micro-architecture in nature. The embedded processor was enabled in these tests so that it would create network packets in memory and then instruct the processing complex to send those packets to the switch. In these tests, an internal monitor was used to monitor this interface, because the test would fail because the switch checker would not be able to find this injected packet in its queues. This internal monitor would observe these created packets and notify the switch scoreboard.

The wrap test scenarios combined the ingress and egress tests. This combination became a complete test suite for a single blade system. In this test scenario, all packets originated from the ingress. The same mechanism was followed as in the ingress scenario. However, once checked, the packet was queued into the switch stimulus protocol component (as opposed to the frame formatter generating it). At this point, the egress flow occurred.

The verification team needed to run the ingress, egress, and wrap tests against the various PNI configurations. The team could have run the complete (or a subset) suite of tests against the various bench configurations to ensure the different physical network chips worked with the DUV. Instead of creating multiple test benches, the verification team used randomness to their advantage; they allowed the PNI stimulus component to randomly choose a physical network chip to emulate. Based on this emulation mode, the PNI stimulus component would then configure internal registers of the network processor so that the two would work together. Because the total number of physical network protocols was limited, this was feasible. Using coverage, it was easy to analyze what physical network configurations were used. Because of the sheer number of test scenarios that were run, no configurations were missed.

Test Bench Performance

The overall performance of any of the above test scenarios was slow, especially in the wrap scenarios. To improve overall performance, the chip verification team used some methods described in Chapter 10. The verification team removed internal units that did not affect the flow of the specific test scenarios.

As shown in Figures 15.15 and 15.16, for ingress and egress test scenarios, internal components were removed to increase the simulation performance. The HDL language was VHDL, so the verification team created different architectures to replace some of the internal units. The only requirement was that these architectures were to drive all outputs to an inactive state, and if the unit had to respond on some internal bus, it would respond with a "no resource available." These architectures were then selected via VHDL configurations (consider these as new test benches).

One could consider that there were four test benches: ingress, egress, full configuration, and initialization test benches. The ingress test scenarios were run with the ingress test bench configuration, the egress test scenarios with the egress configuration, the wrap tests used the full configuration, and the initialization tests used the initialization test bench. The ingress and egress test scenarios were run most often. The initialization, control point, and wrap test scenarios were kept to a minimum. Because the initialization and control point test scenarios were directed, it only made sense to run these once the logic was changed. The wrap

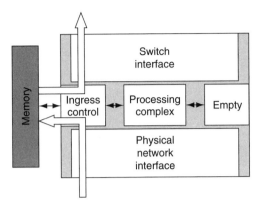

■ **FIGURE 15.15**

Ingress test bench with egress control subsystem "stubbed out." For performance reasons, tests that only focused on ingress flow used a test bench where the egress components were not instantiated in the chip.

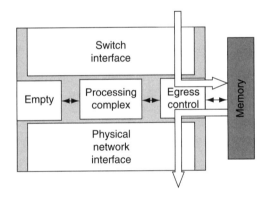

■ **FIGURE 15.16**

Similar to the ingress scenarios, the egress scenarios "stubbed-out" internal components to achieve better simulation performance.

test scenarios were slow and they were run for completeness, because the ingress and egress exercised the same function.

Systems Test Bench

The only difference between the system level simulation test bench and the chip level test bench was that the switch was no longer a verification component. The real switch chip was now contained in the environment and with multiple blades attached. The verification team did it this way primarily to validate the connectivity and interaction of the system with

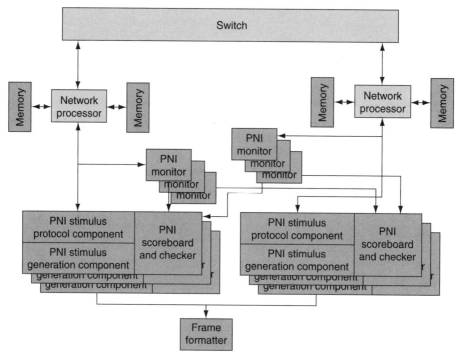

■ **FIGURE 15.17**

System level test bench where a real switch chip was used to route traffic to another network processor.

the real switching fabric, thus validating any assumptions made when the switch behavioral verification component was created. This was not done with the physical interface chips because of the sheer number of chips that could be used within the system. The network processor was designed to interface to any number of physical interface chips that support an industry standard protocol. The switch chip is proprietary; thus, there was only one. Therefore, a system level effort that used the real switch chip was feasible (Figure 15.17).

Not many things changed in the system environment versus the wrap scenario environment. The PNI components, as in the wrap environment, inspected the signature that is part of the packet to determine the destination port. Then, instead of the expect data being sent to the switch scoreboard for checking, the expect data were sent to the receivers PNI scoreboard. Everything else functioned as a normal wrap test.

As before, at the end of every test, the checking components verified that all the queues were empty. This included the DUV queues as well as the verification components (scoreboards and stimulus components). This validated that all the network traffic sent had been received and that the system was in a clean state.

Emulation Environment

In addition to a simulation-based environment, the network processor also had a complex emulation environment as well. The main purpose was so that some of the boot and mainline software that was written for the processor was exercised and debugged before receiving fabricated hardware (hardware/software co-simulation).

The emulation team faced several complexities. First, they had to slow down all the interfaces to match what the chip could support. Second, because the emulation team could run so many more packets through the system than the verification teams could, they could not do any data reliability checking. This was because the tools available to them for emulation did not support this (mainly because of data storage problems). All they could do was check that the number of packets injected into the chip matched the number received. They had to rely on the simulation verification teams to ensure no data corruption.

Emulation started just as the chip and system verification teams were starting. As emulation progressed, and some of the real system software was being developed and debugged, situations were encountered that required the software team to interlock with the hardware team to get a better understanding of the interaction. This allowed the software team to optimize their code for the system. Also, after receiving the fabricated hardware, the system bring-up team had the entire system up and operational running with product level software in about 2 weeks, so the investment in emulation proved to be worthwhile.

An Escape

During the system bring-up in the lab, there was one bug that proved to be catastrophic. The bug presented itself in that a particular PNI port would hang-no packets would be received or transmitted. After weeks of debugging the problem, the lab bring-up team could reliably cause the failure. The team found that by plugging and unplugging the network cable, they could hang the port.

The unit PNI verification and design team was called on to understand and re-create the problem in simulation (as discussed in Chapter 13). After many intense weeks in the lab, they found that the problem was that the PNI unit would get itself into a hang state when the network interface was configured for Ethernet and the input packet it received was less than 64 bytes.

The unit team then ran all their tests that were labeled as "short packet," that is, tests where some of the packet lengths were less than 64 bytes. The entire test suite passed, hinting that something else was going on. Because this team did not implement functional coverage, the team started investigating what could be wrong. The team picked one test that was supposed to only deal with short packets. On looking at a waveform of the simulation, they found all packets were exactly 64 bytes.

The team now knew they had a stimulus component error. On looking at the verification code for these stimulus components, they noticed that if the constraint for the test was less than 64 bytes, the frame formatter should be called with a length equal to 64 bytes. The comment in the code hinted to the fact that the designer had informed a verification engineer that packets less than 64 bytes were illegal. So the verification engineer had decided that because they were illegal, they could never occur. The engineer did not think of the fact that if a network cable was to be unplugged, the size could not be guaranteed.

On fixing the stimulus component, many tests now failed, thus re-creating the hardware bug. The bug was fixed in the HDL, the new HDL was regressed, and new chips where produced without the bug.

15.3.3 Results

System level simulation may affect functions contained within re-usable unit verification components. The unit level models had to support system level functionality. Specifically, they had to support the communication to various scoreboards based on the test benches being used. The chip and system verification team could have created separate verification components, thus adding to the overall cost of chip and system simulation (in terms of either schedule or resource).

In addition to re-using the verification components from the unit environments, the chip and system verification team had to manage various test bench configurations. This was primarily due to performance reasons. They needed to run more tests, and the full chip configuration was not allowing enough tests to run. So the team was faced with either acquiring (purchase, borrow, rent, or lease) more computer hardware and then finding additional funds for licenses for that hardware or finding some other mechanism to push the simulation through. They then looked at the test scenarios that needed to be run the most and then maximized their performance. They removed unnecessary logic (by creating alternate VHDL architectures) to achieve better performance. The drawback was that they had to now manage more configurations.

The verification strategy also used emulation technology. The teams planned to use emulation to perform hardware/software co-verification. The emulation strategy was a success: Using emulation to validate the system software proved to be worth the effort. Once the lab bring-up team received the fabricated parts, they had the chips mounted on boards and were performing basic tests in a matter of weeks.

Even with all the re-use and with the validation of the system software, all it takes is one false assumption to throw everything into a tail-spin. The false assumption regarding packet sizes incapacitated the chip when a network cable was unplugged. This was an expensive lesson that the whole verification team learned from.

15.4 SUMMARY

In this chapter we presented three studies that illustrated different complexities that verification teams encounter. The first was the usage of verification levels within the verification teams. Different verification teams decided what levels were required to validate certain functions.

In the line delete case study, different levels were required to validate different functions. A unit level verification environment was created to isolate the individual functions that comprised the line delete function. A chip level verification environment was used to validate assumptions that the unit's teams had in terms of the behavior of the stimulus components. The system verification team followed the chip effort to validate the software that was to use the function.

In the BHT case study, the verification teams decided that the chip and system levels were not the place to validate the function because they could not guarantee that the function was actually used. The teams decided that to correctly validate this function, a unit level environment was required.

The network processor case study illustrated that the different levels were used to validate different functions. This team utilized unit, chip, system, and an emulation environment to validate the required functions.

Stimulus component robustness was also illustrated in this chapter. In the line delete and the network processor case studies, the stimulus components were not robust enough. In one case, the stimulus component did not drive the appropriate scenarios. In the other case, the verification engineer made an assumption and automatically corrected the constraints for the stimulus component, thus not allowing it to drive the correct scenario. The BHT case study illustrated how the verification team had to rely on both pre-generation and on-the-fly generation to ensure they could hit the scenarios efficiently. Had they not chosen to do a combination of the two approaches, they would not have been able to drive the proper scenarios to hit the state space. Most of the tests would not exercise the function.

In addition to the stimulus component robustness, checking component robustness can also affect the verification effort. The line delete case study illustrated how the checker had missed a function. This simple escape caused a bug to make it to the test floor. The BHT verification team was required to implement a cycle accurate reference model due to the function that was being validated. The BHT function was a performance enhancement. The verification team needed to accurately validate that it was performing as intended. Their best approach was to model DUV with a cycle accurate reference model.

In this chapter we also illustrated how coverage assists the verification team. The BHT verification team used their coverage results from their regression. They analyzed areas of the DUV that were not exercised. This analysis then yielded new biasing parameters that were applied in the form of new test cases. After adding these test cases to the regression suite, they continually analyzed the coverage to ensure these new areas of function were now being exercised. This process repeated until they had a high confidence in their coverage.

As discussed in Chapter 10, re-use causes additional requirements on the verification teams. The network processor verification team desired a high degree of re-use. They architected a verification environment where most unit and the chip and system verification test benches relied on a common verification component-the frame formatter. In addition, the chip and system teams relied on the units to promote their stimulus, monitor, and checking components to the chip and system verification test benches. This drove additional modes and functions into the various verification components.

In addition to re-use, in Chapter 10 we also discussed how the application of different configurations can assist the verification team. The network processor verification team used multiple configurations to speed up simulation time. They used the knowledge that the DUV had some independent flows contained within it, so they carved out units and replaced them with "null" units that drove inactive signals. This created a simulation environment that had less activity (less events) and a smaller memory footprint. These two reductions allowed for a faster simulation.

The last item illustrated in this chapter is how verification teams can bootstrap a test bench to put the DUV into a state that is easier to validate, as discussed in Chapter 14. The line delete verification team utilized this technique to emulate how the software in the system would use the hardware. By doing this, they did not need the real software. The BHT verification team used this technique to put both the DUV and the checking component (because it was cycle accurate) into a state that had higher potential to cause corner conditions than if the bootstrapping had not occurred.

VERIFICATION GLOSSARY

A

ABIST: [Array Built-In Self Test] An automated engine inside of a chip that sends patterns through an array for testability and for array initialization. [Chapter 9]

Acceleration: Utilization of a high-speed simulation engine to run large system models. The simulation engine, or "accelerator", is a hardware system made specifically for simulations. Relative to a cycle-based simulation engine (which runs on a general-purpose computer or workstation), the accelerator can run 1000s of times faster on a given model size. [Chapter 10] *See also:* Cycle Simulation, Emulation

Architectural tests: Verification suites or test cases written with the intent of proving that the design-under-test conforms to the intended instruction set or published design specification. These tests can be deterministic, random, or created by a test case generator. The alternative to architectural tests is microarchitectural tests, which are written with the intent of verifying a specific implementation of the hardware design, such as a queue or state machine. [Chapter 2] *See also:* Architecture, Microarchitecture

Architecture: Architecture refers to the instruction set and system level definitions by which the system MUST abide. Architecture covers all instructions, interrupts, exceptions, cache coherency protocols, IO operations, error handling and resets within the system. Architecture does NOT describe how the design is implemented to comply with the architecture; that is described in the "microarchitecture". [Chapter 1]

ASIC: [Application-Specific Integrated Circuit] A customized microchip designed for a specific system application. ASICs follow a well-defined tools flow for implementation. [Chapter 1]

Assertion: Comment-like statements within the DUV that describe properties within the DUV. These assertions are used by the verification team to assist in debug or for formal verification. These assertions formalize assumptions about conditions inside the design that are supposed to hold true at all verification levels and at all times. [Chapter 3]

Assertion based Verification: A technique utilizing assertions to perform verification. [Chapter 3]

Asynchronous: Within verification, asynchronous refers to an interface between two logical units whose source clocks run off a different oscillator. Asynchronous interfaces are especially challenging to verify because the signal arrival times from one unit to the other may cross local cycle boundaries unpredictably. [Chapter 5]

B

Behavioral: [Also called Stimulus Responder] A behavioral is a verification component which models a piece of HDL or function that neighbors the design-under-verification. The behavioral is designed to respond to stimulus from the DUV, and may drive stimulus back into the DUV. [Chapter 3]

Biasing: A method to provide intended probability to decisions made by stimulus components. Biasing allows the verification engineer to adjust probabilities of specific events without recompiling the verification component. [Chapter 7]

Binary Decision Diagram (BDD): A data structure to represent Boolean functions. BDDs build a compact, tree-like graph providing a basis for efficient algorithms for the reasoning on Boolean functions. [Chapter 11]

Black box testing: Black Box Testing refers to a verification philosophy where the drivers and checkers only utilize the external interfaces of the design-under-verification. True black box testing will base all predictions (checks) on the stimulus sent in by the drivers and will not look at any internal latches or signals of the design. [Chapter 2]

Boolean Equivalency Check: Boolean Equivalency Checking is a type of Formal Verification where a tool is used to mathematically prove that two different designs are combinatorial equal. Equivalence checking verifies exhaustively, for all legal input patterns, that a design representation is still functionally equivalent to the design specification even after many manual or automated design transformations. [Chapter 11]

Bug: Functional verification's term for a flaw in the design. The objective of functional verification is to remove all bugs from the design prior to chip fabrication. [Chapter 1]

Bug Curve: The rate of bugs found versus time, usually displayed in a chart, and used for tracking design and verification progress. [Chapter 1]

C

Checking Component: The portion of the verification environment that observes the behavior of the DUV and flags deviations from the expected behavior. Checking components receive direct orders from the test case, or communicate with the scoreboard and other stimulus components to calculate the DUV's expected behaviors. [Chapter 3,8]

Chip Level Verification: One of multiple levels of hierarchical verification. Chip level verification creates a verification environment at the physical boarders of the chip. [Chapter 2]

Clock Domain: A grouping of latches or flip-flops fed from the same clock tree. Designs may have multiple clock domains. See Clocking. [Chapter 5]

Clocking: Toggling of the physical clock tree that enables latch function. Portions of the logic can have clocking enabled or disabled, which, in turn, turns on or off the functionality. Logic connected to different clock trees can be either synchronous or asynchronous, depending on the frequency and the origin of the clock tree generation logic. [Chapter 5]

Computational Tree Logic (CTL): A form of temporal logic used in formal verification that supports the specification sequences of system states over time. CTL formulas operate of a tree graph representing all unfolded states future of a finite state machine [Chapter 11]

Cone of Influence: Using the graph representation of the logic of a DUV, the cone of influence of a signal is the complete portion of logic that drives it, starting from the DUV inputs [Chapter 11]

Constraints: Restrictions on the inputs of the design-under-verification derived from the set of legal signal values and their inter-relationships. There is a range of possible values for each input. However, choosing a particular value for one input may restrict the realm of possible values for another variable. [Chapter 7]

Constraint Solver: A mechanism to resolve input value restrictions so that stimulus components send legal inputs as defined by the specification. Constraint solvers may be complex, general purpose engines built into a verification language, or may be application specific code written for a single interface specification. [Chapter 7]

Corner cases: Unusual design-under-verification input scenarios that fall outside the mainstream cases. These scenarios may be a combination of events that align in an unusual manner, or may be edge conditions on a single event. These scenarios are especially interesting for stimulus generation because bugs often lurk in corner cases. [Chapter 7]

Co-simulation: The mechanism of coordinating and running two or more different simulation technologies together to yield a single simulation run. [Chapter 10]

Coverage: The process of quantifying the amount of verification stimulus performed. There are two major types of coverage, structural and functional. Coverage is one metric that is used to gauge verification completeness. See Functional Coverage and Structural Coverage. [Chapter 3]

Cross Product Coverage: A type of functional coverage whereby the verification team tracks the relationship of single DUV events with respect to each other. The motivation behind cross product analysis is the interest in the occurrence of a group of events in relation to each other. [Chapter 6]

Cycle Accurate Reference Models: A test bench where the reference model calculates all expected outputs on a cycle-by-cycle basis. The reference model re-implements the function of the DUV, and the checking component compares the outputs of both the DUV and the reference mode every cycle. [Chapter 8]

Cycle-based Simulation: Logic simulation algorithm that evaluates the model of a DUV once per clock cycle [Chapter 5]

Cycle Time: The speed in which the clock to the logic toggles once. Functional verification considers this a single cycle. [Chapter 5]

D

Deadlock: A condition where the logic cannot make forward progress due to conflicting resource constraints. Deadlock conditions usually indicate a flaw in the logic, as the effected parts of the logic are bogged down or totally blocked. [Chapter 7]

Debug: The process of locating and correcting problems in the DUV or test bench. [Chapter 8]

Degraded Mode testing: Verification of conditions where a system must bypass a portion of failing logic and still maintain operations. [Chapter 9]

Design Automation Tools: Software that assists the engineer (and verification engineer) in designing the product. Design automation tools provide productivity enhancements to verification, timing, testability, physical design, and most other electronic design disciplines. [Chapter 1]

Design Intent: The anticipated behavior of the design. Typically, this is described in the design specification. This is different from the HDL, which describes the implementation. Verification ensures that the implementation matches the intent. [Chapter 1]

Designer Level Verification: The earliest level of hierarchical verification, where the DUV is a single portion of HDL. This may be simply a "smoke test" type of environment. The engineer may use this level to "certify" the HDL for the next levels of the verification hierarchy. This level of verification ensures that the basic functions are correct. [Chapter 2]

Deterministic test cases: A highly constrained test case that targets a specific scenario in the DUV. Verification teams use deterministic test cases predominantly early in the verification cycle to prove basic DUV functionality. [Chapter 3]

Design-under-Verification (DUV): The HDL targeted by the verification environment. The DUV can be any portion of the logic design, from a single HDL file up to the entire system. The verification environment surrounds the DUV in order to find bugs in it. [Chapter 1]

Driver: Another name for stimulus component within the verification environment. A driver "drives" inputs into the DUV. [Chapter 2]

E

Electronic Design Automation (EDA): The software and hardware tool industry surrounding chip design and manufacturing. EDA tools provide productivity and efficiency gains to engineers and electronics developers. [Chapter 1]

Element Level Verification: A middle level of the verification hierarchy where the verification effort focuses on a functional component, such as a processor core, storage, or IO component. [Chapter 2]

Emulator: Special-purpose hardware device that allows such a fast simulation of a DUV that it can replace the DUV in the target system as an early prototype (also in-circuit emulator). [Chapter 10]

End-of-test-case checking: Checking performed at the completion of the simulation test, either within the simulation or in a separate program or script. [Chapter 8]

Error Checkers: (hardware error checkers): Logic within the design that activates when it detects specific illegal conditions. This logic includes monitor signals to read parity signals or detect if a soft or hard error has flipped a bit. Other error checker logic monitors the functional logic for illegal conditions in the state machines or invalid command values. [Chapter 9]

Error Injection: A verification activity that tests that internal error checkers work properly. Under error injection, the verification engineer flips bit values in the design and observes the logics behavior surrounding the injection. [Chapter 9]

Escape: Escapes refer to problems that verification engineers did not detect and thus are found in the fabricated hardware. These logic bugs "escaped" detection on all levels of verification, from designer simulation through system simulation. [Chapter 1]

Escape Classification: A formal schema with a set of attributes used to characterize problems found in the fabricated hardware (escapes). [Chapter 13]

Event Simulation: A simulation algorithm that evaluates the model of a DUV as a series of events over time. Event-based simulation engines maintain a queue of events over model time. As the engine processes events from the queue, resulting changes to the model create new events. The event-driven engine evaluates only those portions of a model where changes occur during event processing. [Chapter 5]

F

Fencing: Gating off interface signals to a portion of logic. Fencing is used during recovery or reset operations to prevent propagation of unintentional signal values. [Chapter 9]

Formal Checkers: The portion of the formal verification environment that encodes the properties of the DUV, which represent the specification of the design. The properties are the proof target for formal verification. [Chapter 11]

Formal Verification: A segment of the field of functional verification that relies on mathematical methods to prove the correctness of a DUV exhaustively against its specification. [Chapter 11]

Formal Proof Engine: A software program that implements a specific algorithm used in a formal verification tool. In the process to prove functional correctness of a DUV, formal verification tools typically employ a set of different proof engines each optimized for different design and property types. [Chapter 11]

Functional Coverage: A type of coverage that focuses on the semantics of the stimulus (test scenario) or the design implementation. The environment gathers this coverage across all the test scenarios to determine whether the verification environment has exercised all the identified coverage items. See Coverage. [Chapter 3]

Functional Verification: The job of ensuring that the logical design of a chip or system performs the intended task. Functional verification engineers make sure that the logic design obeys the functional specification. [Chapter 1]

Functional Specification: The functional specification describes the desired product. It contains the specification of the interfaces with which it communicates, the function that it must perform, and the conditions that affect the design. [Chapter 1]

G

Gate Level Model: A model of the DUV, which is exclusively structural that only uses instances of a fixed set of elementary Boolean function library blocks. [Chapter 5]

Golden Vector: An environment where some knowledge base of valid output vectors is known prior to running a simulation. At the beginning of the simulation run, the knowledge is loaded into the scoreboard and the checking component compares the DUV results to this knowledge base by calling the scoreboard and requesting the expected vectors, either on every cycle or every transaction. [Chapter 8]

Grey Box Verification: A combination of both black box and white box verification styles. Some verification components monitor internal signals that assist in validating the black box level functional specification, which utilizes only the external interfaces as defined by the specification. [Chapter 3]

H

Hangs: Cases where the logic design does not complete an operation. A hang may be caused by a deadlock or livelock condition, or an error in the design which causes it to inadvertently drop a command or operation. [Chapter 7]

Hard error: A condition in the hardware where a circuit or wire is broken, causing the hardware to persistently give bad results. [Chapter 9]

Hardware-Software Co-verification: An environment intended to analyze the entire system, bringing together hardware and firmware for the first time in a single verification environment. [Chapter 10]

HDL (Hardware Description Language): Formalized, computer-readable language for the specification of hardware design. [Chapter 5]

Hierarchical Design and Verification: The practice of breaking down the design and verification tasks into smaller, more manageable pieces, then building the pieces back together at multiple intervals until the entire system comes together. Hierarchical design and verification not only makes the two jobs manageable, but also enables re-usable design and verification. [Chapter 2]

HLM (High Level Model): Abstract, implementation independent specification of a hardware design. A high-level model contains a functional specification of a DUV and additionally can cover specifications of physical DUV properties like area, timing and electrical power consumption. [Chapter 14]

HLD (High Level Design): Early chip or system design phase. All requirements for the DUV that are relevant for a high-level model are finalized during HLD. [Chapter 1]

HVL (High-Level Verification Language): Domain-specific computer language targeted to support the authoring of simulation environments consisting of stimulus, checking and monitor components. [Chapter 6]

I

Initiator: A type of stimulus component used to drive new commands into the design under verification. [Chapter 3]

Interface Monitor: A verification component that observes the inputs or outputs of the design under verification. An interface monitor may flag protocol and simple errors, or may place observed commands and data into the scoreboard for future checking. [Chapter 3]

Irritators: A class of stimulus components used to drive miscellaneous signals into the design under verification. [Chapter 3]

Issue: An item that needs to be investigated and resolved. It can be a situation where the specification is unclear or ambiguous on a technical matter, an error that must be fixed, or scenarios and functions that must be tested. An issue is anything that needs to be tracked during the chip development cycle. [Chapter 13]

J

K

Knowledge-based test case generation: A software program that creates test cases for a specific type of design. The software has complete understanding of the design's architecture (the knowledge base) which it uses to create functionally correct test cases. [Chapter 3]

L

LBIST: [Logic Built-In Self Test] An automated engine inside of a chip that sends patterns through the circuits for at-speed testability. [Chapter 9]

Livelock: A condition in a chip or system when processing appears to move forward, but irresolvable contention for a shared resource continually causes processing to retry or loop back to an earlier state.

Liveness properties: A desirable property of a DUV, expressed in temporal logic that will occur eventually at some future time. There is no bound on the timeframe until which the property will hold. [Chapter 11]

M

Mainline function: Normal chip or system operations. All other chip or system functions are pervasive. [Chapter 9]

Microarchitecture: The internal structures of the design that implement the specification [Chapter 1]

Miscompare: A condition when a value in the design under verification does not match the value predicted by the test case or by the verification environment. [Chapter 2]

Model Build: Part of the HDL translation that turns a computer-readable specification of a DUV into a simulation model executable by a simulation engine. [Chapter 5]

Model Checking: A method of formal verification that verifies algorithmically that a model of a DUV satisfies the formal specification of properties. At the core of a model checker is usually a FSM model of the DUV. [Chapter 12]

Monitor Component: A verification component that observes the inputs, outputs, or internals of the design under verification. A monitor may flag protocol and simple errors, or may place observed commands and data into the scoreboard for future checking. [Chapter 3]

N

Netlist: A design representation that is the input to the manufacturing process of the VLSI chip. It provides specific information about the chip;

including gates, placement and wiring data. Netlists may be at the transistor-level, switch-level, or gate-level. [Chapter 3]

O

Observation Point: Sites used by monitor and checking components to verify the DUV's behavior. These observation points may be on external outputs (black box), internal signals (white box), or both (grey box). [Chapter 3]

On-the-fly: A style of test case where the verification environment generates stimulus or calculates expected results on a cycle-by-cycle basis while the simulation engine runs against the design under test. On-the-fly test cases use input constraint directives to create stimulus and make decisions.

Open Verification Library (OVL): Standardized, vendor-independent, openly accessible library of assertion monitors implemented in Verilog and VHDL. [Chapter 12]

P

Package: 1. A self-contained structure for the verification components including all design and verification components and documentation that the verification team requires to bring the verification component into production seamlessly. The "complete package" encapsulates the re-usable components (stimulus, monitor, scoreboard, and checker) into one package that behaves differently based on constraints. The "independent component package" has each verification component packaged separately. [Chapter 10] **2.** A card or board design which connects attached chips together. [Chapter 2]

Parameters: A set of biasing controls used with pseudo-random number generation to control the directing of stimulus components. [Chapter 6]

Pervasive function: Operations beyond the normal chip or system operations. Pervasive functions include the resetting of the hardware, Built-in Self Test (automated, hardware driven diagnostics), recovery scenarios, chip level testability, low power modes, and all hardware debug mechanisms. [Chapter 9]

Physical Design: The actual latch, wiring, and circuit layout of a chip. Also, refers to the act of creating a chip circuit layout, using EDA tools for placement, wiring, and chip integration. [Chapter 1]

Power-on-reset: The method for returning the chip or system logic to a known-good state after initially applying power to the hardware. [Chapter 9]

Pre-generated test cases: Test cases where the input stimulus and output checking exist prior to running the simulation job. [Chapter 7]

Properties: Specification of assertions, static or temporal, that the implementation of DUV has to honor. [Chapter 11]

Property checking: Verification that a DUV fulfills its specification, which is formalized with properties. Static property checking uses formal verification technology to prove the compliance of a DUV implementation with its property specification [Chapter 11]

PSL: Industry standard property specification language; computer-readable domain-specific language for the specification of functional properties of DUVs. [Chapter 12]

Q

Quiesce: Ceasing the initiation of new commands or operations. Under verification, quiesce inhibits the on-the-fly stimulus components from sending in new stimulus. [Chapter 7]

Quiesce Cycle: A pre-determined cycle where the on-the-fly stimulus components stop sending new commands or operations. [Chapter 7]

R

Random Driver: A constraint driven, on-the-fly stimulus component that uses biasing parameters and a pseudo-random number generator to derive legal operations to initiate to the design under verification. [Chapter 7]

Recovery: A series of actions that puts the logic into a working functional state after detecting an error in hardware operations. [Chapter 9]

Reference Model: A model implemented by the verification team to make predictions of the test case results based on the test case inputs. It crosschecks the behavior against the design intent. *See also:* Cycle Accurate Reference Model. [Chapter 1]

Regression: A set of test cases run at a predetermined rate (nightly, weekly, release to manufacturing time, etc.) to verify that HDL changes (fixes or new functions) have not broken any existing function that has previously been verified. As a new function is verified on a DUV, the test cases used to verify it are added to a "regression bucket." [Chapter 13]

Reset: Putting logic into a known-good state. May apply to an entire chip or system, as in Power-on-reset, or to a portion of the logic after recovery. [Chapter 9]

Re-use: A technique to leverage verification components across the verification hierarchy. The concept of "create once, use in many places" results in reduced workload and schedule. [Chapter 10]

Re-usable IP: The process of enabling intellectual property (IP), either verification components or design blocks, from another group or vendor in a verification environment. The re-use of this IP has unique issues regarding verification and debug. [Chapter 10]

RTL (Register Transfer Level): An RTL model specifies a DUV in terms of state-holding dataflow elements (registers and storage arrays) and the action that update the DUV state between clock cycles. [Chapter 5]

S

Safety properties: A desirable property of a DUV, expressed in temporal logic that will always hold true. The model time during which a safety property holds is unlimited. However, safety properties are useful even if the verification only cover limited model time because any violation of a safety property is a bug in the DUV. [Chapter 11]

Scanning: Reading or writing the latches in a chip by shifting values throughout by toggling alternative clocks that gate the inputs to the latches. Used for initializing chips under reset, debugging chips, and for testability. [Chapter 9]

Scan Ring: A loop of latches that may be read or written by shifting values by toggling alternative clocks that gate the inputs to the latches. [Chapter 9]

Scoreboard: A temporary holding location for information that the checker will use to perform its function. It can receive its information in various ways: an input monitor component, a stimulus component, or loaded at the beginning of a simulation in a golden vectors environment. [Chapter 3]

Seed: A value used to initialize a pseudo-random number generator that stimulus components use to make input value decisions. Using the same seed allows the verification engineer to re-create "random" test cases. [Chapter 7]

Semi-Formal Verification: Any verification method that ensures consistency of a DUV with the specification for all possible inputs. Semi-Formal verification tools are those that bridge the gap between simulation and formal verification. [Chapter 12]

Service Element: A code-driven engine that supports bring-up and maintenance of robust systems. [Chapter 9]

Simulation: The portion of functional verification where a simulation engine is used. [Chapter 5]

Simulation Engine: A software program that implements a simulation algorithm (like event-driven or cycle-based simulation) and evaluates the HDL specification of a DUV over time. [Chapter 5]

Specification: A document that defines the expected performance (function, behavior, and outputs) for the chip based on inputs. This document should define valid inputs and valid applications for the chip. The verification team verifies the chip against this document. [Chapter 1]

SOC (System-on-a-Chip): An embedded system that is self-contained within one chip, potentially including an embedded processor, memory, Ethernet PHY, USB port, and other application specific logic. [Chapter 10]

Soft Error: A condition in the hardware where a latch or array value is compromised causing the hardware to give bad results on a single instance (temporarily). [Chapter 9]

State Space: The set of all reachable states of a finite state machine specification of a DUV. [Chapter 11]

State Space Traversal: The algorithmic exploration of the reachable state space of the finite state machine specification of a DUV. [Chapter 11]

Stick: Changing the value of a data object in the design under verification in a simulation environment. Sticking a data object to a value will cause it to hold that value until it is stuck to a different value or unstuck. [Chapter 6]

Stimulus Component: A portion of the verification environment that drives inputs or manipulates values inside the design under verification. Also called drivers, behaviorals, irritators, responders. [Chapter 3]

Structural Coverage: A type of coverage that focuses on the representation of the implemented design. This type of coverage is always derived from the composition of the design HDL. A tool gathers the metrics versus a verification engineer having to specify it as in functional coverage. Different sub-types exist for structural coverage. The most popular types are: toggle, statement or line, branch or conditional, and path. See Coverage. [Chapter 3]

Synchronous: Within verification, synchronous refers to an interface between two logical units whose source clocks run off the same oscillator. [Chapter 5]

System Level Verification: A late level in the verification hierarchy where the verification team focuses on the entire system, including all previously verified components of the design. [Chapter 2]

Systems Test: The part of the verification process where the engineering team brings-up, evaluates, and runs applications on the fabricated hardware. [Chapter 1]

T

Tape-Out: A reference to an archaic process when the design team stored the chip's physical design information onto magnetic tape, and sent it to the fabrication facility. [Chapter 1]

Tape-Out Criteria: A checklist of physical and logical items that the design team must complete prior to releasing a chip to the fabrication facility. [Chapter 1]

Temporal Checks: Verification of temporal properties of a DUV. [Chapter 11]

Test and Testability: Manufacturing test checks whether a physical chip functions according to its gate-level specification. Manufacturing test patterns are sets of stimuli designed to expose manufacturing defects in a chip based on a specific metric (stuck-at fault testing). Testability is a measure of how complete the set of test patterns is to expose all possible stuck-at faults. [Chapter 6, Chapter 9]

Test Case: A single verification job using a simulation engine. Test cases vary widely in stimulus and checking approaches and methods. [Chapter 2]

Test case generator: A method for creating multiple verification jobs utilizing a software engine that contains knowledge about the targeted design under verification. [Chapter 2]

Testcase Harvesting: Collection of test cases for regression purposes in a way that tests with higher coverage are preferred, thus minimizing the number of tests contained in the regression suite. [Chapter 13]

Test Matrix: A list of all the test scenarios that will serve to verify the design. The verification team lists the basic required tests first in the verification plan, and then builds upon it throughout the verification process. The plan groups tests with similar features to form test scenarios, whose descriptions designate the targeted function. Last on the matrix is a cross reference to the functional requirements and coverage goals. [Chapter 4]

Testbench: Set of programs that implement components of a verification environment (stimulus, checking, monitor components) of written in HDLs or high-level verification languages [Chapter 6]

Theorem Proving: Sub-discipline of formal verification with the purpose to prove mathematical theorems with the help of computer algorithms. [Chapter 11]

Trace: An output from a simulation engine that shows the behavior within the design. Trace behavior can be used to determine unwanted behavior within a design or verification environment. Also known as a wave form. [Chapter 5]

Trace-back (wave viewer capability): Method for looking at the cone of logic feeding a portion of a design. [Chapter 5]

Transaction: An abstracted view of the inputs and outputs to a DUV. Instead of viewing the inputs and outputs as bits, the verification engineer defines a transaction that is a grouping of bits over time. Examples of transactions would be PCI bus transactions (read, write, burst read, burst write, etc) or Ethernet packets. [Chapter 3]

Transaction Based checking: An environment used for verifying a DUV that has identifiable transactions. The environment acts upon commands and data and forwards them to appropriate output signal checkers, enabling a structured environment based on the transaction nature of the DUV. This type of environment uses a scoreboard to track commands and data driven on the inputs of the DUV. [Chapter 3]

U

Unit Level Verification: An early level in the verification hierarchy where the verification team focuses on a small portion of logical function. Unit level verification usually brings together a few designers' pieces of logic. [Chapter 2]

V

Vacuity: Trivial satisfaction of a formal property typically caused by an error in the specification of a property. For example, the specification that every request is eventually followed by a grant is true even if the system, for example the stimulus component, never generates request. [Chapter 12]

Verilog: Industry standard hardware description language. [Chapter 5]

Verification Engineer: A professional engineer whose role is to uncover problems in the logical design of chips and systems prior to hardware fabrication. [Chapter 1]

Verification Environment: Test cases and software code components surrounding the design under verification. The verification environment, written by verification engineers, is the supporting infrastructure that drives stimulus and checks outputs. [Chapter 2]

Verification Plan: A plan that defines both the functions that the verification team must attack and how they will do their work. It is a living document owned by the entire design team, and enhanced throughout the verification cycle. It covers the verification levels, required tools, risks and dependencies, functions to be verified, specific tests and methods, coverage requirements, test case matrix, resource requirements, and schedule details. [Chapter 4]

VHDL: Industry standard hardware description language. [Chapter 5]

W

Waveform: Graphical representation of the value of one or more signals of a DUV over time. [Chapter 5]

White Box Verification: An environment that has a full insight into the implementation (internal structures) of the DUV. The checking is typically done by observing internal signals. This environment will flag a bug at its source. It is tightly integrated with implementation, so high maintenance levels are required. [Chapter 3]

Window conditions: Obscure cases within the logic design that occur when multiple microarchitectural edge conditions align within a short number of cycles. Window conditions often occur when multiple corner cases align. These scenarios are especially interesting for stimulus generation because bugs often lurk in window conditions. [Chapter 7]

X

Y

Z

REFERENCES

[1] H. Foster, A. Krolnik, D. Lacey. *Assertion-Based Design*, 2nd ed. Kluwer Academic Publishers, New York, NY.

[2] M. Kantrowitz, L. Noack. 1996. "I'm Done Simulating; Now What?: Verification Correctness Checking of the DECchip 21164 Alpha microprocessor." *Proc. Design Automation Conference*, pp. 325–330.

[3] S. Taylor, et al. 1998. "Functional Verification of a Multi-Issue Out-of-Order, Superscalar Alpha Processor-the DEC Alpha 21264 microprocessor." *Proc. Design Automation Conference*, pp. 638–643.

[4] Accellera home page, http://www.accellera.org.

[5] Accellera OVL Technical Committee, Open Verification Library, http://www.eda.org/ovl.

[6] P.J. Ashenden, 2002. *The Designer's Guide to VHDL*, 2nd ed. Morgan Kaufman, San Francisco, CA.

[7] D.E. Thomas, P.R. Moorby, 2002. *The Verilog Hardware Description Language*, Kluwer Academic Publishers, New York, NY.

[8] IEEE Standard VHDL Language Reference Manual (IEEE Std. 1076–2002).

[9] IEEE Standard Description Language Based on the Verilog™ Hardware Description Language (IEEE Std. 1364–2001).

[10] H. Foster, A. Krolnik, D. Lacey, 2004. *Assertion-Based Design*, 2nd ed. Kluwer Academic Publishers, New York, NY.

[11] J. Bergeron, 2003. *Writing Testbenches: Functional Verification of HDL Models*, 2nd ed. Kluwer Academic Publishers, New York, NY.

[12] *Property Specification Language Reference Manual*. Accellera, http://www.eda.org/vfv/docs/PSL-v1.1.pdf.

[13] SystemVerilog home page, http://www.systemverilog.org.

[14] Standard Performance Evaluation Corporation home page, http://www.spec.org/.

[15] John Darringer et al. 2000. "EDA in IBM: Past, Present, and Future", *IEEE Transaction on Computer Aided Design of Integrated Circuits and Systems*, 19(12).

[16] C. Schepens, 2004. "Unified co-verification breaks HW/SW bottlenecks", *EEDesign*, http://www.eedesign.com/article/showArticle.jhtml?articleId=17601270.

[17] Z. Barzilai, I. L. Carter, B.K. Rosen, J.D. Rutledge, 1987. "HSS: A High-Speed Simulator," *IEEE Transaction on Computer Aided Design of Integrated Circuits and Systems*, 6(4), pp. 601–616.

[18] P. Maurer, Z.C. Wang, 1989. "LECSIM: A Levelize Event Driven Compiled Logic Simulator," Technical Report Number DA-20, Baylor University, Waco, TX.

[19] P. Maurer, J.S. Lee, 1995. "MDCSIM: A Compiled Event-Driven Multi-Delay Simulator," Technical Report Number DA-30, Baylor University, Waco, TX.

[20] Advanced Processor Technologies Group home page, http://www.cs.man.ac.uk/apt/tools/gtkwave/.

[21] VHDL-200x, IEEE, http://www.eda.org/vhdl-200x/.

[22] J. Bergeron, 2003. *Writing Testbenches: Functional Verification of HDL Models*, 2nd ed. Kluwer Academic Publishers, New York, NY.

[23] P.J. Ashenden, 2002. *The Designer's Guide to VHDL*, 2nd ed. Morgan Kaufman, San Francisco, CA.

[24] VHDL Random Number Generation Package, http://www.eda.org/rassp/vhdl/models/math/rng2.txt.

[25] Object-Oriented VHDL Study Group, http://www.eda.org/oovhdl/.

[26] SystemVerilog home page, http://www.systemverilog.org.

[27] IEEE Standard Description Language Based on the Verilog™ Hardware Description Language (IEEE Std. 1364–2001).

[28] ModelSim VHDL Foreign Language Interface, http://www.model.com.

[29] IEEE DASC VHDL PLI Task Force, http://www.eda.org/vhdlpli.

[30] OpenVera home page, http://www.open-vera.com.

[31] A.V. Aho, R. Sethi, J.D. Ullman, 1987. *Compilers*. Addison Wesley, Boston, MA.

[32] F. Imdad-Hague, 2001. "The Art of Verification with Vera," Verification Central.

[33] Verisity home page, http://www.verisity.com.

[34] IEEE, P1647, http://www.ieee1647.org/.

[35] Y. Hollander, M. Morley, A. Noy, 2001. "The e Language: A Fresh Separation of Concerns," *Technology of Object-Oriented Languages and Systems*, Zurich, Switzerland, pp. 41–50.

[36] S. Palnitkar, 2003. *Design Verification with e*. Prentice Hall, Upper Saddle River, NJ.

[37] SystemC home page, http://www.systemc.org.

[38] Test Builder home page, http://www.testbuilder.net.

[39] The Perl Scripting Language, http://www.perl.org.

[40] The TCL Scripting Language, http://tcl.sourceforge.net/.

[41] The Python Scripting Language, http://www.python.org.

[42] B. Wile, "Designer-level verification using TIMEDIAG/GENRAND", *IBM Journal of Research and Development*, 41(4/5), p. 581.

[43] Aldec home page, http://www.aldec.com.

[44] TransEDA home page, http://www.transeda.com.

[45] M. Kantrowitz, L. Noack, 1996: "I'm done simulating; Now what?", *Proceedings 33rd Design Automation Conference*.

[46] D. Dill, S. Tasiran, "Simulation Meets Formal Verification", embedded Tutorial at ICCAD 99, http://chicory.stanford.edu/talks.html.

[47] J.M. Galey, R.E. Norby, J.P. Roth, 1961. "Techniques for the diagnosis of switching circuit failures," *Foundations of Computer Science*, pp. 152–160.

[48] R. Grinwald, E. Harel, M. Orgad, S. Ur, A. Ziv, 1998. "User Defined Coverage: A Tool Supported Methodology for Design Verification", *Design Automation Conference*, pp. 158–163.

[49] *Property Specification Language Reference Manual*. Accellera, http://www.eda.org/vfv/docs/PSL-v1.1.pdf.

[50] O. Lachish, E. Marcus, S. Ur, A. Ziv, 2002. "Hole Analysis for Functional Coverage Data," *Design Automation Conference*, pp. 807–812.

[51] A. Chandra, V. Iyengar, D. Jameson, R. Jawalekar, I. Nair, B. Rosen, M. Mullen, J. Yoon, R. Armoni, D. Geist, Y. Wolfsthal, 1995. "AVPGEN-A Test Generator for Architecture Verification," *IEEE Trans. Very Large Scale Integration (VLSI) Syst.* 3, No. 2, pp. 188–200.

[52] A. Aharon, D. Goodman, M. Levinger, Y. Lichtenstein, Y. Malka, C. Metzger, M. Molcho, G. Shurek, 1995. "Test Program Generation for Functional Verification of PowerPC Processors in IBM," *Proceedings of the 32nd ACM/IEEE Conference on Design Automation Conference*, San Francisco, CA, pp. 279–285.

[53] Eyal Bin, Roy Emek, Gil Shurek, Avi Ziv, 2002. "Using a constraint satisfaction formulation and solution techniques for random test program generation," *IBM Systems Journal*, 41(3).

[54] E. Fujiwara, M. Hamada, "Single b-Bit Byte Error Correcting and Double Bit Error Detecting Codes for High Speed Memory Systems," *Proceedings of the 1992 IEEE International Symposium on Information Theory*, pp. 494 ff.

[55] John Darringer et al., "EDA in IBM: Past, Present and Future," *IEEE Transactions on Computer Aided Design of Integrated Circuits and Systems*, Vol. 19, No. 12, Dec. 2000, pp. 1476–1496.

[56] Juergen Haufe, Peter Schwarz, Thomas Berndt, Jens Grosse, "Accelerated Simulation Using Protoype Boards," *Design, Automation and Test in Europe*, Paris, 1998, pp. 183–189.

[57] Edger W. Dijkstra, "Notes on Structured Programming," 1970, http://www.cs.utexas.edu/users/EWD/ewd02xx/EWD249.PDF.

[58] C. Kern, M. Greenstreet, "Formal Verification in Hardware Design: A Survey." *ACM Transactions on Design Automation of Electronic Systems*, Vol. 4, April 1999, pp. 123–193.

[59] Rolf Drechsler (Ed.), "Advanced Formal Verification," Kluwer 2004.

[60] Hans Eveking, "Verifikation digitaler Systeme," Teubner 1991 (in German).

[61] John E. Hopcroft, Rajeev Motwani, Jeffrey D. Ullman, "Introduction to Automata Theory, Languages and Computability," 2nd edition. Pearson Addison Wesley 2000.

[62] K. L. McMillan, "Symbolic Model Checking: an Approach to the State Explosion Problem," CMU Tech. Rpt. CMU-CS-92–131.

[63] D. Russinoff, "A Mechanically Checked Proof of IEEE Compliance of the Floating-Point Multiplication, Division, and Square Root Algorithms of the

AMD-K7* Processor," *London Mathematical Society Journal of Computation and Mathematics*, 1, December 1998, pp. 148–200.

[64] http://www.cs.utexas.edu/users/moore/acl2.

[65] http://www.cl.cam.ac.uk/Research/HVG/HOL.

[66] http://pvs.csl.sri.com.

[67] A. Kuehlmann, A. Srinivasan, D. P. LaPotin, "Verity-A Formal Verification Program for Custom CMOS Circuits," *IBM Journal of Research and Development*, Vol. 39, No. 1/2, January/March 1995, pp. 149–165.

[68] Wolfgang Kunz, Dominik Stoffel, "Reasoning in Boolean Networks," Kluwer Academic Publishers, 1995.

[69] Randall Bryant, "Graph-based Algorithms for Boolean Function Manipulation," *IEEE Transactions on Computers*, Vol. C-35, No. 8, pp. 677–691.

[70] M. Davis, G. Logemann, D. Loveland, "A Machine Program for Theorem Proving," *Communications of the ACM*, Vol. 5, No. 7, pp. 394–397, 1962.

[71] A. Kuehlmann, M. Ganai, V. Paruthi, "Circuit-based Boolean Reasoning," *Proceedings of the 38th Design Automation Conference*, pp. 232–237.

[72] A. Briere, W. Kunz, "SAT and ATPG: Boolean Engines for Formal Hardware Verification," *Proceedings of the 2002 IEEE/ACM International Conference on Computer-Aided Design (ICCAD 2002)*, pp. 782–785.

[73] http://www.satlive.org.

[74] J. Silva, K. Sakallah, "GRASP-A New Search Algorithm for Satisfiability," *Proceedings of the International Conference on Computer Aided Design (ICCAD)*, pp. 220–227, 1996.

[75] M. Moskewicz, C. Madigan, Y. Zhao, L. Zhang, S. Malik, "Chaff: Engineering an Efficient SAT Solver," *Proceedings of 38th Design Automation Conference*, pp. 530–535, 2001.

[76] E. Goldberg, Y. Novikov, "BerkMin: A Fast and Robust SAT-Solver," *Proceedings of the Design Automation and Test in Europe Conference*, 2002, pp. 142–149.

[77] C. L. Berman, L. H. Trevillyan,"Functional Comparisons of Logic Designs for VLSI Circuits," *Digest of Technical Papers of IEEE Intl. Conference on Computer-Aided Design*, IEEE, Nov. 1989, pp. 456–459.

[78] http://www.synopsys.com/products/verification/formality_ds.html.

[79] http://www.cadence.com/products/digital_ic/conformal/index.aspx.

[80] http://mentor.com/products/fv/formal_verification/formal_pro/index.cfm.

[81] http://www.accellera.com.

[82] http://www.pslsugar.org.

[83] Christian Jacobi, Kai Weber, Viresh Paruthi, Jason Baumgartner, "Automatic Formal Verification of Fused-Multiply-Add Floating Point Units," Proceedings DATE 05 Conference 2005.

[84] Hana Chockler, Orna Kupferman, Moshe Y. Vardi, "Coverage Metrics for Formal Verification," *CHARME* 2003, pp. 111–125.

[85] K. L. McMillan, "Lecture Notes for NATO Summer School on Verification of Digital and Hybrid Systems," http://www.cad.eecs.berkeley.edu/~kenmcmil/tutorial/toc.html

[86]   http://www.systemverilog.org.

[87]   http://www.accellera.org/ovl.

[88]   I. Beer, S. Ben-David, D. Geist, R. Gewirtzman, M. Yoeli, "Methodology and System for Practical Formal Verification of Reactive Hardware," *Lecture Notes in Computer Science*, Vol. 818, pp. 182–193, 1994.

[89]   http://www.eda.org/vfv/docs/PSL-v1.1.pdf.

[90]   J. Friedl, " Mastering Regular Expresssions," 2nd edition. O'Reilly, 2002.

[91]   http://www.pslsugar.org.

[92]   B. Cohen, S. Venkataraman, A. Kumari, " Using PSL/Sugar for Formal and Dynamic Verification," 2nd edition. VhdlCohen Publishing, 2004.

[93]   H. Foster, A. Krolnik, D. Lacey, D. Lacey, "Assertion-Based Design," 2nd edition. Kluwer, 2004.

[94]   Y. Aberbanel, I. Beer, L. Gluhovsky, S. Keidar, Y. Wolfsthal, "FoCs—Automatic Generation of Simulation Checkers from Formal Specifications," *CAV*, 2000, pp. 538–532.

[95]   O. Coudert, C. Berthet, J. Madre, "Verification of Synchronous Sequential Machines Based on Symbolic Execution," Automatic Verification Methods for Finite State Systems, International Workshop, Vol. 407, *Lecture Notes in Computer Science*, Springer, 1989.

[96]   http://www.alphaworks.ibm.com/tech/FoCs.

[97]   H. Touati, H. Savoj, B. Lin, R. Brayton, A. Sangiovanni-Vincentelli, "Implicit State Enumeration of Finite State Machines Using BDDs," ICCAD, *Proceedings of the International Conference on Computer Aided Design*, November 1990, pp. 130–133.

[98]   J. Burch, E. Clarke, D. Long, K. MacMillan, D. Dill, "Symbolic Model Checking for Sequential Circuit Verification," *IEEE Transactions on Computer-Aided Design of Integrated Circuits and Systems*, Vol. 13, No. 4, pp. 401–424, 1994.

[99]   A. Biere, A. Cimatti, E. Clarke, Y. Zhu, "Symbolic Model Checking Without BDDs," *Proceedings of the Workshop on Tools and Algorithms for the Construction and Analysis of Systems (TACAS)*, LNCS, Springer, 1999.

[100] S. Skiena, "The Algorithm Design Manual," Springer-Verlag, New York, 1997.

[101] S. Fine, S. Ur, A. Ziv, "Probabilistic Regression Suites for Functional Verification," *Proceedings IEEE 41st Design Automation Conference*, San Diego, 2004.

[102] http://www.platform.com.

[103] http://www.globus.org.

[104] http://www.cmcrossroads.com.

[105] M. Bartley, D. Galpin, T. Blackmore, "A Comparison of Three Verification Techniques: Directed Testing, Pseudo-Random Testing and Property Checking," *Proceedings IEEE 39th Design Automation Conference, New Orleans*, 2002.

[106] B. Bentley, "Validating the Intel Pentium 4 Microprocessor," *Proceedings IEEE 38th Design Automation Conference, Las Vegas*, 2001.

[107] S. S. Mukherjee, S. V. Adve, T. Austin, J. Emer, P. S. Magnusson, "Performance Simulation Tools," *IEEE Computer*, Vol. 35, No. 2, pp. 38–39, 2002.

[108] http://www.systemverilog.org

[109] A. Habibi, S. Tahar, "A Survey on System-On-a-Chip Design Languages," *Proceedings of the 3rd IEEE Intl. Workshop on System-on-Chip for Real-Time Applications*.

[110] http://www.specc.org

[111] http://www.celoxica.org

[112] http://www.bluespec.com

[113] http://verify.stanford.edu/dill/murphi.html

[114] http://www.systemc.org

[115] J. Schoen, "Performance and Fault Modeling with VHDL," Prentice Hall, 1992.

[116] D. Gajski, "Specification and Design of Embedded Systems," Prentice Hall, 1994.

[117] T. Grotker, S. Liao, G. Martin, S. Swan "System Design with SystemC," Kluwer Academic Publishers, 2002.

[118] http://www.openvera.org

[119] http://www.verisity.com

[120] S. Ur, Y. Yadin, "Micro Architecture Coverage Directed Generation of Test Programs," *Proceedings of 36th Design Automation Conference*, 1999, pp. 175–180.

[121] P. Mishra, N. Dutt, "Architecture Description Language Driven Functional Test Program Generation for Microprocessors using SMV," *CECS Technical Report #02-26*, University of California, Irvine.

[122] http://www.haifa.il.ibm.com/dept/svt/simulation.html

[123] http://en.wikipedia.org/wiki/Bayesian_networks

[124] S. Fine, A. Ziv, "Coverage Directed Test Generation for Functional Verification Using Bayesian Networks", *Proceedings of 40th Design Automation Conference*, 2003, pp. 286–291.

[125] J. S. Liptay, "Design of the IBM Enterprise System/9000 High-end Processor," *IBM Journal of Research and Development*, Vol. 36, No. 4, July 1992, pp. 713–731.

[126] C. L. Chen, N. N. Tendolkar, A. J. Sutton, M. Y. Hsiao, D. C. Bossen, "Fault-tolerance Design of the IBM Enterprise System/9000 Type 9021 Processors," *IBM Journal of Research and Development*, Vol. 36, No. 4, July 1992, pp. 765–779.

[127] D. F. Ackerman et al., "Simulation of IBM Enterprise System/9000 Models 820 and 900," *IBM Journal of Research and Development*, Vol. 36, No. 4, July 1992, pp. 751–764.

SUBJECT INDEX

Page numbers followed by "f" indicate figures. Page numbers followed by "t" indicate tables.

A

ABIST, defined, 641
ABIST engine, 367
Acceleration
   defined, 641
   in system simulation, 421–427, 421t, 422f–425f, 427f
Accuracy, speed *vs.*, in HDLs, 160–162, 161f
Architectural tests, defined, 641
Architecture, 18, 641
ASIC, defined, 641
Assert, in verification layer of PSL, 507–508, 509f
Assertion(s)
   in assertion-based verification
      classification of, 94–95
      design intent expressed by, 92–94, 93f
   in debugging process, 342–343
   defined, 641–642
   importance of, 90–92
Assertion re-use, 410–412, 410f, 411f
Assertion-based verification, 89–95
   assertions in
      classification of, 94–95
      design intent expressed by, 92–94, 93f
      importance of, 90–92
   defined, 642
   overview of, 89–90, 89f–91f
Assume, in verification layer of PSL, 508–509
Assume_guarantee, in verification layer of PSL, 509, 510f
Asynchronous, defined, 642
ATPG, 459–463, 460f–462f
Automated coverage-controlled generation, 597–598, 598f
Automatic theorem provers, 447

B

Base infrastructure layer, 214–216
BDD. *See* Binary decision diagram (BDD)
Behavior(s), incorrect, detection of, challenge of, 12–14, 13t

Behavioral, defined, 642
BFM. *See* Bus Functional Model (BFM)
Biasing, defined, 642
Big-O notation, 443–444, 444f
Binary decision diagram (BDD), 456, 457f, 458f
   defined, 642
Black box, checking of, in verification, 55–59, 56f, 57t, 58f, 59f
Black box verification
   Black box testing, defined, 642
   in verification environment, 86–87
Board- and system-level verification, 37f, 40
Boolean algebra applications, in formal verification, 446–447, 447f
Boolean equivalence checking
   combinational, 451–454, 452f, 453f
      core algorithms for, 454–465, 455f–458f, 460f, 462f, 464f, 465f
   defined, 642
   in formal verification, 448–467, 449f, 451f–453f, 455f–458f, 460f–462f, 464f–466f
      blueprint of modern equivalence checking tool, 465–467, 466f
      described, 448
      elements of, 450–451, 451f
      in VLSI design flow, 449–450, 449f
   sequential, 451–454, 452f, 453f
Boolean layer of PSL, 500–503, 501f, 502f
Boolean logic, 147
Boolean-equation level, 172
Bounded model checking, 525–527, 526f
Branch coverage, 248
Branch history table, case study of, 608–624, 610f–613f, 615f, 617f, 620f
Bug(s)
   closure rate, 553, 554f
   costs of, 44–45
   curve, defined, 642
   defined, 642
   discovery rate, 552–553, 553f, 554f

RECEIVED

JUN - 1 2009

ENGINEERING LIBRARY